WEBSTER'S SECRETARIAL HANDBOOK

A Merriam-Webster

WEBSTER'S SECRETARIAL HANDBOOK

ANNA L. ECKERSLEY-JOHNSON · Editor

G. & C. Merriam Company, Publishers
Springfield, Massachusetts 01101

Library of Congress Cataloging in Publication Data
Main entry under title:

Webster's secretarial handbook.

Bibliography: pp. 518-520
Includes index.
1. Office practice—Handbooks, manuals, etc.
2. Secretaries—Handbooks, manuals, etc. I. Eckersley-Johnson, Anna L., 1924- II. Soukhanov, Anne H., 1943-
HF5547.5.W4 651'.4 76-22498
ISBN 0-87779-036-1

Printed and bound in the United States of America

7RMcN80

Design/Carolyn McHenry
Illustrations/Julie A. Collier
Index/Eva Weber

CONTRIBUTORS

W. ARTHUR ALLEE
University of Houston

ANNA L. ECKERSLEY-JOHNSON
Central Connecticut State College

MINA M. JOHNSON
San Francisco State University

ROGER WAYNE JOHNSON
The Stanley Works

CAROL C. JONIC
IBM Corporation

NATHAN KREVOLIN
Central Connecticut State College

GEORGE J. METZLER
Combustion Engineering, Inc.

MELVIN MORGENSTEIN
Nassau Community College

DONALD D. SCRIVEN
Northern Illinois University

JOLENE D. SCRIVEN
Northern Illinois University

ANNE H. SOUKHANOV
G. & C. Merriam Company

DONALD J. TATE
Arizona State University (Tempe)

TABLE OF CONTENTS

PREFACE

The book that you are holding is a product of G. & C. Merriam Company, publishers of the Merriam-Webster dictionaries and reference books. As such, *Webster's Secretarial Handbook* is characterized by the same thorough research, comprehensive content, and careful editing that have distinguished Merriam-Webster publications for over 125 years. *Webster's Secretarial Handbook* is also the result of the Merriam editorial department's collaboration with a number of carefully chosen specialists—both educators and managers—whose combined experience and expertise in business education and private industry have produced the 15 chapters in the book.

Webster's Secretarial Handbook has a number of features that make it an especially practical day-to-day reference source not only for prospective and practicing secretaries but also for executives seeking answers to questions regarding applied secretarial practices, procedures, and techniques. Some of these features are as follows:

Each chapter is an entirely self-contained unit discussing in detail one major aspect of applied secretarial science, such as dictation and transcription, typewriting and word processing, basic accounting and electronic data processing, reprographics techniques, office mail handling, and telephone diplomacy.

Discussions of office equipment systems are centered not on specific products and brands but rather on general types of systems and processes and their advantages and disadvantages in various office applications. Prime examples of this kind of coverage are Chapter 5—"Automated and Specialized Typewriting with Stylization"—a chapter that overviews word processing equipment and offers specific ways by which the equipment can be used most efficiently and effectively, and Chapter 12—"Office Equipment Systems: How to Make Them Work for You"—a chapter that discusses in detail current reprographic processes and techniques and also contains a section dealing with electronic data processing tools for secretaries.

The physical layout of the book offers the reader maximum access to information with a minimum of searching. For example, each chapter is introduced by its own table of contents listing in numerical order all of its main sections. In turn, the subsections of chapters are introduced by highly visible subheadings that alert the reader to particular topics under discussion. Directional cross-references are placed throughout the text to guide the reader from one subject to a related subject or subjects. A detailed index guides the reader quickly to the needed information.

The text is copiously illustrated with line drawings, sketches, diagrams, charts, tables, facsimiles, and lists that offer the reader an abundance of information in a concise, readable form. In this connection, the reader is encouraged to examine the extensive Worldwide Holidays Chart found in Chapter 15, "Travel and the Multinational Character of Modern Business." This chart is essentially a perpetual calendar of hundreds of holidays that occur in countries throughout the world. It is unique to this book, and as such, it is a feature that secretaries will undoubtedly find invaluable in planning and setting up itineraries for executives who travel in other countries.

Both secretaries and executives will find the portion of the book devoted to Business English particularly valuable. Based on the resources of the Merriam-Webster dictionaries and the vast supporting research files containing over 12 million examples of English usage, this part of the book provides detailed discussion of the conventions of English and spells out acceptable alternatives in careful detail. All essential guidelines for such matters as the styling of abbreviations and numerals, capitalization, italicization, and spacing in typewritten documents are presented in chart form. Each guideline is exemplified with at least one verbal illustration. Many of these are quoted illustrations taken from a variety of business and professional sources. Similarly, guidelines to sound and effective composition are explained in a concise, clear fashion and are illustrated with numerous examples of actual usage. In addition, secretaries will find a great variety of recommendations and facsimile models for the styling of various documents such as memorandums, business letters, reports, news releases, and house organs.

Webster's Secretarial Handbook, like other Merriam-Webster publications, represents a collective effort. It would therefore be ungracious and unfair not to recognize those Merriam staff members who have contributed greatly to the value of the book. Mr. Victor W. Weidman, Vice-president, made major contributions during the initial planning stages of the book, as did Dr. H. Bosley Woolf, Editorial Director/Dictionaries (retired). Dr. Mairé Weir Kay and Dr. Frederick C. Mish, Joint Editorial Directors, reviewed the entire manuscript, offered sound advice, and rendered invaluable guidance throughout the project. Grace A. Kellogg, Associate Editor, assisted in proofreading the material. John K. Bollard, Kathleen M. Doherty, James E. Shea, and Raymond R. Wilson, Assistant Editors, assisted at various points with the editing of the manuscript. Thomas L. Coopee, Comptroller, reviewed the sections of the manuscript that concern electronic data processing. Louise E. Swain, Assistant Secretary of the Company, and Claire O. Cody, Secretary to the President, prepared the typewritten illustrative facsimiles. The manuscript was typed by Helene A. Gingold and Frances W. Muldrew under the direction of Evelyn G. Summers.

The Editors

1

CHAPTER ONE

CAREER-PATH DEVELOPMENT

CONTENTS

1.1

THE SECRETARY'S INCREASED RESPONSIBILITIES AND REQUIRED SKILLS: An Overview

It is entirely appropriate to begin a handbook for secretaries with an overview of what it means to be a member of an extremely competitive profession—a profession that by its very nature must reflect the broadened scope and the heightened competition of modern business. It is true that the secretary is now much more than a receptionist-cum-typist, for an increasing number of executives expect their secretaries to function as administrative assistants who can relieve them of many routine and some specialized tasks. Of course, the secretary has always been a vital link between those who make management-level decisions and those who react to and implement the decisions. In the present role of executive extender, however, a competent and responsible secretary is not only a link between management and line personnel but also a supporting adjunct to the executive.

In the past, secretaries have sometimes been criticized for displaying a lack of initiative in seeking out and accepting additional responsibilities; however, it must be remembered that many secretaries have been placed in positions of responsibility without being delegated enough authority to carry out the responsibility. The current global outreach of business and the resultant pressures affecting managers have caused them to rethink the secretarial function and to delegate more responsibility and implementary authority to their secretaries. While the qualifications set down by employers for various job slots vary with the nature of the particular job and with the requirements of each executive, the trend today is toward better-educated secretaries who are willing and qualified to accept and perform with competence as many tasks as can be delegated to them. Some of these tasks are specialized and demanding and require good judgment in their execution; many of them were once considered administrative or executive functions. The executive-extender trend is best exemplified by the results of a recent survey of over one thousand responding members of the National Secretaries Association (International) conducted in the United States and Canada. This survey reveals that about fifty percent of the respondents had had at least one year of college and that over seventy percent of them had received their secretarial training at business colleges or in high schools. Almost three-fourths of the respondents work with one executive only, while the remaining one-fourth supervise at least one or more employees. Approximately three-fourths of the secretaries who replied to the questionnaire perform duties other than taking dictation, answering the telephone, greeting guests, typing communications, and routing the mail. Some of these additional duties are as follows:

1. Preparing rough drafts of executive responses to communications
2. Reading, signing, and sending out some executive correspondence
3. Composing speeches, memorandums, or reports for the executive to edit
4. Composing articles for publication
5. Editing copy prepared and typed by others
6. Consulting reference sources to obtain information desired by the executive
7. Abstracting information from various sources for the executive's use
8. Selecting or recommending office equipment systems and supplies for purchase by the organization

Such duties clearly indicate that the secretarial function is generally being extended to encompass many specialized tasks that the executive may delegate.

Another aspect in the changing role of the secretary is the effect of rapid and continual technological developments especially in office equipment systems. Rather than eliminating the secretary from the office, technological developments have freed her from many time-consuming routine tasks so that she may be better employed in the more specialized areas of office work that have been listed above. For example, a secretary may now retrieve information from a computerized file without having to leave the work station. Desktop and pocket calculators have greatly streamlined and speeded accounting procedures. Sophisticated copying equipment enables secretaries to handle increased paperwork with relative ease. Typewriters with automatic correcting features expedite the processing of written communications. Highly sophisticated telecommunications equipment systems are now available to facilitate and speed oral business communication. And other electronic devices such as dictation and transcription machines increase input and output and markedly decrease turnaround time.

While not every person will aspire to or reach the rank of executive secretary, every member of the secretarial profession can strive to attain a higher level of competence by giving considerable thought to just how far she wants to go in the field and how she can improve her skills and general education in order to become more competitive. Self-evaluation is essential for those who aspire to business careers, for those who are already employed as secretaries, and for those who are considering reentry into the work force. In short, one should make a mental balance sheet of one's assets and liabilities and then decide how the assets can be improved still further and how the liabilities can be eradicated or transformed into assets. For example, a secretary who is weak in English grammar should give serious thought to taking a course in the subject. A secretary who is unfamiliar with a modern electronic calculator but who has to perform routine accounting functions as a part of a job could benefit herself and the company by asking the company to purchase one so that she may learn how to use it efficiently, thereby saving valuable company time. (See Chapter 12, section 12.2, for further details on the use of calculators.) A secretary in a corporation that is involved in international business operations could improve her professional status and her value to the company by learning a foreign language that might be useful in assisting the executive. In the fast-paced business world of this decade, it is too easy just to keep afloat—to do one's job and keep one day or one hour ahead, rather than to take the time to sit down and evaluate oneself. This evaluation is absolutely essential and cannot be overemphasized because the competition for jobs and promotions shows no signs of slackening; rather, it is stiffening. An ambitious secretary owes it to herself and to the employer to have specific career goals and to have the courage and the competence to attain them.

GENERAL ABILITIES AND ESSENTIAL KNOWLEDGE

Prioritizing tasks It is essential that a secretary be able to organize the work to be done so that the most important tasks are carried out first. The executive knows that smooth office work flow depends on the secretary's ability not only to handle routine matters but also to set up sensible work priorities—a skill that demands good judgment. The competent secretary knows those matters that can be handled with prior approval of the executive, recognizes the kinds of problems that should be relayed to other executives for action, and knows what material must be sent directly to the executive for whom she works.

Discovering and pointing out areas for improvement in one's office An attentive secretary also is on the alert for situations that could be improved through the development of new procedures. And she tries to come up with concrete suggestions for the implementation of these improvements.

Complex record-keeping functions The public sector of our economy—government on all levels—has become more and more closely tied in with the business sector. The most obvious example of government influence on private industry is taxation imposed on businesses by federal, state, and local governments. As a result, executives and secretaries have acquired increased responsibilities for maintaining accurately the financial records that are used in the preparation of tax reports. For example, many changes in payroll procedures have evolved as a result of government regulations. The preparation of numerous and often quite complex reports by businesses at the behest of governmental agencies also requires the special attention of top-level secretaries. They must know who will need the information, what type of information will be required, and in what form it should be presented.

Multinational business problems An increasing number of our major U.S. corporations are not only national but also international and multinational in character. Since these companies operate in countries throughout the world, the secretaries to the corporate executives of such firms are involved in planning for international travel by the executives. In addition, a competent executive-level secretary should be sufficiently familiar with pertinent laws and regulations indigenous to a particular country to enable her to assist a manager in researching, interpreting, and applying them. Other desirable skills would include a broad background in the customs and history of the country or countries with which the executive deals and the ability to speak at least one foreign language.

The communication and retrieval of information As the U.S. economy is increasingly affected by more complex relationships between corporations and government as well as by the global reach of modern business, the secretary needs to be able to acquire, handle, store, retrieve, and understand varied types of information as rapidly and as efficiently as possible. Such information may be acquired manually, mechanically, or electronically. Even in an era of automation, manual techniques of recording data are used on certain business forms and communications. On such forms the secretary may record information or instructions which are to be conveyed to others within a company or to other organizations. Examples of this type of record are purchase orders, cost tickets, expense accounts, and credit memorandums. Letters are not only important conduits of information but are also one of the many ways in which the corporate image is projected. Reports are also a vital information medium, as they assist in keeping designated persons abreast of past, present, and future management actions. Secretaries may also acquire data orally (as at conferences or meetings or through telephone conversations).

The handling of data is called *information processing*. In the office, data may be accurately and rapidly obtained through mechanical means by the secretary with the aid of devices such as electronic calculators, photocopying machines, media typewriters, computers, transcribing machines, and microfilm units. These devices assist one in preparing payroll records, in copying personnel records, in transcribing dictated letters, in searching for noncurrent information, and in updating current information.

1.2

THE IMPORTANCE OF SELF-IMPROVEMENT

GENERAL EDUCATION AND ITS FURTHERANCE

It has already been mentioned that the increasing complexity and worldwide interaction of business, industry, and government have led executives as a group to become more conscious of the value of college-educated secretaries. The well-educated secretary has a broader outlook and a more acute awareness of national and international problems. More and more managers are actively seeking secretaries having both strong liberal arts backgrounds and good technical skills. Many companies offer tuition-refund plans that encourage secretaries to continue their formal education in business schools, community colleges, and universities. Company in-service training programs are typically conducted at all levels; in addition, many companies cosponsor special educational seminars with professional, managerial, and secretarial associations.

Top-level secretaries have often indicated that the most important factors contributing to their success are a sound general education especially in social studies and psychology; skill in typewriting, shorthand, and transcription; a strong knowledge of business mathematics and accounting; an ability to use transcribing and other types of office machines; a thorough competence in the use of the English language for editing and composing written communications; an ability to meet and get along with people based on and linked with a sure knowledge of acceptable business etiquette; and maintenance of sensible work habits.

IMPROVEMENT OF TECHNICAL SKILLS

Today, executives emphasize high-level office skills as requisites for secretarial placement and advancement. As a result, some secretaries report that they have had to learn how to implement specialized office procedures and use sophisticated communications equipment while actually being on the job. Firms which administer tests to applicants for office positions frequently include tests of typewriting, shorthand transcription, spelling, business mathematics and English usage, as well as a personality inventory, a general aptitude test, and an inventory of interest preferences in their evaluations of these applicants. The following paragraphs examine specific skills and delineate ways to improve them.

Shorthand and transcription Every secretary should periodically review the basic shorthand manual for the system that she uses—whether it be Gregg, Pitman, or some other. A relearning of theory, rules, and basic shorthand forms helps to prevent one from carelessly distorting outlines when recording rapid dictation. This self-review and relearning of basic shorthand ensures more rapid and accurate transcription of dictation. Personnel directors consider that a secretary at the time of initial employment should be able to take dictation at a rate of 90 to 100 words per minute and should be able to produce an accurate transcript from this dictation. Higher standards are needed, of course, for secretarial positions that demand greater or more specialized dictation skills.

Speed in shorthand can be acquired by obtaining and using the progressive speed dictation cassettes, records, or tapes available from commercial publishers. Dictation training tapes may also be prepared by the individuals for whom the secretary works. The normal types of office communications (such as letters, memorandums, reports, legal briefs, or engineering specifications) recorded at varying speeds will provide excellent skill-building practice for the new or inexperienced secretary.

Typewriting Many companies set down for new employees specific entrance standards for typewriting. The required typing rate varies from 40 to 60 words a minute with the degree of accuracy dependent on the amount of typing involved in the particular job. If a secretary works for a company which does not have its own secretarial manual, she should carefully read Chapters 5, 6, 8, and 9 of this book to obtain detailed information on automated typewriting, on the typing of business letters, on the implementation of special typing projects (as reports), and on writing letters for an executive, respectively. She should also practice timed-writing exercises to improve her typewriting speed. In large offices secretaries should frequently check the company's secretarial manual (usually prepared by the secretarial services division or by the personnel department's training section) for recommended setup of written-communication formats.

Proofreading and editing skills All secretaries need to strive for perfection in proofreading. Extraordinary proficiency in proofreading is usually acquired by being very attentive to details when rereading transcribed dictation to ensure that meaningful information is conveyed to the reader. One way to check for effectiveness of communication is to read aloud parts of typed materials that may at first glance seem meaningless.

Editing skills will depend greatly upon the person for whom the secretary works. Quite often, simple editing is performed by the employer and is easy to follow. As the secretarial position becomes more complex, an understanding of the editing guidelines and symbols that are commonly found in general office manuals will suffice. To attain high-level editing skills, however, one really needs to invest in a journalism course that presents editing techniques in depth. (See also Chapter 8, section 8.8, for further details on the mechanics of proofreading.)

Business mathematics A secretary may conduct a review of basic business mathematics by obtaining a programmed-learning text on the subject. After reviewing the general arithmetical processes, the secretary will then be directed to the types of mathematical operations that may be needed in preparing payrolls and insurance registers.

Listening skills A secretary must be able to follow instructions precisely as given by the executive. She needs to listen carefully to oral instructions in order to comprehend them and convey them to others if necessary. While listening, the secretary should try to get to the heart of the subject or the problem being discussed. Telephone conversations are of such importance that she needs to listen carefully not only for the name of the caller but also for the purpose of the call so that she can handle the call herself or accurately record the message for someone else to handle later. When taking notes in a conference or at a meeting, the secretary cultivates the ability to listen purposefully in order to cull important matters that must be recorded and to screen out extraneous information.

Creativity Professional secretaries who have a high degree of imaginative ability can put it to work in many ways, such as developing interesting and attractive layouts for the office, drafting more efficient forms for work simplification, and devising innovative ways of working with other members of the office staff. The secretary should use initiative in finding original and creative ways to assist the executive.

HUMAN RELATIONS

Good human relations in business basically center around the secretary's ability to react in a positive way to the persons with whom she is working. A good working relationship with the executive is of the utmost importance to the secretary. The secretary's first responsibility in this area is to understand the employer as an individual. In addition, a secretary must also be aware of the particular goals and problems that are associated with an executive's position. A manager often has to accept heavy responsibilities, make demanding corporate decisions, and work under extreme pressure. A secretary's loyalty both to superior and to company is very important if she and the executive are to work together as a team. A secretary must be trustworthy to merit her employer's confidence and to be entrusted with the handling of confidential and personal material such as the executive's business affairs which often must be dealt with responsibly and expeditiously when he or she is away from the office.

A good employer-secretary team will cooperatively develop guidelines to enable the secretary to assume shared administrative responsibility for routine duties, to screen out nonessential from essential interruptions, and to supervise the work of designated co-workers or subordinates. In this way, the secretary may proceed to exercise initiative and creativity in such a way as to complement the overall goals, systems, and policies of the firm.

A secretary should work well with her peers—those individuals holding comparable positions in other offices within the organization. Of equal importance is the secretary's ability to get along with all co-workers, regardless of their professional levels. In doing so, she should display loyalty, dependability, and good judgment. As she works with these individuals, her constant goal is to learn more about the business and to assume a substantial amount of the office workload with maximum competence and at the same time with minimum supervision.

Many secretaries supervise other employees. This may involve planning and organizing work assignments as well as instructing personnel on acceptable office procedures. An effective supervisor tries to foresee unusual situations before they arise. She also should be able to be a temporary substitute for a worker who may be unexpectedly absent. The manner in which a person performs as a supervisor and the relationship maintained with those being supervised have a great deal to do with building and preserving a smooth-working office organization.

Good working relations must be assured with individuals such as visitors, maintenance personnel on call, mailmen, or messengers who have business dealings with an organization. The secretary can be proud of the position she holds in a company if she assists in creating and maintaining a high level of goodwill within the organization and if she works to promote a positive corporate image to outsiders. Her success in this accomplishment paves the way for further advancement within the firm.

1.3

UPWARD MOBILITY WITHIN SECRETARIAL RANKS

Advancement from the position of stenographer to senior stenographer or secretary will depend upon the quality of the work performed, the willingness of the individual to acquire education beyond the high-school level, and an interest in company operations. The following paragraphs examine various general levels of secretarial work and explain methods of advancement.

SECRETARIAL LEVELS WITHIN ORGANIZATIONS

Pre-secretarial The person who works for a junior executive is more likely to function as a receptionist or a clerk-typist rather than a secretary per se. Many duties will center upon people-to-people contacts such as dealing with visitors, handling telephone conversations, and making appointments (see also Chapter 2, pages 15–22). A position of this caliber is often referred to as *pre-secretarial.* The person on the pre-secretarial level enhances the likelihood of promotion to a full secretarial position if she performs competently and desires promotion enough to work for it.

Secretarial A person in a secretarial position will find that stenographic skills will be essential to the position but that additional administrative duties will fall to her as well. Many of these, such as opening and routing the mail, ordering new supplies, daily filing, and answering the telephone, will seem strictly routine; but they represent the first steps in acceptance of individual responsibility since they are performed with little or no supervision. They thus merit the utmost care and attention. Other duties that may be assigned to a secretary include typing correspondence and other written communications, setting up travel itineraries, determining the payroll for a section, or handling a petty cash fund on a regular basis. This kind of secretary functions as a generalist—one who has diverse capabilities and responsibilities.

In large corporations today, the secretary can lend administrative support to the executive by handling many time-consuming details and tasks such as the following: compiling and organizing information for reports and long memorandums, maintaining confidential files, disseminating information relative to administrative policies, researching data for presentations to be given by the executive, composing and dictating certain letters, and performing any other duties so delegated by management. Frequently, the title *administrative secretary* is given to the secretary who functions in an administrative-support capacity, often within the framework of a corporate word processing center.

Corporations using word processing systems usually identify secretarial functions under two major classifications: administrative secretaries and corresponding secretaries. Each of these classifications contains numerous subclassifications representative of career-growth opportunities leading to supervisory-level positions within each division.

Administrative secretarial centers are staffed with a team of two or more secretaries who work closely with a group of executives to lend administrative support in handling three basic functions exclusive of typewriting: business mail, telephone communications, and records/files. In administrative secretarial centers the emphasis is on the use of initiative and creativity in oral and written communication, expert editing and proofreading, efficient planning, organizing and scheduling work priorities, research techniques, and other pertinent areas.

On the other hand, special centers for corresponding secretaries are designed to handle all typewriting in the form of machine transcription, magnetic keyboarding, and other kinds of specialized typewriting. (See Chapter 5 for further details.) Here again, career-path opportunities are available to the corresponding secretary who excels in oral and written communication, effective time management, efficient recording and production of assigned tasks, human relations, and in many other important areas.

In meeting the obligations of a particular job, a secretary will gradually assume as much administrative responsibility as is consistent with her capabilities and with the employer's willingness to delegate duties. When a secretary knows an executive's work thoroughly and has exhibited competence to make some executive decisions, she may be promoted to the position of administrative assistant. This secretary is one considered extremely competent in public relations and one who thus epitomizes the best image of the company.

SPECIALIZED SECRETARIAL POSITIONS

Secretarial employment opportunities are available in specialized fields such as law and medicine as well as in engineering and other technical areas. Secretarial positions may also be secured in other countries through the Foreign Service of the U.S. Department of State or with U.S. multinational corporations.

Those who plan to enter a particular field often prefer to develop general experience in a business or government office before applying for specialized jobs (as in science). A description of some important specialized secretarial positions is given below.

The legal secretary This person performs varied duties depending on the size and nature of the firm for which she works, whether one attorney or a partnership. Also, such a secretary may be employed by a legal division in a large corporation. A general practicing lawyer handles all types of legal transactions. In a large firm, on the other hand, each lawyer usually specializes in one branch of law. Most large corporations have in-house law departments staffed by lawyers qualified in virtually every field of law needed in the company's operations (such as security law, antitrust law, insurance law, or labor law).

Courts on all levels provide a variety of legal secretarial positions. One of the most demanding jobs is that of secretary to a judge whose court docket is extremely crowded. Some secretaries are also employed by officials who are lawyers and who have become members of city councils, or have been elected to state legislatures or to the United States Congress.

A working knowledge of legal terminology and procedures is vital to the competence of a legal secretary. A standard law dictionary such as *Black's Law Dictionary* is an invaluable reference tool. Familiarity with legal matters such as pleadings, deeds, and subpoenas is expected of the legal secretary. She is also called upon to type and format legal documents such as briefs, proxies, wills, rental leases, and abstracts. A legal secretary may need to hold a notary's commission so that she can notarize papers. In a small law office or partnership a legal secretary may assume much of the responsibility for managing the routines of the legal practice. For example, it is vital that she be constantly alert to the lawyer's calendar that indicates dates for pending cases, cases that are current, and other such events. Many legal secretaries also serve as apprentices or paralegal aides as they continue part-time education at a college or law school.

The medical secretary This person has more opportunities than are available in most other areas of secretarial specialization. The secretary who has a strong preparation in medical terminology, medical shorthand, and medical office procedures can choose from a wide variety of jobs. The most obvious positions are those in doctors' or dentists' offices, in hospitals and clinics, and in government health departments. But one should not overlook such additional possibilities as those in corporations having medical departments or in companies manufacturing medical supplies and pharmaceuticals. If one is also interested in editorial work, one should investigate research foundations and companies publishing technical works in the medical field.

The duties of the medical secretary will vary according to the nature and size of the employing organization; also, the diversity of duties will depend on the scope and degree of specialization of the employer. For example, if she works for a large medical insurance company she is involved with claims for hospitalization benefits. If working for doctors in a large joint practice, she makes appointments for their patients as well as transfers of patients to other physicians, arranges with cooperating hospitals for the admission of patients assigned by doctors in the joint practice, and spends a great deal of time typing and filing medical records. In particular, a medical secretary is responsible for typing case histories and patients' records, receiving payments from patients for their medical bills, and ordering office supplies. If qualified, and if such duties are delegated to her, she may be requested to secure personal medical data from patients, take temperatures and pulse rates, prepare patients for examination, or even sterilize some medical instruments.

Preparation for medical secretaryship includes instruction in accounting and in the maintenance of financial records adapted to doctors' and dentists' offices and practice in working with hospital records and insurance forms. Essential qualifications for the medical secretary are a sympathetic grasp of human problems and an ability to guard confidential matters.

If an individual likes working as a medical secretary, she may wish to enroll at a school that prepares its students to become medical assistants. Such preparation gives one a thorough background in the basic sciences, laboratory practice, and the fundamentals of patient care. The graduate medical assistant works closely with physicians in obtaining case-history data, in conducting such laboratory tests as blood counts, and, when requested, in applying and removing surgical dressings. At times a medical assistant may be expected to operate some of the less formidable equipment in the office.

The technical secretary This person specializes in the preparation of technical correspondence and reports (as for engineering firms). Typing tabulations and typing chemical and mathematical formulas featuring special characters are typical tasks. Fundamentals of accounting are also necessary as a background for the technical secretary since she works with often highly complex financial records (such as those associated with research contracts).

If a secretary's company deals with classified information, she may have to be cleared by the U.S. Government to handle such documents, and, if so cleared, she will be expected to follow carefully all security regulations imposed by the Government (see Chapter 6, section 6.9 and Chapter 11, sections 11.6 and 11.9 for specific information on handling classified data).

The person who wishes to become a technical secretary should be well prepared in the physical sciences (such as chemistry and physics) as well as in mathematics and statistics. She should also be familiar with scientific and engineering terminology and ought to be proficient in recording technical dictation.

Employment possibilities in other countries If an individual is interested in foreign-based employment, one of the best sources is a domestically based U.S. corporation that also operates internationally. Although knowledge of a foreign language may not be required for a job abroad, such a skill will increase one's opportunities for obtaining and holding a good position.

The United States Department of State posts its secretaries to more than three hundred foreign countries, where Foreign Service secretaries work in embassies and consulates. General qualifications for such positions include the following:

1. The applicant must be at least twenty-one years of age.
2. The applicant must be a U.S. citizen, and, if he or she is married, the spouse must also be a U.S. citizen.
3. The applicant must be a high-school graduate or hold a high-school equivalency certificate.
4. The applicant and the applicant's dependents (if any) must successfully pass a medical examination.
5. The applicant must pass clerical, shorthand, and typing tests given by a U.S. Civil Service Examiner.
6. The applicant must have appropriate work experience.

Additional factors that are considered when an applicant is being evaluated include whether or not he or she exhibits an interest in foreign affairs and is willing to learn a foreign language if necessary. Of course, the applicant who already speaks a foreign language has an additional advantage.

A Foreign Service secretary must be willing to serve anywhere in the world. Although the State Department will consider one's choice of posting, there is no guarantee that the choice will be fulfilled. Successful applicants are assigned to the Foreign Service Institute for an orientation and training period, after which they receive their assignments. Those persons interested in applying for Foreign Service secretarial positions should write to the Recruitment Branch, Employment Division, U.S. Department of State, Washington, DC 20520.

POST-SECRETARIAL OPPORTUNITIES

College graduates aspiring to certain professional and executive jobs frequently find that their best entrance is by way of a secretarial position. This may be the case in such areas as publishing, fashion design, personnel, and television. If office assistants perform satisfactorily, they may be given assignments related, for example, to television programming or news writing for a city newspaper. These "glamour" fields offer secretaries an opportunity to use their creative talents.

An increasing number of secretaries are qualifying for positions as personnel directors, production coordinators, editors, advertising executives, office managers, programmers, and systems analysts. Although the career path from secretarial to nonsecretarial managerial posts is not common, there is, nevertheless, a trend toward filling managerial positions by promotion from within a company or an industry. Thus, talented individuals entering the secretarial field can realistically aspire to post-secretarial positions at a higher level. They do, however, need a few years' experience to learn as well as possible the total operations of their companies and to prove that they are capable of assuming administrative duties.

The corporate secretary occupies a unique position in business society. In theory he or she reports directly to the Board of Directors, but in practice answers to the president or chief executive officer of the company. The corporate secretary of a company holds such important responsibilities as these: organizing corporate meetings, recording minutes of these meetings, maintaining a record of activities in stocks and bonds, improving stockholder relations, keeping records of trademark information, and handling corporate books, records, and reports.

PROFESSIONAL CERTIFICATION AS AN AID TO ADVANCEMENT

The Certified Professional Secretary In 1951, the National Secretaries Association (International) inaugurated the program for the Certified Professional Secretary (CPS), which is administered by the Institute for Certifying Secretaries. To qualify as a CPS, a secretary must have successfully completed a two-day examination that is given each year in May at approved colleges and universities throughout the United States.

The CPS examination is based on an analysis of secretarial work, with emphasis on judgment, understanding, and administrative ability gained through education and work experience. The Institute has indicated that the examination includes skills, techniques, and knowledge in the following specific areas:

Part I: Environmental Relationships in Business
Principles of human relations and understanding of self, subordinates, peers, and superiors. Fundamentals of one's own needs and motivations, nature of conflict problem-solving techniques, essentials of supervision and communication, leadership styles, and understanding of the informal organization.

Part II: Business and Public Policy
Major elements of business law involved in the secretary's daily life, particularly contracts and bailments, law of agency and sales, insurance, negotiable instruments, real property, and public policy for governmental regulatory legislation.

Part III: Economics and Management
Applied economics, principles of management, and elements of business operation. Management of personnel, finance, production, and marketing.

Part IV: Financial Analysis and the Mathematics of Business
Principles of financial and managerial accounting. Computations necessary for the analysis and interpretation of financial reports and statistical data.

Part V: Communications and Decision Making
Performance test to establish job priorities involving descriptions of actions to be taken and specifications of how the work is to be completed. Dictation and typewriting abilities and skills required in editing, listening, composing, abstracting, and appraising work.

Part VI: Office Procedures
Knowledge of the basic concepts of current secretarial procedures, office and records management, and business and data processing.

Successful candidates are awarded a certificate from the Institute for Certifying Secretaries. The professional status of a secretary holding this certificate is definitely enhanced. Further information on the Certified Professional Secretary rating may be obtained by writing to the National Secretaries Association (International), 2440 Pershing Road, Kansas City, MO 64108.

The Certified Administrative Manager A new avenue of professional recognition in the form of the C.A.M. (Certified Administrative Manager) designation is now available to those secretaries who later aspire to supervisory or management-level positions in the business world. This new program was initiated in September, 1970, by the AMS, Administrative Management Society (International) for qualified persons in the area of administrative management. (Program eligibility does not depend on AMS membership.) Basically, the plan calls for the candidate to make application for the C.A.M. candidacy and then to meet the C.A.M. program standards within a ten-year period. These standards are as follows:

1. The successful candidate must pass a five-part C.A.M. examination in the fields of personnel management; financial management, control, and economics; administrative services; systems and information management; and managerial skill applied to an in-depth case problem.
2. The successful candidate must have two years of experience at the administrative management level.
3. The successful candidate must have high standards of personal and professional conduct.
4. The successful candidate must provide satisfactory evidence of active participation and/or leadership, within recent years in voluntary organizations.
5. The successful candidate must show evidence of having made contributions to effective administrative management ideas and principles through oral and/or written communications.

The candidate who successfully completes the C.A.M. program becomes a member of the Academy of Certified Administrative Managers with all its rights and privileges including the right to use the initials *C.A.M.* after his or her name on letterheads and after his or her name in signature blocks. Inquiries regarding C.A.M. may be sent to: Director of Professionalization, AMS Headquarters, Willow Grove, PA 19090.

1.4

KNOWING ONE'S COMPANY

The truly forward-thinking secretary assumes the role of the executive extender while working with, rather than for, an executive. The executive's job has become more difficult and yet more challenging because of increased interrelationships between corporations and government, because of skyrocketing labor and production costs, and for many other complex reasons. Automation and other technological advances have occasioned changes in routine operations. Management is now much more sophisticated. Forecasting techniques and market analysis have become more complicated as business competition has become more and more acute. The global thrust of modern business has so broadened the role of the operational executive that he or she needs dependable secretaries and assistants to perform routine tasks whenever possible. Most executives would like to turn larger and larger amounts of routine work over to their secretaries. But to prepare for such increased responsibilities the secretary must truly know her company. The secretary must become thoroughly familiar with the corporate structure, the products, the goals, the achievements, and the basic advertising and marketing strategies of the company. With regard to personnel policies, the secretary must be well acquainted with employer-employee relationships within the corporate hierarchy as well as with company employee benefits. Those company manuals that are pertinent to the secretary's job should be studied thoroughly. She should make a real effort also to understand the people for and with whom she works, as well as the individuals she may supervise.

As a competent secretary advances from one level to another, her associations with the key personnel of the company increase. Few individuals in a company have so great an opportunity to work with top management and thereby learn so much about the operations of the company. Such associations are stimulating and rewarding. As the secretary working at this level is given many associate executive responsibilities, she soon knows more about the company and its operations than many of the department heads and junior executives do.

In a small business operation, a secretary's work is so varied that she has a chance to gain broad experience. In a larger enterprise, on the other hand, she often is assigned to a particular department (such as one specializing in marketing, production, personnel, or law). In such a situation, she may not be so likely to gain company-wide experience unless she remains secretary to an executive who moves up through various departments and managerial levels of the business. However, an in-depth knowledge of one particular aspect of company operations can be invaluable if later on she decides to specialize, for example, as a technical secretary.

Thus, it is clear that the secretary is an integral part of the American business team. It has been pointed out that the pressures on management are acute and that the degree to which a secretary can relieve these pressures effectively is the degree to which she is a successful executive extender. The person who will reach the top and who will remain at the top of the executive secretarial profession is the one who takes the time and makes the extra effort required to continue to grow in general knowledge, technical skills, and human understanding.

NOTE: A brief illustrated guide to the preparation of job application letters and résumés is found on pages 521–524 of the Appendix.

2

CHAPTER TWO

BUSINESS OFFICE INTERFACE: Effective Communication with People

CONTENTS

2.1

ONE-TO-ONE COMMUNICATION

One-to-one communication abounds in business—in using the telephone, in setting up appointments, in greeting visitors, in making introductions, in conversing with others, and in working closely with an executive. Communication with groups of people is also a part of your job—in your receptionist duties, in conference situations, in hosting business social events, in giving directions, and in committee work. Then there are situations in which communication may involve several people or just one person—instructing someone on the details of a job, working with support staff, or chatting with fellow employees.

Success or failure at work depends to a large extent upon the way you communicate. Numerous studies have shown that it is less often a lack of skill that causes people to lose their jobs or to stagnate than it is their inability to communicate and get along with people. In your communicating, does what you send reach the receiver the way you meant it to? Are you constantly thinking about what effect your message will have on the person who is listening to or observing you? Are you aware of the importance of working graciously with and through people? Discussion in this chapter centers on specific ways to communicate more effectively in the areas just mentioned.

TELEPHONE USAGE

The correct use of the telephone can speed business, build goodwill, project the best possible image of your company, elevate your office in the eyes of your superiors, and thus be important to your own success. If you train your ear to recognize at once frequent callers' voices so that you can address them by name, you will gain the reputation of being exceptionally keen.

Knowing your equipment is of first priority. Telephone company representatives will be glad to answer questions about card dialers, Call-A-Matic equipment, the Call Director or the Call Commander, Centrex, exclusion buttons, key telephones, and Magicall equipment. They will explain special signaling devices such as gongs for noisy areas, tone ringers for persons with hearing impairment, buzzers or chimes instead of rings, and signal light attachments—any one of which may be secured for your telephone (see also Chapter 14 for more discussion of telecommunications equipment).

Of second priority is developing the habit of picking up a pen and reaching for a pad to write on as the phone rings. Simultaneously, you should put that smile into your voice which will make just the right impression on the caller. An alert, pleasant, well-modulated, cordial, cheerful voice is a necessity. Tact, courtesy, and a genuine attempt to help the caller are basic to good telephone usage.

Incoming calls Try to answer at the end of the first ring: Not only is it discourteous to the caller to let the phone ring and ring, but it also will irritate both him and any executive who happens to be near enough to hear your phone ringing several times without being answered. Under no circumstances should you continue to talk to someone in the office after you have picked up the receiver and not yet spoken into it. It is also best to speak directly into the instrument, keeping the mouth from about one-half inch to one inch from it.

Some offices are equipped with the Spokesman or a speakerphone, which allow you to have both hands free to look for a file, to compute amounts on your calculator, or to flip through the pages of a book while carrying on a conversation with the caller. If you are having a conference and everyone present needs to hear both sides of a conversation, a speakerphone will make this possible since it amplifies the caller's voice; for convenience, the volume may be adjusted. For private conversations, the instrument may be used as a conventional telephone.

Identify your office and/or yourself (depending upon office preference). But avoid saying things like, "Mr. Bonn's desk," because desks don't talk! And if you give your name, it isn't necessary to add, "Speaking." Never address a woman as "Madam," as it is often taken to be uncomplimentary.

If you must screen calls in order to find out who is calling, the best words to use are, "May I ask who's calling, please?" On the other hand, if you say, "May I tell him (*or* her) who's calling, please?" or "May I say who's calling?" you have indicated to the caller that the person he or she is trying to reach is there; such a situation might be embarrassing if the one being called chose <u>not</u> to take the call at that particular moment.

In transferring calls, be sure to tell the caller what you are going to do; otherwise, the caller will think that you have hung up on him or that the line is dead. You also should give the caller the proper number for returning the call in case your connection is broken during the transfer.

If you must leave the phone to obtain authorized information, get back to the caller before thirty seconds have elapsed. To the caller, thirty seconds will seem interminable. If it becomes clear that your task will take more than thirty seconds (and most tasks do), return to the phone and ask the caller if he cares to wait longer or if you may return the call later.

When you take a message, beware of saying, "I'll have him (*or* her) call you." The proper words are something like, "I'll ask him to call" or "I'll give him the message the moment he comes in." (After all, you really don't have an executive do things!) The next thing to do is to write down the message; don't attempt to remember it. Many expert secretaries keep carbon copies of telephone messages clipped together so that they can be referred to for telephone numbers, amounts, sizes, quantities, names, and other important information should the original message be misplaced. This material also serves as an informal record of telephone messages over a period of time. A listing or logging of calls is a helpful procedure; an *action* column will also provide valuable information. Books containing duplicate telephone message forms are also available.

Each message should be dated and should contain the time that the message was received. Of course, telephone numbers and names should be unfailingly correct. You should always indicate by initials or in some other manner that you took the message. It's a good idea to repeat a message—especially a complex one—so that you will be sure that you have taken it down correctly. If a message must be repeated to a caller while there are others present who may overhear the conversation, ask the caller to repeat the message to you. In this way, you preserve confidentiality and ensure accuracy. Precise messages are very important; vague messages only confuse.

If it is necessary to spell names, a standard code for indicating letters could be used. This code, which is handy for differentiating often-confused letters such as *B* and *D, F* and *S,* or *B* and *V,* is as follows:

A-Alfa	G-Golf	M-Mike	S-Sierra	Y-Yankee
B-Bravo	H-Hotel	N-November	T-Tango	Z-Zulu
C-Charlie	I-India	O-Oscar	U-Uniform	
D-Delta	J-Juliett	P-Papa	V-Victor	
E-Echo	K-Kilo	Q-Quebec	W-Whiskey	
F-Foxtrot	L-Lima	R-Romeo	X-X-ray	

When you repeat numbers to a caller, the proper articulation is: 415-334-2541 pronounced: *Area Code four one five* pause *three three four* pause *two five* pause *four one.* 702-469-2500 pronounced: *Area Code seven oh two* pause *four six nine* pause *two five hundred.*

If a caller dials you by mistake, be courteous and never say, "Wrong Number" and abruptly hang up. Instead, you can say, "You've reached the wrong number, I believe." The caller might be a customer who has confused your number with the one above or below it in his own listing.

Should the caller ask for someone who is already using another line of the telephone, you could say, "I'm sorry, he's talking on another line," but not "He's on another line." (Is he hanging there???) And follow this statement with "May I help you or would you care to speak to someone else?" Of course, you would never say, "She hasn't come back from lunch yet" (and it's 3 p.m.) or "He's playing golf today," or "I don't know where he went" or "He isn't in," without elaboration. Telephone courtesy requires that you give correct information but at the same time that you do not state facts that could lead to a misunderstanding and that you do not divulge information you are not authorized to give. Discretion is important. Be helpful but not too revealing—learn to be courteously noncommittal.

Always end a call with "Goodbye," but be sure to let the caller hang up first. After the caller has hung up, replace your own receiver gently. If the caller persists in talking, you might have to say, "I'm sorry, but I have a call on another line," or "I'd like to talk longer, but I'm due at a meeting now," or "We must continue this at another time, for I have an important letter I must finish before the next mail pickup," or "Excuse me, but Mr. Nichols has just buzzed for me to take dictation."

You and your executive should set up a priority list for his or her accepting calls. It might look something like this:

First—internal calls from superiors
Second—calls from customers or clients
Third—internal calls from others
Fourth—calls from suppliers or salesmen
Fifth—calls from civic, trade, and service organizations
Last—personal calls

You might want to arrange a buzzer signal with the executive to let him know of especially urgent phone calls that are waiting for his attention.

You may be asked to take dictation over the telephone. Because you have just one hand free (unless you have one of the hands-free telephone devices that have been referred to previously in this section), you may have to ask that some things be repeated. It is wise to read the entire dictation back to the dictator when he is finished. If you are asked to monitor a telephone conversation and to take notes on it, get the main points as you would do if you were taking notes at a lecture.

Some secretaries refuse to put a call through to their executive until the caller is ready to speak. If this happens to you, don't react stubbornly—perhaps the secretary is following orders. And perhaps your executive may, at some time, request that a call not be put through until you have made certain that the caller is already on the line; or, if your executive is making a call, he or she may wish to make sure that the person being called is on the line first.

Outgoing calls When you make calls for an executive, always be sure that he or she is available before you actually place the call. Sometimes an executive will ask you to make a call for him; then for some reason, he will step out of the office for a minute or two. You don't want to be left holding the call with the person whom you have just dialed waiting impatiently on the other end of the line. Such a situation can be embarrassing for the secretary and the executive, and it needlessly wastes the time of the individual being called—not to mention irritating him.

Having looked up the correct number in a directory (calls to the Directory Assistance Operator should be avoided unless absolutely necessary), you then dial the number. Correct dialing can be assured if you follow this procedure: dial the number by inserting your finger or a dialer into the proper number hole (if you are using a dial telephone), pull it to the stop bar, and then remove your finger or the dialer to allow the mechanism to return to the starting position by itself. If you leave your finger in the dial and allow finger and dial to return together to the starting point, you may cause the telephone to malfunction. You should allow the telephone to ring at least six or seven times (the telephone company recommends that you let it ring as many as ten times if necessary). When the telephone is answered, identify yourself and state your business in a clear, coherent, polite way.

Some local listings in the telephone directory are often difficult to find. These items may include:

Buildings found under "Office Buildings" in the Yellow Pages

City offices under the name of the city

Company names beginning with letters at the beginning of their respective alphabetical listings

Consulates under the letter C or under the name of the country or the nationality or in the Yellow Pages under "Consulates & Other Foreign Government Representatives"

County offices under the name of the county

Emergency numbers in the front of the directory

Federal Government offices under "United States Government"

Information (labeled "Directory Assistance") usually 411—to be sure, look in the front of the directory

Internal Revenue Service sometimes under the letter *I* but more often under "United States Government"

Libraries in the White Pages under the name of the city, under the letter *P* for *Public Library,* under the first letter of the name of the library if it is privately owned, or under a college or a university listing if it is a part of such an institution; or in the Yellow Pages under "Libraries."

Long-distance numbers 0 or 211 or 110 or 1—look in the front of the directory

Post Office under "United States Government"

Radio stations under the call letters at the first of their alphabetical listing; they may also be listed under "Radio Station . . ." and in the Yellow Pages under "Radio Stations & Broadcasting Companies"

State offices under the name of the state

Telegram service under "Western Union"

Television stations under their call letters at the first of their alphabetical listing; they may also be under "Television Station . . ." and in the Yellow Pages under "Television Stations & Broadcasting Companies"

Long-distance calls may be of two kinds. Station-to-station calls are less expensive and are made when the caller is willing to talk with anyone who answers. Consult your directory to ascertain the times and rates for "station" calls. If, for instance, you are on the West Coast and need to call someone on the East Coast in the morning, a call before 8 a.m. costs considerably less than it would after 8 a.m., since it's already 11 a.m. in the East, of course. Be sure to always check time zones before making long-distance calls to be sure you are within usual working hours. Remember, too, that not all states change to daylight saving time; be sure to check with the Operator about this. "Station" calls may be dialed directly on many phones by dialing the ten digits. In some states it is necessary to dial 1 first to get into the long-distance mode—check your directory when uncertain.

Person-to-person calls are made when the caller wants to talk only to one specific person. These calls are made in one of two ways:

1. Dial the Operator and say "This is a call to (name of *city* being called) at (number of telephone) to speak personally to (name of person)." If information is given in this order, the Operator can be starting the call while you are continuing to supply information.
2. Use direct-distance dialing (DDD), in which you dial 0 first followed by the complete telephone number; the Operator will answer, and while your call goes through the system, you give the Operator the name of the person to whom you want to speak. If you do not have the number you want to call, you obtain it by dialing the appropriate area code and 555-1212 anywhere in the United States. This is a Directory Assistance number and there is usually no charge for this call.

Most secretaries keep a record of all out-of-town and toll calls that have been made so that telephone charges can be checked against this list and costs can be allocated to customers, clients, or projects. If you are required to get the charges immediately after a call has been completed, you do so by asking the Operator before you say anything else when you place the call, as "Operator, please quote T and C on this call." (*T and C* mean *time and charges.*)

A variety of long-distance calls are available to you:

1. Appointment calls are made with the Operator. You ask to have a call placed at a certain time, which is done. The Operator then calls you when the caller is ready to converse.

2. Collect calls follow the person-to-person routine. The first thing you say to the Operator is, "This is a collect call," and then you give your name. The Operator will ask the called person if he wishes to accept the charges; if he declines, the call is not completed (unless you are willing to pay for it) and no charge is made.
3. Conference calls can be arranged whereby three to fourteen long-distance points are connected at one time. Ask for the Conference Operator and explain the setup that you desire. All of the persons connected in this manner can talk with one another as if they were around a conference table. Up to forty-nine points can be connected for a one-way conference call where only the speaker can be heard.
4. A credit card call permits a traveler to charge long-distance or toll calls from any telephone by means of a credit card which is issued by the telephone company. The call is placed through the Operator, with your first words being, "This is a credit card call. My card number is . . ." If you want your call charged to another number, say first of all, "Please bill to (area code and telephone number to which the call is to be billed)" and follow with the usual long-distance information.
5. Sequence calls are person-to-person calls handled by the Operator as rapidly as possible in the order you have indicated on the list that you have provided him or her.
6. Messenger calls are used when it is necessary to reach someone who does not have a phone. A messenger is dispatched by the Operator at the distant place to notify the person that there is a call for him.
7. Mobile calls may be made to or from a telephone installed in a car or other vehicle (as a train, a plane, or a truck). The mobile number is ordinarily listed in the telephone directory; otherwise, you can ask for the Mobile Service Operator.
8. Overseas calls (including Alaska and Hawaii) require the assistance of the Overseas Operator. Give the Operator the same information that you would give to a regular Long-distance Operator. There may be a delay, but it is possible to call practically every telephone in the world by this method; some direct-distance dialing will soon be available.
9. Shore-to-ship calls are possible if the ship is within calling range and is equipped to accept telephone calls. Ask a Long-distance Operator for the Marine Operator. Give the name of the ship, the name of the person being called, his stateroom number and his telephone number if known. If the ship is in port, it may be possible to use regular telephone lines to call: check with the steamship line office. A written message service to ships, initiated by telephone, is also available. The message is telephoned to an international carrier (as ITT World Communications or RCA Communications) or to Western Union International which will then transfer the message to the international carrier that you designate.

Specialized services at an additional charge are also available from the telephone company. Some of them are:

1. Bellboy—a personalized signaling service within a 40-mile radius. A lightweight unit is worn by the person and when his number is called, the unit buzzes. The wearer immediately goes to any telephone and calls his office to get whatever message is there for him. A variation of this system is called Pageboy, where the wearer may have a choice of the buzzer alone or a combination of the buzzer and a voice message.
2. Extended Area Service (EAS)—a service available to businesses in metropolitan areas. Companies can arrange to have calls to nearby suburbs billed as local rather than as long-distance calls.
3. Federal Telecommunications System (FTS)—a system available to federal government agencies only. This is a nationwide direct-dial system linking the network of government agencies.
4. Foreign-Exchange Service (FX)—a service used when a local telephone number is listed for a company that is not locally based but is situated in a nearby city. The call goes through as locally dialed rather than as long-distance.
5. Private Automatic Branch Exchanges (PABX's)—a system used by hotels, motels, and other organizations requiring special features.

6. Picturephone—a device first used in 1964. Few are in operation now in the United States; but as customer demand rises, they will be more generally used. A small television screen mounted on one's desk can be activated to televise the speaker or show the documents that the speaker may wish to discuss; both participants in the call have the privilege of turning the screen off or on so as to be seen or unseen.
7. Tie-line or Leased Line Telephone Service—a service affording direct contact between branches of business offices.
8. Touch-Tone Telephone—a device used in the conventional way or linked to a computer that may be consulted for such matters as bank balances, billing, credit authorizations, inventory control, ordering, or making reservations. (See also Chapter 14.)
9. Wide Area Telephone Service (WATS)—a system convenient for businesses that make and receive many long-distance calls. A special nationwide access line or just one line within a state or an area is available at a charge for the time the line is in use; individual calls are not charged separately. Inward WATS service (identified by 800 as the prefix to the number) is free to the caller. WATS service is either full-time or measured time and is offered only on a station-to-station basis.

New services and devices are constantly being marketed to make telephone communication better. Message-taking services, call transferrers (or switchers), and recording machines are examples of this type of technological development. If you have an answering service to take calls when the office is closed or the telephones are unmanned, you should establish good rapport with the service and be sure to check with them on a daily basis immediately upon arriving at the office. (For a detailed discussion of telecommunications, see Chapter 14.)

You will find that a list of frequently called numbers is extremely helpful. It is usually typed and attached to the pullout ledge of your desk. It may also be put on cards on a wheel or a rotary file, or it may be written on the pages of a flip-up index pad. The following example illustrates a skeleton file of frequently called numbers. Of course, such a file will vary with one's office requirements:

Accountant
Airlines
Attorney
Building manager or superintendent
Business associates regularly called
Car rental agency
Committee members
Emergency numbers (as ambulance, fire, or police)
Family and friends
Hotels and motels used for company business
Insurance agent
Library information desk
Messenger service
Personal services (as bank, barber, club, dentist, doctor, dry cleaner, garage, organizations of which your executive is a member, stockbroker, stores, tailor, or theater ticket agency)
Post Office information
Railroads
Stationer and office supply store
Time check (exact up-to-the-minute report)
Trade and/or professional associations
Travel agency
Union information
Unlisted numbers
Weather information

A private list of home phone numbers of executives, office employees, and important clients or customers is also very helpful. This list should be considered confidential and should be kept out of sight.

If your office is one in which many long-distance calls are frequently made to certain cities, a file of out-of-town directories may be helpful. You may also find a street-address telephone directory valuable; this type of directory is available for large cities and may be rented from the telephone office.

Your city telephone directory contains much useful information in addition to the regular alphabetical listings. Learn to use the Yellow Pages. Look for the maps showing postal zones and telephone area codes. Some directories have perpetual calendars and a list of numbers to call for the correct time, for current weather information, and for postal rate information. Special instructions for making calls are contained in the front of each directory. A helpful practice is to underline lightly, or to mark with a yellow felt-tip pen any number you look up, thus making it easier to find the next time you need it. Of value, too, is the current city-directory for your locale. This book shows the addresses that have telephones, although telephone numbers are not contained therein.

APPOINTMENTS

Another kind of one-to-one or one-to-more-than-one communication involves making appointments for an exeuctive. Just as extreme diplomacy should be practiced when using the telephone, so too accuracy and attention to detail should be stressed in setting up appointments.

The importance of calendars and reminders A daily calendar for your desk, one for your executive's desk, and a small pocket diary for the executive to carry with him or her are basic to scheduling appointments. Some executives like to use month-at-a-glance or year-at-a-glance calendars, too. One type of permanent calendar is called a tickler file. It may be a small card file or a rotary file having tabs showing the months of the current year and a set of 1–31 date tabs. Tabs for years beyond the current one are also typically used. Two types of information that are put on these cards are extremely important to you as you set up your appointment book each year: (1) special meeting or convention dates in the future years, and (2) weekly events such as departmental conferences, monthly events such as executive committee meetings, and yearly events such as a stockholders' meeting. These reminders often come to your notice near the end of the year, alerting you to record both on your calendar and on your executive's calendar for the following year whatever recurring meetings need to be put there. These items should be entered on the calendars before any other appointments are made.

Efficient scheduling of appointments When making appointments, you will want to keep in mind the following guidelines:

1. If your employer has been away, don't schedule appointments for the day of return.
2. If you make an outside appointment for your executive, telephone before he is ready to leave the office to reconfirm the appointment.
3. Schedule appointments lightly for Monday mornings, Friday afternoons, and days before and after vacations and holidays.
4. Allow time in the morning for the set routines of the day to be accomplished before appointments begin.
5. Avoid late-afternoon appointments so that the work of the day can be completed more easily.
6. Be alert to see that you do not make appointments on weekends or holidays! Remember that other faiths have holidays that may not coincide with yours.
7. When <u>you</u> schedule an appointment, be sure to explain that it is subject to the approval of the executive.
8. Suggest times instead of asking open-ended questions such as "When would you like to see Mr. Nichols?"
9. If you know there may be a delay in keeping an appointment, explain that you will telephone the person involved to reconfirm the date and time.
10. When an appointment is scheduled for someone who is at your desk, type a reminder note for him with the date and time of the appointment and the office number indicated on it.

11. Obtain the telephone number of the person or persons for whom you make an appointment in case the appointment later has to be canceled or rescheduled.

Appointments may be made in several ways:

1. Your executive schedules an appointment, he or she tells you about it, and you make sure it is recorded both on your calendar and on his or her desk calendar.
2. You schedule an appointment with someone over the telephone or in person, you check with the executive to confirm it, and then you add it to both calendars.
3. Someone writes to secure a definite time for an appointment. Once the time is set, you notify the one seeking the appointment of the date and time designated, and you also record it on both calendars.
4. While your executive is conferring with someone, he may call you and ask that you schedule an appointment in the future with that person. When you do so, you make sure the person receives a written or verbal reminder of the appointment, and enter it on both calendars.
5. You or your executive may schedule by mail tentative appointments with out-of-town visitors. These appointments should be entered in pencil on both calendars since they are subject to change.

You may discover, much to your embarrassment, that the executive has scheduled appointments that you know nothing about because he or she has forgotten to tell you about them. Therefore, it is extremely important that you ask your executive each morning to check the pocket diary for any appointments you may not be aware of. Be smilingly persistent about this, for your calendar and your executive's must coincide.

As you get to know your executive better, you will be aware of his attitude toward individuals who seek his time. You will then be able to screen and classify visitors according to his preferences.

Executive reminders Executives need to be reminded of their appointments even though they have a marked calendar before them each day. Some prefer to be reminded by a typed and detailed list of the day's appointments which is already on the desk when they arrive at the office in the morning. Others prefer that an abbreviated list of the next day's appointments be typed on a 3″ × 5″ card and given to them before they leave the office the night before. A quick glance at a typed reminder often is more efficient than reading the handwriting on the daily calendar. Make a copy of the reminder list, check it at the end of the day for correctness, delete all appointments that were not kept, and insert any that were added. It's wise to keep these reminder lists as a log of visitors seen and as a record of places the executive went during the year. Such records are invaluable to substantiate claims for expenses incurred, trips taken, and charges made in case of tax reviews.

2.2

RECEPTION AND VISITORS

Although it will be impossible to find time for everyone who asks to see your employer, all callers must be treated with unfailing courtesy and consideration. You should deal with everyone—visitor, custodian, chief accountant, secretary in the next office, Vice-president for Marketing, mail messenger, Chairman of the Board—with equal kindness because you realize that each one plays an important part in the successful operation of your organization. From the time you greet the visitor to the time he or she leaves the office, you are the official host for your organization —usually the first and last person that the visitor sees.

GENERAL GUIDELINES

If you work in an organization where a receptionist or switchboard operator sees the visitor first, give her a list of the names of persons who have appointments on any given day so that she may recognize them. You will then be notified that a certain visitor is on his way to your office. If the visitor sees you first, your responsibility is greater. In either case, however, cordial and gracious treatment is important no matter what the appearance of the visitor may be. Although some of the most important people to your organization may appear in your eyes to be far-out, this subjective opinion should not affect your professional attitude toward them.

Greeting visitors and remembering names Your greeting of visitors will range from normal courtesy to flattering attention, depending on their importance to your organization. No matter who the visitor is, you should look up from your work immediately and recognize him or her with a smile and a pleasant but not effusive greeting. Mention the name if you possibly can. Remembering faces is sometimes far easier than remembering names. If, however, the visitor has an appointment, you should have carefully reviewed his name in your mind and its correct pronunciation before his arrival at your desk. The first time you heard the visitor's name, you should have made a note of it with the correct spelling and a note on its pronunciation beside it if necessary. (Such a notation could have been made on the business card he gave you before, or on another small card that you have kept in your card file.) For instance, if the name is Tunny, you've written "rhymes with Rooney" beside it; Ratto "rhymes with Motto"; Histed "sounds like Highstead."

You, as a top-notch secretary, should keep a 3" × 5" card file with the names of frequent visitors on separate cards. As news stories mention their names, you make a note of the pertinent facts; if the visitor has sent your executive something special or if he always lunches with the visitor at a special place, you jot these items down on the card also. Before the visitor comes to his appointment, you and the executive review this card for a quick update. Business cards may be stapled or glued to this card and filed by the name of the company represented or by the name of the person. You should date a person's business card on the day you receive it so that you know how up-to-date your information about the individual is. Sometimes a note in shorthand about a person's distinctive features will help you to recall him or her after months have passed.

Remembering names takes effort and a positive attitude—you can train yourself to remember them by repeating them frequently, by reviewing in your own mind at the day's end the names of all the individuals who have come to your desk that day, and by making it a practice to use people's names when you speak with them.

Some executives like to have their secretaries keep a "contact file" in loose-leaf form, the pages of which are arranged by the names of persons whom he or she has met at various functions. Such a file will help the executive to recall individuals especially if he meets great numbers of people regularly. The executive's cooperation is necessary to make this file valuable since he must supply the details of where and when contacts were made and what special information should be recorded. Perhaps the person sent a special beverage for Christmas or for another holiday, perhaps he is a member of a particular organization, perhaps he has had a complimentary copy of a book sent to your executive, or perhaps your employer met him at a prestigious gathering. When this person makes an appointment to see your superior, a quick glance at the book will refresh the latter's memory about the visitor.

Priority visitors Certain visitors will have priority access to your executive: his own superiors and their secretaries, peers with whom he often confers, his immediate staff, and designated relatives. You will learn in time who these people are. There are some callers your executive may prefer to see only at certain times; e.g., all salesmen between 10 a.m. and noon on Wednesdays. Some executives have an open-door policy, which means that they will see anybody at any time. Often a secretary will merely greet the visitor as a public relations gesture and then either announce him on the intercom or indicate that he may go right in. For those visitors who arrive by appointment, a courteous "Good morning, Ms. Linn," or "Good afternoon, Mr. Wood," said with a genuine smile, is the proper greeting.

Receiving and entertaining visitors You neither make the first move to shake hands nor do you rise from your chair unless the caller is extremely distinguished or unusually elderly. Be alert, however; if the visitor takes the lead and offers his hand, don't let it dangle! If the visitor is wearing a coat and hat, show him where to put them or offer to do so yourself. In inclement weather, umbrellas and rainwear should be accommodated before the visitor sees the executive. If you must request that the visitor wait, be sure to ask him to be seated and then provide him with current magazines or newspapers if he wishes them. If coffee is easily available, you might offer it; or you might call attention to an especially attractive view from the office window in order to keep the visitor occupied while waiting.

If the visitor asks to make a telephone call, you of course graciously show him to a private telephone if there is one at hand and you make sure he knows how to operate it. You may offer the use of your own telephone, if necessary, and then give every appearance of not listening to the conversation. If it appears to be personal, quietly leave your desk (being sure that the work on it is covered) for the time the visitor is talking.

Never direct a visitor to the employer's office to wait if your executive is not there unless you have been specifically instructed to do so. If the visitor is an important friend who has never seen the inner office before and you do not expect the executive to be able to see him, you might want to show the caller around the office briefly just as a courteous gesture.

If the visitor wants to converse, let <u>him</u> initiate the conversation. Be careful about offering opinions about people or events that are connected with your organization. Talk should be directed to noncontroversial topics. In other words, the conversation is best confined to something that will be of interest to the visitor—a vacation he has recently had, current news stories about his product or his company, or a trip. If the visitor asks questions about your organization, answer only in generalities. If a visitor is extremely talkative, you may excuse yourself after a few minutes to return to your work. You might say, "You'll have to excuse me as I have these reports (*or* letters *or* memos) that must be done by (specify the time) today."

Problem visitors Some visitors are difficult to be courteous to: they may be gruff, unresponsive, glaring, irritating, aggressive, condescending, or even rude. To be gracious to such people requires much self-discipline and willpower. These visitors are often the ones without appointments, too!

The visitor who has no appointment can be a problem. If you do not know the visitor, a polite "May I help you?" and "May I ask your name and company?" are legitimate ways to greet him. If you are approached by one who has every intention of getting past you to see the executive even though he will neither divulge his name nor tell you the purpose of his visit in spite of the fact that you have already told him there is no possibility of his seeing the executive, you must be extremely firm. You might say any of the following:

1. "I'm sorry, but Mr. Nichols sees visitors only by appointment and he has asked me to find out what you wish to discuss with him before I can schedule an appointment."
2. "Won't you please write your name on this card with a short note to Mr. Nichols and I'll take it in to him?"
3. "I'm carrying out Mr. Nichols' instructions and he'll be very unhappy with me and with you if I disobey them. I suggest that you let him know in writing what you want to discuss with him and I'm sure you'll accomplish a lot more that way than this way."
4. "If you'll let me know what you want, I'll be sure to see that Mr. Nichols hears about it. He'll give me his opinion; you can call me later and I'll give you his answer."
5. "I wish I could be more helpful but Mr. Nichols is working on some very important matters and will be for some time. He's asked that I limit his appointments to those matters directly connected with this present situation and I know it will be some time before this situation changes. The only thing I can suggest is that you write to him."
6. "I'm sorry, but Mr. Nichols has told me that we are not contemplating changing our procedures (*or whatever*) and it would be a waste of your valuable time to wait to see him. I'd suggest that you write to Mr. Nichols and then he will decide whether there is any point in the two of you meeting."

Talking to reporters One of the visitors to your office may be a news reporter who has what he or she thinks is a tip about something relating to your company or to one of its employees. He may have heard of a new development and may want details about it if he thinks it may be newsworthy. Treat him cordially and exhibit a desire to be helpful but do not display knowledge either pro or con that will give out any information that is not ready for official release. A newspaper reporter is quick to see fear, indecision, antagonism, secretiveness, stalling, and the like, and often will misinterpret such actions to the detriment of your organization. A cooperative attitude, complete command of the situation, straightforward answers, and confidence are necessary in dealing with this particular situation. You should immediately direct the reporter to the public relations person in your organization or, in his or her absence, to a company officer. Although you may be very sure there is no truth in what the reporter is saying, denial of it should not come from you—check privately with your executive to be certain of the proper response to make.

If you are authorized to give information, it should be prepared in the manner indicated in Chapter 8, section 8.3. Unless you have been told to answer to the best of your ability questions that may then arise, you should suggest that your employer will be glad to discuss any questions with the news reporter. Your role is to be helpful in setting up an appointment for such a discusssion.

At times new products or services may be announced to the public and news reporters may be invited to attend such special occasions. The arrangements made for such a meeting are outlined beginning on page 27 of this chapter.

ANNOUNCING A VISITOR AND MAKING INTRODUCTIONS

If more than one caller is waiting, you must indicate which one is to have the first appointment. When the executive is ready to see a visitor who has been waiting, you may make any one of the following statements that best fits your situation:

1. "Mr. Nichols will see you now. Won't you go right in?" indicating the nearby door. This approach is appropriate when you are confident that the visitor is well known to the executive.
2. If this is the person's first visit to the office, you rise and accompany the visitor into the executive's office and say, "Mr. Nichols, this is Mr. Yuen." Note that you give the name of the one you consider more important first. Business position rather than sex or age determines whose name is mentioned first.
3. You might want to refresh your executive's memory by saying, "Mr. Nichols, this is Mr. Yuen of Associated Chemical, who has an appointment with you."

Remember that when you make introductions, you should face each person as you give the other person's name; i.e., look at Mr. Yuen when you say "Mr. Nichols" and look at Mr. Nichols when you say "Mr. Yuen" so that each person hears the other's name distinctly and clearly. It's senseless to give each person his own name!

Groups of visitors If more than one person shares a single appointment with your executive, you should make sure that enough chairs, pencils, and note pads have been provided; that ashtrays are within reach; and that the room arrangement is comfortable for easy conversation within the group. If the people arrive separately, you might ask each visitor to be seated and to wait for the others before you ask the group to go in to meet with the executive. Whether you do this or not depends of course on the work load and on the personal preferences of your employer. In any case, you will graciously introduce the people to each other as they assemble.

Interrupting and terminating visits At times you will have to interrupt your executive while a visitor is in the office. For example, an urgent call may come for the executive or the visitor, and the caller may insist that he does not want to leave a message. In a situation like this, you may call on the intercom or type a message and take it into the inner office. A knock is seldom necessary—it is less interruptive just to enter and put the note where the person can see it easily. Wait to see if there is any response or question. If it is necessary to announce a very important caller while the executive is busy with another visitor, take the caller's business card in to the executive and let him decide what to do.

Some visitors do not seem to know when to terminate their visits. You can sometimes reduce overlong visits by saying something like this to the caller before he enters the executive's office: "Mr. Nichols has another appointment in fifteen minutes; we've scheduled appointments quite closely today."

It is helpful if you and your employer have a signaling system to assist in getting a visitor who has overstayed to leave. Any one of the following systems is effective in this situation:

1. Take a note to the executive that may contain a request for him to go elsewhere.
2. Enter the executive's office and apologetically say that it's time for him to leave for his next engagement (be sure he does plan to leave).
3. Telephone the executive from an outer office and ask him if he wants to be interrupted so that the visitor will leave.
4. Enter the office and softly announce that the person who has an appointment for this time is waiting.

BUSINESS DIPLOMACY

Gifts In the eyes of some visitors, you, the secretary, have great influence in your office—you make the appointments, you cancel them, you screen telephone calls, you guard the files, you share the executive's plans. Therefore, they may try to win your approval and perhaps extra favors for themselves through gifts and luncheon invitations. The wise secretary realizes that accepting these gestures of so-called goodwill will make it difficult and embarrassing to refuse that person an appointment with the executive later on. Of course, the type of business gift (calendar, notebook, pencil dialer, erasure shield, etc.) that is given to all is perfectly legitimate, since no feeling of obligation is involved. If an inappropriate gift does arrive at your desk, returning it to the sender with an appreciative note is always in good taste, especially if you explain that company regulations prohibit you from accepting it.

Business social functions As secretary/assistant to an important executive, you may be called on to host a business social function. Communication then becomes a one-to-many art. In this role you are even more of a representative of your company. Remember—at every moment during the social function, someone will be watching you; your conduct must not only appear to be above reproach, but it must be so. The competent professional secretary follows the laws of etiquette. Not a hint of scandal should be associated with your name as the result of any noisy or exuberant behavior at a business-related social function.

Your duties will include being gracious to all, remembering names, greeting people whom you know or don't know with equal warmth, circulating to see that no one is neglected, and keeping an eye on details. If the event is held in a hotel facility or a restaurant, your responsibilities will be lighter than if it is a catered function and you are helping to order the food and beverages, overseeing the setting up of the room arrangements, and keeping the ashtrays emptied! If you are responsible for details, make a checklist that will include the following questions that should be answered beforehand:

1. What place or room is to be used?
2. Are firm reservations made in writing with date and hours of room use specified?
3. How many people are expected?
4. Are there any special diet requests?
5. Are name tags to be used? If so, who will provide them?
6. Is the menu selected or is the food to be catered?
7. Has a letter of confirmation been signed by the caterer?
8. When will the food and beverages be delivered? What number should be called if the food and beverages are late in arriving? Are arrangements for food storage needed?
9. Where will the food and beverages be delivered?
10. Is there a special theme or are special decorations to be used? If so, who is responsible for these?
11. Who will see that tables are properly set up and covered and that all necessary accessories (as napkins, plates, cups, glasses, utensils, or ashtrays) are in place?
12. Are centerpieces needed for all tables or for the speaker's table?
13. Is bar service provided? By whom? Are any special arrangements needed?
14. Is there a plan for the disposal of dishes after the meal?
15. Is background music needed?
16. Is a head table needed? How will it be set up? Are place cards to be used? What will be the seating arrangement?
17. Is a receiving line planned? Where? When? Who will be in it?
18. Is entertainment planned? Are there union restrictions?
19. Are out-of-town guests coming? If so, are there any of the following needed:
    Hotel reservations?
    Transportation?
    Welcome gifts in rooms?
    Guest cards for local clubs?
    Tickets to local attractions and special events?
    Special activities for spouses? Sightseeing tours?
    Theater or concert tickets?
20. Will the executive need notes for making introductions?
21. Are seating arrangements needed for the group?
22. Has provision been made for coat checking or is there a safe place for hanging wraps?

These items can be written or typed in a checklist format which might include one column for each item or task, a second column for confirmation or fulfillment of the task, a third column for comments or reminders regarding the task, and a fourth column for indicating those tasks that still must be carried out.

A few days before the event, check by phone to make sure that all is going according to plan, and on the day of the event make a personal on-site check to see if there are any last-minute problems. Since your organization is sponsoring this social event, your prime responsibility is to see that it runs smoothly. You must be on guard to spot potential problems and to solve them before they become realities; you must be ready to take care of the difficulties that may arise with mature good judgment and composure.

2.3

DESK AND OFFICE ARRANGEMENT FOR EFFICIENT FUNCTIONING

In order to accomplish the varied tasks you are called upon to do and to project the image your executive has a right to expect, your desk and office arrangement are important. Your work station and immediate surroundings will reveal what kind of person you basically are. Of course, you will organize your working tools to suit your own work requirements and personality. However, you may improve your image if you give careful thought to desk organization, supply cabinet arrangement, your office area in general, and your housekeeping duties. Just what is the overall picture that your work environment presents to those who see it daily as part of the total office landscape?

YOU AND YOUR WORK ENVIRONMENT

Although you may now make no decisions about furniture selection and placement and office decor, an awareness of efficient work flow, a knowledge of sensible use of space, and a realization of the importance of appearance will make you valuable in the future. When your executive consults you and you feel unsure of yourself in a particular situation, remember that professional assistance may be obtained from outside sources if you feel you need help. Many studies of the effect of light, noise, color, and furniture arrangement have been made to determine the most productive situations; you should take advantage of these findings if you are faced with having to make decisions about them. (See the Appendix for some suggested references on office studies and office landscape.)

Your work station Even if you cannot control major office-design decisions, your desk and the office space immediately adjacent to it is yours to organize for maximum efficiency and attractiveness. Whatever desk you have is the place to begin. Try this: Sit in your desk chair and face your working surface; stretch your arms straight out over it about six inches off the top surface, with both thumbs side by side. Now swing your arms carefully out to each side, making a wide arc. Watch to see what areas of your desk your arms cover. This is the area of your desk top on which you should have all of the articles that you work with frequently. The far corners which you cannot reach without extreme effort or without getting up from your chair should be clean and free from clutter and may house your name plate or even a plant or a small unobtrusive decorative item or two.

If your telephone is not installed where it is handy for you to use (on the right side if you are left-handed and on the left side if you are right-handed), request permission to have it changed. Your reference books should be readily available on your desk top or in a drawer that you can reach within your "working arc." A lazy Susan can be purchased or made to hold several books in a small space. Although you may like a glass top or a plastic sheet, a nonglare working surface will be easier on your eyes.

You should have a work organizer of some kind on your desk in which to put papers. You might have an expanding portfolio—a holder with heavy separator leaves or one with metal slots in which to put dictation to be transcribed, items ready for your executive to sign, reading to be done, projects in process of completion, or other materials.

As you work, the attention that you pay to the placement of papers, notebook, and supplies on your desk will label you as an organized or a disorganized person. While pristine bareness seldom denotes efficiency, absolute chaos does not necessarily characterize it either. You may be the most efficient somewhere in the realm of "organized chaos"!

Your typewriter is an important part of your desk top. If you use an eraser, fasten an emery board or a small piece of sandpaper to the side of your machine, on which to clean your eraser before you use it; better still, it is well to form the habit of cleaning the eraser <u>after each use</u>. Other accessories for your typewriter should include a charcoal white pencil, some white correction tape or patches, and white correction fluid. (These things are especially useful in helping to camouflage certain difficult corrections, e.g., deep punctuation marks and others. Erasing the error or errors <u>before</u> applying the whitener aids will prevent later bleed-through onto the document from heavily inked ribbons or carbonized tapes. If used discreetly, correction fluids have a place in eradicating deeply impressed characters such as periods which are often hard to remove. However, it cannot be overemphasized that the top-notch secretary is an expert with an abrasive eraser or a small knife in order to render her corrections invisible especially on material that is being disseminated outside the firm.) Remember to keep your typewriter covered at night so that dust will not get into it.

Store all loose papers at the day's end <u>in</u> your desk. If these papers must be left on top of your desk, put them out of sight in your work organizer. Locking your desk may not keep out determined thieves, but it will keep normally inquisitive eyes from seeing things that should not be seen.

Not only is the organization of your desk top desirable, but of equal importance is your organization of the contents of its drawers. The large center drawer that holds small things is the one most likely to become jumbled unless you corral loose items in box tops, spray-can tops, or something similar. Sticky tape or a dab of glue will hold the containers together well and keep them in order in your drawer. Store your stamp pad upside down to keep the ink at the top of the pad and to keep you from jangling the nerves of your co-workers whenever you must use a rubber stamp.

Desks usually contain a slotted drawer in which you can place your letterhead, carbon paper, and copy sheets in that order so that you can pull all three out in a ready-to-use stack. Place your envelopes in their own slots so that when you remove one, you can drop it immediately into your typewriter without having to twist or turn the envelope in any fashion. Keep your personal items at the back of the lowest drawer where they are the least accessible. You will therefore be using the least valuable working space in your desk for nonessential personal belongings. A careful check of the contents of each drawer may indicate that you have stored items there that you <u>never</u> use. This is a waste of valuable space that should be reserved for the materials you use daily to do your work well. Get rid of those white elephants by finding a spot for them somewhere far from your desk drawers.

Because most offices have a supply cabinet of some kind, you may be charged with keeping it orderly too. If several people have access to your supply cabinet, keeping things in order there can be a problem. Labeling its shelves will probably help, as will grouping similar things together. Store items that will spill such as duplicator fluid, ink, and copy machine fluids on the bottom shelves. Paper and other heavy supplies should occupy lower shelves; make sure that the labels on these items face the front. Smaller items should be on the higher shelves at easy eye level and should be stored in labeled boxes. Do not allow small loose items to scatter about on the shelves. Open a ream of paper on the end that has no printing and remove what you need. In this way you will preserve the label so that everyone knows what kind of paper remains in that package. Some copy paper must be stacked in a certain manner—check the arrows on the ends of the reams. Store carbon paper flat—not on end—and as far from a heat source as possible. As supplies are replenished, place the newer items to the back and use the older items first.

Housekeeping tasks Organization includes a certain amount of housekeeping that no expert secretary will hesitate to perform. You will want to dust your own desk top including the area around the typewriter and your books. Check each morning to see if other office surfaces need dusting, too, and do it! Keep the tops of file cabinets clean and uncluttered. If it is necessary to store items on top of these cabinets, consider requisitioning matching boxes that can be labeled discreetly.

Office atmosphere and landscaping In situations where extensive cleaning is required, you may have to call the individual in charge of custodial services to let him know that the office is not being cleaned properly. Another tactic is to leave on your desk at day's end a polite note to the cleaners asking them to be a bit more thorough in their cleaning of hard-to-reach areas (as light fixtures which often accumulate cobwebs). Phone dials and receiver ends frequently need cleaning. A soaped cotton swab dipped in a disinfectant works wonders. Books in bookcases must present a neat appearance—bookends can help. If the bookcases are open, an occasional dusting is important. Magazines to be kept should be housed in cabinets or boxes because they tend to slip and create unsightly piles.

Other housekeeping niceties include adjusting blinds so that all of them are uniform. You should also be alert to changing light patterns for the readjustment of blinds. Sometimes you may have to rearrange wastebaskets that may have been left helter-skelter by the night crew. You also should wash and put away coffee cups and related articles as soon as possible.

No heating, ventilating, or music system pleases everyone. If something drastically out of line occurs—too much heat or cold or a sudden increase in music volume—you must notify the proper department or manager at once. If you have permission to suggest furniture arrangement, arrange the desks so that you do not face another person—not even your executive across a room. Such an arrangement is distracting. You should be able to see visitors easily as they approach and you ought to be so located as to form a natural but yet not a formidable barrier to the executive's office. Desks, chairs, and especially visitors' chairs should not be placed so that they face directly into a light source.

A very modern approach to office arrangement is called *office landscaping.* In this system the office becomes a large open space with no walls except movable panels and screens of various heights to give some privacy. Colorful furniture in a variety of modules is put together to create whatever working arrangement best suits a special worker. Carpeting and modern decor abound, real or artificial plants create a pleasing effect, and complete rearrangement of working space is usually the result. To be effective, a careful study of work flow must be made before this change takes place. Handbooks and textbooks in office management have a wealth of information for you if you want to study office layouts and work with space and furniture templates made to exact scale. Such a study is beyond the scope of this handbook. However, some reference sources on this subject will be found in the Appendix.

In the more traditional office, many companies rent paintings and works of art which may be exchanged at intervals for other items. If no effort is made by your organization to provide other than the basic furniture needed to do your job, some type of colorful hanging or art form may be a welcome relief from monotony. It should be emphasized, however, that decals, amateur artwork, overly elaborate floral arrangements, pictures drawn by a five-year-old niece, and brightly colored inexpensive "junque" will make your office surroundings appear gaudy and cheap. Your object is to create a restful impression on visitors and to favorably affect other employees and the executive for whom you work, while at the same time retaining a businesslike atmosphere in which you can work effectively.

2.4

ESSENTIALS OF HUMAN RELATIONS IN THE OFFICE ENVIRONMENT

The importance of working well with people and thinking how you affect them have been themes running through every section of this chapter. No office is an island unto itself. Your skill in being the catalyst, the "person in the middle," is basic to your success. You must have congenial relationships with your executive and other superiors, with your peers, with your subordinates, and with the outsiders who visit your organization. Nothing can take the place of a secretary who keeps everyone happy while getting her own work done correctly, on time, and cheerfully.

POSITIVE TRAITS OF TOP SECRETARIES

Lists of the desirable traits of a top-notch secretary have appeared frequently in many publications; none agree but all have features in common. As you read the following list, consider honestly the degree to which you possess each of these traits. Listed order has no significance since all are important. As you think about each one, resolve to increase your strengths and decrease your weaknesses; this becomes your responsibility.

To be effective in your dealings with people, you must be:

Polite It's easy to be polite to nice people but it takes the skill of a professional to be gracious to one who is somewhat offensive. Politeness is remembering to praise in public and to reprimand or criticize constructively in private. Politeness can be construed as patronization if your voice inflection is not right. Tact and politeness go hand in hand.

Pleasant Using a genuine smile even if you do not feel much like smiling is important. Everyone has personal problems that can be unpleasant, but you should not bring those problems to the office. In short, do not entwine your business and your personal life. Your ready smile when asked to do something difficult will be appreciated tremendously. A cheerful greeting in the morning to your executive and to the co-workers whom you meet is expected. Even if you do not get an answer, continue the practice. And a cordial "good night" as you leave is proper.

Friendly Be equally friendly to everyone in the office; do not have favorites and do not join cliques. Although you may have an especially good friend in your office, do not share business information with that person.

Fair While you should take credit for your own work, you also should give credit to others for their ideas and their help with your work. In addition, you should mention to your executive the helpfulness of co-workers and pass along to them any compliments or words of appreciation your executive shares with you about them.

Thoughtful Opinions that others have are important. It's wise to remember that in any argument or discussion between you and another, there may be your side, his or her side, and "the right side." Thoughtfulness is closely linked with courtesy. Stopping at another secretary's desk before going in to see the executive; carefully considering word choice when giving instructions to be sure that your words reflect your executive's thinking and direction and are not merely your authoritative delegation of work—these are examples of professional thoughtfulness.

Cooperative You and your executive must work together comfortably and happily. Your executive is the most important person in your business life. He or she too is a human being with traits and behavior that are not always perfect. When he lets off steam and you are around to bear the brunt of the remarks, do not take the words personally and vow inwardly to get even or, worse, hold a grudge. Cooperation extends to working with others to get a job done even though some of the tasks you are asked to do are not "your job." It is always right to offer to help a fellow employee who is overloaded with work when you have time to assist unless you have been given specific instructions not to do so. When your employer asks you to perform a task that you consider to be of a personal nature or to run a personal errand, you should cooperate willingly because you realize that by taking care of these time-consuming details, you free the executive to make the policies and decisions that are his or her job. If your executive is a woman, your cooperation is exactly the same as that which you would accord a man; your executive's sex makes no difference.

Humble Humility means being able to accept justified criticism well and to look at it objectively for what it is meant to be: a signal to you to help you increase your value to your superior and to your organization. Humility also includes the ability to accept praise and compliments gracefully and with a genuine "thank you" as the response.

Tolerant and considerate People differ in mental ability, interests, goals, personality and character, appearance, physical and mental health, and behavior. How dull this world would be if everyone were alike! Consideration of these differences will make your office a more livable place for everyone. Patience, pity, sympathy, empathy, and kindness are traits of the tolerant and considerate person.

Loyal Dedication to your superior and to your organization is absolutely necessary in your business life. If you cannot be loyal to either, you should seriously consider finding another position. Confidential matters <u>must</u> remain so—not a hint may you give that you have privileged information that you cannot share. A loyal employee never criticizes company policies to other persons. If you are loyal, you also are <u>proud</u> of your position, and you take pride in what your organization is, does, or produces.

Sensitive Sensitivity to those around you will develop on the job. You must be constantly aware, alert, and observant. You learn by trial and error and by experience what pleases and what displeases your executive, when he or she wants to be interrupted and when he would rather be alone, when his actions speak louder than his words, where he prefers that you sit for dictation or consultation, and where and in what form he likes finished work to be presented to him. You thus begin to anticipate his needs before he asks. You are sensitive to the likes and dislikes of your co-workers in the same manner. And you are sensitive to your own foibles, knowing that the tendency exists to look at the self through rose-colored glasses while severely criticizing others who have the same traits. (If someone else oversteps the bounds of etiquette, he's rude; but if you do so, you're original!)

Courageous You are not afraid to accept responsibility and you reach out for additional duties that you know you can be responsible for. You give your opinions or ideas when you have sufficient background and experience to have formed a reliable opinion that can be backed up with facts and figures if necessary. You do not wait to be asked to do something you know you can do—you try it, realizing that you may be reprimanded if it does not go well but realizing, too, that this is the way to grow on your job.

Honest In your dealings with everyone, never lie. If your executive is playing golf and his superior asks where he is, your answer might be, "He's with a group of men." If the superior asks, "Where?" your answer should be, "I'm not sure exactly (and you aren't—he could be teeing off, at the 6th hole, or elsewhere on the course) but I believe I can get in touch with him. Would you like me to try?" Honesty also extends to not appropriating company supplies for your personal use. As a trustworthy secretary, you admit your mistakes and neither make excuses for them nor shift the blame for them to others. You also can be depended upon never to feed the office grapevine.

Self-controlled Self-control is a mark of maturity but not every mature individual is self-controlled! Self-discipline, the engaging of one's brain before putting one's mouth in motion, thinking of the consequences of one's words or acts before saying or doing them, keeping one's temper in check at all times, never resorting to tears in the office—these are the attributes of self-control.

Flexible and adaptable The ability to accept change willingly is of inestimable value. Changes in work surroundings, procedures, equipment, and company structure may come quickly. A flexible and adaptable secretary accepts changes with a let's-give-it-a-try attitude and then does everything possible to see that the new arrangement works. Only the person set in his or her ways will say, "Why change? It works fine the way it is," or "We've always done it that way," and then grudgingly tries the new way with no intention of making it work.

Diplomatic and observant of etiquette If first names are customarily used in your office, you must remember to use courtesy titles and last names when visitors are present. Keep personal phone calls and personal visitors to a minimum. Remember your manners in the parking lot—in the mad dash to get to or from work, some employees are safety hazards. You should be careful neither to interrupt others' conversations nor to finish their sentences for them. You should not whistle, hum, chew gum, or mumble and talk to yourself at your desk. If you smoke, you should be careful to see that the smoke does not go directly into the face of someone else, and you should not smoke while others are eating. You ought not to be nosy—mind your own business! And you should not bring your miniature radio into the office to be played "softly."

Well-groomed You watch what the top-level secretaries wear as a guide. Your appearance and clothes should always be such that you could be asked to take an important visitor to lunch, sit in at a meeting for your executive, or greet an arriving dignitary at the airport. Remember that the image you present of your organization should be a businesslike one. Because you are considerate of others, you comb your hair, adjust articles of your clothing, and clean your fingernails only in the lounge or at home.

Punctual Observe your office hours scrupulously. If you have permission to begin work at a later hour some day or take an extra-long lunch break or leave early, be sure to let others in your area know the reason. Morale deteriorates speedily when workers see their co-workers supposedly getting special privileges that they don't get. Punctuality also means getting work done when you've promised it; if this is not possible, you notify the person for whom you are doing the work sufficiently far in advance that his or her plans can be adjusted.

Willing to train another to take your place If you are inwardly secure in your job, you will see that someone else knows what you do and how you do it. This means training a co-worker or subordinate to take over when you must be absent due to illness or travel for your organization, when you are on vacation, or when the opportunity for advancement comes to you. This foresightedness is advantageous to you because your work will not pile up while you are gone, and it is advantageous to your executive who will not panic at the thought of your being away. Because you recognize the value of a desk manual in the training process, you keep yours up to date and use it as a training aid. The contents of your loose-leaf desk manual should include current information on instructions and procedures relative to your duties. A well-organized manual appropriately indexed for ready reference might include topics such as: addresses, business associates, clients or customers, correspondence, data processing, forms, filing, office supplies, news releases, personal data, public relations, subscriptions, telegrams, telephone numbers, travel, and word processing.

Endowed with a sense of humor A sense of humor can make a tense situation less formidable. Stories in poor taste may be told in your presence. If you act as though you have never heard a lewd phrase or a suggestive word, you will be the target of those who deliberately try to shock you. A holier-than-thou attitude is not considered appropriate for the office.

Enthusiastic Although you may score well on the other traits mentioned above, if you are not enthusiastic about what you do, about where you work, and about the possibilities for the future, you are like a cake without frosting—something superb is missing!

Responsible Responsibility is *personal*. *You* are responsible for getting things done on time and correctly. *You* are responsible for the careful proofreading and checking of dates, figures, and spellings of names. Responsibility has two forms: explicit (things you have been delegated or told to do or that were part of your job description when you were hired) and implicit (things you have taken upon yourself to do and which you have done so well that you are now responsible for them although no one has explicitly told you to be). Performing your explicit jobs well is expected of you; performing your implicit tasks well makes you grow on your job and causes your executive to say when someone asks him or her to release you for a more important job, "If you can find me somebody *to take her place* (not *to do her job*), I'll let her go."

As you become known as one who can handle responsibility beautifully, you may be called upon to be a problem solver. In every office things go wrong between human beings. Although you may not always be able to help right the wrongs, you may sometimes be able to help solve the problems by (1) keeping calm (2) getting all the facts from every side (3) talking and listening to everyone involved (4) sifting the emotional statements from factual ones (5) seeking solutions from others as well as trying to brainstorm them yourself (6) considering the advisability of a cooling-off period before suggesting anything, and (7) recommending solutions but not forcing them on anyone.

In any discussion of responsibility, the concepts of authority and accountability must also be considered. Authority is the right and/or obligation to command with the expectation of being obeyed. If someone is given the responsibility of doing something, then he must be given an equal amount of authority to get it done. Authority can be full (authority to decide something and carry it out) or limited (authority to carry something out only). When you give people full authority to decide how, when, or where, they will try to do their job in the best way possible to prove their judgment was good.

A word often misunderstood is *accountability*. You are always accountable for everything you do yourself and for the things anybody to whom you have delegated responsibility and authority does. In other words, you can be called to account for your actions, for those of your subordinates, and for those of your delegates. For that reason, accountability and control or supervision are inseparably linked. Several excellent books on supervision are available for your further study; these are listed in the Appendix.

3

CHAPTER THREE

MEETING AND CONFERENCE ARRANGEMENTS

CONTENTS

3.1

KINDS OF BUSINESS MEETINGS, CONFERENCES, AND CONVENTIONS

The scope of secretarial responsibility in assisting with meeting and conference arrangements is diversified. Depending on the size of the event, the time required for preparations may be brief or extensive. Above all, flexibility and adaptability are necessary to cope with the needed or last-minute changes that frequently occur. *Webster's New Collegiate Dictionary* defines *meeting* as follows:

meeting . . . *n* **1:** an act or process of coming together: as **a:** an assembly for a common purpose . . .

and *conference* as:

conference . . . *n* **1a:** a usually formal interchange of views: CONSULTATION **b:** a meeting of two or more persons for discussing matters of common concern . . .

Essentially, then, a conference is a meeting for discussion but its scope varies from the narrow intra-office meeting for discussion of purely local problems to meetings on a national or international scale to treat matters of world import.

By contrast, the term *convention* regularly and unmistakably refers to large formal meetings such as state, regional, national, or international gatherings of representatives from business firms. Regardless of the scope of the event, the secretary will often be assigned duties such as helping to get ready for the meeting, providing services during the meeting, and assisting with post-meeting follow-ups.

The major classifications of business meetings and conferences are these:

In-house Business Meetings and Conferences—held on the company premises and usually relating to normal business activity.

Satellite (Off-premises) Meetings and Conferences—held at sites that may or may not be company-owned, but nonetheless company-sponsored events.

Outside Business Meetings, Conferences, and Conventions—held outside the company but sponsored by other business firms and attended by company representatives.

Local Business Meetings—held as a rule within the local community and having local participation.

The following drawing illustrates the Worldwide Classifications of Business Meetings, Conferences, and Conventions. The interplay of individuals and groups within

Worldwide Classification of Business Meetings, Conferences, and Conventions

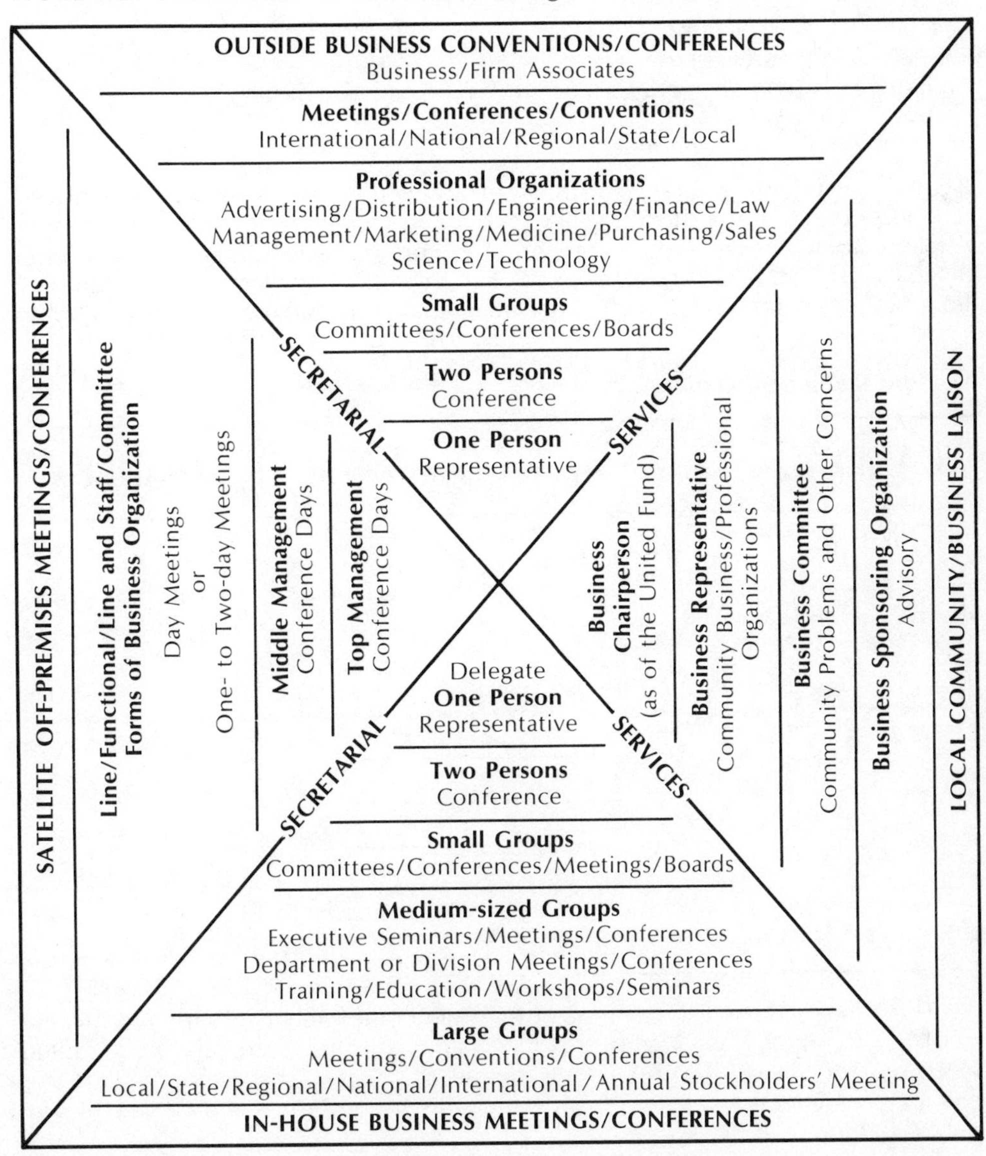

the business framework is shown by the merging triangles in the illustration. The narrowed and pointed end of the triangle represents the movement of key executives, managers, or chairpersons to and from meetings along with their counterparts from other firms in order to transact business. As one looks at the other levels of the triangular configuration, greater involvement of company personnel is evident. The bisecting lines represent the wide range of secretarial services that support all aspects of business activity both at home and abroad.

INVITATIONS TO IN-HOUSE BUSINESS MEETINGS, CONFERENCES, AND OTHER FUNCTIONS

The secretary plays a key role in getting the right people together at the right time for business meetings. Executive secretaries frequently say that their most difficult task is to find enough time in the busy schedules of three or four top managers to arrange special meetings among them. The major kinds of in-house invitations that are prepared by the secretary are these:

Regular executive meetings
Special executive meetings
Annual stockholders' meetings (and proxies)
Corporate directors' meetings
Other meetings and conferences

Regular executive meetings For those meetings that are locked into executives' schedules (as on a monthly or weekly basis), the secretary should remind the participants about the meeting by preparing an interoffice memorandum or a letter timed to arrive the day before the event. See the following illustration. (Additional information on interoffice memorandum preparation may be found in Chapters 8 and 9).

Meeting Reminder Memorandum

HANLEY INTER-OFFICE CORRESPONDENCE **HANLEY**

TO: Lottie G. Wolfe, Vice-president DATE: April 16, 19—

SUBJECT: Public Affairs Meeting

This note will confirm that the Public Affairs Meeting will be held on Monday, April 30 at 9:00 a.m. in the Purchasing Conference Room. Agenda is as follows:

____

____

____

Signature

The administrative secretary may often telephone executive offices to make a quick check on the availability of officers or managers for regularly scheduled meetings. The person who is chairing the meeting should then be notified of any member's anticipated absence. In this way, the voting process on key issues will not be hampered by lack of a quorum.

Special executive meetings Executives often find themselves in crisis situations which call for fast decision-making. As a result, special meetings may be required to deal with these situations. The secretary can best arrange such a meeting by contacting the appropriate officers quickly and in person to explain the situation, or by simply telephoning the individuals. If the meeting is not to be held immediately, a follow-up written reminder should also be prepared indicating the day of the week, the time of day, the location, and the subject of the meeting. In addition, an agenda should be included if available beforehand.

Annual stockholders' meetings (and proxies) Invitations to the annual meeting of the stockholders of a corporation are formal and are issued in printed form by the corporate secretary. A proxy statement is mailed with the annual meeting notice about three or four weeks before the event, or in accordance with the time stipulated in the corporate bylaws.

Corporate directors' meetings Individual corporate bylaws may stipulate the provisions for notifying the directors of upcoming meetings. Even though written notification for regular meetings may not be required, it is nonetheless advisable to remind the directors in this way. The secretary may have to notify directors of special meetings by telephoning them. It is also important to have a list of the directors' names available for each meeting and to indicate on it whether or not they will be present. A prepared form as shown below will be a time-saver.

Directors' Meeting Notification and Attendance Form

WATERMAN ENTERPRISES, INC.
BOARD OF DIRECTORS

Name of Chairperson: William Theodore Waterman, Presiding Officer

Meeting Date: October 19, 19— Time: 9:30 a.m.

Meeting Place: Board Room

Names of Board Members (Listed in order of years on the Board)	Date Notice Sent	Will Attend	Will Not Attend
Charles France	10/5/19—	X	
Henry G. Johnson	"	X	
Willard Hazelett	"	X	
Ralph Knepshield	"	X	
Mark McKallip	"	X	
Myron Klingensmith	"	X	
Andrew Konietzko	"	X	
Harald Rasmusson	"	X	
Roger Wayne Johnson	"	X	
William Kiersey	"		X
Inga Konietzko	"	X	
Elmer Wolfe	"	X	
Lawrence Slack	"	X	
Leonard Wolfe	"	X	
Cuvier Best	"	X	

Total Members to Attend 14
Regular Meeting X
Special Meeting ______

Quorum Assured: X Yes ______ No

____
Secretary

Other meetings and conferences Meeting notices that are sent to large groups of company personnel are normally printed or duplicated. The secretary's initial task is to assemble all pertinent data and frequently to arrange it in an attractive format. Notices of in-house committee meetings and other routine meetings may be set up on interoffice correspondence paper. (See Chapters 8 and 9 for additional information on composing memorandum messages.) All-inclusive captions such as the following ones may be used to address a particular group: "Marketing Representatives," "Personnel Staff," or "Department/Division Managers." Frequently a request is made on an invitation that the recipient telephone the chairperson if he cannot attend.

The secretary will want to be certain that the day of the week, the time of day, the location, and the subject of the meeting are clearly spelled out in the distribution copies. Invitations to seminars, workshops, training sessions, and other specialized in-house business activities may have unusual eye-catching formats, including the use of color and design to spark interest and attention.

Depending upon the size of the group and the importance of the event, the secretary may be requested to send original typewritten letters to specific individuals. (See also Chapter 5 for detailed information on automated and specialized letter preparation.)

INVITATIONS TO OUTSIDE BUSINESS MEETINGS, CONFERENCES, AND OTHER FUNCTIONS

Modern business reaches out to many parts of the globe and to many areas of civic, professional, and educational endeavor. Coordinated and detailed planning is reflected in the many and varied styles that one sees used for the announcements of outside business meetings and functions. These invitations range from those for formal and informal events to those for complex business conventions and conferences, and finally to those that are mere semi-business and social functions.

Specific information on invitations to outside business meetings and functions is presented in this order:

Outside conventions and conferences
Outside professional and community meetings
Outside social/business functions

Outside conventions and conferences Printed invitations designed and set up in an original way are useful in attracting attention and in developing interest in large-scale conventions or conferences. In preparing the invitations, the secretary should double-check the day of the week, the date, the time of day, the room location, and the names of the chairpersons, speakers, panelists, guests, and others involved in the various programs and sectional meetings held during a convention or conference. All details of the event should be correctly and completely reflected on the invitations. No participant should have to telephone the sponsors for vital information inadvertently omitted from these invitations.

Outside professional and community meetings The secretary whose employer is a leader in professional and community affairs may be asked to include informal meeting notices as part of a newsletter. An illustration of this kind of meeting notice is given at the top of the next page.
A self-addressed postal card may also be included so that the participants in the meeting can respond to the invitation or announcement quickly. These cards will later serve as a list of names for the reservation list (as for a luncheon or dinner meeting.) The second figure illustrates the message side of a reservation card.

Newsletter Meeting Notice

J A N U A R Y   M E E T I N G

Monday, January 19, 19—

TOPIC: "The Office of Tomorrow"

PANEL:

Ruth Anderson, Berlin Industries
Arline Basarab, Hanley Works, Inc.
Cecelia Dul, Tate Products
Vivian Klingensmith, Clarion Mowers, Inc.
Ola Knepshield, Leechburg Associates
Alice Ralph, Latch Insurance Company

CHAIRPERSON: Alta Hazelett, Past President
Arnold Chapter, Secretary's Forum;
Supervisor, Secretarial Services
Arnold Stainless Steel Corporation

PLACE: Devon Country Club

TIME: 6:00 p.m. Social

6:30 p.m. Dinner

MENU: Smorgasbord

COST: $6.50

RETURN: Enclosed reservation card by January 12, please

Reservation Postal Card

PLEASE—

Send this reservation card to our Secretary on or before Wednesday of this week.

___ Yes, I plan to attend the next Forum dinner meeting.

___ Yes, I'll bring ___ guests.

Guest Names: ____________________

___ Sorry, I'll miss the Forum this month.

Signature ______________

Company ________________

Outside social/business functions The secretary is often involved in preparing and issuing formal and informal invitations to social/business functions. Many of these events are part of convention activities extending over one or more days. At such meetings, invitations are usually extended to the executive and the executive's spouse. Here, R.S.V.P. (please reply) cards may be used advantageously. Today the handwritten reply to a business invitation is infrequently used, although such replies are conventional for formal social invitations. (See also Chapter 9 for additional information on invitations and replies).

USE OF MAILING LISTS FOR INVITATIONS AND NOTICES

The secretary ought to devise a system for keeping mailing lists current. If name and address changes are infrequent, correction notations may be made directly on the list. With a list requiring frequent changes, however, a card system is helpful. An alphabetical listing of address information by geographical region or country; by organization or firm name; by individual name, title, or position; or by address should be included on the card.

Individually typed addresses may be prepared within the firm for small- or medium-sized group functions. Volume envelope addressing is normally done by addressing machines or other automated processes. On computerized name and address lists, changes should be reported on special cards in order to update future printouts.

3.2

MEETING, CONFERENCE, OR CONVENTION ACTIVITIES

There are three major aspects of meeting, conference, or convention activities in which the secretary may contribute greatly to the success of the event:

1. Preparations for meetings, conferences, or conventions
2. Duties during meetings, conferences, or conventions
3. Follow-up after meetings, conferences, or conventions

PREPARATIONS FOR MEETINGS, CONFERENCES, OR CONVENTIONS

The administrative secretary may work closely with the executive who leads, directs, chairs, or sponsors a meeting, convention, or conference. These are the principal areas of secretarial preplanning involvement:

Meeting site and speaker confirmation
Editing and preparing conference materials
Special arrangements for services

Meeting site and speaker confirmation The secretary should contact the site manager for block reservations of rooms for the conference participants. Room size (single or double) and price range should be specified. Also, the catering manager should be asked to reserve the appropriate meeting rooms, including both general-session auditorium and "break-up" rooms for smaller group sessions. In addition, seating plans should be discussed. (See page 43 for an illustration of seating arrangements.) Provision should be made for smoking if it is to be permitted at the meeting. A thermos or a water pitcher and glasses should be available for the speakers, panelists, or board members. Arrangements for coat checking may also have to be made.

Sample Meeting/Conference Seating Arrangements

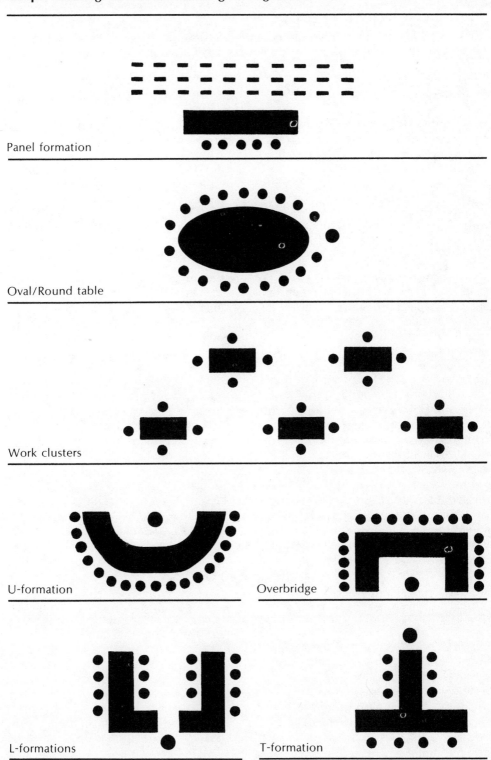

Panel formation

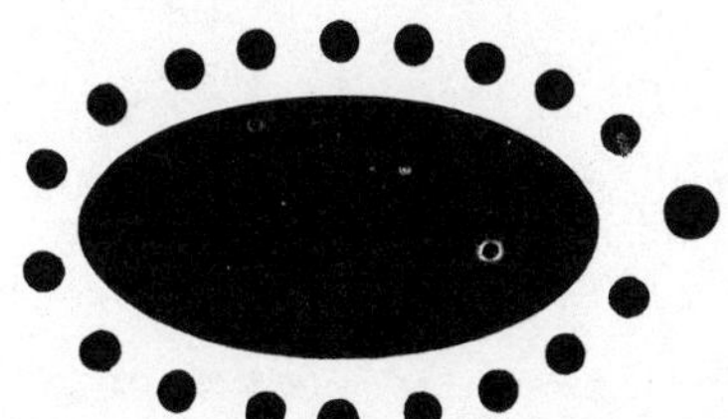

Oval/Round table

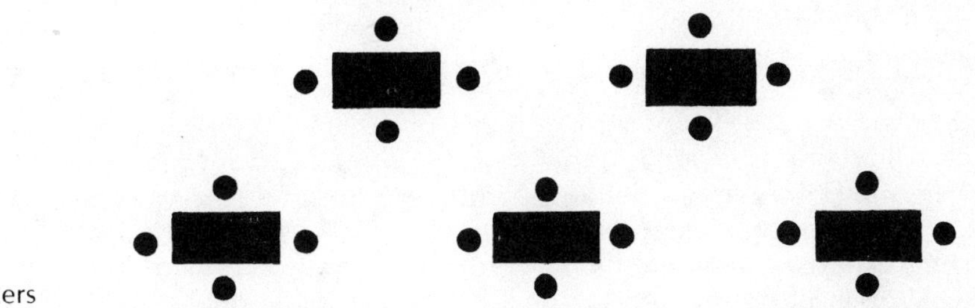

Work clusters

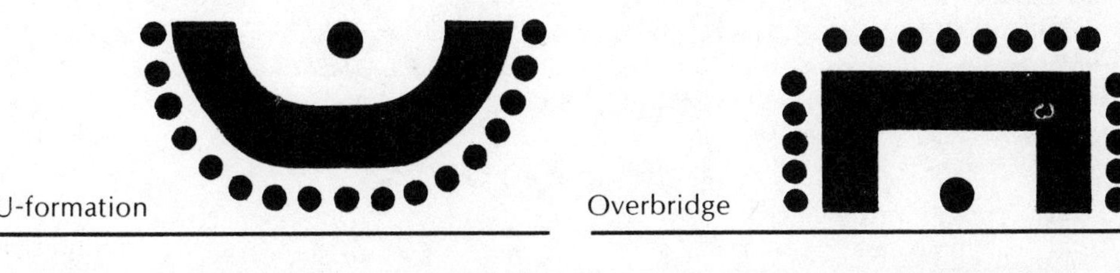

U-formation

Overbridge

L-formations

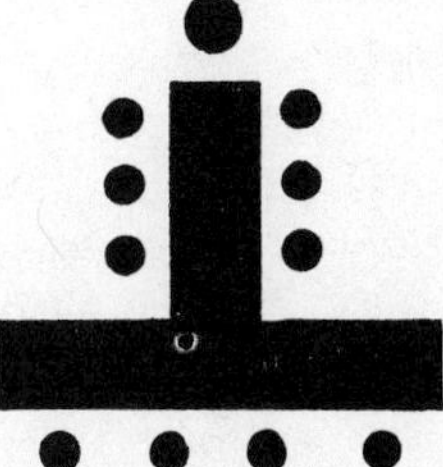

T-formation

Advance arrangements for large or small meetings or conferences are important. It is a good idea to inspect unfamiliar meeting sites if possible to be certain that there is adequate space for the event. Firsthand knowledge of the meeting or conference layout will be helpful in planning for the placement of the registration desk, in locating needed lighting and electrical outlets for audiovisual equipment, and in directing guests to the meeting area. A letter confirming the reservation of all pertinent meeting or conference facilities should be sent to the site manager. In the case of in-house requests, this may be done by telephone and confirmed by a written memorandum.

Prompt notation of the month, the day of the week, the year, and the time of day should be made on both secretarial and executive calendars to reserve time for the event and to serve as a reminder for the manager participating in it.

After the meeting date is set, letters of invitation to speakers may be composed or dictated. An executive will often telephone the invitations to the speakers. Such invitations should be taken care of as soon as possible. If the invitation is accepted, a follow-up letter requesting information about the speaker's background and experience may then be sent. Glossy prints of the speaker are frequently requested for inclusion with news releases.

Editing and preparing meeting and conference materials The preparation of an agenda is basic to business-meeting procedure. A sample workshop agenda is shown on page 46. Supporting materials such as tables, reports, financial statements, or advertisements may be needed at some meetings, too. The secretary may be asked to prepare a copy of each of these items for the meeting participants. These items are often assembled and placed in a folder or envelope for later distribution.

The program planning for formal conferences and conventions is complex. Careful editing is needed in the assembly of program information to ensure that the names, titles, topics, sections, and meeting times are correct.

When a conference speaker has submitted his résumé, vita, or autobiographical sketch, a news release may then be prepared. If the firm has a public relations office, the secretary forwards this information to that department; if the firm does not have such an office, the secretary may be asked to draft a news release. (See Chapter 8 for details concerning the setup of a news release.)

The preparation of trip itineraries is necessary for meetings and conferences held outside the firm. The figure on page 47 exemplifies a typical itinerary. Several copies of the itinerary are needed: one for the executive's travel folder, a copy for the executive's spouse, and at least one office copy. (See also Chapter 15 for more information on travel.)

Special arrangements for services Large-scale conventions and conferences require a wide variety of special services. For example, the secretary may be asked to do the following:

Attend to printing and engraving arrangements
Organize tours and special events for conferees and/or spouses
Arrange for refreshments and meals
Handle pre-registration and registration arrangements
Assemble conference folders or packets
Request audiovisual equipment and materials
Arrange for translation service (as for international conferences)
Mail pre-work conference materials

Ship supplies and printed materials to conference site
Arrange for press coverage
Inform security officers and parking attendants of pertinent conference details
Prepare meeting file folders

Assembling all the information needed for a complete convention program is a demanding task. The secretary will often have to coordinate all the information, type the final copy, and send it to the printer on time. This material usually includes programs, booklets, reports, brochures, name tags, tickets, and others. Banquet and special event tickets should be ready early. The pre-numbering of tickets will aid in setting up an accounting system later on. Special office numbering machines may be secured for this purpose. Orders for special items (as award plaques and other engraved items) should be placed well ahead of time.

Wives of executives sometimes accompany their husbands to conventions or conferences extending over a period of several days. Special activities (as tours or social events) may be arranged for the wives. In these situations, it is helpful to print brochures for wives only. A Ladies' Entertainment Committee headquarters may be established at the convention site. A group of hostesses who are familiar with the city must be organized and made available to assist the guests with information on shopping tours, restaurants, theaters, and other matters of interest.

Arrangements must be made with the catering manager for refreshment and meal selection. It is most important to confirm the number of conference participants for refreshments, social hours, luncheons, and banquets.

A card system is a real boon to the secretary in the handling of pre-registration information. As conference reservations and registration fees come in, each conferee's name, title, firm, address, and other important information may be typed on a card. Conference-fee payment may be recorded on the card for accounting purposes. Later, the cards may be grouped and filed by geographical areas, by committees, or by some other system.

After the cutoff date for pre-registration, and usually one week before the meeting, the rooming list of conference participants should be sent to the conference manager.

One should arrange the staffing of the registration desk well in advance. A telephoned reminder to registration assistants the day before the conference will assure no break in the continuity of plans made for handling duties at the registration desk. Personnel at the registration desk may be responsible for accepting registrations by alphabetical divisions, by regions, by countries, or by some other system on the day of the convention. Decisions must be made about the organization and placement of the registration desk. Attractive and readable signs at the desk will enable those registering to find information quicker. Orders should be placed early for signs and other such supplies.

Whenever possible, conference name tags or badges should be prepared ahead of time and arranged in a system that will facilitate easy distribution. These items are often included in the conference packets. All convention- or conference-related materials should be assembled in packets for the participants. These items include the convention program, appropriate brochures, relevant reports, minutes, and other materials. Individual names may be typed on the packets of those who have pre-registered and have paid all necessary fees; name tags, tickets for meals and other special events are generally included too. Alphabetical arrangement of these packets will facilitate distribution. Special conference program packages will be needed for speakers and honored guests. These packages normally include complimentary tickets to luncheons, banquets, and other special events, as well as conference or convention badges or name tags.

A Sample Workshop Agenda

A Workshop in Multi-Media Training

International Management Society

September 24, 19—

SCHEDULE

8:00 a.m.	Arrive Doyle, Inc.	
8:15 a.m.	Breakfast	Conference Room B
9:00 a.m.	Workshop	Conference Room 6 Education Center
10:00 a.m.	Plant Tour (Optional) or Departure	
11:00 a.m.	Departure	

WORKSHOP AGENDA

9:00 a.m.	Welcome	Stella Willins School Department Manager
9:05 a.m.	Introduction, Management Development Skills Training	Stanley Lindberg Public Relations Manager
9:20 a.m.	Sales Training	Elwin Young Sales Training Supervisor
9:35 a.m.	Service Training	Peter Lawson Service Training Supervisor
9:50 a.m.	Discussion	All

A Sample Itinerary

ITINERARY

MANAGEMENT EXECUTIVES' SOCIETY MEETING—HOBE SOUND, FLORIDA

April 10 - 12

Wednesday, April 9

Lv. Bradley Field	1:12 p.m.	EA #193	F/C	(1 stop in NY. Snack served)
Ar. West Palm Beach	5:12 p.m.			

Transportation to Coral Island Club: Perkins Transfer

Accommodations: Coral Island Club
Hobe Sound, Florida
Tel: (305) 546-2751
April 9-12, 19—

Sunday, April 13

Lv. West Palm Beach	3:55 p.m.	DL #252	F/C	(stops in Tampa and Phila.
Ar. Bradley Field	8:27 p.m.			Dinner served)

Driver at airport to meet flight

Arrangements should be made with the catering manager or with another designated person for audiovisual equipment and its operators if needed. Some of the frequently used items are as follows:

Chalkboards	Overhead projector
Feltboard	Projection screen (specify size)
Filmstrip projector	Record player
Hook-and-loop board	Simultaneous translation headsets and control boxes
Lectern or podium	Slide projector (specify tray design)
Microphones (floor or lapel)	Tape recorder (specify cassette size)
Movie projector (specify size)	Television (specify screen size)
Newsprint with easel	Videotape machine

Use of a reservation request form will simplify the procedure for ordering audio-visual aids and other items. The equipment and services desired are simply checked off on this form. It also is wise to order stands or dollies of the proper height for the correct placement of projectors. The secretary should ensure that extra projector bulbs and extension cords are provided. The person chairing the meeting should be familiar with the location of all electrical outlets and light switches to assure smooth presentations. The secretary may convey this information to the appropriate individuals.

International conferences will probably require simultaneous translation services similar to those available at the United Nations. When the decision is reached concerning the official languages to be used at the conference, language specialists with simultaneous translation skills can then be sought. During conference addresses and lectures, international conference participants will need individual listening headsets and control boxes so that each one may tune in to the language he feels most comfortable with. Translators may be required for special activities (as banquets and tours) also.

Training conferences such as those for sales training often require the participants to study advance materials relating to the forthcoming event. In this case the secretary will have to mail these pre-work materials to the conference participants at least two weeks before the event.

General conference supplies, booklets, and other information will have to be shipped to the conference site at least two weeks before the meeting. It will be necessary to call the catering manager and request that the conference supplies be held for pickup by the chairperson on the conference date. A follow-up letter to this effect would be added insurance against later mix-ups.

News releases concerning the conference should be prepared for distribution to the media either before or after the event. (See Chapter 8 for detailed information on news release preparation.) Arrangements also should be made for any photographs that will be taken during the conference. Summaries of addresses or lectures may be needed for distribution to the media. Whenever possible, copies of these summaries should be prepared in advance.

Security police or other such personnel ought to be alerted about forthcoming conventions and conferences. They should know the general agenda and the locations and times of meetings. They should also be informed if VIP guests (as high government officials requiring extra protection) will be in attendance. In-house events create special problems if large numbers of persons are involved. Extra parking facilities frequently must be made available. If one informs parking attendants of the approximate number of meeting participants, they will be able to offer the guests more assistance. It is also helpful to prepare maps showing various driving routes to the conference site and to send them along with printed directions to each participant in advance.

Executive file folders should contain all pertinent information about the conference or convention. A copy of all programs, reports, brochures, minutes of previous meetings, correspondence, and other important information should be included. Of course, for outside conferences, the folders should contain travel information and the itinerary. The executive file folder should be labeled with the name of the conference, the place where it is being held, the dates, and any other pertinent information. The secretary will find it useful to have separate file folders relating to arrangements for segments of large functions in which the employer is a leader. The file labels should contain the name or abbreviation of the conference, topics relating to the conference, the city where the event will be held, and the applicable dates.

Travel expense sheets or booklets are needed by executives for recording travel and conference expenses. These booklets or sheets contain ledger space for recording items such as the following: principal reason for the trip, transportation, personal mileage, taxi fare and fares for other local transport, room, meals including tips, telephone calls that are business-related, and so forth. There are also pages or space for recording cash advances and the total amounts of money expended from such advances.

DUTIES DURING MEETINGS, CONFERENCES, OR CONVENTIONS

At the actual event, the secretary's competence meets one of its severest tests. In her hands rests the responsibility for the meticulous checking that alone can ensure that all the carefully laid plans for the event are carried through to the letter. Good organization and follow-through are the keynotes to effective meetings and conferences.

In-house meeting room readiness An early personal visit to the conference room of the in-house meeting will give the secretary extra time to make a final check of room arrangements and to distribute printed materials to the participants. Since correct lighting and proper heating and ventilation will contribute to the comfort of the participants, these items should be double-checked. The secretary should ensure that the room is arranged as desired. Its cleanliness should be checked. Fresh water and glasses should be available for speakers or panelists. The secretary should place pens, note pads, pencils, and conference folders containing agenda, minutes, reports, and other data at each place at the conference table for management-level meetings. The availability and the proper placement of requested audiovisual equipment and materials should also be checked. If any of the arrangements are not in order, a quick telephone call should immediately solve minor problems.

Checklist of arrangements for outside meetings Conference-day inspection of meeting room arrangements, audiovisual equipment delivery, and other items may be expedited by the use of a checklist which the secretary should prepare and give to the catering manager for each day of a conference. This list serves as a summary of items needed for each program as well as of desired food services, menus, and other details. A sample conference arrangements checklist is illustrated on page 50.

The secretary greets conference guests A pleasant welcome to conference members and/or guests is extremely important to the goodwill of the firm. (Before a meeting the secretary should present a list of guests to the company's receptionist. In some instances, an identification badge can then be prepared and given to each visitor for security reasons.) The secretary should be the epitome of the perfect hostess when she greets guests and introduces one to another. If there are only a few guests, they may be met personally by the executive secretary and individually escorted to the meeting room. On the other hand, large numbers of guests may be directed to the coat-check rooms, then to the registration desk, and finally to the conference room. Assistants might also be made available as guides to direct conference participants to designated areas.

Secretarial services during meetings and conferences Certain special duties may be delegated to a secretary during those days when meetings, conferences, or conventions are held. The following list identifies some of the services that a secretary or secretarial staff may provide on these occasions:

1. Supervise registration desk procedures. Alert registration desk personnel as to the identity and the arrival time of speakers, honored guests, or dignitaries so that complimentary tickets may be presented to them for luncheons, banquets, and other events. Conference badges, name tags, and programs may also be provided for them.
2. Be ready to provide statistics on the number of participants who will attend each event.
3. Prepare a list of participants as well as the names and addresses of the companies they represent. This list is often duplicated and distributed to other participants and members.

Daily Conference/Convention Checklist

DAILY CONFERENCE/CONVENTION ARRANGEMENTS CHECKLIST

TO: Catering Manager

FROM: Beatrice Pomerance
Administrative Secretary

DATE: October 19, 19—

KIND OF MEETING: Sentinel Chemicals Sales Training Conference

MEETING SITE: Kansas Hotel, Kansas City, MO

MEETING DATES: October 19-21, 19—

DATE	TIME	AM	PM	NAME OF ROOM	NAME OF FUNCTION	ROOM SET UP	NO. OF GUESTS	MENUS/AUDIOVISUAL AIDS
10/19/19—	9-12	AM		McKenzie	Sentinel Sales Training Conf.	U-Formation Tables for 30 Trainees	30	1 Lectern 1 Overhead Projector 1 Cassette Recorder 1 Easel with News-print Paper
	10:30-10:45	AM		McKenzie	Coffee Break	Serving Table Self-Service	30	Coffee Danish
	12:15-1:15		PM	Kansas Star	Luncheon	5 Tables of 6 each	30	French Onion Soup Chicken a la King Green Beans Almondine Butternut Squash Apple Pie a la Mode Coffee/Tea
	1:30-4:30		PM	McKenzie	Sales Training	6 Tables of 5 each		Same as 9-12
	3:00-3:15		PM	McKenzie	Coffee Break	Self-Service	30	Coffee Donuts

4. Take minutes of certain meetings, either in shorthand or by tape recording. (See also the section of this chapter entitled "The Secretary Takes Minutes."
5. Handle specific correspondence requests for convention officers, executive personnel, or special guests.
6. Assemble and typewrite information for a convention news sheet.
7. Coordinate duplicating services and distribute convention news sheets to participants.
8. Place important telephone calls related to conference activities.
9. Coordinate and synchronize convention events, as by facilitating the transmittal of messages or by reaching individuals sought by others.
10. Meet and direct media representatives and photographers to room locations for group pictures and other events. Distribute prepared news releases to media representatives.
11. Arrange place cards for seating officers and guests on the dais or at the head table for luncheons and banquets.
12. Assign guides or hostesses to escort guests to the dais.

FOLLOW-UP AFTER MEETINGS, CONFERENCES, OR CONVENTIONS

The follow-up duties after a meeting, conference, or convention often become the secretary's responsibility. If an executive is the chairperson of the meeting, his or her secretary may be asked to perform the following duties at the meeting site:

1. Remove any surplus meeting- or conference-related literature (as reports or minutes) from the room where the meeting was held.
2. Notify the catering manager to collect water glasses and any food service items from the meeting room.
3. Request that audiovisual equipment be transferred to locked storage areas. For security reasons, await the arrival of authorized representatives to store this equipment.
4. Return any lost-and-found items to the company receptionist or to the appropriate convention authorities.

Upon return to the office, the secretary will make notations on her desk calendar and on the executive's calendar of further meeting dates, reports, appointments, and other meeting- or conference-related information.

Conference correspondence, reports, minutes, and notations Letters of appreciation will have to be written to those officers and chairpersons who assisted with the conference. Letters of congratulations may also be in order for newly elected officers, directors, or chairpersons. Minutes taken at the conference should be transcribed as soon as possible. (See Chapter 8 for details on the typewriting of minutes.) Particular attention should be paid to specific tasks assigned to committee members. Follow-up dates should be recorded in a tickler file. Also, the secretary will want to remind the executive of any unassigned tasks which are spelled out in the minutes.

3.3

THE SECRETARY TAKES MINUTES

Serving as recording secretary and taking minutes or notes at meetings, conferences, or conventions may be a major portion of a secretary's responsibility.

PREPAREDNESS FOR THE MEETING

The secretary should arrive early at the meeting and should organize the area in which minutes will be taken. Preparedness for complete note-taking is essential.

The secretary will want a sufficient number of pens, pencils, notebooks, and an adequate supply of paper available for manual note-taking. An adequate supply of paper tape should be on hand for machine shorthand writers. Recording machines are often used to supplement secretarial note-taking when verbatim minutes are required. In the latter case, the secretary will need to have a good supply of recording tapes available, either reels or cassettes of the proper size to fit the particular recording equipment being used at the time.

Regular and special meeting materials The presiding officer and the secretary should discuss the materials which will be needed at a meeting. There should be an understanding concerning what materials the secretary must provide. These items might include the minutes book or books, the bylaws, the membership and committee lists, extra copies of the agenda and printed minutes, a reference book on parliamentary law, and other materials.

The corporate secretary will need to take some or all of the following items to the annual stockholders' meeting, directors' meetings, and other special meetings:

Current meeting file (current papers relating to the meeting)
Minutes book or books
Corporate seal
Copy of published meeting notice to stockholders with a notation of the mailing date
Copy of corporation laws of the state in which the firm is incorporated
Copy of the certificate of incorporation, including amendments
Copy of the corporate bylaws, plus amendments
Meeting regulation information, if any
Blank forms, i.e., those for affidavits, oaths, and other purposes

KNOWLEDGE OF MEETING PROCEDURES

Having adequate knowledge of meeting procedures is essential to the secretary. Reading and referring to previous minutes and talking with secretaries who have taken notes at similar meetings will aid the secretary in her own note-taking. Before a meeting, it is also a good idea to consult the presiding officer about a means of having motions or statements clarified or repeated.

Meetings may be conducted on an informal or a formal basis. At informal meetings the presiding officer joins in the discussion and some of the formalities of the application of parliamentary procedures (*Robert's Rules of Order*) are waived. Committee meetings are examples of this.

On the other hand, formal meetings call for strict adherence to the rules of parliamentary procedure and the bylaws governing the meeting. (See the section of this chapter "The Secretary Chairs a Meeting.") Annual stockholders' meetings, board of directors' meetings, and professional association meetings are typical examples of formal meetings.

Familiarity with the order of business A meeting agenda or order of business may or may not be used at informal meetings; however, it is required for formal meetings and it is a great help to both the presiding officer and the recording secretary.

The items in an agenda follow a set pattern established by the official group or organization. A comprehensive list of possible agenda items follows (starred * items apply only to certain meetings, i.e., an actual board of directors' meeting):

Agenda (Order of Business)

1. Call to order
2. Roll call or verification of members or stockholders present
3. Minutes of the previous meeting (changes/approval)

4. Reading of correspondence
5. Report of treasurer
* 6. Report of board of directors
7. Report of officers
8. Report of standing committees
* 9. Report of special committees
*10. Unfinished business (from previous meeting or meetings)
11. New business (normally items submitted in advance to the presiding officer)
*12. Appointment of committees
*13. Nominations and elections
14. Program, if appropriate
15. Announcements (including date of next meeting)
16. Adjournment

Recording basic facts about the meeting It is essential for the secretary to record the following basic facts concerning a meeting:

1. The date, location, and time of day that the meeting was held.
2. The name of the presiding officer.
3. The kind of meeting (as regular, special, board, executive, or committee).
4. The names of members present for small groups of under 20 persons; the names of members absent. A quorum check is needed for larger groups. (Majority representation at corporate stockholders' meetings is usually based upon shares of stock and not upon the number of individual stockholders. Thus, it is necessary to have information about the number of shares owned by each listed stockholder.)
5. The order of business as indicated on the agenda.
6. The motions made, their adoption or rejection, and the names of the originators of the motions. (It is not necessary to record the names of those who second motions unless one is requested to do so.)

See also the Chapter 4 section on the use of the stenographic notebook (pages 66–69) for suggestions on handling additions, changes, corrections in the taking of minutes.

Actual wording of minutes The wording of minutes should be factual, brief, and devoid of editorial opinion and comments. An illustration of the way in which the secretary might word the minutes of a meeting is shown in the following illustration on this page and overleaf.

Sample Minutes of a Board Meeting

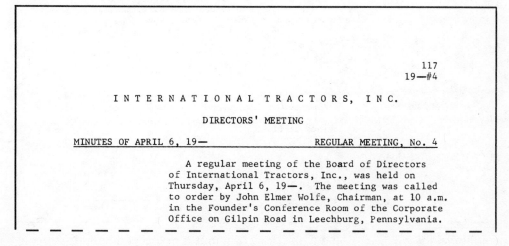

117
19—#4

INTERNATIONAL TRACTORS, INC.

DIRECTORS' MEETING

MINUTES OF APRIL 6, 19— REGULAR MEETING, No. 4

A regular meeting of the Board of Directors of International Tractors, Inc., was held on Thursday, April 6, 19—. The meeting was called to order by John Elmer Wolfe, Chairman, at 10 a.m. in the Founder's Conference Room of the Corporate Office on Gilpin Road in Leechburg, Pennsylvania.

PRESENT — Thirteen members of the Board were present: Pauline Alt, Charles Filip, Glenn France, Robert Hazer, Joseph Latina, Richard Linamen, Lorraine Perejda, Ismail Perez, Ethel Rasmusson, Irene Stanick, Elizabeth Walden, Forest Wolfe, and John Zalesny. These members constitute a quorum.

ABSENT — One member was absent: Louis Jones.

MINUTES APPROVED — The minutes of the March 5, 19—, special Directors' meeting were read and approved.

REPORT OF THE CHAIRMAN — The chairman reported on the period of growth in sales during the last quarter, especially in international business with a 12 percent increase as compared with a year ago. However, mention was made of the increasing difficulties in bidding for critical material supplies against strong and affluent foreign competitors.

A plan for Organizing for Growth was submitted to the Board for study:

First, decentralize from our corporate headquarters into each operating company responsibility for its sales, marketing, and accounting operations.

Next, reinstitute the dual management posts of chairman and chief executive officer and of president and chief operating officer. This will assure that undivided attention will be given to current operations and to future growth.

118

MINUTES OF APRIL 6, 19— — 19—#4

REPORT OF THE TREASURER — James McKallip, Treasurer, submitted a quarterly profit and loss statement, dated March 31, 19—, with a net profit of $........ The surplus available for dividends is $........ as determined by a general balance sheet, dated March 31, 19—. These reports were accepted and placed on file.

ADJOURNMENT — A motion for adjournment was made by Mr. France and seconded by Ms. Stanick. The meeting was adjourned at 11:45 a.m.

Charlotte Charpnak, Secretary — John Elmer Wolfe, Chairman

Additional information on the typewriting of minutes may be found in Chapter 8.

3.4

THE SECRETARY CHAIRS A MEETING

Today's secretary can take an active role as the presiding officer or president of some professional, civic, or community organizations; thus, many firms have organizations of secretaries for the purpose of developing certain skills. An example is a Secretarial Forum organized to assist secretaries in developing the ability to speak before small groups and large audiences. Before stepping to the podium to conduct a meeting, the secretary should be well-versed in parliamentary procedure.

PLANNING AHEAD FOR THE MEETING

The president or presiding officer of a meeting needs to do some organizing and planning before the meeting. An agenda should be prepared to serve as a guide to conducting the meeting. While the presiding officer certainly should have a copy of the agenda, copies of it may also be distributed to the members. Members of the organization may contribute topics for the agenda in advance according to the time limits set down in the bylaws of the organization or by mutual agreement of the membership.

Thinking through the agenda items in advance The items on the agenda should be carefully thought through by the presiding officer before the meeting. Perhaps file folders will have to be organized to hold the various reports and other items that will be discussed. If one-fifth-cut file folders are used, they may be arranged alphabetically by topic and placed in a small case for easy reference. Being able to locate material quickly at the meeting results in a well-organized and productive session.

APPLICATION OF PARLIAMENTARY PROCEDURES

It is especially important for the presiding officer to know how to handle the order of business efficiently. The presiding officer (known as the Chair) remains impartial in discussions, maintains order in considering one topic at a time, recognizes the rights of members to express themselves, and assures equitable treatment for all members.

Opening the meeting Usually, a gavel is tapped once on a desk to bring the members to attention at the start of the meeting. The presiding officer says, "The meeting will now come to order."

Making a quorum check One should verify the number of members necessary for a quorum according to the bylaws of the organization or group. If there is no quorum, an attempt may be made to secure one. If the required number of members cannot be found, the only proper action is to fix the time to adjourn and to adjourn.

Announcing the reading of the minutes The Chair remarks, "The minutes of the previous meeting will be read by the secretary." If copies of the minutes were distributed in printed form to the membership in advance, the Chair asks, "Are there any additions or corrections in the minutes?"

There should be a pause for membership reflection or response. If there is no response, the Chair continues, "If not, the minutes stand approved [*or* approved as read]."

If there is a correction, the Chair may informally direct that it be made. If there is an objection by a member, a formal vote is needed for the correction.

If an error is discovered in the minutes after their approval, an amendment must be made and a vote taken.

Calling for reports The presiding officer calls for organization reports in this order:

1. Officers, e.g., Vice-president, Treasurer
2. Executive Board (Board of Directors)
3. Standing Committees
4. Special Committees

For example, the presiding officer might ask, "May we now have the Treasurer's Report?"

After the report is read or presented, the Chair may add, "The Treasurer's Report may now be filed for audit."

At this point in the meeting, the report of the Executive Board may be made. Action may be taken on it at this time, or it may be recalled under new business. (Note that Board minutes are not read since they are the property of the Board.) Normally, reports of the other officers may be made at the annual meeting or at the end of the term of office.

Procedure for handling reports The presiding officer will call for the appropriate report from an officer, a board, a standing committee, or a special committee by saying, "Will the chairperson of the Ways and Means Committee please present her report?"

The chairperson of the Ways and Means Committee presents the report. A motion is needed to accept (or adopt) the report.

Processing a motion Following a report, if there is no response from the membership in the form of a motion, the presiding officer may comment, "Is there a motion that this report be accepted?"

Here it is important that the presiding officer accept only motions that are worded affirmatively. Often rewording is necessary to avoid a negative motion.

One of the members will remark, "I move that the Ways and Means Committee Report be accepted."

Another member will state, "I second the motion."

The Chair will then comment, "It has been moved and seconded that the Ways and Means Committee Report be accepted. Is there any discussion?"

The presiding officer opens the discussion; however, it is not proper to enter into the discussion at a formal meeting, except to process the order of business.

Undoubtedly, there will be questions from the floor. When there is an appropriate lull in the discussion, the presiding officer might remark, "Is there further discussion?"

If no discussion ensues, the presiding officer then says, "If not, are you ready to put the question?" or "Are you ready to vote?"

If the members are ready to vote, the presiding officer will call for a voice vote. This is the usual procedure; however, a show of hands, a rising vote, a roll call, or a ballot will provide an accurate count if needed.

"All those in favor, please signify by saying aye. Those opposed, please signify by saying no."

The Chair then states, depending upon the outcome, "The motion is carried," or "The motion is lost."

Introducing new business The presiding officer refers to an agenda item of new business and introduces the item. Discussion by the membership follows. If a motion is made and seconded, the presiding officer should restate the motion so that all may hear and understand it. After a reasonable time for discussion, a member may call, "Question."

Also it is appropriate for the Chair to say, "Are you ready for the question?" The vote may then be taken.

Some types of motions Main motions are made to present a resolution, a recommendation, or other proposal for consideration by the members. No other main motion may be brought before the assembly when a main motion is already on the floor.

Subsidiary motions are those that modify the principal or the main motion; therefore, such motions must be decided before the main motion. (However, subsidiary motions are considered after privileged and incidental motions.) Examples of subsidiary motions are these:

to postpone indefinitely The purpose is to suppress action, or to prevent a vote on the question.

to amend The purpose is to modify the main notion; it must be germane to the subject which is to be amended.

to refer to committee The purpose is to provide for more consideration on the question. In effect, it delays action.

to postpone to a certain day or time The purpose is to defer action to a specific day or time.

to limit or extend debate The purpose is to modify the freedom of debate.

to move the previous question or *call the question* The purpose is to stop debate at once.

to lay on the table or *to table* The purpose is to make way for more important business. In effect, it delays action.

Incidental motions are those which come incidentally as other motions are being considered. Action must be taken on the incidental motion before the main motion or a subsidiary motion can be considered. Examples of incidental motions are:

to suspend the rules The purpose is to permit an action which would otherwise be impossible according to the rules that govern the order of business or admission to the meeting. (A motion to suspend the rules cannot be made to suspend the bylaws or constitution of the organization, however.)

to withdraw a motion The purpose is to remove the motion from the floor; this can only be done *before* the voting has started. The members must give their consent if the motion was stated by the chairperson, though.

to read a paper The purpose is to provide the opportunity to object to a member's reading from a certain book, paper, or other document without permission of the assembly.

to object to the consideration of a question The purpose is to prevent the discussion of a question which is irrelevant or contentious. Before debate begins, the mover says, "Madam Chairperson; I object to its consideration."

to appeal a decision from the Chair The purpose is to call for a vote to reverse the Chair's decision on an issue.

to raise a question of order The purpose is to halt a disorderly or unparliamentary procedure. It may be made at any time by saying, "Madam Chairperson. I rise to a point of order."

Privileged motions relate to the well-being of the group or of any individual member. These motions are undebatable and take precedence over all questions. Examples of privileged motions are:

to call for the orders of the day The purpose is to demand the adherence to the order of business or to the program at hand.

to raise a question of privilege The purpose relates to the rights or privileges of the members of the group. The member would rise and say, "Madam Chairperson: I rise to a question of personal privilege." The Chairperson must then decide if it is a question of privilege or not.

to take a recess The purpose is to make a break in the proceedings of the meeting, e.g., for counting ballots.

to adjourn The purpose is to bring the meeting to a close. Before bringing this motion to a vote, the presiding officer should be certain that no important items or announcements have been overlooked. The motion to adjourn may be made by a member who has been recognized by the Chair. All business should cease after an affirmative vote on this motion.

to fix the time to adjourn The purpose of this motion is to fix the exact time that the meeting shall end.

THE SECRETARY ADDRESSES AN AUDIENCE

There are increasing opportunities for secretaries to assume leadership roles through speaking to groups, large or small. A good beginning is to learn the guidelines for reaching your audience and the basic elements of public speaking:

1. Investigate information for your address to be certain of the facts. Document any information which may be needed in answering questions from the audience.
2. Clearly think through in advance what you are going to say. Jot down an outline of your remarks; cards are helpful for this purpose.
3. Practice what you have to say before a mirror. Be particularly mindful of facial and body expressions and gestures.
4. Record your message on a tape recorder so that you may listen back to check points that might need improvement.
5. Use language that is easy to understand. Keep sentence structure simple and uncomplicated.
6. Maintain poise, stand erect, maintain a pleasant expression, be relaxed, and glance across the audience to gain their attention.
7. Time your message to keep it within a specified time limit.
8. Speak in a normal, well-modulated voice. Project your voice by directing your comments to the people in the last row of the audience.
9. Pace your rate of speech: it should be neither too fast nor too slow.
10. Pause during appropriate points in your message to allow your audience to follow the trend of thought that you are illustrating.
11. Avoid mannerisms, i.e., fumbling with papers, or excessive movement of the feet, arms, or hands. If necessary, hold something such as a card or a piece of paper to keep your hands still.
12. Create the right frame of mind toward your presentation—one of assurance that you are thoroughly prepared, that you know exactly what you want to say and how you want to say it, and that your message is worthy of the time and the attention of your audience.

4

CHAPTER FOUR

DICTATION AND TRANSCRIPTION: Input and Output

CONTENTS

4.1

OFFICE COMMUNICATION: Systems for Linking the Voice to Paper

The use of modern technology in office dictation and transcription systems enables the secretary to reflect the corporate image in correspondence most quickly, efficiently, and effectively. Attractive letters may be swiftly returned to the dictator by the use of these special systems. Turnaround time for correspondence—the completed letter on the dictator's desk—may be within minutes or an hour or two from the actual time of live dictation, if necessary. Same-day service is standard with many corporations for dictation that has been completed by a designated hour in the morning.

It is advantageous for the secretary to understand and know how to utilize the company's dictation system and to have knowledge of the machine-transcription process in addition. For instance, the experienced secretary may have the responsibility for dictating responses to routine and/or special correspondence on a regular basis, at peak-load times, or when the employer is away from the office for several days. (See Chapter 9 for additional information on letters written by the secretary.) This continuous dictation service will expedite the office work flow and will reduce the backlog of mail to be answered by the executive. Thus, the secretary becomes an executive extender, demonstrating capabilities in a vital communications area.

THE NATURE OF DICTATION SYSTEMS

An overview of dictation systems should deepen the secretary's understanding of their use within a firm. Also, knowledge of a system places one in a position to utilize it to good advantage as individual opportunities occur.

An analysis of office dictation system location and use reveals three general classes of equipment: portable machines, desktop models, and centralized units which interact with the mobile and the stationary units. The current trend is toward interchangeability of discrete recording media (cassettes, mini-cassettes, belts, cartridges, discs, and others) used on portable and/or desktop units. For example, a dictation system can have maximum flexibility if a recorded message (perhaps a cassette) can be fed into a central (perhaps an endless-loop) recording system or if it can be inserted into a transcribing machine for direct use by the secretary. Thus, the great virtue of any given dictation system is its compatibility with other systems within the corporate structure.

Portable machines The small, comparatively lightweight (10–25 ounce) portable dictation unit which fits easily into a pocket, handbag, or attaché case has won wide acceptance from busy executives. It is the "go anywhere" unit that permits its user to dictate freely when telephones are not available. Portables are particularly useful at conventions and conferences, in travel, and in field work.

The recording time available on portable dictation machines ranges from 15 to 90 minutes depending upon the medium (as standard cassette, mini-cassette, mag belt, or visible belt) being used.

The versatility of modern portable dictation machines is evidenced by their capabilities in providing varied transcription possibilities for the secretary:

Prerecorded discrete media from the portable dictator (cassette, mini-cassette, and others) can be inserted into a companion unit for direct transcription.

A headset jack may be inserted into the portable dictation unit itself for direct transcription.

A special transcribe module adapter can be used to input the recorded information into any company centralized endless-loop system.

Special features of some portable dictation units include a wide range of useful controls, some of which are listed here:

The digital counter pinpoints the amount of tape available on the machine and it also helps to locate correspondence quickly. Some units have an instant reset feature.

Side thumb-touch controls order the machine to stop, rewind, and play back.

Direct visual indication of document length and location eliminates the need for log pads and index strips.

A pause button permits the user to dictate at any desired pace.

Through the use of a recorder coupler, a dictator may prerecord the message in a remote area and immediately transmit it to the office by dialing the office. The information is transmitted from the portable's cassette to a cassette in the office for direct transcription.

Note: Not all of the features described above are available on all equipment models.

Desktop models Standard or desktop models of dictation machines are extremely useful in large corporate offices having a heavy dictation flow. The skillful secretary can provide quick correspondence turnaround with the companion model of a transcribing machine equipped with sophisticated and sensitive tone, speed, and volume controls.

Smaller offices may be equipped with a combination machine to be used for both dictation input and transcription output on a smaller scale. However, during times of peak work load a combination dictation-transcription unit can present a problem, for it can perform only one operation at a time: It either records or plays back dictation. To prevent a backlog in the company's work load, it is necessary to have additional compatible systems that can be made accessible by departmental loan.

Centralized dictation systems Continuous service is the most characteristic feature of large corporate centralized dictation systems—24-hour service seven days a week, with input from almost anywhere. The component parts of the central recording system in a firm may vary widely from in-house operations—private-wire phone/recorder installations, for example, to PBX (private branch exchange) systems which direct the dictation flow into banks of endless-loop tanks.

Standardization is another important feature of centralized dictation systems. As job requirements of the firm change and as dictation needs vary, the system can be enlarged or modified.

The capabilities of some centralized dictation systems are illustrated to show their potential for adaptation within various firms having special or limited dictation needs:

Sample System 1: In-house, Private-wire System
Ten remote microphone input stations.
Only one dictator may dictate at any given time.
Input stations are installed within 500 feet of the central recorder or recorders.

Sample System 2: Private-wire and PBX Systems
Recorder automatically loads and records.
Nine hours of recording time.
Filled cassettes drop out of the recorder.
Empty cassettes are automatically positioned.

Sample System 3: Pushbutton Phones or Private-wire Systems
Private-wire input through special desk phones which give access to a cassette recorder.
Remote-location access to a central recorder through use of a phone coupler and a small four-button, hand-held terminal.

4.2

THE USE OF MACHINE DICTATION SYSTEMS

Executives or their designated assistants are the prime users of office dictation systems that link their voices to various kinds of communications. Frequently, when working for top-echelon management, a secretary may originate many letters (as to assist the president of a firm). On the other hand, secretaries involved in middle management today find that their role is also extended to encompass dictation of certain letters. For instance, the administrative secretary now may assist three or more executives instead of one. In this role, the secretary engages in office administration: She may be involved in handling some dictation, telephone communications, office mail, filing, research, travel arrangements, and other duties.

The administrative secretary may dictate through a telephone or a microphone to a dictation system in a word processing center or a secretarial services center for transcription by a corresponding secretary.

STEPS IN PREPARATION FOR DICTATION

After receiving from an executive correspondence designated to be answered, an administrative secretary should follow this procedure as soon as possible:

1. Get ready to dictate.
2. Instruct the transcriber.
3. Proceed to dictate.

Get ready to dictate Readiness to dictate involves five preparatory steps that will minimize time loss:

1. Plan ahead—dictation early in the day means quicker turnaround.
2. Contact the word processing or secretarial services center supervisor for any priority or rush work.
3. Position the telephone or the microphone of the dictating machine; have extra input media (as cassettes or belts) available.
4. Review the correspondence to be answered or the material to be dictated.
5. Outline the replies briefly; organize thoughts about secretarial instructions.

Instruct the transcriber It is important to remember that the transcriber needs some special cues from the dictator in order to produce acceptable transcripts. Following these instructions produce better work:

Record the dictator's identification by name, title, and location.

Give directions to erase *confidential* information immediately after transcribing.

Identify the nature of the message (as a telegram, a letter, an outline, a memorandum, or a report) and the stationery to be used; indicate the appropriate spacing also.

Suggest the insertion of attached illustrations or drawings in reports, as needed.

Specify the number of copies needed.

Indicate priority or rush work.

Dictate numbers slowly, numeral by numeral, i.e., *zero, one, five, eight.*

Spell out names and difficult or technical words.

Mention paragraphs, capitalization, underlining, and unusual punctuation.

Give instructions about letter closing, title if desired, and whether or not envelopes are needed.

Proceed to dictate The art of effective dictation involves the correct tone of voice, naturalness of expression, sufficient volume to project the message, proper enunciation, and the avoidance of mannerisms. For example, the tap of a pencil, the squeak of a chair, the chewing of gum, or a chance personal remark to the transcriber can later confuse the transcriber.

A SIMULATION OF THE USE OF A DESKTOP DICTATING MACHINE

A simulation of dictation preparations, of instructions for the transcriber, and of actual dictation is given in the following illustration.

How to get ready to dictate The dictation machine is positioned on the desk and is connected to an electrical outlet; the microphone, if detached, should be connected. Next, the machine should be turned on. The operation panel of the machine should be checked to ensure that the tone, volume, and speed controls are set correctly. These instructions should then be followed:

a. Insert the mini-cassette into the holder; close the holder: This will cause an automatic rewind of the mini-cassette, if needed. As new dictation is added, previous dictation will be automatically removed.

b. Place a new index strip into the compartment provided. The index strip is divided into 15 one-minute time zones for the 15 minutes of dictation time available on one side of the mini-cassette; total capacity is 30 minutes for quick transcription turnaround time.

c. Lift the microphone from its bracket; the machine is thus automatically activated. Hold the microphone three or four inches away. Speak across the face of the microphone rather than directly into it.

d. Depress the *Dictate* switch: The pilot light will then illuminate. Slide the *Start/Stop* switch down to begin dictating. Speak in a natural tone of voice.

How to instruct the transcriber The dictator moves the *Secretarial Instructions* switch up and dictates needed secretarial transcription information, i.e., special instructions or corrections.

Secretarial instructions

Secretary: This is Lois McKallip, Secretarial Services Supervisor. Today's dictation is a continuation of the manuscript of our new SECRETARIAL PROCEDURES MANUAL. Please place this title in all-capital letters on the sixth line of each page at the left margin. Indicate the page number on the same line at the right margin. Use double-spacing, a 60-spaced line, and a five-space indention for paragraphs. Three copies are needed. Please use the copy machine instead of carbons.

How to dictate The dictator lifts the microphone off its bracket, slides the *Start/Stop* switch down, and begins to dictate. When dictation is completed, the dictator slides the end-of-letter switch up to mark the length of the page.

In the following samples of machine dictation, the terms to be transcribed are shown in Roman type while interspersed directions are printed in italics.

Dictation A

all capitals Secretarial Procedures Manual *align page at right margin* page 31

Transcription A

SECRETARIAL PROCEDURES MANUAL 31

Secretarial instructions

Secretary: Triple-space after the main title. Underscore the side heading to follow.

Dictation B

capital E efficiency and *capital O* organization *no period double-space capital R* research tells us that efficient secretaries spend only one third as much time handling the *quote* extras *comma unquote* such as carbon and stationery *comma* as do the less efficient ones *period capital O* organization spells success for thoughtful and careful office personnel *period capital S* some suggestions for desirable work habits and procedures follow *colon*

Transcription B

Efficiency and Organization

Research tells us that efficient secretaries spend only one third as much time handling the "extras," such as carbon and stationery, as do the less efficient ones. Organization spells success for thoughtful and careful office personnel. Some suggestions for desirable work habits and procedures follow:

Secretarial instructions

Secretary: Please indent the following ten enumerated items five spaces from each margin. Single-space within each item and double-space between items. Use Arabic numbers to identify each item; use a period and two spaces after each number. Capitalize the first letter of the first word after each number. Line up all words at the left at the point where the first word begins; do not typewrite beneath the numbers.

Dictation C

number one period two horizontal spaces capital O organize your work *period capital D* decide on the most important task *semicolon* complete it *semicolon* then *comma* start on a second task *period capital A* a good motto is *colon quote capital P* plan your work and work your plan *period unquote double-space down number two period two horizontal spaces capital P* place only those materials needed for a given task on your desk at any one time *period capital R* remove excess materials when a project is finished *period double-space down number three period two horizontal spaces capital T* try to take expeditious action on each paper that comes to your desk *period double-space down number four period two horizontal spaces capital M* maintain a system for arranging stationary and other supplies in your desk *period capital K* keep your desk neat at all times *period correction*

Secretarial instructions

Secretary: Reword the last sentence to read *capital K* keep your desk and work area neat at all times *period*

Special note to the dictator

An alternative procedure would be to rewind the tape and redictate the sentence with the correction, thus eliminating the need for the last Secretarial Instruction.

Transcription C
(including correction given above)

1. Organize your work. Decide on the most important task; complete it; then, start on a second task. A good motto is: "Plan your work and work your plan."

2. Place only those materials needed for a given task on your desk at any one time. Remove excess materials when a project is finished.

3. Try to take expeditious action on each paper that comes to your desk.

4. Maintain a system for arranging stationery and other supplies in your desk. Keep your desk and work area neat at all times.

Dictation D

double-space down number five period two horizontal spaces capital C check and double *hyphen* check all communications which you prepare *period capital B* be sure of your accuracy *period double-space down number six period two horizontal spaces capital A* avoid guessing about the spelling of a word *comma* the division of a word *comma* or a point of grammar *period capital C* check a recent secretarial reference book or dictionary *period double-space down number seven period two horizontal spaces capital S* see your supervisor about pertinent questions relative to company procedures *period double-space down number eight period two horizontal spaces capital A* after typewriting *open parenthesis* or writing *close parenthesis* a communication *comma* place it *quote* face down *unquote* on your desk to protect vital company information *dash* to screen these data from visitors to your office *period*

Transcription D

5. Check and double-check all communications which you prepare. Be sure of your accuracy.

6. Avoid guessing about the spelling of a word, the division of a word, or a point of grammar. Check a recent secretarial reference book or dictionary.

7. See your supervisor about pertinent questions relative to company procedures.

8. After typewriting (or writing) a communication, place it "face down" on your desk to protect vital company information—to screen these data from visitors to your office.

Secretarial instructions

Secretary: Item nine will have four subdivisions. Place a period and two horizontal spaces after each lettered item. Use single-spacing for this listing, *a* through *d*. Continuation lines should start two horizontal spaces beneath the words in the first line.

Dictation E

number nine period two horizontal spaces capital D do the following *quote* housekeeping *unquote* tasks at the day *apostrophe* s end *colon double-space once here indent five spaces from each margin lowercase letter a period two horizontal spaces capital C* clean your typewriter *period single-space down lowercase b period two horizontal spaces capital C* clear your desktop of papers *period single-space down lowercase c period two horizontal spaces capital C* cover appropriate office machines *period single-space down lowercase d period two horizontal spaces capital S* straighten the contents of your desk drawers *comma* cabinets *comma* and bookcases *period*

Transcription E

9. Do the following "housekeeping" tasks at the day's end:

   a. Clean your typewriter.
   b. Clear your desktop of papers.
   c. Cover appropriate office machines.
   d. Straighten the contents of your desk drawers, cabinets, and bookcases.

Secretarial instructions

Secretary: The abbreviation of the Latin expression *id est* meaning *that is* and abbreviated *i.e.* will be dictated in item 10. At that point, please listen to the instructions carefully before typewriting it.

Dictation F

number ten period two horizontal spaces capital M maintain a *quote* businesslike *unquote* office atmosphere by avoiding a *quote* cluttered *unquote* work module *comma lowercase letter i period no space lowercase letter e period comma* needless quantities of art objects and pictures *comma* postal cards *comma* and so on *comma* at any one time *period*

Transcription F

10. Maintain a "businesslike" office atmosphere by avoiding a "cluttered" work module, i.e., needless quantities of art objects and pictures, postal cards, and so on, at any one time.

THE USE OF THE SHORTHAND MACHINE

Specialized dictation needs in fields such as medicine, law, or science frequently call for above-normal secretarial recording ability in the range of from 140 to over 200 words per minute. The secretary who knows how to use a shorthand machine can fulfill this specialized need as well as other dictation requirements at lower rates.

The secretary records notes on a shorthand machine equipped with prefolded paper note tape. As notes are taken, this tape emerges in an A-frame configuration and folds into a tray behind the machine.

A careful check should be made of the amount of paper tape available in the machine for a given dictation session. Extra tape should be at hand in case it is needed. Machine shorthand paper tape is available in two sizes—100-folds and 300-folds per package.

The shorthand machine may be placed on a separate table beside the executive's desk; also, a pullout shelf from this desk may be used. Or, during lengthy dictation sessions, an executive's personal secretary may prefer a shorthand machine mounted on a tripod. The tripod should be adjusted for correct height; also, a comfortable, attractive posture should be maintained by sitting slightly to the right of the tripod. Sometimes the secretary will hold the shorthand machine on her lap.

During pauses in dictation, the secretary may use the pencil from the top of the shorthand machine to cross out changed notes on the tape. Special attention to the notes during dictation will result in smoother transcription. For example, rush or priority items may be flagged for quick reference. The secretary should not gaze directly at the dictator or dictators (as in a conference), since this may interrupt the person's train of thought.

Adjusting the inking of the machine shorthand ribbon is essential if the notes are to be readable. Before a dictation session, a few lines of sample notes should be written, an inspection of which will reveal whether or not a few drops of ink should be added to the top of the ink spool by means of the special ink applicator bottle.

One who dictates to a secretary using a shorthand machine should follow the general procedures for dictation found on pages 61–65. These procedures also apply to the machine shorthand medium.

4.3

INPUT: Dictation for the Secretary/Stenographer

Dictation rates may vary from 80 to 140 words per minute. Even though average dictation normally ranges at the lower end of this scale—i.e., between 90 to 110 words per minute—the secretary/stenographer needs reserve speed for fast spurts of dictation.

As a rule, correspondence, reports, and manuscripts form the major portion of executive stenographic dictation. However, secretaries may also take notes at staff meetings. In this situation the reporting process is selective: Unimportant information can be screened out and only essential information recorded. Also, the secretary can readily take notes by hand in a rather noisy environment. A secretary may also be of invaluable assistance at conferences by recording hastily given instructions that the executive can follow through on later.

THE USE OF THE STENOGRAPHIC NOTEBOOK

The secretary needs to devise a system for use of the stenographic notebook. Any method used will, of course, be tailor-made to meet individual circumstances; however, it is of prime importance to have the notebook, pens, and other items readily at hand, so that one may respond immediately to the dictation call of the executive. Some basic procedures for handling the notebook are these:

Use several elastic bands around the top cover of the notebook in order to bind off transcribed notes.

Attach several paper clips at the side of the notebook cover for use in flagging rush or important items to be transcribed first.

Assemble a work folder or binder consisting of a stationery pocket inside each cover. The stenographic notebook will fit easily in the right-hand pocket. The left-hand pocket will be useful for reference copies of correspondence, reports, or other items related to the day's dictation.

Place several pens, colored or black pencils, and a small ruler in the pocket of the folder beside the stenographic notebook.

Dictation Folder

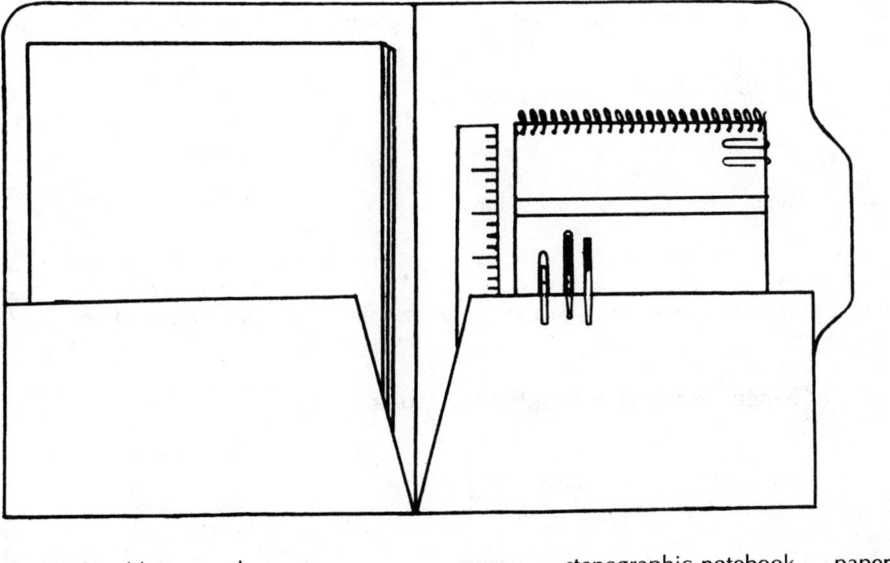

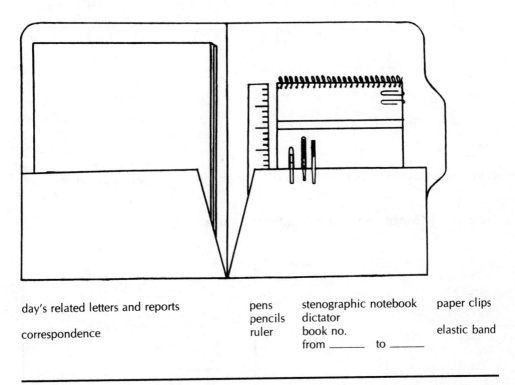

day's related letters and reports	pens	stenographic notebook	paper clips
	pencils	dictator	
correspondence	ruler	book no.	elastic band
		from ______ to ______	

Notebook identification systems If the secretary takes dictation from several persons, a separate notebook should be maintained for each one. Label each notebook cover with the name of the dictator and the date on which the notebook was last used. Completed notebooks may then be filed chronologically under the name of each dictator. It is important to check with the employer concerning how long filled notebooks are to be kept: this time may vary from one year to a number of years, especially for law firms.

Paper clips, a triangularly folded notebook page corner, or colored pencil markings may be used to identify rush items that must be transcribed first.

Space planning in the notebook Intelligent use of notebook space will enable the secretary to add information with ease or to write in changes or instructions with care, either during or after dictation. Each item in a day's dictation series should bear an identifying number. Allow several blank lines before and after each numbered dictation item: This will normally provide enough space for last-minute changes and instructions. However, if the executive is prone to make extensive revisions, it is well to record notes only in the left column of the notebook and to reserve the right column for major revisions.

Coding the stenographic notebook Changes in dictation are part of the normal course of events in any stenographic recording session. The secretary ought to be familiar with symbols to code these changes. Some example are:

- Delete or remove a word or phrase.
- Add a word or a short phrase.
- Use at the beginning and at the end of a change or an instruction.
- Marks the first lengthy insert. (Each subsequent insert bears the letter b, c, and so on.)
- Indicates a priority transcription item.
- Strike out this section of the notes.
- Shows a transposition; invert the order of the words.
- Move this sentence or section to the new position indicated by the arrow.

Illustrations of some ways in which these stenographic codes may be useful are found below.

Examples of Changes in the Stenographic Notebook

Addition:
The Editor called yesterday to remind all chairpersons that Newsletter copy will be due on September 23.

Please add after the word *copy*: *of 200 words.*

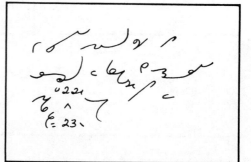

Correction:
William Masden, National Sales Manager for Abbot Industries, is scheduled to attend the international sales meeting in Miami on February 19, at the Foster House.

Let's change that to the *Turf House*—I just remembered the site correction that came in yesterday.

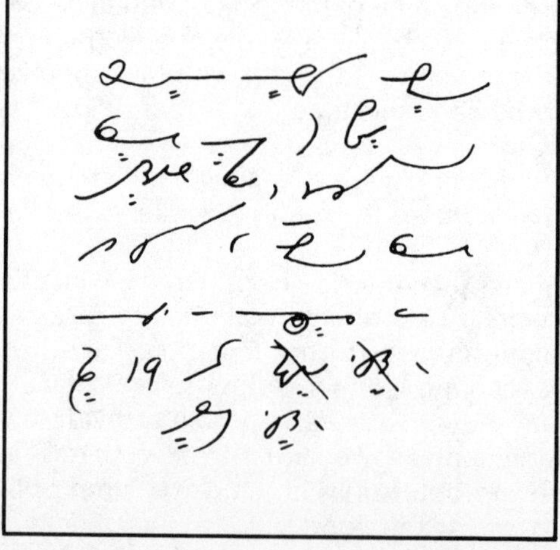

Deletion:
The annual banquet will feature Mr. James Everett, former President of Paterson Lines, who will speak on "Restructuring of the Railroads."

Please omit: *Mr.*

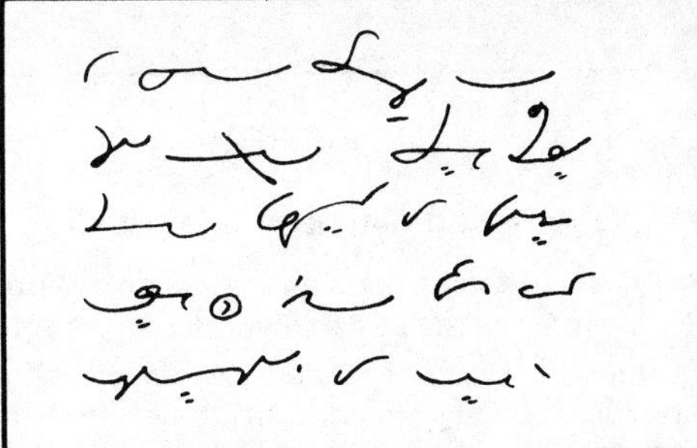

Restoration:
Mr. Austin Bower of the Hinsdale Insurance Company will be here on Wednesday, October 19, at 2 p.m. to meet with any interested staff member.

Let's make that: *confer with;* on second thought, let it stand as: *to meet with.*

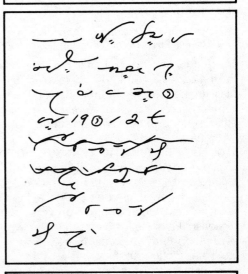

Insertion:
Betty Best has earned the title, Pennsylvania's Secretary of the Year. This is an outstanding honor for Mrs. Best and Randall Industries.

Please insert this sentence after the word *year: The announcement was made at the CPS Banquet today.*

The secretary should seek opportunites to utilize stenographic skills in order to maintain high performance levels. If office dictation is infrequent, it is helpful to write personal notes and reminders in shorthand. Also, note-taking at lectures and from radio and television addresses is beneficial. In addition, records and tapes may be secured for additional practice at desired speeds, ranging in ten-word increases.

The suggestions outlined in the section "Steps in Preparation for Dictation" on pages 61 and 62 will assist a secretary/stenographer in planning ahead for dictation.

4.4

OUTPUT: Transcription Systems

The transcription output system usually parallels that of the dictation input:

a. Machine transcription by the secretary from belts, cassettes, discs, tapes, and other media results from the dictator's initial decision to use such discrete media.

b. Transcription from machine shorthand notes results from the dictator's selection of a secretary who is highly skilled in machine shorthand, perhaps in technical, specialized, or scientific fields. (Computer transcription is available to qualified reporters for the production of depositions and appellate transcripts. In this system, the computer translates from machine shorthand notes.)

c. Conventional transcription from the stenographic notebook results from the dictator's decision to use this form of recording business messages.

The production of accurate professional output papers (as letters, reports, or drafts) is the major goal of all transcribers, regardless of the particular method used. In fact, work measurement of this output is a valid determinant of the net worth of the transcribers in many firms. An alert secretary can combine her knowledge, skill, and intellect to attain success in transcription production.

THE NATURE OF THE TRANSCRIPTION PROCESS

The product or output of the transcription process is the transcript. *Webster's New Collegiate Dictionary* defines *transcript* as ". . . a written, printed, or typed copy; *esp* : a usually typewritten copy of dictated or recorded material."

The actual transcription process involves three phases of secretarial/transcriber responsibility for effective output:

1. Pretranscription preparations
2. Transcription functions
3. General post-transcription procedures

PRETRANSCRIPTION PREPARATIONS

Organization and planning play a major part in pretranscription preparations. The work module should be arranged efficiently, and the typewriter checked regularly.

The work module organization Those items (as the transcribing machine, the stenographic notebook, or machine shorthand notes) that are essential to specialized transcription ought to be assembled and arranged for easy use on the transcriber's desk. Reference books should be within easy reach; these are a dictionary, a secretarial handbook, applicable company manuals, postal references, directories, and other such material. The basic kinds of stationery should be readily accessible in the stationery drawer; they include letterhead, forms, continuation sheets (plain bond), carbon (regular, film, or snap-out), envelopes, and other items of this type.

Correction tools (as tapes, liquids, or pencils) should be placed beside the typewriter work station. The right-handed secretary will usually place erasing tools at the right side of the typewriter; the left-handed secretary will, as a rule, choose the left-side placement for convenience. Of course, if the secretary has a self-correcting typewriter, there is little if any need for basic correction substances and materials.

Chair adjustment Chair adjustment is important so that the transcriber can maintain a good, comfortable posture. Chairs with adjustable backrests should fit the small of the back for support. Correct chair and desk height definitely affect a typist's transcription production. For example, the typist's forearm slope should only equal that of the typewriter keyboard—i.e., there should be less slope for electric machines.

Typewriter condition Careful attention to the condition of the typewriter before transcription will often save valuable time later. First of all, an inspection should be made to ensure a clean typeface. Daily brushing is vital to good typescript. Liquid cleaners may be used only on conventional manual or electric machines with type bars. One may use plastic cleaners and brushes on elements or fonts; however, on electric typewriter components, liquid cleaners are definitely harmful.

A ribbon check before transcription will indicate whether or not a new fabric ribbon is needed; in this way, a uniform, dark typescript will be ensured. Checking machines that use film ribbon will indicate whether a replacement ribbon will be required soon; having a spare cartridge or spool at hand in advance will ensure minimal interruption at the point when the ribbon change is needed.

TRANSCRIPTION FUNCTIONS

Machine transcription is the identifying label usually given to the processing through typewriting of information located on discrete media (as belts, cassettes, discs, tapes, and others). The term *transcription* alone encompasses the typewriting of machine shorthand tape notes and stenographic notes.

There are many manufacturers of transcribing machines. These companies provide helpful booklets with each new machine to assist the transcriber. If pertinent operating instructions are unavailable, the secretary need only telephone the company's local educational representative for information and assistance.

A machine transcription simulation function The following steps comprise a general outline of some basic procedures that are adaptable to the majority of transcribing machines found in modern offices. A simulation of the work flow of a machine transcriber is illustrated:

1. Place the recorded medium into the transcribing machine.
2. Put the earpiece or headset in place.

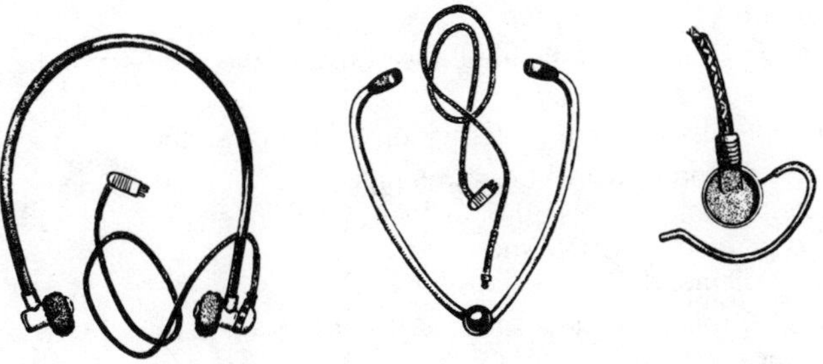

3. Position the foot control or the thumb control panel.

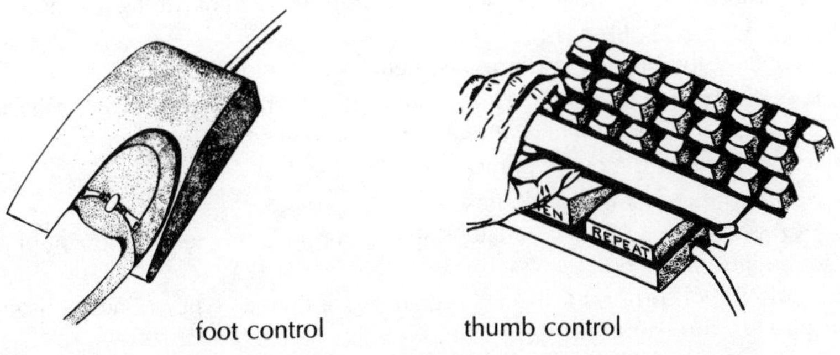

foot control thumb control

4. Check the machine controls for proper settings.

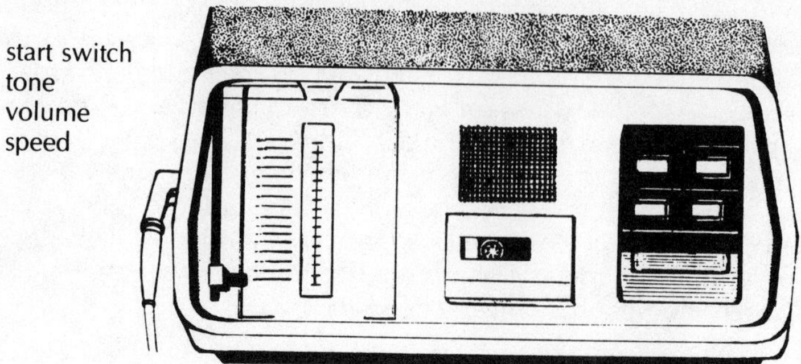

5. Install an index strip.

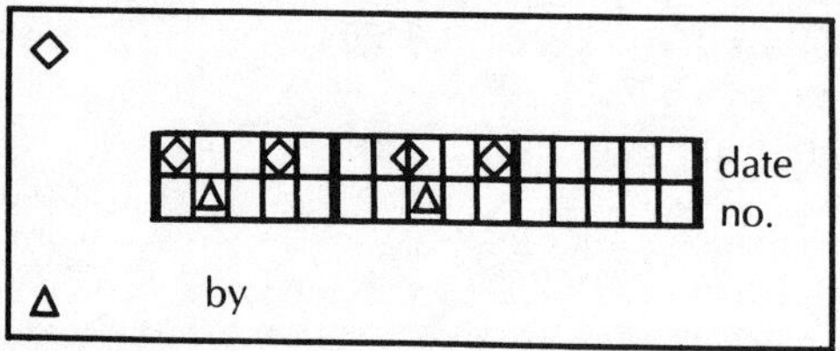

There are 15 calibrations on the above index strip.
Each calibration represents one minute of dictation.
One minute of dictation is equal to ten typewritten lines.
The diamond ◇ mark above the horizontal line indicates the end of a letter.
The triangle △ below the horizontal line represents an instruction or a correction. (ALWAYS LISTEN TO THESE SECTIONS BEFORE TRANSCRIBING.)

6. Move the index strip scanner (or pointer) to the first priority or rush item.
7. Depress the foot control or the thumb control to activate the machine for listening. (Adjustments may be needed in tone, volume, or speed.)
8. Look at the index strip and determine the estimated line length of the first letter to be transcribed.

   The sample index strip provides the following information to the transcriber:
   Item 1, marked by the first diamond ◇ is five lines in length.
   Item 2, marked by the second diamond ◇ is 30 lines long.
   Item 3, marked by the third diamond ◇ is 35 lines long.
   Item 4, marked by the fourth diamond ◇ is 25 lines long.
9. Refer to the *Letter Placement Table* on page 74 to find the suggested marginal settings for the letter for either elite or pica spacing.
10. Set the typewriter margins, tabular stops, and correct vertical setting.
11. Find the triangle markings △ on the index strip, position the scanner at each triangle, and listen to the instructions and/or corrections of the dictator before transcribing. Doing so will avoid retyping because of changes.
12. Position the scanner at the beginning of the first item to be transcribed.
13. Use the *Triple-Form Typewriting Copy Guide* on page 73 (the secretary can easily construct a copy) to insert the appropriate stationery into the typewriter.
14. Listen to the first transcription thought phrase.
15. Type only a *portion* of the first thought phrase.
16. Listen to the second thought phrase as typewriting is completed on the first thought phrase. Please refer to the illustration on page 74.
17. Continue the transcription process toward the goal of continuous typewriting, as listening continues in spurts by thought phrases.

Triple-Form Typewriting Copy Guide

Baronial (half-sheet) stationery
Monarch (executive) stationery
Standard (full-sized) stationery

Baronial (half-sheet)	Monarch (executive)	Standard (full-sized sheet)
1	1	1
2	2	2
3	3	3
4	4	4
5	5	5
6	6	6
7	7	7
8	8	8
9	9	9
10	10	10
11	11	11
12	12	12
13	13	13
14	14	14
15	15	15
16	16	16
17	17	17
18	18	18
19	19	19
20	20	20
21	21	21
22	22	22
23	23	23
24	24	24
25	25	25
26	26	26
27	27	27
28	28	28
29	29	29
30	30	30
31	31	31
32	32	32
33	33	33
34	34	34
35	35	35
36	36	36
37	37	37
38	38	38
39	39	39
40	40	40
41	41	41
42	42	42
43	43	43
44	44	44
45	45	45
46	46	46
47	47	47
48	48	48
49	49	49
50	50	50
51	51	51
52	52	52
53	53	53
54	54	54
55	55	55
56	56	56
	57	57
	58	58
	59	59
	60	60
	61	61
	62	62
	63	63
		64
		65
		66

Suggestions for Copy Guide Use: A triple-form typewriting copy guide may easily be constructed on colored paper for ready identification. This vertical placement device can then be positioned behind the page or behind the carbon pack on which typewriting is to be done. The numbers on the copy guide should be exposed at the right-hand side. In this way, the typist may be guided as to the remaining lines on a page. A red pencil may be advantageously used to mark the copy guide at significant points such as the starting point of a date line, the place where the bottom margin is to begin, the length of an executive or half-page letter, and so on.

Letter Placement Table
Three Sizes of Stationery

Lines in Letter Body	Words in Letter Body	Starting Line for Inside Address*	Typewriter Marginal Stops Elite/Pica	Length in Inches of Typing Line
Half-sheet Stationery: Assume Letterhead takes 7 vertical lines. (Baronial—center No. 36 for Elite; No. 30 for Pica)				
9–10	60–66	17**	15–60/10–50	4
11–12	67–73	16**	15–60/10–50	4
13–14	74–80	15**	15–60/10–50	4
15–16	81–87	14**	15–60/10–50	4
17–18	88–94	13**	15–60/10–50	4
19–20	95–100	12**	15–60/10–50	4
Executive-size Stationery: Assume Letterhead takes 8 lines. Monarch—center No. 44, Elite; No. 35, Pica)				
13–14	95–115	19**	15–75/10–60	5
15–16	116–135	18**	15–75/10–60	5
17–18	136–155	17**	15–75/10–60	5
19–20	156–175	16**	15–75/10–60	5
Full-size Stationery: Assume Letterhead takes 9 lines. (Standard—center No. 50, Elite; No. 42, Pica)				
11–14	175–200	20**	15–90/12–72	6
15–18	201–225	19**	15–90/12–72	6
19–22	226–250	18**	15–90/12–72	6
23–26	251–275	17**	15–90/12–72	6
27–30	276–300***	16**	15–90/12–72	6

*Begin to count at the very top edge of the stationery.
**The date should be typed three lines below the last line of the letterhead on all letters.
***Letters consisting of more than 300 words should be two-page letters.

An Illustration of the Listen/Type Transciption Process

TYPExxxxxxxxxxxxxxTYPExxxxxxxxxxxxxxxTYPExxxxxxx
LISTEN))))))))))))))/LISTEN))))))))))))))/LISTEN)))))))))))/
The Corporate Office of The Hanley Works is in New Britain;

xxxxxxxxxxxxxTYPExxxxxxxxxxxxxxxxxxxxxxxxxxxxxTYPExxxxxxxxxxxxxxxxxxxxxxx
LISTEN))))))))))))))/LISTEN))))))/LISTEN))))))))))))))/LISTEN))))))))))))/LISTEN)))))
Field Sales Offices are located in Atlanta, Georgia; Chicago, Illinois;

Machine shorthand transcription Converting and interpreting machine shorthand English letter abbreviations and symbols into readable typewritten format involves some new procedures and some that are similar to those of machine transcription.

A description of the machine shorthand transcription process follows:

1. Remove the tape notes at the platen of the shorthand machine.

2. Place the note tape into a transcription box so that two lengths of notes are readily visible at a given time.
3. Scan the notes for priority or rush work.
4. Edit the notes to find corrections, deletions, additions, or other changes; mark these sections with a colored pencil for ready reference.
5. Cross out notes not to be included in the transcript. Often, after a letter is dictated, there will need to be a change in a sentence. Identify the change by recording three asterisks and a number 2; record the new sentence as a substitution for the first one, as shown:

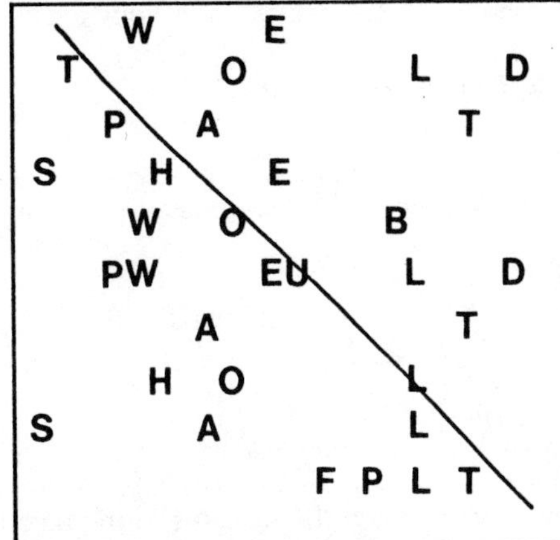

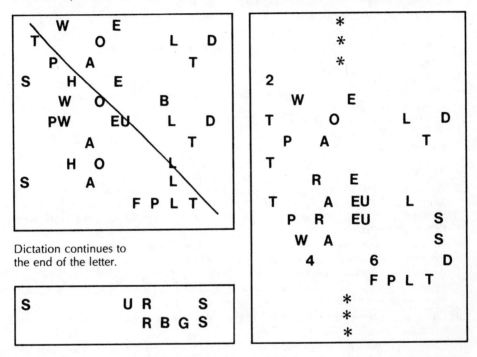

Dictation continues to the end of the letter.

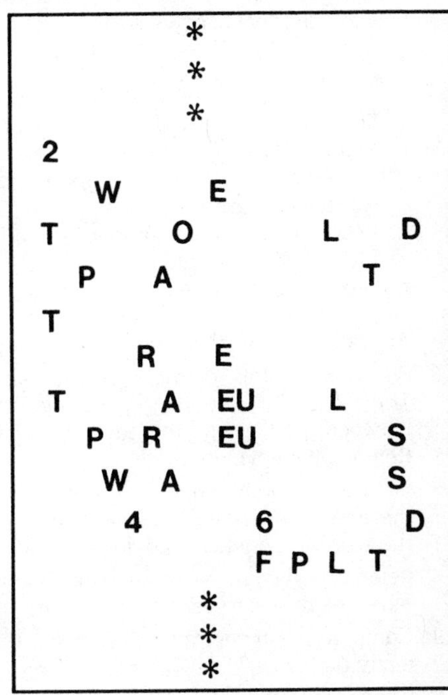

6. Estimate the number of actual words found in one fold of machine shorthand notes. Multiply this number by the number of prefolded sections in the recorded notes for a given letter. This will produce an estimated word count.
7. Refer to the *Letter Placement Table*, page 74, for marginal typewriter information; set margins and tabular stops; also, prepare the typewriter for correct spacing.
8. Place an envelope on the typewriter paper table. Assemble the appropriate stationery on top of the *Triple-Form Typewriting Copy Guide* (see sample on page 73). Place these pages between the envelope flap. Spin this packet into the machine to prevent slippage.
9. Remove the envelope and begin to transcribe while focusing attention on the machine shorthand notes; read by phrases.
10. Strive for smooth continuous typewriting by coordinating the reading of a phrase ahead of the typewriting. (See the illustration of the listen/type process on page 74; substitute the word *read* for the word *listen* when studying this illustration.)

Post-transcription procedures for machine shorthand The following procedures will be helpful in identifying completed machine shorthand notes:

Remove the completed tape from the transcription box. Place an elastic band around the notes and write the date on them.

Transcribed tape notes may also be filed in long envelopes ($4^1/_8" \times 9^1/_2"$) for future reference. Identifying information written on the face of the envelope might include the date, the dictator, the file number, and other data.

Stenographic transcription While the stenographic-notebook transcription process differs in various ways from other forms of transcription, it also shares similarities with them. A typical work-flow pattern which may be used by a secretary/stenographer is outlined below:

1. Elevate the stenographic notebook to preclude eye fatigue. A copyholder may be used for this purpose.
2. Look for signaling devices (as paper clips, folded corners of the notebook, or colored pencil notations) that are often used to flag rush items for priority transcription.
3. Edit the shorthand notes so that changes, insertions, and special instructions are clearly understood.
4. Determine as follows the marginal settings needed for the first letter:
   a. Select ten full lines of shorthand notes.
   b. Make an exact count of the number of words contained in these lines.
   c. Take the total word count and divide it by ten (lines) to obtain an average number of words per line.
   d. Record this average number for ready reference.
   e. Multiply this average number by the lines of recorded shorthand in a given letter.
   f. See the *Letter Placement Table* on page 74 for the marginal settings.
5. Adjust the marginal settings, tabular stops, and spacing as necessary.
6. Place an envelope on the typewriter paper table. Insert the letterhead (and carbons) and the *Triple-Form Typewriting Copy Guide* (a sample of which appears on page 73) into the space between the flap and the envelope. Spin the envelope into the machine to the date line. Remove the envelope.
7. Strive for smooth continuous typewriting by coordinating the reading of a phrase ahead of the typewriting. (See the listen/type illustration on page 74; substitute the word *read* for the word *listen* when studying this illustration).
8. Refer to a dictionary for spelling. Use a secretarial handbook or a company manual and other references to verify data as transcription progresses.
9. Compare the typescript with the shorthand notes to be certain that nothing was inadvertently omitted.
10. Cancel the letter in the notebook by drawing a vertical line through it to show that it is transcribed.

GENERAL POST-TRANSCRIPTION PROCEDURES

Regardless of the transcription method used—be it machine transcription, shorthand machine, or stenographic—the following procedures, if used by the secretary, will assure quality work:

Proofread and correct any previously undetected errors before removing the letter from the typewriter.

If possible, enlist the aid of a proofreading assistant to help check statistical or technical data on a transcript.

Make certain that any enclosures are attached to the letter.

Present the letter to the executive for signature.

5

CHAPTER FIVE

AUTOMATED AND SPECIALIZED TYPEWRITING WITH STYLIZATION

CONTENTS

5.1

AUTOMATED TYPEWRITING

INTRODUCTION

A revolution in typewriting began in the 1930s with the availability of the Autotypist®, a technological advancement which assisted the secretary in the production of routine, repetitive letters. The revolution manifested itself more dramatically in the mid 1960s with the introduction of media typewriters of a technologically far more advanced nature—typewriters coupled with recording media for the purpose of editing and correcting copy, information storage and retrieval, and overall increase in typewriting productivity, efficiency, and quality. Since that time, more advancements in typewriter technology have taken place and undoubtedly will continue to do so in future years.

Media typewriters are manufactured and marketed by many office machine companies. Classification of equipment is usually by media type, i.e., paper tape, magnetic tape, magnetic card, cassette, disk, memory, etc. Some media typewriters have a built-in capability to communicate with other similar devices in the same location or anywhere in this country or abroad. Some are designed to operate on-line with computers, mainly for the purpose of high-volume text editing—the typographical and editorial revision of typewritten copy.

Cathode-ray tube units (CRT) whose function is the electronic display of typewritten material stored in a computer are available with some advanced typewriter technologies.

A Typical Media Typewriter Includes an Input/Output Writer and a Console

The kind of media typewriter installed in an office is determined by the kind of work to be done—e.g., nature, volume, and quality requirements. Media typewriters are appropriate for use in office environments of all sizes and categories (as legal, medical, commercial, educational, financial, or sales).

With the installation of media typewriters, smaller business offices may have to change some procedures and eliminate others that have been found through work analysis to be unnecessary, in order to create an efficient work flow. Management of large offices may choose to reorganize entire departments or functional areas, they may wish to have secretaries specialize in typewritten communication or administration, and they may open new management opportunities to secretaries as a result of the installation of automated typewriting equipment and related devices and the implementation of vastly changed procedures. *Word processing* is a term used with reference to such changes in offices of all sizes and types.

Basic typing skills and related knowledge acquired by personnel working in offices equipped with media typewriters have now gained new importance and emphasis. Speed and accuracy are still the keys to typing productivity and quality; however, proofreading, editing, and applying the rules of English grammar have equal importance.

This chapter will build the secretary's knowledge of media typewriters and will help increase efficiency in using them. The suggestions presented here deal with methods and techniques of accomplishing work rather than descriptions of specific machine functions.

THE PRINCIPLE OF MEDIA

Media typewriters are designed to make secretarial tasks easier. The principle is a simple one. Everything the secretary types at the input/output writer or computer terminal (typewriter-like portion of the equipment installation) is simultaneously stored on media (as paper tape, magnetic tape, magnetic card, cassette, or memory) or directly into computer memory. That is, as typewriting takes place, each keystroke, space, tab, and carrier return is electronically inscribed on the media or sent over wires to a computer. Through the use of special recorded codes, the material

Media Typewriter with CRT Display Unit

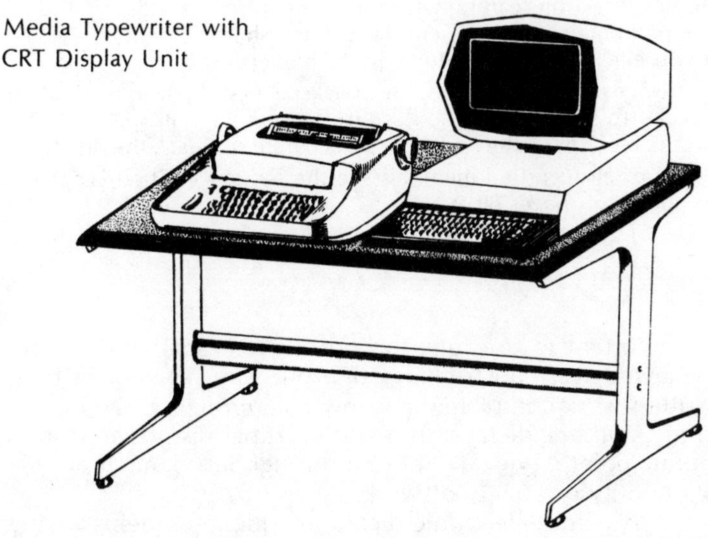

can be located quickly and easily and played back on paper (known as *hard copy*) in draft or final form. Typographical errors are corrected in almost all instances by a simple backspace/strikeover process. Playback speeds range from 150 words per minute to over 300 words per minute depending on the brand and sophistication of equipment. The fundamentals of single-element typewriter technologies make this possible.

Such typewriters accompanied by a cathode-ray tube display unit eliminate the need for hard copy when one is making revisions, since all reworking of the copy can be done from keyboard to computer with the display unit making each function visible. A final hard copy is produced (played back from computer memory) after all changes have been made or when the copy is required.

All typewritten work can be done on a media typewriter. Even a single envelope or label can be typed by using the capabilities offered by the recording media or computer memory. The secretary decides when to engage the media or memory capability in these applications. There are very few instances when the media portion of the typewriter should be deactivated and the keyboard used strictly as a non-media typewriter, as media capability is designed to aid in the processing of virtually all office typewriting.

TRAINING AND FOLLOW-UP

Most manufacturers of media typewriters offer complete training in machine function and the application of the equipment to specific work. Some companies offer self-paced programmed instruction in the operation of their equipment. Such instruction can take place in the work environment where the equipment is installed. Other manufacturers offer classroom instruction on their premises. It is vital that the media typewriter company commit itself to training as well as to any follow-up assistance that may be needed after installation.

TRANSITION PERIOD

After training, the secretary is likely to require from two to four weeks to become fully adjusted to a media typewriter. This is a very important period, since it is the time when the basis for efficiency and high productivity is established. The following points will help make transition easy:

1. Follow the manufacturer's directions carefully for recording, playback, editing, and all other functions of the equipment. As experience is gained, shortcuts will be discovered which will increase efficiency and productivity to higher levels.
2. Record media "perfectly" each time; that is, the backspace/strikeover method of correcting typographical errors should be used as errors occur, and all special codes should be included in the recording which will create accurate playback the first time.
3. Keep an accurate record of all recorded material (see the section entitled "Logging, Filing, and Record Keeping" on pages 89–90).
4. Be consistent in the use of all machine functions and activities related to the media typewriter.

WORK FLOW

A smooth work flow is important to use fully the productive capabilities of the media typewriter and to avoid wasteful backlogs of work. The segment of time taken to process typewritten work completely is known as *throughput* and comprises the time from *input* (author's dictation) to *output* (final distribution). It is desirable from an economic point of view to shorten throughput as much as posible without sacrificing quantity or quality of work.

In addition to media typewriters, electronic dictation equipment helps greatly in reducing throughput time (see also Chapter 4, "Dictation and Transcription:

Input and Output"). This equipment permits the author's input speed to be relatively high, while allowing the secretary to remain productive at the work station.

SUGGESTED METHODS FOR BUILDING EFFICIENCY

Standard writing line Select a writing line appropriate in length for all correspondence and documents which are typed on 8½" × 11" paper, e.g., six inches. Adjust for document body length by recording fewer or additional carrier returns (referred to as *carriage returns* on standard typebar typewriters) before the first line of typing or in another appropriate area. The establishment of a standard writing line length for the majority of work will save time and effort and will avoid unnecessary duplication of machine setup activities, which are costly.

Tab grid (standard tabs) Set tab stops every five spaces across the writing line; do not remove tab stops except for very unusual formatting or for documents prepared on paper of an unusual size. Tabbing through several tab stops to arrive at a desired location on the writing line saves considerable time and effort as compared with clearing and resetting tab stops for every new document. Thus, all material containing tabs can be played back from media without concern for changing or resetting tab stops manually.

Standard tabs are useful in typing tables and statistical columns as well: Either space forward one, two, or three spaces or backspace once, twice, or three times from the nearest tab stop to arrive at any given location on the writing line; if recording, be sure to use the special code for this kind of backspacing.

Page beginnings When the beginning of a page is the starting point of a document, insert the paper to a point two carrier returns above the first line of type and begin recording with two carrier returns.

```
Insert paper to here ⊥ Turn to record mode
2 CR's ——
          January 15, 197_




          Mr. John Adams
          123 Main Street
          Southbury, CT 06488
```

This procedure will ensure that the typing element will begin playback from the left margin regardless of its position on the writing line just before playback. Consistent use of this procedure will avoid false starts in playback. For example, if the beginning of the page is not the starting point of the document, begin recording with the first character of type after the page heading or page number.

```
          Stevens and Stevens          -2-          June 4, 197__

Begin recording
here ———— rental of equipment from your company.  We can justify the
          installation of two Model 16-AZs and one Model 16-AW.  Please
```

Page endings When the end of the page is also the end of the document, record end-of-page codes—e.g., stop, media eject, repeat—according to the kind of document in process and according to the manufacturer's instructions.

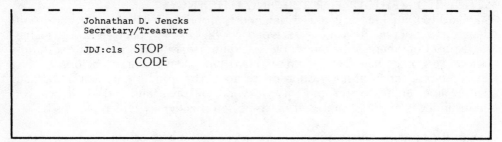

```
Johnathan D. Jencks
Secretary/Treasurer

JDJ:cls  STOP
         CODE
```

When the end of the page is not the end of the document, record the number of carrier returns normally required after the last line typed.

```
Since you have expressed a high level of interest in our
products, we would like to hear from you soon in regard to
ordering our latest model.  CR
                            CR
```

It is imperative to be consistent in the end-of-page recording procedure. Carrier-return codes, tab codes, and other page-end codes are not generally visible on the hard copy. Consistent adherence to standardized coding procedures will assure accurate playback of recorded information.

Pagination and subsequent page headings When recording one-time documents which will not be edited extensively by the author, record the page numbers and the subsequent page headings as part of the body of the document. If, however, extensive revision is anticipated, these page numbers and page headings (with the exception of the page-one heading lines) should not be recorded. These items should be inserted manually from the typewriter keyboard during playback, with the secretary being certain that this identifying information is not inadvertently recorded on the media. In this way, only the body of the document is recorded and the secretary need not be concerned that a page number may appear from playback at an inappropriate place on the page during the revision process.

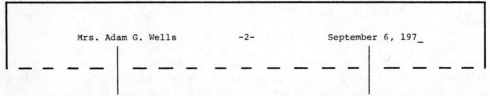

```
Mrs. Adam G. Wells            -2-            September 6, 197_
```

Record heading if one-time document with little or no author revision anticipated.

Do not record heading if extensive editing is anticipated. Change to record mode for 1st character after heading line.

Fingering techniques A secretary experienced in the use of a media typewriter touch-types the control keys and code keys related to the functions of the media with the same speed and skill as an experienced secretary handles the familiar alphabetical and numerical keys of the typewriter keyboard. In order to master efficient fingering techniques, one should (1) determine which fingers facilitate the quickest and easiest reach to the control and code keys, and (2) practice the use of these keys with the appropriate fingers without looking at the I/O keyboard or media console. Speed will soon develop and accuracy will become established.

Touch-typing the Control Keys

Preparation of media for editing Review the initial machine instructions for the special procedures and codes that are necessary when recording material subsequently to be edited and corrected on hard copy as well as on media. For example, hyphenation, underscoring, and centering are usually subject to special handling. Always record material while utilizing these necessary procedures and codes. Very frequently, copy thought to be final the first time it is typed is later edited and therefore must be retyped. Inclusion of all special codes at the time when the material is first recorded will eliminate confusion when revisions are later made. Consistency in this practice is imperative.

Work grouping The term *work grouping* refers to the organization and prioritizing of work according to task. The many advantages of work grouping include increased productivity and efficiency, a heightened sense of accomplishment, and reduced fatigue. Work grouping takes only a few minutes and can be accomplished in the following ways:

1. At the beginning of the workday and at various intervals during the day, review the tasks to be done.
2. Sort the tasks into categories (as proofreading, filing, copying, recording, or playback).
3. Decide which categories must be completed first, second, third, and so on according to their importance and urgency. Of course, any single task which must take priority over all others should be handled first.
4. Whenever possible, complete all tasks in each category before going on to the next one.

A well-organized approach to accomplishing tasks is always the best. Work grouping is of great assistance in completing work accurately and on time.

Proofreading Every secretary is responsible for proofreading the materials that she has typed. The importance of this task should never be underestimated. Each word should be read carefully to ensure that the spelling is correct, and each sentence should be read to make sure that no words or punctuation marks have been omitted. An efficient method of proofreading copy which has just been recorded on media is as follows: Read the first few lines of the hard copy produced during the recording function, then start playback, keeping the fingers over the playback control keys and continuing to read ahead of playback. When an error is detected, control playback by line, word, or character to the point of change. Make the correction and resume the procedure. When proofreading copy away from the media typewriter, the secretary or the author must mark the copy where errors exist or changes are to be made. The list of proofreader's marks shown in Chapter 8 will aid in this process. Authors and secretaries should use the same marks for consistency and also for complete understanding of the revisions to be made.

Developing a procedures manual Ideally, any office should standardize its operational procedures in order to attain peak efficiency. Otherwise, confusion, duplication of effort, and great amounts of wasted time can result. Therefore, with the installation of media typewriter equipment, standardization and uniform procedures are highly recommended. A procedures manual is an invaluable aid to standardization efforts. Such a manual should include at least all of the following items:

1. Examples of company correspondence format (including recorded codes which are not readily visible on hard copy)
2. Manuscript format (including recorded codes which are not readily visible on hard copy)
3. Procedures for typing envelopes, labels, cards, and other miscellaneous documents
4. Filing procedures (both media and copy)
5. Work flow chart
6. Copying and duplicating procedures
7. Distribution procedures
8. Administrative procedures (e.g., with respect to petty cash, messages, etc.)

A good procedures manual covers every task performed by a secretary in a given office environment. Such a manual can be used as a training tool for new secretarial personnel as well as a reference for presently employed secretaries.

SPECIAL APPLICATIONS OF MEDIA TYPEWRITERS

Drafts A media typewriter is invaluable in the preparation of drafts—typed information which will be edited once or several times before being prepared in final form. It is suggested that most work be prepared in draft form during the record process. This makes a working copy of each document available to the author for review and editorial change if necessary. If material is known to be editorially correct at the time of input, then the secretary need only submit a final typed copy.

Drafts can be typed in the desired format on hard-copy paper of the same size and quality as the final copy, or more economically on paper of lesser quality. If a draft is prepared on slightly larger paper and double-spaced, ample white space will be available for the author's editing, changes, and/or marginal notes. Prenumbered draft paper facilitates accounting for the number of lines in a document and coordinating page lines to media lines. It is important that the vertical space between the numbers at the left edge of the draft paper be identical to the vertical (double) spacing of the I/O writer so that registration of typewritten lines and printed numbers will remain constant from the top of the page to the bottom.

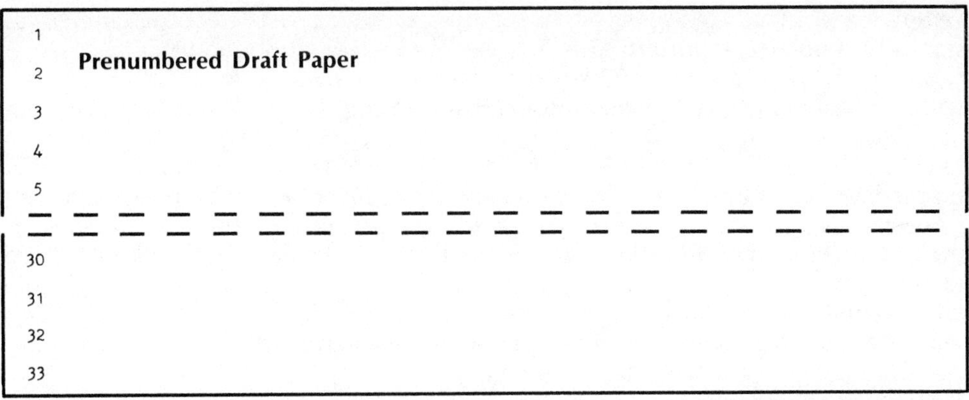

Specially designed continuous-form draft paper is available for high-volume draft work. It minimizes the consumption of time when rough drafts are in process. This type of paper (sometimes packaged in roll form) is perforated at the end of each sheet. The free edge of the first sheet is inserted into the typewriter. When this sheet is fully typed, the secretary rolls the second sheet into place without detaching the first, and so on until the last page of the draft is completed. The secretary then tears off and separates the sheets of the finished draft.

If the first draft of a document returned to the secretary is revised more than 30 percent, it is suggested that the secretary rerecord the entire draft at top keyboarding speed since the time required to process the revisions will probably exceed rerecording time. It is most likely that any subsequent revision of the document by the author will be less extensive than the previous one; therefore, the material should be revised using the benefits provided by the media. Henceforth, the document need not be typed in its entirety again—use of the media for each new revision and the final playback will result in peak productivity.

Guide letters (form letters) Oftentimes, a guide letter program is appropriate when an office initiates or responds to high volumes of routine correspondence. Media typewriters are ideal for this purpose. Each guide letter is recorded once and played back the necessary number of times, letter-perfect and at high speed. Letters can be programmed on the media to play back on continuous-form letterhead without stopping until the last letter is completed, or one at a time on individual sheets of letterhead paper.

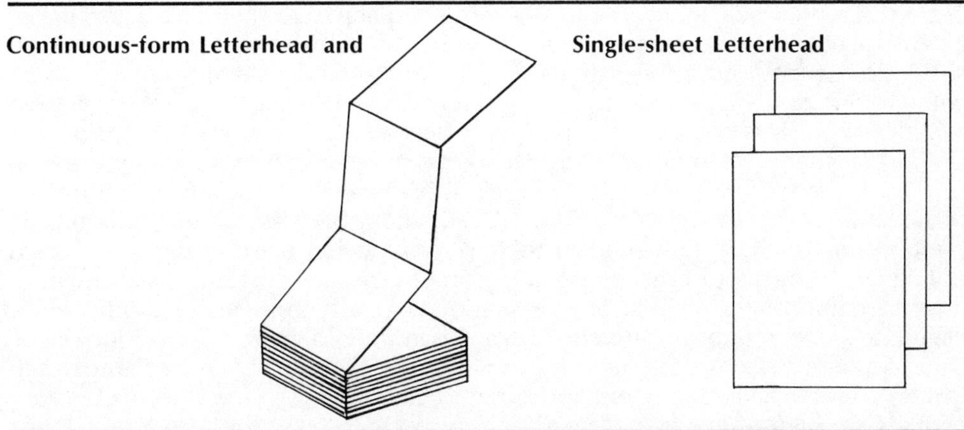

Letters containing varying information for each recipient are programmed to stop at the point(s) of insertion of the varying information. The variables can be typed in manually from the I/O keyboard during playback or, in some media typewriters, programmed to play out automatically. In some cases, inside addresses can be played back automatically on envelopes. When continuous-form envelopes are used, the process becomes fully automatic. Guide letters are stored permanently on media or until they are no longer useful. For specific instructions in recording guide letters, one should refer to the directions provided by the manufacturer of the equipment. A guide letter logbook ought to be maintained as a directory to letters recorded on media. A file folder or binder should house copies of the guide letters showing any special codes or indicating any special instructions for machine setup activities. The reference initial line can include coding which indicates the location of the letter on media.

Media Codes in Reference Initial Area of a Letter

```
Rochelle M. Parkes
President

RMP:cnj306A
```

special coding to indicate location of document on media

Forms The preparation of forms on a media typewriter is a quick, easy process. Place a sheet of onionskin or other lightweight, tissue-like paper over a working copy of each form that is to be completed. The boxes and lines of the form will show through the onionskin paper, thus allowing accurate placement of the information to be filled in and creating a draft at the same time. For each such form, use the same working copy and a new sheet of onionskin. When there are several copies of the same form to be completed, each with varying information, the secretary simply proceeds as just described—i.e., recording document separation codes between each set of variables according to the manufacturer's recommendations. It is significant that in selecting or designing business forms to be processed via media typewriter equipment, one should not overlook the vertical spacing between lines, boxes, and blank areas to be filled in. The space should be equal to multiples of the vertical single-spacing of the I/O writer. This requirement is important to the complete and automatic registration (alignment) of fill-in information on lines and in boxes and blanks during playback.

If the vertical spacing of the form is not comparable to the vertical spacing of the I/O writer, it is necessary to record stop codes at the points where manual readjustment for accurate registration is required. Manual readjustment is made with the variable-spacing device of the I/O writer—usually a feature of the left cylinder knob. This device is designed to disengage the vertical-line spacing (indexing) mechanism temporarily so that the secretary can turn the platen upward or downward freely and change the vertical placement of the line of writing.

When all of the drafts are recorded, play them back from the media on the printed (final copy) forms. If all of the typographical errors have been corrected during recording, all of the forms will then be letter-perfect and the placement of information in the boxes and on the lines will be accurate. This method is especially useful when one is completing several-part forms separated by carbon paper, since no erasures will be required during the final-copy process and since each carbon copy of the form (up to approximately eight copies) will be legible because of the firm, even impression created during playback from the media.

Columnar format Typing alphabetical and numerical information in columnar format is facilitated by media for two important reasons: (1) easy correction of typographical errors, and (2) high-speed, error-free playback. Recording tabular material is an easy process with some special consideration given to backspacing, centering, aligning numbers, and underscoring. The manufacturer's instructions and/or training materials should be reviewed to ensure proper recording procedures and accurate playback. Some media typewriters are equipped with automatic number and decimal-point alignment features for columnar formatting. This technological advancement should be considered for high-volume statistical work, as this kind of machine capability increases statistical typing productivity.

Legal format Typewritten work in the law office is highly specialized and requires particular care. Elements of legal documentation which make it special are:

1. Very high quality requirements—usually letter-perfect typing without erasures
2. Strict adherence to preestablished (and, in some instances, ruled) left and right margins
3. High revision rate
4. High volume of constant material which calls for the insertion of varying information

Legal documents of all kinds can be produced quickly and easily by using media typewriter equipment. The backspace/strikeover method of error correction is the means by which high-quality error- and erasure-free copy can be produced.

The mechanical adjustment to the right margin of each recorded line of information, in the playback mode with or without revisions or variables, automatically places copy between the vertical rulings found on many legal documents. When line lengths must change due to editorial revision or the insertion of variable information or when preestablished margin settings must be honored, a simple mechanical adjustment (usually the depression of a special key button) and the implementation of some special record and playback rules will provide the copy required. Reference to the manufacturer's instructions will aid in achieving the desired results. Revision procedures for legal documents are carried out just as those for any other communications (see "Drafts," pages 84–85). Equipment instruction materials should also be reviewed for further assistance.

Paragraph selection is a term often used to describe a method of preparing large volumes of information that is similar in content but can be varied in paragraph sequence. The entire resource of paragraphs is recorded containing appropriate coding to facilitate the insertion of variable information where it is required. Special coding at the end of each paragraph is necessary to avoid the playback of unwanted paragraphs. The paragraphs can be permanently stored and played back in any desired sequence, any number of times. Great increases in productivity can be realized through this procedure. As information becomes outdated, revision of the media should take place to ensure the correctness of all final documents. External correspondence prepared in the law office is often repetitive. Thus, the principles for structuring a guide letter program (see pages 85–86 of this chapter) are applicable to it. These same principles can be adapted to other legal documents (as wills, trusts, or briefs) that are similar in content and that are almost always prepared in the same sequence of paragraphs.

MEDIA MANAGEMENT

The work station The following illustration depicts an effectively organized work station where a media typewriter is installed. Note the close proximity of all supplies, references, communication devices, and other items to the actual secretarial seating area. An efficiently arranged work area will significantly increase productivity and at the same time decrease fatigue.

The Work Station

The following environmental considerations are important when creating or modifying the work station area:

Furniture
Lighting
Heating, air-conditioning, and ventilation
Electrical outlets
Space
Safety and security
Accessibility

Media supply Most manufacturers of media typewriters offer the media for purchase in any quantity. Some companies offer a lower price for large orders. Although paper tape media is less expensive initially, magnetic media is more practical since it is reusable indefinitely. It is wise to have extra supplies of media on hand in the event that an unusually large volume of work must be processed, or in case a special project is to be done at the media typewriter. A notation of the reorder number of media should be kept close at hand to facilitate quick replenishment of supply. A reorder number file located at the work station is very useful.

Media utilization Media should be separated into three categories for efficient use: Daily, Temporarily-stored, and Permanently-stored.

Daily media is that which is used repeatedly for one-time documents, items which do not need to be stored for long periods of time. The benefit of reserving media for each workday, e.g., Monday tapes, Tuesday tapes, is in allowing five workdays for the editing, revising, and final processing of the recorded materials before revising the media for other work.

Temporarily-stored media should contain those documents such as some guide letters, reports, and manuscripts which have short-term usefulness. These materials may be played back repeatedly or revised over an extended period of time.

Permanently-stored media should contain materials which are useful over a long period. Guide letters (see the section entitled "Guide Letters," pages 85–86), basic formats of reports and other documents which seldom change in content, address lists, and manuscripts which are in a constant process of revision are among the kinds of documents that are permanently stored.

Media storage Daily media should be stored within fingertip reach of the secretary. Since this media is used most often, it should be kept in the secretary's desk or in a portable file that is in the immediate area of the work station for quick, easy access. Temporarily-stored media may be kept in a file drawer located in an area close to the work station but it need not be within immediate reach. The same principle applies to permanently-stored media. It is advisable to retain all media within drawers or files which can be locked. This is important for security purposes, especially where recorded classified information is involved.

Logging, filing, and record keeping It is important to maintain a system of control that permits the rapid location of all recorded material and hard copies of that material. In designing a logging/filing/record keeping system, one should keep in mind simplicity and convenience. The specific design of such a system is determined in every instance by the nature and volume of the work itself. The following suggestions, however, will aid in establishing effective controls:

1. Identify cassettes, cartridges, magnetic cards, magnetic tapes, etc., by means of numbers or other identifying codes. Some media are pre-numbered by the manufacturer and adapt easily to any control system.

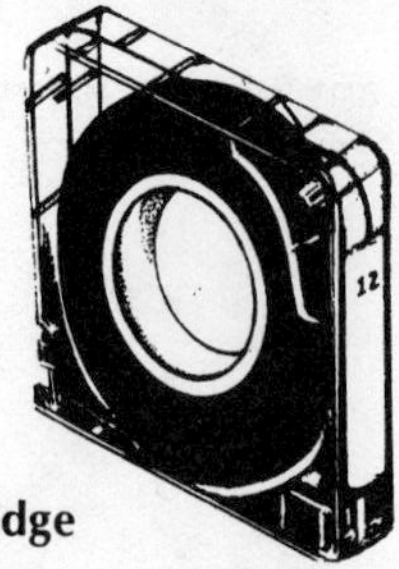

Tape Cartridge

Magnetic Card

2. Create a brief coding system to appear on hard copy indicating the media and the location on the media of that document.
3. File one copy of each one-time document in a daily file folder in the order of its location on the media. Store the folder in the secretarial desk or within immediate reach in the work station area.
4. File in a special drawer or binder copies of temporarily- and permanently-stored documents, showing all special codes and typewriter setup information. Use transparent page protectors or page lamination (a mechanically applied plastic coating) to protect copies of permanently-stored documents and to ensure a long storage life for them.
5. Keep files and binders up-to-date; that is, once the stored information is out-of-date or no longer useful, eliminate the obsolete copies. Update media according to the manufacturer's instructions, omitting old or unused information, and adding any new material. File updated hard copies in the file or binder.

Media care and maintenance With normal use, most magnetic media is virtually indestructible and is indefinitely reusable for recording and playing back information. Paper media is recordable once and may be played back an indefinite number of times. Paper media, however, requires special handling because of its inherent susceptibility to tearing and wear.

Regardless of the physical makeup of media, it is necessary to maintain its serviceability through proper care and maintenance:

Paper media

Store the media where the possibility of physical damage is minimized.

If the media is torn, investigate the feasibility of splicing or repairing it. If repair is impossible, discard the old media and rerecord the information on new media.

Magnetic media

Store the media where there is as little dust as possible. Wipe visible dust from media with a clean, dry cloth.

Fingerprints may impair record and playback functions of some media. To remedy, wipe the affected area or areas with a clean, dry cloth.

Store and handle media in such a manner that the possibility of physical damage is minimized. If irreparable damage occurs, discard the media and rerecord information on new media.

Media typewriter care and maintenance To ensure the greatest serviceability of media typewriter equipment, the secretary should:

1. Call for service if equipment is not functioning properly.
2. Clean the typefaces with a clean dry cloth as needed, unless instructed otherwise by the manufacturer.
3. Use the acoustical hood (the clear plastic cover in the area of the typehead) as a dust cover as well as a noise reducer.
4. Keep food and beverages away from the equipment.
5. Cover the I/O writer when the equipment is not in use.

6. Discourage the use of the equipment by personnel who are not properly trained in its use.
7. Be sure that the On/Off switch is set at "Off" at the end of the workday or when the equipment is to be idle for long periods of time.

On the other hand, the manufacturer should:

1. Instruct the customer in the use and care of equipment.
2. Offer a regularly scheduled maintenance program to ensure cleaning, lubrication, and replacement of parts as needed.
3. Respond quickly to service calls.

Ordering typewriter (I/O writer) ribbons Media typewriter ribbons are generally available in either fabric or film design. The following list shows the significant characteristics of each.

Fabric	**Film**
Medium to high quality print	Highest quality print
Durable	Durable*
Reusable until inking intensity is no longer effective	Disposable* after single use
Multicolors available from some manufacturers	Multicolors available from some manufacturers

**Note regarding the durability of film ribbons:* Film ribbons are durable even though they are disposable after one use. This kind of ribbon, usually made of plastic that is coated with ink on one side, must be durable to withstand the striking of typebars or a typehead. Such ribbons are disposable because of their makeup: when the typebar or typehead strikes the ribbon, the ink in the shape of whatever character that has been struck is removed from the ribbon and is impressed onto the paper. This leaves a blank (or uninked) place on the ribbon in the shape of the struck character, thus preventing its reuse.

Most companies make ribbons available for the media typewriter equipment that they manufacture and market. Ribbons can usually be ordered and paid for singly or in quantity. The cost per ribbon is often less when a sizable quantity is ordered. Some companies offer an ordering plan that features automatic, periodic shipment of and billing for necessary supplies. Prepared-coupon systems are also available from some manufacturers of ribbons and other office supplies, whereby reorders are processed when a coupon is forwarded to the company with whom the ribbon order was placed. This coupon contains all the information necessary to ensure delivery of the proper items. Other convenient methods for ordering and reordering materials may be offered to the media typewriter customer and may warrant consideration, depending on individual office needs.

5.2

SPECIALIZED TYPEWRITING WITH STYLIZATION

GENERAL

The dynamics of today's business office has created the need for improvement, change, and versatility in the preparation of those typewritten documents that are to be distributed both internally and externally. Special effects, unique stylization, and a positive impact on the recipients of these documents can all be achieved by use of technologies now available.

SPECIALIZATION THROUGH TYPESTYLES

A very large variety of typestyles and sizes is available today from most typewriter and media typewriter manufacturers. The typestyles are designed to suit the needs of any office. For the sake of consistency, it is suggested that a standard typestyle be used for all general typing such as correspondence, manuscripts, reports, or notices. Special typestyles for specialized work such as mathematical equations, legal documents, library materials, and foreign languages are available as well. Single-element technology has made it possible to interchange typestyles while using only one typewriter. Most styles are available in two sizes: ten spaces to the inch (pica), and twelve spaces to the inch (elite). It is possible in some instances to use both elite and pica type on the same typewriter, thus providing great flexibility and economy in the production of typewritten material having strict copy fit requirements. Some standard typebar typewriters are designed so that selected typebars can be changed by the secretary to facilitate the use of special symbols or characters.

A variety of typestyles and sizes also exists for use with proportionally-spacing typewriters (both media and non-media). Composition typewriters provide a very wide selection of styles, sizes, and weights from which one may choose.

COPY JUSTIFICATION AND PROPORTIONAL SPACING

Copy with symmetrically even left and right margins is called *justified.* This format is desirable when special effects are desired and when the copy must fit precisely between two given points, for example, in a columnar format or on a full-width page (e.g., a six-inch line). Justified copy is found most often in books such as this one, in periodicals, in newspapers, and in advertising literature. It is also appropriate in correspondence, in legal documents, and in forms design. Standard typewriter characters (pica and elite) are rarely used for justified material because of their inflexibility; that is, each character fits into an equal amount of space without variation. Adjustment to compensate for justification must occur in spaces between words (see the illustration below) which creates an awkward appearance. Copy arranged in such a way is often difficult to read.

Justified Copy Prepared on a Pica-typeface Typewriter

It is often desirable to prepare
typewritten copy in "justified"
format. This format provides pre-
cisely even left and right margins;
and each line within the document
is precisely the same length as in
this sample of several lines. When
justified copy is prepared on a
pica (or elite) typewriter as in
this sample, the copy tends to look
awkward and is often difficult to
read.

Compare the above illustration with the following sample of the same material prepared on a typewriter designed to produce proportionally-spaced characters.

Justified Copy Prepared on a Proportionally-spacing Typewriter

It is often desirable to prepare typewritten
copy in "justified" format. This special for-
mat provides precisely even left and right
margins; and each line within the document
is precisely the same length as in this sample
of five and one half lines.

Proportionally-spaced characters occupy just the space they need according to their varying widths. Also, each character and each space consists of a number of "units" (the number varies among manufacturers) facilitating a pleasing appearance, excellent readability, and, when desired, justified copy.

Proportional Spacing Compared with Pica/Elite Typefaces

elite type	Many mornings are spent mailing materials to Madison.
pica type	Many mornings are spent mailing materials to Madison.
proportional spacing	Many mornings are spent mailing materials to Madison.

Proportionally-spacing typewriters are available in both media and non-media versions. Proportional spacing requires that the secretary pay special attention to setting tab stops, centering, error correction, typing numbers in columns, spacing, and setting margins. Instruction in these areas should be given by the typewriter manufacturer. Quick reference to an operator's manual will also aid in successful use of a proportionally-spacing typewriter the first time it is used.

Special effects can be produced through the versatility of proportionally-spacing typewriters. For example, the double printing of headings gives extra emphasis and variation to copy format.

A Double-typed Heading Prepared on a Proportionally-spacing Typewriter

MONTHLY REPORT - JULY

This special effect is accomplished by typing the information twice with a space between each character and two spaces between each word, with the second impression of the characters appearing superimposed over the first and misregistered by one unit of space. Other creative ways of producing attractive copy can be discovered through continued use of such specialized typewriters. Manufacturers of proportionally-spacing typewriters provide a variety of typestyles and sizes from which to choose in order to customize type to user needs.

Justified and non-justified copy of the highest quality can be produced through the use of desk model and media-related composition equipment. This equipment is used widely in the field of graphic arts and in business offices where highly specialized copy is required.

Sample of Copy Prepared on a Composition Typewriter

Justified Format

Several years before, the group had toured the area by bus. This time, half of the group rented cars, and the other half toured by bicycle. Places of interest included the French Riveria, Pisa (in Italy), Rome, and Florence. Each member of the group touring by bicycle expressed a great deal of enthusiasm for this means of travel.

Non-justified Format

Several years before, the group had toured the area
by bus. This time, half of the group rented cars, and
the other half toured by bicycle. Places of interest
included the French Riveria, Pisa (in Italy), Rome,
and Florence. Each member of the group touring
by bicycle expressed a great deal of enthusiasm
for this means of travel.

SPECIAL DOCUMENTS

Labels and cards Adhesive and nonadhesive labels as well as cards of various sizes are available in continuous form for ease in typing. The continuous form may be more efficient than separate labels or cards if many such items must be processed. Continuous-form materials are particularly effective when used with media typewriters but are also useful with standard non-media typewriters.

Secretarial procedures for the use of continuous-form labels and cards are as follows:

1. Insert the first of the continuous-form labels or cards behind the center of the platen with the bulk of the remainder attached and stacked behind the typewriter.
2. Move the page edge guide to the right until it is properly located to guide the left edge of the labels or cards. Roll the first label or card into position for typing.
3. Move two bail rollers so that they are located on the face of the first label or card. Set the left margin stop at a point which will allow accurate placement of typed information.

Pin-feed platens are available for most standard non-media and media typewriters. The purpose of this special platen is to guide continuous-form documents through the typewriter mechanism without slippage.

The typing of individual labels or cards (not in continuous form) is facilitated by the use of a sheet of 8½" × 11" paper pleated horizontally in the center. The pleat forms a pocket to hold the edge (bottom or top) of the label or card while it is positioned for typing. Follow the illustrations which are pictured below to construct the pleated sheet.

Procedure for the Construction of a Pleated Sheet

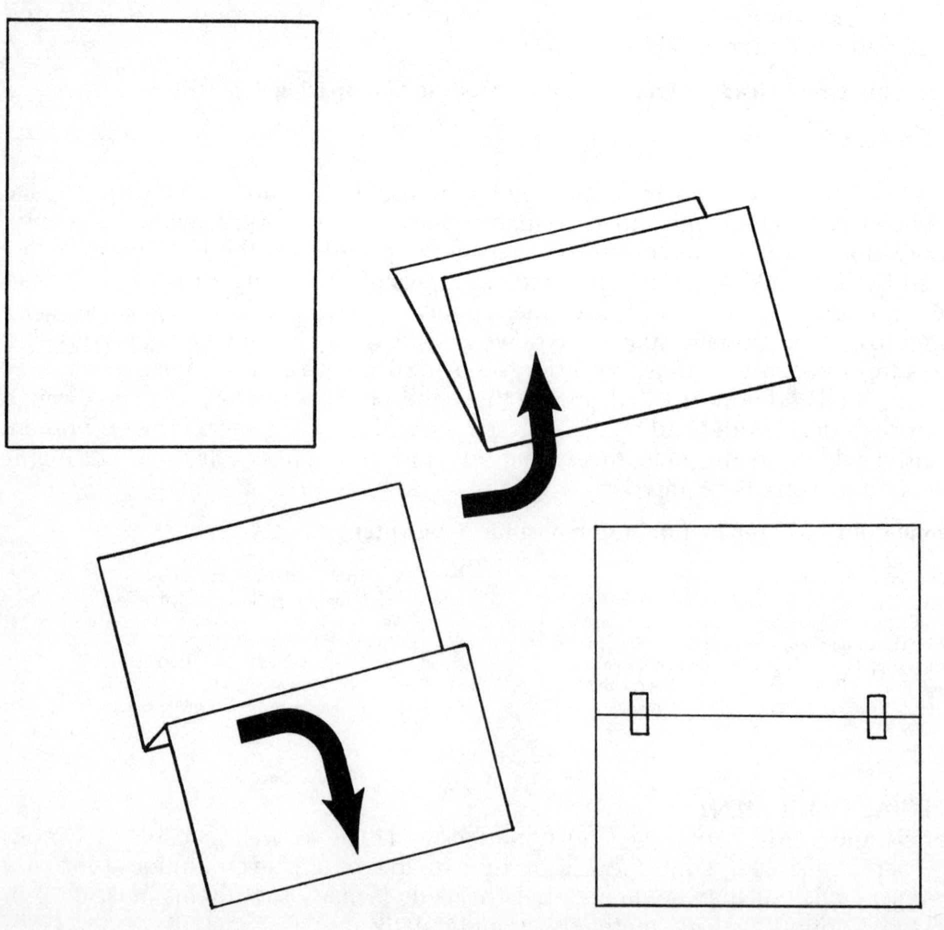

Once the sheet is prepared, roll it into the typewriter to a point where the pleat is exposed in front of the platen. To type in the center of the label or card, place the bottom edge of the label or card in the pleat on the front of the sheet. The margin stops, tab stops, paper-edge guide, bail rollers, and other mechanisms should be set appropriately. Roll the pleated sheet with card or label inserted in it toward the front of the typewriter into place for typing.

When the typing has been completed, remove the card or label by rolling the platen knobs toward the back of the typewriter until the lower edge of the label or card is freed from beneath the platen. Do not remove the pleated sheet until the last card or label is completed.

To type at the top edge of the card or label, follow the procedure for typing in the center portion of cards and labels described above.

To type at the bottom edge of the card or label, invert the pleated sheet, roll it into the typewriter to a point above the type guide (the area of typewriter mechanism where the type is impressed on the paper). Insert the top edge of the label or card into the pleat and roll the platen toward the front of the typewriter until the bottom edge of the card is in position for typing. Type the required information.

Envelopes Envelopes for business correspondence are available in continuous form as well as individually. Continuous-form envelopes are a time-saver when large numbers must be addressed. The procedure for typing on continuous-form envelopes is similar to that for typing continuous-form cards and labels.

Chain feeding increases productivity when one is typing individual envelopes. This method is useful when a large number of envelopes must be typed and continuous-form envelopes are not to be used. Follow the steps outlined below to accomplish chain feeding with the front-feed method:

1. Place a stack of blank envelopes to the right (or left) of the typewriter for quick, easy access. They should be placed in the normal reading position.
2. Set margins and tab stops where required.
3. Roll the first envelope into the typewriter and type the desired information.
4. Roll the platen knobs toward the front of the typewriter until the top edge (about ¾″) of the envelope remains visible in front of the platen.
5. Place a blank envelope, bottom edge first, behind the top edge of the typed envelope and roll the platen knobs toward the front of the typewriter until it is in position for typing. Type the required information.
6. Roll the platen knobs toward the front of the typewriter until the top edge of the second envelope is exposed ¾″.
7. Place the next envelope behind the one in the typewriter and proceed as with the second envelope.

The completed envelopes will accumulate at the rear of the platen. When six to ten typed envelopes have accumulated, remove them and continue the procedure.

METHODS OF DUPLICATING ORIGINAL DOCUMENTS

Today's secretary should be well-informed about the availability and use of various means of duplicating office documents: carbon paper, electronic copying, and playback from media. Offset reproduction as well as spirit and stencil processes are available according to the criteria described in Chapter 12. Office management usually determines the method to be used. If the decision-making responsibility is delegated to the secretary, the choice should be based on an examination of such factors as quantity and quality of copies required, time and equipment availability, expense, and other similar considerations. Copy for electronic duplication can be prepared on a non-media typewriter as well as on a media typewriter.

Carbon paper In order to produce several copies of a document at the same time that the original is being typed, carbon paper and lightweight tissue-like copy paper are appropriate. This method of duplication is used when a minimum number of copies is required (one to eight is a common recommendation), and when the quality of the copies is not an important factor. A typewriter rendering a firm, even impression will produce legible copies because of the firmness with which the type head or typebars strike the paper (an adjustment mechanism is available on most typewriters to increase or decrease type pressure as needed). A media typewriter is particularly capable of producing legible carbon copies.

To prevent slippage of loose carbons and copy paper, place the top edge of the assembled carbon pack into the flap of an envelope with the back of the envelope and the back of the pack facing forward. Place the envelope carrying the carbon pack behind the platen and roll, or index, the entire assembly into place. Remove the envelope and position the pack to begin typing (standard typewriter), recording, or playing back (media typewriter).

Preassembled carbon sets are useful for saving time. Make ready time is significantly reduced as the carbon paper and copy sheets are prepacked in tablet form. The secretary tears off the number of carbons and copy sheets required, places the original copy paper on top of the pack, and inserts all items into the typewriter.

Prepacked Tablet-form Carbon Sets

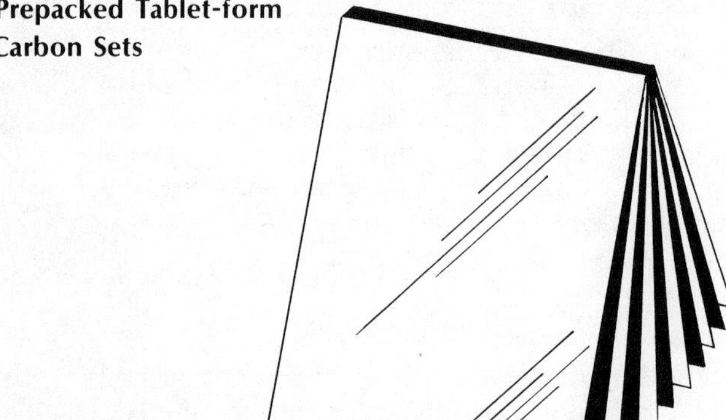

When typing is completed, the carbon paper is then snapped out of the pack and discarded. The copy sheets are simultaneously released from the pack and are ready for distribution or filing. One should always give consideration to the quality of carbon paper and copy paper. Supplies of poor quality are virtually useless in today's progressive business office.

Electronic copying equipment For moderate- to high-copy volume and quality requirements, electronic duplication of originals may be most effective and efficient. Today, electronic copiers are available in various configurations to produce volumes of copies from one to several thousand. Some copiers are capable of producing duplicates of mailable quality—that is, the copies are so clean and clear that some authors sign them and send them out in the same manner as actual originals.

Also available is equipment ranging from low-volume desktop copiers to sophisticated high-volume floor models capable of copying, enlarging, and reducing the original copy; collating; reproducing on materials other than paper (e.g., clear plastic transparencies) as well as on letterhead, colored paper, plain bond, and others. Because of the broad versatility of equipment available today, it is important to give very careful thought to the copying needs of one's office before deciding on or suggesting a model for purchase, lease, or rental. Many manufacturers will analyze copier needs to help the user make the right equipment decision. Installation of an appropriate model will ensure the capability to copy at a minimum cost.

Playback from media If more than one copy of a document having original quality is required, one can produce additional originals by repeated playback of recorded material. This method is ideal when the document to be reproduced is brief (i.e., one to two pages) and the number of required originals is relatively low.

MECHANIZED TYPOGRAPHICAL ERROR CORRECTION

In an effort to make the typewriting job as streamlined and efficient as possible, technical designers of typewriter equipment have devoted time and attention to the problem of typographical errors. As a result, the capability for error correction has been built into some standard electric typewriters and into some media typewriters. Secretarial procedures in general terms are as follows:

Assumption

The word to be typed is *home*.
The secretary has typed *hi*.

Procedure for Correction

Backspace to the *i* according to manufacturer's instructions.

Restrike the *i* to automatically remove or cover the character (this depends on the design of the typewriter).

Type the *o* where the *i* had been.

Proceed with the typewriting.

A review of the operator's manual for specific instruction in the use of the correction feature is necessary, since the operation varies from typewriter to typewriter.

TECHNIQUE REVIEW OF SELECTED TYPING PROCEDURES

Alignment The term *alignment* refers to the proper placement of characters (words, numbers, or symbols) within a text after the paper has been removed from the typewriter and reinserted.

Procedure

1. Insert a sheet of scrap paper into the typewriter.
2. Type the alphabet without spacing between letters.
3. Make a mental note of the spatial relationship of rulings on the alignment scale of the typewriter to the letters of the alphabet typed on the paper.
4. Remove the scrap paper from the typewriter.
5. Reinsert the page to be corrected while maintaining the original paper-edge guide location. Straighten the paper if necessary.
6. Roll the paper into the typewriter to the point of correction.
7. Adjust the spatial relationship of the rulings on the alignment scale to the typed information surrounding the correction area (both horizontally and vertically) as noted in step 3.
8. (Optional) Test the accuracy of the resulting alignment before typing the actual correction by setting the ribbon position lever at "stencil," and typing the correction. The inkless impression made on the paper will show whether alignment is accurate or not. If so, reengage the ribbon mechanism. If not, readjust and retest.
9. Type the correction.

Result

. . . Sales for the month totaled $20,000.
corrected to
. . . Sales for the month totaled $200,000.

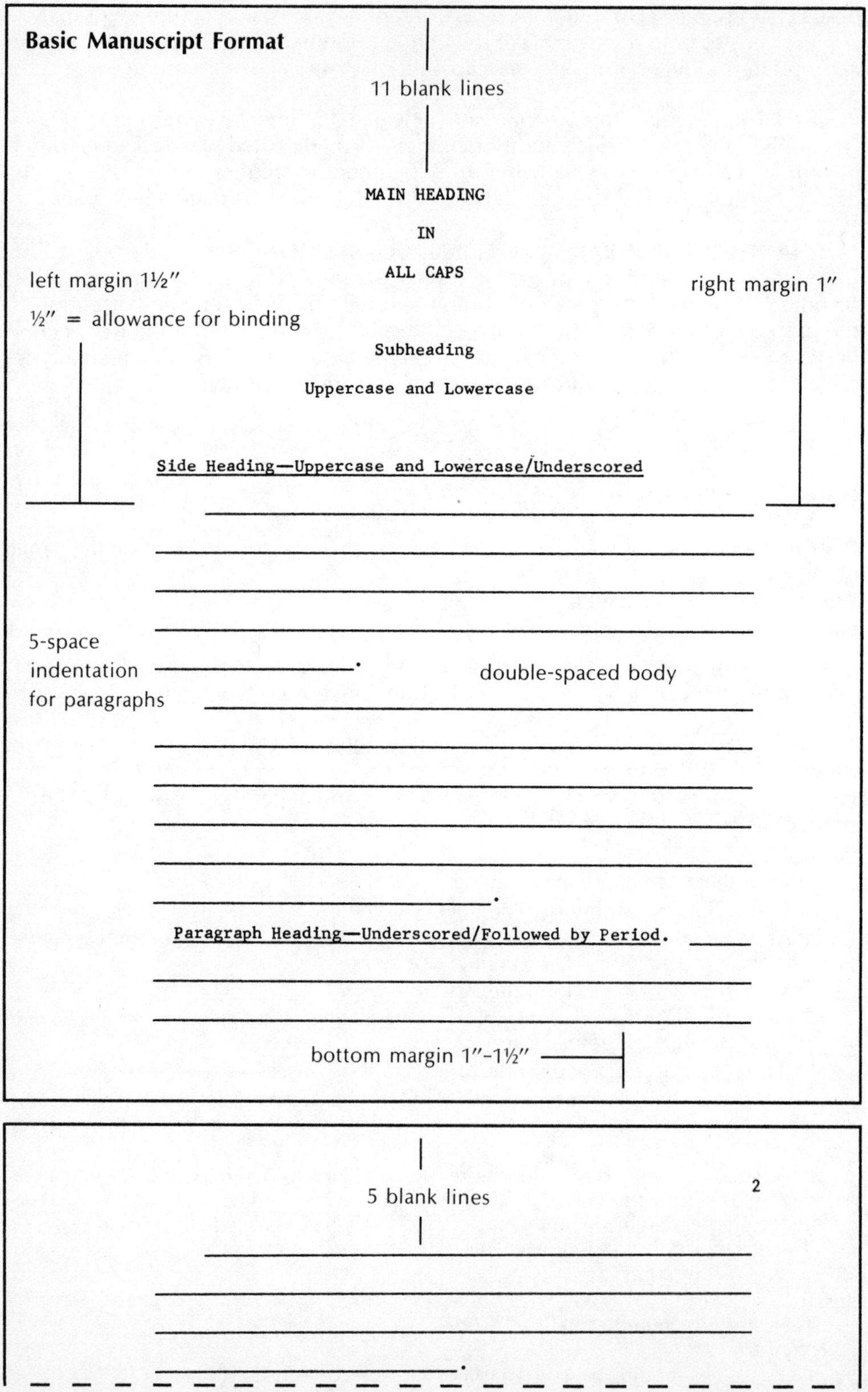

Basic Manuscript Format

11 blank lines

MAIN HEADING

IN

ALL CAPS

left margin 1½"

½" = allowance for binding

right margin 1"

Subheading

Uppercase and Lowercase

Side Heading—Uppercase and Lowercase/Underscored

5-space indentation for paragraphs

double-spaced body

Paragraph Heading—Underscored/Followed by Period.

bottom margin 1"–1½"

5 blank lines

2

Centering (horizontal) Horizontal centering of information can be accomplished in any specified area of a page—on the writing line, in a column, in a boxed area, or in other areas.

Procedure

1. Position the typewriter at the center point of the area in which the centered information is to appear.
2. Backspace once for every two characters and spaces <u>within</u> the information to be centered.
3. Type the information.

Centering (vertical) Careful planning will result in the accurate vertical placement of the material to be typed.

Procedure

1. Count the number of lines and blank lines <u>within</u> the material to be typed.
2. Determine the number of available lines on the paper; one vertical inch usually equals six horizontal lines; a standard sheet (8½" × 11") has 66 lines.
3. Subtract the number of lines in the material to be typed from the available lines.
4. Divide the remainder found in step 3 by two. This quotient represents the top and bottom margins which will appear above and below the information to be typed.
5. Position the typewriter on the first line to be typed: Do this by carrier returning from the top edge of the paper the number of times determined in step 4 plus one. This procedure will assure that the planned amount of space will appear in the top and bottom margins.
6. Type the information.

Crowding characters The term *crowding* refers to the typing of a word, longer by one character, in a space previously occupied by an incorrectly typed word. The principles described below can also be applied to correcting numbers and symbols where one additional character is needed. This procedure is not appropriate for use with a media typewriter.

Assumption

Desired information
. . . at this convention.

Typed in error
. . . at the convention.

Problem
Crowd *this* into the space where *the* was typed.

Procedure

1. Remove *the* by erasing or other means of eliminating the incorrect word.
2. Position the typewriter where the *t* in *the* had been typed.
3. a. *Manual typewriter*
   Partially depress the backspace key to move the carriage back one half space; hold the backspace key in this position and at the same time type the *t* in *this*.
   Release the backspace key. Space forward once; repeat the half-backspace procedure described above; type the *h*.
   Repeat the process for each remaining character in the word.
   Type the next word or character.
   b. *Electric typewriter (typebar model)*
   Follow the procedure described in 3a above with the following exception:
   To move the carriage back one half space, press against the left cylinder knob until the carriage moves the desired distance.

c. *Electric typewriter (single-element type)*
Follow the procedure described in 3a above with the following exception:
To move the carrier back one half space, place the edge of the index finger of the right hand against the right side of the carrier and manually push the carrier to the left the desired distance.

d. *Typewriter equipped with a half-backspace key*
Follow the directions provided by the typewriter manufacturer.

Result
. . . at the convention.
corrected to
. . . at this convention.

Spreading characters The term *spreading* refers to the typing of a word, shorter by one character, in a space previously occupied by an incorrectly typed word. The principles described below can also be applied to correcting numbers and symbols where one less character is needed. This procedure is not appropriate for use with a media typewriter.

Assumption
Desired information
. . . is being transferred to Denver on May 1.
Typed in error
. . . is being transferred to Detroit on May 1.
Problem
Spread *Denver* into the space where *Detroit* was typed.

Procedure
Follow the above procedure for crowding characters with the following exception:
Position the typewriter at the point where the second letter of the incorrect word was typed.

Result
. . . is being transferred to Detroit on May 1.
corrected to
. . . is being transferred to Denver on May 1.

Basic steps in typing tables To type a three-column table, follow this procedure:

1. Clear tab stops.
2. Remove margin stops.
3. Insert paper.
4. Determine precise center of the page. Set a tab stop at center.
5. Determine the number of lines contained in the table from the heading through the last line. Include all blank lines where no typing is to appear.
6. Subtract the total in Step 5 from the total lines available on the page.
7. Divide the remainder determined in step 6 by two. The quotient represents the margins to appear above and below the table.
8. Position the typewriter on the line which equals the quotient determined in step 7 plus one to assure that the planned amount of space will appear in the top and bottom margins.
9. Tab to the center tab stop.
10. Backspace once for every two characters and spaces in the first line of the main heading; type the line.
11. Find the placement of a main heading with more than one line by following the procedure described in step 10 for each subsequent line.

12. Position the typewriter in the center of the first line of the table (this may be the columnar-heading line).
13. Count the blank spaces appearing between the longest lines of each column.
14. Backspace half of the number of spaces determined in step 13.
15. Backspace once for every two characters and spaces in the longest line of each of the columns. This may be a heading over one of the columns (space between columns is accounted for in steps 13 and 14).
16. Set the left margin stop.
17. Space forward once for each character and space in the first column plus the space between column one and column two. Set a tab stop for column two.
18. Space forward once for each character and space in the longest line of the second column plus the space between column two and column three. Set a tab stop for column three.
19. Return the carrier (carriage) to the left margin, on the same line.
20. Space forward one-half the number of characters and spaces in the longest line of the first column. Backspace once for each two characters and spaces in the heading over the first column. Type the heading.
21. Tab to the second column. Repeat step 20 to position and type the heading over column two. Repeat the procedure for the heading over column three.
22. Carrier (carriage) return and type the information in each column line for line while tabbing from the end of one column entry to the beginning of the next column.

Specialized alignment The typing of degree symbols (32°), exponents (A^2), double underscores (‗), and other specialties in formatting may require a temporary deviation from the original writing line. Most typewriters (non-media) are equipped with a mechanism which, when engaged, will assist the secretary in placing special characters and symbols by allowing temporary movement away from the established writing line. When the mechanism is disengaged, the original writing line location is found with a slight turning of the cylinder knob (right or left) thus creating perfect alignment of all typing on the page. Some media typewriters are equipped with a mechanical feature which allows for easy recording of technical typing and the automatic accurate indexing during playback for the accommodation of superior and subordinate numbers and symbols.

5.3

TERMINOLOGY

The following short glossary is entered as an aid to those readers who may not be familiar with the specialized vocabulary of media typewriting.

acoustical hood
a clear plastic device located over the typehead area of most late model media typewriters and used to reduce noise

alignment
the proper placement of characters (letters, figures, or symbols) or groups of characters (as words or numbers) within a text after the paper has been removed from the typewriter and reinserted

bold type
characters of high inking density that appear darker than type of average weight

carrier return
the repositioning of the typehead of a single-element typewriter at the left margin stop; this automatically occurs upon activation of the carrier return key located on the I/O keyboard

codes
electronic impulses recorded on magnetic media, into computer memory, or perforations in paper media; the codes produce identical alpha/numeric/symbolic copy during playback that match what was created during the recording process

composition typewriter
a typewriter that produces type with the characteristics of print

constant information
information in a document (as a guide letter or a legal instrument) intended to be read by each of many recipients; *compare* VARIABLE INFORMATION

continuous-form documents
paper supplies such as letterhead, carbon packs, forms, and envelopes separated by top- and bottom-edge perforations that afford quick efficient processing through the typewriter by eliminating the need to insert individual documents when processing large volumes of such material

continuous-form draft paper
sheets of draft paper separated by perforations

CRT
cathode-ray tube

draft
typed information that will be edited one or more times before being typed in final form

draft/record mode
functional condition of a media typewriter during which time all keystrokes including alpha/numeric/symbolic characters, tabs, spaces, carrier returns, and special codes are recorded on media

external correspondence
correspondence sent to or received from organizations or individuals outside of one's own organization

final/playback mode
functional condition of a media typewriter during which time recorded information can be played back

flowchart
a diagram or outline showing the sequence of operations in a process

format
physical presentation of a typed document

guide letter
a standardized letter designed to initiate or respond to high-volume routine correspondence but often planned to allow insertion of individually relevant matter—called also *form letter*

hard copy
typewritten copy produced at the input/output writer during record or playback functions

index
vertical incrementation of a page in a typewriter

input
the first step in the processing of typewritten work; it usually refers to the author's dictation; *compare* THROUGHPUT

input/output writer
the typewriter-like portion of a media typewriter—called also *I/O writer*

justification
a format whereby typed lines fit precisely on a writing line of a preestablished length, thus producing symmetrically even left and right margins

keyboarding
typing at rough-draft speed, correcting typographical errors as they occur by means of a backspace/strikeover method, and simultaneously recording on media or into computer memory

lamination
a mechanical method of coating paper with plastic (as by heating)

log
a record of recorded material

makeready time
the time consumed in preparatory activities (as setting margins and tab stops, inserting paper, or determining format) before the typing of a document

media
the material (as magnetic tape) on which typewritten material is recorded

media typewriter
an electronic typewriter usually featuring single-element technology that is coupled with recording media

one-time document
material (as a letter, a memo, a report, an outline, or a manuscript) typed only once for one recipient

on-line
of or relating to the direct connection to and interaction with a computer

output
the final distribution of typewritten material; *compare* THROUGHPUT

page-edge guide
a device located to the back of the platen of most typewriters and I/O writers whose purpose is to assist in the insertion of paper into the typewriter

paragraph selection
a media-typewriter method of preparing large volumes of information in paragraphs that are similar in content but can be varied in sequence

permanently-stored document
material (as a guide letter) recorded on media and utilized periodically in the same format and with the same content

permanently-stored documents with variables
material (as some guide letters, legal instruments, or reports with variables) recorded on media including special codes for automatic playback stop at points where variable information is to be inserted

pin-feed platen
a platen designed especially to guide continuous-form documents through the typewriter without slippage or misalignment

placement
the location of information at any given point on a document

playback
high-speed typewriting of information from recorded media

playback/final mode
—see FINAL/PLAYBACK MODE

prenumbered draft paper
draft paper with preprinted numbers in ascending order at the left edge of each page that assist in accounting for the number of lines in a document and that facilitate the coordination of page lines to media lines

prioritizing
determining the order of priority in which work will be processed

proportional spacing
typewriter spacing and characters whose widths vary in size

record process
the recording of information on media

registration
precise vertical and horizontal alignment

retrieval
mechanical selection of recorded material for playback

self-paced programmed instruction
a method of learning whereby the student proceeds through carefully structured written or audiovisual training materials at an individual speed; in some situations, the student may request assistance of a monitor or an instructor as needed

single-element technology
typewriter design featuring, for example, a sphere- or wheel-like device where all alpha/numeric/symbolic characters are located, versus the typebar design found in standard typewriters

special codes
electronic impulses or perforations recorded on media but usually invisible on hard copy that cause desired playback, with examples of special codes being stop codes, underscore codes, backspace codes, tab codes, and others; some media typewriters have a special code-print feature to aid in proofreading

tab grid
tab stops set at equally spaced intervals (usually four to five spaces apart) across a writing line—called also *standard tabs*

temporarily-stored document
material played back more than once or

revised at least one time by its author after being recorded and not having a permanent storage requirement

text editing
typographical and/or editorial revision of typewritten copy

throughput
a segment of time consumed in processing typewritten work from the author's dictation to final distribution

touch-typing
the quick, efficient activation of typewriter keys and control/code keys of a media typewriter without the operator's looking at the keyboard

typestyle
a design of type

update media
to revise and/or correct recorded information on media

variable information
information within a document (as a guide letter or a legal instrument) that pertains to a specific recipient or recipients; *compare* CONSTANT INFORMATION

variables
—*see* VARIABLE INFORMATION

vertical incrementation
the top-to-bottom/bottom-to-top spacing created by rotation of the typewriter platen —a function that is accomplished by activating the carrier-return key, by activating a special key designed for this purpose that is found on many typewriters and I/O writers, or by manually turning the cylinder knobs

work grouping
organizing and prioritizing tasks to maximize efficiency and expedite work flow

work station
the immediate physical environment where one's tasks are accomplished

6

CHAPTER SIX

STYLE IN BUSINESS CORRESPONDENCE

CONTENTS

6.1

THE BUSINESS LETTER AS AN IMAGE-MAKER

The word *style* as applied to business-letter writing encompasses format, grammar, stylistics, and word usage. All of these elements conjoin in a letter to produce a tangible reflection on paper not only of the writer's ability and knowledge and the typist's competence, but also of an organization's total image. For example, a corporation may spend considerable sums on advertising to promote its products and services and to advance a positive image; yet, this image may be seriously eroded or negated altogether by massive output of carelessly prepared letters especially when produced over a long time span. On a smaller scale, a few letters of that kind may create such negative impressions on their recipients that they will have second thoughts about pursuing business relationships with the writer or his organization —a situation that has special impact on small businesses. The letter, then, is actually an exponent of overall organizational style, regardless of the size of the firm. And if there appears to be no pride in or concern for the quality of something as basic as one's business correspondence, how then can there be concern for or pride in the quality of one's products and services? Thus, the initial impression created by an attractively and accurately typed, logically oriented, and clearly written letter can be a crucial factor in its ultimate effectiveness.

Letters—whether mass-produced by word processors or typed individually—are still the most personal method of written business communication. An executive may devote as much as 50 percent or more of the workday to correspondence, be it planning and thinking out the direction, tone, and content of his or her own letters or reading and acting on incoming letters. Secretaries spend even more of their time on correspondence. And time costs money.

Therefore, if both writer and typist keep in mind the following simple aids to good letter production, the time and money involved will have been well spent:

1. Stationery should be of high-quality paper having excellent correcting or erasing properties.
2. Typing should be neat and accurate with any corrections or erasures rendered invisible.
3. The essential elements of a letter (such as the date line, inside address, message, and signature block) and any other included parts should conform in page placement and format with one of the generally acceptable, up-to-date business-letter stylings (as the Simplified Letter, the Block Letter, the Modified Block Letter, the Modified Semi-block Letter, or the Hanging-indented Letter).
4. The language of the letter should be clear, concise, grammatically correct, and devoid of padding and clichés.
5. The ideas in the message should be logically oriented, with the writer always keeping in mind the reader's reaction.
6. All statistical data should be accurate and complete.

Style in business correspondence, like language itself, is not a static entity: it has changed over the years to meet the varying needs of its users, and it is continuing to change today. For example, the open punctuation pattern and the Simplified Letter have gained wide currency. On the other hand, the closed punctuation pattern and the Indented Letter, once considered standard formats, are now little used in the United States. General diversification and the multinational character of modern business have rendered fast, clear, lean communication in all media essential. The following two chapters have been prepared with all of these factors in mind.

6.2

TOTAL-LETTER CONSIDERATIONS

It has often been said that an attractive letter should look like a symmetrically framed picture with even margins working as a frame for the typed lines that are balanced under the letterhead. But how many letters really do look like framed pictures? Planning ahead before starting to type is the real key to letter symmetry:

1. Estimate the approximate number of words in the letter or the general length of the message by looking over the writer's rough draft or one's shorthand notes, or by checking the length of a dictated source.

2. Make mental notes of any long quotations, tabular data, long lists or footnotes, or of the occurrence of scientific names and formulas that may require margin adjustments, a different typeface, or even handwork within the message.
3. Set the left and right margin stops according to the estimated letter length: about one inch for very long letters, about one and one-half inches for medium-length ones, and about two inches for very short ones.
4. Use a guide sheet (see Chapter 4, page 73) as a bottom margin warning.
5. Continuation-sheet margins should match those of the first sheet, and at least three lines of the message should be carried over to the continuation sheet.

The following illustrations show how letters of varying sizes may be balanced on a page. See also Chapter 4, page 74 for a Letter Placement Table.

A Quick Guide to Attractive Letter Placement on the Page

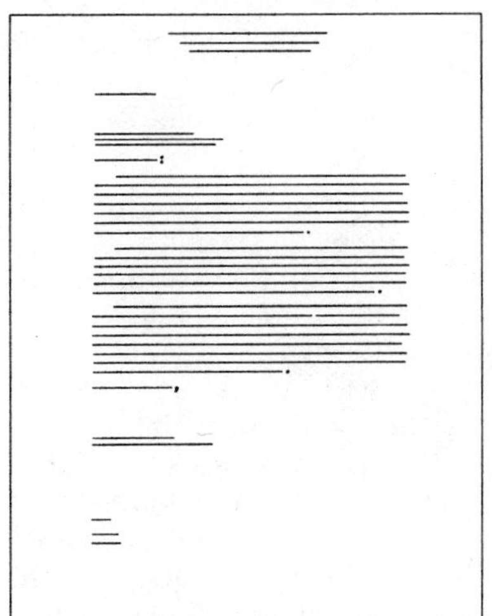

The Short Letter
100 words or less

side margins: about 2″

paragraphs may be double-spaced throughout

The Medium-length Letter
about 100–300 words

side margins: about 1½″

single-spacing within paragraph

double-spacing between paragraphs

The Long Letter
300 words or more
(should comprise at least 2 pages)

side margins: about 1–1¼″

6.3

LETTERHEAD DESIGN AND LETTER BALANCE

Letterhead designs vary with one's organization. Some letterheads are positioned dead-center at the top of the page, others are laid out across the top of the page from the left to the right margin, and still others are more heavily balanced right or left of center. Sometimes a company's name and logo appear at the top of the page, while its address and other data are printed at the bottom.

Regardless of layout and design, a typical business letterhead contains all or some of the following elements, with the asterisked items being essential:

logo
*full legal name of the firm, company, corporation, institution, or group
*full street address
suite, room, or building number, if needed—post office box number, if applicable
*city, state, and ZIP Code
Area Code and telephone number(s)
other data (as telex or cable references)

The names of particular departments, plants, groups, or divisions may be printed on the letterhead of extremely large or diversified companies or institutions. Other organizations such as large law firms may have the full names of their partners and staff attorneys all listed on the letterhead. Elaborate letterhead layouts require especially careful letter planning to avoid an unbalanced look.

Personalized or executive letterhead for high corporate officers is widely used: the standard company letterhead design is supplemented with the name of the office (as "Office of the President") or with the full name and business title of the officer (as "John M. Jones, Jr., President") printed or engraved in small letters one or two lines beneath the letterhead at or near the left margin. The officer's business title may appear on the same line as his or her name if space permits and if both name and title are short, or it may be blocked directly below the name. Executive stationery is often not printed but instead engraved on a better grade of paper than that of the standard, printed company stationery. Executive stationery is also smaller than the standard, as shown in the table on page 109.

6.4

ALL ABOUT PAPER

Paper and envelope size, quality, and basis weight vary according to application. The table on page 109 lists various paper and envelope sizes along with their uses.

Good-quality paper is an essential element in the production of attractive, effective letters. When one assesses paper quality, one should ask these questions:

1. Will the paper withstand corrections and erasures without pitting, buckling, or tearing?
2. Will the paper accept even and clear typed characters?
3. Will the paper permit smooth written signatures?
4. Will the paper perform well with carbons and in copying machines?
5. Will the paper withstand storage and repeated handling and will its color wear well over long time periods?

Stationery and Envelope Sizes and Applications

Stationery	Stationery Size	Application	Envelope	Envelope Size
Standard	8½" × 11" *also* 8" × 10½"	general business correspondence	*commercial*	
			No. 6¾	3⅝" × 6½"
			No. 9	3⅞" × 8⅞"
			No. 10	4⅛" × 9½"
			window	
			No. 6¾	3⅝" × 6½"
			No. 9	3⅞" × 8⅞"
			No. 10	4⅛" × 9½"
			airmail	
			No. 6¾	3⅝" × 6½"
			No. 10	4⅛" × 9½"
Executive *or* Monarch	7¼" × 10½" *or* 7½" × 10"	high-level corporate officers' correspondence; usually personalized	*regular* Executive *or* Monarch	3⅞" × 7½"
			window Monarch	3⅞" × 7½"
Half-sheet *or* Baronial	5½" × 8½"	extremely brief notes	*regular* Baronial	3⅝" × 6½"

An important characteristic of paper is its fiber direction or grain. When selecting paper, one should ensure that the grain will be parallel to the direction of the typewritten lines, thus providing a smooth surface for clear and even characters, an easy erasing or correcting surface, and a smooth fit of paper against the typewriter platen. Every sheet of paper has what is called a felt side: this is the top side of the paper from which a watermark may be read, and it is from this side of the sheet that the letterhead should be printed or engraved. The table below illustrates various paper weights according to their specific uses.

Weights of Paper for Specific Business Correspondence Applications

Application: letter papers and envelopes	**Basis Weight:** letter papers and envelopes
Standard (*i.e., corporate correspondence*)	24 *or* 20
Executive	24 *or* 20
Airmail (*especially for overseas correspondence*)	13
Branch-office *or* salesmen's stationery	20 *or* 16
Form letters	20 *or* 24
Continuation sheets	match basis weight of first sheet
Half-sheets	24 *or* 20

Continuation sheets, although blank, must match the letterhead sheet in color, basis weight, texture, size, and quality. Envelopes should match both the first and continuation sheets. Therefore, these materials should be ordered along with the letterhead to ensure a good match.

6.5

GENERAL PUNCTUATION PATTERNS IN BUSINESS CORRESPONDENCE

As with letterhead designs, the choice of general punctuation patterns in business correspondence is usually determined by the organization. However, it is important that specific punctuation patterns be selected for designated letter stylings, and that these patterns be adhered to for the sake of consistency and fast output. The two most common patterns are *open punctuation* and *mixed punctuation.* Their increased popularity in recent years is yet another reflection of the marked trend toward streamlining correspondence, for these patterns have all but totally replaced the older and more complex *closed punctuation* requiring a terminal mark at the end of each element of a business letter—a pattern that was used most often with the now outmoded Indented Letter styling.

OPEN PUNCTUATION PATTERN

1. The end of the date line is unpunctuated, although the comma between day and year is retained.
2. The ends of the lines of the inside address are unpunctuated, unless an abbreviation such as *Inc.* terminates a line, in which case the period after the abbreviation is retained.
3. The salutation if used is unpunctuated.
4. The complimentary close if used is unpunctuated.
5. The ends of the signature block lines are unpunctuated.
6. This pattern is always used with the Simplified Letter (see pages 136–137) and is often used with the Block Letter (see pages 138–139).

Open Punctuation Pattern

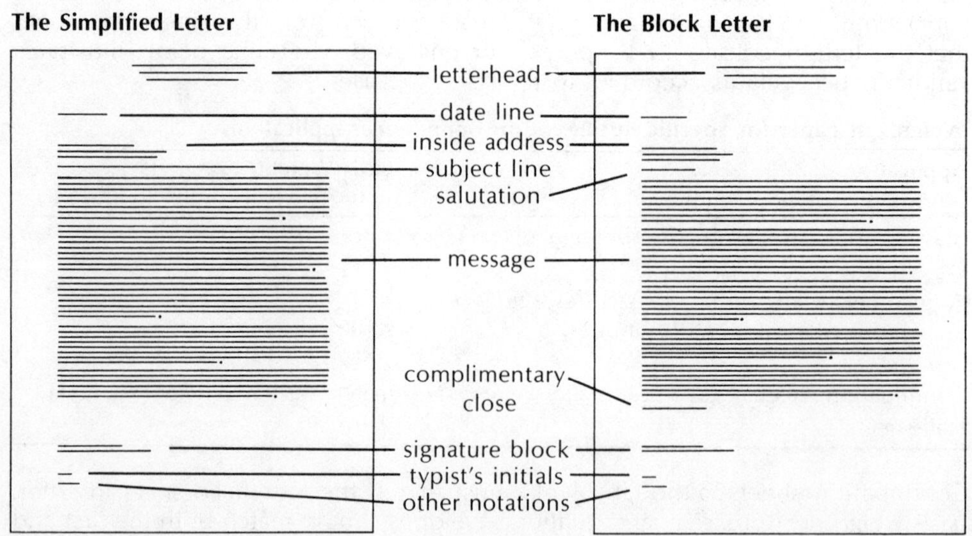

MIXED PUNCTUATION PATTERN

1. The end of the date line is unpunctuated, although the comma between the day and year is retained.
2. The ends of the lines of the inside address are unpunctuated unless an abbreviation such as *Inc.* terminates a line, in which case the period after the abbreviation is retained.
3. The salutation is punctuated with a colon.
4. The complimentary close is punctuated with a comma.
5. The end(s) of the signature block line(s) are unpunctuated.
6. This pattern is used with either the Block, the Modified Block, Modified Semiblock, or the Hanging-indented Letters.

Mixed Punctuation Pattern Illustrated in Four Letter Stylings

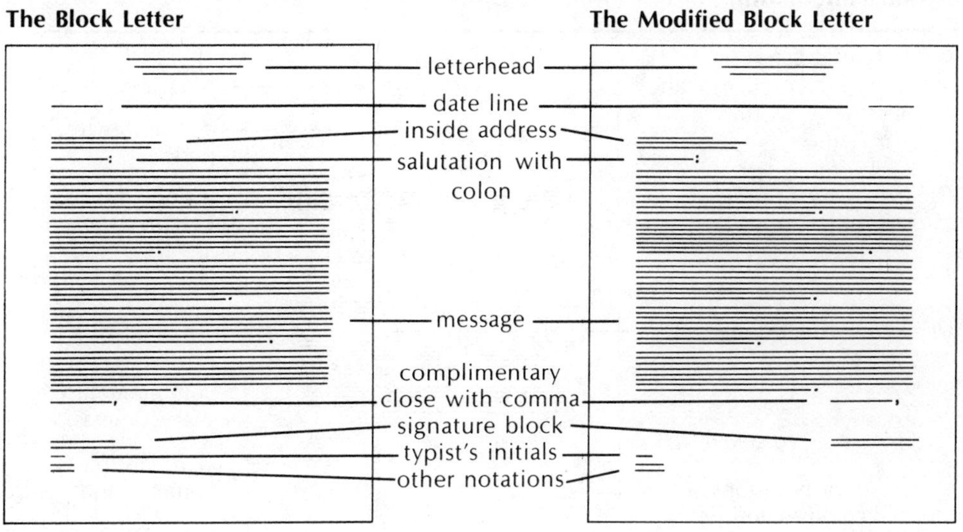

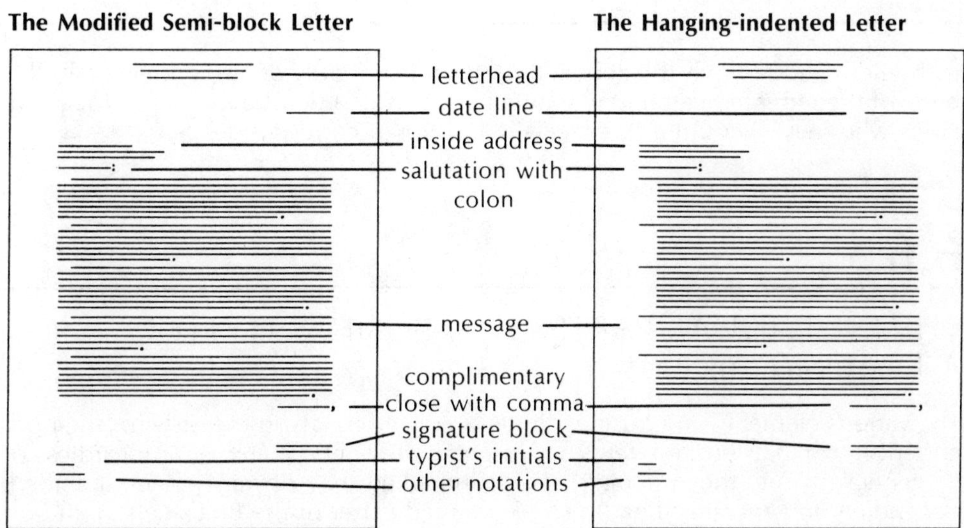

CLOSED PUNCTUATION PATTERN

Although the closed punctuation pattern is not used in the United States today, it is, nevertheless, employed in some European business correspondence. This pattern exhibits these characteristics:

1. A period terminates the date line.
2. A comma terminates each line of the inside address except the last which is ended by a period.
3. A colon punctuates the salutation.
4. A comma punctuates the complimentary close.
5. A comma terminates each line of the signature block except the last which is terminated by a period.
6. This pattern is used chiefly with the Indented Letter.

Closed Punctuation Pattern

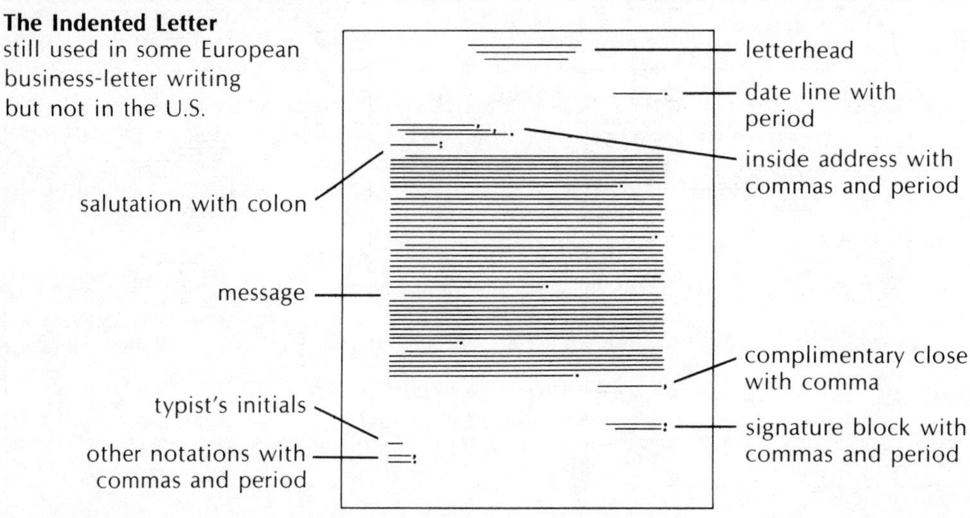

It should be added that the above illustration is the only description given in this book of the Indented Letter. It is shown here only as a point of reference for secretaries who may encounter it, especially in foreign correspondence.

6.6

THE INDIVIDUAL PARTS OF A BUSINESS LETTER: A Discussion of Each

The various elements of a business letter are listed below in the order of their occurrence. While asterisked items are essential elements of any letter regardless of its general styling, those items that are unmarked may or may not be included, depending on general styling (as the Simplified Letter or the Block Letter) and on the nature of the letter itself (as general or confidential correspondence):

DATE LINE

The date line may be typed two to six lines below the last line of the printed letterhead; however, three-line spacing is recommended as a standard for most letters. Spacing may be expanded or contracted, depending on letter length, space available, letterhead design, and organization policy. In the Simplified Letter, the date is typed six lines below the letterhead at the left margin. The date line consists of the month, the day, and the year: January 1, 19--

The use of an abbreviation or an Arabic numeral for the month is not permitted in date lines, although the day and the month may be reversed and the comma dropped in United States Government correspondence or in British correspondence, where this styling is common: 1 January 19--

The following page placements of date lines are all acceptable, and the choice depends on the general letter styling or the letterhead layout; however, the date line should never overrun either right or left margins.

date line blocked flush with the left margin used with the Block Letter (see letter facsimile, pages 138–139 for full-page views).

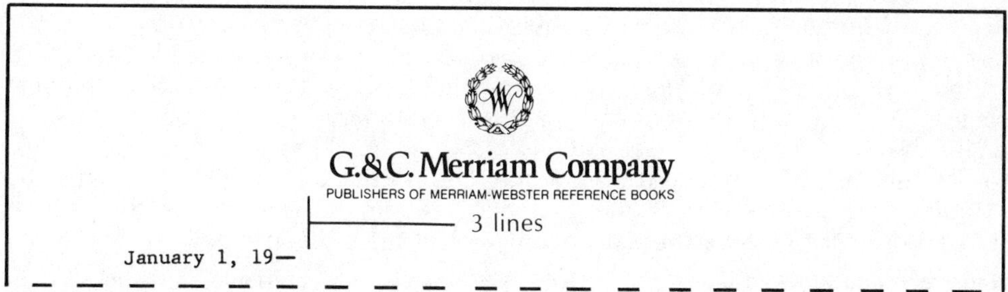

date line blocked flush with the right margin so that the last digit of the date is aligned exactly with the margin: may be used with the Modified Block, the Modified Semi-block, and the Hanging-indented Letters (see pages 135 and 142–143).

In order to align a date at the right margin, the typist moves the typewriter carriage to the right margin stop and then backspaces once for each keystroke and space that will be required in the typed date. The secretary can then set the tab stops when typing the first of several letters that will bear the same date.

date line centered directly under the letterhead may be used with the Modified Block or the Modified Semi-block Letters.

G.&C. Merriam Company
PUBLISHERS OF MERRIAM-WEBSTER REFERENCE BOOKS
3 lines
January 1, 19—

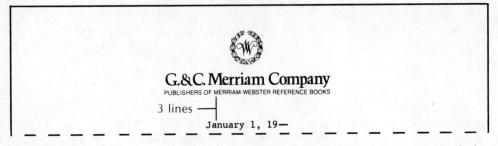

date line positioned about five spaces to the right of dead center may be used with the Modified Block or the Modified Semi-block Letters (see page 140).

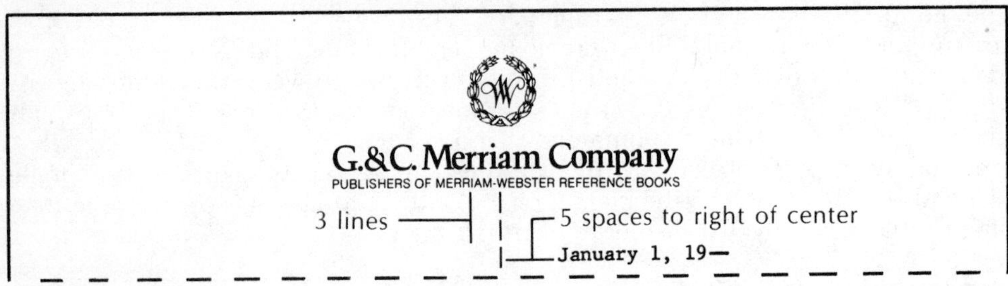

REFERENCE LINE

A reference line with file, correspondence, control, order, invoice, or policy numbers is included in a letter when the addressee has specifically requested that correspondence on a subject contain a reference, or when it is needed for filing. It may be centered and typed one to four lines below the date, although some offices require that it be typed and single-spaced directly above or below the date. With the Block Letter, the reference line should be aligned flush left, regardless of its position either above or below the date. With the Modified Block and the Modified Semi-block Letters, the reference line may be centered on the page or blocked under or above the date line wherever it has been typed.

reference line blocked left

January 1, 19--
X-123-4
or
X-123-4
January 1, 19--

reference line blocked right

January 1, 19--
X-123-4
or
X-123-4
January 1, 19--

Reference Line Blocked with Date Line to Right of Dead Center

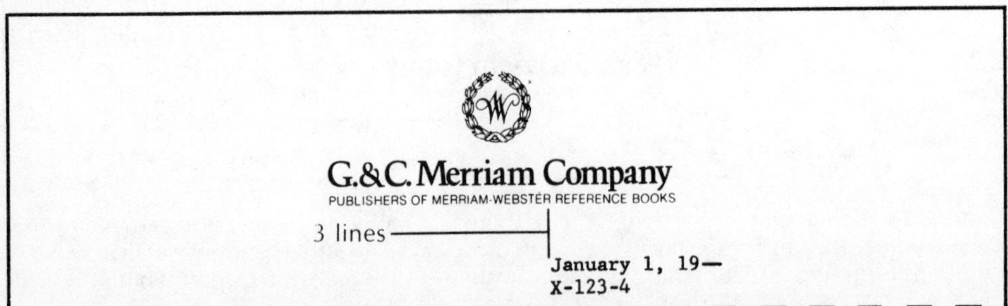

Reference Number Centered on Page Four Lines Beneath Date Line

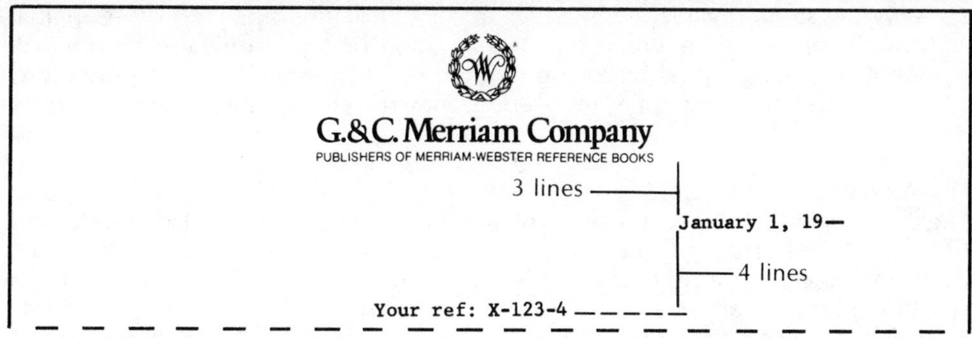

Reference lines on the first sheet must be carried over to the heading of a continuation sheet or sheets. The styling of the date line and the reference line on a continuation sheet should match the one on the first page as closely as possible; for example, if the reference line appears on a line below the date on the first sheet, it should be so typed on the continuation sheet. The first setup below illustrates a continuation-sheet reference line as used with the Simplified or Block Letters:

Mr. John B. Jones
January 1, 19--
X-123-4
Page 2

The second example illustrates the positioning of a reference line on the continuation sheet of a Modified Block, a Modified Semi-block, or a Hanging-indented Letter:

Mr. John B. Jones	-2-	January 1, 19--
		X-123-4

See page 123 for continuation-sheet facsimiles.

SPECIAL MAILING NOTATIONS

If a letter is to be sent by any method other than by regular mail, that fact is indicated on the letter itself and on the envelope (see pages 145–148 for details on envelope styling). The all-capitalized special mailing notation (as CERTIFIED MAIL or SPECIAL DELIVERY) is aligned flush left about four lines below the line on

Special Mailing Notation vis-à-vis Inside Address and Date Line

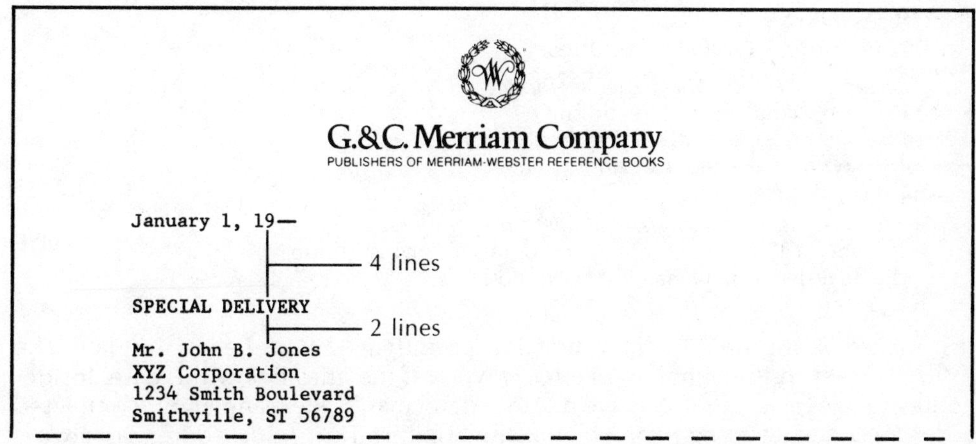

which the date appears, and about two lines above the first line of the inside address. While some organizations prefer that this notation appear on the original and on all copies, others prefer that the notation be typed only on the original.

Vertical spacing (as between the date line and the special mailing notation) may vary with letter length, i.e., more space may be left for short or medium letter lengths.

ON-ARRIVAL NOTATIONS

The on-arrival notations that may be included in the letter itself are PERSONAL and CONFIDENTIAL. The first indicates that the letter may be opened and read only by its addressee; the second, that the letter may be opened and read by its addressee and/or any other person or persons authorized to view such material. These all-capitalized notations are usually positioned four lines below the date line and usually two but not more than four lines above the first line of the inside address. They are blocked flush left in all letter stylings. If a special mailing notation has been used, the on-arrival notation is blocked one line beneath it. Spacing between the date line and the on-arrival notation may be increased to as much as six lines if the letter is extremely brief.

If either PERSONAL or CONFIDENTIAL appears in the letter, it must also appear on the envelope (see pages 145–148 for envelope styling).

On-arrival Notation vis-à-vis Date Line, Special Mailing Notation, and Inside Address

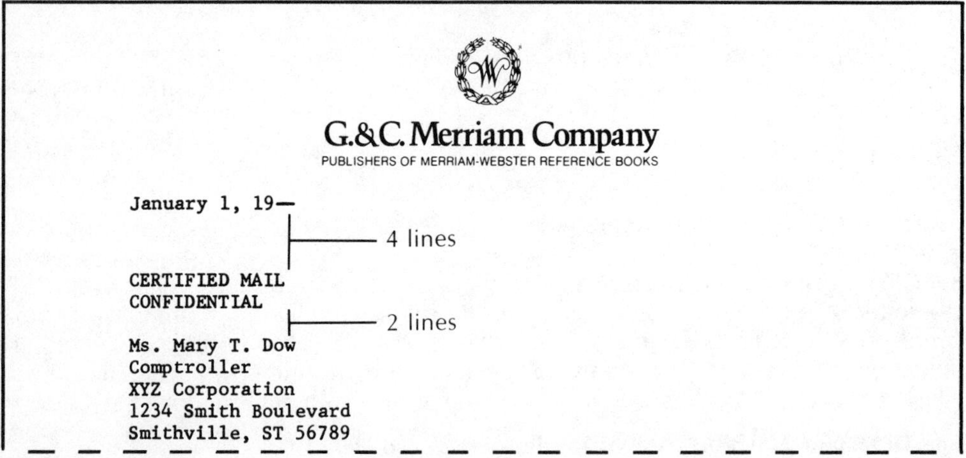
G.&C. Merriam Company
PUBLISHERS OF MERRIAM-WEBSTER REFERENCE BOOKS

January 1, 19—

4 lines

CERTIFIED MAIL
CONFIDENTIAL

2 lines

Ms. Mary T. Dow
Comptroller
XYZ Corporation
1234 Smith Boulevard
Smithville, ST 56789

INSIDE ADDRESS

An inside address typically includes:

1. *if letter is directed to a particular individual*
   addressee's courtesy title + full name
   addressee's business title if required
   full name of addressee's business affiiliation
   full geographical address
2. *if letter is addressed to an organization in general*
   full name of the firm, company, corporation, or institution
   individual department name if required
   full geographical address

It is placed about three to eight, but not more than 12 lines below the date. The inside address in the Simplified Letter is typed three lines below the date. Inside-address page placement relative to the date may be expanded or contracted according to letter length or organization policy. The inside address is always single-spaced internally. In all of the letters discussed in this book, the inside address is blocked flush with the left margin. See pages 133–144 for full-page views.

Inside Address Styling Used with the Block Letter

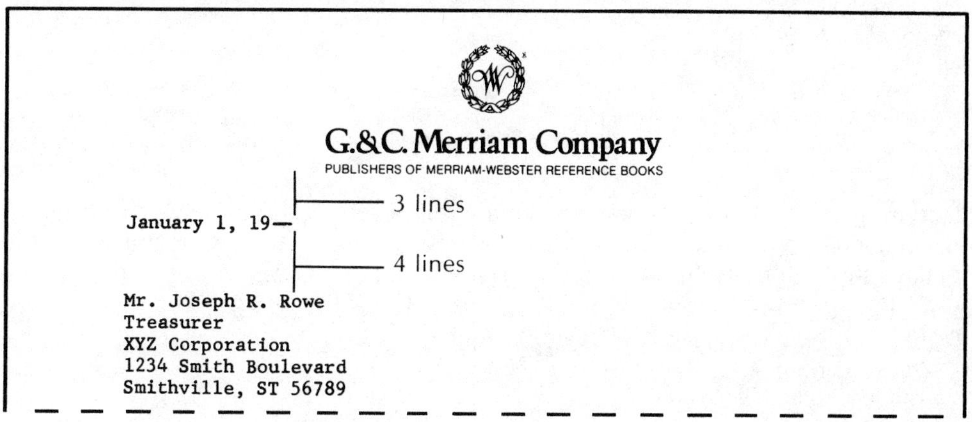

A courtesy title (as *Mr., Ms., Mrs., Miss,* or *Dr.*) should always be typed before the addressee's full name, even if a business title (as *Treasurer*) is also included after the surname (see the Forms of Address chart on pages 149–179 of this chapter for a full list and discussion of special titles).

Before typing the addressee's full name, the secretary should, if possible, refer to the signature block of previous correspondence from that individual to ascertain the exact spelling and styling of the name. This information may also be obtained from printed executive letterhead. A business title, if included, should also match the styling in previous correspondence or in official literature (such as an annual report). Business titles should not be abbreviated. If an individual holds several offices (as *Vice-president and General Manager*) within an organization, the title shown in the signature block of previous correspondence should be copied, or the title of the individual's highest office (in this case, *Vice-president*) may be selected. If a business title is so long that it might overrun the center of the page, it may be typed on two lines with the second line indented two spaces, as

Mr. John P. Hemphill, Jr.
Vice-president and Director
  of Research and Development

The following are acceptable inside-address stylings for business titles; however, care should be taken to choose the one that will enhance and not detract from the total balance of the letter on the page:

Mr. Arthur O. Brown
News Director
Radio Station WXYZ
1234 Peters Street
Jonesville, ZZ 56789

In the above example, the business title forms line 2 of the inside address. This format is acceptable with all letter styles.

Ms. Ann B. Lowe, Director
Apex Community Theater
67 Smith Street
North Bend, XX 12345

Here, the business title ends line 1 and is separated from the addressee's surname by a comma—a format recommended for short names and titles that may be used with all letter styles: the Simplified, the Block, the Modified Block, the Modified Semi-block, and the Hanging-indented Letters.

Mrs. Joyce A. Cavitt
President, C & A Realty
Johnson Beach, ZZ 56789

The business title heads line 2 and is separated from the addressee's business affiliation by a comma. This format is recommended for short titles and short business-affiliation names, and may be used with all letter styles: the Simplified, the Block, the Modified Block, the Modified Semi-block, and the Hanging-indented Letters.

If an individual addressee's name is unknown or irrelevant and the writer wishes to direct a letter to an organization in general or to a unit within that organization, the organization name is typed on line 1 of the inside address, followed on line 2 by the name of a specific department if required. The full address of the organization is then typed on subsequent lines, as

XYZ Corporation
Consumer Products Division
1234 Smith Boulevard
Smithville, ST 56789

The organization name should be styled exactly as it appears on the letterhead of previous correspondence, or as it appears in printed sources (as annual reports or business directories).

Street addresses should be typed in full and not abbreviated unless window envelopes are being used (see Chapter 10, "Addressing for Automation"). Arabic numerals should be used for all building and house numbers except *one,* which should be typed out in letters, as

One Bayside Drive
but
6 Link Road
1436 Freemont Avenue

and Arabic numerals should be used for all numbered street names above *twelve,* as

145 East 14th Street

but numbered street names from *one* through *twelve* should be spelled out:

167 West Second Avenue   One East Ninth Street

If a numbered street name over *twelve* follows a house number with no intervening word or words (as a compass direction), a spaced hyphen is inserted between the house number and the street-name number, as

2018 - 14th Street

An apartment, building, or suite number if required should follow the street address on the same line with two spaces or a comma separating the two:

62 Park Towers Suite 9   62 Park Towers, Suite 9

Names of cities (except those following the pattern of *St. Louis* or *St. Paul*) should be typed out in full. The name of the city is followed by a comma and then by the name of the state and the ZIP Code. Names of states (except for the District of Columbia which is always styled *DC* or *D.C.*) may or may not be abbreviated: if a window envelope is being used, the all-capitalized, unpunctuated two-letter Postal Service abbreviation followed by <u>one space</u> and the ZIP Code must be used; on the other hand, if a regular envelope is being used, the name of the state may be typed out in full followed by one space and the ZIP Code, or the two-letter Postal Service abbreviation may be used. For the sake of fewer keystrokes and consistency, it is recommended that the Postal Service abbreviations be used throughout the material. See Chapter 10 for a complete list of these abbreviations.

An inside address should comprise no more than five typed lines. No line should overrun the center of the page. Lengthy organizational names, however, like lengthy business titles, may be carried over to a second line and indented two spaces from the left margin.

ATTENTION LINE

If the writer wishes to address a letter to an organization in general but also to bring it to the attention of a particular individual at the same time, an attention line may be typed two lines below the last line of the inside address and two lines above the salutation if there is one. The attention line is usually blocked flush with the left margin; it must be so blocked in the Simplified and Block Letters. On the other hand, some organizations prefer that the attention line be centered on the page: this placement is acceptable with all letters except the Simplified and the Block. However, for the sake of fast output, it is generally recommended that the attention line be aligned with the left margin. This line should be neither underlined nor entirely capitalized; only its main elements are capitalized. Placement of a colon after the word *Attention* is optional unless the open punctuation pattern is being followed throughout the letter, in which case the colon should be omitted:

Attention Mr. John P. Doe *or* Attention: Mr. John P. Doe

The salutation appearing beneath the attention line should be "Gentlemen" even though the attention line routes the letter to a particular person. Such a letter is actually written to the organization; hence, the collective-noun salutation.

Page Placement of an Attention Line in a Block Letter with Open Punctuation

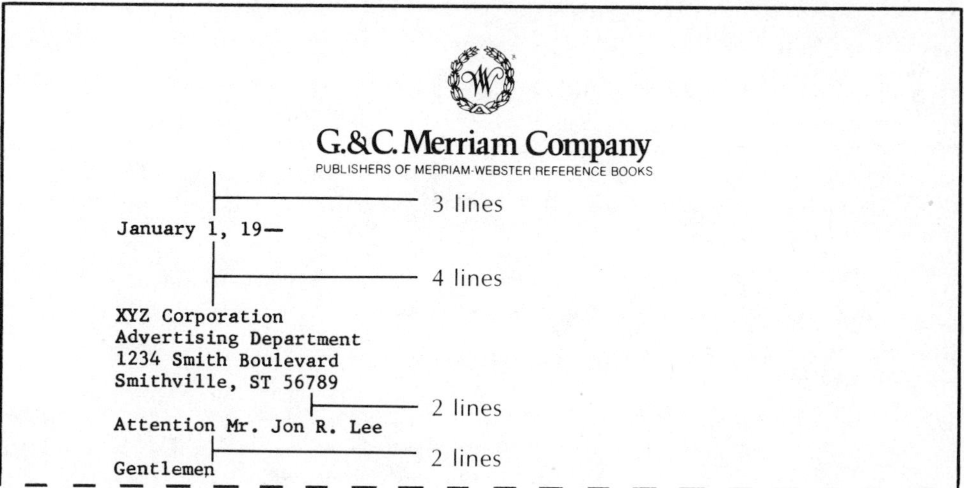
G.&C. Merriam Company
PUBLISHERS OF MERRIAM-WEBSTER REFERENCE BOOKS

3 lines

January 1, 19—

4 lines

XYZ Corporation
Advertising Department
1234 Smith Boulevard
Smithville, ST 56789

2 lines

Attention Mr. Jon R. Lee

2 lines

Gentlemen

SALUTATION

The salutation—used with all letter stylings except the Simplified—is typed flush with the left margin, usually two to four lines beneath the last line of the inside address or two lines below the attention line if there is one. Additional vertical lines of space may be added after the inside address of a short letter which is to be enclosed in a window envelope. The first letter of the first word of the salutation is capitalized, as are the first letters of the addressee's courtesy title and surname.

If the mixed punctuation pattern is being followed in the letter, the salutation is followed by a colon; if open punctuation is being observed, the salutation is unpunctuated. The following are typical examples of various salutations, the last four of which are used in letters to high-level personages (as in the government, the diplomatic corps, or the clergy):

most commonly used
Gentlemen
Dear Mr. (*or* Ms., Mrs., Miss, Dr., Professor) Smith
Dear Bob

reserved for high-level personages
My dear Justice Roberts
Your Excellency
Excellency
Right Reverend and dear Father

The salutation "Dear Sir" is rarely used today except in form letters and in letters to high-level personages (as the President-elect of the U.S.). Although the salutation "Dear Sirs" is now considered archaic in American business writing, it is still used in Great Britain.

With the advent of the Women's Rights Movement and the ensuing national interest in equal rights and equal opportunity, some writers—both male and female—have discarded the conventional salutation "Gentlemen" and have coined what they feel are more neutral, non-sexist replacements for letters addressed to organizations whose officers may be both male and female. Although a number of writers have used the following salutations, widespread general usage over a long time span has not yet been achieved and these expressions are therefore still not considered conventional:

Gentlepeople   Gentlepersons   Dear People   Dear Sir, Madam, or Ms.

The most conventional way of addressing a male-female group is to write

Ladies and Gentlemen *or* Dear Sir or Madam

although the latter expression has become less popular in recent years since the use of *Madam* in a letter to an unmarried woman may offend her. The most convenient way to avoid the problem of sexual semantics altogether is to use the salutationless Simplified Letter styling (see the facsimile on pages 136–137).

When a letter is addressed to an all-female organization, the following salutations may be used:

Ladies *or* Mesdames

The salutation for a married couple is styled as

Dear Mr. and Mrs. Hathaway
Dear Dr. and Mrs. Simpson

Salutations for letters addressed to two or more persons having the same or different surnames may be found in the Forms of Address section, page 179. Salutations in letters addressed to persons with specialized titles may also be found in the Forms of Address section, pages 149–178.

SUBJECT LINE

A subject line gives the gist of the letter. Its phrasing is necessarily succinct and to the point: it should not be so long as to require more than one line. The subject line serves as an immediate point of reference for the reader as well as a convenient filing tool for the secretaries at both ends of the correspondence.

In the salutationless Simplified Letter, the subject line (an essential element) is positioned flush left, three lines below the last line of the inside address. The subject line may be entirely capitalized and not underlined. As an alternative, the main words in the subject line may be capitalized and every word underlined.

If a subject line is included in a letter featuring a salutation, it is positioned flush left, two lines beneath the salutation, and may be entirely capitalized. Also, the word *subject* may be used to introduce the line as follows:

SUBJECT: CHANGE IN TRAFFIC ROUTE

Page Placement of the Subject Line in the Simplified Letter

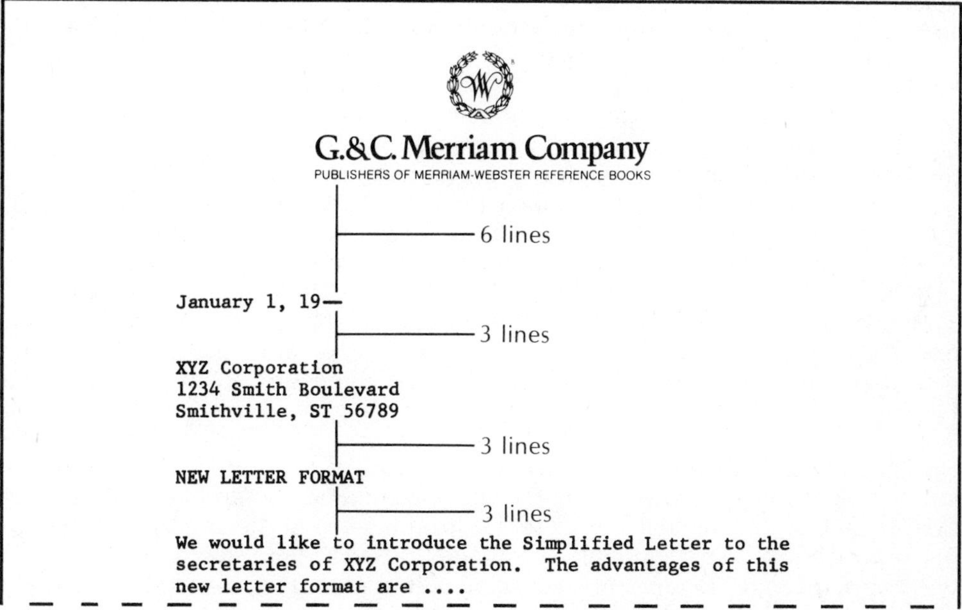

G.&C. Merriam Company
PUBLISHERS OF MERRIAM-WEBSTER REFERENCE BOOKS

6 lines

January 1, 19—

3 lines

XYZ Corporation
1234 Smith Boulevard
Smithville, ST 56789

3 lines

NEW LETTER FORMAT

3 lines

We would like to introduce the Simplified Letter to the secretaries of XYZ Corporation. The advantages of this new letter format are ....

Page Placement of the Subject Line with a Short Block Letter, Open Punctuation

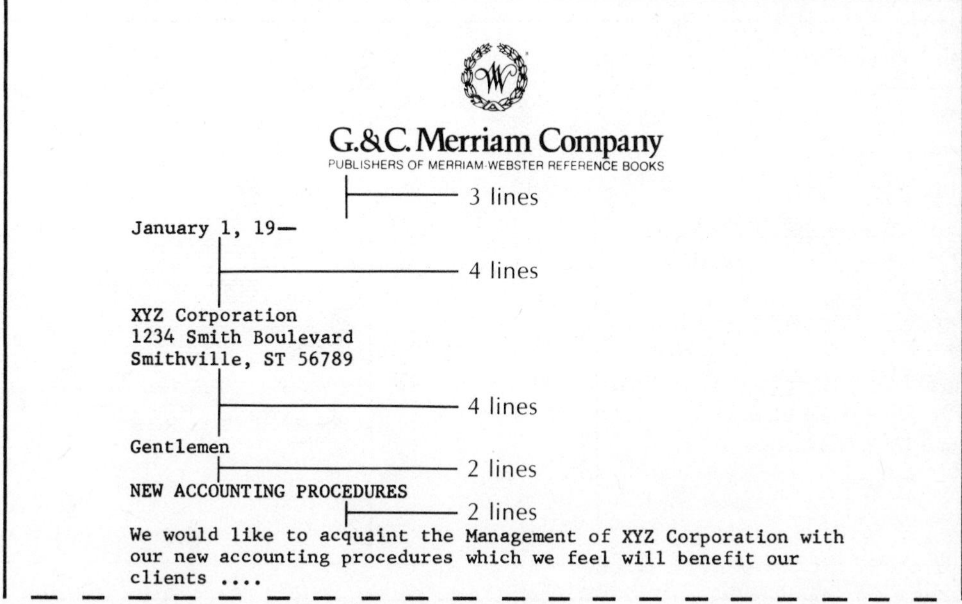

G.&C. Merriam Company
PUBLISHERS OF MERRIAM-WEBSTER REFERENCE BOOKS

3 lines

January 1, 19—

4 lines

XYZ Corporation
1234 Smith Boulevard
Smithville, ST 56789

4 lines

Gentlemen

2 lines

NEW ACCOUNTING PROCEDURES

2 lines

We would like to acquaint the Management of XYZ Corporation with our new accounting procedures which we feel will benefit our clients ....

While the subject-line headings *In re* and *Re* are now seldom recommended for general business letters, they are nevertheless often used in legal correspondence. Some offices still prefer use of the headings

SUBJECT: *or* Subject: *or* Reference:

followed by the rest of the subject line, but the unheaded line is the most common except in government and military correspondence (see pages 188 and 191). Headings should not be used if one is following the Simplified Letter styling.

MESSAGE

The body of the letter—the message—should begin about two lines below the salutation or two lines below the subject line if there is one in all letter stylings except the Simplified Letter, where the message is typed three lines below the subject line.

Paragraphs are single-spaced internally and double-spaced between each other. If a letter is extremely brief, its paragraphs may be double-spaced throughout the letter. Indentations then identify paragraphs.

Equal margins measuring one inch for long letters, about one and one-half inches for medium-length letters, and at least two inches for short letters should be kept (see Section 6.2 for a discussion of attractive letter page placement).

The first lines of indented paragraphs (as in the Modified Semi-block Letter) should begin five to ten spaces from the left margin; however, the five-space pattern is the most common. With the Hanging-indented Letter, the first lines of the paragraphs are blocked flush left, while subsequent lines are indented and blocked five spaces from the left margin. All other letter stylings require flush-left paragraph alignment.

Long quotations should be indented and blocked five to ten spaces from the left and right margins with internal single-spacing and top-and-bottom double-spacing so that the material will be set off from the rest of the message. Long enumerations should also be indented: enumerations with items requiring more than one line apiece may require single-spacing within each item, followed by double-spacing between items. Tabular data should be centered on the page.

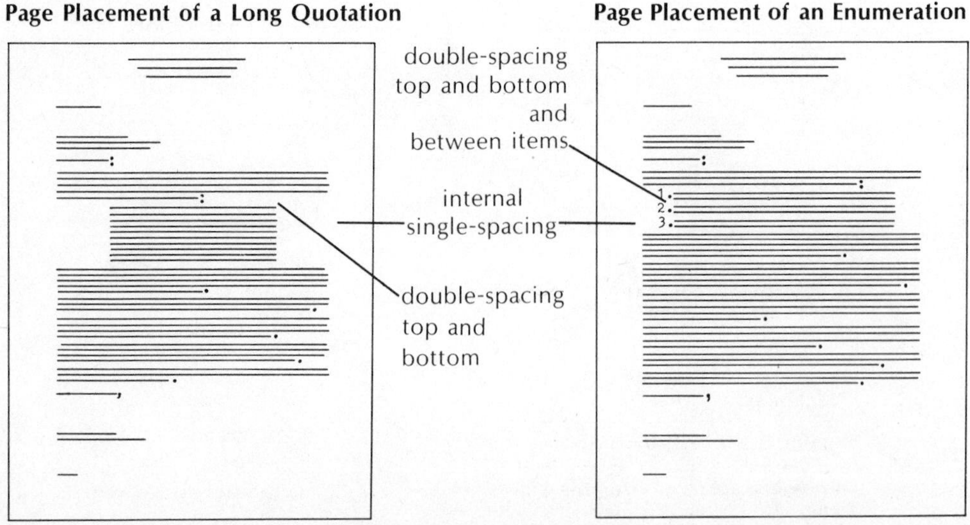

If a letter is long enough to require a continuation sheet or sheets, at least three message lines must be carried over to the next page. The complimentary close and/or typed signature block should never stand alone on a continuation sheet. The last word on a page should not be divided. Continuation-sheet margins should match those of the first sheet. At least six blank lines equaling one inch should be maintained at the top of the continuation sheet. The two most common continuation-sheet headings are described below.

Continuation-sheet Heading: Simplified and Block Letters

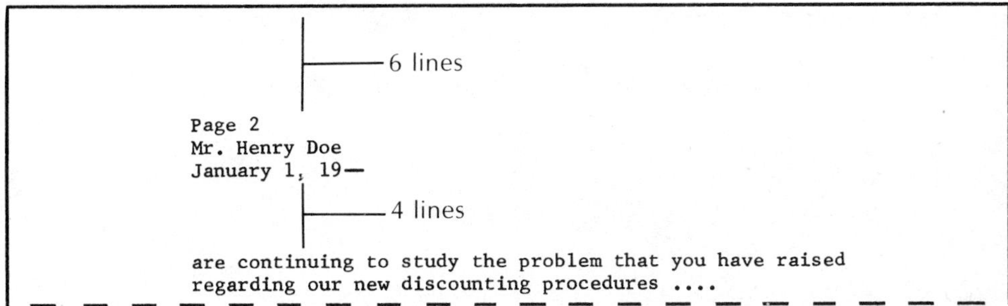

The format shown above is used with the Simplified and Block Letters. It features a flush-left heading beginning with the page number, followed on the next line by the addressee's courtesy title and full name, and ending with the date on the third line. Some companies prefer that the page number appear as the last line of the continuation-sheet heading, especially if a reference number is included.

Another way to type the heading of a continuation sheet is to lay the material out across the page, six lines down from the top edge of the sheet. The addressee's name is typed flush with the left margin, the page number in Arabic numerals is centered on the same line and enclosed with spaced hyphens, and the date is aligned flush with the right margin—all on the same line. This format is often used with the Modified Block, the Modified Semi-block, and the Hanging-indented Letters.

Continuation-sheet Heading: Used with Modified Block, Modified Semi-block, and Hanging-indented Letters

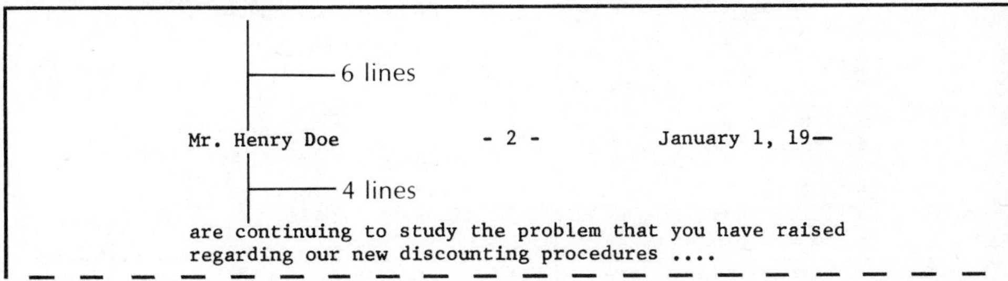

COMPLIMENTARY CLOSE

There is no complimentary close in the Simplified Letter. However, a complimentary close is used with the Block, Modified Block, Modified Semi-block, and Hanging-indented Letters. The complimentary close is typed two lines below the last line of the message in all letters. Its page placement depends on the general letter styling being used:

complimentary close with the Block Letter the complimentary close is blocked flush with the left margin.

Open Punctuation Pattern Shown in Block Letter Format for Complimentary Close

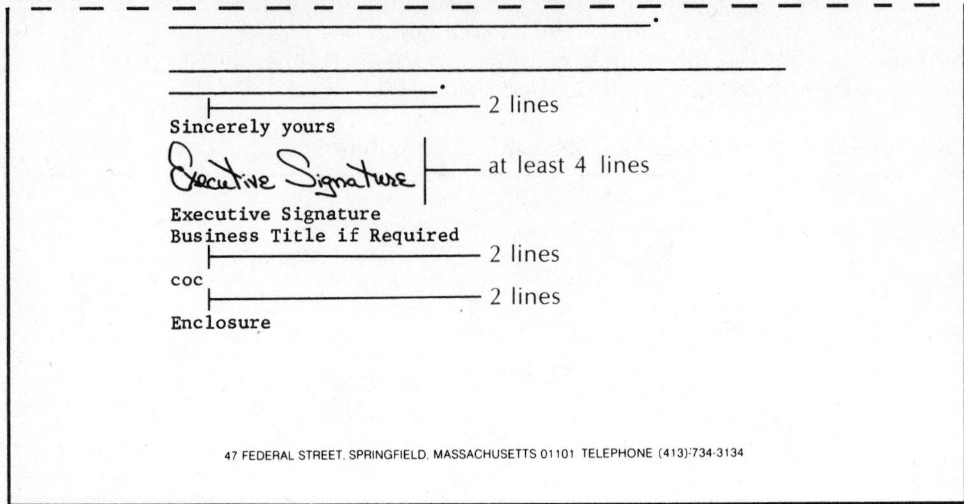

complimentary close with the Modified Block, the Modified Semi-block, and the Hanging-indented Letters the complimentary close may be aligned directly under the date line (e.g., about five spaces to the right of dead center, or flush with the right margin) or under some particular part of the printed letterhead. It should never overrun the right margin.

Complimentary Close Five Spaces to Right of Center as in a Modified Block Letter with Mixed Punctuation

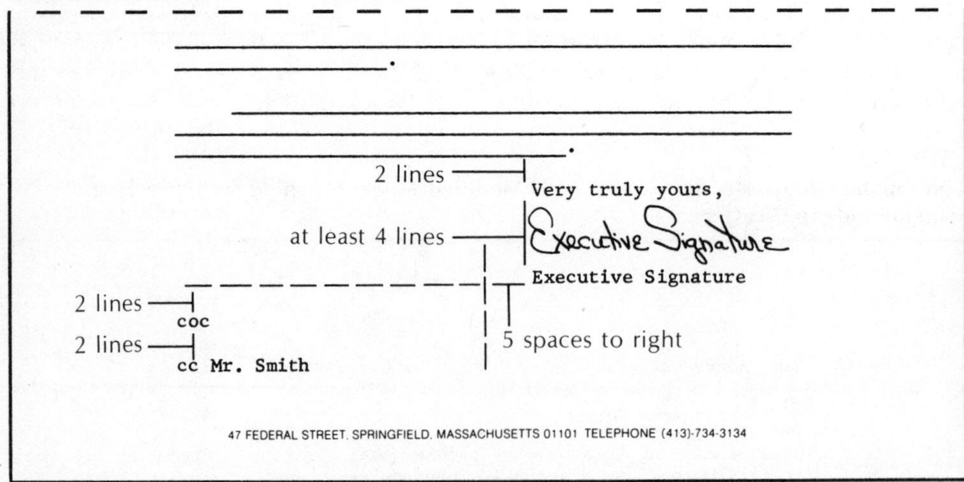

Only the first word of the complimentary close is capitalized. If the open punctuation pattern is being followed, the complimentary close is unpunctuated. If the mixed punctuation pattern is being followed, a comma terminates the complimentary close. The following chart lists the most often used complimentary closes, and also groups them according to general tone and degree of formality. For a complete list of complimentary closes for letters addressed to high-level officials and to persons with specialized titles, see Forms of Address, pages 149–178.

General Tone & Degree of Formality	Complimentary Close
highly formal—usually used in diplomatic, governmental, or ecclesiastical correspondence to show respect and deference to a high-ranking addressee	Respectfully yours Respectfully Very respectfully
politely neutral—usually used in general correspondence	Very truly yours Yours very truly Yours truly
friendly and less formal—usually used in general correspondence	Most sincerely Very sincerely Very sincerely yours Sincerely yours Yours sincerely Sincerely
more friendly and informal—often used when writer and reader are on a first-name basis but also often used in general business correspondence	Most cordially Yours cordially Cordially yours Cordially
most friendly and informal—usually used when writer and reader are on a first-name basis	As ever Best wishes Best regards Kindest regards Kindest personal regards Regards
British	Yours faithfully Yours sincerely

The typist should always use the complimentary close that is dictated because the writer may have a special reason for the choice of phrasing. If the dictator does not specify a particular closing, the typist may wish to select the one that best reflects the general tone of the letter and the state of the writer-reader relationship.

SIGNATURE BLOCK

With the Simplified Letter, the name of the writer is typed entirely in capitals flush left at least five lines below the last line of the message. If the writer's business title is not included in the printed letterhead, it may be typed on the same line as the name entirely in capitals and separated from the last element of the name by a spaced hyphen, as

JOHN P. HEWETT - DIRECTOR

although some organizations prefer to use a comma in place of the hyphen, as

JOHN P. HEWETT, DIRECTOR

or a combination of the two punctuation marks may be used if the title is complex, as

JOHN P. HEWETT - DIRECTOR, TECHNICAL INFORMATION
or
JOHN P. HEWETT - DIRECTOR
TECHNICAL INFORMATION CENTER

Page Placement of Signature Block, Simplified Letter

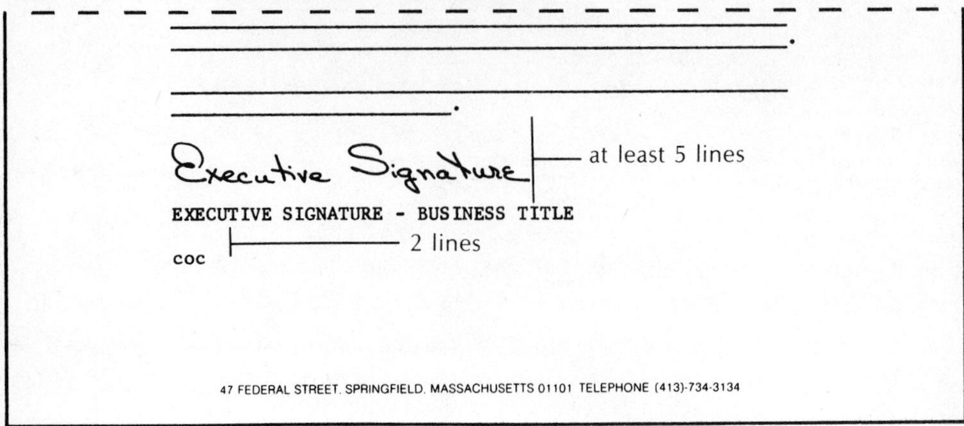

With the Block Letter, the signature block is aligned flush left at least four lines below the complimentary close. Only the first letter of each element of the writer's name is capitalized, and only the first letter of each major element of the writer's business title and/or department name are capitalized if they are included. The business title and the department name may be omitted if they appear in the printed letterhead:

John D. Russell, Director Consumer Products Division	*if title and department name are needed for identification*
or	
John D. Russell Director	*if department name is already printed on the letterhead*
or	
John D. Russell	*if both title and department name appear in printed letterhead*

Signature Block in the Block Letter

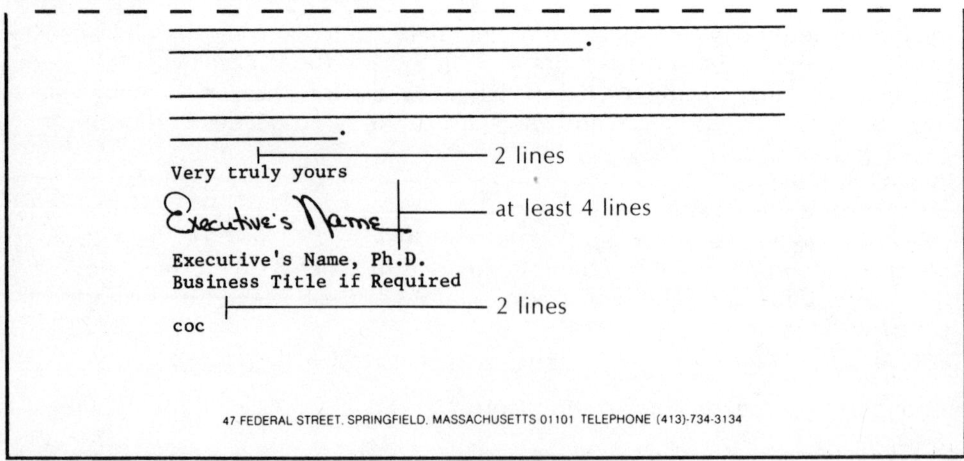

With the Modified Block, the Modified Semi-block, and the Hanging-indented Letters, the signature block begins with the name of the writer typed at least four lines below the complimentary close. The first letter of the first element of each line in the signature block is aligned directly below the first letter of the first element of the complimentary close, unless this alignment will result in an overrunning of the right margin, in which case the signature block may be centered under the complimentary close. Only the first letter of each of the major elements of the writer's name, title (if used), and department name (if used) are capitalized:

(Ms.) Sarah L. Talbott, Director *or* (Ms.) Sarah L. Talbott *or* (Ms.) Sarah L. Talbott
Marketing Division Director

Signature Block Five Spaces to Right of Center as in a Modified Block Letter with Mixed Punctuation

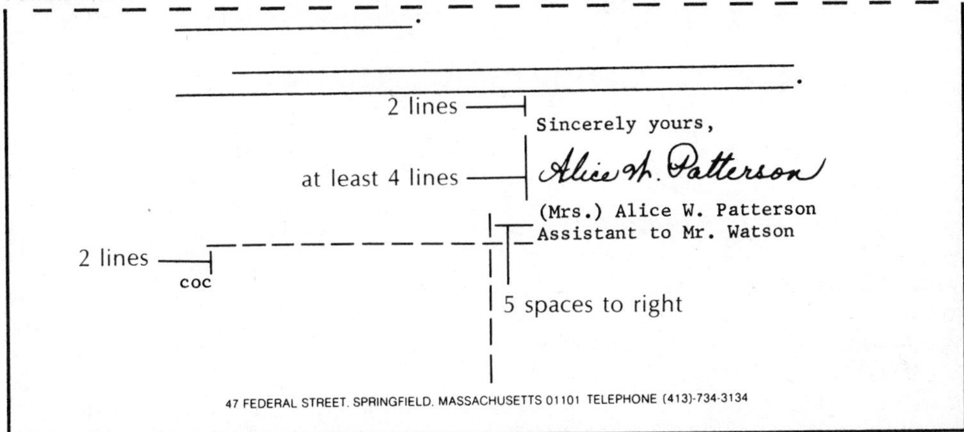

Complimentary Close and Signature Block Flush Right as in the Modified Block Letter

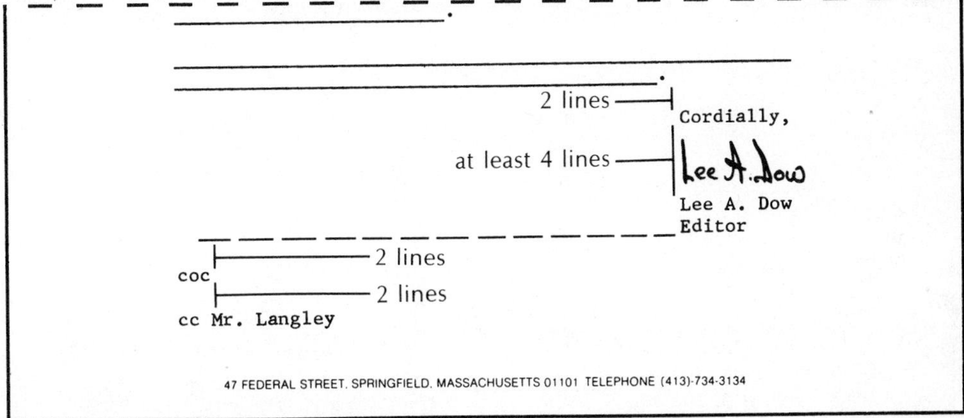

If printed letterhead is being used, the name of the firm should never appear below the complimentary close. If printed letterhead is not being used, the name of the firm may be typed all in capitals two lines beneath the complimentary close with the first letter of the firm's name aligned directly underneath, as

Very truly yours,

AJAX VAN LINES, INC.

Samuel O. Lescott
Dispatcher

with the writer's name typed in capitals and lowercase at least four lines below the firm's name. The writer's title if needed is typed in capitals and lowercase on a line directly underneath the signature line.

If the company name is long enough to overrun the right margin, it may be centered beneath the complimentary close in the Modified Block and the Modified Semi-block Letters, as

---

Very truly yours,

JOHNSON AEROSPACE ENGINEERING ASSOCIATES

Sidney C. Johnson, Ph.D.
President

Regardless of page placement and letter styling, the name of the writer should be typed exactly as he signs his name. If applicable, any academic degrees (as *Ph.D.*) or professional ratings (as *P.E.*) that the writer holds should be included after his surname so that the recipient of the letter will know the proper form of address to use in his or her reply. For example:

Typed Signature	**Salutation in Reply**
Francis E. Atlee, M.D.	Dear Dr. Atlee:
Ellen Y. Langford, Ph.D. Dean of Women	Dear Dr. Langford *or* Dear Dean Langford
Carol I. Etheridge, C.P.A. *or* (Mrs.) Carol I. Etheridge, C.P.A.	Dear Ms. Etheridge Dear Mrs. Etheridge

These academic and professional degrees and ratings need not be repeated in the signature line if they are already included in the printed letterhead, and they are never included in the written signature.

The only titles that may precede a typed signature are *Ms., Mrs.,* and *Miss,* even though they are not included in the writer's written signature. These titles are enclosed in parentheses and are blocked flush left in the Simplified and the Block Letters, and they are aligned with or centered under the complimentary close in the Modified Block, the Modified Semi-block, and the Hanging-indented Letters.

Signature Stylings for Unmarried Women	**or**	**or**
Sincerely yours	Sincerely yours	Sincerely yours
Joan Dunn Vice-president	(Ms.) Joan Dunn Vice-president	(Miss) Joan Dunn Vice-president

Signature Stylings for Women who Consider their Marital Status Irrelevant

Sincerely yours (Ms.) Joan Dunn Vice-president	or	Sincerely yours Joan Dunn Vice-president

Signature Stylings for Married Women Using Given Name + Maiden Name Initial + Husband's Surname

Sincerely yours (Mrs.) Joan M. Dunn Vice-president	or	Sincerely yours (Ms.) Joan M. Dunn Vice-president

Signature Stylings for Married Woman Using her Husband's Full Name

Sincerely yours

Mrs. Robert A. Dunn
Vice-president

A widow may use either her first name and her maiden name initial and her late husband's surname with the courtesy title *Mrs.* or *Ms.* enclosed in parentheses, or she may use her husband's full name with *Mrs.*, as

Sincerely yours (Mrs.) Joan M. Dunn or (Ms.)	Sincerely yours Mrs. Robert A. Dunn

A divorcee may use her maiden name if it has been legally regained, along with the courtesy title *Ms.* or *Miss* enclosed by parentheses or she may omit the title:

Sincerely yours (Ms.) Joan M. Dunn or (Miss)	Sincerely yours Joan M. Dunn

or she may use her maiden name and her former husband's surname with *Mrs.*:

Sincerely yours

Mrs. Matthews Dunn

If the secretary signs a letter for the dictator or writer, his name is followed by the typist's initials immediately below and to the right of the surname, or centered under the full name, as

lc lc

If the secretary signs a letter in her own name for someone else, that individual's courtesy title and surname <u>only</u> are typed directly below, as

---

Sincerely yours

(Miss) Janet A. Smith
Assistant to Mr. Wood

Sincerely yours

Seymour T. Barnes
Assistant to Senator Ross

Sincerely yours

Lee L. Linden
Secretary to Ms. Key

IDENTIFICATION INITIALS

The initials of the typist and sometimes those of the writer are placed two lines below the last line of the signature block, and are aligned flush left in all letter stylings. There is a marked trend towards complete omission of the writer's initials if the name is already typed in the signature block or if it appears in the printed letterhead. In the Simplified Letter, the writer and/or dictator's initials are usually omitted, and the typist's initials if included on the original are typed in lowercase. Many organizations indicate the typist's initials only on carbons for record-keeping purposes, and they do not show the dictator's initials unless another individual signs the letter. These are common stylings:

FCM/HL
FM/hl

hol
hl

FCM:HL
FCM:HOL

FCM:hl
FCM:hol
fcm:hol

Franklin C. Mason:HL

Franklin C. Mason
HL

A letter dictated by one person (as an administrative secretary), typed by another (as a corresponding secretary), and signed by yet another person (as the writer) may show (1) the writer/signer's initials entirely in capitals followed by a colon and (2) the dictator's initials entirely in capitals followed by a colon and (3) the transcriber/typist's initials in lowercase, as AWM:COC:ls

ENCLOSURE NOTATION

If a letter is to be accompanied by an enclosure or enclosures, one of the following expressions should be aligned flush left and typed one to two lines beneath the identification initials, if there are any, or one to two lines beneath the last line of the signature block, if there is no identification line:

Enclosure *or if more than one* Enclosures (3)

or

enc. *or* encl. *or if more than one* 3 encs.

If the enclosures are of special importance, each of them should be numerically listed and briefly described with single-spacing between each item:

Enclosures: 1. Annual Report (19--), 2 copies
2. List of Major Accounts
3. Profit and Loss Statement (19--)

The following type of notation then may be typed in the top right corner of each page of each of the enclosures:

Enclosure (1) to company name letter No. 1-234-X,
dated January 1, 19--, page 2 of 8
(if enclosure has more than one page)

If the enclosure is bound, a single notation attached to its cover sheet will suffice.

CARBON COPY NOTATION

A carbon copy notation showing the distribution of courtesy copies to other individuals should be aligned flush left and typed two lines below the signature block if there are no other notations or initials, or two lines below any other notations. If space is very tight, the carbon copy notation may be single-spaced below the above-mentioned items. The most common stylings are:

cc   cc: Copy to   Copies to

This notation may appear on the original and all copies or only on the copies.

Multiple recipients of copies should be listed alphabetically. Sometimes only their initials are shown, as

cc: WPB
TLC
CNR

or the individuals' names may be shown, especially if the writer feels that such information can be useful to the addressee:

cc: William L. Carton, Esq.
45 Park Towers, Suite 1
Smithville, ST 56789

Dr. Daniel I. Maginnis
1300 Dover Drive
Jonesville, ZZ 12345

or

cc: Ms. Lee Jamieson

Copy to Mr. John K. Long

Copies to Mr. Houghton
Mr. Ott
Mr. Smythe

If the recipient of the copy is to receive an enclosure or enclosures as well, that individual's full name and address as well as a description of each enclosure and the total number of enclosed items should be shown in the carbon copy notation:

cc: Ms. Barbra S. Lee (2 copies, Annual Report)
123 Jones Street
Smithville, ST 56789
Ms. Sara T. Tufts
Ms. Laura E. Yowell

If the writer wishes that copies of the letter be distributed without this list being shown on the original, the blind carbon copy notation bcc *or* bcc: followed by an alphabetical list of the recipients' initials or names may be typed on the carbons in the same page position as a regular carbon copy notation. The *bcc* notation may also appear in the upper left-hand corner of the carbon copies.

Page Placement of Identification and Enclosure Notations

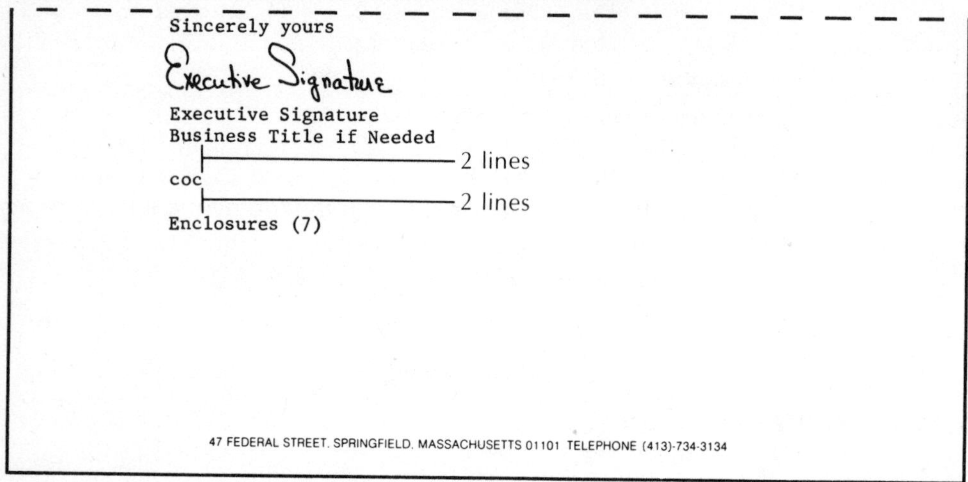
Sincerely yours

Executive Signature

Executive Signature
Business Title if Needed

coc

Enclosures (7)

47 FEDERAL STREET, SPRINGFIELD, MASSACHUSETTS 01101 TELEPHONE (413)-734-3134

POSTSCRIPT

A postscript is aligned flush left and is typed two to four lines (depending on space available) below the last notation. If the letter's paragraphs are strict-block, the postscript reflects this format. If the paragraphs within the letter are indented, the first line of the postscript is also indented. If the Hanging-indented Letter styling is used, the first line of the postscript is flush left and all subsequent lines are indented five spaces. All postscripts are single-spaced. Their margins conform with those maintained in the letters themselves. The writer should initial a postscript. While it is not incorrect to head a postscript with the initials *P.S.* (for an initial postscript) and *P.P.S.* (for subsequent ones), these headings are redundant and require extra keystrokes; therefore, it is recommended that they be omitted.

6.7

ESSENTIAL LETTER STYLES FOR TODAY'S BUSINESS CORRESPONDENCE

LETTER FACSIMILES

The following pages contain full-page letter facsimiles of the five most often used business-letter formats:

In addition, the section contains facsimiles of the following letters:

Each facsimile contains a detailed description of letter format and styling.

The Official Letter Styling with Printed Executive Letterhead

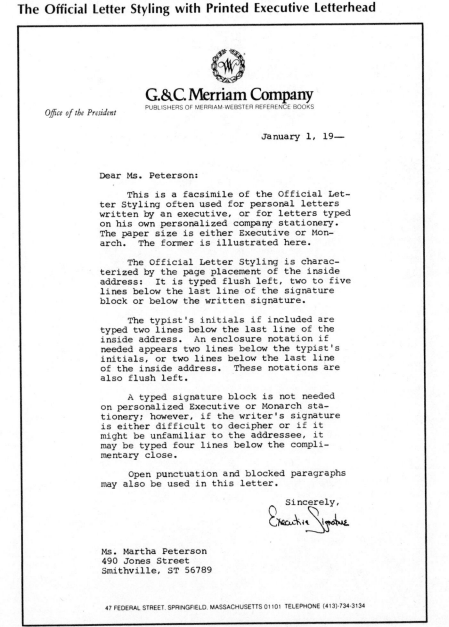

G.&C. Merriam Company
PUBLISHERS OF MERRIAM-WEBSTER REFERENCE BOOKS

Office of the President

January 1, 19—

Dear Ms. Peterson:

This is a facsimile of the Official Letter Styling often used for personal letters written by an executive, or for letters typed on his own personalized company stationery. The paper size is either Executive or Monarch. The former is illustrated here.

The Official Letter Styling is characterized by the page placement of the inside address: It is typed flush left, two to five lines below the last line of the signature block or below the written signature.

The typist's initials if included are typed two lines below the last line of the inside address. An enclosure notation if needed appears two lines below the typist's initials, or two lines below the last line of the inside address. These notations are also flush left.

A typed signature block is not needed on personalized Executive or Monarch stationery; however, if the writer's signature is either difficult to decipher or if it might be unfamiliar to the addressee, it may be typed four lines below the complimentary close.

Open punctuation and blocked paragraphs may also be used in this letter.

Sincerely,

Executive Signature

Ms. Martha Peterson
490 Jones Street
Smithville, ST 56789

47 FEDERAL STREET. SPRINGFIELD. MASSACHUSETTS 01101 TELEPHONE (413)-734-3134

The Official Letter Styling with Plain Executive Letterhead

4400 Ambler Boulevard
Smithville, ST 56789
January 1, 19—

Dear Bob

This is a facsimile of a letter typed on plain Executive or Monarch stationery. The basic format is the same as that of the Official Letter Styling. The block paragraphs and the open punctuation pattern are illustrated here.

The heading which includes the writer's full address and the date may be positioned six lines from the top edge of the page and flush with the right margin as shown here. Approximately six vertical lines may be placed after the date line down to the salutation.

The complimentary close is typed two lines below the last line of the message. The inside address is flush left, two to five lines below the last line of the signature block or below the written signature.

Typist's initials, if included, should be positioned two lines beneath the last line of the inside address. An enclosure notation or any other notation if required should be typed two lines below the typist's initials or two lines below the last line of the inside address if there are no initials.

Sincerely

Executive Signature

Mr. Robert Y. Owens
123 East Second Avenue
Jonesville, ST 45678

The Hanging-indented Letter

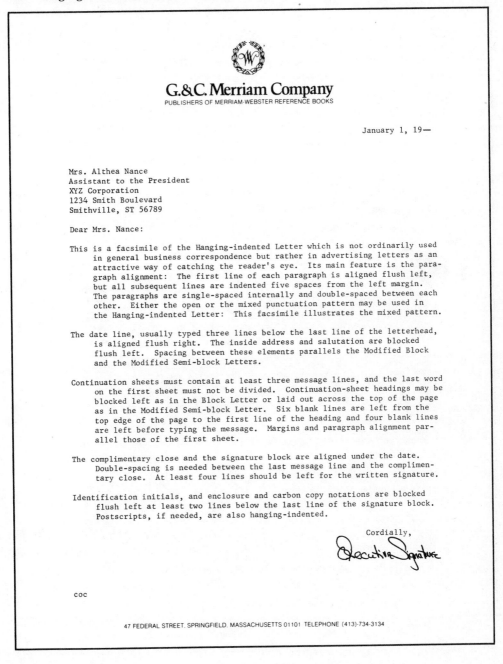

G.&C. Merriam Company
PUBLISHERS OF MERRIAM-WEBSTER REFERENCE BOOKS

January 1, 19—

Mrs. Althea Nance
Assistant to the President
XYZ Corporation
1234 Smith Boulevard
Smithville, ST 56789

Dear Mrs. Nance:

This is a facsimile of the Hanging-indented Letter which is not ordinarily used in general business correspondence but rather in advertising letters as an attractive way of catching the reader's eye. Its main feature is the paragraph alignment: The first line of each paragraph is aligned flush left, but all subsequent lines are indented five spaces from the left margin. The paragraphs are single-spaced internally and double-spaced between each other. Either the open or the mixed punctuation pattern may be used in the Hanging-indented Letter: This facsimile illustrates the mixed pattern.

The date line, usually typed three lines below the last line of the letterhead, is aligned flush right. The inside address and salutation are blocked flush left. Spacing between these elements parallels the Modified Block and the Modified Semi-block Letters.

Continuation sheets must contain at least three message lines, and the last word on the first sheet must not be divided. Continuation-sheet headings may be blocked left as in the Block Letter or laid out across the top of the page as in the Modified Semi-block Letter. Six blank lines are left from the top edge of the page to the first line of the heading and four blank lines are left before typing the message. Margins and paragraph alignment parallel those of the first sheet.

The complimentary close and the signature block are aligned under the date. Double-spacing is needed between the last message line and the complimentary close. At least four lines should be left for the written signature.

Identification initials, and enclosure and carbon copy notations are blocked flush left at least two lines below the last line of the signature block. Postscripts, if needed, are also hanging-indented.

Cordially,

Executive Signature

coc

47 FEDERAL STREET, SPRINGFIELD, MASSACHUSETTS 01101 TELEPHONE (413)-734-3134

The Simplified Letter

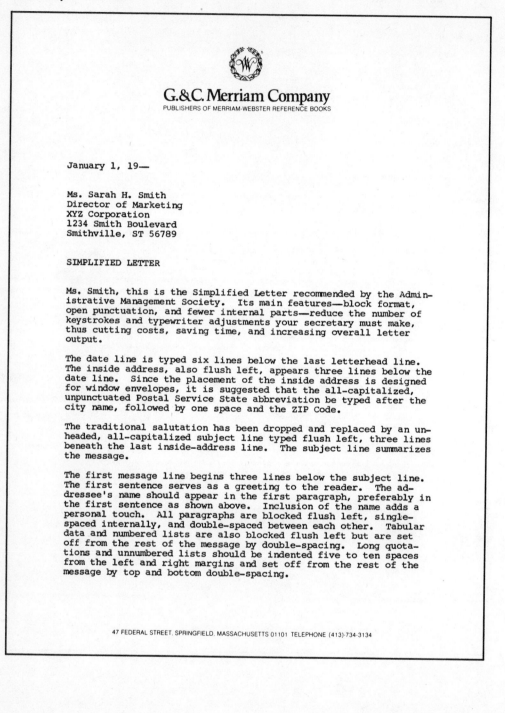

G.&C. Merriam Company
PUBLISHERS OF MERRIAM-WEBSTER REFERENCE BOOKS

January 1, 19—

Ms. Sarah H. Smith
Director of Marketing
XYZ Corporation
1234 Smith Boulevard
Smithville, ST 56789

SIMPLIFIED LETTER

Ms. Smith, this is the Simplified Letter recommended by the Administrative Management Society. Its main features—block format, open punctuation, and fewer internal parts—reduce the number of keystrokes and typewriter adjustments your secretary must make, thus cutting costs, saving time, and increasing overall letter output.

The date line is typed six lines below the last letterhead line. The inside address, also flush left, appears three lines below the date line. Since the placement of the inside address is designed for window envelopes, it is suggested that the all-capitalized, unpunctuated Postal Service State abbreviation be typed after the city name, followed by one space and the ZIP Code.

The traditional salutation has been dropped and replaced by an unheaded, all-capitalized subject line typed flush left, three lines beneath the last inside-address line. The subject line summarizes the message.

The first message line begins three lines below the subject line. The first sentence serves as a greeting to the reader. The addressee's name should appear in the first paragraph, preferably in the first sentence as shown above. Inclusion of the name adds a personal touch. All paragraphs are blocked flush left, single-spaced internally, and double-spaced between each other. Tabular data and numbered lists are also blocked flush left but are set off from the rest of the message by double-spacing. Long quotations and unnumbered lists should be indented five to ten spaces from the left and right margins and set off from the rest of the message by top and bottom double-spacing.

47 FEDERAL STREET, SPRINGFIELD, MASSACHUSETTS 01101 TELEPHONE (413)-734-3134

Ms. Smith
Page 2
January 1, 19—

If a continuation sheet is required, at least three message lines must be carried over. Continuation-sheet format and margins match those of the first sheet. At least six blank lines are left from the top edge of the page to the first line of the heading which is blocked flush left, single-spaced internally, and typically composed of the addressee's courtesy title and name, the page number, and the applicable date. The rest of the message begins four lines beneath the last heading line.

There is no complimentary close in the Simplified Letter, although closing sentences such as "You have my best wishes," and "My best regards are yours" may end the message. The writer's name (and business title if needed) is aligned flush left and typed all in capitals at least five lines below the last message line. Although the Administrative Management Society uses a spaced hyphen between the writer's surname and his business title, some companies prefer a comma. The writer's department name may be typed flush left all in capitals, one line below the signature line.

The identification initials, flush left and two lines below the last line of the signature block, comprise the typist's initials only. An enclosure notation may be typed one line below the identification initials and aligned flush left. Carbon copy notations may be typed one or two lines below the last notation, depending on available space. If only the signature block and/or typist's initials appear before it, the carbon copy notation is typed two lines below.

Executive Signature

EXECUTIVE SIGNATURE - BUSINESS TITLE

coc
Enclosures (12)

cc Dr. Alice L. Barnes

The Block Letter

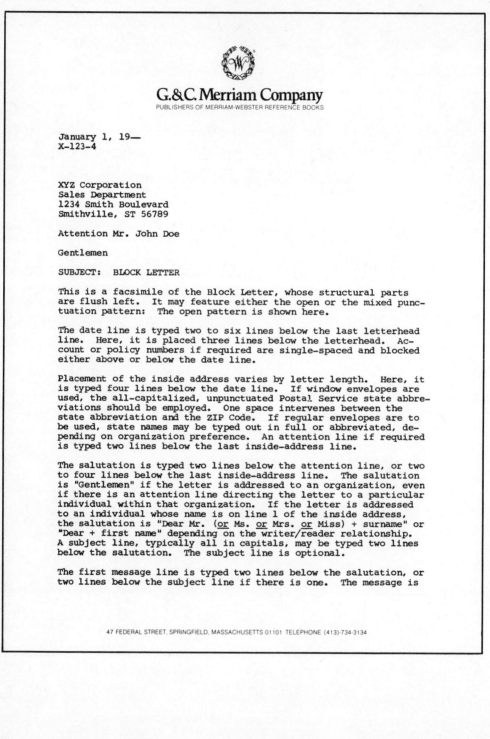

G.&C. Merriam Company
PUBLISHERS OF MERRIAM-WEBSTER REFERENCE BOOKS

January 1, 19—
X-123-4

XYZ Corporation
Sales Department
1234 Smith Boulevard
Smithville, ST 56789

Attention Mr. John Doe

Gentlemen

SUBJECT: BLOCK LETTER

This is a facsimile of the Block Letter, whose structural parts are flush left. It may feature either the open or the mixed punctuation pattern: The open pattern is shown here.

The date line is typed two to six lines below the last letterhead line. Here, it is placed three lines below the letterhead. Account or policy numbers if required are single-spaced and blocked either above or below the date line.

Placement of the inside address varies by letter length. Here, it is typed four lines below the date line. If window envelopes are used, the all-capitalized, unpunctuated Postal Service state abbreviations should be employed. One space intervenes between the state abbreviation and the ZIP Code. If regular envelopes are to be used, state names may be typed out in full or abbreviated, depending on organization preference. An attention line if required is typed two lines below the last inside-address line.

The salutation is typed two lines below the attention line, or two to four lines below the last inside-address line. The salutation is "Gentlemen" if the letter is addressed to an organization, even if there is an attention line directing the letter to a particular individual within that organization. If the letter is addressed to an individual whose name is on line 1 of the inside address, the salutation is "Dear Mr. (or Ms. or Mrs. or Miss) + surname" or "Dear + first name" depending on the writer/reader relationship. A subject line, typically all in capitals, may be typed two lines below the salutation. The subject line is optional.

The first message line is typed two lines below the salutation, or two lines below the subject line if there is one. The message is

47 FEDERAL STREET, SPRINGFIELD, MASSACHUSETTS 01101 TELEPHONE (413)-734-3134

XYZ Corporation
Sales Department
January 1, 19—
X-123-4
Page 2

single-spaced internally and double-spaced between paragraphs. At least three message lines must be carried over to a continuation sheet: At no time should the complimentary close and the signature block stand alone. The last word on a sheet should not be divided. The continuation-sheet heading is typed six lines from the top edge of the page. Account or policy numbers if used on the first sheet must be included in the continuation-sheet headings. The message begins four lines below the last line of the heading.

The complimentary close is typed two lines below the last message line, followed by at least four blank lines for the written signature, followed by the writer's name in capitals and lowercase. The writer's business title and/or name of his department may be included in the typed signature block, if they do not appear in the printed letterhead.

Identification initials may comprise only the typist's initials if the same person dictated and signed the letter. These initials are typed two lines below the last signature-block line. The enclosure notation if used is typed one line below the identification line. The carbon copy notation if needed is placed one or two lines below any other notations, depending on available space.

Sincerely yours

Executive Signature

Executive Signature
Business Title

coc
Enclosures (2)

cc Mr. Howard T. Jansen

The Modified Block Letter

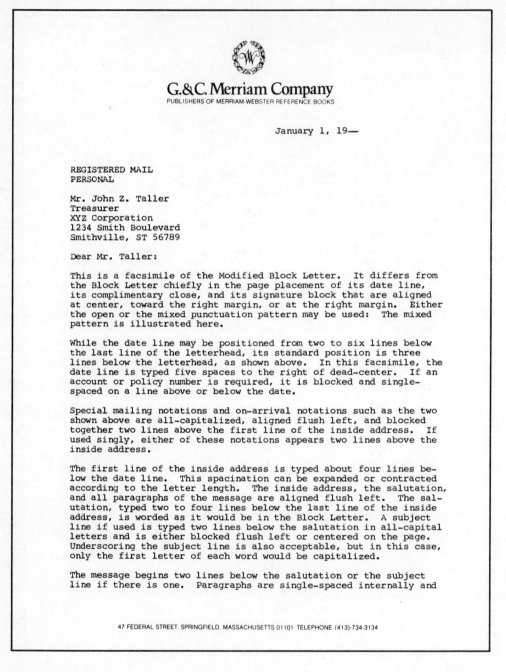

G.&C. Merriam Company
PUBLISHERS OF MERRIAM-WEBSTER REFERENCE BOOKS

January 1, 19—

REGISTERED MAIL
PERSONAL

Mr. John Z. Taller
Treasurer
XYZ Corporation
1234 Smith Boulevard
Smithville, ST 56789

Dear Mr. Taller:

This is a facsimile of the Modified Block Letter. It differs from the Block Letter chiefly in the page placement of its date line, its complimentary close, and its signature block that are aligned at center, toward the right margin, or at the right margin. Either the open or the mixed punctuation pattern may be used: The mixed pattern is illustrated here.

While the date line may be positioned from two to six lines below the last line of the letterhead, its standard position is three lines below the letterhead, as shown above. In this facsimile, the date line is typed five spaces to the right of dead-center. If an account or policy number is required, it is blocked and single-spaced on a line above or below the date.

Special mailing notations and on-arrival notations such as the two shown above are all-capitalized, aligned flush left, and blocked together two lines above the first line of the inside address. If used singly, either of these notations appears two lines above the inside address.

The first line of the inside address is typed about four lines below the date line. This spacination can be expanded or contracted according to the letter length. The inside address, the salutation, and all paragraphs of the message are aligned flush left. The salutation, typed two to four lines below the last line of the inside address, is worded as it would be in the Block Letter. A subject line if used is typed two lines below the salutation in all-capital letters and is either blocked flush left or centered on the page. Underscoring the subject line is also acceptable, but in this case, only the first letter of each word would be capitalized.

The message begins two lines below the salutation or the subject line if there is one. Paragraphs are single-spaced internally and

47 FEDERAL STREET, SPRINGFIELD, MASSACHUSETTS 01101 TELEPHONE (413)-734-3134

Mr. Taller - 2 - January 1, 19—

double-spaced between each other; however, in very short letters, the paragraphs may be double-spaced internally and triple-spaced between each other.

Continuation sheets should contain at least three message lines. The last word on a sheet should not be divided. The continuation-sheet heading may be blocked flush left as in the Block Letter or it may be laid out across the top of the page as shown above. This heading begins six lines from the top edge of the page, and the message is continued four lines beneath it.

The complimentary close is typed two lines below the last line of the message. While the complimentary close may be aligned under some portion of the letterhead, directly under the date line, or even flush with but not overrunning the right margin, it is often typed five spaces to the right of dead-center as shown here.

The signature line is typed in capitals and lowercase at least four lines below the complimentary close. The writer's business title and department name may be included if they do not already appear in the printed letterhead. All elements of the signature block must be aligned with each other and with the complimentary close.

Identification initials need include only those of the typist, providing that the writer and the signer are the same person. These initials appear two lines below the last line of the signature block. An enclosure notation is typed one line below the identification line, and the carbon copy notation if required appears one or two lines below any other notations, depending on space available.

Very truly yours,

Executive Signature

Executive Signature
Business Title

coc
Enclosures (5)

cc Mr. Doe
Mr. Franklin
Mr. Mason
Ms. Watson

The Modified Semi-block Letter

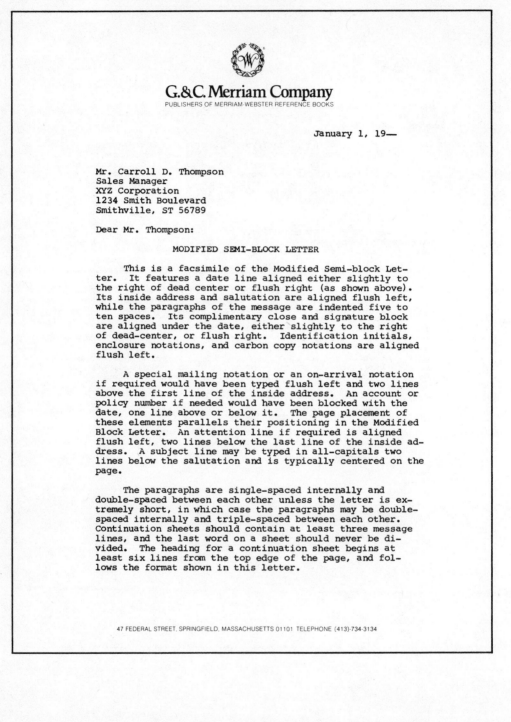

G.&C. Merriam Company
PUBLISHERS OF MERRIAM-WEBSTER REFERENCE BOOKS

January 1, 19—

Mr. Carroll D. Thompson
Sales Manager
XYZ Corporation
1234 Smith Boulevard
Smithville, ST 56789

Dear Mr. Thompson:

MODIFIED SEMI-BLOCK LETTER

This is a facsimile of the Modified Semi-block Letter. It features a date line aligned either slightly to the right of dead center or flush right (as shown above). Its inside address and salutation are aligned flush left, while the paragraphs of the message are indented five to ten spaces. Its complimentary close and signature block are aligned under the date, either slightly to the right of dead-center, or flush right. Identification initials, enclosure notations, and carbon copy notations are aligned flush left.

A special mailing notation or an on-arrival notation if required would have been typed flush left and two lines above the first line of the inside address. An account or policy number if needed would have been blocked with the date, one line above or below it. The page placement of these elements parallels their positioning in the Modified Block Letter. An attention line if required is aligned flush left, two lines below the last line of the inside address. A subject line may be typed in all-capitals two lines below the salutation and is typically centered on the page.

The paragraphs are single-spaced internally and double-spaced between each other unless the letter is extremely short, in which case the paragraphs may be double-spaced internally and triple-spaced between each other. Continuation sheets should contain at least three message lines, and the last word on a sheet should never be divided. The heading for a continuation sheet begins at least six lines from the top edge of the page, and follows the format shown in this letter.

47 FEDERAL STREET, SPRINGFIELD, MASSACHUSETTS 01101 TELEPHONE (413)-734-3134

Mr. Thompson - 2 - January 1, 19—

The complimentary close is typed at two lines below the last line of the message. The signature line, four lines below the complimentary close, is aligned with it if possible, or centered under it if the name and title will be long. In this case, it is better to align both date and complimentary close about five spaces to the right of dead-center to ensure enough room for the signature block which should never overrun the right margin. The writer's name, business title and department name (if not already printed on the stationery), are typed in capitals and lowercase.

Although open punctuation may be followed, the mixed punctuation pattern is quite common with the Modified Semi-block Letter, and it is the latter that is shown here.

Sincerely yours,

Executive Signature
Business Title

coc

Enclosures: 2

cc: Dr. Bennett P. Oakley
Addison Engineering Associates
91011 Jones Street
Smithville, ST 56789

A postscript if needed is typically positioned two to four lines below the last notation. In the Modified Semi-block Letter, the postscript is indented five to ten spaces to agree with message paragraphing. It is not necessary to head the postscript with the abbreviation P.S. The postscript should be initialed by the writer.

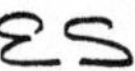

The Half-Sheet

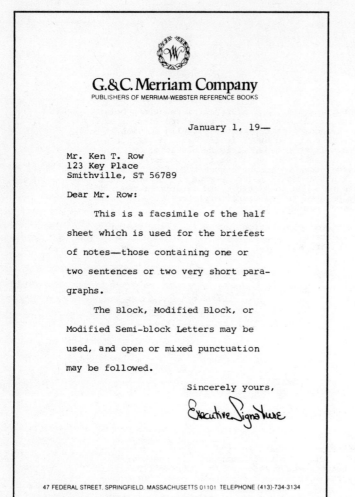

G.&C. Merriam Company
PUBLISHERS OF MERRIAM-WEBSTER REFERENCE BOOKS

January 1, 19—

Mr. Ken T. Row
123 Key Place
Smithville, ST 56789

Dear Mr. Row:

This is a facsimile of the half sheet which is used for the briefest of notes—those containing one or two sentences or two very short paragraphs.

The Block, Modified Block, or Modified Semi-block Letters may be used, and open or mixed punctuation may be followed.

Sincerely yours,

Executive Signature

47 FEDERAL STREET, SPRINGFIELD, MASSACHUSETTS 01101 TELEPHONE (413)-734-3134

ENVELOPES

The following information may appear on any envelope regardless of its size. Asterisked items are essential and those that are unmarked are optional, depending on the requirements of the particular letter:

*1. The addressee's full name and full geographical address typed approximately in the vertical and horizontal center
2. Special mailing notation or notations typed below the stamp
3. On-arrival notation or notations typed about nine lines below the top left
*4. Sender's full name and geographical address printed or typed in the upper left corner.

The typeface should be block style. The Postal Service does not recommend unusual or italic typefaces. The typewriter keys should be clean.

The address block on a regular envelope should encompass no more than 1½″ × 3¾″ of space. There should be ⅝″ of space from the bottom line of the address block to the bottom edge of the envelope. The entire area from the right and left bottom margins of the address block to the right and left bottom edges of the envelope as well as the area under the center of the address block to the bottom center edge of the envelope should be free of print. With regular envelopes, most address blocks are begun about five spaces to the left of horizontal center to admit room for potentially long lines. The address block should be single-spaced. Block styling should be used throughout.

If a window envelope is being used, all address data must appear within the window space, and at least ¼″ margins must be maintained between the address and the right, left, top, and bottom edges of the window space.

Address-block data on a regular envelope should match the spelling and styling of the inside address. Address-block elements are positioned as follows:

first line

If the addressee is an individual, that person's courtesy title + full name are typed on the first line.

If the addressee is an organization, its full name is typed on the first line.

If an individual addressee's business title is included in the inside address, it may be typed either on the first line of the address block with a comma separating it from the addressee's name, or it may be typed alone on the next line, depending on length of title and name.
If a particular department within an organization is specified, it is typed on a line under the name of the organization.

Examples:
Mr. Lee O. Idlewild, President
or
Mr. Lee O. Idlewild
President
or, addressed for automation
MR LEE O IDLEWILD
PRES
or
MR L O IDLEWILD
PRES
and
XYZ Corporation
Sales Department
or, addressed for automation
XYZ CORP
SALES DEPT

next line

The full street address should be typed out (although it is acceptable to abbreviate such designations as *Street, Avenue, Boulevard,* etc.). In mass mailings that will be presorted for automated handling, it is correct to capitalize all elements of the address block and to use the unpunctuated abbreviations for streets and street-designations that are recommended by the U.S. Postal Service. Room, suite, apartment, and building numbers are typed immediately following the last element of the street address and are positioned on the same line with it.

last line

The last line of the address block contains the city, state, and the ZIP Code number. Only one space intervenes between the last letter of the state abbreviation and the first digit of the ZIP Code. The all-capitalized, unpunctuated, two-letter Postal Service state abbreviations are mandatory, as is the ZIP Code.

Examples:

Mr. John P. Smith
4523 Kendall Place, Apt. 8B
Smithville, ST 56789

or

Mr. John P. Smith
4523 Kendall Pl., Apt. 8B
Smithville, ST 56789

or, addressed for automation

MR J P SMITH
4523 KENDALL PL APT 8B
SMITHVILLE ST 56789

or

CAMERON CORP
ATTN MR J P SMITH
765 BAY ST ROOM 100
SMITHVILLE ST 56789

When typing a foreign address, the secretary should refer first to the return address on the envelope of previous correspondence to ascertain the correct ordering of the essential elements of the address block. Letterhead of previous correspondence may also be checked if an envelope is not available. If neither of these sources is available, the material should be typed as it appears in the inside address of the dictated letter. The following guidelines may be of assistance:

1. All foreign addresses should be typed in English or in English characters: if an address must be in foreign characters (as Russian), an English translation should be interlined in the address block.
2. Foreign courtesy titles may be substituted for the English; however, it is unnecessary.
3. The name of the country should be typed in all-capital letters. Canadian addresses always carry the name CANADA, even though the name of the province is also given.
4. When applicable, foreign postal district numbers should be included.

Some samples of foreign corporate abbreviations are shown in the following table.

Foreign Corporate Abbreviations: A Brief Sampling of Commonly Used Terms

Language	Type of Business	Abbreviation
Danish	Partnership	I/S
	Limited Partnership	K/S
	Limited-liability Company	A/S
	Private Limited-liability Company	Ap/S
Dutch	Private Company	B.V.
	Public Corporation	N.V.
French	Limited-liability Company	SARL
	Corporation	SA
German	Partnership	OHG
	Limited Partnership	KG
	Limited-liability Company	G.m.b.H.
	Corporation	AG
Italian	Corporation	S.p.A.
	Limited-liability Company	S.r.l.
Portuguese	Corporation	SARL
Spanish	Stock Company	SA
	Corporation	S/A
	Company	CIA
Swedish	Joint Stock Company	SA

On-arrival notations such as PERSONAL or CONFIDENTIAL must be typed entirely in capital letters, about nine lines below the left top edge of the envelope. Any other on-arrival instructions such as Hold for Arrival or Please Forward may be typed in capitals and lowercase, underlined, and positioned about nine lines from the left top edge of the envelope.

If an attention line is used in the letter itself, it too must appear on the envelope. Attention lines are typed in capitals and lowercase for regular mailings using commercial envelopes, and they are typed entirely in capitals for mass mailings that will be presorted for automatic handling. The attention line may be placed anywhere in the address block so long as it is directly above the next-to-last line, as

XYZ Corporation
Sales Department
Attention Mr. E. R. Bailey
1234 Smith Boulevard
Smithville, ST 56789

XYZ CORP
SALES DEPT
ATTN MR E R BAILEY
1234 SMITH BLVD
SMITHVILLE ST 56789

Facsimile of a Commercial Envelope Showing On-arrival and Special Mailing Notations

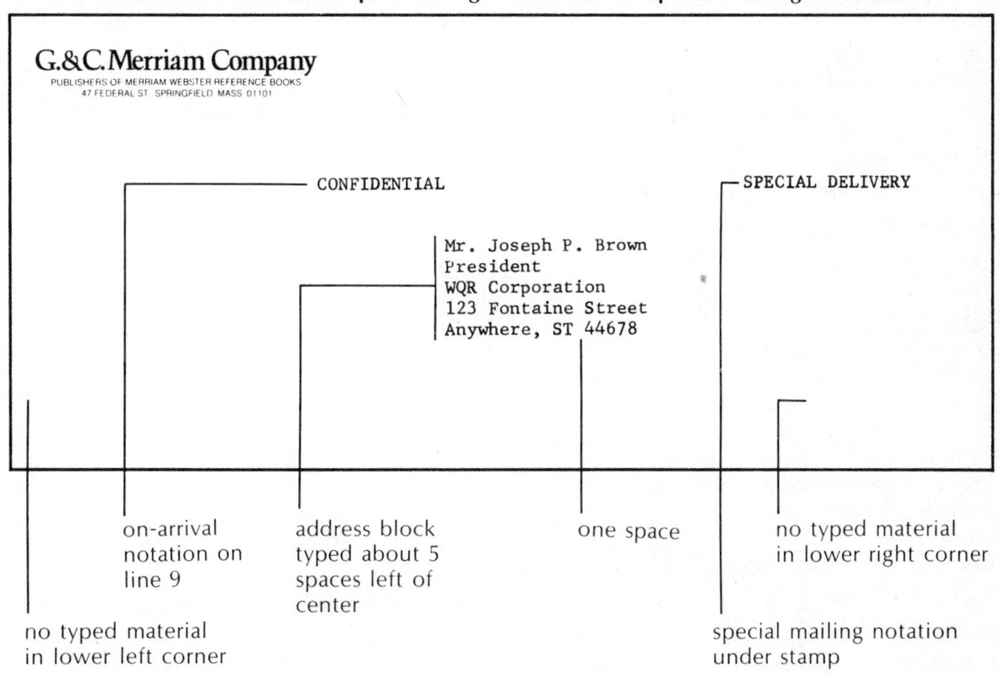

A special mailing notation (as CERTIFIED, REGISTERED MAIL, or SPECIAL DELIVERY) is typed entirely in capitals just below the stamp or about nine lines from the right top edge of the envelope. It should not overrun a ½″ margin.

The printed return address (as of a company) may be supplemented by the name of the writer typed in at the top. The return address on a plain envelope should be styled as

Stephen P. Lemke
123 Ann Street
Jonesville, XX 12345

with at least two blank lines between the return address and the left and top edges of the envelope.

See page 109 for a chart showing stationery and envelope sizes and applications. See Chapter 10 for detailed treatment of mailing procedures.

6.8

FORMS OF ADDRESS

It has already been emphasized that the initial impression created by a letter is vital to the letter's ultimate effectiveness. It follows that proper use of the conventional forms of address is essential, especially since these forms appear in conspicuous areas of the letter: on the envelope, in the inside address, and in the salutation.

FORMS OF ADDRESS CHART

The following pages contain a chart of alphabetically grouped and listed forms of address for individuals whose offices, ranks, or professions warrant special courtesy titles, salutations, and complimentary closes. The chart also indicates in its last column how these individuals should be addressed orally (as in an introduction or in a conversation) and how they should be referred to in a written text (such as in a letter, a report, or an article).

The main categories covered in the chart are listed below in the order of their appearance:

Clerical and Religious Orders
College and University Faculty and Officials
Consular Officers
Diplomats
Foreign Heads of State
Government Officials
Military Ranks
Miscellaneous Courtesy, Business, and Professional Titles
United Nations Officials

A special chart headed "Multiple Addressees" immediately follows the Forms of Address Chart.

When two or more stylings are shown in the Forms of Address Chart, it should be understood by the reader that the most formal styling appears first. It should also be understood that male and female addressees (as in the clergy and in the armed forces) are addressed alike unless stated otherwise. An acute space problem within this chart has precluded mention of both male and female addressees in every single instance. The fact that female addressees are not shown throughout the material in no way suggests that women may not hold these positions or ranks.

Addressee	Form of Address	Salutation	Complimentary Close	(*1*) **Oral Reference** (*2*) **Written Reference**
CLERICAL AND RELIGIOUS ORDERS				
abbot	The Right Reverend John R. Smith, O.S.B. Abbot of ----	Right Reverend and dear Father Dear Father Abbot Dear Father	Respectfully yours Sincerely yours	(*1*) Father Abbot (*2*) Father Smith
apostolic delegate	His Excellency, The Most Reverend John R. Smith Archbishop of ---- The Apostolic Delegate	Your Excellency My dear Archbishop	Respectfully yours Respectfully	(*1*) Your Excellency (*2*) the Apostolic Delegate
	or The Apostolic Delegation	Gentlemen	Sincerely yours	(*1 and 2*) the Apostolic Delegation
archbishop	The Most Reverend Archbishop of ----	Your Excellency	Respectfully yours	(*1*) Your excellency (*2*) the Archbishop of ----
	or The Most Reverend John R. Smith Archbishop of ----	Your Excellency Dear Archbishop Smith	Respectfully yours Sincerely yours	(*1*) Archbishop Smith (*2*) Archbishop Smith
archdeacon	The Venerable The Archdeacon of ----	Venerable Sir	Respectfully yours	(*1*) Archdeacon Smith (*2*) the Archdeacon of ----
	or The Venerable John R. Smith	Venerable Sir My dear Archdeacon	Respectfully yours Sincerely yours	(*1 and 2*) Archdeacon (*or if having doctorate* Dr.) Smith
bishop, Catholic	The Most Reverend John R. Smith Bishop of ----	Your Excellency Dear Bishop Smith	Respectfully yours Sincerely yours	(*1 and 2*) Bishop Smith

Addressee	Form of Address	Salutation	Complimentary Close	(*1*) **Oral Reference** (*2*) **Written Reference**
bishop, Episcopal Presiding	The Most Reverend John R. Smith Presiding Bishop	Most Reverend Sir Dear Bishop Dear Bishop Smith	Respectfully yours Sincerely yours	(*1 and 2*) Bishop Smith
bishop, Episcopal	The Right Reverend The Bishop of ---- *or* The Right Reverend John R. Smith Bishop of ----	Right Reverend Sir Right Reverend Sir Dear Bishop Smith	Respectfully yours Respectfully yours Sincerely yours	(*1*) Bishop Smith (*2*) the Episcopal Bishop of ----
bishop, Methodist	The Reverend John R. Smith Methodist Bishop	Reverend Sir Dear Bishop Smith	Respectfully yours Sincerely yours	(*1 and 2*) Bishop Smith
brotherhood, member of	Brother John, S.J.	Dear Brother John	Respectfully yours Sincerely yours	(*1*) Brother John (*2*) Brother John, S.J.
brotherhood, superior of	Brother John, S.J., Superior	Dear Brother John	Respectfully yours Sincerely yours	(*1*) Brother John (*2*) Brother John, S.J., Superior of ----
canon	The Reverend John R. Smith Canon of ---- Cathedral	Dear Canon Smith	Respectfully yours Sincerely yours	(*1 and 2*) Canon Smith
cardinal	His Eminence John Cardinal Smith Archbishop of ---- *or* His Eminence Cardinal Smith Archbishop of ----	Your Eminence My dear Cardinal Smith Dear Cardinal Smith	Respectfully yours Sincerely yours	(*1*) Your Eminence *or* Cardinal Smith (*2*) His Eminence Cardinal Smith *or* Cardinal Smith

chaplain, college or university—*see* COLLEGE AND UNIVERSITY FACULTY AND OFFICIALS				
clergyman, Protestant (excluding Episcopal)	The Reverend John R. Smith	Dear Mr. Smith	Respectfully yours Sincerely yours	(*1*) Mr. Smith (*2*) The Reverend Mr. Smith *or* The Reverend John R. Smith *or* Mr. Smith
	or if having doctorate The Reverend Dr. John R. Smith	Dear Dr. Smith	Respectfully yours Sincerely yours	(*1*) Dr. Smith (*2*) The Reverend Dr. Smith *or* Dr. Smith
dean (of a cathedral)	The Very Reverend John R. Smith ---- Cathedral	Very Reverend Sir Dear Dean Smith	Respectfully yours Sincerely yours	(*1 and 2*) Dean (*or if having doctorate* Dr.) Smith
	or Dean John R. Smith ---- Cathedral	Very Reverend Sir Dear Dean Smith	Respectfully yours Sincerely yours	
moderator, Presbyterian	The Moderator of ----	Reverend Sir My dear Sir	Respectfully yours Sincerely yours	(*1 and 2*) the Moderator of ----
	or The Reverend John R. Smith	Dear Mr. Moderator My dear Mr. Smith	Respectfully yours Sincerely yours	(*1 and 2*) Mr. Smith
	or if having doctorate Dr. John R. Smith	My dear Dr. Smith	Respectfully yours Sincerely yours	(*1 and 2*) Dr. Smith
monsignor				
domestic prelate	The Right Reverend Monsignor John R. Smith	Right Reverend and dear Monsignor Smith	Respectfully yours	(*1 and 2*) Monsignor Smith
	or The Rt. Rev. Msgr. John R. Smith	Dear Monsignor Smith	Sincerely yours	
papal chamberlain	The Very Reverend Monsignor John R. Smith	Very Reverend and dear Monsignor Smith	Respectfully yours	(*1 and 2*) Monsignor Smith
	or The Very Rev. Msgr. John R. Smith	Dear Monsignor Smith	Sincerely yours	

Addressee	Form of Address	Salutation	Complimentary Close	(*1*) **Oral Reference** (*2*) **Written Reference**
patriarch (of an Eastern Orthodox Church)	His Beatitude the Patriarch of ----	Most Reverend Lord	Respectfully yours	(*1*) Your Beatitude (*2*) John R. Smith, the Patriarch of ---- *or* The Patriarch
pope	His Holiness the Pope *or* His Holiness Pope ----	Your Holiness Most Holy Father	Respectfully yours	(*1*) Your Holiness (*2*) His Holiness the Pope *or* His Holiness, Pope ---- *or* The Pope
president, Mormon	The President Church of Jesus Christ of Latter-Day Saints	My dear President Dear President Smith	Respectfully yours Sincerely yours	(*1 and 2*) Mr. Smith
priest, Catholic	The Reverend John R. Smith	Dear Father Smith	Respectfully yours Sincerely yours	(*1 and 2*) Father Smith
	or if having doctorate The Reverend Dr. John R. Smith	Dear Father Smith	Respectfully yours Sincerely yours	(*1 and 2*) Father Smith
priest, Episcopal	The Reverend John R. Smith	Dear Mr. Smith Dear Father Smith	Respectfully yours Sincerely yours	(*1 and 2*) Mr. (*or* Father) Smith
	or if having doctorate The Reverend Dr. John R. Smith	Dear Dr. Smith Dear Father Smith	Respectfully yours Sincerely yours	(*1 and 2*) Dr. (*or* Father) Smith
priest/president—*see* COLLEGE AND UNIVERSITY FACULTY AND OFFICIALS (of a college or university)				
rabbi	Rabbi John R. Smith	Dear Rabbi Smith	Respectfully yours Sincerely yours	(*1 and 2*) Rabbi Smith
	or if having doctorate Rabbi John R. Smith, D.D.	Dear Dr. Smith		(*1 and 2*) Dr. (*or* Rabbi) Smith

sisterhood, member of	Sister Mary Angelica, S.C.	Dear Sister Dear Sister Mary Angelica	Respectfully yours Sincerely yours	(*1 and 2*) Sister Mary Angelica
sisterhood, superior of	The Reverend Mother Superior, S.C.	Reverend Mother Dear Reverend Mother	Respectfully yours Sincerely yours	(*1*) Reverend Mother (*2*) The Reverend Mother Superior *or* The Reverend Mother
COLLEGE AND UNIVERSITY FACULTY AND OFFICIALS				
chancellor (of a university)	Dr. John / Amelia } R. Smith Chancellor	Sir Madam Dear Dr. Smith	Very truly yours Sincerely yours	(*1*) Dr. Smith (*2*) Dr. Smith *or* John / Amelia } R. Smith, Chancellor of ---- University
chaplain (of a college or university)	The Reverend John / Amelia } R. Smith Chaplain	Dear Chaplain Smith Dear Mr. / Miss / Mrs. } Smith Dear Father Smith	Respectfully Sincerely yours	(*1 and 2*) Chaplain Smith *or* Mr., Miss, Mrs. Smith *or* Father Smith
dean (of a college or university)	Dean John / Amelia } R. Smith *or* Dr. John / Amelia } R. Smith Dean	Sir Madam Dear Dr. Smith Dear Dean Smith	Very truly yours Sincerely yours	(*1*) Dean *or* Dr. Smith (*2*) Dean *or* Dr. Smith *or* Dr. Smith, Dean of ----
instructor	Mr., Dr. John R. Smith Ms., Miss, / Mrs., Dr. } Amelia R. Smith Instructor	Dear Mr., Dr. Smith Dear Ms., Miss, Mrs., Dr. Smith	Very truly yours Sincerely yours	(*1 and 2*) Mr., Ms., Miss, Mrs., Dr. Smith

Addressee	Form of Address	Salutation	Complimentary Close	(*1*) **Oral Reference** (2) **Written Reference**
president	Dr. John / Amelia } R. Smith President *or* President John / Amelia } R. Smith	Sir Madam Dear Dr. Smith Dear President Smith	Very truly yours Sincerely yours Very truly yours Sincerely yours	(*1*) Dr. Smith (2) Dr. Smith *or* Dr. Smith, the President of ----
president/priest	The Very Reverend John R. Smith, S.J. President	Sir Dear Father Smith	Respectfully yours Sincerely yours	(*1*) Father Smith (2) Father Smith, President of ----
professor, assistant or associate	Mr., Dr. John R. Smith Ms., Mrs., Miss, Dr. Amelia R. Smith Assistant/Associate Professor of ----	Dear Mr., Dr. Smith Dear Ms., Mrs., Miss, Dr. Smith *or* Dear Professor Smith	Very truly yours Sincerely yours	(*1*) Mr., Ms., Mrs., Miss, Dr. Smith (2) Professor Smith
professor, full	Professor John / Amelia } R. Smith *or* Dr. John / Amelia } R. Smith Professor of ----	Dear Professor Smith Dear Dr. Smith	Very truly yours Sincerely yours	(*1 and 2*) Professor *or* Dr. Smith
CONSULAR OFFICERS				
consulate, American	The American Consulate (foreign city, country) *or if in Central or South America* The Consulate of the United States of America (foreign city, country)	Gentlemen Gentlemen	Very truly yours Very truly yours	(*1*) ---- (2) the American Consulate in ---- (*1*) ---- (2) the United States Consulate in ----

consuls, American (covers all consular grades such as *Consul General, Consul, Vice-Consul* and *Consular Agent*)	The American Consul (foreign city, country) *or if in Central or South America*	Sir	Respectfully yours Very truly yours	(*1*) ---- (*2*) the American Consul in ----
	The Consul of the United States of America (foreign city, country) *or if individual name is known*	Sir	Respectfully yours Very truly yours	(*1*) ---- (*2*) the United States Consul in ----
NOTE: Since these officers are frequently transferred it is advisable to address letters to the office and not to the individual.	John / Amelia R. Smith, Esq. American Consul *or if in Central or South America* Consul of the United States of America	Sir / Madam Dear Mr. / Ms. / Mrs. / Miss Smith	Respectfully yours Very truly yours	(*1*) Mr., Ms., Mrs., Miss Smith (*2*) the American *or* United States Consul in ----
consulate, foreign	The ---- Consulate *or* The Consulate of ---- (U.S. city, state, ZIP)	Gentlemen	Very truly yours	(*1*) ---- (*2*) the ---- Consulate *or* the Consulate of ----
consuls, foreign (covers all consular grades)	The ---- Consul *or* The Consul of ---- (U.S. city, state, ZIP) *or if individual name is known*	Sir	Respectfully yours Sincerely yours	(*1*) ---- (*2*) the ---- Consul in (*city*) *or* the Consul of ---- in (*city*)
NOTE: Since these officers are frequently transferred it is advisable to address letters to the office and not to the individual.	The Honorable John / Amelia R. Smith ---- Consul *or* Consul of ---- (U.S. city, state, ZIP)	Sir / Madame Dear Mr. / Ms. / Mrs. / Miss Smith	Respectfully yours Sincerely yours	(*1*) Mr., Ms., Mrs., Miss Smith *or* Mr., Ms., Mrs., Miss Smith, the ---- Consul (*2*) Mr., Ms., Mrs., Miss Smith, the ---- Consul in (*city*)

Addressee	Form of Address	Salutation	Complimentary Close	(*1*) **Oral Reference** (2) **Written Reference**
DIPLOMATS				
ambassador, American	The Honorable John / Amelia R. Smith American Ambassador *or if in Central or South America* The Ambassador of the United States of America	Sir Madam Dear Mr. / Madam Ambassador	Very truly yours Sincerely yours	(*1*) Mr., Madam Ambassador *or* Mr., Ms., Mrs., Miss Smith (2) the American Ambassador *or* the Ambassador of the United States *or* the United States Ambassador *or* Mr., Ms., Mrs., Miss Smith, the American Ambassador *or* the Ambassador
ambassador, foreign	His / Her Excellency John / Amelia R. Smith Ambassador of ---- *or if from Great Britain* His Excellency The Right Honorable John R. Smith British Ambassador	Excellency Dear Mr. / Madame Ambassador Excellency Dear Mr. Ambassador	Respectfully yours Sincerely yours Respectfully yours Sincerely yours	(*1*) Mr., Madame Ambassador (2) the Ambassador of ---- *or* the Ambassador *or* Mr., Ms., Mrs., Miss Smith (*1*) Mr. Ambassador (2) the British Ambassador *or* The Honorable Mr. Smith, the British Ambassador
chargé d'affaires ad interim, American	John / Amelia R. Smith, Esq. American Chargé d'Affaires ad Interim *or if in Central or South America* United States Chargé d'Affaires ad Interim	Sir Madam Dear Mr. / Ms. / Mrs. / Miss Smith	Very truly yours Sincerely yours	(*1*) Mr., Ms., Mrs., Miss Smith (2) the American Chargé d'Affaires in ---- *or* the United States Chargé d'Affaires in ---- *or* Mr., Ms., Mrs., Miss Smith

chargé d'affaires ad interim, foreign	Mr. / Ms. / Mrs. / Miss } John / Amelia } R. Smith Chargé d'Affaires ad Interim of ----	Sir Madame Dear Mr. / Ms. / Mrs. / Miss } Smith	Respectfully yours Sincerely yours	(*1*) Mr., Ms., Mrs., Miss Smith (*2*) the ---- Chargé d'Affaires *or* Mr., Ms., Mrs., Miss Smith
chargé d'affaires (de missi), foreign	Mr. / Ms. / Mrs. / Miss } John / Amelia } R. Smith Chargé d'Affaires of ----	Sir Madame Dear Mr. / Ms. / Mrs. / Miss } Smith	Respectfully yours Sincerely yours	(*1*) Mr., Ms., Mrs., Miss Smith (2) the ---- Chargé d'Affaires *or* Mr., Ms., Mrs., Miss Smith
minister, American	The Honorable John / Amelia } R. Smith American Minister *or if in Central or South America* Minister of the United States of America	Sir Madam Dear Mr. / Madam } Minister	Very truly yours Sincerely yours	(*1*) Mr., Madam Minister *or* Mr., Ms., Mrs., Miss Smith (*2*) the American (*or* the United States) Minister, Mr., Ms., Mrs., Miss Smith *or* the Minister *or* Mr., Ms., Mrs., Miss Smith
minister, foreign	The Honorable John / Amelia } R. Smith Minister of ----	Sir Madame Dear Mr. / Madame } Minister	Respectfully yours Sincerely yours	(*1*) Mr., Madame Minister *or* Mr., Ms., Mrs., Miss Smith (*2*) the Minister of ---- *or* the Minister *or* Mr., Ms., Mrs., Miss Smith

Addressee	Form of Address	Salutation	Complimentary Close	(*1*) **Oral Reference** (*2*) **Written Reference**
FOREIGN HEADS OF STATE: A BRIEF SAMPLING				
premier	His/Her Excellency John/Amelia R. Smith Premier of ----	Excellency Dear Mr./Madame Premier	Respectfully yours Sincerely yours	(*1*) Your Excellency *or* Mr., Ms., Mrs., Miss Smith (*2*) the Premier of ---- *or* the Premier *or* Mr., Ms., Mrs., Miss Smith
president of a republic	His/Her Excellency John/Amelia R. Smith President of ----	Excellency Dear Mr./Madame President	Respectfully yours Sincerely yours	(*1*) Your Excellency (*2*) President Smith *or* Mr., Ms., Mrs., Miss Smith
prime minister	His/Her Excellency John/Amelia R. Smith	Excellency Dear Mr./Madame Prime Minister	Respectfully yours Sincerely yours	(*1*) Mr., Madame Prime Minister *or* Mr., Ms., Mrs., Miss Smith (*2*) the Prime Minister of ---- *or* the Prime Minister *or* Mr., Ms., Mrs., Miss Smith
GOVERNMENT OFFICIALS–*FEDERAL*				
attorney general	The Honorable John R. Smith The Attorney General	Sir Dear Mr. Attorney General	Very truly yours Sincerely yours	(*1*) Mr. Attorney General *or* Attorney General Smith *or* Mr. Smith (*2*) the Attorney General, Mr. Smith *or* the Attorney General *or* Mr. Smith

cabinet officer(s) addressed as "Secretary"	The Honorable The Secretary of ---- *or* The Honorable John / Amelia R. Smith Secretary of ---- *or* The Secretary of ----	Sir Madam Sir Madam Dear Mr. / Madam Secretary Sir Madam	Very truly yours Very truly yours Sincerely yours	(*1*) Mr., Madam Secretary *or* Secretary Smith *or* Mr., Ms., Mrs., Miss, Dr. Smith (*2*) the Secretary of ----, John / Amelia R. Smith *or* the Secretary *or* Mr., Ms., Mrs., Miss, Dr. Smith
cabinet officer, former	The Honorable John / Amelia R. Smith	Dear Mr. / Ms. / Mrs. / Miss Smith	Very truly yours Sincerely yours	(*1 and 2*) Mr., Ms., Mrs., Miss Smith
chairman of a (sub) committee, U.S. Congress (stylings shown apply to House of Representatives & Senate)	The Honorable John / Amelia R. Smith Chairman Committee on ---- United States Senate	Dear Mr. / Madam Chairman Dear Senator Smith	Very truly yours Sincerely yours	(*1*) Mr., Madam Chairman *or* Senator Smith *or* Senator (*2*) (*title*) Smith, the Chairman of the ---- Committee on ---- *or* the Chairman *or* Senator Smith
chief justice—*see* SUPREME COURT, FEDERAL; STATE				
commissioner	*if appointed* The Honorable John / Amelia R. Smith Commissioner *if career* Mr. / Ms. / Mrs. / Miss John / Amelia R. Smith Commissioner	Dear Mr. / Madam Commissioner Dear Mr. / Ms. / Mrs. / Miss Smith Dear Mr. / Ms. / Mrs. / Miss Smith	Very truly yours Sincerely yours Very truly yours Sincerely yours	(*1*) Mr., Ms., Mrs., Miss Smith (*2*) Mr., Ms., Mrs., Miss Smith, the ---- Commissioner *or* the Commissioner of ---- (*1*) Mr., Ms., Mrs., Miss Smith (*2*) Mr., Ms., Mrs., Miss Smith *or* the Commissioner of ----

Addressee	Form of Address	Salutation	Complimentary Close	(1) Oral Reference (2) Written Reference
congressman—*see* REPRESENTATIVE, U.S. CONGRESS				
director (as of an independent federal agency)	The Honorable John / Amelia R. Smith Director ---- Agency	Dear Mr. / Ms. / Mrs. / Miss Smith	Very truly yours Sincerely yours	(1) Mr., Ms., Mrs., Miss Smith (2) John / Amelia R. Smith Director of ---- Agency *or* The Honorable Mr., Ms., Mrs., Miss Smith
district attorney	The Honorable John / Amelia R. Smith District Attorney	Dear Mr. / Ms. / Mrs. / Miss Smith	Very truly yours Sincerely yours	(1) Mr., Ms., Mrs., Miss Smith (2) District Attorney Smith *or* the District Attorney *or* Mr., Ms., Mrs., Miss Smith
federal judge	The Honorable John / Amelia R. Smith Judge of the United States District Court for the ---- District of ----	Sir Madam My dear Judge Smith Dear Judge Smith	Very truly yours Very sincerely yours	(1) Judge Smith (2) the Judge *or* Judge Smith
justice—*see* SUPREME COURT, FEDERAL; STATE				
librarian of congress	The Honorable John R. Smith Librarian of Congress	Sir Dear Mr. Smith	Very truly yours Sincerely yours	(1) Mr. Smith (2) the Librarian of Congress *or* the Librarian *or* The Honorable Mr. Smith *or* Mr. Smith

postmaster general	The Honorable John R. Smith The Postmaster General	Sir Dear Mr. Postmaster General	Very truly yours Sincerely yours	(*1*) Mr. Postmaster General *or* Postmaster General Smith *or* Mr. Smith (*2*) the Postmaster General, Mr. Smith *or* the Postmaster General *or* Mr. Smith
president-elect of the United States	The Honorable John R. Smith President-elect of the United States (local address)	Dear Sir Dear Mr. Smith	Very truly yours Sincerely yours	(*1*) Mr. Smith (*2*) the President-elect *or* President-elect Smith *or* Mr. Smith
president of the United States	The President The White House *or* The Honorable John R. Smith President of the United States The White House	Mr. President My dear Mr. President Dear Mr. President Mr. President My dear Mr. President Dear Mr. President	Respectfully yours Very respectfully yours Respectfully yours Very respectfully yours	(*1*) Mr. President (*2*) The President *or* President Smith *or* The Chief Executive *or* Mr. Smith
president of the United States (former)	The Honorable John R. Smith (local address)	Sir Dear Mr. Smith	Respectfully yours Very truly yours Sincerely yours	(*1*) Mr. Smith (*2*) former President Smith *or* Mr. Smith
press secretary to the President of the United States	Mr. John R. Smith Press Secretary to the President The White House	Dear Mr. Smith	Very truly yours Sincerely yours	(*1*) Mr. Smith (*2*) the President's Press Secretary, John Smith *or* Presidential Press Secretary John Smith *or* White House Press Secretary John Smith *or* Mr. Smith

Addressee	Form of Address	Salutation	Complimentary Close	(*1*) **Oral Reference** (*2*) **Written Reference**
representative, United States Congress	The Honorable John / Amelia R. Smith United States House of Representatives	Dear Sir Dear Madam Dear Representative Smith Dear Mr. / Ms. / Mrs. / Miss Smith	Very truly yours Sincerely yours	(*1*) Mr., Ms., Mrs., Miss Smith (*2*) John / Amelia R. Smith, U.S. Representative from ---- *or* Congressman, Congressperson, Congresswoman ---- Smith
representative, United States Congress (former)	The Honorable John / Amelia R. Smith (local address)	Dear Mr. / Ms. / Mrs. / Miss Smith	Very truly yours Sincerely yours	(*1 and 2*) Mr., Ms., Mrs., Miss Smith
senator, United States Senate	The Honorable John / Amelia R. Smith United States Senate	Sir Madam Dear Senator Smith	Very truly yours Sincerely yours	(*1*) Senator Smith *or* Senator (*2*) Senator Smith *or* the Senator from ---- *or* the Senator
senator-elect	The Honorable John / Amelia R. Smith Senator-elect (local address)	Dear Mr. / Ms. / Mrs. / Miss Smith	Very truly yours Sincerely yours	(*1*) Mr., Ms., Mrs., Miss Smith (*2*) Senator-elect Smith *or* Mr., Ms., Mrs., Miss Smith
senator (former)	The Honorable John / Amelia R. Smith (local address)	Dear Senator Smith	Very truly yours Sincerely yours	(*1*) Senator Smith *or* Senator *or* Mr., Ms., Mrs., Miss Smith (*2*) Senator Smith *or* former Senator Smith

speaker, United States House of Representatives	The Honorable The Speaker of the House of Representatives *or* The Honorable Speaker of the House of Representatives *or* The Honorable John R. Smith Speaker of the House of Representatives	Sir Sir Sir Dear Mr. Speaker Dear Mr. Smith	Very truly yours Very truly yours Very truly yours Sincerely yours	(*1*) Mr. Speaker *or* Mr. Smith (2) the Speaker, Mr. Smith *or* Speaker of the House John R. Smith *or* John R. Smith, Speaker of the House *or* the Speaker *or* Mr. Smith
speaker, United States House of Representatives (former)	The Honorable John R. Smith (local address)	Sir Dear Mr. Smith	Very truly yours Sincerely yours	(*1*) Mr. Smith (*2*) Mr. Smith *or* John R. Smith, former Speaker of the House
supreme court, associate justice	Mr. Justice Smith The Supreme Court of the United States	Sir *or* Mr. Justice My dear Mr. Justice Dear Mr. Justice Dear Mr. Justice Smith	Very truly yours Sincerely yours	(*1*) Mr. Justice Smith *or* Justice Smith (*2*) Mr. Justice Smith *or* John R. Smith, an associate Supreme Court justice *or* John R. Smith, an associate justice of the Supreme Court
supreme court, chief justice	The Chief Justice of the United States The Supreme Court of the United States *or* The Chief Justice The Supreme Court	Sir My dear Mr. Chief Justice Dear Mr. Chief Justice Sir My dear Mr. Chief Justice Dear Mr. Chief Justice	Respectfully Very truly yours Respectfully Very truly yours	(*1*) Mr. Chief Justice (*2*) the Chief Justice *or* Chief Justice John R. Smith *or* John R. Smith, Chief Justice of the U.S. Supreme Court

Addressee	Form of Address	Salutation	Complimentary Close	(*1*) **Oral Reference** (*2*) **Written Reference**
supreme court, retired justice	The Honorable John R. Smith (local address)	Sir Dear Justice Smith	Very truly yours Sincerely yours	(*1*) Mr. Justice Smith *or* Justice Smith (*2*) Mr. Justice Smith *or* retired Supreme Court Justice John R. Smith
special assistant to the President of the United States	Mr. / Ms. / Mrs. / Miss } John / Amelia } R. Smith	Dear Mr. / Ms. / Mrs. / Miss } Smith	Very truly yours Sincerely yours	(*1 and 2*) Mr., Ms., Mrs., Miss Smith
territorial delegate	The Honorable John / Amelia } R. Smith Delegate of ---- House of Representatives	Dear Mr. / Ms. / Mrs. / Miss } Smith	Very truly yours Sincerely yours	(*1*) Mr., Ms., Mrs., Miss Smith (*2*) Mr., Ms., Mrs., Miss Smith, Territorial Delegate of ----
undersecretary of a department	The Honorable John / Amelia } R. Smith Undersecretary of ----	Dear Mr. / Ms. / Mrs. / Miss } Smith	Very truly yours Sincerely yours	(*1*) Mr., Ms., Mrs., Miss Smith (*2*) Mr., Ms., Mrs., Miss Smith *or* ---- Smith, Undersecretary of ---- *or* the Undersecretary of ----, ---- Smith
vice president of the United States	The Vice President of the United States United States Senate *or* The Honorable John R. Smith Vice President of the United States Washington, DC ZIP	Sir My dear Mr. Vice President Sir My dear Mr. Vice President Dear Mr. Vice President	Respectfully Very truly yours Respectfully Very truly yours	(*1*) Mr. Vice President *or* Mr. Smith (*2*) the Vice President *or* the Vice President, Mr. Smith *or* Vice President Smith *or* John Smith, Vice President of the United States

GOVERNMENT OFFICIALS—*LOCAL*				
alderman	The Honorable John / Amelia R. Smith Alderman	Dear Mr. / Ms. / Mrs. / Miss Smith Dear Alderman Smith	Very truly yours Sincerely yours	(*1 and 2*) Mr., Ms., Mrs., Miss Smith
	or Alderman John / Amelia R. Smith	Dear Alderman Smith Dear Mr. / Ms. / Mrs. / Miss Smith	Very truly yours Sincerely yours	
city attorney (includes city counsel, corporation counsel)	The Honorable John / Amelia R. Smith	Dear Mr. / Ms. / Miss / Mrs. Smith	Very truly yours Sincerely yours	(*1 and 2*) Mr., Ms., Mrs., Miss Smith
councilman—*see* ALDERMAN				
county clerk	The Honorable John / Amelia R. Smith Clerk of ---- County	Dear Mr. / Ms. / Mrs. / Miss Smith	Very truly yours Sincerely yours	(*1 and 2*) Mr., Ms., Mrs., Miss Smith
county treasurer—*see* COUNTY CLERK				
judge	The Honorable John / Amelia R. Smith Judge of the ---- Court of ----	Dear Judge Smith	Very truly yours Sincerely yours	(*1 and 2*) Judge Smith
mayor	The Honorable John / Amelia R. Smith Mayor of ----	Sir Madam Dear Mayor Smith	Very truly yours Sincerely yours	(*1*) Mayor Smith (*2*) Mayor Smith *or* the Mayor *or* ---- Smith, Mayor of ----

Addressee	Form of Address	Salutation	Complimentary Close	(*1*) **Oral Reference** (2) **Written Reference**
selectman—*see* ALDERMAN				
GOVERNMENT OFFICIALS—*STATE*				
assemblyman—*see* REPRESENTATIVE, STATE				
attorney (*as* commonwealth's attorney, state's attorney)	The Honorable John / Amelia R. Smith (*title*)	Dear Mr. / Ms. / Mrs. / Miss Smith	Very truly yours Sincerely yours	(*1 and 2*) Mr., Ms., Mrs., Miss Smith
attorney general	The Honorable John / Amelia R. Smith Attorney General of the State of ----	Sir Madam Dear Mr. / Madam Attorney General	Very truly yours Sincerely yours	(*1*) Mr., Ms., Mrs., Miss Smith *or* Attorney General Smith (2) the Attorney General, Mr., Ms., Mrs., Miss Smith *or* the state Attorney General
clerk of a court	John / Amelia R. Smith, Esq. Clerk of the Court of ----	Dear Mr. / Ms. / Mrs. / Miss Smith	Very truly yours Sincerely yours	(*1 and 2*) Mr., Ms., Mrs., Miss Smith
delegate—*see* REPRESENTATIVE, STATE				
governor	The Honorable The Governor of ---- *or* The Honorable John / Amelia R. Smith Governor of ---- *or in some states*	Sir Madam Sir Madam Dear Governor Smith	Respectfully yours Very sincerely yours Respectfully yours Very sincerely yours	(*1*) Governor Smith *or* Governor (2) Governor Smith *or* the Governor *or* the Governor of ---- (*only used outside his or her state*)

governor (continued)	His / Her Excellency, the Governor of ----	Sir Madam Dear Governor Smith	Respectfully yours Very sincerely yours	(*1 and 2*) same as above
governor (acting)	The Honorable John / Amelia R. Smith Acting Governor of ----	Sir Madam Dear Mr. / Ms. / Mrs. / Miss Smith	Respectfully yours Very sincerely yours	(*1 and 2*) Mr., Ms., Mrs., Miss Smith
governor-elect	The Honorable John / Amelia R. Smith Governor-elect of ----	Dear Mr. / Ms. / Mrs. / Miss Smith	Very truly yours Sincerely yours	(*1*) Mr., Ms., Mrs., Miss Smith (*2*) Mr., Ms., Mrs., Miss Smith, the Governor-elect
governor (former)	The Honorable John / Amelia R. Smith	Dear Mr. / Ms. / Mrs. / Miss Smith	Very truly yours Sincerely yours	(*1*) Mr., Ms., Mrs., Miss Smith (*2*) John / Amelia R. Smith, former Governor of ----
judge, state court	The Honorable John / Amelia R. Smith Judge of the ---- Court	Dear Judge Smith	Very truly yours Sincerely yours	(*1 and 2*) Judge Smith

judge/justice, state supreme court—*see* SUPREME COURT, STATE

Addressee	Form of Address	Salutation	Complimentary Close	(*1*) **Oral Reference** (*2*) **Written Reference**
lieutenant governor	The Honorable The Lieutenant Governor of ---- *or* The Honorable John / Amelia R. Smith Lieutenant Governor of ----	Sir Madam Sir Madam Dear Mr. / Ms. / Mrs. / Miss Smith	Respectfully yours Respectfully yours Sincerely yours	(*1*) Mr., Ms., Mrs., Miss Smith (*2*) Lieutenant Governor Smith *or* the Lieutenant Governor *or* ---- Smith, Lieutenant Governor of ---- (*only used outside his or her state*) *or* the Lieutenant Governor of ---- (*only used outside his or her state*)
representative, state (includes assemblyman, delegate)	The Honorable John / Amelia R. Smith House of Representatives (*or* The State Assembly *or* The House of Delegates)	Sir Madam Dear Mr. / Ms. / Mrs. / Miss Smith	Very truly yours Sincerely yours	(*1*) Mr., Ms., Mrs., Miss Smith (*2*) Mr., Ms., Mrs., Miss Smith *or* ---- Smith, the state Representative (*or* Assemblyman *or* Delegate) from ----
secretary of state	The Honorable The Secretary of State of ---- *or* The Honorable John / Amelia R. Smith Secretary of State of ----	Sir Madam Sir Madam Dear Mr. / Madam Secretary	Very truly yours Very truly yours Sincerely yours	(*1*) Mr., Ms., Mrs., Miss Smith (*2*) Mr., Ms., Mrs., Miss Smith *or* ---- Smith, Secretary of State of ----

senate, state, president of	The Honorable John / Amelia R. Smith President of the Senate of the State (*or* Commonwealth) of ----	Sir Madam Dear Mr. / Ms. / Mrs. / Miss / Senator Smith	Very truly yours Sincerely yours	(*1 and 2*) Senator, Mr., Ms., Mrs., Miss Smith
senator, state	The Honorable John / Amelia R. Smith The Senate of ----	Sir Madam Dear Senator Smith	Very truly yours Sincerely yours	(*1*) Senator Smith *or* Senator (*2*) Senator Smith *or* ---- Smith, the state Senator from ----
speaker, state assembly, house of delegates, or house of representatives	The Honorable John / Amelia R. Smith Speaker of ----	Sir Madam Dear Mr. / Ms. / Mrs. / Miss Smith	Very truly yours Sincerely yours	(*1*) Mr., Ms., Mrs., Miss Smith (*2*) the Speaker of the ---- *or* ---- Smith, Speaker of the ----
supreme court, state, associate justice	The Honorable John / Amelia R. Smith Associate Justice of the Supreme Court of ----	Sir Madam Dear Justice Smith	Very truly yours Sincerely yours	(*1*) Mr., Madam Justice Smith *or* Judge Smith (*2*) Mr., Madam Justice Smith *or* Judge Smith *or* ---- Smith, associate justice of the ---- Supreme Court
supreme court, state, chief justice	The Honorable John / Amelia R. Smith Chief Justice of the Supreme Court of ----	Sir Madam Dear Mr. / Madam Chief Justice	Very truly yours Sincerely yours	(*1*) Mr., Madam Chief Justice *or* Chief Justice Smith *or* Judge Smith (*2*) Chief Justice Smith *or* ---- Smith, Chief Justice of the ---- Supreme Court

Addressee	Form of Address	Salutation	Complimentary Close	(*1*) **Oral Reference** (*2*) **Written Reference**
supreme court, state, presiding justice	The Honorable John } R. Smith Amelia } Presiding Justice ---- Division Supreme Court of ----	Sir Madam Dear Mr. } Justice Madam }	Very truly yours Sincerely yours	(*1*) Mr., Madam Justice Smith *or* Judge Smith (*2*) Mr., Madam Justice Smith *or* Judge Smith *or* ---- Smith, Presiding Justice of ----
MILITARY RANKS—A TYPICAL BUT NOT EXHAUSTIVE LIST: TITLES APPLY TO BOTH MALE AND FEMALE MEMBERS OF THE ARMED FORCES—BOTH FULL TITLES AND ABBREVIATIONS SHOWN				
admiral (coast guard or navy)	Admiral *or* ADM John R. Smith, USN	Dear Admiral Smith	Very truly yours Sincerely yours	(*1 and 2*) Admiral Smith
rear admiral	Rear Admiral *or* RADM John R. Smith, USCG	Dear Admiral Smith	Very truly yours Sincerely yours	(*1 and 2*) Admiral Smith
vice admiral	Vice Admiral *or* VADM John R. Smith, USN	Dear Admiral Smith	Very truly yours Sincerely yours	(*1 and 2*) Admiral Smith
airman *as*				
airman basic	AB } John R. Smith, USAF	Dear Airman Smith	Sincerely yours	(*1 and 2*) Airman Smith
airman	AMN } John R. Smith, USAF	Dear Airman Smith	Sincerely yours	(*1 and 2*) Airman Smith
airman first class	A1C } John R. Smith, USAF	Dear Airman Smith	Sincerely yours	(*1 and 2*) Airman Smith
brigadier general—*see* GENERAL				
cadet				
U.S. Air Force Academy	Cadet John } R. Smith Amelia }	Dear Cadet Smith	Sincerely yours	(*1 and 2*) Cadet Smith
U.S. Military Academy	Cadet John } R. Smith Amelia }	Dear Cadet Smith	Sincerely yours	(*1 and 2*) Cadet Smith

captain				
air force	Captain *or* CPT John R. Smith, USAF	Dear Captain Smith	Sincerely yours	(*1 and 2*) Captain Smith
army	Captain *or* CPT John R. Smith, USA	Dear Captain Smith	Sincerely yours	(*1 and 2*) Captain Smith
coast guard	Captain *or* CAPT John R. Smith, USCG	Dear Captain Smith	Sincerely yours	(*1 and 2*) Captain Smith
marine corps	Captain *or* Capt. John R. Smith, USMC	Dear Captain Smith	Sincerely yours	(*1 and 2*) Captain Smith
navy	Captain *or* CAPT John R. Smith, USN	Dear Captain Smith	Sincerely yours	(*1 and 2*) Captain Smith
colonel (air force, army)	Colonel *or* COL John R. Smith, USAF (*or* USA)	Dear Colonel Smith	Sincerely yours	(*1 and 2*) Colonel Smith
(marine corps)	Colonel *or* Col. John R. Smith, USMC	Dear Colonel Smith	Sincerely yours	(*1 and 2*) Colonel Smith
commander (coast guard or navy)	Commander *or* CDR John R. Smith, USCG (*or* USN)	Dear Commander Smith	Sincerely yours	(*1 and 2*) Commander Smith
corporal (army)	Corporal *or* CPL John R. Smith, USA	Dear Corporal Smith	Sincerely yours	(*1 and 2*) Corporal Smith
lance corporal (marine corps)	Lance Corporal *or* L/Cpl. John R. Smith, USMC	Dear Corporal Smith	Sincerely yours	(*1 and 2*) Corporal Smith
ensign (coast guard, navy)	Ensign *or* ENS John R. Smith, USN (*or* USCG)	Dear Mr. Smith *or if female* Dear Ensign Smith	Sincerely yours	(*1*) Mr. Smith; Ensign Smith (*if female*) (*2*) Ensign Smith
first lieutenant (air force, army)	First Lieutenant *or* 1LT John R. Smith, USAF	Dear Lieutenant Smith	Sincerely yours	(*1 and 2*) Lieutenant Smith
(marine corps)	First Lieutenant *or* 1st. Lt. John R. Smith, USMC	Dear Lieutenant Smith	Sincerely yours	(*1 and 2*) Lieutenant Smith

Addressee	Form of Address	Salutation	Complimentary Close	(*1*) **Oral Reference** (2) **Written Reference**
general (air force, army)	General *or* GEN John R. Smith, USAF (*or* USA)	Dear General Smith	Very truly yours Sincerely yours	(*1 and 2*) General Smith
(marine corps)	General *or* Gen. John R. Smith, USMC	Dear General Smith	Very truly yours Sincerely yours	(*1 and 2*) General Smith
brigadier general (air force, army)	Brigadier General *or* BG John R. Smith, USAF (*or* USA)	Dear General Smith	Very truly yours Sincerely yours	(*1 and 2*) General Smith
(marine corps)	Brigadier General *or* Brig. Gen. John R. Smith, USMC	Dear General Smith	Very truly yours Sincerely yours	(*1 and 2*) General Smith
lieutenant general (air force, army)	Lieutenant General *or* LTG John R. Smith, USAF (*or* USA)	Dear General Smith	Very truly yours Sincerely yours	(*1 and 2*) General Smith
(marine corps)	Lieutenant General *or* Lt. Gen. John R. Smith, USMC	Dear General Smith	Very truly yours Sincerely yours	(*1 and 2*) General Smith
major general (air force, army)	Major General *or* MG John R. Smith, USAF (*or* USA)	Dear General Smith	Very truly yours Sincerely yours	(*1 and 2*) General Smith
(marine corps)	Major General *or* Maj. Gen. John R. Smith, USMC	Dear General Smith	Very truly yours Sincerely yours	(*1 and 2*) General Smith
lieutenant (coast guard, navy)	Lieutenant *or* LT John R. Smith, USCG (*or* USN)	Dear Mr. Smith *or if female* Dear Lieutenant Smith	Sincerely yours	(*1*) Mr. Smith; Lieutenant Smith (*if female*) (2) Lieutenant Smith

lieutenant colonel (air force, army)	Lieutenant Colonel *or* LTC John R. Smith, USAF (*or* USA)	Dear Colonel Smith	Sincerely yours	(*1*) Colonel Smith (*2*) Lieutenant Colonel Smith
(marine corps)	Lieutenant Colonel *or* Lt. Col. John R. Smith, USMC	Dear Colonel Smith	Sincerely yours	(*1*) Colonel Smith (*2*) Lieutenant Colonel Smith
lieutenant commander (coast guard, navy)	Lieutenant Commander *or* LCDR John R. Smith, USCG (*or* USN)	Dear Commander Smith	Sincerely yours	(*1*) Commander Smith (*2*) Lieutenant Commander Smith
lieutenant, first—*see* FIRST LIEUTENANT				
lieutenant general—*see* GENERAL				
lieutenant junior grade (coast guard, navy)	Lieutenant (j.g.) *or* LTJG John R. Smith, USCG (*or* USN)	Dear Mr. Smith *or if female* Dear Lieutenant Smith	Sincerely yours	(*1*) Mr. Smith; Lieutenant Smith (*if female*) (*2*) Lieutenant (j.g.) Smith
lieutenant, second—*see* SECOND LIEUTENANT				
major (air force, army)	Major *or* MAJ John R. Smith, USAF (*or* USA)	Dear Major Smith	Sincerely yours	(*1 and 2*) Major Smith
(marine corps)	Major *or* Maj. John R. Smith, USMC	Dear Major Smith	Sincerely yours	(*1 and 2*) Major Smith
major general—*see* GENERAL				
midshipman (Coast Guard and Naval Academies)	Midshipman John / Amelia } R. Smith	Dear Midshipman Smith	Sincerely yours	(*1 and 2*) Midshipman Smith

Addressee	Form of Address	Salutation	Complimentary Close	(*1*) **Oral Reference** (*2*) **Written Reference**
petty officer and chief petty officer ranks (coast guard, navy)	Petty Officer *or* PO John R. Smith, USN (*or* USCG)	Dear Mr. Smith	Sincerely yours	(*1*) Mr. Smith (*2*) Mr. Smith *or* Petty Officer Smith
	Chief Petty Officer *or* CPO John R. Smith, USN (*or* USCG)	Dear Mr. Smith		(*1*) Mr. Smith *or* Chief Smith *or* Chief Petty Officer Smith
private (army)	Private *or* PVT John R. Smith, USA	Dear Private Smith	Sincerely yours	(*1 and 2*) Private Smith
(marine corps)	Private *or* Pvt. John R. Smith, USMC	Dear Private Smith	Sincerely yours	(*1 and 2*) Private Smith
private first class (army)	Private First Class *or* PFC John R. Smith, USA	Dear Private Smith	Sincerely yours	(*1 and 2*) Private Smith
seaman (coast guard, navy)	Seaman *or* SMN John R. Smith, USCG (*or* USN)	Dear Seaman Smith	Sincerely yours	(*1 and 2*) Seaman Smith
seaman first class	Seaman First Class *or* S1C John R. Smith, USCG (*or* USN)	Dear Seaman Smith	Sincerely yours	(*1 and 2*) Seaman Smith
second lieutenant (air force, army)	Second Lieutenant *or* 2LT John R. Smith, USAF (*or* USA)	Dear Lieutenant Smith	Sincerely yours	(*1 and 2*) Lieutenant Smith
(marine corps)	Second Lieutenant *or* 2nd. Lt. John R. Smith, USMC	Dear Lieutenant Smith	Sincerely yours	(*1 and 2*) Lieutenant Smith
sergeant (a cross section of sergeant ranks)				

first sergeant (army)	First Sergeant *or* 1SG John R. Smith, USA	Dear Sergeant Smith	Sincerely yours	(*1 and 2*) Sergeant Smith
(marine corps)	First Sergeant *or* 1st. Sgt. John R. Smith, USMC	Dear Sergeant Smith	Sincerely yours	(*1 and 2*) Sergeant Smith
gunnery sergeant (marine corps)	Gunnery Sergeant *or* Gy. Sgt. John R. Smith, USMC	Dear Sergeant Smith	Sincerely yours	(*1 and 2*) Sergeant Smith
master sergeant (air force)	Master Sergeant *or* MSGT John R. Smith, USAF	Dear Sergeant Smith	Sincerely yours	(*1 and 2*) Sergeant Smith
(army)	Master Sergeant *or* MSG John R. Smith, USA	Dear Sergeant Smith	Sincerely yours	(*1 and 2*) Sergeant Smith
senior master sergeant (air force)	Senior Master Sergeant *or* SMSGT John R. Smith, USAF	Dear Sergeant Smith	Sincerely yours	(*1 and 2*) Sergeant Smith
sergeant (army, air force)	Sergeant *or* SGT John R. Smith, USA (*or* USAF)	Dear Sergeant Smith	Sincerely yours	(*1 and 2*) Sergeant Smith
sergeant major (army)	Sergeant Major *or* SGM John R. Smith, USA	Dear Sergeant Major Smith	Sincerely yours	(*1 and 2*) Sergeant Major Smith
(marine corps)	Sergeant Major *or* Sgt. Maj. John R. Smith, USMC	Dear Sergeant Major Smith	Sincerely yours	(*1 and 2*) Sergeant Major Smith
staff sergeant (air force)	Staff Sergeant *or* SSGT John R. Smith, USAF	Dear Sergeant Smith	Sincerely yours	(*1 and 2*) Sergeant Smith
(army)	Staff Sergeant *or* SSG John R. Smith, USA	Dear Sergeant Smith	Sincerely yours	(*1 and 2*) Sergeant Smith
technical sergeant (air force)	Technical Sergeant *or* TSGT John R. Smith, USAF	Dear Sergeant Smith	Sincerely yours	(*1 and 2*) Sergeant Smith

Addressee	Form of Address	Salutation	Complimentary Close	(*1*) **Oral Reference** (*2*) **Written Reference**
specialist (army) *as* specialist fourth class	Specialist Fourth Class *or* S4 John R. Smith, USA	Dear Specialist Smith	Sincerely yours	(*1 and 2*) Specialist Smith
warrant officer (army) as warrant officer W1	Warrant Officer W1 *or* WO1 John R. Smith, USA	Dear Mr. Smith	Sincerely yours	(*1*) Mr. Smith (*2*) Mr. Smith *or* Warrant Officer Smith
chief warrant officer (army) *as* chief warrant officer W4	Chief Warrant Officer W4 *or* CWO4 John R. Smith, USA	Dear Mr. Smith	Sincerely yours	(*1*) Mr. Smith (*2*) Mr. Smith *or* Chief Warrant Officer Smith
other ranks not listed	full title + full name + comma + abbreviation of branch of service	*Dear* + rank + surname	Sincerely yours	(*1 and 2*) rank + surname
MISCELLANEOUS PROFESSIONAL TITLES				
attorney	Mr./Ms./Mrs./Miss John/Amelia R. Smith Attorney-at-Law *or* John/Amelia R. Smith, Esq.	Dear Mr./Ms./Mrs./Miss Smith	Very truly yours	(*1*) Mr., Ms., Mrs., Miss Smith (*2*) Mr., Ms., Mrs., Miss Smith *or* Attorney (*or* Atty.) Smith
dentist	John/Amelia R. Smith, D.D.S. *or* Dr. John/Amelia R. Smith	Dear Dr. Smith	Very truly yours Sincerely yours	(*1 and 2*) Dr. Smith

physician	John / Amelia R. Smith, M.D. *or* Dr. John / Amelia R. Smith	Dear Dr. Smith	Very truly yours Sincerely yours	(*1 and 2*) Dr. Smith
veterinarian	John / Amelia R. Smith, D.V.M. *or* Dr. John / Amelia R. Smith	Dear Dr. Smith	Very truly yours Sincerely yours	(*1 and 2*) Dr. Smith
UNITED NATIONS OFFICIALS				
representative, American (with ambassadorial rank)	The Honorable John / Amelia R. Smith United States Permanent Representative to the United Nations (address)	Sir Madam My dear Mr. / Madam Ambassador Dear Mr. / Madam Ambassador	Respectfully Sincerely yours	(*1*) Mr., Madam Ambassador *or* Mr., Ms., Mrs., Miss Smith (*2*) Mr., Ms., Mrs., Miss Smith *or* the United States Representative to the United Nations *or* UN Representative ---- Smith
representative foreign (with ambassadorial rank)	His / Her Excellency John / Amelia R. Smith Representative of ---- to the United Nations (address)	Excellency My dear Mr. / Madame Ambassador Dear Mr. / Madame Ambassador	Respectfully Sincerely yours	(*1*) Mr., Madame Ambassador *or* Mr., Ms., Mrs., Miss Smith (*2*) Mr., Ms., Mrs., Miss Smith *or* the Representative of ---- to the United Nations *or* UN Representative ---- Smith

Addressee	Form of Address	Salutation	Complimentary Close	(*1*) **Oral Reference** (*2*) **Written Reference**
secretary-general	His Excellency John R. Smith Secretary-General of the United Nations (address)	Excellency	Respectfully	(*1*) Mr. Smith *or* Sir (*2*) the Secretary-General of the United Nations *or* UN Secretary-General Smith *or* The Secretary-General *or* Mr. Smith
		My dear Mr. Secretary-General Dear Mr. Secretary-General	Sincerely yours	
undersecretary	The Honorable John / Amelia R. Smith Undersecretary of the United Nations (address)	Sir / Madam / Madame	Very truly yours	(*1*) Mr., Ms., Mrs., Miss Smith (*2*) Mr., Ms., Mrs., Miss Smith *or* the Undersecretary of the United Nations *or* UN Undersecretary ---- Smith
		My dear Mr. / Ms. / Mrs. / Miss Smith	Sincerely yours	
		Dear Mr. / Ms. / Mrs. / Miss Smith	Sincerely yours	

Multiple Addressees (See also discussion on pages 180–186)

Inside Address Styling	Salutation Styling
two or more men with same surname	
Mr. Arthur W. Jones Mr. John H. Jones	Gentlemen
or	*or*
Messrs. A. W. and J. H. Jones *or* The Messrs. Jones	Dear Messrs. Jones
two or more men with different surnames	
Mr. Angus D. Langley Mr. Lionel P. Overton	Gentlemen *or* Dear Mr. Langley and Mr. Overton
or	
Messrs. A. D. Langley and L. P. Overton *or* Messrs. Langley and Overton	Dear Messrs. Langley and Overton
two or more married women with same surname	
Mrs. Arthur W. Jones Mrs. John H. Jones	Mesdames
or	*or*
Mesdames A. W. and J. H. Jones *or* The Mesdames Jones	Dear Mesdames Jones
two or more unmarried women with same surname	
Miss Alice H. Danvers Miss Margaret T. Danvers	Ladies
or	*or*
Misses Alice and Margaret Danvers *or* The Misses Danvers	Dear Misses Danvers
two or more women with same surname but whose marital status is unknown or irrelevant	
Ms. Alice H. Danvers Ms. Margaret T. Danvers	Dear Ms. Alice and Margaret Danvers
two or more married women with different surnames	
Mrs. Allen Y. Dow Mrs. Lawrence R. Frank	Dear Mrs. Dow and Mrs. Frank
or	*or*
Mesdames Dow and Frank	Mesdames *or* Dear Mesdames Dow and Frank
two or more unmarried women with different surnames	
Miss Elizabeth Dudley Miss Ann Raymond	Ladies *or* Dear Miss Dudley and Miss Raymond
or	*or*
Misses E. Dudley and A. Raymond	Dear Misses Dudley and Raymond
two or more women with different surnames but whose marital status is unknown or irrelevant	
Ms. Barbara Lee Ms. Helen Key	Dear Ms. Lee and Ms. Key

SPECIAL TITLES, DESIGNATIONS, AND ABBREVIATIONS: A GUIDE TO USAGE

Doctor If *Doctor* or its abbreviation *Dr.* is used before a person's name, academic degrees (as *D.D.S., D.V.M., M.D.,* or *Ph.D.*) are not included after the surname. The title *Doctor* may be typed out in full or abbreviated in a salutation, but it is usually abbreviated in an envelope address block and in an inside address in order to save space. When *Doctor* appears in a salutation, it must be used in conjunction with the addressee's surname:

Dear Doctor Smith *or* Dear Dr. Smith *not* Dear Doctor

If a woman holds a doctorate, her title should be used in business-related correspondence even if her husband's name is also included in the letter:

Dr. Ann R. Smith and
  Mr. James O. Smith
Dear Dr. Smith and Mr. Smith

If both husband and wife are doctors, one of the following patterns may be followed:

Dr. Ann R. Smith and
  Dr. James O. Smith
or
The Drs. Smith
or
The Doctors Smith
or
Drs. Ann R. and James O. Smith
or
Ann R. Smith, M.D.
James O. Smith, M.D.
more formal
My dear Doctors Smith
informal
Dear Drs. Smith
Dear Doctors Smith

Address patterns for two or more doctors associated in a joint practice are:

Drs. Francis X. Sullivan and
  Philip K. Ross
or
Francis X. Sullivan, M.D.
Philip K. Ross, M.D.
more formal
My dear Drs. Sullivan and Ross
informal
Dear Drs. Sullivan and Ross
Dear Doctors Sullivan and Ross
Dear Dr. Sullivan and Dr. Ross
Dear Doctor Sullivan and Doctor Ross

Esquire The abbreviation *Esq.* for *Esquire* is used in the United States after the surnames of professional persons such as architects, attorneys, and consuls, regardless of their sex. In Great Britain, it is generally used after the surnames of people who have distinguished themselves in professional, diplomatic, or social circles. For example, when addressing a letter to a high corporate officer of a British firm, one should include *Esq.* after his surname, both on the envelope and in the inside address. Under no circumstances should *Esq.* appear in a salutation. This rule applies to both American and British correspondence. If a courtesy title such as *Dr., Hon., Miss, Mr., Mrs.,* or *Ms.* is used before the addressee's name, *Esq.* is omitted. The plural of *Esq.* is *Esqs.* and is used with the surnames of multiple addressees.

Examples:

Carolyn B. West, Esq.
American Consul

Dear Ms. West

Samuel A. Sebert, Esq.
Norman D. Langfitt, Esq.
or
Sebert and Langfitt, Esqs.
or
Messrs. Sebert and Langfitt
Attorneys-at-Law

Gentlemen
Dear Mr. Sebert and Mr. Langfitt
Dear Messrs. Sebert and Langfitt

Simpson, Tyler, and Williams, Esqs.
or
Scott A. Simpson, Esq.
Annabelle W. Tyler, Esq.
David I. Williams, Esq.

Dear Ms. Tyler and Messrs. Simpson
and Williams

British

Jonathan A. Lyons, Esq.
President

Dear Mr. Lyons

Honorable In the United States, *The Honorable* or its abbreviated form *Hon.* is used as a title of distinction (but not rank) and is accorded elected or appointed (but not career) government officials. Neither the full form nor the abbreviation is ever used by its recipient either in written signatures, letterhead, business or visiting cards, or in typed signature blocks. While it may be used in an envelope address block and in an inside address of a letter addressed to him or her, it is never used in a salutation. *The Honorable* should never appear before a surname standing alone: there must always be an intervening first name, an initial or initials, or a courtesy title:

The Honorable John R. Smith
The Honorable J. R. Smith
The Honorable J. Robert Smith
The Honorable Mr. Smith
The Honorable Dr. Smith

If *The Honorable* is used with a full name, a courtesy title should not be added. *The Honorable* may also precede a woman's name:

The Honorable Jane R. Smith
The Honorable Mrs. Smith

However, if the woman's full name is given, a courtesy title should not be added. When an official and his wife are being addressed, his full name should be typed out, as

The Honorable John R. Smith
and Mrs. Smith

or

The Honorable and Mrs. John R. Smith
Dear Mr. and Mrs. Smith

The stylings "Hon. and Mrs. Smith" and "The Honorable and Mrs. Smith" should never be used. If, however, the official's full name is unknown, the styling is:

The Honorable Mr. Smith and Mrs. Smith

If a married woman holds the title and her husband does not, her name appears first on business-related correspondence addressed to both persons. However, if the couple is being addressed socially, the woman's title may be dropped unless she has retained her maiden name for use in personal as well as business correspondence:

business correspondence

The Honorable Harriet M. Johnson and Mr. Johnson	Dear Mrs. (*or* Governor, etc.) Johnson and Mr. Johnson

social correspondence

Mr. and Mrs. Robert Y. Johnson	Dear Mr. and Mrs. Johnson

if maiden name retained:

business correspondence

The Honorable Harriet A. Mathieson and Mr. Robert Y. Johnson	Dear Ms. Mathieson and Mr. Johnson

social correspondence

Ms. Harriet A. Mathieson Mr. Roger Y. Johnson	Dear Ms. Mathieson and Mr. Johnson

If space is limited, *The Honorable* may be typed on the first line of an address block, with the recipient's name on the next line:

The Honorable
John R. Smith
and Mrs. Smith

When *The Honorable* occurs in a running text or in a list of names in such a text, the *T* in *The* is then lowercased:

. . . a speech by the Honorable Charles H. Patterson, the American Consul in Athens. . . .

In informal writing such as newspaper articles, the plural forms *the Honorables* or *Hons.* may be used before a list of persons accorded the distinction. However, in official or formal writing either *the Honorable Messrs.* placed before the entire list of surnames or *the Honorable* or *Hon.* repeated before each full name in the list may be used:

formal . . . was supported in the motion by the Honorable Messrs. Clarke, Goodfellow, Thomas, and Harrington.

. . . met with the Honorable Albert Y. Langley and the Honorable Frances P. Kelley.

informal . . . interviewed the Hons. Jacob Y. Stathis, Samuel P. Kenton, William L. Williamson, and Gloria O. Yarnell—all United States Senators.

Jr. and **Sr.** The designations *Jr.* and *Sr.* may or may not be preceded by a comma, depending on office policy or writer preference; however, one styling should be selected and adhered to for the sake of uniformity:

John K. Walker Jr.
or
John K. Walker, Jr.

Jr. and *Sr.* may be used in conjunction with courtesy titles, and with academic degree abbreviations or with professional rating abbreviations, as

Mr. John K. Walker[,] Jr.
Dr. John K. Walker[,] Jr.
General John K. Walker[,] Jr.
The Honorable John K. Walker [,] Jr.
Hon. John K. Walker[,] Jr.
John K. Walker[,] Jr., Esq.
John K. Walker[,] Jr., M.D.

Formation of the possessive with either *Jr.* or *Sr.* follows this pattern:

singular possessive
John K. Walker, Jr.'s hospitality suite is open.

plural possessive
The John K. Walker, Jrs.' house is on this street.

Plural patterns for *Jr.* and *Sr.* are:

The John K. Walkers Jr. are here.
The John K. Walkers, Jr. are here.
The John K. Walker Jrs. are here.
The John K. Walker, Jrs. are here.

Madam and **Madame** The title *Madam* should be used only in salutations of highly impersonal or high-level governmental and diplomatic correspondence, unless the writer is certain that the addressee is married. The French form *Madame* is recommended for salutations in correspondence addressed to foreign diplomats and heads of state. See Forms of Address Chart for examples.

Mesdames The plural form of *Madam, Madame,* or *Mrs.* is *Mesdames,* which may be used before the names of two or more married women associated together in a professional partnership or in a business. It may appear with their names on an envelope and in an inside address, and it may appear with their names or standing alone in a salutation:

Mesdames T. V. Meade and P. A. Tate
Mesdames Meade and Tate

Dear Mesdames Meade and Tate
Mesdames

Mesdames V. T. and A. P. Stevens
The Mesdames Stevens

Dear Mesdames Stevens
Mesdames

See also the Multiple Addressees Chart, page 179.

Messrs. The plural abbreviation of *Mr.* is *Messrs.* It is used before the surnames of two or more men associated in a professional partnership or in a business. *Messrs.* may appear on an envelope, in an inside address, and in a salutation when used in conjunction with the surnames of the addressees; however, this abbreviation should never stand alone. Examples:

Messrs. Archlake, Smythe, and Dabney
Attorneys-at-Law

Dear Messrs. Archlake, Smythe, and Dabney
Gentlemen

Messrs. K. Y. and P. B. Overton
Architects

Dear Messrs. Overton
Gentlemen

Messrs. should never be used before a compound corporate name formed from two surnames:

Lord & Taylor
Woodward & Lothrup

For correct use of *Messrs.* + *The Honorable* or + *The Reverend,* see pages 182 and 186, respectively.

Misses The plural form of *Miss* is *Misses,* and it may be used before the names of two or more unmarried women who are being addressed together. It may appear on an envelope, in an inside address, and in a salutation. Like *Messrs., Misses* should never stand alone but must occur in conjunction with a name or names. Examples:

Misses Hay and Middleton
Misses D. L. Hay and H. K. Middleton

Dear Misses Hay and Middleton
Ladies

Misses Tara and Julia Smith
The Misses Smith

Dear Misses Smith
Ladies

For a complete set of examples in this category, see the Multiple Addressees Chart, page 179.

Professor If used with a surname, *Professor* should be typed out in full; however, if used with a given name and initial or a set of initials as well as a surname, it may be abbreviated to *Prof.* It is, therefore, usually abbreviated in envelope address blocks and in inside addresses, but typed out in salutations. *Professor* should not stand alone in a salutation. Examples:

Prof. Florence C. Marlowe
Department of English

Dear Professor Marlowe
or
Dear Dr. Marlowe
or
Dear Miss Marlowe
Mrs. Marlowe
Ms. Marlowe
but not
Dear Professor

When addressing a letter to a professor and his wife, the title is usually written out in full unless the name is unusually long:

Professor and Mrs. Lee Dow
Prof. and Mrs. Henry Talbott-Smythe

Dear Professor and Mrs. Dow
Dear Professor and Mrs. Talbott-Smythe

Letters addressed to couples of whom the wife is the professor and the husband is not may follow one of these patterns:

Professor Diana Goode and Mr. Goode	*business correspondence*
Mr. and Mrs. Lawrence F. Goode	*business or social correspondence*
Professor Diana Falls Mr. Lawrence F. Goode	*if wife has retained maiden name*

Dear Professor Goode and Mr. Goode	*business correspondence*
Dear Mr. and Mrs. Goode	*business or social correspondence*
Dear Professor (*or* Ms.) Falls and Mr. Goode	*wife having retained her maiden name*

When addressing two or more professors—male or female, whether having the same or different surnames—type *Professors* and not "Profs.":

Professors A. L. Smith and C. L. Doe

Dear Professors Smith and Doe
Dear Drs. Smith and Doe
Dear Mr. Smith and Mr. Doe
Dear Messrs. Smith and Doe
Gentlemen

Professors B. K. Johns and S. T. Yarrell

Dear Professors Johns and Yarrell
Dear Drs. Johns and Yarrell
Dear Ms. Johns and Mr. Yarrell

Professors G. A. and F. K. Cornett
The Professors Cornett

Dear Professors Cornett Dear Drs. Cornett	*acceptable for any combination*
Gentlemen	*if males*
Ladies *or* Mesdames	*if females*
Dear Mr. and Mrs. Cornett Dear Professors Cornett Dear Drs. Cornett	*if married*

Reverend In formal or official writing, *The* should precede *Reverend;* however, *The Reverend* is often abbreviated to *The Rev.* or just *Rev.* especially in unofficial or informal writing, and particularly in business correspondence where the problem of space on envelopes and in inside addresses is a factor. The typed-out full form *The Reverend* must be used in conjunction with the clergyman's full name:

The Reverend Philip D. Asquith
The Reverend Dr. Philip D. Asquith
The Reverend P. D. Asquith

The Reverend may appear with just a surname only if another courtesy title intervenes:

The Reverend Mr. Asquith
The Reverend Professor Asquith
The Reverend Dr. Asquith

The Reverend, The Rev., or *Rev.* should not be used in the salutation, although any one of these titles may be used on the envelope and in the inside address. In salutations, the following titles are acceptable for clergymen: *Mr.* (or *Ms., Miss, Mrs.*), *Father, Chaplain,* or *Dr.* See the Forms of Address Chart under the section entitled "Clerical and Religious Orders" for examples. The only exceptions to this rule are salutations in letters addressed to high prelates of a church (as bishops, monsignors, etc.). See the Forms of Address Chart. When addressing a letter to a clergyman and his wife, the typist should follow one of these stylings:

The Rev. and Mrs. P. D. Asquith
or
The Rev. and Mrs. Philip D. Asquith
or

The Reverend and Mrs. P. D. Asquith
or
The Reverend and Mrs. Philip D. Asquith
but never
Rev. and Mrs. Asquith
Dear Mr. (*or, if having a doctorate,* Dr.) and Mrs. Asquith

Two clergymen having the same or different surnames should not be addressed in letters as "The Reverends" or "The Revs." or "Revs." They may, however, be addressed as *The Reverend* (or *The Rev.*) *Messrs.* or *The Reverend* (or *The Rev.*) *Drs.*, or the titles *The Reverend, The Rev.,* or *Rev.* may be repeated before each clergyman's name; as

The Reverend Messrs. S. J. and D. V. Smith
The Rev. Messrs. S. J. and D. V. Smith
The Reverend Messrs. Smith
The Rev. Messrs. Smith

and, as

The Rev. S. J. Smith and
The Rev. D. V. Smith
Rev. S. J. Smith and
Rev. D. V. Smith

with "Gentlemen" being the correct salutation. When writing to two or more clergymen having different surnames, the following patterns are acceptable:

The Reverend Messrs. P. A. Francis
and F. L. Beale
The Rev. Messrs. P. A. Francis
and F. L. Beale
The Rev. P. A. Francis
The Rev. F. L. Beale
Gentlemen
Dear Mr. Francis and Mr. Beale
Dear Father Francis and Father Beale

In formal texts, "The Reverends", "The Revs.", and "Revs." are not acceptable as collective titles (as in lists of names). *The Reverend* (or *Rev.*) *Messrs.* (or *Drs.* or *Professors*) may be used, or *The Reverend* or *The Rev.* or *Rev.* may be repeated before each clergyman's name. If the term *clergymen* or the expression *the clergy* is mentioned in introducing the list, a single title *the Reverend* or *the Rev.* may be added before the list to serve all of the names. While it is true that "the Revs." is often seen in newspapers and in catalogs, this expression is still not recommended for formal, official writing. Examples:

. . . were the Reverend Messrs. Jones, Smith and Bennett, as well as. . . .
Among the clergymen present were the Reverend John G. Jones, Mr. Smith, and Dr. Doe.
Prayers were offered by the Rev. J. G. Jones, Rev. Mr. Smith, and Rev. Dr. Doe.

Second, Third These designations after surnames may be styled as Roman numerals:

II
III
IV

or as ordinals:

2nd / 2d
3rd / 3d
4th

Such a designation may or may not be separated from a surname by a comma, depending on office policy or writer perference:

Mr. Jason T. Johnson III (*or* 3rd *or* 3d)
Mr. Jason T. Johnson, III (*or* 3rd *or* 3d)

Plural patterns for such designation are:

The Samuel Z. Watsons III (*or* 3rd *or* 3d) are here.
The Samuel Z. Watson IIIs (*or* 3rds *or* 3ds) are here.

Possessive patterns are:

Samuel Z. Watson III's (*or* 3rd's *or* 3d's) house is for sale.
The Samuel Z. Watson IIIs' (*or* 3rds' *or* 3ds') house is for sale.

The following illustrates the proper order of occurrence of initials representing academic degrees, religious orders, and professional ratings that may appear after a name and that are separated from each other by commas:

religious orders (as *S.J.*)
theological degrees (as *D.D.*)
academic degrees (as *Ph.D.*)
honorary degrees (as *Litt.D.*)
professional ratings (as *C.P.A.*)

Examples:

John R. Doe, B.S., M.S., P.E.

John R. Doe, B.S., Ph.D., D.V.M.

John R. Doe, M.D., Ph.D.
Chief of Staff
——— Hospital

John R. Doe, B.A., M.A., Ph.D., Litt.D.
Professor of English

The Rev. John R. Doe, S.J., D.D., LL.D.
Chaplain
——— College

6.9

CORRESPONDENCE WITH UNITED STATES GOVERNMENT AGENCIES: Letter Format and Security Precautions

Increasing government and private industry tie-ins have made it necessary that civilian contractors be familiar with special correspondence and security procedures. While it is true that letter format and security precautions vary with the policies of each government contracting agency and with the nature of each contract, the following overview should nevertheless be an adequate orientation and point of departure for the secretary heretofore unfamiliar with these matters.

The two most basic problems are: (1) ensuring that all material regardless of its classification be marked in such a way that it will be speedily delivered to its intended addressee and that copies of it are readily retrievable in company files, and (2) ensuring that all classified material be safeguarded according to government guidelines so that unauthorized persons may not gain access to it.

CORRESPONDENCE FORMAT

Letters to government agencies should conform to the guidelines of the agency with which one's firm is working. Letters incorrectly set up and addressed may be delayed, lost, rejected, or returned—a situation that at the least may cause costly production delays, or at the most may result in loss of a contract especially if bidding is going on under a deadline.

When writing to a nonmilitary government agency, it is correct to use any one of the generally accepted business letter stylings that have been discussed in this chapter, providing that a subject line and a reference line are included. These data are necessary for proper interagency routing of the letter. Elected and appointed officials should be correctly addressed, and their forms of address may be found in this chapter in the Forms of Address Chart.

The following general principles are applicable to correspondence directed to the Department of Defense:

1. A general Modified Block Letter style with numbered paragraphs is recommended.

2. If any section of the letter is classified, the highest classification category therein must be stamped at the top and the bottom of each page. This stamp is affixed above the printed letterhead and below the last line of the message on the first sheet, and above the heading and below the last notation on a second sheet. The CLASSIFIED BY and NATIONAL SECURITY INFORMATION stamps must be affixed at the bottom of the letterhead sheet (see the letter facsimile on pages 191–192).

3. A special mailing notation, if needed, is typically typed in all-capital letters or stamped in the upper left corner of the letterhead sheet and in the upper left corner of a continuation sheet or sheets.

4. The writer's courtesy title and surname, followed by a slash, followed by the typist's initials and another slash, followed by his telephone extension (if not already included in the printed letterhead) may be typed in the upper right corner of the first sheet.

5. An inverted date (day, month, year) forms the date line, blocked flush left about three lines from the last line of the letterhead. The date may be styled as
   1 January 19--
   or
   1 Jan -- (last 2 digits of year)
   but one styling should be used consistently throughout the letter. Abbreviations for the twelve months are:

Jan	May	Sep
Feb	Jun	Oct
Mar	Jul	Nov
Apr	Aug	Dec

6. Companies contracted to the government for specific projects usually assign control numbers to files and correspondence related to the project. This number should be included in the date line block, one line below the date.

7. The next element of the letter—whether it be the SUBJECT block or the TO block (the order varies according to agency)—is typed about three lines below the last line of the date block and is blocked flush left. The SUBJECT block, shown first in this book, consists of:
   line 1. contract number
   line 2. name of program or project
   line 3. subject of the letter + appropriate security classification expressed as a parenthetical abbreviation, as (C) = Confidential, (S) = Secret, or (TS) = Top Secret.

8. The TO block which is really the inside address, is typed about three lines below the date block or the SUBJECT block (order varies with agency policy). Its internal elements are:
   line l. initials or name of office
   line 2. name of applicable administrator (the addressee)
   line 3. name of organization
   line 4. geographical address + ZIP Code

9. The THROUGH or VIA block (caption varies with agency policy) is typed about three lines below any other blocks that precede it. This block is used in letters that must be sent through designated channels before reaching the addressee. Each agency, office, or individual should be named and addressed as in the TO block.

10. The REFERENCE block is typed about three lines below the last typed block. It contains a list of material or previous correspondence that must be consulted before the letter can be acted on by the addressee. This information is listed alphabetically or by numerals.

Note: Regardless of the order of the items discussed above, the captions SUBJECT, TO, THROUGH, and REFERENCE should <u>not</u> be visible in the window area of a window envelope. Only the address in the TO block should be visible in such an envelope. The styling of these captions varies; they may be entirely in capitals, they may be in capitals and lowercase, or they may be abbreviated to SUBJ, THRU, etc. Use the styling recommended by the agency with which your company is dealing.

11. There is no salutation.

12. The message begins flush left, two lines below the last line of the REFERENCE block. Paragraphs are numbered consecutively and are single-spaced internally but double-spaced between each other. Subparagraphs are alphabetized, are single-spaced internally, and are double-spaced between each other:

    1. xxxxxxxxxxxxxxxxxxxxxxxxxxxxxxxxxxxxxxxxxxxxxxxxxxxxxxxxxxxxxxxxxxxxxxxxxxxxxx
    xxxxxxxxxxxxxxxxxxxxxxxxxxxxxxxxxxxxxxxxxxxxxxxxxxxxxxxxxxxxxxxxxxxxxxxxxxxxxx

        a. xxxxxxxxxxxxxxxxxxxxxxxxxxxxxxxxxxxxxxxxxxxxxxxxxxxxxxxxxxxxxxxxxxxxxxxxxxxx
        xxxxxxxxxxxxxxxxxxxxxxxxxxxxxxxxxxxxxxxxxxxxxxxxxxxxxxxxxxxxxxxxxxxxxxxxxxxx

        b. xxxxxxxxxxxxxxxxxxxxxxxxxxxxxxxxxxxxxxxxxxxxxxxxxxxxxxxxxxxxxxxxxxxxxxxxxxxx
        xxxxxxxxxxxxxxxxxxxxxxxxxxxxxxxxxxxxxxxxxxxxxxxxxxxxxxxxxxxxxxxxxxxxxxxxxxxx

            1. xxxxxxxxxxxxxxxxxxxxxxxxxxxxxxxxxxxxxxxxxxxxxxxxxxxxxxxxxxxxxxxxxxxxxxxxxx
            xxxxxxxxxxxxxxxxxxxxxxxxxxxxxxxxxxxxxxxxxxxxxxxxxxxxxxxxxxxxxxxxxxxxxxxxxx

            2. xxxxxxxxxxxxxxxxxxxxxxxxxxxxxxxxxxxxxxxxxxxxxxxxxxxxxxxxxxxxxxxxxxxxxxxxxx
            xxxxxxxxxxxxxxxxxxxxxxxxxxxxxxxxxxxxxxxxxxxxxxxxxxxxxxxxxxxxxxxxxxxxxxxxxx

    2. xxxxxxxxxxxxxxxxxxxxxxxxxxxxxxxxxxxxxxxxxxxxxxxxxxxxxxxxxxxxxxxxxxxxxxxxxxxxxx
    xxxxxxxxxxxxxxxxxxxxxxxxxxxxxxxxxxxxxxxxxxxxxxxxxxxxxxxxxxxxxxxxxxxxxxxxxxxxxx

If there is a paragraph *1,* there must be a *2,* if there is an *a,* there must be a *b,* and so on.

13. There is no complimentary close.

14. The company name is typed flush left entirely in capital letters two lines beneath the last line of the message. The writer's name is typed in capitals and lowercase at least four lines below the company name, also flush left. His title and department name, if not already appearing on the printed letterhead, may be included beneath his name in capitals and lowercase, also flush left.

15. The typist's initials if not already included in the top right corner of the first sheet may be typed flush left, two lines below the last element of the signature block.

16. Enclosures are listed and identified two lines below the typist's initials. The numeral stylings 1. or (1) may be used. The appropriate headings are *Enclosure*(s), *Encl.*, or *Enc.* for the Air Force and Navy; and *Inclosure*(s), *Inc.* for the Army. Classification categories should be noted at the beginning of each applicable enclosure description as shown in enclosure (3) below. Example:

    Enc.: (1) 3 copies of Test Procedure Report
    WXYzz dated 1 January 19--
    (2) 1 copy of Contract AF 45(100)-1147
    (3) (C) 2/c ea. specifications mentioned
    in paragraph 7

    Some government agencies require that enclosures be noted in a block two or three spaces below the REFERENCE block.

    If enclosures are to be mailed under separate cover, they still must be listed on the letter and their classification categories noted.

17. The carbon copy notation *cc:* or *Copy to* is typed flush left two lines below any other notations. It includes an alphabetical listing of all individuals or persons not associated with the company who will receive copies. Addresses should be included. Internal copies should contain a complete list of external and internal recipients of copies. Example:

    cc: COL John K. Walker, + address
    (w/enc. (1)–2 copies)

18. In some correspondence, an approval line may be the last typed item on the page if the contracting agency must approve the material and return it to the contractor. In this case, two copies of the letter must be enclosed in the envelope. Example:

    APPROVED:

    ____

    (addressee's title)

    date

    This material may be typed two to four lines beneath the last notation and blocked with the left margin.

19. Continuation-sheet headings are typed six lines from the top edge of the page. The message is continued four lines beneath the heading. Continuation-sheet headings should include the SUBJECT block data as well as the company control number, the appropriate date, and the page number. See the following facsimile for setup.

CLASSIFIED MATERIAL

Both the United States government and its civilian contractors are responsible for the security of sensitive material passing between them—responsibility that specifically means the safeguarding of classified material against unlawful or unauthorized dissemination, duplication, or observation. Each employee of a firm that handles or has knowledge of classified material shares responsibility for protecting it while it is in use, in storage, or in transit. The Department of Defense has established an Information Security Program to implement its security regulations. These regulations are outlined in DoD 5200.1-R *Information Security Program Regulation* for sale by the Superintendent of Documents, U.S. Government Printing Office, Washington, DC 20402.

Letter Styling for Department of Defense Correspondence

CONFIDENTIAL

CERTIFIED MAIL

Mr. Exec/tp/413-734-4444

G.&C. Merriam Company
PUBLISHERS OF MERRIAM-WEBSTER REFERENCE BOOKS

1 January 19—
76TRANS123

SUBJECT: Contract AF 45(100)-1147
Foreign Technology Program
Life Sciences Translation QC (C)

TO: Initials or Name of Office
Name of Applicable Administrator
Organization
Geographical Address + ZIP Code

THROUGH: Applicable Channels
and Addresses
Listed and Blocked

REFERENCE: (a) WXYZ letter ABCD/EF dated 1 December 19—
(b) EFGH letter IJKL/MN dated 1 November 19—

1. This is a typical format for letters directed to the Department of Defense. Styling varies with the agency or department one is writing to; thus, a format consensus is shown here.

2. In letters containing classified information, the highest classification category of any included information must be noted at the top and bottom of each page.

   a. Since the subject of this letter is supposed to be CONFIDENTIAL, it is so stamped above the letterhead and at the bottom of the page.

   b. The parenthetical abbreviation (C) for CONFIDENTIAL is typed at the end of the subject line.

   c. Appropriate classification stamps are affixed at the bottom of the first page.

3. Special mailing notations if required are typically typed in the upper left corner of the page.

CLASSIFIED BY: ____________
EXEMPT FROM GENERAL DECLASSIFICATION
SCHEDULE OF EXECUTIVE ORDER 11652
EXEMPTION CATEGORY
DECLASSIFY on

CONFIDENTIAL

NATIONAL SECURITY INFORMATION
Unauthorized disclosure subject to criminal sanctions.

47 FEDERAL STREET. SPRINGFIELD. MASSACHUSETTS 01101 TELEPHONE (413)-734-3134

CONFIDENTIAL

CERTIFIED MAIL

Contract AF 45(100)-1147
Foreign Technology Program
Life Sciences QC (C)

1 January 19—
76TRANS123
Page 2

4. If the writer's name and telephone number are not on the printed letterhead, they may be typed with the typist's initials in the upper right corner of the first page.

5. The date line featuring an inverted date and the company control number are flush left, with the date line three lines below the letterhead.

6. The SUBJECT block, sometimes placed after the TO and/or THROUGH blocks depending on agency preference, contains the contract number, project name, and subject of the letter.

7. The TO block is really the inside address. The THROUGH or VIA block lists the designated channels through which the letter must pass before it reaches the addressee.

8. The REFERENCE block lists related material or previous correspondence that must be referred to before action can be taken.

9. The SUBJECT, TO, THROUGH, and REFERENCE blocks are separated by triple-spacing, and are internally single-spaced.

10. There is no salutation. The message, comprising numbered paragraphs and alphabetized subparagraphs, begins two lines below the last line in the REFERENCE block.

11. Continuation-sheet headings begin six lines from the top edge of the page and contain subject data, date, pagination, and control number. The classification category must be stamped at the top and bottom of each continuation sheet.

12. There is no complimentary close. The company name is typed all in capitals two lines below the last message line, followed four lines down by the writer's name, title, and department in capitals and lowercase.

13. Typist's initials if not shown at the top of the first page may appear two lines below the signature block. Enclosures should be listed numerically and identified, as should carbon-copy recipients. Only external distribution lists appear on the original.

G. & C. MERRIAM COMPANY

Executive Signature

Executive Signature
Project Manager

Enclosures (1) (C) 3 copies of Translation
Printout dated 30 December 19—

(2) 1 copy of Contract AF 44(100)-1147

CONFIDENTIAL

Classification in industrial operations is based on government security guidance. Private sector management does not make original security classification decisions or designations but does implement the decisions of the government contracting agency with respect to classified information and material developed, produced, or handled in the course of a project. Management also designates persons within the firm who will be responsible for assuring that government regulations are followed. Each system and program involving research, development, testing, and evaluation of technical information is supported by its own program security guide.

What is classified information and material? The following mini-glossary adapted from Department of Defense definitions should give the secretary some insight:

classified information official information which requires, in the interests of national security, protection against unauthorized disclosure and which has been so designated

national security a collective term encompassing both the national defense and the foreign relations of the United States

information knowledge which can be communicated by any means

official information information which is owned by, produced for or by, or is subject to the control of the United States government

material any document, product, or substance on or in which information may be recorded or embodied

document any recorded information (as written or printed material, data processing cards and tapes, graphics, and sound, voice, or electronic recordings in any form) regardless of its physical form or characteristics

upgrade to determine that certain classified information requires, in the interest of national security, a higher degree of protection against unauthorized disclosure than currently provided, and to change the classification designation to reflect this higher degree

downgrade to determine that certain classified information requires, in the interest of national security, a lower degree of protection against unauthorized disclosure than currently provided, and to change the classification designation to reflect this lower degree

declassify to determine that certain classified information no longer requires, in the interest of national security, any degree of protection against unauthorized disclosure, and to remove or cancel the classification designation

The classification categories

Unclassified referring to information or material requiring, in the interests of national security, no protection against unauthorized disclosure

Confidential referring to information or material requiring protection because its unauthorized disclosure could cause damage to the national security

Secret referring to information requiring a substantial degree of protection because its unauthorized disclosure could cause serious damage (as a serious disruption of foreign relations) to the national security

Top Secret referring to information or material requiring the highest degree of protection because its unauthorized disclosure could cause exceptionally grave damage (as armed hostilities against the U.S.) to the national security

are designated on correspondence and other matter by the stamps (not less than ¼″ in height)

UNCLASSIFIED **SECRET**

CONFIDENTIAL **TOP SECRET**

They may also be represented before individual paragraphs, in subject lines, and in enclosure notations by the parenthetical abbreviations

(U) (C) (S) (TS)

The following general marking procedures are required by the government:

1. The overall classification of a document whether or not permanently bound or any copy or reproduction thereof must be conspicuously marked or stamped at the top and bottom on the outside of the front cover (if any), on the title page (if any), on the first page, on the last page, and on the outside of the back cover (if any). Each inside page of the document will be marked or stamped top and bottom with the highest classification category applicable to the information appearing there.
2. Each section, paragraph, subparagraph, or part of a document will be marked with the applicable parenthetical classification abbreviation (TS), (S), (C), or (U) when there are several degrees of classified information therein.
3. Large components of complex documents which may be used separately should be appropriately marked. These components include: attachments and appendices to a memorandum or a letter, annexes or appendices to a plan or program, or a major part of a report.
4. Files, folders, or packets for classified documents should be conspicuously marked on both front and back covers with the highest category of classification occurring in documents they enclose.
5. Transmittal documents including endorsements and comments should carry the highest classification category applicable to the information attached to them.

Basic mailing procedures for classified documents are outlined below. For detailed information on mailing and on hand-carrying such documents, see DoD publication 5200.1-R:

1. Classified material must be enclosed in two sealed opaque envelopes before it may be mailed through the U.S. Postal Service or by means of a commercial carrier.
2. Both envelopes must contain the names and addresses of the sender and the receiver.
3. The inner envelope must contain the appropriate classification category stamp, which must not be visible through the outer envelope.
4. The classified information should be protected from the inner envelope by being folded inward, or by use of a blank cover sheet.
5. The inner envelope must contain an appropriate classified-material receipt.
6. Confidential material is sent by CERTIFIED MAIL and Secret information is sent by REGISTERED MAIL. Top Secret documents require specialized transit procedures.

Classified material is downgraded and declassified as soon as there is no longer any national-security reason for it to be classified. The Department of Defense makes these judgments. An automatic schedule of downgrading has been set up for the three categories:

TOP SECRET will be downgraded automatically to SECRET at the end of the second full calendar year in which it was originated; downgraded to CONFIDENTIAL at the end of the fourth full calendar year in which it was originated; and declassified at the end of the tenth full calendar year in which it was originated.

SECRET will be downgraded automatically to CONFIDENTIAL at the end of the second full calendar year following the year in which it was originated, and will be declassified at the end of the eighth full calendar year following the year in which it was originated.

CONFIDENTIAL will be automatically declassified at the end of the sixth full calendar year following the year it was originated.

Classified documents therefore must be conspicuously marked or stamped to indicate the intended automatic downgrading timephase. This information is typed or stamped on the first or title page of a document immediately below or adjacent to the classification stamp.

Exemptions to the General Declassification Schedule will bear the following information affixed immediately below or adjacent to the classification stamp on the first or title page:

```
CLASSIFIED BY: ________________
EXEMPT FROM GENERAL DECLASSIFICATION
SCHEDULE OF EXECUTIVE ORDER 11652
EXEMPTION CATEGORY
DECLASSIFY on
```

See the letter facsimile in this section for the positioning of the above information on a confidential document.

7

CHAPTER SEVEN

A GUIDE TO EFFECTIVE BUSINESS ENGLISH

CONTENTS

7.1

INTRODUCTION

The importance of cleanly typed business correspondence is discussed in Chapter 6, and special typing projects (as memorandums and reports) are treated in Chapter 8. However, the mechanics of typing attractive-looking material is only one factor contributing to effective written communication. Other equally important elements are standard grammar, correct spelling, felicitous style, and sound presentation of ideas within logically constructed sentences and paragraphs. While the physical appearance and mechanical setup of the material will impress a reader at first glance, these other factors will create even more lasting impressions as a reader studies the material carefully and reflects on its content.

Thus, all of the interrelated elements illustrated in the diagram are vital to effective communication: If the grammar is substandard, if the spelling is incorrect, if the sentence structure is contorted, if the paragraph orientation is cloudy or irrational, and if the text is riddled with padding and clichés, one can reasonably anticipate negative reader reaction. Although the writer or dictator does bear the prime re-

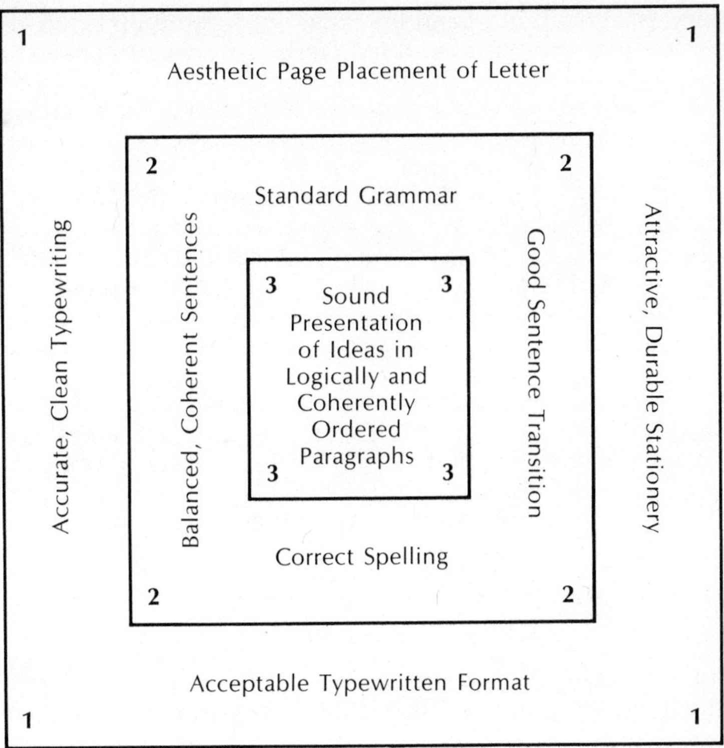

1. Physical appearance of the material creates a first-glance impression on the reader

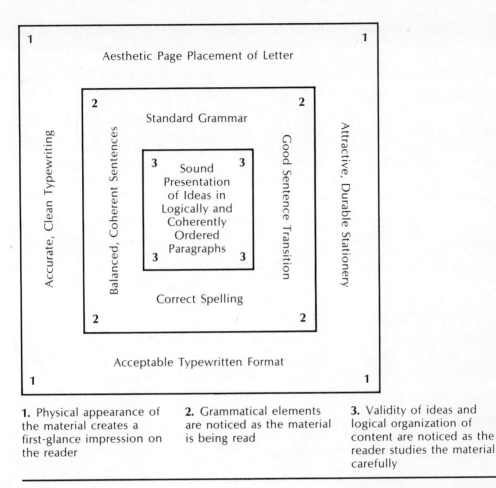

2. Grammatical elements are noticed as the material is being read

3. Validity of ideas and logical organization of content are noticed as the reader studies the material carefully

---

sponsibility for his or her own grammar, diction, and usage, the secretary still should be competent enough in these areas to recognize basic grammatical and stylistic infelicities. Before typing questionable material, the secretary should research any doubtful points and then tactfully query the writer. The following sections have been prepared as a quick reference tool for just this sort of situation. Highly specialized questions may be answered by consulting a current book on English grammar (see the Appendix for a list of titles).

7.2

ABBREVIATIONS

The occurrence of abbreviations in typed or printed material is directly related to the nature of the material itself. For example, technical literature (as in the fields of aerospace, engineering, data processing, and medicine) abounds in abbreviations, but formal literary writing features relatively few such terms. By the same token, the presence or absence of abbreviations in business writing depends on the nature of the business. A secretary in a university English department and one in an electronics firm each will encounter widely different abbreviations.

Abbreviation styling (as capitalization and punctuation) is, unfortunately, inconsistent and at the same time arbitrary. No rules can be set down to cover all possible variations, exceptions, and peculiarities. Abbreviation styling depends most often on the writer's preference or the organization's policy; for example, some companies style the abbreviations for *cash on delivery* as *COD,* but others prefer *C.O.D.* It can be said, however, that some abbreviations (as *a.k.a., e.g., etc., f.o.b., i.e., No.,* and *viz.*) are backed by a strong punctuation tradition, and that others (as *GATT, LIFO, MIRV, PAYE,* and *SCAT*) that are pronounced as solid words tend to be all capitalized and unpunctuated. Styling problems can be alleviated by (1) consulting an adequate dictionary especially for capitalization guidance (2) following the guidelines of one's own organization, and (3) consulting an abbreviations dictionary for answers to highly specialized questions (see the Appendix for a list of titles).

Abbreviations are used (1) to avoid repetition of long words and phrases that may distract the reader (2) to save space and time (3) to reduce keystrokes and increase output, and (4) to reflect statistical data in limited space. When using an abbreviation that may be unfamiliar or confusing to the reader, one should give the full form first, followed by the abbreviation in parentheses, as

I shall address the American Bar Association (ABA) meeting in . . . .

followed in subsequent references by just the abbreviation, as

At this particular ABA meeting, I intend to . . . .

The chart on the following pages offers abbreviation guidelines with applicable illustrations. These guidelines are listed alphabetically by key words in boldface type.

ABBREVIATIONS

Guideline	Illustration
1. **a** or **an** before an abbreviation; *see page* 241.	
2. **A.D.** and **B.C.** are usually styled in printed matter as small punctuated unspaced capitals, but in typed material as punctuated unspaced capitals.	[41 B.C.] [41 B.C.] [A.D. 185 *also* 185 A.D.] [A.D. 185 *also* 185 A.D.] [fourth century A.D.] [fourth century A.D.]
3. **Beginning a sentence with an abbreviation** should be avoided unless the abbreviation represents a courtesy title.	[Page 22 contains . . . .] *but not* [P. 22 contains . . . .] *however* [Dr. Smith is here.] *or* [Doctor Smith is here.]
4. **Capitalization** of abbreviations; *see page* 202.	
5. **Compass points** are abbreviated when occurring after street names, and they can be unpunctuated; *however* compass points are usually typed out in full when they form essential internal elements of street names.	[2122 Fourteenth Street, NW] [192 East 49th Street]

6. **Dates** (as days and months) should not be abbreviated in running texts; months should not be abbreviated in general business-letter date lines but they may be abbreviated in government or military correspondence.	[I expect to meet with you in Chicago on Monday, June 1, 19--.] *general business-letter date line* [June 1, 19--] *military date line* [1 Jun --]
7. **Division of an abbreviation** either at the end of a line or between pages should be avoided.	[received his M.B.A. degree . . . .] *but not* [received his M.B.- A. degree . . . .]
8. **Company names** are not abbreviated unless abbreviations comprise their official names; *and* the words *Airlines, Associates, Consultants, Corporation, Fabricators, Manufacturing,* and *Railroad* should not be abbreviated when part of proper names.	[Ginn and Company] [The Bailey Banks and Biddle Company] *but* [Gulf + Western Industries, Inc.] [Harwood Engineering Co., Inc.] [Crompton & Knowles Corporation] [Eastern Airlines]
9. **Footnotes** are sometimes introduced by abbreviations.	[[4] Ibid.]
10. **Geographical and topographical names.** U.S. Postal Service abbreviations for states are all-capitalized and unpunctuated, as are the Postal Service abbreviations for streets and localities when used on envelopes addressed for automated mass handling, *and* ordinals are abbreviated in some street addresses *also* names of countries are typically abbreviated in tabular data, but are typed in full in running texts (exception: *U.S.S.R.*) *and* *United States* is often abbreviated when it modifies names of federal agencies, policies, or programs; when it is used as a noun, it is usually typed in full.	[Smithville, ST 56789] *addressed for automated handling* [1234 SMITH BLVD SMITHVILLE, ST 56789] *regular address styling* [1234 Smith Blvd. (or Boulevard) Smithville, ST 56789] [147 East 31st Street] [147 East 3d Avenue] [147 East 3rd Avenue] *in a table* [U.A.R. *or* UAR] *in a text* [The United Arab Republic and the U.S.S.R. announced the trade agreement.] [U.S. Information Agency] [U.S. foreign policy] *but* [The United States has offered to. . . .]
11. **Latin words and phrases** commonly used in general writing are often abbreviated.	[etc.] [i.e.] [e.g.] [viz.]
12. **Latitude and longitude** are abbreviated in tabular data, but are typed in full in running texts.	*in a table* [lat. 10°20′N *or* lat. 10-20N] *in a text* [from 10°20′ north latitude to 10°30′ south latitude. . . .]

Rule	Examples
13. Laws and bylaws when first quoted are typed in full; however, subsequent references to them in a text may be abbreviated.	*first reference* [Article I, Section 1] *subsequent references* [Art. I, Sec. 1]
14. Measures and weights may be abbreviated in figure + unit combinations; however, if the numeral is written out, the unit must also be written out.	[15 cu ft] *or* [15 cu.ft.] *but* [fifteen cubic feet]
15. Number when part of a set unit (as a contract number), when used in tabular data, or when used in bibliographic references may be abbreviated to *No.* (sing.) or *Nos.* (plural).	[Contract No. N-1234-76-57] [Policy No. 123-5-X] [Publ. Nos. 12 and 13]
16. Period with abbreviations; *see* PERIOD, RULE 3, *page* 223.	
17. Personal names should not be abbreviated; however, initials of famous persons are sometimes used in place of their full names.	[George S. Patterson] *not* [Geo. S. Patterson] *but* [J.F.K. *or* JFK]
18. Plurals of abbreviations may be formed by addition of *-s* *or* by the addition of *-'s* especially if the abbreviation is internally punctuated, except for a few such terms that are punctuated only with terminal periods, in which case the apostrophe is omitted *or* by repeating a letter of the abbreviation *or* by no suffixation.	[MLDs] [MPs] [PNs] [f.o.b.'s] *but* [Nos. 3 and 4] [Figs. A and B] [p. → pp.] [f. → ff.] [1 sec → 30 sec] [1 ml → 24 ml]
19. Possessives of abbreviations are formed in the same way as those of nouns: the singular possessive is signaled by addition of *-'s* *and* the plural possessive, by addition of *-s'*.	[the British PM's decision] [British Commonwealth PMs' decisions]
20. Saint may be abbreviated when used before the name of a saint; however, it may or may not be abbreviated when it forms part of a surname, depending on the name.	[St. Peter] *or* [Saint Peter] *but* [Ruth St. Denis] [Augustus Saint-Gaudens]
21. Scientific terms In binomial nomenclature a genus name may be abbreviated after the first reference to it is typed out.	[(first reference) *Escherichia coli*] [(subsequent references) *E. coli*]

22. Time When time is expressed in figures, the abbreviations that follow may be set in unspaced punctuated lowercase letters; if capitals or small capitals are used, one space should separate the letters (the writer's or organization's preference will dictate the particular style used)

[8:30 a.m. *or* 8:30 A. M. *or* 8:30 A. M.]

and

standard measurements of time (as in tabular data) are expressed in figures and typically unpunctuated abbreviations.

[10 sec] [18 min] [24 hr]
[17 yr] [52 wk] [19 mo] [100 da]

---

23. Titles The only titles that are invariably abbreviated are *Mr., Ms., Mrs.,* and *Messrs.* Other titles (except for *Doctor* which may be written out or abbreviated) are given in full form in business-letter salutations;

[Ms. Lee A. Downs]
[Messrs. Lake, Mason, and Nambeth]
[Dear Doctor Howe] *or*
[Dear Dr. Howe]
but
[Dear Professor Howe]
[Dear General Howe]
[Dear Private Howe]

but

titles may be abbreviated in envelope address blocks and in inside addresses;

[Dr. John P. Howe]
[COL John P. Howe, USA]
[GEN John P. Howe, USA]
[PVT John P. Howe, USA]

also

Honorable and *Reverend* when used with *The* are typed out, but if used without *The,* they may be abbreviated; *see also pages* 181–182; 185–186.

[The Reverend Samuel I. O'Leary]
[The Honorable Samuel I. O'Leary]
but
[Rev. Samuel I. O'Leary]
[Hon. Samuel I. O'Leary]

---

24. Versus is abbreviated as the lowercase Roman letter *v.* in legal contexts; it is either typed in full or abbreviated as lowercase Roman letters *vs.* in general contexts.

in a legal context
[*Smith* v. *Vermont*]
in a general context
[honesty versus dishonesty]
or
[honesty vs. dishonesty]

7.3

CAPITALIZATION

Capitals are used for two broad purposes in English: They mark a beginning (as of a sentence) and they signal a proper noun or adjective. The following eighty-one principles, each with a bracketed example or examples, describe the most common uses of capital letters. These principles are alphabetically ordered under the following headings:

When uncertain about the capitalization of a term not shown below, the secretary should consult a dictionary such as *Webster's New Collegiate Dictionary.*

CAPITALIZATION

Abbreviations

1. Abbreviations are capitalized if the words they represent are proper nouns or adjectives; consult a dictionary when in doubt of styling.	[98 F for *Fahrenheit*] [Nov. for *November*] [NBC for *N*ational *B*roadcasting *C*ompany] *but* [a.k.a. for *a*lso *k*nown *a*s]
2. Most acronyms are capitalized unless they have been assimilated into the language as parts of speech, and as such are lowercased; consult a dictionary when in doubt of styling.	[OPEC] [CREEP] [MIRV] [GATT] *but* [quasar] [laser] [radar] [sonar] [scuba] [snafu]
3. Abbreviations of government agencies, military units, and corporate names are usually capitalized.	[CIA] [FBI] [HEW] [USIA] [USAF] [MAAG] [RCA] [ITT]
4. Abbreviations of air force, army, coast guard, and navy ranks are all-capitalized; those of the marine corps are capitalized and lowercased; *see* FORMS OF ADDRESS, *pages* 170–176.	[BG John T. Dow, USA] [LCDR Mary I. Lee, USN] [Col. S. J. Smith, USMC]
5. Abbreviations of compass points are capitalized; punctuation styling depends on the writer's or organization's preference.	[lat. 10°20′N] [2233 Fourteenth Street, N.W. 2233 Fourteenth Street, NW. 2233 Fourteenth Street, NW]
6. Abbreviations of academic degrees and professional ratings may be all-capitalized or capitalized and lowercased, depending on the word; consult a dictionary when in doubt of styling.	[D.D.S.] [M.B.A.] [P.E.] [C.P.A.] [Ph.D.] [Litt.D.]

Beginnings

7. The first word of a sentence, of a sentence fragment, or of a complete sentence enclosed in parentheses is capitalized; *however* the first word of a parenthetical phrase or sentence enclosed by parentheses and occurring within another sentence is lowercased.	[The meeting was postponed.] [No! I cannot do it.] [Will you go?] [Prices. Nothing has gone down. —*Audio-Visual Communications*] [The meeting ended. (The results were not revealed.)] *but* [She studied economics under Dr. Heller (he wrote this text, you know) at the university.]
8. The first word of a direct quotation is capitalized *but* a split direct quotation tightly bound to the rest of a sentence may be lowercased at the beginning of its continued segment or segments.	[He said, "We must consider the sales problems."] ["The Administration has denied the story," the paper reports, and goes on to say that "the President feels the media are irresponsible."]
9. The first word of a direct question within a sentence or of a series of questions within a sentence may be capitalized.	[That question is this: Is man an ape or an angel? —*Benjamin Disraeli*] [Is there someone standing behind you? On your right? On your left? —*Management World*]
10. The first word following a colon may be lowercased or capitalized if it introduces a complete sentence; while the former is the more usual styling, the latter is common especially when the sentence introduced by the colon is fairly lengthy and distinctly separate from the preceding clause.	[The advantage of this particular system is clear: it's inexpensive.] [The situation is critical: This company cannot hope to recoup the fourth-quarter losses that were sustained in five operating divisions.]
11. The first words of run-in or blocked enumerations that form complete sentences are capitalized as are the first words of phrasal lists and enumerations blocked beneath running texts;	[The advantages of the task inventories are . . . as follows: 1. The technique is economical. 2. The information . . . is quantifiable. —*Business Education World*] [Occupations are divided into the following . . . areas: Business, marketing, and management Personal and public services Health . . . . —*Business Education World*]
however phrasal enumerations run-in with the introductory text are lowercased.	*but* [. . . the following sequence of activities has proven . . . satisfying . . . (1) teacher demonstration; (2) performance by students; (3) diagnosis of errors. . . . —*Business Education World*]

12. The words *Whereas* and *Resolved* are capitalized in minutes and legislation, as is the word *That* or an alternative word or expression which immediately follows either.

[Resolved, That. . . .]
[Whereas, Substantial benefits. . . .]
[Whereas, The Executive Committee. . . .]
[Resolved by the ----, the ---- concurring, That. . . .]

---

13. The first letter of the first word in an outline heading is capitalized.

[I. Editorial tasks
II. Production responsibilities
A. Cost estimates
B. Bids]

---

14. The first letter of the first word in a salutation and a complimentary close is capitalized as is the first letter of each noun following SUBJECT and TO headings (as in memorandums).

[Dear Bob] [Gentlemen] [My dear Dr. Smith] [Very truly yours]
[Yours very truly] [SUBJECT: Pension Plan]
[TO: All Department Heads]

---

15. The first word of a line of poetry is conventionally capitalized.

[Yet this abundant issue seem'd to me
But hope of orphans and unfather'd fruit;
For summer and his pleasures wait on thee,
And, thou away, the very birds are mute. . . .
—William Shakespeare]

Proper Nouns, Pronouns, and Adjectives

Armed Forces

16. Branches and units of the armed forces are capitalized as are easily recognizable short forms of full branch and unit designations.

[United States Army] *and* [a contract with the Army]
[Corps of Engineers] *and* [a bridge built by the Engineers]

Awards

17. Awards and prizes are capitalized.

[the Nobel Prize for Literature]
[Nobel Peace Prize] [Nobel Prize winners]
[Academy Award] [Oscar] [Emmy]

Deity

18. Words designating the Deity are usually capitalized; *compare* RULE 55.

[An anthropomorphic, vengeful Jehovah became a spiritual, benevolent Supreme Being.
—A. R. Katz]

Epithets

19. Epithets used in place of names or titles are capitalized.

[the Big Board] [the Fleet Street boys]
[No. 10 Downing Street announced . . . .]
[The White House has verified . . . .]

Geographical and Topographical References

20. Divisions of the earth's surface and names of distinct areas, regions, places, or districts are capitalized, as are adjectives and some derivative nouns and verbs; consult a dictionary when in doubt.

[the Middle East] [the Middle Eastern situation] [Eastern Hemisphere]
[the Great Divide] [Tropic of Cancer]
[Geneva] [Texas]
[Vietnam] [Vietnamization]
[Vietnamize] *but* [sovietism *often* Sovietism] [sovietize *often* Sovietize]

Rule	Examples
21. Compass points are capitalized when they refer to a geographical region or when they are part of a street name, but are lowercased when they refer to simple direction.	[out West] [back East] [down South] [up North] [the South] [the Middle West] [the West Coast] [157 East 92nd Street] *but* [west of the Rockies] [traveling east on I-84] [the west coast of Florida]
22. Adjectives derived from compass points and nouns designating the inhabitants of some geographical regions are capitalized; when in doubt of the proper styling, consult a dictionary.	[a Southern accent] [a Western drawl] [members of the Eastern Establishment] [Northerners]
23. Popular names of localities are capitalized.	[the Corn and Wheat Belts] [the Gold Coast] [the Loop] [the Eastern Shore] [City of Brotherly Love] [Foggy Bottom] [the Village]
24. Topographical names are capitalized, as are generic terms (as *channel, lake, mountain*) that are essential elements of total names.	[the English Channel] [Lake Como] [the Blue Ridge Mountains] [Atlantic Ocean] [Great Barrier Reef] [Mississippi River] [Black Sea] [Bering Strait] [Strait of Gilbraltar] [Ohio Valley]
25. Generic terms occurring before topographical names are capitalized except when *the* precedes them, in which case the generic term is lowercased.	[Lakes Michigan and Superior] [Mounts Whitney and Rainier] *but* [the rivers Don and Volga] [the river Thames]
26. Plural generic terms occurring after multiple topographical names are lowercased, as are singular or plural generic terms that are used descriptively or alone.	[the Himalaya and Andes mountains] [the Don and Volga rivers] [the valley of the Ohio] [the Ohio River valley] [the river valley] [the valley]
27. Words designating global, national, regional, or local political divisions are capitalized when they are essential elements of specific names; however, they are usually lowercased when they precede a proper name or stand alone.	[the British Empire] *but* [the empire] [Oregon State] *but* [the state of Oregon] [Bedford County] *but* [the county of Bedford] [New York City] *but* [the city of New York] [Ward 1] *but* [fires in three wards]
28. Terms designating public places are capitalized when they are essential elements of specific names; however, they are lowercased when they occur after multiple names or stand alone.	[Fifth Avenue] [Brooklyn Bridge] [Empire State Building] [St. John's Church] [the Dorset Hotel] [Central Park] [Washington Square] [Bleecker Street] [Ford Theater] *but* [on the bridge] [Fifth and Park avenues] [the Dorset and the Drake hotels] [St. John's and St. Mark's churches]
29. Well-known short forms of place names are capitalized.	[Fifth Avenue → the Avenue] [Wall Street → the Street] [New York Stock Exchange → the Exchange]

Governmental, Judicial, and Political Bodies

30. The terms *administration* and *government* are capitalized when they are applicable to a particular government in power.	[The Administration announced a new oil and gas program.] [the Ford Administration] *but* [White House parties vary from one administration to another.]
31. The names of international courts are capitalized.	[the International Court of Arbitration]
32. The U.S. Supreme Court and the short forms *Supreme Court* and *Court* referring to it are capitalized.	[the Supreme Court of the United States] [the United States Supreme Court] [the U.S. Supreme Court] [the Supreme Court] [the Court]
33. Official and full names of higher courts are capitalized; however, the single designation *court* is usually lowercased when referring to them.	[the United States Court of Appeals for the Second Circuit] [the Michigan Court of Appeals] [the Virginia Supreme Court] [the Court of Queen's Bench] *but* [the federal courts] [the court of appeals ruled that . . . .] [the state supreme court] [the court]
34. Names of city and county courts are usually lowercased.	[the Lawton municipal court] [the Owensville night court] [police court] [the county court] [juvenile court]
35. The single designation *court* when specifically applicable to a judge or a presiding officer is capitalized.	[It is the opinion of this Court that. . . .] [The Court found that. . . .]
36. The term *federal* is capitalized only when it is an essential element of a name or title, when it identifies a specific government, or often when it refers to a particular principle of government.	[the Federal Bureau of Investigation] [. . . efforts made by the Federal Government. . . .] [the Federal principle of government] *but* [federal court] [federal district court] [federal agents] [federal troops]
37. Full names of legislative, deliberative, executive, and administrative bodies are capitalized as are the easily recognizable short forms of these names; however, nonspecific noun and adjective references to them are usually lowercased.	[United Nations Security Council] *and* [the Security Council] *but* [the council] [United States Congress] *and* [the Congress] *but* [congressional elections] [the Maryland Senate] *but* [the state senate] [Department of State] *and* [the State Department] *and* [State] *but* [the department]
38. The term *national* is capitalized when it precedes a capitalized word or when it forms a part of a specific name or title; however, it is lowercased when used as a descriptive word or as a noun.	[National Socialist Party] *but* [in the interests of national security] [the screening of foreign nationals]

39. The names of political parties and their adherents are capitalized, but the word *party* may or may not be capitalized, depending on the writer's or organization's preference.	[Democrats] [Republicans] [Liberals] [Tories] [the Democratic party] *or* [the Democratic Party]

Names of Organizations

40. Names of firms, corporations, organizations, and other such groups are capitalized.	[G. & C. Merriam Company] [EXXON Corporation] [Rotary International]
41. Common nouns used descriptively and occurring after two or more organization names are lowercased.	[American and Allegheny airlines] [the ITT and IBM corporations]
42. The words *company* and *corporation* are capitalized when they refer to one's own organization even when the full organization name is omitted; however, they are lowercased when they refer to another organization.	[It is contrary to the policies of our Company to. . . .] *but* [He works for a company in Delaware.] [Give me the name of your company.]
43. Words such as *group, division, department, office,* or *agency* that designate corporate units are capitalized when used with a specific name.	[The Plastics Molding and Fabrication Division is in charge of the project.] *but* [The memorandum was sent to all operating divisions.]

Names of Persons

44. The names of persons are capitalized.	[John W. Jones, Jr.]
45. Words designating peoples and their languages are capitalized.	[Canadians] [Turks] [Swedish] [Welsh] [Iroquois] [Ibo] [Vietnamese]
46. Derivatives of proper names are capitalized when used in their primary sense; consult a dictionary when in doubt of styling.	[Saudi Arabian oil interests] [Keynesian economics] [Manhattanite] [Orwellian society] *but* [manila envelope] [pasteurize] [bohemian tastes]

Numerical Designations

47. Monetary units typed in full (as in legal documents and on checks) are capitalized.	[Your fee is Two Thousand Dollars ($2,000.00), payable upon receipt of. . . .]
48. Nouns introducing a set number (as on a policy) are usually capitalized.	[Order 123] [Policy 123-4-X] [Flight 409] [Regulation 15] [Stock Certificate X12345] [Exhibit A] [Form 2E] [Catalog No. 65432]
49. Nouns used with numbers or letters to designate major reference headings (as in a literary work) are capitalized; however, minor reference headings and subheads are typically lowercased.	[Book II] [Volume V] [Division 4] [Section 3] [Article IV] [Table 5] [Figure 8] [Appendix III] [Plate 16] [Part 1] *but* [footnote 14] [page 101] [line 8] [note 10] [paragraph 6.1] [item 16] [question 21]

Particles and Prefixes

50. Particles forming initial elements of surnames may or may not be capitalized, depending on the styling of the individual name; however, if a name with a lowercase initial particle begins a sentence, the particle is capitalized.

[Du Pont] [D'Albert] [De Camp]
[de la Mare] [de Tocqueville]
[du Maurier] [Von Braun] [von Kleist]

[The novels of du Maurier are. . . .]
but
[Du Maurier's novels are. . . .]

---

51. Elements of hyphened compounds are capitalized in running texts if they are proper nouns or adjectives; consult a dictionary when in doubt of styling.

[East-West trade] [U.S.-U.S.S.R. détente]
[Arab-Israeli relations]
but
[a nineteenth-century poet]
[. . . said the idea was un-American.]

---

52. Prefixes occurring with proper nouns or adjectives are capitalized if they are essential elements of the compounds or if they begin headings or sentences; they are lowercased in other instances. NOTE: If a second element in a two-word compound modifies the first element or if both elements constitute a single word, the second element is lowercased.

[Afro-American customs] [nationalism of the Pan-Slavic variety]
[Pro-Soviet sentiments were voiced.]
but
[The pro-Soviet faction objected.]

[French-speaking peoples]
[an A-frame house]

Personifications

53. Personifications are capitalized.

[We have Mr. and Ms. Entropy among us . . . bent on breaking down civilized discourse.
—Alan Harrington]

[The Chair recognized the Senator from. . . .]

Pronouns

54. The pronoun *I* is capitalized.

[He and I will attend the meeting.]

55. Pronouns referring to the Deity are capitalized; *compare* RULE 18.

[. . . that when God chose to save the heathen He could do it by Himself.
—Elmer Davis]

Scientific Terms

56. Names of geological eras, periods, epochs, and strata and of prehistoric ages are capitalized, but the generic nouns which they modify are lowercased except when those generic nouns appear <u>before</u> the names of eras, periods, epochs, strata, or divisions, in which case they are capitalized.

[Silurian period] [Pleistocene epoch]
[Neolithic age]
but
[Age of Reptiles]

---

57. Names of planets, constellations, asteroids, stars, and groups of stars are capitalized, but *sun, earth,* and *moon* are lowercased unless they are listed with other astronomical names.

[Venus] [Big Dipper] [Sirius] [Pleiades]
but
[sun] [earth] [moon]
[unmanned space probes to the Moon and to Mars]

---

58. Meterological phenomena are lowercased.	[northern lights] [aurora borealis]
59. Genera in binomial nomenclature in zoology and botany are capitalized; however, species names are lowercased.	[a cabbage butterfly (*Pieris rapae*)] [a common buttercup (*Ranunculus acris*)] [the robin (*Turdus migratorius*)] [the haddock (*Melanogrammus aeglefinus*)]
60. New Latin names of classes, families, and all groups above genera in zoology and botany are capitalized; however, their derivative nouns and adjectives are lowercased in American English.	[Gastropoda] *but* [gastropod] [Thallophyta] *but* [thallophyte]
61. Proper names forming essential elements of terms designating diseases, syndromes, signs, tests, and symptoms are capitalized.	[Parkinson's disease] [syndrome of Weber] [German measles] [Rorschach test] *but* [mumps] [measles] [herpes simplex]
62. Proprietary (i.e., brand and trade) names of drugs are capitalized, but generic names of drugs are lowercased.	[. . .was tranquilized with Thorazine.] *but* [. . .recommended chlorpromazine—a generic name for. . . .]
63. Proper names forming essential elements of scientific laws, theorems, and principles are capitalized; however, the descriptive nouns *law, theorem, theory,* and the like are lowercased.	[Boyle's law] [the Pythagorean theorem] [Planck's constant] [Einstein's theory of relativity] [the second law of thermodynamics]
Time Periods, Zones, and Divisions	
64. Names of the seasons are capitalized if personified.	[the gentle touch of Spring] *but* [The book will be published in the spring.]
65. Days of the week, months of the year, holidays, and holy days are capitalized.	[Tuesday] [July] [Independence Day] [Good Friday] [Easter]
66. Historic periods are capitalized, but latter-day periods are often lowercased.	[Christian Era] [Golden Age of Greece] [Roaring Twenties] [Augustan Age] *often* [nuclear age] [the atomic age] [space age]
67. Numerical designations of historic time periods are capitalized when they are essential elements of proper names; otherwise, they are lowercased.	[the Roaring Twenties] *but* [the seventeenth century] [the twenties]
68. Historical events and appellations referring to particular time periods or events in time are capitalized.	[the Reign of Terror] [the Cultural Revolution] [Prohibition] [the Great Depression] [the New Frontier] [the Third Reich] [the Fourth Republic]
69. Time zones are capitalized when abbreviated, but lowercased when written out.	[EST] *but* [eastern standard time]

Titles of Persons

70. Corporate titles are capitalized when referring to specific individuals; when used in general or plural contexts, they are lowercased.

[Mr. John M. Jones, Vice-president]
and
[Mr. Carl T. Yowell, Sales Manager]
but
[The sales manager called me.]
[All of our district managers will be here.]

---

71. Specific corporate and governmental titles may be capitalized when they stand alone or when they are used in place of particular individuals' names.

[The Executive Committee approved the Treasurer's report.]
[The Secretary of State gave a news conference. The Secretary said . . . .]
[The Judge will respond to your request when he returns to chambers.]

---

72. All titles preceding names are capitalized.

[President Roosevelt] [Archbishop Makarios] [Queen Elizabeth] [Dr. Doe] [Professor Doe] [The Honorable John M. Doe] [The Very Reverend John M. Doe] [Chief Justice Warren Burger]

---

73. Words of family relationship preceding names are capitalized.

[Aunt Laura] *but* [His aunt, Mrs. W. P. Jones, is the beneficiary.]

Titles of Printed Matter

74. Words in the titles of printed matter are capitalized except for internal conjunctions, prepositions (especially those having less than four letters), and articles;

[*Writing and Communicating in Business*] [*Before the Fall*] [an essay entitled "Truth Instead of Falsity"] [*War and Peace*]

also

verb segments (as *be* in *to be*) in infinitives, and particles (as *off* in *take off*) in two-word verbs are capitalized.

[*What is to Be Done?*]
[*Go Down, Moses*]

---

75. Major sections (as a preface, an introduction, or an index) of books, long articles, or reports are capitalized when they are specifically referred to within the same material.

[The Introduction explains the scope of the book.]

---

76. The first word following a colon in a title is capitalized.

[*CBS: Reflections in a Bloodshot Eye*]
[*The Dead of Winter: A Novel of Modern Scotland*]

---

77. The *the* before a title of a newspaper, magazine, or journal is capitalized if considered an essential element of the title; otherwise, it is lowercased,

[*The Wall Street Journal*]
but
[the New York *Times*]

and

descriptive nouns following publication titles are also lowercased.

[*Time* magazine]

---

78. Constitutional amendments are capitalized when referred to by title or number, but are lowercased when used as general terms.

[I took the Fifth Amendment]
but
[states ratifying constitutional amendments]

---

79. Formal titles of accords, pacts, plans, policies, treaties, constitutions, and similar documents are capitalized.	[The Geneva Accords] [Kellogg-Briand Pact] [the first Five Year Plan] [New Economic Policy] [Treaty of Versailles] [the United States Constitution] [the North Carolina Constitution] *but* [gun-control legislation] [various new economic policies] [the state constitution]
Trademarks **80.** Brand names, trademarks, and service marks are capitalized.	[the IBM Selectric] [Xerox] [Wite-Out correction fluid] [Air Express] [Laundromat]
Transport **81.** The names of ships, airplanes, and often spacecraft are capitalized.	[M. V. *West Star*] [Lindbergh's *Spirit of St. Louis*] [*Apollo 13*]

7.4

ITALICIZATION

The following are usually italicized in print and underlined in typescript or manuscript:

1. foreign words and phrases that have not been naturalized in English	[*aere perennius*] [*che sarà, sarà*] [*sans peur et sans reproche*] [*ich dien*] *but* [quid pro quo] [pasta] [enfant terrible] [a priori]
2. legal citations, both in full and shortened form, except when the person involved rather than the case itself is being discussed, in which instance the reference is typed in Roman letters without underlining	[*Jones* v. *Massachusetts*] [the *Jones* case] [*Jones*] *but* [the Jones trial and conviction]
3. letters when used as run-in enumerations (as in printed matter)	[. . . provided examples of (*a*) typing (*b*) transcribing (*c*) formatting (*d*) graphics . . . .]
4. names of ships and airplanes and often spacecraft	[M. V. *West Star*] [Lindberg's *Spirit of St. Louis*] [*Apollo 13*]
5. New Latin scientific names of genera, species, subspecies, and varieties (but not groups of higher rank such as phyla, classes, or orders, or derivatives of any of these) in botanical and zoological names	[a thick-shelled American clam *Mercenaria mercenaria*] [a cardinal (*Richmondena cardinalis*)] *but* [looked like an amoeba] [felid]

6. **titles** of books (but not chapter titles), magazines, newspapers, plays, movies, (but not radio or TV programs), works of art, and long musical compositions (but not symphonies)	[T. S. Eliot's *The Waste Land*] [the magazine *Business Week*] [*The Wall Street Journal*] [Shakespeare's *Othello*] [the movie *Gone With the Wind*] [Gainsborough's *Blue Boy*] [Mozart's *Don Giovanni*]
NOTE 1: Titles of essays, short stories, short poems, and unpublished works are not italicized but are enclosed by quotation marks.	*but* [CBS's "Sixty Minutes"] [the Ninth Symphony] ["Strangers in the Night"] [Pushkin's "Queen of Spades"] [Robert Frost's "Dust of Snow"] [his unpublished dissertation "Problems in Cost Accounting Procedures"]
NOTE 2: Plurals of such italicized titles have Roman-type inflectional endings.	[. . . had two *Business Week*s under his arm.]
7. **words, letters, and figures** when referred to as words, letters, or figures	[The word *stationery* meaning "paper" is often misspelled.] [The *g* key on my typewriter sticks.] [The first *2* and the last *0* in that ZIP code are illegible.]

7.5

NUMERALS

In modern business writing, most numerals—and especially exact numbers above *ten*—are expressed in figures. However, general usage allows all numbers below 100 to be styled as words. Therefore, if material is being prepared for publication (as in a professional journal), the writer and the typist should familiarize themselves with the particular style guidelines of the publication to which the manuscript will be submitted. The most important suggestion that can be offered is this: one should be consistent. For example, if one decides to use a figure in expressing a monetary unit, one should not use a written-out numerical designation in expressing a similar monetary unit within the same text. Since usage is divided on some points, the following alphabetically arranged guidelines sometimes show alternative stylings.

NUMERALS

1. **Compounds** When two numbers comprise one item or unit, one of the numbers (usually the first) should be expressed in words, and the other (usually the second) should be expressed in figures; if, however, the second number is the shorter, it may be expressed in words instead.	[two 7-drawer files] *but* 20 ten-drawer files]
2. **Compounds adjacent to other figures** Two sets of figures (except for those in monetary units) should not be typed in direct succession in a text unless they comprise a series; *compare* MONETARY UNITS; SERIES	[By 1976, one hundred shares of stock will be . . . .] *but not* [By 1976, 100 shares of stock will be . . . .]

3. **Date lines** Figures are used to express days and years in business-letter date lines.	[January 1, 19--]
4. **Enumerations** Run-in and vertical enumerations are often numbered.	[felt that she should (1) accept more responsibility (2) increase her overall production (3) maintain security precautions (4) . . . .] [. . . . responsibilities include: 1. Taking dictation 2. Transcribing dictated matter 3. Typing correspondence 4. Routing the mail]
5. **Exact amounts** Exact amounts are usually expressed in figures unless they begin sentences, in which case they are expressed in words.	[We have processed your order for 300 copies of *Webster's Medical Speller*. . . .] *but* [Three hundred copies of *Webster's Medical Speller* have been shipped. . . .]
6. **Figures** Figures are usually used to indicate policy, catalog, contract, and page numbers; street, apartment, room, or suite numbers; sizes, weights, and measures; shares, mixed amounts, percentages, and fractions.	[Policy No. 1-234-X] [page 67] [Room 1000] [Apt. 1A] [Suite 40] [1234 Smith Boulevard] [size 7] [120 lb] [9′ x 12′] [17 1/4] [14,280 shares] [78.654] [10 percent *or* 10%]
7. **Footnotes** Unspaced superscript numerals follow footnoted text material and superscript numerals followed by one space introduce the footnotes themselves.	[. . .is a prime factor in successful management."[2]] [[2] Ibid., p. 300.]
8. **Four-digit numbers** A number of four or more digits has each set of three digits separated by a comma except in set combinations such as policy, contract, check, street, room, or page numbers, which are unpunctuated; *see also* COMMA, RULE 14	[15,000 keystrokes] [assets of $12,500] [a population of 1,500,000] [4,600 words] *but* [Check 34567] [page 4589] [the year 1980] [Room 6000] [Policy No. 3344]
9. **Fractions** Single fractions and fractions occurring with whole numbers are expressed in words in running texts; however, fractions occurring in series and in tabulations are expressed in figures. NOTE: When some figure fractions in a text or table are not included on the keyboard, all fractions should be made up. Do not mix made-up and keyboard fractions.	[About three fourths of the budget has been used.] [The book weighs three and one-half pounds.] *but* [item 1 . . . . . 3 1/4 lb item 2 . . . . . 5 1/6 lb item 3 . . . . . 8 1/3 lb] [1 1/2″ x 1 1/8″] *not* [1½″ x 1 1/8″]
10. **Market quotations** are expressed in figures.	[16 bid–20 asked]

11. Measures and weights may be styled as figure + abbreviated unit combinations (as in tables); however, if the unit of measure or weight is typed out in full, the number is expressed in words.

[15 cu ft] *or* [15 cu.ft.]
but
[fifteen cubic feet]

12. Monetary units when containing both mixed and even-dollar amounts and typed in series should each contain: decimal point + 2 ciphers for the even-dollar amounts; also, the $ should be repeated before each unit. Units of less than one dollar are usually typed in running texts as: figure + *cents* (or ¢). Monetary units of one dollar or more or of less than one dollar are usually typed in vertical tabulations as: $ + decimal + figures on the first line, followed by decimals and figures only.

[The price of the book rose from $7.95 in 1970 to $8.00 in 1971 and to $8.50 in 1972.]
but
[The bids were $80, $100, and $300.]
[$10–$20]
[The pencil costs 15 cents.]
or
[The pencil costs 15¢.]

```
[$16.95
    .06
 ------
 $17.01]
```

13. No. *or* **#** should be avoided when a descriptive word appears before a figure, except for catalog or contract numbers, which may be so labeled.

[periscope lens 345] [page 12]
but
[Stock No. 1234]

14. Ordinals are expressed in words in running texts, but they may be expressed in figure and abbreviation combinations in some street addresses; *see also page* 118.

[the twentieth century] [The fifteenth applicant is in the outer office.]
but
[167 East 93rd (*or* 93d) Street]

15. Percentages are usually styled in running text as: figure + *percent,* but in tabulations as: figure + %.

[. . .reported 55 percent of the editing complete. . . .]
but

```
[completed copy editing   60%
 completed proofreading   10%
 completed graphics       70%]
```

16. Roman numerals (as those used in outlines) should be aligned to the right for uniformity in the appearance of the typescript that follows the numerals. Horizontal strokes should not be added to the numerals I–X, since this multiplies the numbers by 1,000.

```
[   V.
   VI.
  VII.
 VIII.
   IX.
    X.]
```

17. Round numbers and approximations are usually expressed in words, although some writers prefer to express them in figures for added emphasis. Numbers over one million are often expressed in figures + words to save keystrokes and to facilitate the reader's interpretation; *compare* EXACT AMOUNTS

[about thirty to fifty applicants]
or for added emphasis
[processed more than 3,000 citations]

[a $10 million profit] *or*
[a 10 million-dollar profit]

18. Series Figures are usually used to express a series of numbers that occur in a sentence even if the amounts are less than ten or are rounded off.

[We need 4 desks, 3 chairs, and 5 typewriters.] [They ordered about 15 pen sets, 7 blotters, and 9 legal pads.]

19. Short numbers Numbers expressible in one or two short words may be written in words.

[. . . interviewed two new applicants.]
but
[. . . received 24 dozen job applications.]

20. Time Time of day is expressed in words when it is followed by the contraction *o'clock* or when *o'clock* is understood; when time is followed by the abbreviations *a.m.* or *p.m.,* it is expressed in figures.

[He left for the day at four o'clock.]
[He left for the day at four.]
[We shall arrive at a quarter to ten.]
but
[He left for the day at 4:30 p.m.]
[We shall arrive at 9:45 a.m.]

21. Weights—*see* MEASURES AND WEIGHTS

7.6

PUNCTUATION

The English writing system uses punctuation marks to separate groups of words for meaning and emphasis; to convey an idea of the variations of pitch, volume, pauses, and intonation of speech; and to help avoid contextual ambiguity. Punctuation marks should be used sparingly: overpunctuating often needlessly comlicates a passage and also increases keystrokes. English punctuation marks, together with general rules and bracketed examples of their use, follow in alphabetical order. At the end of the section, a Punctuation-Spacination Chart will be found.

' APOSTROPHE

1. indicates the possessive case of singular and plural nouns and indefinite pronouns, as well as of surname and terminal title combinations

[Mr. Wilson's store] [Senator Ceccacci's office] [the boy's mother] [the boys' mothers] [anyone's guess] [everyone's questions] [his father-in-law's car] [their father-in-laws' cars] [John Burns' *or* Burns's insurance policy] [the Burnses' insurance policy] [Jay Adams' *or* Adams's boat] [the Adamses' boat] [a witness' *or* witness's testimony] [John K. Walker Jr.'s house] [the John K. Walker Jrs.' house]

NOTE: The use of an apostrophe + *s* with words ending in /s/ or /z/ sounds usually depends on the pronounceability of the final syllable: if the syllable is pronounced, the apostrophe + *s* is usually used; if the syllable is silent, the apostrophe is retained but an *s* is usually not appended to the word.

[Mr. Gomez's store]
[Knox's products]
[the class's opinion]
but
[Degas' paintings]
[Moses' laws]
[for righteousness' sake]

2. indicates joint possession when appended to the last noun in a sequence

[Appleton and Delaney's report]
[Doyle Dane Bernbach's advertisement]

3. indicates individual possession when appended to each noun in a sequence	[Appleton's and Delaney's report] [John's, Bill's, and Tim's boats] [Benton & Bowles' and Doyle Dane Bernbach's advertisements]
4. indicates possession when appended to the final element of a compound construction	[Norfolk, Virginia's newest shopping center contains a wide variety of stores.] [XYZ Corporation's order]
5. indicates understood possession	[The book is at your bookseller's.]
6. marks omissions in contractions	[isn't] [you're] [aren't] [o'clock]
7. marks omissions of numerals	[the class of '67]
8. often forms plurals of letters, figures, or words especially when they are referred to as letters, figures, or words	[His *1*'s and *7*'s looked alike.] [She has trouble pronouncing her *the*'s.] [five YF-16's] [the 1970's] *also* [the 1970s]
9. is often used with *s* in expressions of time, measurement, and money *but* is not used with a plural noun used as a modifier	[a dollar's worth of gas] [a year's subscription] [ten cents' worth] [six weeks' vacation] *but* [earnings statement] [sales projection]
10. is used with *s* before a gerund or gerund phrase	[She objected to the editor's changing her material.]

[ ] BRACKETS

1. set off extraneous data (as editorial comments especially within quoted material)	[He wrote, "I recieved [sic] your letter."]
2. function as parentheses within parentheses	[Bowman Act (22 Stat., Ch. 4, § [or sec.] 4, p. 50)]

: COLON

1. introduces a clause or phrase that explains, illustrates, amplifies, or restates what has gone before	[The sentence was poorly constructed: it lacked both unity and coherence.]
2. directs attention to an appositive	[He had only one pleasure: eating.]
3. introduces a series	[Three countries were represented: England, France, and Belgium.]
4. introduces lengthy quoted matter set off from a running text by blocked indentation but not by quotation marks	[I quote from Part I of the market study:]

5. separates elements in statements of time and in bibliographic and biblical references	[8:30 a.m.] [New York: Smith Publishing Company] [John 4:10]
6. separates titles and subtitles (as of books)	[*CBS: Reflections in a Bloodshot Eye*]
7. punctuates the salutation in a business letter featuring the mixed punctuation pattern	[Gentlemen:] [Dear Bob:] [Dear Mr. Smith:]
8. punctuates memo and government correspondence headings, and some subject lines in general business letters	[TO:] [THROUGH:] [VIA:] [SUBJECT:] [REFERENCE:]
9. separates writer/dictator/typist initials in the identification lines of business letters	[WAL:coc] [WAL:WEB:coc]
10. separates carbon copy or blind carbon copy abbreviations from the initials or names of copy recipients in business letters	[cc: RWP JES] [bcc: MWK FCM]

, COMMA

1. separates main clauses joined by coordinating conjunctions (such as *and, but, for, nor, or,* and sometimes *so* and *yet*) and very short clauses not so joined NOTE: Two very brief and tightly connected clauses joined by a coordinating conjunction and two predicates also so joined may be unpunctuated.	[She knew very little about him, and he volunteered nothing.] [He wanted to see her, so she went to his office.] [She knew, she was there, she saw it.] [He had found the motive, anyone could.] *but* [We have tested the computer and we are pleased.] [He discussed several important marketing problems in great detail and followed them with an appraisal of current sales.]
2. sets off an adverbial clause that precedes a main clause	[When she found that her friends had deserted her, she sat down and cried.] [Although the airport was shut down for an hour, I was still able to fly home that night.]
3. sets off an introductory phrase (as a participial, infinitive, or prepositional phrase) that precedes a main clause NOTE: If a phrase or a noun clause is the subject of the sentence, it is unpunctuated.	[Having made that decision, he turned to other matters.] [To understand this situation fully, you have to be familiar with the background.] [On Monday, he left early.] *but* [To have followed your plan would have been dishonest.] [Whatever is worth doing is worth doing well.]

4. sets off from the rest of a sentence interrupting transitional words and expressions (such as *on the contrary, on the other hand*), conjunctive adverbs (such as *consequently, furthermore, however*), and expressions that introduce an illustration or example (such as *namely, for example*)	[Your second question, on the other hand, is unanswerable.] [The market predictions, however, remain fluid.] [He expects to travel through two countries, namely, France and England.] [He believes in responsibility, i.e., corporate responsibility.]
5. often sets off contrasting and opposing expressions within sentences	[I note that he has changed his style, not his ethics.] [The cost is not $65.00, but $56.65.] [A holiday, but not a vacation day, is still open.] *but*
NOTE: When *and, or, either . . . or,* or *neither . . . nor* join items in a pair or in a series, the series is internally unpunctuated.	[The cost is either $65.00 or $56.65.] [A holiday and a vacation day are still open.] [He has changed neither his style nor his ethics nor his attitude.]
6. separates words, phrases, or clauses in series joined at the end by a coordinating conjunction	[Men, women, and children crowded into the square.] [He was young, eager, and restless.] [It requires one to travel constantly, to have no private life, and to need no income. . . . —Sara Davidson]
NOTE: The final comma before the conjunction in a series is optional; its purpose is to clarify meaning; *compare* COMMA, RULE 13	[The hors d'oeuvres consisted of celery, pâté, olives, onions, and mushrooms.] *but meaning could be different* [The hors d'oeuvres consisted of celery, pâté, olives, onions and mushrooms.]
7. separates coordinate adjectives and phrases modifying the same word; *see also page* 232 NOTE: Two or more tightly connected adjectives in series each of which modifies the same word or a whole phrase may not require punctuation.	[It was a bright, beautiful, sunny day.] [They prepared a thorough, organized, in-depth study of the sales figures.] *but* [The company rented office space in a new 90-story concrete and glass building.] [a 15-cu.ft. upright freezer]
8. sets off from the rest of a sentence parenthetic elements (as nonrestrictive modifiers and nonrestrictive appositives) NOTE: The comma does not set off restrictive or essential modifiers or appositives required to give a sentence or a phrase meaning.	[Our guide, who wore a blue beret, was an experienced traveler.] [We visited Gettysburg, the site of a famous battle.] [The Manufacturing Manager, Joseph Dowd, attended the meeting.] *but* [the late astronaut Gus Grissom]
9. introduces a direct quotation, terminates a direct quotation that is neither a question nor an exclamation, and encloses segments of a split quotation	[Jim said, "I am leaving."] ["I am leaving," Jim said.] ["I am leaving," Jim said with determination, "even if you want me to stay."]
10. sets off words in direct address, absolute phrases, and mild interjections	[We would like to discuss your account, Mr. Baker.] [I fear the encounter, his temper being what it is.] [Ah, that's my idea of a sensible man.]

11. separates a tag question from the rest of a sentence	[It's been a fine sales conference, hasn't it?]
12. indicates the omission of a word or words, and especially a word or words used earlier in a sentence	[Common stocks are favored by some investors; bonds, by others.]
13. is used to avoid ambiguity and also to emphasize a particular phrase; *compare* COMMA, RULE 6, NOTE	[To Mary, Jane was someone special.] [The more accessories on a car, the higher the price.]
14. groups numerals into units of three in separating thousands, millions, etc.; it is generally not used with numbers of four or more digits in set combinations; *see also* NUMERALS, RULE 8	[Smithville, pop. 100,000] *but* [3600 rpm] [the year 1980] [page 1411] [1127 Smith Street] [Room 3000]
15. punctuates the date line of a business letter, an informal letter, and the expression of dates in running texts	[January 1, 19--] [On January 1, 19--, this company reported net profits of. . . .]
16. follows a personal-letter salutation	[Dear Bob,]
17. follows the complimentary close of a business letter or of an informal letter featuring the mixed punctuation pattern	[Very truly yours,] [Affectionately,]
18. sometimes separates names from corporate titles in envelope address blocks, inside addresses, and signature blocks	[Mr. John P. Dow, President SWC Corporation Smithville, ST 56789] [Very truly yours, Lee H. Cobb, Editor General Reference Books]
19. may separate elements within some official corporate names	[Leedy Manufacturing Co., Inc.] [Manville Rubber Products, Inc.]
20. punctuates an inverted name	[Smith, John W.]
21. separates a surname from a following academic, honorary, religious, governmental, or military title	[John W. Smith, M.D.] [John W. Smith, Esq.] [The Reverend John W. Smith, S.J.] [General John W. Smith, USA]
22. sets off geographical names (as that of a state or county from that of a city), items in dates, and addresses from the rest of a running text	[Shreveport, Louisiana, is the site of a large air base.] [On December 7, 1941, Pearl Harbor was attacked.] [Mail your check to: XYZ Corporation, 1234 Smith Boulevard, Smithville, ST 56789.]

DASH

1. usually marks an abrupt change or break in the continuity of a sentence	[When in 1960 the stockpile was sold off—indeed, dumped as surplus —natural-rubber sales were hard hit. —Barry Commoner]
2. is sometimes used in place of other punctuation (as the comma) when special emphasis is required (as in advertising)	[Mail your subscription—now!]
3. introduces a summary statement that follows a series of words or phrases	[Oil, steel, and wheat—these are the sinews of industrialization.]
4. often precedes the attribution of a quotation	[The next question was . . . how many administrative secretaries to a zone. —Samuel T. Rose]
5. may occur inside quotation marks if considered part of the quoted matter	["I'm just not going to—" and then he broke off very abruptly.]
6. may be used with the exclamation point or the question mark	[The faces of the crash victims—how bloody!—were shown on TV.] [Your question—was it on our proposed merger?—just can't be answered.]

● ● ● ELLIPSIS *or* SUSPENSION POINTS ● ● ● ●

1. indicates by three periods the omission of one or more words within a quoted passage	[The figures are accumulated for a month . . . and then the department's percentage of effectiveness is calculated. —Joyce B. Jewell]
2. indicates by four periods (the last of which represents a period) the omission of one or more sentences within a quoted passage or the omission of a word or words at the end of a sentence	[That recovering the manuscripts would be worth almost any effort is without question. . . . The monetary value of a body of Shakespeare's manuscripts would be almost incalculable. —Charlton Ogburn] [It will take scholars years to determine conclusively the origins, the history, and, most importantly, the significance of the finds. . . . —Robert Morse]
3. is used as a stylistic device especially in advertising copy to catch and hold the reader's attention	[An indispensable survival manual for job seekers . . . must reading for personnel managers. . . . —*Publishers Weekly*]
4. indicates halting speech or an unfinished sentence in dialogue	["I'd like to . . . that is . . . if you don't mind. . . ." He faltered and then stopped speaking.]

5. may be used as leaders (as in tables of contents) when spaced and extended for some length across a page NOTE: leaders should be in perfect alignment vertically and should end precisely at the same point.	[Punctuation . . . . page 1 Capitalization . . . . page 10]
6. usually indicates omission of one or more lines of poetry when extended the length of a line	[Thus driven By the bright shadow of that lovely dream, ... He fled. —Percy Bysshe Shelley]

! EXCLAMATION POINT

1. ends an emphatic phrase or sentence	[Mail your subscription—now!]
2. terminates an emphatic interjection	[Encore!]

- HYPHEN

1. marks division at the end of a line concluding with a syllable of a word that is to be carried over to the next line	[mill- stone] [pas- sion]
2. is used between some prefix and root combinations, such as prefix + proper name; some prefixes ending with vowels + root; sometimes prefix + word beginning often with the same vowel; stressed prefix + root word, especially when this combination is similar to a different word	 [pre-Renaissance art] [re-ink] *but* [reissue] [co-opted] *but* [cooperate] [re-cover a sofa] *but* [recover from an illness]
3. is used in some compounds, especially those containing prepositions; consult a dictionary when in doubt of styling	[president-elect] [attorney-at-law] [air-conditioned his house] *but* [bought an air conditioner]
4. is often used between elements of a compound modifier in attributive position in order to avoid ambiguity	[He is a small-business man.] *but* [He is a man who owns a small business.]
5. suspends the first part of a hyphened compound when joined with another hyphened compound in attributive position	[a six- or eight-cylinder engine] *but* [an engine of six or eight cylinders]

6. is used in expressing written-out numbers between 21 and 99	[forty-one] [one hundred twenty-eight]
7. is used between the numerator and the denominator in writing out fractions especially when they are used as modifiers; however, fractions used as nouns are usually styled as open compounds	[a two-thirds majority of the stockholders] *but* [used two thirds of the stationery]
8. serves as an arbitrary equivalent of the phrase "(up) to and including" when used between numbers and dates	[pages 40–98] [the decade 1960–1970]
9. is used in the compounding of two or more capitalized names *but* is not used when a single capitalized name is in attributive position	[caught a New York-Chicago flight] [U.S.-U.S.S.R. détente] *but* [a New York garbage strike] [Middle East exports]

( ) PARENTHESES

1. set off supplementary, parenthetic, or explanatory material when the interruption is more marked than that usually indicated by commas and when the inclusion of such material does not essentially alter the meaning of the sentence; *see also* CAPITALIZATION, RULE 7	[Three old typewriters (all broken) will be scrapped.] [He is hoping (as we all are) that the economy will turn around.] [We appreciate your nice remarks (especially your reference to our New York salesman).]
2. enclose Arabic numerals confirming a typed-out number in a general text or in a legal document	[Delivery will be made in thirty (30) days.] [The fee for your services is Two Thousand Dollars ($2,000.00), payable. . . .]
3. may enclose numbers or letters separating and heading individual elements or items in a series	[We must set forth (1) our long-term goals, (2) our immediate objectives, and (3) the means at our disposal.]
4. enclose abbreviations synonymous with typed-out forms and occurring after those forms	[. . . whose chief products are polyethylene and polyvinyl chloride (PVC) bottles and containers. . . . —Ethyl Corporation *Annual Report*]
5. indicate alternate terms and omissions (as in form letters)	[Please sign the enclosed form(s) and return. . . .] [On (date) we mailed you. . . .]
6. are used as follows with other punctuation: **a.** If the parenthetic expression is an independent sentence standing alone at the end of another sentence, its first word is capitalized and a period is typed <u>inside</u> the last parenthesis.	 [The discussion was held in the boardroom. (The results are still confidential.)]

b. Parenthetic material within a sentence may be internally punctuated by a question mark, a period after an abbreviation only, an exclamation point, or a set of quotation marks.	[Years ago, someone (who?) told me. . . .] [The conference was held in Vancouver (that's in B.C.).] [Sales this year have been better (knock on wood!), but. . . .] [He was depressed ("I must resign") and refused to promise anything.]
c. No punctuation mark should be placed directly before parenthetic material in a sentence; if a break is required, the punctuation should be placed after the final parenthesis.	[I'll get back to you tomorrow (Monday), when I have more details.]

• PERIOD

1. terminates sentences or sentence fragments that are neither interrogative nor exclamatory	[Take dictation.] [She took dictation.] [She asked whether he wanted her to take dictation.]
2. often terminates polite requests especially in business correspondence	[Will you please return these forms as soon as possible.]
3. punctuates some abbreviations and some contractions, as	[f.o.b.] [a.k.a.] [sec'y.] [Ass'n.]
a. courtesy titles and honorifics backed by a strong tradition of punctuation	[Mr.] [Mrs.] [Ms.] [Dr.] [Prof.] [Rev.] [Hon.] [Esq.] [Jr.] [Sr.] [Ph.D.] [Litt.D.]
b. some abbreviations (as of measure) especially when absence of punctuation could cause misreading	[98.6° F.] *also* [98.6° F] [p. 20] [Paper, 521 ff.] [18 in.] [No. 2 pencils] [fig. 15]
c. abbreviations of Latin words and phrases commonly used in texts	[etc.] [i.e.] [e.g.] [c. *or* ca. *or* circ.] [q.v.] [viz.]
d. abbreviations of Latin phrases used in footnotes	[Ibid.] [Op. cit.] [Loc. cit.]
e. compass points NOTE: Punctuation styling varies.	[1400 Sixteenth Street, N.W.] *or* [1400 Sixteenth Street, NW.] *or* [1400 Sixteenth Street, NW]
f. some geographical-name abbreviations NOTE: Punctuation styling varies.	[U.S.-U.S.S.R. détente] *or* [US-USSR détente] *but not* [U.S.-USSR détente] *and not* [US-U.S.S.R. détente]
g. abbreviated elements of some official corporate names	[Dowden, Hutchinson & Ross, Inc.]
4. is used with an individual's initials	[Mr. W. A. Morton]

5. is used after Roman numerals in enumerations and outlines but not with Roman numerals used as part of a title	[I. Objectives] *but* [Queen Elizabeth II]
6. is often used after Arabic numerals in enumerations whose numerals stand alone	[Required skills are: 1. Shorthand 2. Typing 3. Transcription]

QUESTION MARK

1. terminates a direct question	[Who signed the memo?] ["Who signed the memo?" he asked.]
2. punctuates each element of an interrogative series that is neither numbered nor lettered; however, only one such mark punctuates a numbered or lettered interrogative series	[Can you give us a reasonable forecast? back up your predictions? compare them with last-quarter earnings?] *but* [Can you (1) give us a reasonable forecast (2) back up your predictions (3) supply enough figures (4) compare them with last-quarter earnings?]
3. indicates the writer's ignorance or uncertainty	[John Jones, the President (?) of that company said. . . .] [Omar Khayyám, Persian poet (?–?1123)]

“ ” QUOTATION MARKS, DOUBLE

1. enclose direct quotations in conventional usage	[He said, "I am leaving."] *but* [He said that he was leaving.]
2. enclose fragments of quoted matter when reproduced exactly as originally stated	[The agreement makes it quite clear that he "will be paid only upon receipt of an acceptable manuscript."]
3. enclose words or phrases borrowed from others, words used in a special way, and often a word of marked informality when it is introduced into formal writing	[As the leader of a gang of "droogs," he is altogether frightening, as is this film. —Liz Smith] [He called himself "emperor," but he was just a cheap tinhorn dictator.] [He was arrested for smuggling "smack."]
4. enclose titles of reports, catalogs, short poems, short stories, articles, lectures, chapters of books, songs, short musical compositions, and radio and TV programs; *compare* ITALICIZATION, RULE 6	[the report "College Graduates and Their Employers"] [the catalog "Automotive Parts and Accessories"] [Robert Frost's "Dust of Snow"] [Pushkin's "Queen of Spades"] [The third chapter of *Treasure Island* is entitled "The Black Spot."] ["America the Beautiful"] [Ravel's "Bolero"] [NBC's "Today Show"]

5. are used with other punctuation marks in the following ways:	
the period and the comma fall within the quotation marks	[He was arrested for smuggling "smack."] ["I am leaving," he said.] [His camera was described as "waterproof," but "moisture-resistant" would have been a better description.]
the semicolon falls outside the quotation marks	[He spoke of his "little cottage in the country"; he might have called it a mansion.]
the dash, question mark, and the exclamation point fall within the quotation marks when they refer to the quoted matter only; they fall outside when they refer to the whole sentence	[He asked, "When did you leave?"] [What is the meaning of "the open door"?] [The sergeant shouted, "Halt!"] [Save us from his "mercy"!]
6. are not used with quoted material comprising more than three typed lines and only one paragraph: such material is blocked and single-spaced internally but double-spaced top and bottom to set it off from the rest of the text	[An article entitled "The Secretary in the Management Function" on page 9 of the December, 1975, issue of *The Secretary* makes this point: Good supervision comes from good planning before trying to meet goals, knowing the work and duties of each subordinate, carefully assigning the work, communicating both orally and through written facilities, and evaluating the work and correcting the deviations. This, then, summarizes the major aspects of secretarial supervision.]
7. are used with long quoted matter comprising more than three typed lines and having two or more paragraphs: double quotation marks are typed at the beginning of each paragraph and at the end of the final paragraph	[*U.S. News & World Report* offers these economic predictions: "Recession, marked by sharp cutbacks in jobs and output, will continue into spring. "Economic activity will then show little change—and no real improvement—for about three months, with one possible exception: Home building may experience a little recovery before summer. "After the middle of the year, a broad upturn in business will develop, very sluggish at first, but gaining speed by the end of the year." This material is included in an article entitled "Uphill Road for Business" on page 13 of the February 17, 1975, issue of the magazine.]

‘ ’ QUOTATION MARKS, SINGLE

1. enclose a quotation within a quotation in conventional English	[The witness said, "I distinctly heard him say, 'Don't be late,' and then I heard the door close."]

2. are sometimes used in place of double quotation marks especially in British usage NOTE: When both single and double quotation marks occur at the end of a sentence, the period typically falls within both sets of marks.	[The witness said, 'I distinctly heard him say, "Don't be late," and then I heard the door close.'] [The witness said, "I distinctly heard him say, 'Don't be late.'"]

; SEMICOLON

1. links main clauses not joined by coordinating conjunctions	[Some people are good managers in their willingness to accept responsibility and delegate authority with wisdom; others do not measure up.]
2. links main clauses joined by conjunctive adverbs (as *consequently, furthermore, however*)	[Speeding is illegal and dangerous; furthermore, it is uneconomical in view of current gasoline prices.]
3. links clauses which themselves contain commas even when such clauses are linked by coordinating conjunctions; *see page 236 for a list of coordinating conjunctions*	[Thus our search was for people who could think in very fundamental ways, who could buttress their views with careful analysis; people who were able to hang in during deliberations. . . . —Frank Newman]
4. often occurs before phrases or abbreviations (as *for example, for instance, that is, that is to say, namely, e.g.*, or *i.e.*) that introduce expansions or series	[We are pleased with your performance; for example, the large number of sales calls, the sizable orders. . . .]

/ VIRGULE

1. separates alternatives	[. . . designs intended for high-heat and/or high-speed applications. —F. S. Badger, Jr.]
2. separates successive divisions (as months or years) of an extended period	[the fiscal year 1975/76]
3. often represents *per* in numeral + abbreviation combinations	[9 ft/sec] [20 km/hr] [4000 bbl/da] [200 gal/min]
4. often is an arbitrary punctuation mark within an abbreviation	[B/L] [L/C] [C/D]
5. serves as a dividing line between run-in lines of poetry in quotations	[Say, sages, what's the charm on earth/ Can turn death's dart aside? —Robert Burns]

PUNCTUATION-SPACINATION SUMMARY

Position	Example
Degree of Spacination **No Space**	
1. between any word and the punctuation immediately following it	[Here is the car.] [Is the car here?] [Here is the car!] [The car is here, isn't it?] [The car is here; however, I don't need it now.] [The car is here: now, do I get in, or not?] [The car is here. . . .]
2. between quotation marks and the quoted matter	["I am leaving," he said.] [He said, "I am leaving."]
3. between parentheses and the words or figures they enclose	[He is (should I say it?) just a bit peculiar.] [(1)]
4. between brackets and the words or figures they enclose	[had recieved [sic] the gift]
5. between initials comprising punctuated or unpunctuated abbreviations	[f.o.b.] [A.D.] [i.e.] [p.m.] [GATT] [MIRV] [CREEP] [PhD *or* Ph.D.]
6. between elements in figure + abbreviation or other word combinations when they are in attributive position	[a 200-hp engine] [a $15-million project]
7. between ellipses in leaders except for initial and terminal ellipsis points which are preceded & followed by one space, respectively; *compare* ONE SPACE, RULE 13	[Item 1 .... page 1]
8. between elements of hyphened compounds	[to air-condition a room] [$10-$20] [United States-Canadian tariffs]
9. before or after an apostrophe within or attached to a word	[isn't] [o'clock] [the boys' story]
10. on either side of a dash	[If she understands the contract—and I'm sure she does—we'll have no trouble.]
11. between words, letters, or figures separated by a virgule	[1976/77] [and/or]
12. between figures and symbols	[$12.95] [75%] [90°F] [7.654] [8¢] [$.08]
13. within units expressing time of day	[9:30 a.m.] [9:30 p.m.]
14. in identification lines, and in carbon copy notations indicating only one recipient designated by initials	[FCM:hol] [MWK:FCM:hol] [cc:FCM] [bcc:MWK]
15. between footnoted textual material and the footnote symbol or number	[. . . is a prime factor in successful management"*] *or* [. . . is a prime factor in successful management."[1]]
Degree of Spacination **One Space**	
1. after a comma	[The car is here, isn't it?] [Scarsdale, New York] [January 1, 19—]

Position	Example
Degree of Spacination One Space	
2. after a semicolon	[The car is here; however, I don't need it now.]
3. after a period following an initial	[Mr. H. C. Matthews]
4. before and after *x* meaning "by" or "times"	[a 3 x 5 card] [3 x 5 = 15]
5. after a suspended hyphen	[the long- and short-term results]
6. on each side of a hyphen in the Simplified Letter signature block	[SAMUEL T. LEE - SENIOR EDITOR]
7. on each side of a hyphen in some street addresses	[2135 - 71st Street, NW]
8. between a question mark and the first letter of the next word in a series question	[Are you coming today? tomorrow? the day after?]
9. between Postal Service state abbreviations and ZIP Codes	[Smithville, ST 56789]
10. after the heading cc that is unpunctuated in letters following the open punctuation pattern and that introduces a list of names	[cc Mr. Slaughter Mr. Tate Mr. Watson]
11. between a final quotation mark and the rest of a sentence	["I am leaving," he said.]
12. in a footnote entry between the superscript figure and the first letter of the first word following it	[[1] Albert H. Marckwardt, *American English* (New York: Oxford University Press, 1958), p. 94.]
13. between ellipses in leaders except for initial and terminal ellipsis points which are preceded and followed by at least two spaces, respectively (this styling is optional); *compare* NO SPACE, RULE 7	[Item 1 . . . . . page 1]
Degree of Spacination Two Spaces	
1. after a period ending a sentence	[Here is the car. Do you want to get in?]
2. after a question mark or an exclamation point ending a sentence	[Get out of here! Well, what are you waiting for? I've said enough.]
3. after a colon in running texts, in bibliographic references, in publication titles, and in letter or memorandum headings	[The car is here: Now, do I get in, or not?] [New York: Macmillan, 1976] [*Typewriting: A Guide*] [SUBJECT: Project X]
4. after a carbon copy notation punctuated with a colon + a full name	[cc: Mr. Johnson]
5. after a figure + a period that introduces an item in an enumeration	[The following skills are essential: 1. typing 2. shorthand]

7.7

WORD DIVISION

In the United States more time and energy have been spent worrying about the division of words at the end of a printed or typed line than the subject merits. The very fact that widely used and respected dictionaries published by different houses indicate different points at which to divide many words is evidence enough that there is no absolute right or wrong, and that for numerous words there are acceptable end-of-line division alternatives. The best policy to follow in individual instances is to consult an adequate dictionary whose main entries indicate points of division. End-of-line division is not based solely upon pronunciation, and in any case there is great variety in pronunciation throughout the English-speaking world. The question of end-of-line division occurs only in written contexts, and it is perhaps unreasonable to expect the spoken form of the language to dictate a consistent set of principles for an essentially mechanical problem.

Common sense suggests some guidelines which will help to minimize the time spent consulting a dictionary. For instance, the division of a single letter at the beginning or end of a word should be avoided. On the one hand, in typed material a single letter hanging onto the end of a line with a hyphen may be dropped to the next line without leaving unsightly right-hand margins, and in printed material the space required for two characters (the letter and the hyphen) is, in most circumstances, easily filled. On the other hand, if there is room for a hyphen at the end of a line, there is room for the last letter of a word in its place. Thus, *ablaze* and *oleo* should not be divided, for such divisions as

a- *o-* *ole-*
blaze *leo* *o*

would detract from rather than add to the appearance of the page.

Compounds containing one or more hyphens will cause a reader less trouble if divided after the hyphen. For the words *bumper-to-bumper, smoking-room,* and *vice-president* the divisions

bumper- *bumper-to-* *smoking-* *vice-*
to-bumper *bumper* *room* *president*

are less obtrusive than such divisions as

bum- *bumper-to-bum-* *smok-* *vice-pres-*
per-to-bumper *per* *ing-room* *ident*

although there are no "rules" against the latter set of examples, and such divisions may occasionally prove necessary especially in narrow columns.

Similarly, closed compounds are best divided between component elements; thus, the divisions

every- *may-* *speaker-*
one *flower* *phone*

appear more natural and will cause the reader less trouble than

ev- *mayflow-* *speak-*
eryone *er* *erphone*

though divisions such as the ones above may be required in exceptional circumstances.

For words that are not compound, it is best to consult a dictionary or a guide to word division, and in order to maintain greatest consistency it is preferable always to consult the same source. Another general principle is to avoid end-of-line division altogether whenever possible, especially in successive lines.

There are, in addition, some specific instances in which one should avoid end-of-line division if at all possible. These are as follows:

1. The last word in a paragraph should not be divided.
2. The last word on a page (as of a business letter or a memorandum) should not be divided.
3. Items joined by *and/or* and the coordinating conjunction *and/or* itself should not be divided.
4. Proper names, courtesy titles, and following titles (as *Esq.*) should not be divided either on envelopes, in inside addresses, or in running texts:

correct	*incorrect*
. . . to Mr. J. R. Smith.	. . . to Mr. J. R. Smith.

The one exception to this rule is the separation of long honorary titles from names especially in envelope address blocks and in inside addresses where space is often limited:

correct	*incorrect*
The Honorable John R. Smith	The Honorable John R. Smith

5. If dates must be divided (as in running texts), the division should occur only between the day and the year:

correct	*incorrect*
. . . arrived on January 1, 19--.	. . . arrived on Jan- uary 1, 19--.
. . . arrived on January 1, 19--.	. . . arrived on January 1, 19--.

6. Set units (as of time and measure) as well as single monetary units should not be divided:

correct	*incorrect*
. . . at 10:00 a.m.	. . . at 10:00 a.m.
. . . had a temperature of 98.6°F.	. . . had a temperature of 98.6° F.
. . . a fee of $4,900.50.	. . . a fee of $4,900.- 50.

7. Abbreviations should not be divided:

correct	*incorrect*
. . . received the M.B.A. from Harvard.	. . . received the M.B.- A. from Harvard.

8. Compound geographic designations (as city + state combinations) should not be divided:

correct	*incorrect*
. . . to St. Paul, Minnesota.	. . . to St. Paul, Minnesota.

7.8

COMPONENTS OF DISCOURSE

The word *discourse* is defined in *Webster's New Collegiate Dictionary* as "formal and orderly and usually extended expression of thought. . . ." Thus, no guide to effective communication can ignore the fundamental components of discourse: the word, the phrase, the clause, the sentence, and the paragraph. Each of these increasingly complex units contributes to the expression of a writer's points, ideas, and concepts.

The word, of course, is the simplest component of discourse. Words have been traditionally classified into eight parts of speech. This classification system is determined chiefly by a word's inflectional features, its general grammatical functions, and its positioning within a sentence. On the following pages, the parts of speech—the adjective, adverb, conjunction, interjection, noun, preposition, pronoun, and verb—are alphabetically listed and briefly discussed. Each part of speech is introduced by an applicable definition from *Webster's New Collegiate Dictionary*. The phrase, the clause, the sentence, and the paragraph are discussed later in this section.

PARTS OF SPEECH

Adjective

[2]**adjective** *n* **:** a word belonging to one of the major form classes in any of numerous languages and typically serving as a modifier of a noun to denote a quality of the thing named, to indicate its quantity or extent, or to specify a thing as distinct from something else

The main structural feature of an adjective is its ability to indicate degrees of comparison (positive, comparative, superlative) by addition of the suffixal endings *-er/-est* to the base word (*clean, cleaner, cleanest*), by addition of *more/most* or *less/least* before the base word (*meaningful, more meaningful, most meaningful; less meaningful, least meaningful*), or by use of irregular forms (*bad, worse, worst*). Some adjectives are compared in two ways (as *smoother, smoothest/more smooth, most smooth*), while still others (as *prior, optimum,* or *maximum*), called "absolute adjectives," are ordinarily not compared since they are felt to represent ultimate or highest conditions.

Adjectives may occur in the following positions within sentences:

1. preceding the nouns they modify, as
   the *black* hat
   a *dark brown* coat
2. following the nouns they modify, as
   an executive *par excellence*
   I painted my room *blue.*
3. following the verb *to be* in predicate-adjective position, as
   The hat is *black.*
   and following other linking (or "sense") verbs in predicate-adjective position, as
   He seems *intelligent.*
   The food tastes *stale.*
   I feel *queasy.*
4. following some transitive verbs used in the passive voice, as
   The room was painted *blue.*
   The passengers were found *dead* at the crash site.

Adjectives may describe something or represent a quality, kind, or condition (a *sick* man); they may point out or indicate something (*these* men); or they may convey the force of questions (*Whose* office is this?). Some adjectives (as *Orwellian, Churchillian, Keynesian,* and others) are called "proper adjectives." They are derived from proper nouns, take their meanings from what characterizes the nouns, and are capitalized.

The following are general points of adjective usage:

Absolute adjectives Some adjectives (as *prior, maximum, optimum, minimum, first,* and the like) ordinarily admit no comparison because they represent ultimate conditions. However, printed usage indicates that many writers do compare and qualify some of these words in order to show connotations and shades of meaning that they feel are less than absolute. The word *unique* is a case in point:

. . . we were fairly *unique*. . . .
—J. D. Salinger

. . . a rather *unique* concept. . . .
—E. Ohmer Milton

. . . some of the more *unique* and colorful customs. . . .
—Ernest Osborne

. . . the most *unique* human faculty. . . .
—Robert Plank

The more we study him, the less *unique* he seems. . . .
—James Joyce

While many examples may be found of qualification and/or comparison of *unique,* it is difficult to find printed evidence showing comparison of a word like *optimum.* When one is in doubt about the inflection of such an adjective, one should consult a dictionary.

Coordinate adjectives Adjectives that share equal relationships to the nouns they modify are called coordinate adjectives and are separated from each other by commas:

a *concise, coherent, intelligent* essay

However, in the following locution containing the set phrase *short story*

a *concise, coherent* short story

the adjectives *concise* and *coherent* are neither parallel nor equal in function or relationship with *short* which is an essential element of the total compound *short story.* The test to use before inserting commas is to insert *and* between questionable adjectives, and then to decide whether the sentence still makes sense. Whereas *and* could fit between *coherent* and *intelligent* in the first example, it could not work between *coherent* and *short* in the second example.

Adjective/noun agreement The number (singular or plural) of a demonstrative adjective (*this, that, these, those*) should agree with that of the noun it modifies:

these kinds of typewriters *not* these kind of typewriters
those sorts of jobs *not* those sort of jobs
this type of person *not* these type of people

Double comparisons Double comparisons should be avoided since they are considered nonstandard:

the easiest
or
the most easy solution *not* the most easiest solution

an easier
or
a more easy method *not* a more easier method

Incomplete or understood comparisons Some comparisons are left incomplete because the context clearly implies the comparison; hence, the expressions

Get *better* buys here!
We have *lower* prices.

These are commonly used especially in advertising. It should be understood, however, that the use of incomplete comparisons is often considered careless or illogical especially in formal writing.

Adverb

[1]**ad•verb.** . . *n* . . . : a word belonging to one of the major form classes in any of numerous languages, typically serving as a modifier of a verb, an adjective, another adverb, a preposition, a phrase, a clause, or a sentence, and expressing some relation of manner or quality, place, time, degree, number, cause, opposition, affirmation, or denial

An adverb admits three degrees of comparison (positive, comparative, superlative) ordinarily by addition of *more/most* or *less/least* before the base word (*quickly, more quickly, most quickly*). However, a few adverbs (such as *fast, slow, loud, soft, early, late,* and *quick*) may be compared in two ways: by the method described above, or by the addition of the suffixal endings *-er/-est* to the base word (*quick, quicker, quickest*).

Adverbs may occur in the following positions within sentences:

1. before the subject, as
   Then he announced his resignation.
2. after the subject, as
   He *then* announced his resignation.
3. before the predicate, as
   He praised the committee's work and *then* announced his resignation.
4. at the end of the predicate, as
   He announced his resignation *then.*
5. in various other positions (as before adjectives or other adverbs), as
   He also made an *equally* important announcement—that of his resignation.
   He adjourned the meeting *very* abruptly.

Adverbs answer the following questions: "when?" (Please reply *at once*), "how long?" (She wants to live here *forever*), "where?" (I work *there*), "in what direction?" (Move the lever *upward*), "how?" (The staff moved *expeditiously* on the project), and "how much?" or "to what degree?" (It is *rather* hot).

Adverbs modify verbs, adjectives, or other adverbs, as

He studied the balance sheet *carefully.*

He gave the balance sheet *very* careful study.

He studied the balance sheet *very* carefully.

and may also serve as clause joiners or sentence connectors, as

clause joiner
You may share our car pool; *however,* please be ready at 7:00 a.m.

sentence connector
He thoroughly enjoyed the symposium. *Indeed,* he was fascinated by the presentations.

In addition, adverbs may be essential elements of two-word verb collocations commonly having separate entry in dictionaries, such as

He looked *over* the figures.
He looked the figures *over.*

The waiter took the tray *away.*
The waiter took *away* the tray.

See also page 237 for a discussion of conjunctive adverbs, words like *however* in the example on page 233 that are adverbs functioning as conjunctions in sentences. The following are general points of adverb usage:

Placement within a sentence Adverbs are generally positioned as close as possible to the words they modify if such a position will not result in misinterpretation by the reader:

unclear
The project that he hoped his staff would support completely disappointed him.

Does the writer mean "complete staff support" or "complete disappointment"? Thus, the adverb may be moved to another position or the sentence may be recast, depending on intended meaning:

clear
The project that he hoped his staff would completely support had disappointed him.
or
He was completely disappointed in the project that he had hoped his staff would support.

Emphasis Adverbs (such as *just* and *only*) are often used to emphasize certain other words. Thus, a writer should be aware of the various reader reactions that may result from the positioning of an adverb in a sentence:

strong connotation of curtness
He just nodded to me as he passed.
but
emphasis on timing of the action
He nodded to me *just* as he passed.

In some positions and contexts these adverbs can be ambiguous:

I will only tell it to you.

Does the writer mean that he will only tell it, not put it in writing, or does he mean that he will tell no one else? If the latter interpretation is intended, a slight shift of position would remove the uncertainty, as

I will tell it only to you.

Adverbs vs. adjectives: examples of misuse

a. Adverbs but not adjectives modify action verbs:
not He answered very harsh.
but He answered very harshly.

b. Complements referring to the subject of a sentence and occurring after linking verbs conventionally take adjectives but not adverbs:
questionable I feel badly.
The letter sounded strongly.
acceptable I feel bad.
The letter sounded strong.
but
acceptable He looks good these days.
He looks well these days.

In the last two examples, either *good* or *well* is acceptable, because both words may be adjectives or adverbs, and here they are functioning as adjectives in the sense of "being healthy."

c. Adverbs but not adjectives modify adjectives and other adverbs:
not She seemed dreadful tired.
but She seemed dreadfully tired.

Double negatives A combination of two negative adverbs (as *not* + *hardly, never, scarcely,* and the like) used to express a single negative idea is considered substandard:

not We cannot see scarcely any reason why we should adopt this book.

but We can see scarcely any reason why we should adopt this book.

We can't / cannot } see any reason why we should adopt this book.

Conjunction

con•junc•tion . . . *n* . . . **4 :** an uninflected linguistic form that joins together sentences, clauses, phrases, or words **:** CONNECTIVE

Conjunctions exhibit no characteristic inflectional or suffixal features. They may occur in numerous positions within sentences; however, they ordinarily do not appear in final position unless the sentence is elliptical. Three major types of conjunctions are listed and illustrated according to their functions in the table on page 236.

A comma is traditionally used before a coordinating conjunction linking coordinate clauses especially when these clauses are lengthy or when the writer desires to emphasize their distinctness from one another:

The economy is in serious condition, and it shows few signs of improvement.

Shall we consider this person's application, or shall we consider that one's?

We do not discriminate between men and women, but we do have high professional standards and qualifications that the successful applicant must meet.

In addition to the three main types of conjunctions in the table on page 236, the English language has transitional adverbs and adverbial phrases called "conjunctive adverbs" that express relationships between two units of discourse (as two independent clauses, two complete sentences, or two or more paragraphs), and that function as conjunctions even though they are customarily classified as adverbs. The table on page 237 groups and illustrates conjunctive adverbs according to their functions.

Occurrence of a comma fault especially with conjunctive adverbs indicates that the writer has not realized that a comma alone will not suffice to join two sentences, and that a semicolon is required. The punctuation pattern with conjunctive adverbs is usually as follows:

clause + semicolon + conjunctive adverb + comma + clause

The following two sentences illustrate a typical comma fault and a rewrite that removes the error:

comma fault	*rewrite*
The company had flexible hours, however its employees were expected to abide by the hours they had selected for arrival and departure.	The company had flexible hours; however, its employees were expected to abide by the hours they had selected for arrival and departure.

Three Major Types of Conjunctions and their Functions

Type of Conjunction	Function	Example
coordinating conjunctions link words, phrases, dependent clauses, and complete sentences	*and* joins elements and sentences	[He ordered pencils, pens, *and* erasers.]
	but, yet exclude or contrast	[He is a brilliant *but* arrogant man.]
	or, nor offer alternatives	[You can wait here *or* go.]
	for offers reason or grounds	[The report is poor, *for* its data are inaccurate.]
	so offers a reason	[Her diction is good, *so* every word is clear.]
subordinating conjunctions introduce dependent clauses	*because, since* express cause	[*Because* she is smart, she is doing well in her job.]
	although, if, unless express condition	[Don't call *unless* you have the information.]
	as, as though, however express manner	[He looks *as though* he is ill.] [We'll do it *however* you tell us to.]
	in order that, so that express result	[She routes the mail early *so that* they can read it.]
	after, before, once, since, till, until, when, whenever, while express time	[He kept meetings to a minimum *when* he was president.]
	where, wherever express place or circumstance	[I don't know *where* he has gone.] [He tries to help out *wherever* it is possible.]
	whether expresses alternative conditions or possibilities	[It was hard to decide *whether* I should go or stay.]
	that introduces several kinds of subordinate clauses including those used as noun equivalents (as a subject or an object of a verb, or a predicate nominative)	[Yesterday I learned *that* he has been sick for over a week.]
correlative conjunctions work in pairs to link alternatives or equal elements	*either . . . or, neither . . . nor,* and *whether . . . or* link alternatives	[*Either* you go *or* you stay.] [He had *neither* looks *nor* wit.]
	both . . . and and *not only . . . but also*	[*Both* typist *and* writer should understand style.]
	link equal elements	[*Not only* was there inflation, *but* there was *also* unemployment.]

Conjunctive Adverbs Grouped According to Meaning and Function

Conjunctive Adverbs	Functions	Examples
also, besides, furthermore, in addition, in fact, moreover, too	express addition	[This employee deserves a substantial raise; *furthermore,* she should be promoted.]
indeed, that is [to say], *to be sure*	add emphasis	[He is brilliant; *indeed,* he is a genius.]
anyway, however, nevertheless, on the contrary, on the one hand/on the other hand	express contrast or discrimination	[The major responsibility lies with top management; *nevertheless,* line officers should be competent in decision-making.] [*On the one hand,* we must consider the editorial function; *on the other hand,* manufacturing procedures and costs.]
e.g., for example, for instance, i.e., namely, that is	introduce illustrations or elaborations	[Losses were due to several negative factors; *namely,* inflation, competition, and restrictive government regulation.] [He is highly competitive—*i.e.,* he goes straight for a rival's jugular vein.]
accordingly, as a result, consequently, hence, therefore, thus, so	express or introduce conclusions or results	[This division had an outstanding year; *as a result,* operating income increased 131% to a record $30.1 million.] [Government overregulation in that country reached a prohibitive level in the last quarter. *Thus,* we are phasing out all of our operations there.]
first, second, further on, later, then, in conclusion, finally	orient elements of discourse as to time or space	[*First,* we can say that the account is long overdue; *second,* that we must consider consulting our attorneys if you do not meet your obligation.] [The road is straight here; *further on,* it is winding.]

The following are general points of conjunction usage:

Conjunctions as meaning clarifiers Properly used conjunctions ensure order and coherence in writing since they often serve to pinpoint shades of meaning, place special emphasis where required, and set general tone within sentences and paragraphs. Improperly used conjunctions may result in choppy, often cloudy writing, and in incoherent orientation of ideas. Therefore, the purpose of a conjunction is totally defeated if it creates ambiguities rather than makes things clear. The often misused conjunction-phrase *as well as* is an example:

ambiguous
Jean typed the report *as well as* Joan. (Does the writer mean that both women typed the report together, or that both women typed the report equally well?)

clear
Jean typed the report just *as well as* Joan did.
Jean and Joan typed the report equally well.
or
Both Jean and Joan typed the report.
Jean typed the report; so did Joan.
Jean typed the report, and so did Joan.

Coordinating conjunctions: proper use These terms should link equal elements of discourse—e.g., adjectives with other adjectives, nouns with other nouns, participles with other participles, clauses with other equal-ranking clauses, and so on. Combining unequal elements may result in unbalanced sentences:

unbalanced
Having become disgusted *and* because he was tired, he left the party.

balanced
Because he was tired *and* disgusted, he left the party.
or
He left the party because he had become tired *and* disgusted.
or
Having become tired *and* disgusted, he left the party.

Coordinating conjunctions should not be used to string together excessively long series of elements, regardless of their equality.

strung-out
We have sustained enormous losses in this division, and we have realized practically no profits even though the sales figures indicate last-quarter gains and we are therefore reorganizing the entire management structure as well as paring down personnel.

tightened
Since this division has sustained enormous losses and has realized only insignificant profits even with its last-quarter sales gains, we are totally reorganizing its management. We are also cutting its personnel.

Choice of just the right coordinating conjunction for a particular verbal situation is important: the right word will pinpoint the writer's true meaning and intent, and will highlight the most relevant idea or point of the sentence. The following three sentences exhibit increasingly stronger degrees of contrast through the use of different conjunctions:

neutral	He works hard *and* doesn't progress.
more contrast	He works hard *but* doesn't progress.
stronger contrast	He works hard, yet he doesn't progress.

The coordinating conjunction *and/or* linking two elements of a compound subject often poses a problem as to the number (singular or plural) of the verb that follows. A subject comprising singular nouns connected by *and/or* may be considered singular or plural, depending on the meaning of the sentence:

singular
All loss and/or damage *is* to be the responsibility of the sender. [one or the other and possibly both]

plural
John R. Jones and/or Robert B. Flint *are* hereby *appointed* as the executors of my estate. [both executors are to act, or either of them is to act if the other dies or is incapacitated]

Subordinating conjunctions: proper use Subordinating conjunctions introduce dependent clauses, and also deemphasize less important ideas in favor of more important ideas. Which clause is made independent and which clause is made subordinate has great influence in determining the effectiveness of a sentence. Notice how differently these two versions strike the reader:

When the building burst into flames, we were just coming out of the door.

Just as we were coming out of the door, the building burst into flames.

The writer must take care that the point he or she wishes to emphasize is in the independent clause and that the points of less importance are subordinated.

Faulty clause subordination can render a sentence impotent. Compare the following examples:

faulty subordination	*improved*
Because the government of that country has nationalized our refineries, and since overregulation of prices had already become a critical problem, we decided to withdraw all our operations when the situation became intolerable.	Since that country's government has over-regulated prices and has nationalized our refineries, we have decided to withdraw our operations altogether.

Correlative conjunctions: proper use These pairs of words also join equal elements of discourse. They should be placed as close as possible to the elements they join:

misplaced	*repositioned*
Either I must send a telex *or* make a long-distance call.	I must *either* send a telex *or* make a long-distance call.

The negative counterpart of *either . . . or* is *neither . . . nor.* The conjunction *or* should not be substituted for *nor* because its substitution will destroy the negative parallelism. However, *or* may occur in combination with *no.* Examples:

He received *neither* a promotion *nor* a raise.

He received *no* promotion *or* raise.

Interjection

in•ter•jec•tion . . . *n* . . . **3 a :** an ejaculatory word (as *Wonderful*) or form of speech (as *ah*) **b :** a cry or inarticulate utterance (as *ouch*) expressing an emotion

Interjections exhibit no characteristic features or forms. As independent elements not having close grammatical connections with the rest of a sentence, interjections may often stand alone.

Interjections may be stressed or ejaculatory words, phrases, or even short sentences, as

Absurd!

Quickly!

Right on!

Get out!

or they may be so-called "sound" words (such as those representing shouts, hisses, etc.):

Ouch! That hurts.

Shh! The meeting has begun.

Psst! Come over here.

Ah, that's my idea of a terrific deal.

Oh, you're really wrong there.

Noun

noun . . . *n* . . . **1 :** a word that is the name of a subject of discourse (as a person, animal, plant, place, thing, substance, quality, idea, action, or state) and that in languages with grammatical number, case, and gender is inflected for number and case but has inherent gender **2 :** a word except a pronoun used in a sentence as subject or object of a verb, as object of a preposition, as the predicate after a copula, or as a name in an absolute construction

Nouns exhibit these characteristic features: they are inflected for possession, they have number (singular, plural), they are often preceded by determiners (as *a, an, the; this, that, these, those; all, every,* and other such qualifiers; *one, two, three,* and other such numerical quantifiers; *his, her, their,* and other such pronominal adjectives), a few of them still have gender (as the masculine *host,* the feminine *hostess*), and many of them are formed by suffixation (as with the suffixes *-ance, -ist, -ness,* and *-tion*).

The only noun case indicated by inflection is the possessive which is normally formed by addition of *-'s* (singular) or *-s'* (plural) to the base word. (See Apostrophe, pages 215–216, for other examples.)

Number is usually indicated by addition of *-s* or *-es* to the base word, although some nouns (as those of foreign origin) have irregular plurals:

regular plurals

dog→dogs	grass→grasses
race→races	dish→dishes
guy→guys	buzz→buzzes
monarch→monarchs	branch→branches

irregular and zero plurals

army→armies
ox→oxen
foot→feet
phenomenon→phenomena
libretto→librettos *or* libretti
curriculum→curricula *also* curriculums
memorandum→memorandums *or* memoranda
alga→algae
corpus delicti→corpora delicti
sergeant major→sergeants major *or* sergeant majors
sheep→sheep
encephalitis→encephalitides
pediculosis→pediculoses

When in doubt of a plural spelling, the secretary should consult a dictionary. Nouns may be subgrouped according to type and function within a sentence as shown in the table on page 242.

Nouns may be used as follows in sentences:

1. as subjects
   The *office* was quiet.
2. as direct objects
   He locked the *office.*

3. as objects of prepositions
   The file is in the *office.*
4. as indirect objects
   He gave his *wife* a ring.
5. as retained objects
   His wife was given a *ring.*
6. as predicate nominatives
   Mr. Dow is the *president.*
7. as subjective complements
   Mr. Dow was announced *president.*
8. as objective complements
   They made Mr. Dow *president.*
9. as appositives
   Mr. Dow, the *president,* wrote that memorandum.
10. in direct address
   Mr. Dow, may I present Mr. Lee?

Compound nouns Since English is not a static and unchanging entity, it experiences continuous style fluctuations because of preferences of its users. The styling (open, closed, or hyphened) variations of noun and other compounds reflect changing usage. No rigid rules can be set down to cover every possible variation or combination, nor can an all-inclusive list of compounds be given here. The secretary should consult a dictionary when in doubt of the styling of a compound.

Use of indefinite articles with nouns The use of *a* and *an* is not settled in all situations. In the examples below, some words or abbreviations beginning with a vowel letter nevertheless have a consonant as the first sound (as *one, union,* or *US*). Conversely, the names of some consonants begin with a vowel sound (as *F, H, L, M, N, R, S,* and X).

a

a. Before a word (or abbreviation) beginning with a consonant sound, *a* is usually spoken and written: *a BA degree, a COD package, a door, a hat, a human, a one, a union, a US senator.*

b. Before *h-* in an unstressed (unaccented) or lightly stressed (lightly accented) first syllable, *a* is more frequently written, although *an* is more usual in speech whether or not the *h-* is actually pronounced. Either one certainly may be considered acceptable in speech or writing: *a historian—an historian, a heroic attempt—an heroic attempt, a hilarious performance—an hilarious performance.*

c. Before a word beginning with a vowel sound, *a* is occasionally used in speech: *a hour, a inquiry, a obligation.* (In some parts of the United States this may be more common than in others.)

an

a. Before a word beginning with a vowel sound, *an* is usually spoken and written: *an icicle, an FCC report, an hour, an honor, an MIT professor, an nth degree polynomial, an orange, an Rh factor, an SAT, an unknown.*

b. Before *h-* in an unstressed or lightly stressed syllable, *an* is more usually spoken whether or not the *h-* is pronounced, while a is more frequently written. Either may be considered acceptable in speech or writing. (See the examples above at point b.)

c. Sometimes *an* is spoken and written before a word beginning with a vowel in its spelling even though the first sound is a consonant: *an European city, an unique occurrence, such an one.* This is less frequent today than in the past and it is more common in Britain than in the United States.

d. Occasionally *an* is used in speech and writing before a stressed syllable beginning with *h-* in which the *h-* is pronounced: *an huntress, an heritage.* This is regularly the practice of the King James Version of the Old Testament.

Nouns Subgrouped According to Type and Function

Type of Noun	Function	Example
common nouns	identify general classes of things	[valley] [college] [company] [author]
proper nouns	identify particular members of classes of things, and are capitalized	[the Ohio Valley] [Amherst College] [The Macmillan Company] [Shakespeare]
abstract nouns	name qualities and ideas that do not have physical substance or configuration	[good] [evil] [honesty] [dishonesty] [science] [philosophy] [ruthlessness] [compassion]
concrete nouns	name animate and inanimate objects	[desk] [typewriter] [chair] [building] [floor] [ceiling] [finger] [stomach]
mass nouns	identify things that are not ordinarily thought of in terms of numbered elements; they are usually singular in form, although in a few contexts the plural is appropriate especially when *types* of items within a class are being differentiated	[paper] [fruit] [water] [rice] [cotton] [Paper is costly today.] [Fruit is healthful.] [Water was scarce there.] [Rice grows in the Deep South.] [Cotton is raised in South Carolina.] *but* [Not all cottons have the same texture.]
count nouns	identify things considered as separate units that can be enumerated or counted	[paper clip] [peach] [desk] [chair] [five hundred paper clips] [many peaches] [two desks and various types of chairs]
	NOTE: Many nouns have both count and non-count senses.	[Their firm manufactures the cloth for our book covers.] *but* [She used two cloths to polish the silver.]
collective nouns	identify things that can be construed either in terms of number or collectively; collective nouns are singular in form but are sometimes or always plural in construction	[The family was proud of her.] [The committee have been debating among themselves for an hour.] *but* [The group has decided.] [The mob was running wild.] [That audience was impolite.]

prep•o•si•tion . . . *n* . . . **:** a linguistic form that combines with a noun, pronoun, or noun equivalent to form a phrase that typically has an adverbial, adjectival, or substantival relation to some other word

Preposition

Prepositions are not characterized by inflection, number, case, gender, or identifying suffixes. Rather, they are identified chiefly by their positioning within sentences and by their grammatical functions.

Prepositions may occur in the following positions:

1. before nouns or pronouns
   below the desk
   beside them
2. after adjectives
   antagonistic *to*
   insufficient *in*
   symbolic *of*
3. after the verbal elements of idiomatically fixed verb + preposition combinations
   take *for*
   get *after*
   come *across*

Prepositions may be simple, i.e., composed of only one element (as *of, on, out, from, near, against,* or *without*); or they may be compound, i.e., composed of more than one element (as *according to, by means of,* or *in spite of*). Prepositions are chiefly used to link nouns, pronouns, or noun equivalents to the rest of a sentence:

He expected continued softness *in* the economy.
He sat down *beside* her.

Prepositions may also be used to express the possessive:

one fourth *of* the employees
the top drawer *of* my desk

The following are general points of preposition usage:

Prepositions and conjunctions: confusion between the two The words *after, before, but, for,* and *since* may function as either prepositions or conjunctions. Their positions within sentences clarify whether they are conjunctions or prepositions:

preposition	I have nothing left *but* hope. (*but* = "except for")
conjunction	I was a bit concerned *but* not panicky. (*but* links 2 adjectives)
preposition	The device conserves fuel *for* residual heating. (*for* + noun)
conjunction	The device conserves fuel, *for* it is battery-powered. (*for* links 2 clauses)

Implied or understood prepositions If two words combine idiomatically with the same preposition, that preposition need not be repeated after both of them:

We were antagonistic [to] and opposed *to* the whole idea.
but
We are interested *in* and anxious *for* raises.

Prepositions terminating sentences There is no reason why a preposition cannot end a sentence, especially when it is an essential element of an idiomatically fixed verb phrase:

One cannot look back on industrialization without being shocked by many of its manifestations, by many of the things we put up *with*.
—August Heckscher

Vietnam was incredibly mismanaged. It was easier to get into than to get out *of*.
—Nancy Kissinger

Use of *between* and *among* The preposition *between* is ordinarily followed by words representing two persons or things:

between you and me

détente *between* the United States and the Soviet Union

and *among* is ordinarily followed by words representing more than two persons or things:

among the three of us

among various nations

However, *between* sometimes may be used to express an interrelationship between more than two things when those things are being considered individually rather than collectively:

. . . travels regularly *between* New York, Baltimore, and Washington.

---

pro•noun . . . *n* . . . **:** a word belonging to one of the major form classes in any of a great many languages that is used as a substitute for a noun or noun equivalent, takes noun constructions, and refers to persons or things named or understood in the context

Pronoun

Pronouns exhibit all or some of the following characteristic features: case (nominative, possessive, objective), number (singular, plural), person (first, second, third person), and gender (masculine, feminine, neuter). Pronouns may be grouped according to major types and functions, as shown in the table on the next page. The following paragraphs discuss points of pronoun usage.

Personal pronouns A personal pronoun agrees in person, number, and gender with the word it refers to; however, the case of a pronoun is determined by its function within a sentence:

Everybody had *his* own office.

Everybody was given an office to *himself*.

Each employee was given an office to *himself*.

You and *I* thought the meeting was useful.

Just between *you* and *me*, the meeting was useful but far too lengthy.

My assistant and *I* attended the seminar.

The vice-president told my assistant and *me* to attend the seminar.

The nominative case (as in the locutions "It is I" and "This is she") after the verb *to be* is considered standard English and is preferred by strict grammarians; however, the objective case (as in the locution "It's me") also may be used without criticism especially in spoken English.

When a personal pronoun occurs in a construction introduced by *than* or *as*,

Types and Functions of Pronouns

Type of Pronoun	Function	Example
personal pronouns (such as *I, we, you, he, she, it, they*)	refer to beings and objects and reflect the person and gender of those antecedents	[Put the book on the table and close *it.*] [Put the baby in *his* crib and cover *him* up.]
reflexive pronouns (such as *myself, ourselves, yourself, yourselves, himself, herself, itself, themselves*)	express reflexive action on the subject of a sentence or add extra emphasis to the subject	[He hurt *himself.*] [They asked *themselves* if they were being honest.] [I *myself* am not afraid.]
indefinite pronouns (*all, another, any, anybody, anyone, anything, both, each, each one, either, everybody, everyone, everything, few, many, much, neither, nobody, none, no one, one, other, several, some, somebody, someone, something*)	are indistinguishable by gender, are chiefly used as third-person references, and do not distinguish gender	[*All* of the people are here.] [*All* of them are here.] [Has *anyone* arrived?] [*Somebody* has called.] [Does *everyone* have his paper?] [*Nobody* has answered.] [A *few* have offered their suggestions.]
reciprocal pronouns	indicate interaction	[They do not quarrel with *one another.*] [Be nice to *each other.*]
demonstrative pronouns (*this, that, these, those*)	point things out	[*This* is your seat.] [*That* is mine.] [*These* belong to her.] [*Those* are strong words.]
relative pronouns (*who, whom, which, what, that, whose*) or combinations with *-ever* (as *whoever, whosever, whichever, whatever*)	introduce clauses acting as nouns or as modifiers	[The thrust of this memorandum is *that* there will be no cost overruns.] [I'll do *what* you want.] [I'll do *whatever* you want.]
interrogative pronouns (as *who, which, what, whoever, whichever, whatever*)	phrase direct questions	[*Who* is there?] [*What* is his title?] [His title is *what*?] [*Whom* did the article pan?] [*Whatever* is the matter?]

it should be in the nominative case:

He received a bigger bonus than *she* [did].
She has as much seniority as *I* [do].

The suffixes *-self* and *-selves* combine only with the possessive case of the first- and second-person pronouns (*myself, ourselves, yourself, yourselves*) and with the objective case of the third-person pronouns (*himself, herself, itself, themselves*). Other combinations (as "hisself" and "theirselves") are considered nonstandard and should not be used.

When one uses the pronoun *I* with other pronouns or with other peoples' names, *I* should be last in the series:

Mrs. Smith and *I* were trained together.

He and *I* were attending the meeting.

The memorandum was directed to Ms. Montgomery and *me*.

Some companies prefer that writers use *we* and not *I* when speaking for their companies in business correspondence. *I* is more often used when a writer is referring only to himself or herself. The following example illustrates use of both within one sentence:

We [i.e., the writer speaks for the company] have reviewed the manuscript that you sent to *me* [i.e., the manuscript was sent only to the writer] on June 1, but *we* [a corporate or group decision] feel that it is too specialized a work to be marketable by *our* Company.

While the personal pronouns *it, you,* and *they* are often used as indefinite pronouns in spoken English, they can be vague or even redundant in some contexts and therefore should be avoided in precise writing:

vague	*explicit*
They said at the seminar that the economy would experience a third-quarter upturn. (The question is: Who exactly is *they?*)	The economists on the panel at the seminar predicted a third-quarter economic upturn.
redundant	*lean*
In the graph *it* says that production fell off by 50%.	The graph indicates a 50% production drop.

Notwithstanding recent concern about sexism in language, the personal pronoun *he* and the indefinite pronoun *one* are still the standard substitutes for antecedents whose genders are mixed or irrelevant:

Each employee should check *his* W-2 form.

Present the letter to the executive for *his* approval.

If *one* really wants to succeed, *one* can.

Indefinite pronouns: agreement Agreement in number between indefinite pronouns and verbs is sometimes a problem especially in contexts where the actual number of individuals represented by the pronoun is unclear. In some instances, there is also a conflict between written and spoken usage.

The following indefinite pronouns are clearly singular, and as such take singular verbs:

another	*much*	*other*
anything	*nobody*	*someone*
each one	*no one*	*something*
everything	*one*	

And these are clearly plural:

both
few
many
several

But depending on whether they are used with mass or count nouns, the following may be either singular or plural:

all
any
each
none
some

with mass noun *All* of the *property is* entailed.
with count noun *All* of our *bases are* covered.

The following are singular in form, and as such logically take singular verbs; however, because of their plural connotations, informal speech has established the use of plural pronoun references to them:

anybody
anyone
everybody
everyone
somebody

The following citations illustrate usage variants involving indefinite pronouns:

Anyone who tries to discuss the problem . . . is at once met with the suggestion that *he* is unaware . . . .
—Wendell L. Willkie

but

. . . it may be difficult for *anyone* to find *their* path through . . . a sort of maze.
—Ford Madox Ford

. . . a small Mid-Western town where *everybody* knows you!
—William A. Tyson, Jr.

Everybody drives just where *they* want to.
—F. Scott Fitzgerald

Everybody has a right to describe *their* own party machine as *they* choose.
—Winston Churchill

Everybody fights for *their* own team . . . .
—Stuart Symington

I was calling *everybody* by *their* first names.
—Marshall McLuhan

and

Everyone from the time *he* is first conscious of *himself* until *he* dies, is continually comparing *himself* with others . . . .
—William J. Reilly

Somebody is always putting down a table of specifications for the good salesman.
—*Printers' Ink*

but

Now that *everyone* goes to the Mediterranean for *their* holidays . . . .
—*Times Literary Supplement*

. . . the minute *somebody* opens *their* mouth. . . . .
—Robert A. Hall, Jr.

The question of number in pronoun phrases such as *each* + *of* + noun(s) or other pronoun(s), *none* + *of* + noun(s) or other pronoun(s), *either/neither* + *of* + noun(s) or other pronoun(s), and *some* + *of* + noun(s) or other pronoun(s), depends on the number of the headword. For example, when *either* means "one of two or more" or "any one of more than two," it is usually singular in construction and thus takes a singular verb. However, when *of* after *either* is followed by a plural, the verb that follows the whole phrase is often plural. This decision is really a matter of writer preference:

Either of the two pronunciations *is* standard.
Either of these pronunciations *is/are* standard.
or
Either of the two *is* satisfactory.
Either of them *are* satisfactory.

The word *none* involves similar variations:

. . . *none* [i.e., *not any*] of them *were* intellectually absorbing . . . .
—Winthrop Sargeant

None [i.e., *not any*] of those statements *are* particularly disputable . . . .
—Tom Wicker

but

. . . *none* [i.e., *not one*] of our scholars *has* written a monograph on him . . . .
—Norman Douglas

. . . *none* [i.e., *not one*] *is* identifiably more expert in foreign than domestic affairs, or vice versa.
—Tom Wicker

The indefinite pronoun *any* when used in comparisons The indefinite pronoun *any* is conventionally followed by *other(s)* or *else* when it forms part of a comparison of two individuals in the same class. Examples:

not He is a better researcher than any in his field.
(Is he a better researcher than all others including himself?)
but He is a better researcher than any others in his field.
He is a better researcher than anyone else in his field.
not Boston is more interesting than any city in the U.S.
but Boston is more interesting than any other city in the U.S.

Demonstrative pronouns One problem involving demonstrative pronouns occurs when a demonstrative introduces a sentence referring to an idea or ideas contained in a previous sentence or sentences. One should be sure that the reference is definite and not cloudy:

a cloudy sentence
The heir's illness, the influence of a faith healer at court, massive military setbacks, general strikes, mass outbreaks of typhus, and failed crops contributed to the revolution. *This* influenced the course of history.

The question is: What exactly influenced the course of history? All of these factors, some of them, or the last one mentioned?

an explicit sentence
None of the participants in the incident kept records of what they said or did. *That* is quite unfortunate, and it should be a lesson to us.

When demonstrative pronouns are used with the words *kind, sort,* and *type* + *of* + nouns, they should agree in number with both nouns:

not We want these kind of pencils.
but We want *this kind* of *pencil.* *or* We want *these kinds* of *pencils.*

Relative pronouns While a relative pronoun itself does not exhibit number, gender, or person, it does determine the number, gender, and person of the relative-clause elements that follow it because of its implicit agreement with its antecedent:

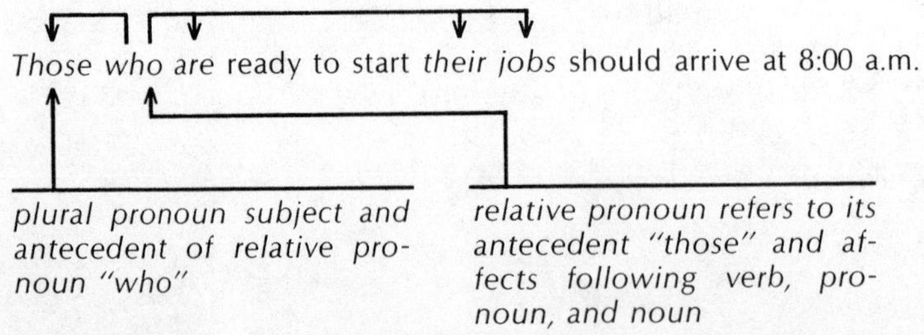

Those who are ready to start *their jobs* should arrive at 8:00 a.m.
plural pronoun subject and antecedent of relative pronoun "who"
relative pronoun refers to its antecedent "those" and affects following verb, pronoun, and noun

When the antecedent of a relative pronoun is compound (as two noun subjects, one of which is singular and the other plural), the number of the verb may vary according to the writer's preference. If a plural noun antecedent is closer to the verb, the writer may choose a plural verb. Examples:

He's one of those executives who *worry* a lot.
or
He's an executive who *worries* a lot.

The relative pronoun *who* typically refers to persons and some animals; *which,* to things and animals; and *that,* to both beings and things:

a man *who* sought success

. . . a hummingbird *who* came to the bushes in front must have got very slim pickings.
—Edmund Wilson

a book *which* sold well
a dog *which* barked loudly

a book *that* sold well
a dog *that* barked loudly
a man *that* we can trust

Relative pronouns can sometimes be omitted for the sake of brevity:

The man *whom* I was talking to is the president.
or
The man I was talking to is the president.

The relative pronoun *what* may be substituted for the longer and more awkward phrases "that which," "that of which," or "the thing which" in some sentences:

stiff He was blamed for *that which* he could not have known.

easier He was blamed for *what* he could not have known.

The problem of when to use *who* or *whom* has been blown out of proportion. The situation is very simple: standard written English makes a distinction between the nominative and objective cases of these pronouns when they are used as relatives or interrogatives, as

Who is she?
Who does she think she is, anyway?
She thinks she is the one *who* ought to be promoted.
She's the one individual *who* I think should be promoted.
Give me a list of the ones *who* you think should be promoted.
but
Whom are you referring to?
To *whom* are you referring?
He's a man *whom* everyone should know.
He's a man with *whom* everyone should be acquainted.

In speech, however, case distinctions and boundaries often become blurred, with the result that spoken English favors *who* as a general substitute for all uses of *whom* except in set phrases as "*To whom* it may concern." *Who,* then, may be used without criticism as the subject of the clause it introduces, as

I serve *who* I like.
—*Irish Digest*

and *who* may be used as the object of a verb in a clause that it introduces, as

. . . old peasants . . . *who,* if isolated from their surroundings, one would expect to see in a village church. . . .
—John Berger

Then I would have him select *who* he thought would make the best . . . candidate.
—Joseph Napolitan

Who is used less frequently, however, as the object of a preceding or following preposition in the clause that it introduces:

. . . of *who* I know nothing.
—Raymond Paton

Who are you going to listen to, anyway. . . .
—*National Review*

The relative pronoun *whoever* likewise lends itself without criticism to flexible grammatical relationships:

. . . sells eggs to *whoever* has the money to buy. . . .
—J. R. Chamberlain

Whoever he picks has to have the stature of a collaborator, not a subordinate. . . .
—*Time*

or

. . . so that she could help *whomever* she married. . . .
—Lillian Ross

. . . *whomever* this alleged autobiography . . . is about, it is a real life. . . .
—*Springfield* (Mass.) *City Library Bulletin*

Verb

verb . . . *n* . . . **:** a word that characteristically is the grammatical center of a predicate and expresses an act, occurrence, or mode of being, that in various languages is inflected for agreement with the subject, for tense, for voice, for mood, or for aspect, and that typically has rather full descriptive meaning and characterizing quality but is sometimes nearly devoid of these esp. when used as an auxiliary or copula

Verbs exhibit the following characteristic features: inflection (*help, helps, helping, helped*), person (first, second, third person), number (singular, plural), tense (present, past, future), aspect (time relations other than the simple present, past, and future), voice (active, passive), mood (indicative, subjunctive, imperative), and suffixation (as by the typical suffixal markers *-ate, -en, -ify,* and *-ize*).

Regular verbs have four inflected forms signaled by the suffixes *-s* or *-es, -ed,* and *-ing*. The verb *help* as shown in the first sentence above is regular. Most irregular verbs have four or five forms, as

bring *see*
brings *sees*
bringing *seeing*
brought *saw*
seen

but some, like *can, ought, put,* and *spread,* have fewer forms, as

can *ought* *put* *spread*
could *puts* *spreads*
putting *spreading*

and one, the verb *be*, has eight:

be *being*
is *was*
am *were*
are *been*

When one is uncertain about a particular inflected form, one should consult a dictionary that indicates not only the inflections of irregular verbs but also those inflections resulting in changes in base-word spelling, as

blame; blamed; blaming
spy; spied; spying
picnic; picnicked; picnicking

in addition to variant inflected forms, as

bias; biased or *biassed; biasing* or *biassing*
counsel; counseled or *counselled; counseling* or *counselling*
diagram; diagramed or *diagrammed; diagraming* or *diagramming*
travel; traveled or *travelled; traveling* or *travelling*

all of which may be found at their applicable entries in *Webster's New Collegiate Dictionary.*

There are, however, a few rules that will aid one in ascertaining the proper spelling patterns of certain verb forms. These are as follows:

1. Verbs ending in a silent -e generally retain the -e before consonant suffixes (as *-s*) but drop the -e before vowel suffixes (as *-ed* and *-ing*):

   arrange; arranges; arranged; arranging
   hope; hopes; hoped; hoping
   require; requires; required; requiring
   shape; shapes; shaped; shaping

   Other such verbs are: *agree, arrive, conceive, grieve, imagine,* and *value.*

   NOTE: A few verbs ending in a silent -e retain the -e even before vowel suffixes in order to avoid confusion with other words:

   dye; dyes; dyed; dyeing (vs. *dying*)
   singe; singes; singed; singeing (vs. *singing*)
2. Monosyllabic verbs ending in a single consonant preceded by a single vowel double the final consonant before vowel suffixes (as *-ed* and *-ing*):

   brag; bragged; bragging
   grip; gripped; gripping
   pin; pinned; pinning
3. Polysyllabic verbs ending in a single consonant preceded by a single vowel and having an accented last syllable double the final consonant before vowel suffixes (as *-ed* and *-ing*):

   commit; committed; committing
   control; controlled; controlling
   occur; occurred; occurring
   omit; omitted; omitting

   NOTE: The final consonant of such verbs is not doubled when

   a. two vowels occur before the final consonant, as

      daub; daubed; daubing
      spoil; spoiled; spoiling

   b. two consonants form the ending, as

      help; helped; helping
      lurk; lurked; lurking
      peck; pecked; pecking
4. Verbs ending in *-y* preceded by a consonant regularly change the *-y* to *-i* before all suffixes except those beginning with *-i* (as *-ing*):

   carry; carried; carrying
   marry; married; marrying
   study; studied; studying

   NOTE: If the final *-y* is preceded by a vowel, it remains unchanged in suffixation, as

delay; delayed; delaying
enjoy; enjoyed; enjoying
obey; obeyed; obeying

5. Verbs ending in -c add a *-k* when a suffix beginning with -e or *-i* is appended, as
   mimic; mimics; mimicked; mimicking
   panic; panics; panicked; panicking
   traffic; traffics; trafficked; trafficking

   And words derived from this type of verb also add a *k* when such suffixes are added to them, as
   panicky
   trafficker

English verbs exhibit their two simple tenses by use of two single-word grammatical forms:

simple present = *do*
simple past = *did*

The future is expressed by *shall/will* + verb infinitive:

I *shall do* it.
He *will do* it.

or by use of the present or progressive forms in a revealing context, as

I *leave* shortly for New York. (present)
I *am leaving* shortly for New York. (progressive)

Aspect is a property that allows verbs to indicate time relations other than the simple present, past, or future tenses. Aspect covers these relationships:

action occurring in the past and continuing to the present	has seen	*present perfect tense*
action completed at a past time or before the immediate past	had seen	*past perfect tense*
action that will have been completed by a future time	will have seen	*future perfect tense*
action occurring now	is seeing	*progressive*

In contexts that require it, the perfective and the progressive aspects can be combined to yield special verb forms, as

had been seeing

Voice enables a verb to indicate whether the subject of a sentence is acting (he *loves* = active voice) or whether the subject is being acted upon (he *is loved* = passive voice).

Mood indicates manner of expression. The indicative mood states a fact or asks a question (He *is* here. *Is* he here?). The subjunctive mood expresses condition contrary to fact (I wish that he *were* here). The imperative mood expresses a command or request (*Come* here. Please *come* here).

Verbs may be used transitively; that is, they may act upon direct objects, as

She *contributed* money.

or they may be used intransitively; that is, they may not have direct objects to act upon, as

She *contributed* generously.

There is another group of words derived from verbs and called *verbals* that deserve added discussion. The members of this group—the gerund, the participle, and the infinitive—exhibit some but not all of the characteristic features of their parent verbs.

A gerund is an *-ing* verb form, but it functions mainly as a noun. It has both the active (*seeing*) and the passive (*being seen*) voices. In addition to voice, a gerund's verbal characteristics are as follows: it conveys the notion of a verb—i.e., action of some sort; it can take an object; and it can be modified by an adverb. Examples:

Typing tabular *data daily* is a boring task.
gerund *noun object* *adverb*

He liked *driving cars fast.*
gerund *noun object* *adverb*

Nouns and pronouns occurring before gerunds are expressed by the possessive:

Her typing is good.
She is trying to improve *her typing.*
We objected to *their telling* the story all over town.
We saw the *boy's whipping.* (i.e., the boy being whipped)
We expected the *senator's coming.* (i.e., his arrival)

Participles, on the other hand, function as adjectives and may occur alone (a *broken* typewriter) or in phrases that modify other words (*Having broken the typewriter,* she gave up for the day). Participles have active and passive forms like gerunds. Examples:

active-voice participial phrase modifying "he"
Having failed to pass the examination, he was forced to repeat the course.

passive-voice participial phrase modifying "he"
Having been failed by his instructor, he was forced to repeat the course.

Participles, unlike gerunds, are not preceded by possessive nouns or pronouns:

We saw the *boy whipping* his dog. (i.e., we saw the boy doing the whipping)
We saw the *senator coming.* (i.e., we saw him arrive)

Infinitives may exhibit active (*to do*) and passive (*to be done*) voices and they may indicate aspect (*to be doing, to have done, to have been doing, to have been done*).

Infinitives may take complements and may be modified by adverbs. In addition, they can function as nouns, adjectives, and adverbs in sentences. Examples:

noun use
To be known is *to be castigated.*
(subject) (subjective complement)
He tried everything except *to bypass his superior.*
(object of preposition *except*)

adjectival use
They had found a way *to increase profits* greatly.
(modifies the noun *way*)

adverbial use
He was too furious *to speak.*
(modifies *furious*)

Although *to* is the characteristic marker of an infinitive, it is not always stated but may be understood:

He helped [to] complete the marketing report.

The following are general points of verb and verbal usage:

Sequence of tenses If the main verb in a sentence is in the present tense, any other tense or compound verb form may follow it in subsequent clauses, as

I *realize* that you *are leaving.*
I *realize* that you *left.*
I *realize* that you *were leaving.*
I *realize* that you *have been leaving.*
I *realize* that you *had left.*
I *realize* that you *had been leaving.*
I *realize* that you *will be leaving.*
I *realize* that you *will leave.*
I *realize* that you *will have been leaving.*
I *realize* that you *can be leaving.*
I *realize* that you *may be leaving.*
I *realize* that you *must be leaving.*

If the main verb is in the past tense, that tense imposes time restrictions on any subsequent verbs in the sentence, thus excluding use of the present tense, as

I *realized* that you *were leaving.*
I *realized* that you *left.*
I *realized* that you *had left.*
I *realized* that you *had been leaving.*
I *realized* that you *would be leaving.*
I *realized* that you *could be leaving.*
I *realized* that you *might be leaving.*
I *realized* that you *would leave.*

If the main verb is in the future tense, it imposes time restrictions on subsequent verbs in the sentence, thus excluding the possibility of using the simple past tense, as

He *will see* you because he *is going* to the meeting too.
He *will see* you because he *will be going* to the meeting too.
He *will see* you because he *will go* to the meeting too.
He *will see* you because he *has been going* to the meetings too.
He *will see* you because he *will have been going* to the meetings too.

In general, most writers try to maintain an order of tenses throughout their sentences that is consistent with natural or real time, e.g., present tense = present-time matters, past tense = past matters, and future tense = matters that will take place in the future. However, there are two outstanding exceptions to these principles:

a. If one is discussing the contents of printed or published material, one conventionally uses the present tense, as

In *Etiquette,* Emily Post *discusses* forms of address.

This analysis *gives* market projections for the next two years.

In his latest position paper on the Middle East, the Secretary of State *writes* that . . . .

b. If one wishes to add the connotation of immediacy to a particular sentence, one may use the present tense instead of the future, as

I *leave* for Tel Aviv tonight.

c. The sequence of tenses in sentences which express contrary-to-fact conditions is a special problem frequently encountered in writing. The examples below show the sequence correctly maintained:

If he *were* on time, we *would leave* now.

If he *had been* (not *would have been*) on time, we *would have left* an hour ago.

Subject-verb agreement Verbs agree in number and in person with their grammatical subjects. At times, however, the grammatical subject may be singular in form, but the thought it carries—i.e., the logical subject—may have plural connotations. Here are some general guidelines:

a. Plural and compound subjects take plural verbs even if the subject is inverted. Examples:

Music, theater, and painting *are* grouped under the heading "fine arts."

Both dogs and cats *were* tested for the virus.

b. Compound subjects or plural subjects conveying a unitary idea take singular verbs in American English. Examples:

Lord & Taylor *has* stores in the New York area.

Five hundred dollars *is* a stiff price for a coat.

c. Compound subjects expressing mathematical relationships may be either singular or plural. Examples:

One plus one *makes* (or *make*) two.

Six from eight *leaves* (or *leave*) two.

d. Singular subjects joined by *or* or *nor* take singular verbs; plural subjects so joined take plural verbs. Examples:

A freshman or sophomore *is* eligible for the scholarship.

Neither freshmen nor sophomores *are* eligible for the scholarship.

If one subject is singular and the other plural, the verb usually agrees with the number of the subject that is closer to it. Examples:

Either the secretaries or the supervisor *has* to do the job.

Either the supervisor or the secretaries *have* to do the job.

e. Singular subjects introduced by *many a, such a, every, each,* or *no* take singular verbs, even when several such subjects are joined by *and:*

Many an executive *has* gone to the top in that division.

No supervisor and no assembler *is* excused from the time check.

Every chair, table, and desk *has* to be accounted for.

f. The agreement of the verb with its grammatical subject ordinarily should not be skewed by an intervening phrase even if the phrase contains plural elements. Examples:

One of my reasons for resigning *involves* purely personal considerations.

The president of the company, as well as members of his staff, *has* arrived.

He, not any of the proxy voters, *has* to be present.

g. The verb *to be* agrees with its grammatical subject, and not with its complement:

His mania *was* fast cars and beautiful women.

Military skirmishes between China and the Soviet Union *is* an interesting field for study.

In addition, the verb *to be* introduced by the word *there* must agree in number with the subject following it. Examples:

There *are* many complications here.
There *is* no reason to worry about him.

NOTE: For discussion of verb agreement with indefinite-pronoun subjects, see pages 246–248. For discussion of verb number as affected by a compound subject whose elements are joined by *and/or*, see page 238.

Linking and *sense* verbs Linking verbs (as the various forms of *to be*) and the so-called "sense" verbs (as *feel, look, taste, smell,* as well as particular senses of *appear, become, continue, grow, prove, remain, seem, stand,* and *turn*) connect subjects with predicate nouns or adjectives. The latter group often cause confusion, in that adverbs are mistakenly used in place of adjectives after these verbs. Examples:

He *is* a vice-president.
He *became* vice-president.
The temperature *continues* cold.
The future *looks* prosperous.
I *feel* awful.
This perfume *smells* nice.
The meat *tastes* good.
He *remains* healthy.

Split infinitives The writer who consciously avoids splitting infinitives regardless of resultant awkwardness or changes in meaning is as immature in his or her position as the writer who consciously splits all infinitives as a sort of rebellion against convention. Actually, the use of split infinitives is no rebellion at all, because this construction has long been employed by a wide variety of distinguished English writers—Wycliffe, Byron, Coleridge, Browning (at least 23 times, according to one scholarly source), and Spenser—to name a few. Indeed, the split infinitive can be a useful device for the writer who wishes to delineate a shade of meaning or direct special emphasis to a word or group of words—emphasis that cannot be achieved with an undivided infinitive construction. For example, in the locution

to *thoroughly* complete the physical examination

the position of the adverb as close as possible to the verbal element of the whole infinitive phrase strengthens the effect of the adverb on the verbal element—a situation that is not necessarily true in the following reworded locutions:

to complete *thoroughly* the physical examination
thoroughly to complete the physical examination
to complete the physical examination *thoroughly*

In other instances, the position of the adverb may actually modify or change the entire meaning, as

original	*recast with new meanings*
. . . arrived in New York to *unexpectedly* find it in print. —Harrison Smith	. . . arrived in New York *unexpectedly* to find it in print. . . . arrived in New York to find it in print *unexpectedly.*

The main point is this: If the writer wishes to stress the verbal element of an infinitive or wishes to express a thought that is more clearly and easily shown with *to* + adverb + infinitive, such split infinitives are acceptable. However, very long adverbial modifiers such as

He wanted to *completely and without mercy* defeat his competitor.

are clumsy and should be avoided or recast, as

He wanted to defeat his competitor *completely and without mercy.*

Dangling participles and infinitives Careful writers avoid danglers (as participles or infinitives occurring in a sentence without having a normally expected syntactic relation to the rest of the sentence) that may create confusion for the reader or seem ludicrous. Examples:

dangling	Walking through the door, her coat was caught.
recast	While walking through the door, she caught her coat.
	Walking through the door, she caught her coat.
	She caught her coat while walking through the door.
dangling	Caught in the act, his excuses were unconvincing.
recast	Caught in the act, he could not make his excuses convincing.
dangling	Having been told that he was incompetent and dishonest, the executive fired the man.
recast	Having told the man that he was incompetent and dishonest, the executive fired him.
	Having been told by his superior that he was incompetent and dishonest, the man was fired.

Participial use should not be confused with prepositional use especially with words like *concerning, considering, providing, regarding, respecting, touching,* etc., as illustrated below:

prepositional usage
Concerning your complaint, we can tell you. . . .
Considering all the implications, you have made a dangerous decision.
Touching the matter at hand, we can say that. . . .

Having examined the eight parts of speech individually in order to pinpoint their respective characteristics and functions, we now view their performance in the broader environments of the phrase, the clause, and the sentence.

PHRASES

A phrase is a brief expression that consists of two or more grammatically related words and that may contain either a noun or a finite verb (i.e., a verb that shows grammatical person and number) but not both, and that often functions as a particular part of speech within a clause or a sentence. The table on page 258 lists and describes seven basic types of phrases.

CLAUSES

A clause is a group of words containing both a subject and a predicate and functioning as an element of a compound or a complex sentence (see pages 260–265 for discussion of sentences). The two general types of clauses are:

independent	*It is hot,* and *I feel faint.*
dependent	*Because it is hot,* I feel faint.

Like phrases, clauses can perform as particular parts of speech within a total sentence environment. The table on page 259 describes such performance.

Clauses that modify may also be described as restrictive or nonrestrictive. Whether a clause is restrictive or nonrestrictive has direct bearing on sentence punctuation.

Types of Phrases

Type of Phrase	Description	Example
noun phrase	consists of a noun and its modifiers	[*The concrete building* is huge.]
verb phrase	consists of a finite verb and any other terms that modify it or that complete its meaning	[She *will have arrived too late* for you to talk to her.]
gerund phrase	is a nonfinite verbal phrase that functions as a noun	[*Sitting on a patient's bed* is bad hospital etiquette.]
participial phrase	is a nonfinite verbal phrase that functions as an adjective	[*Listening all the time in great concentration,* he lined up his options.]
infinitive phrase	is a nonfinite verbal phrase that may function as a noun, an adjective, or an adverb	[*To do that* will be stupid.] [This was a performance *to remember.*] [It would be highly improper *to bypass your superior.*]
prepositional phrase	consists of a preposition and its object(s) and may function as a noun, an adjective, or an adverb	[Here is the desk *with the extra file drawer.*] [He now walked *without a limp.*] [*Out of here* is where I'd like to be!]
absolute phrase	is also called a nominative absolute, consists of a noun + a predicate form (as a participle), and acts independently within a sentence without modifying a particular element of the sentence	[He stalked out, *his eyes staring straight ahead.*]

Restrictive clauses are the so-called "bound" modifiers. They are absolutely essential to the meaning of the word or words they modify, they cannot be omitted without the meaning of the sentences being radically changed, and they are unpunctuated. Examples:

Women who aren't competitive should not aspire to high corporate office.

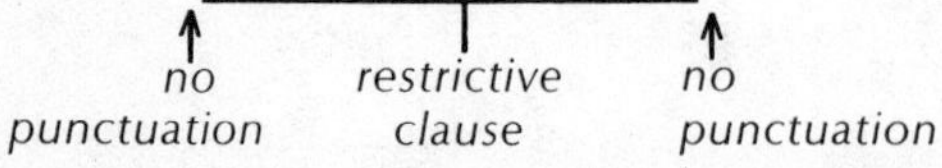

In this example, the restrictive clause limits the classification of women, and as such is essential to the total meaning of the sentence. If, on the other hand, the restrictive clause is omitted as shown below, the classification of women is now not limited at all, and the sentence conveys an entirely different notion:

Women should not aspire to high corporate office.

Basic Types of Clauses with Part-of-speech Functions

Type of Clause	Description	Example
noun clause	fills a noun slot in a sentence and thus can be a subject, an object, or a complement	[*Whoever is qualified* should apply.] [I do not know *what his field is*.] [Route that journal to *whichever department you wish*.] [The trouble is *that she has no ambition*.]
adjective clause	modifies a noun or pronoun and typically follows the word it modifies	[His administrative assistant, *who was also a speech writer,* was overworked.] [I can't see the reason *why you're uptight*.] [He is a man *who will succeed*.] [Anybody *who opts for a career like that* is crazy.]
adverb clause	modifies a verb, an adjective, or another adverb and typically follows the word it modifies	[They made a valiant effort, *although the risks were great*.] [I'm certain *that he is guilty*.] [We accomplished less *than we did before*.]

Nonrestrictive clauses are the so-called "free" modifiers: They are not inextricably bound to the word or words they modify but instead convey additional information about them, they may be omitted altogether without the meaning of the sentence being radically changed, and they are set off by commas. Examples:

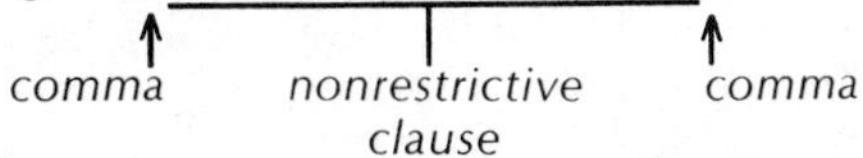
Our guide, who wore a green beret, was an experienced traveler.
comma
nonrestrictive clause
comma

Obviously, the guide's attire is not essential to his experience as a traveler. Removal of the nonrestrictive clause does not affect the meaning of the sentence:

Our guide was an experienced traveler.

The following are basic points of clause usage:

Elliptical clauses Some clause elements may be omitted if the context makes clear the understood elements:

I remember the first time [that] we met.
This typewriter is better than that [typewriter is].
When [she is] on the job, she is always competent and alert.

Clause placement In order to achieve maximum clarity and to avoid the possibility that the reader will misinterpret what he reads, one should place a modifying clause as close as possible to the word or words it modifies. If intervening words cloud the overall meaning of the sentence, one must recast it. Examples:

cloudy A memorandum is a piece of business writing, less formal than a letter, which serves as a means of interoffice communication.

The question is: Does the letter or the memorandum serve as a means of interoffice communication?

recast A memorandum, less formal than a letter, is a means of interoffice communication.

Tagged-on *which* clauses Tagging on a "which" clause that refers to the total idea of a sentence is a usage fault that should be avoided by careful writers. Examples:

tagged-on	*recast*
The company is retooling, which I personally think is a wise move.	The company's decision to retool is a wise move in my opinion. *or* I believe that the company's decision to retool is wise.

SENTENCES

A sentence is a grammatically self-contained unit that consists of a word or a group of syntactically related words and that expresses a statement (declarative sentence), asks a question (interrogative sentence), expresses a request or command (imperative sentence), or expresses an exclamation (exclamatory sentence). A sentence typically contains both a subject and a predicate, begins with a capital letter, and ends with a punctuation mark. The following table illustrates the three main types of sentences classified by their grammatical structure.

Sentences Classified by their Grammatical Structure

Description	Example
simple sentence is a complete grammatical unit having one subject and one predicate, either or both of which may be compound	[*Paper* is costly.] [*Bond* and *tissue* are costly.] [*Bond* and *tissue are* costly and *are* sometimes scarce.]
compound sentence comprises two or more independent clauses	[*I could arrange to arrive late,* or *I could simply send a proxy.*] [*This commute takes at least forty minutes by car,* but *we can make it in twenty by train.*] [*A few of the executives had Ph.D.'s, even more of them had B.A.'s,* but *the majority of them had both B.A.'s and M.B.A.'s.*]
complex sentence combines one independent clause with one or more dependent clauses (dependent clauses are italicized in examples)	[The executive committee meeting began *when the board chairman and the president walked in.*] [*Although the czar made some reforms,* his changes came so late that they could not preserve him in power.]

How to construct sentences The following paragraphs outline general guidelines for the construction of grammatically sound sentences.

One should maintain sentence coordination by use of connectives linking phrases and clauses of equal rank. Examples:

faulty coordination with improper use of "and"
I was sitting in on a meeting, and he stood up and started a long rambling discourse on a new pollution-control device.

recast with one clause subordinated
I sat in on a meeting during which he stood up and rambled on about a new pollution-control device.

or—recast into two sentences
I sat in on that meeting. He stood up and rambled on about a new pollution-control device.

faulty coordination with improper use of "and"
This company employs a full-time research staff and was founded in 1945.

recast with one clause subordinated
This company, which employs a full-time research staff, was founded in 1945.

or—recast with one clause reworded into a phrase
Established in 1945, this company employs a full-time research staff.

One should also maintain parallel, balanced sentence elements in order to achieve good sentence structure. Examples illustrating this particular point are as follows:

unparallel
The report gives market statistics, but he does not list his sources for these figures.

parallel
The report gives market statistics, but it does not list the sources for these figures.

unparallel
We are glad to have you as our client, and please call us whenever you need help.

parallel
We are glad to have you as our client and we hope that you will call on us whenever you need help.

or recast into two sentences
We are glad to have you as our client. Please do call on us whenever you need help.

Loose linkages of sentence elements such as those caused by excessive use of *and* should be avoided by careful writers. Some examples of this type of faulty coordination are shown below:

faulty coordination/excessive use of "and"
This company is a Class 1 motor freight common carrier of general commodities and it operates over 10,000 tractors, trailers, and city delivery trucks through 200 terminals, and serves 40 states and the District of Columbia.

recast into three shorter, more effective sentences
This company is a Class 1 motor freight common carrier of general commodities. It operates over 10,000 tractors, trailers, and city delivery trucks through 200 terminals. The company serves 40 states and the District of Columbia.

In constructing one's sentences effectively, one should choose the conjunction that best expresses the intended meaning. Examples:

not
The economy was soft *and* we lost a lot of business.

but
We lost a lot of business *because* the economy was soft.
The economy was soft, *so* we lost a lot of business.

or recast to
The soft economy has cost us a lot of business.

Good writers avoid unnecessary grammatical shifts that interrupt the reader's train of thought and needlessly complicate the material. Some unnecessary grammatical shifts are shown below, and improvements are also illustrated:

unnecessary shifts in verb voice
Any information you *can give* us *will be* greatly *appreciated* and we *assure* you that discretion *will be exercised* in its use.

rephrased (note the italicized all-active verb voice)
We *will appreciate* any information that you *can give* us. We *assure* you that we *will use* it with discretion.

unnecessary shifts in person
One can use either erasers or correcting fluid to remove typographical errors; however, *you* should make certain that *your* corrections are clean.

rephrased (note that the italicized pronouns are consistent)
One can use either erasers or correcting fluid to eradicate errors; however, *one* should make certain that *one's* corrections are clean.
or
You can use either erasers or correcting fluid to eradicate errors; however, *you* should make certain that *your* corrections are clean.

unnecessary shift from phrase to clause
Because of the current parts shortage and *we are experiencing a strike,* we cannot fill any orders now.

rephrased
Because of a parts shortage and a strike, we cannot fill any orders now.
or
Because we are hampered by a parts shortage and we are experiencing a strike, we cannot fill any orders now.

Always keeping in mind the reader's reaction, the writer should strive for a rational ordering of sentence elements. Closely related elements, for example, should be placed as close together as possible for the sake of maximum clarity. Examples:

not
We would appreciate your sending us the instructions on manuscript copy editing by mail or cable.
but
We would appreciate your sending us by mail or by cable the manuscript copy-editing instructions.
or
We would appreciate your mailing or cabling us the manuscript copy-editing instructions.
or
We would appreciate it if you would mail or cable us the manuscript copy-editing instructions.

One should ensure that one's sentences form complete, independent grammatical units containing both a subject and a predicate, unless the material is dialogue or specialized copy where fragmentation may be used for particular reasons (as to reflect speech or to attract the reader's attention). Examples:

poor
During the last three years, our calculator sales soared. While our conventional office machine sales fell off.
better
During the last three years, our calculator sales soared, but our conventional office machine sales fell off.

or, with different emphasis
While our conventional office machine sales fell off during the last three years, our calculator sales soared.

sentences fragmented for special effects
(dialogue)
"Have you hand grenades?"
"Plenty."
"How many rounds per rifle?"
"Plenty."
"How many?"
"One hundred fifty. More maybe."
—Ernest Hemingway

(advertising)
See it now. The car for the Seventies . . .
A car you'll want to own.

Sentence length Sentence length is directly related to the writer's purpose: there is no magic number of words that guarantees a good sentence. For example, an executive covering broad and yet complex topics (as in a long memorandum) may choose concise, succinct sentences for the sake of clarity, impact, fast dictation, and reading. On the other hand, a writer wishing to elicit the reader's reflection upon what is being said may employ longer, more involved sentences. Still another writer may juxtapose long and short sentences to emphasize an important point. The longer sentences may build up to a climactic and forceful short sentence.

Sentence strategy Stylistically, there are two basic types of sentences—the periodic and the cumulative or loose. The periodic sentence is structured so that its main idea or its thrust is suspended until the very end, thereby drawing the reader's eye and mind along to an emphatic conclusion:

buildup — While the Commission would wish to give licensees every encouragement to experiment on their own initiative with new and different means of providing access to their stations for the discussion of important public issues, it cannot justify the imposition of a specific right of access by government fiat. — *thrust*

—*Television/Radio Age*

The cumulative sentence, on the other hand, is structured so that its main thought or its thrust appears first, followed by other phrases or clauses expanding on or supporting it:

main point — The solution must be finely honed, lest strategists err too much on the side of sophistication only to find that U.S. military forces can be defeated by overwhelming mass. — *supporting phrase*

—William C. Moore

The final phrase in a cumulative sentence theoretically could be deleted without skewing or destroying the essential meaning of the total sentence. A cumulative sentence is therefore more loosely structured than a periodic sentence.

A writer may employ yet another strategy to focus the reader's attention on a problem or an issue. This device is the rhetorical question—a question that requires no specific response from the reader but often merely sets up the introduction of the writer's own views. In some instances, a rhetorical question works as a topic sentence in a paragraph; in other instances, a whole series of rhetorical questions may spotlight pertinent issues for the reader's consideration. The following excerpts illustrate rhetorical questions in action:

rhetorical question as a topic sentence	Why all the mystery about factoring? It has a lot to do with the concentration of this service in the textile business for the past hundred years.
author answers question posed earlier	Because of this, many businessmen have had little contact with the service, and worse, have succumbed to the mythology surrounding factoring. —William R. Gruttemeyer
series of rhetorical questions focus on specific issues	Will automatic vtr's [video tape recorders] be hooked to computers? Is this the next step in automation? What comes next in tape libraries? When will it all happen? —*Television/Radio Age*

A writer uses either coordination or subordination or a mixture of both to create different stylistic effects. As shown in the subsection on clauses, coordination links independent sentences and sentence elements by means of coordinating conjunctions, while subordination transforms elements into dependent structures by means of subordinating conjunctions. While coordination tends to promote rather loose sentence structure which can become a fault, subordination tends to tighten the structure and to focus attention on a main clause. Examples of these two strategies are shown below:

coordination
During the balance of 1976, this Company expects to issue $100,000,000 of long-term debt and equity securities *and* may guarantee up to $200,000,000 of new corporate bonds.
subordination
While this Company expects to issue $100,000,000 of long-term debt and equity securities during the balance of 1976, it may also guarantee up to $200,000,000 of new corporate bonds.

A reversal of customary or expected sentence order is yet another effective stylistic strategy, when used sparingly, because it injects a dash of freshness, unexpectedness, and originality into the prose. Examples:

customary or expected order
I find that these realities are indisputable: the economy has taken a drastic downturn, costs on all fronts have soared, and jobs are at a premium.
reversal
That the economy has taken a drastic downturn; that costs on all fronts have soared; that jobs are at a premium—these are the realities that I find indisputable.

Interrupting the normal flow of discourse by inserting comments is a strategy that some writers employ to call attention to an aside, to emphasize a word or phrase, to render special effects (as forcefulness), or to make the prose a little more informal. Since too many interrupting elements may distract the reader and disrupt his train of thought, they should be used with discretion. The following are typical interrupted sentences:

an aside	His evidence, if reliable, could send our client to prison.
emphasis	These companies—ours as well as theirs—must show more profits.
forcefulness	This, gentlemen, is the prime reason for your cost overruns. I trust it will not happen again?

While interruption breaks up the flow of discourse, parallelism and balance work together toward maintaining an even rhythmic flow of thoughts. Parallelism means a similarity in the grammatical construction of adjacent phrases and clauses that are equivalent, complementary, or antithetical in meaning. Examples:

These ecological problems are of crucial concern *to* scientists, *to* businessmen, *to* government officials, and *to* all citizens.

Our attorneys have argued *that* the trademark is ours, *that* our rights have been violated, and *that* appropriate compensation is required.

He was respected not only *for his intelligence* but also *for his integrity.*

Balance is the juxtaposition and equipoise of two or more syntactically parallel constructions (as phrases and clauses) that contain similar, contrasting, or opposing ideas:

To err is human; to forgive, divine.

—Alexander Pope

Ask not what your country can do for you—ask what you can do for your country.

—John F. Kennedy

And finally, a series can be an effective way to emphasize a thought and to establish a definite rhythmic prose pattern:

The thing that interested me . . . about New York . . . was the . . . contrast it showed between the dull and the shrewd, the strong and the weak, the rich and the poor, the wise and the ignorant. . . .

—Theodore Dreiser

PARAGRAPHS

The underlying structure of any written communication—be it a memorandum, a letter, or a report—must be controlled by the writer if the material is to be clear, coherent, logical in orientation, and effective. Since good paragraphing is a means to this end, it is essential that the writer be facile when using techniques of paragraph development and transition between paragraphs. While the writer is responsible for the paragraphing system, the secretary still should be able to recognize various kinds of paragraphs and their functions as well as the potential problems that often arise in structuring a logical paragraph system. In this way, the secretary can assist the writer, especially by pointing out possible discrepancies that might result in misinterpretation by the reader or that might detract from the total effect of the communication.

A paragraph is a subdivision in writing that consists of one or more sentences, that deals with one or more ideas, or that quotes a speaker or a source. The first line of a paragraph is indented in reports, studies, articles, theses, and books. However, the first line of a paragraph in business letters and memorandums may or may not be indented, depending on the style being followed. See Chapter 6, section 6.7, for business-letter styling; see also Chapter 8, sections 8.2 and 8.5, for memorandum and report styling.

Uses of paragraphs Paragraphs should not be considered as isolated entities that are self-contained and mechanically lined up without transitions or interrelationship of ideas. Rather, paragraphs should be viewed as components of larger groups or blocks that are tightly interlinked and that interact in the sequential development of a major idea or cluster of ideas. The overall coherence of a communication depends on this interaction.

Individual paragraphs and paragraph blocks are flexible: their length, internal structure, and purpose vary according to the writer's intention and his own style. For example, one writer may be able to express his point in a succinct, one-sentence paragraph, while another may require several sentences to make his point. Writers' concepts of paragraphing also differ. For instance, some writers think of paragraphs as a means of dividing their material into logical segments with each unit developing one particular point in depth and in detail. Others view paragraphs as a means of emphasizing particular points or adding variety to long passages.

Writers use paragraphs in the following ways:

1. To support a generalization with facts or examples
2. To give a reason or reasons
3. To define something
4. To classify—i.e., to present something as a member of a particular class and then to explain the characteristics of that class
5. To delineate (as facts) or to list (as details) usually in support of a proposition
6. To set forth points of comparison and contrast, or pros and cons
7. To describe (as a situation or a thing)
8. To limit, expand, elaborate, or restate (as an idea)
9. To narrate (as an anecdote or story)
10. To paraphrase or to quote (an individual or a source)
11. To analyze or summarize (as a situation)
12. To summarize (as findings)

There are two general types of paragraphs: the expository—a unit of facts, details, or ideas brought together to explain or describe; and the argumentative—a unit of facts, details, or ideas brought together to persuade or convince. A writer may use or modify one or both of these prototypes, depending on the major thrust.

Paragraph development and strategy Depending on the writer's intentions, paragraph development may take any of these directions:

1. The paragraph may move from the general to the specific.
2. The paragraph may move from the specific to the general.
3. The paragraph may exhibit an alternating order of comparison and contrast.
4. The paragraph may chronicle events in a set temporal order—e.g., from the beginning to the end, or from the end to the beginning.
5. The paragraph may describe something (as a group of objects) in a set spatial order—e.g., the items being described may be looked at from near-to-far, or vice versa.
6. The paragraph may follow a climactic sequence with the least important facts or examples described first followed by a buildup of tension leading to the most important facts or examples then followed by a gradual easing of tension. Other material can be so ordered for effectiveness; for example, facts or issues that are easy to comprehend or accept may be set forth first and followed by those that are more difficult to comprehend or accept. In this way the easier material makes the reader receptive and prepares him to comprehend or accept the more difficult points.
7. Anticlimactic order is also useful when the writer's intent is to persuade the reader. With this strategy, the writer sets forth the most persuasive arguments first so that the reader, having then been influenced in a positive way by that persuasion, moves along with the rest of the argument with a growing feeling of assent.

Keys to effective paragraphing The following material outlines some ways of building effective paragraphs within a text.

A topic sentence—a key sentence to which the other sentences in the paragraph are related—may be placed either at the beginning or at the end of a paragraph. A lead-in topic sentence should present the main idea in the paragraph, and should set the initial tone of the material that follows. A terminal topic sentence should be an analysis, a conclusion, or a summation of what has gone before it.

Single-sentence paragraphs can be used to achieve easy transition from a preceding to a subsequent paragraph (especially when those are long and complex), if it repeats an important word or phrase from the preceding paragraph, if it contains a pronoun reference to a key individual mentioned in a preceding paragraph, or if it is introduced by an appropriate conjunction or conjunctive adverb that tightly connects the paragraphs.

Since the very first paragraph sets initial tone, introduces the subject or topic under discussion, and leads into the main thrust of a communication, it should be worded so as to immediately attract the reader's attention and arouse interest. These openings can be effective:

a. a succinct statement of purpose or point of view
b. a concise definition (as of a problem)
c. a lucid statement of a key issue or fact

But these openings can blunt the rest of the material:

a. an apology for the material to be presented
b. a querulous complaint or a defensive posture
c. a rehash of ancient history (as a word-for-word recap of previous correspondence from the individual to whom one is writing)
d. a presentation of self-evident facts
e. a group of sentences rendered limp and meaningless because of clichés

The last paragraph ties together all of the ideas and points that have been set forth earlier and reemphasizes the main thrust of the communication. These can be effective endings:

a. a setting forth of the most important conclusion or conclusions drawn from the preceding discussion
b. a final analysis of the main problem or problems under discussion
c. a lucid summary of the individual points brought up earlier
d. a final, clear statement of opinion or position
e. concrete suggestions or solutions if applicable
f. specific questions asked of the reader if applicable

But the following endings can decrease the effectiveness of a communication:

a. apologies for a poor presentation
b. qualifying remarks that blunt or negate incisive points made earlier
c. insertion of minor details or afterthoughts
d. a meaningless closing couched in clichés

The following are tests of good paragraphs:

1. Does the paragraph have a clear purpose? Is its utility evident, or is it there just to fill up space?
2. Does the paragraph clarify rather than cloud the writer's ideas?
3. Is the paragraph adequately developed, or does it merely raise other questions that the writer does not attempt to answer? If a position is being taken, does the writer include supporting information and statistics that are essential to its defense?
4. Are the length and wording of all the paragraphs sufficiently varied, or does the writer employ the same types of locutions again and again?
5. Is the sentence structure coherent?
6. Is each paragraph unified? Do all the sentences really <u>belong</u> there; or does the writer digress into areas that would have been better covered in another paragraph or that could have been omitted altogether?
7. Are the paragraphs coherent so that one sentence leads clearly and logically to another? Is easy, clear transition among the paragraphs effected by a wise selection of transitional words and phrases which indicate idea relationships and signal the direction in which the author's prose is moving?
8. Does one paragraph simply restate in other terms what has been said before?

The following essay, reproduced from page 11 of the 1974 *Annual Report* of Pacific Power & Light Company, is an example of effective paragraphing.

Our Source of Coal . . . and Pride

This is the story of your company's attempt to reconcile the energy demands of America's civilization with the necessity of preserving her great beauty, a story of Pacific's mining operation at Glenrock, Wyoming.

Energy shortage is among the most critical problems facing our country. America needs more domestic energy supply, but some don't want to mine coal, construct coal-fired plants, or use nuclear technology. People may dream of solar and geothermal energy, but without utilizing the resources and technology available to us today, exotic energy supplies in meaningful quantities will remain only a dream.

Coal, which our nation has in great supply, is one of the prime answers to this country's energy problems for the next quarter century. Under the prairielands of the Northern Great Plains lie billions of tons of coal with an energy equivalent greater than Saudi Arabia's oil reserves. Much of this coal is found in thick seams that lie close to the earth's surface, seams that can easily and economically be surface mined. This mining method maximizes the efficient use of this resource by recovering a much greater percentage than is possible by underground methods. There is virtually no waste. Safety factors are an important benefit. Surface miners have substantially less frequency and severity of accidents than underground miners. This is human conservation, an often ignored aspect of ecology. In addition to achieving a high level of productivity, safety is always at the top of corporate priorities.

The mining process begins with scrapers lifting off the layer of topsoil and piling it aside for respreading later. Then draglines remove the subsoil that covers the coal seam. After the coal is broken up with explosives, it is loaded into trucks and carried to a railhead. Now comes a technically difficult and most controversial part of the mining operation—reclamation. Bulldozers recontour the subsoil to the existing lay of the land. Scrapers then replace the original topsoil. This **reclaimed** portion is then mulched with small grained straw, seeded with special perennial grasses, and fertilized with nitrogen.

paragraph block 1
paragraph 1 functions as a topic sentence for the entire essay

paragraph 2 topic sentence sets forth a fact and occurs first in that paragraph

subsequent sentences support and expand topic sentence

paragraph block 2
paragraph 3 topic sentence offers a solution to the problem posed in paragraph 2

subsequent sentences explain in depth the solution offered in the topic sentence

last two sentences summarize and make pertinent points

paragraph 4 is ***descriptive:*** *it lists in temporal order the steps in a process*

paragraph transition is achieved by the repetition of key words in paragraphs 4, 5, 6, and 7

Our **reclamation** processes have undergone many years of research and experimentation so that **reclaimed** areas now exceed the native terrain in productivity. Nature herself can prove this. The number of animals which can feed in any given area is regulated by nature balance. On our 550 **reclaimed** acres of the Wyoming plains, the herds of deer and antelope are increasing markedly, positive proof that the productivity of the land has also increased.

The whole cycle of surface mining, from the time the topsoil is removed to the final seeding, takes about 2½ years and costs about $2,000 per acre. Though the surface acre may be valued at only $30, we proportion the **reclamation** cost to the value of the coal mined. The final bill will amount to about 5 cents a ton. Our commitment to **reclamation** is total. If ever the value of the coal will not support **reclamation** costs, the land will not be disturbed.

paragraph block 3

last sentence of paragraph 5 contains support for preceding arguments

paragraph 6 is ***expository:*** *it gives facts and figures*

The myth that corporations are pro-pollution, relentlessly exploiting the earth, must be disclaimed. Many are often at the forefront in the struggle to preserve the environment, and preserve the land entrusted to them. Pacific has been **reclaiming** Wyoming land since 1965, four years before it became state law. There were many technical problems, but most of them are solved now. There may be more problems, but the recognition of that fact is the best assurance that we will overcome them. The responsibility to serve necessitates the obligation to keep trying.

An environmentalist is one who has learned to live in harmony with his surroundings, not be controlled by them. As the advance of society must not be made at the expense of nature, so the preservation of nature must not be achieved at the destruction of society. They must coexist, and in man's technology, ever alert and ever advancing, lies our only answer.

If man would strive for knowledge and understanding, reason, not emotion, must be the guidepost. Performance, not talk, must be the touchstone. We believe our performance speaks clearly. Pacific Power is uncovering one of nature's great resources, is supplying one of America's vital needs, and is revitalizing part of the prairielands of Wyoming. Both man and nature are benefiting from our recovery of necessary fossil fuel. That's our story . . . our source of pride.

paragraph block 4

paragraph 7 is ***argumentative:*** *it begins with its major point of argument in its topic sentence, followed in subsequent sentences by supporting arguments, and supporting figures and facts*

paragraph 8 begins with a definition to which the rest of the arguments continuing from paragraph 7 are keyed

paragraph 9 offers general solutions to problems discussed throughout the essay; the tone is intentionally upbeat

last sentence neatly ties in with the title, thus exemplifying coherence

7.9

TONE IN WRITING

The tone of a communication is usually set in the first paragraph and is ordinarily maintained throughout the subsequent paragraphs to the end. Of course, tone depends on a number of factors:

1. the underlying reason or reasons why something (as a memorandum or a letter) is being written in the first place
2. the personal attitude of the writer toward his reader and his subject matter.
3. the content (as general vs. technical) of the material itself

Thus, a communication may be formal or informal, neutral or biased, friendly or critical, or it may reflect any number of other feelings and attitudes.

THE IMPORTANCE OF TONE IN COMMUNICATIONS

The effect of the tone of a communication on its reader cannot be overemphasized. A letter, for example, may feature excellent layout, clean typewriting, attractive stationery, good sentence structure, correct spelling, and easy transition from one paragraph to another. It may contain complete, logically presented data. Yet, if the tone of the letter is needlessly abrupt or indeed rude, the effect of the material on the reader will be negative, of course. Reader responses should therefore be kept in mind at all times. Some principles relevant to tone in general business communications are outlined and discussed briefly in the following paragraphs. For further examples of varying tone in business letters, the reader may consult Chapter 9 where several kinds of letters are illustrated.

A communication should be reader-oriented. When one is intent on setting forth one's own objectives, especially under pressure, one often unfortunately forgets the reader's point of view and possible responses. Compare the following two approaches:

abrupt
We have read with interest your article on HDPE pipe in the October 12 issue of *Plastics.* Since our marketing division is preparing a multiclient study on plastic pipe applications, we will need offprints of the following papers you have written on this subject: . . . .

polite
We have read with interest your article on HDPE pipe in the October 12 issue of *Plastics.* Our marketing division is preparing a multiclient study on plastic pipe applications—a study that will not be complete without reference to your outstanding research. We'd therefore be pleased if you'd send us offprints of the following papers you've written on the subject: . . . .

The writer should not assume automatically that the reader has the same degree of familiarity with the matter to be discussed as he has. He should consciously pitch his presentation at an appropriate level, neither writing down to experts nor writing over the heads of nonexperts.

Use of the personal pronoun *you* can personalize a communication and thus make the reader feel more involved in the discussion. Compare the following pairs of examples:

impersonal
The enclosed brochure outlining this Company's services may be of interest.
This Company is gratified when its clients offer useful suggestions.

personal
We've enclosed a brochure outlining our services, which we hope will interest you.
We appreciate your taking the time to offer such a useful suggestion.

In the same way, the personal pronouns *I* and *we* should not be consciously avoided in favor of passive or impersonal constructions that, when overused, can depersonalize a communication. Examples:

impersonal	*personal*
Reference is made to your May 1 letter received by this office yesterday.	We are referring to your May 1 letter which we received yesterday.
Enclosed is the requested material.	We're enclosing the material you requested.
It is the understanding of this writer that the contract is in final negotiation stages.	I understand that the contract is in final negotiation stages.

Common courtesy and tactfulness can be exercised without resort to obsequiousness. Considerate writers use polite expressions whenever possible.

7.10

ACHIEVEMENT OF A MORE ORIGINAL WRITING STYLE

The effectiveness and overall output of communications can be markedly increased if one avoids the padding and clichés that can blunt what otherwise might be incisive writing. These expressions, sometimes called *business static,* have become fixtures in the vocabularies of far too many writers. Some of the locutions (as "enclosed please find") are best avoided because they are stale. Others (as "aforesaid"), while common to legal documents, are stiff and awkward in general business contexts. Still others (as "beg to respond") have an antique ring. And then there are some expressions (as "forward on") that are redundant, and others (as "acknowledge receipt of") that are overlong.

Unfortunately, these verbal tics seem to occur most often in conspicuous areas of a text: either at the very beginning where initial tone is being set or at the very end where summations are being made, or at the beginnings and ends of individual sentences and paragraphs where particular ideas and points are being set forth. Needless to say, a busy reader can become quite annoyed when he or she must wade through superfluous or hackneyed expressions to get at the gist of a communication.

While this section does not presume to prescribe word choice, it does attempt to spotlight ways to shave away verbal fat so that the main ideas and points in a piece of writing will stand out. The following alphabetically ordered mini-glossary is a representative list of expressions better avoided by writers who seek more clarity, brevity, and originality in their business communications.

abeyance
hold in abeyance

stilted We are holding our final decision in abeyance. . . .

easier We are deferring / delaying / holding up our final decision. . . .

above

While use of this word as a noun ("see the above"), an adjective ("the above figure shows"), and an adverb ("see above") is indeed acceptable, its overuse within one document can distract a reader. Alternative expressions are:

See the figure on page --.
See the figure at the top of the page.
This (that) figure shows. . . .
See the material illustrated earlier.

above-mentioned

is overlong and is often overworked within a single document.

longer The above-mentioned policy. . . .

shorter This (That) policy. . . .

acknowledge receipt of
requires 22 keystrokes, but the alternative expression *have received* is a 13-stroke synonym. Why not use the shorter of the two?

longer We acknowledge receipt of your check. . . .

shorter We have / We've } received your check. . . .

advise
has been overworked when meaning "to inform." Since "to inform" can be expressed by either of the shorter verbs *say* or *tell,* why not use one of them?

longer We regret to advise you that the book is out of stock.

shorter We must tell you that the book is out of stock.
Unfortunately, the book is out of stock.
We're sorry to say that the book is out of stock.

advised and informed
is redundant, since the two conjoined words simply repeat each other.

redundant He has been advised and informed of our position.
We have advised and informed him of our position.

lean He has been told of our position.
We have told him of our position.
We have outlined our position to him.
He knows our position.

affix (one's) **signature to**
is padding, and can be reduced to *sign.*

padded Please affix your signature to the enclosed documents.

lean Please sign these documents.
Please sign the enclosed documents.

aforementioned/aforesaid
are commonly used in legal documents but sound verbose and pointlessly pompous in general business contexts. The same idea may usually be conveyed by one of the demonstrative adjectives (*this, that, these, those*).

verbose The aforementioned company. . . .

natural This (that) company. . . .
or
The company in question. . . .
The company (we) mentioned earlier. . . .

verbose . . . must reach a decision regarding the aforesaid dispute.

natural . . . must make a decision about this (that) dispute.

amplify to a maximum
may be pared down to *maximize.*

padded . . . expect all salesmen to amplify to a maximum their sales calls next month.

lean . . . expect all salesmen to maximize their next month's sales calls.

—*compare* REDUCE TO A MINIMUM

and etc.
is redundant, because *etc.* is the abbreviation of the Latin *et cetera* meaning "and the rest." Omit the *and.*

not . . . carbon packs, onionskin, bond, and etc.

but . . . carbon packs, onionskin, bond, etc.

as per
has been overworked when meaning "as," "in accordance with," and "following." It is a tired and formulaic way to begin a letter, paragraph, or sentence.

overworked As per your request of. . . .
As per our telephone conversation of. . . .
As per our agreement. . . .

more natural As you requested. . . .
According to your request. . . .
In accordance with your request. . . .
As a follow-up to our telephone conversation. . . .
In accordance with our telephone conversation. . . .
As we agreed. . . .
In accordance with our agreement. . . .
According to our agreement. . . .

as regards
can also be expressed by the terms *concerning* or *regarding*.

stiff As regards your complaint. . . .
easier Concerning your complaint. . . .
or
Let's talk about your complaint.

as stated above
can be more naturally expressed as:
As we (I) have said. . . .

assuring you that
is an outmoded participial-phrase ending to a business letter that should not be used.

outmoded Assuring you that your cooperation will be appreciated, I remain
Sincerely yours
current I will appreciate your cooperation.
Sincerely yours

as to
has been as overworked as the phrase *as per*. Here are some alternatives for *as to:*
regarding
concerning
about
of

overworked As to your second question. . . .
fresher Regarding your second question. . . .
Coming to your second question. . . .
or
Now for your second question.
Let's look at your second question.
overworked We have no means of judging as to the wisdom of that decision.
fresher We cannot (can't) judge the wisdom of that decision.

—*compare* AS PER

at about
is meaningless because *at* is explicit but *about* is indefinite. Thus, when conjoined, they cancel each other's meaning.

meaningless I'll get back to you at about 9:30 a.m. tomorrow.
explicit I'll get back to you at 9:30 a.m. tomorrow.
or
I'll get back to you about 9:30 a.m. tomorrow.

at all times
may be shortened to *always*.

longer We shall be glad to meet with you at all times.
shorter We'll always be glad to meet with you.

at an early date
is both long and vague. If the writer means "immediately," or "by (*date*)," he should say as much; if he means "when convenient," he should specify it.

at once and by return mail
when conjoined are repetitious: either *at once* or *immediately* will suffice.

repetitive Please send us your check at once and by return mail.
succinct Please send us your check at once (*or* immediately).

—*see also* RETURN MAIL

attached hereto/herewith
is quite impersonal and may be expressed in a more personal way as:
Attached is/are
We are attaching
We have attached
You'll see attached
—*compare* ENCLOSED HEREWITH

at this point in time/at this time
may be shortened to
now
presently
at (the) present

at this writing
may be shortened to *now*

at your earliest convenience
manages to convey nothing in 28 keystrokes; however, the alternative *as soon as you can* requires only 18 strokes and states the case explicitly. Still other expressions, as
now
immediately
by (*date*)
within (*number of days*)
may also be used, depending on context.

basic fundamentals
is redundant. One of the following may be substituted:

the basics
the fundamentals

beg
beg to acknowledge
beg to advise
beg to state
and other such *beg* combinations sound antique. The following may be used instead:
We acknowledge. . . .
We've received. . . .
Thank you for. . . .
We're pleased to tell you. . . .
We can say that. . . .
We can tell you that. . . .

brought to our notice
is overlong and may be recast to:

We note . . . .
We notice . . . .
We see . . . .

contents carefully noted
contributes little or no information and should be omitted.

not Yours of the 1st. received and contents carefully noted.

but We've read carefully your June 1 letter.

We've read your June 1 letter.

The instructions in your June 1 letter have been followed.

We've read your June 1 letter and have followed its instructions.

dated
is unnecessary when used in locutions like "your letter dated June 1." The word may be omitted:

your June 1 letter
your letter of June 1

deem (it)
is a stiff way of saying *think* or *believe.*

stiff We deem it advisable that you . . . .

easier We think you ought to . . . .

We think it advisable that you . . . .

demand and insist
when conjoined are redundant; however, the use of just one of the following at a time will suffice: *demand* or *insist* or *require*

despite the fact that
may be pared down to *although* or *though*

due to
due to the fact that
are both stiff and may be reduced to:

because (of)
since

duly
is meaningless in expressions like

Your order has been duly forwarded.

and thus should be omitted:

Your order has been forwarded.
We've forwarded your order.

earnest endeavor
is cloying when used in this type of sentence:

It will be our earnest endeavor to serve our customers . . . .

It should be replaced with more direct, straightforward phrasing:

We'll (*or* We shall) try to serve our customers . . . .

enclosed herewith/enclosed please find
are impersonal and stilted expressions better worded as:

We enclose . . . .
We are enclosing . . . .
We have enclosed . . . .
Enclosed is/are . . . .
—*compare* ATTACHED HERETO/HEREWITH

endeavor
is an eight-letter verb that can be replaced by the three-letter verb *try,* which is synonymous and not pompous.

pompous and longer
We shall endeavor to . . . .
direct and shorter
We'll (*or* We shall) try to . . . .
or
We'll make a real effort to . . . .
We'll make every effort to . . . .
We'll do everything we can to . . . .
We'll do our best to . . . .

esteemed
is effusive when used in a sentence like

We welcome your esteemed favor of June 9.

and therefore should not be used. The sentence may be recast to:

Thank you for your June 9 letter.

favor
should never be used in the sense of a letter, an order, a check, or other such item.

not your favor of April 14
but your April 14 letter

for the purpose of
may be more succinctly worded as *for.*

padded . . . necessary for purposes of accounting.
lean . . . necessary for accounting.

forward on
is redundant, since *forward* alone conveys the meaning adequately.

redundant We have forwarded your complaint on to the proper authorities.
explicit We have forwarded your complaint to the proper authorities.

hand (one) **herewith**
as in the locution

We are handing you herewith an invoice for . . . .

is an inflated way of saying

We're (*or* We are) enclosing
Enclosed is/are

have before me
is superfluous. Obviously, the writer has previous correspondence at hand when responding to a letter.

not I have before me your letter of June 1 . . . .
but In reply / response / answer } to your June 1 letter . . . .

hereto
—*see* ATTACHED HERETO/HEREWITH

herewith
—*see* ATTACHED HERETO/HEREWITH
ENCLOSED HEREWITH/ENCLOSED PLEASE FIND

hoping for the favor (*or* to hear)
and other such participial-phrase endings for business letters are now outmoded and should be omitted. Instead of

Hoping for the favor of a reply,
I remain

one of these alternatives may be selected:
I (We) look forward to hearing from you.
I (We) look forward to your reply.
May I (we) hear from you soon?

I am/I remain
as in the expression

Looking forward to a speedy reply from you,
I am (*or* remain)

should never be used as lead-ins to complimentary closes; however, the writer might choose one of the following expressions:

I (We) look forward to your immediate reply.
I (We) are looking forward to a reply from you soon.
May I (we) please have an immediate reply?
Will you please reply soon?

immediately and at once
when conjoined are redundant; however, each element of the expression may be used separately, as

May we hear from you immediately (*or* at once)?

incumbent
it is incumbent upon (one)
is more easily expressed as

I/we must . . . .
You must . . . .
He/she/they must . . . .

in re
should be avoided in general business letters, although it is often used in legal documents. Adequate substitutes are:

regarding
concerning
in regard to
about

stiff In re our telephone conversation of . . . .
easier Concerning our telephone conversation of . . . .

institute the necessary inquiries
is overlong and overformal, and may be reworded as follows:

We shall inquire . . . .
We'll find out . . . .
We are inquiring . . . .

in the amount of
is a long way to say *for.*

longer . . . are sending you a check in the amount of $50.95.
shorter . . . are sending you a check for $50.95.
. . . are sending you a $50.95 check.

in the course of
may be more concisely expressed by *during* or *while.*

longer In the course of the negotiations . . . .

shorter During the negotiations . . . . While we were negotiating. . . .

in the event that
may be more concisely expressed by *if* or *in case.*

longer In the event that you cannot meet with me next week, we shall . . . .

shorter If you cannot meet with me next week, we shall . . . .

in view of the fact that
may be shortened to *because* (*of*) or *since.*

longer In view of the fact that he is now president of . . . .

He was terminated in view of the fact that he had been negligent.

shorter Since he is now president of . . . .

He was terminated because of negligence.

it is incumbent upon
—*see* INCUMBENT

it is within (one's) **power**
—*see* POWER

line
is a vague substitute for one of the following more explicit terms:

merchandise
line of goods (*or* merchandise)
goods
product(s)
service(s)
system(s)

meet with (one's) **approval**
is a stiff phrase more easily expressed as:

is (are) acceptable
I (we) accept (*or* approve)

stiff If the plan meets with Mr. Doe's approval . . . .

easier If the plan is acceptable to Mr. Doe . . . .

If Mr. Doe accepts (*or* approves) the plan . . . .

note
we note that
you will note that
often constitute padding and thus should be dropped.

padded We note that your prospectus states . . . .

You will note that the amount in the fourth column . . . .

lean Your prospectus states . . . .

The amount in the fourth column . . . .

Or, if a word of this type is required, a more natural substitute is *see:*

We see that you have paid the bill in full.

oblige
is archaic in the following locution:

Please reply to this letter and oblige.

The sentence should be recast to read:

Please reply to this letter immediately.

of recent date
—*see* RECENT DATE

of the opinion that
is a stiff way of saying:

We think (*or* believe) that . . . .
Our opinion is that . . . .
Our position is that . . . .

our Mr., Ms., Miss, Mrs. + (surname)
is best omitted.

not Our Mr. Lee will call on you next Tuesday.

but Our sales representative, Mr. Lee, will call on you next Tuesday.

Mr. Lee, our sales representative, will call on you next Tuesday.

party
while idiomatic in legal documents, is nevertheless awkward in general business contexts when the meaning is "individual" or "person."

awkward We understand that you are the party who called earlier.

smoother We understand that you are the person (*or* individual *or* one) who called earlier.

pending receipt of
while used in legal documents is, in general contexts, a stiff way of saying "until we receive."

stiff We are holding your order, pending receipt of your check.

easier We'll ship your order as soon as we receive your check.

permit me to remain
is outmoded and should not be used as part of the last sentence in a business letter.

place an order for
takes 18 keystrokes, but the verb *order* takes only 5 strokes. Why not try the shorter of the two?

position
be in a position to
The locutions

We are not in a position to
We are now in a position to

are unnecessarily long and may be recast to the shorter and more personal phrases

We cannot/can't
We are unable/aren't able
We can
We are now able

power
it is (not) **within** (one's) **power to**
is a lengthy way of saying

We can (*or* are able to)
We cannot/can't
We are unable to

longer It is not within our power to back such an expensive project.

It is now within our power to help you.

shorter We cannot back such an expensive project.

We can help you now.

prepared to offer
is a set phrase that can be reworded in a number of more original ways as shown below.

set We are prepared to offer you the following discounts: . . . .

varied We can offer you these discounts: . . . .

Our discount schedule is: . . . .

We're ready to offer you these discounts: . . . .

We offer the following discounts: . . . .

The discounts we're now offering are:

prior to
is a stiff way to say *before*.

stiff Prior to receipt of your letter of July 1, we . . . .

easier Before we received your July 1 letter, we . . . .

Before receipt of your July 1 letter, we . . . .

Before receiving your July 1 letter, we . . . .

—*compare* SUBSEQUENT TO

pursuant to
is a stiff phrase that unfortunately occurs in the very beginnings of many follow-up letters and memorandums. It should be reworded to read:

In accordance with
According to
Following up (*or* As a follow-up to)

stiff Pursuant to our telephone conversation of June 1, let me say that . . . .

easier Following up our June 1 telephone conversation, I can say that . . . .

reason is because
is ungrammatical, because the noun *reason* + the verb *is* call for a following noun clause and not an adverbial clause introduced by *because*.

The reason is:
The reason is that
This is the reason:
Because (*or* since)

receipt
—*see* PENDING RECEIPT OF

receipt is acknowledged
is an unnecessarily impersonal passive construction more concisely expressed as

We received
We have received
We've received

recent date
of recent date
is an unwieldy way to indicate an undated letter; the alternatives

your recent letter
your undated letter

are smoother. If the letter is dated, it is best to repeat the exact date.

reduce to a minimum
may be pared down to *minimize*.

wordy This product reduces to a minimum the air pollution in work areas.

succinct This product minimizes air pollution in work areas.

—*compare* AMPLIFY TO A MAXIMUM

refer back to
is a phrase in which *back* is redundant because the word element *re-* means "back."

redundant We must refer back to last year's figures before we can answer your inquiry.

lean We must refer to last year's figures before we can answer your inquiry.

refuse and decline
when conjoined are redundant; however, the use of one but not both will suffice: *refuse* or *decline*

redundant We must refuse and decline any further dealings with your company.

lean We must refuse any further dealings . . . .
or
We must decline to have any further dealings . . . .

—*compare* DEMAND AND INSIST

reiterate again
the adverb *again* is redundant, since the verb *reiterate* carries the total meaning by itself.

redundant Let me reiterate our policy again.

succinct Let me reiterate / restate / repeat } our policy.
May I reiterate / restate / repeat } our policy?
or
Let me state our policy again.
May I state our policy again?

return mail
by return mail
is a hackneyed and meaningless way of saying
immediately
promptly
at once
by (*explicit date*)

hackneyed Please send us your check by return mail.

fresher Won't you mail (us) your check immediately?
Please send us your check at once.
We'd like to have your check by (*date*).

said
is idiomatic in legal documents; however, it sounds stiff in general business contexts.

stiff . . . a discussion of said matters.

easier . . . a discussion of those (these) matters.

same
is an awkward substitute for the pronoun *it* or *them,* or for the applicable noun.

awkward We have your check and we thank you for same.
Your July 2 order has been received and same has been shipped.

easier Thank you for your check which arrived yesterday.
Your July 2 order has been received and shipped.

sells at a price of
is a 19-keystroke phrase more concisely expressed as:
costs
sells for
is priced at

separate cover
under separate cover
is a tired, overlong, vague phrase. If a specific mailing method (as SPECIAL DELIVERY) is not to be indicated, the adverb *separately* should be substituted.

hackneyed We are mailing you our 1976 Annual Report under separate cover.

fresher We're sending you separately our 1976 *Annual Report.*

subsequent to
is longer than its synonyms *after* or *following.* Why not opt for fewer keystrokes?

longer Subsequent to the interview, she . . . .

shorter After the interview, she . . . .

—*compare* PRIOR TO

take the liberty
is overlong and sounds somewhat obsequious.

longer We are taking the liberty of sending you free samples of. . . .

shorter We are sending you free samples of. . . .

thanking you in advance
is an outmoded participial-phrase ending that should not be used in modern business letters. A writer who uses this phrase is also cavalier enough to presume that his request will be honored.

not Thanking you in advance for your help, I am
Sincerely yours

but Your help (*or* assistance) will be appreciated.
I'll appreciate your help.
Any help you may give me will be greatly appreciated.
I'll appreciate any help you may give.
If you can help me, I'll appreciate it.
I'll be grateful for your help.
Won't you help me?

therefor/therein/thereon
are commonly used in legal documents, but sound stiff in general business contexts.

stiff The order is enclosed herewith with payment therefor.
The safe is in a secure area with the blueprints kept therein.
Enclosed please find Forms X, Y, and Z; please affix your signature thereon.

easier We're enclosing a check with our order.
The blueprints are kept in the safe which is located in a secure area.
Please sign Forms X, Y, and Z which we have enclosed.

trusting you will
is an outmoded participial-phrase ending that should not be used in business letters. A writer who uses this phrase is also cavalier enough to presume that his request will be honored.

not Trusting that you will inform me of your decision soon, I am
Sincerely yours

but I hope that you'll give me your decision soon.
Will you please give me your decision soon?
Won't you give me your decision soon?

under date of
is an awkward locution that should be omitted.

not . . . your letter under date of December 31. . . .

but . . . your December 31 letter. . . .
. . . your letter of December 31. . . .

—*compare* DATED

under separate cover
—*see* SEPARATE COVER

(the) **undersigned**
is awkward and impersonal.

awkward Please return these photographs to the undersigned.
The undersigned believes that. . . .

easier Please return these photographs to me.
I believe that. . . .

up to the present writing
is padding and should be omitted.

padded Up to the present writing, we do not seem to have received. . . .

lean We have not yet received. . . .
As of now we have not received. . . .
We still have not received. . . .
We haven't received. . . .

valued
is redundant when used after the verb *appreciate* which carries the idea itself.

redundant We appreciate your valued order of. . . .

lean We appreciate your order of. . . .
Your order is, of course, appreciated. . . .

8

CHAPTER EIGHT

SPECIAL TYPING PROJECTS: The Practical Application of Business English

CONTENTS

8.1

INTRODUCTION

This chapter concerns those special typing projects that exemplify Business English in action: the preparation of and the formats for interoffice memorandums, news releases, reports, minutes of meetings, and articles for house organs. Special attention is given to the use of library resources, the assembling of data for reports, the style and format of formal reports, the preparation of graphic aids, the proper styling of footnotes and bibliographies, and the techniques of proofreading.

8.2

FORMAT OF INTEROFFICE MEMORANDUMS

The interoffice memorandum or memo is a means of informal communication within a firm or organization. Its special arrangement replaces the salutation, complimentary close, and written signature of the letter with identifying headings.

Although a memorandum may be typed on a plain sheet of paper, it is usually typed on special prepared forms, which are most often full sheets. The forms may be in pads or in special carbon packs to facilitate preparation and distribution of carbon copies. Some carbon packs have the file copy printed on a sheet of colored paper. Space is provided for the message which is typically informal in style and routine in content. Since many companies design their own interoffice memorandum forms, the variety of sizes, styles, and arrangements is great. Generally, the format is simple and comprises two major parts: (1) the *heading* consisting of the printed guide words *To, From, Date,* and *Subject,* and (2) the *body* or *message.*

THE MAIN PARTS OF A MEMORANDUM

The heading Although the heading usually contains only the guide words shown just above, other guide words such as *Telephone Extension, Department,* or *Agency* may be added. The *To* line identifies the individual(s) or group(s) intended to receive the memorandum. It includes the addressee's name (courtesy titles such as *Mr., Ms., Mrs., Miss,* and *Dr.* are optional; they are more likely to be used when addressing a person of higher rank), job title (optional), and department (especially in large organizations). Several names may be listed after *To* if the memorandum is being sent to several people. A check is placed after the name of each person on his or her copy to facilitate handling. Multiple distribution may also be achieved by listing several names in the carbon copy notation which may appear at the bottom of the memorandum and then checking each name off. The *From* line indicates the name of the writer. A courtesy title is generally not used, but the writer's job title or department may be included. Some forms feature guide words for job titles and department designations. The *Date* line contains the full date, which should not be abbreviated or appear in all-numerical form. The *Subject* line pinpoints the gist of the memorandum and thus serves to orient its recipient before he begins to read. It is usually one line in length and should be as brief as possible. Since this line is often used for filing purposes, it must be accurate.

The guide words are usually followed by a colon. The typist begins insertions two spaces after the colon. The guide words are often but not always aligned at the right on a printed form to make typing easier for the secretary:

```
      TO:               TO:
    FROM:      or       FROM:
 SUBJECT:               SUBJECT:
```

Since the guide word or words and the insertions must align horizontally, the variable line spacer or the ratchet release lever on the typewriter is used:

Incorrect	*Correct*
FROM: Thomas Kingsford	FROM: Thomas Kingsford

The body or message The body or message of the memorandum is separated from the subject line by two or three blank lines. It may be typed in block style (with no indentations for paragraphs), it is usually single-spaced (with double-spacing between paragraphs), and it normally has one-inch side margins. It is also appropriate to double-space short memorandums. The tone or degree of formality of a memorandum message varies with the level of management it will reach, with the subject being discussed, and with the reader-writer relationship. The basic organization of the message usually follows one or the other of these patterns: *direct*—where the main idea is presented first and followed by explanations or facts, and *indirect*—where the explanations and facts are given first and the main idea is set forth last.

Interoffice Memorandum Typed on a Printed Form

MEMORANDUM

To: Cynthia A. Barnes
William P. Cook
Joan T. Davis

Date: May 20, 19—

From: Roger N. Taylor

Subject: Interoffice Memorandum Format

If the printed words To, From, and Subject are aligned to the right, leave two blank spaces after the colons and then proceed to typewrite the fill-in data. If, however, the guide words are aligned to the left as shown here, block the fill-ins so that they will be vertically aligned with the body of the memorandum. Set a tab stop two spaces after the guide word Date and then type the fill-in which should not be abbreviated. Thus, if the writer's initials are to be typed at the end of the message, the first letter of the typed date and the first letter of the initials will be vertically aligned later on.

All fill-ins should be horizontally aligned with their guide words. Horizontal alignment is accomplished by use of the variable line spacer or the ratchet release lever on the typewriter.

If the memorandum is confidential, type the word confidential in the center of the page about three lines below the top edge of the sheet or about two lines below the printed heading Memorandum. This designation may be typed all in capital letters or in underscored capital and lower case letters.

Maintain side margins of at least one inch. Leave three blank lines between the subject line and the first message line. Block all paragraphs flush left. Single-space the paragraphs internally; double-space between paragraphs.

Type the writer's initials two lines below the last message line and align them with the date.

R. T.

coc

G. & C. Merriam Company - 47 Federal Street, Springfield, Mass. 01101

Interoffice Memorandum Typed on a Plain Sheet of Paper

```
TO:        Alison Paige
           Marketing Department

FROM:      Maria Rodriguez
           Personnel Department

DATE:      November 21, 19—

SUBJECT:   Format for Interoffice Memorandums on Plain Paper


          Leave top and side margins of at least one inch when
typing memorandums on plain paper.  Align all guide words at the
left margin.  For easier typing, use a ten-space tab stop to
align the fill-in data.

          Leave two or three blank lines after the subject line.
Indent all paragraphs of the message by ten spaces or use the
blocked paragraph style illustrated in the printed memorandum
facsimile.

          Type the writer's initials two spaces beneath the last
line of the last paragraph and position them slightly to the
right of dead center.

                                   M. R.

coc

cc Wesley Torrence
   Annette Roberts
```

Although there is no formal closing to a memorandum form, the writer's initials are usually typed at the end. Some writers prefer to initial or sign a memorandum. The typist's initials as well as enclosure and carbon copy notations also appear at the bottom in the same position as those in a regular letter.

Since the memorandum form is an informal communication tool, it is common for the respondent to pen a reply directly on the form. One form in use even states, "SAVE TIME: If convenient, handwrite reply to sender on this same sheet." As has already been mentioned, some memorandum forms are in convenient carbon packs to facilitate the typing of multiple copies. Another typical practice is use of the preprinted reply section on the memorandum form itself.

The envelope A memorandum may be distributed unfolded without an envelope; however, many companies have special envelopes for interoffice memorandums. These envelopes may be in color to help the mail clerks differentiate them from outgoing mail. If a regular envelope is used, the notation *Company Mail* is typed in the place where a stamp would have been affixed. Some memorandum forms may have a fold line to aid in folding for envelope insertion. The fold line is particularly helpful if a window envelope is used. The conveyor location is listed (usually in a letter and number code) on the envelope to facilitate delivery. It might cite a particular department, a specific floor, or a certain wing of a building.

8.3

PREPARATION OF A NEWS RELEASE

It is a journalistic convention that news releases be written in inverted pyramidal form—the main idea is set forth first, followed by an exposition of the major details relating to that idea, and concluding with the minor details or supplementary ideas that are related to the main topic but that are not essential in an explanation or discussion of it. If the article is so written, it can be cut from the bottom by an editor without destroying its essential meaning. An acceptable article from a journalistic standpoint contains all the vital information at the beginning: the five *W*'s—who, what, when, where, and why—as well as an important *H*—how. The article should be factual, interesting, and informative. Since accuracy is very important, the secretary should proofread the article before it is submitted for publication. All details, especially spelling and numbers, must be checked and verified.

FORMAT OF A NEWS RELEASE

Paper and setup A news release may be typed on plain paper measuring 8½" x 11" or on a special news-release form. Double-spacing is preferred, as it facilitates editing later on. Top and side margins are usually one inch in width. At the discretion of the secretary, the bottom margin may be somewhat wider to allow for editorial comments. Frequently the words N E W S R E L E A S E are typed conspicuously all in spaced capital letters at the top of the page if a preprinted form is not being used.

The heading The heading contains what is called *source data:* the name of the individual and/or company issuing the release and the appropriate address of that individual or company, a telephone number if desired, and specific release information (as the phrases For Immediate Release; June 26, 19--, or IMMEDIATE RELEASE typed all in capitals).

The title line The title line, centered on the page and typed all in capital letters, tells the reader at first glance what the article is about.

The article The article itself starts with an indented date line consisting of the city and the date. The city name is typed all in capital letters; the date is typed in capital and lowercase letters and is followed by a dash. Example:

NEW YORK CITY, January 1—

The name of the state is given only if the city has a very common name (for instance, the *Directory of Post Offices* lists twenty-four cities with the name *Springfield*) or if the city is not well known.

Continuation sheets If there is more than one page, the word MORE is typed all in capital letters at the bottom of the first sheet either in the center or on the right side. Continuation sheets are numbered and feature a brief caption typed flush with the left margin near the top of the page:

```
AWARD—2
```

The end of the article One of the following devices typically positioned in the center of the page signals the end of the article:

or
-30-
-end- *or* (END)

A facsimile of a news release is shown in the following illustration.

A News Release

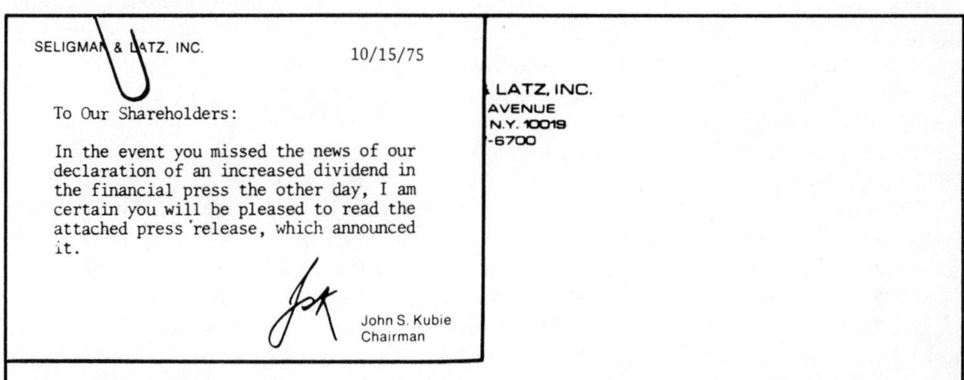

SELIGMAN & LATZ, INC. 10/15/75

LATZ, INC.
AVENUE
N.Y. 10019
-6700

To Our Shareholders:

In the event you missed the news of our declaration of an increased dividend in the financial press the other day, I am certain you will be pleased to read the attached press release, which announced it.

John S. Kubie
Chairman

main idea

NEW YORK--Seligman & Latz, Inc. (AMEX) today declared an increased quarterly cash dividend of 25 cents per share, up from the prior rate of 20 cents, and declared a 5 per cent stock dividend, as well.

major details

The increase in the cash dividend is the second in this fiscal year. Last April, the board of directors increased the quarterly dividend to 20 cents from 15 cents. At that time, the company also declared a 5 per cent stock dividend.

The cash dividend will be paid on the increased number of shares resulting from the stock dividend.

Both dividends will be paid November 28, 1975, to stockholders of record at the close of business on October 31, 1975. Cash will be paid in lieu of the issuance of fractional shares resulting from the stock dividend.

minor details

Seligman & Latz, Inc. engages in the operation of leased beauty salons in department stores here and abroad. It also operates Finlay fine jewelry departments in department stores and owns Adrien Arpel, Inc., a distributor and retailer of beauty and skin care products and services.

Last month, Seligman & Latz, Inc. reported increased earnings for the third quarter and nine months of fiscal 1975. Third quarter profit was $767,000 or 47 cents per share. Nine-month income was $2,714,000 or $1.69 per share.

#####

8.4

REPORT RESEARCH: Use of Library Resources

Two kinds of information gathering are employed in the business world: primary research and secondary research. Primary research entails gathering information or data firsthand: the researcher may study company records, he may experiment, and he may use observational techniques or interviewing procedures. Primary research is often complex, time-consuming, and costly. Secondary research entails the use of library resources. If information is available from a library, it is usually easier and less costly to retrieve than information available only from primary sources. It is therefore wise to refer to a library or libraries at the outset of an investigation in order to avoid needless duplication of effort. Although library investigation often provides no more than a basis for primary research, on occasion it may yield all the needed data.

Libraries are of two basic types—the general and the specialized. The former includes public, college, and university libraries whose collections afford researchers information in fairly broad areas. The latter contains selective and often highly specialized collections that may be maintained by a company, a research organization, a group, or an individual. For example, an oil company may have an excellent library containing an extensive collection of books relating to geology as well as a broad collection of chemical- and petroleum-engineering literature. Since specialized libraries or resources may be difficult to locate, researchers should consult such guide books as *Research Centers Directory, Special Libraries Directory,* or *Directory of Special Libraries and Information Centers.*

USING A GENERAL LIBRARY

the most expeditious method of finding information at the library is to consult the card catalog, the available reference works, and the periodical indexes.

The card catalog The card catalog lists the library's holdings by author's name, title, and subject. Each title is subject-classified by a *call number* which is used to locate it. These call numbers are based on one of two classification systems:

Dewey Decimal		Library of Congress	
000	General works	A	General Works—Polygraphy
100	Philosophy	B	Philosophy—Religion
200	Religion	C	History—Auxiliary Sciences
300	Social Sciences	D	History and Topography (except America)
400	Language	E–F	America
500	Pure Science	G	Geography—Anthropology
600	Technology	H	Social Sciences
700	The Arts	J	Political Science
800	Literature	K	Law
900	History	L	Education
		M	Music
		N	Fine Arts
		P	Language and Literature
		Q	Science
		R	Medicine
		S	Agriculture—Plant and Animal Husbandry
		T	Technology
		U	Military Science
		V	Naval Science
		Z	Bibliography and Library Science

Reference works An unabridged dictionary such as *Webster's Third New International Dictionary* will aid the writer in determining the meanings of terms. General encyclopedias such as the *Encyclopaedia Britannica* or the *Encyclopedia Americana* provide broad information and good points of departure for some investigations. Specialized encyclopedias such as the *Encyclopedia of Banking and Finance* and the *Accountant's Encyclopedia* may be particularly helpful to business people. The biographical directories such as *Who's Who in America, Who's Who of American Women, American Men and Women of Science,* and others provide information about distinguished individuals. *Who's Who in Commerce and Industry* and *Poor's Register of Corporations, Directors and Executives* are specialized publications that may be of value to business people.

Trade directories (as *Trade Directories of the World, Guide to American Directories, The Million Dollar Directory,* or *Thomas Register*), almanacs (as *World Almanac and Book of Facts* or *Economic Almanac*), government publications (as *Current Population Reports* or *Census of Business*), and business publications (as *Moody's Manuals* or *Corporate Records*) are all additional sources of information.

Periodical indexes Periodical indexes list articles published in journals, magazines, and other serials. *Business Periodicals Index, The Wall Street Journal Index,* and *The Reader's Guide to Periodical Literature* are good guides for the businessman.

GETTING READY TO WRITE A REPORT

To avoid confusion, an orderly research procedure is essential. First, a working bibliography should be prepared; next, a systematic method of note taking should be employed. To accomplish this, two sets of cards (bibliography and information) need to be carefully assembled.

Bibliography cards Small 3" x 5" cards can be used to record the bibliographic description of each reference. The cards are numbered sequentially in the upper right corner and notes are keyed to their sources by means of these numbers.

Bibliography Card for a Book

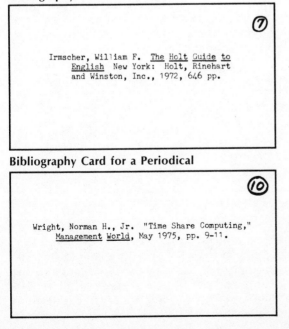

Irmscher, William F. The Holt Guide to English New York: Holt, Rinehart and Winston, Inc., 1972, 646 pp.

Bibliography Card for a Periodical

Wright, Norman H., Jr. "Time Share Computing," Management World, May 1975, pp. 9-11.

Information cards In addition to the bibliography cards, researchers usually keep a set of larger 5″ x 7″ cards to record findings. These information cards are also called *note cards.* Pertinent information is accurately recorded on these cards, which are keyed to the bibliography cards by the code number assigned to the bibliography card.

Information or Note Card

III. Computer time sharing 

p. 9 ". . . the computer to be a device capable of receiving data, processing the data prescribed by a program, and supplying the results of the processed data."

p. 10 "Some computers process data in nanoseconds, waiting time is mostly a function of peripheral equipment allocation, or busy time with maximum user activity."

Photocopying findings In place of cards, the researcher may choose to make use of photocopying machines to record complicated research findings for future reference. If so, permission must first be secured in advance from the publisher of copyrighted materials; failure to do so results in copyright violation. The secretary may secure additional information about copyright laws by writing for a copy of "General Information on Copyright," Circular 1, Copyright Office, Library of Congress, Washington, DC 20559. Copying machines are available in most offices and libraries. The sheets of copy can be keyed to bibliography cards by the code number assigned to the bibliography card. Photocopying research findings is fast, accurate, and efficient.

8.5

MANUSCRIPT AND REPORT STYLE

Modern business practice necessitates that reports, like other business communications, be well organized and coherent. Therefore, the secretary should become familiar with conventional formats in order to be of maximum assistance to the writer during the research, writing, typing, and proofreading stages of the report-preparation process and in order to avoid asking the writer unnecessary questions while the material is being typed.

STYLES OF BUSINESS REPORTS

The styling of business reports is extremely varied. The chosen style has a direct relationship with the content of the report. Some company manuals offer the secretary guidelines for report styling; however, the normal pattern is to give the writer of the report wide latitude in the selection of a style that will best suit the company's purpose. The style or format that the writer selects may then be indicated to the secretary. Typewriting guidelines concerning the four basic kinds of reports based on the degree of formality that is required and on the scope of information that is to be covered are presented in this section in the following order: the memorandum report, the letter report, the short report, and the formal report.

Depending on the nature of the business venture, the characteristics of report format may range from informal to formal, from short to long, from periodic to special, from informational to statistical, from in-house to outside, from private to public, from illustrated to unillustrated, and from progress to investigative.

The memorandum report The *memorandum report* is an in-house report or communication that is generally of a routine, informal nature. The weekly sales report and the report from an assistant manager to a manager are typical examples of this kind of communication. Since the memorandum report is an internal communication, it can be objective and impersonal in tone or wording; the letter openings and closings used on external communications may be deleted. In fact, introductory comment is normally very brief in this report; however, when a report of this type accompanies a lengthy formal report, an introductory paragraph or two is appropriate. Headings may be used for quick reference and to highlight certain aspects of the report.

Standardization of in-house communications, an important goal of most firms, is achieved in part through the use of interoffice correspondence stationery, which is less costly than letterhead paper. Use of the familiar *To, From, Date,* and *Subject* lines on the interoffice form reduces typing time and effort. Some firms have modernized their interoffice correspondence stationery by omitting these guide words on the printed forms, and typists are instructed to omit them also.

Even though the first draft of the memorandum report may be double-spaced for editorial purposes, the final draft is usually single-spaced to provide a more compact appearance and to give more information in less space. When in doubt about memorandum report headings and styling, the secretary should seek the employer's advice. If a choice is given to the secretary, the styling may be altered to suit the particular situation in accordance with normal practices in report writing, e.g., the use of double-spacing for extremely short memorandum reports.

Unless instructed otherwise, the secretary should use matching plain bond paper for continuation sheets of memorandum reports. An appropriate heading of a two-page memorandum report is illustrated here:

```
Memorandum                    - 2 -                 May 14, 19—

A list of the participants for the Sales Training Seminar in
Pittsburgh, Pennsylvania on June 26 is as follows:

                Corvair, Ted
                Gordon, Sidney
                Lawson, Peter
```

The writer may wish to have a typed signature line four lines below the end of the report; the signature would then be placed above this line. (Some authors prefer to place their initials after their names in the headings of the reports; often the memorandum report is not signed at all.)

The letter report A report that is presented in letter format is known as a *letter report.* As a general rule, a letter report is directed to or from persons or groups outside a company. Letter-report format would typically be used by an outside consultant to present analyses and recommendations. Normally, factual data would be presented with headings to highlight this information. Also, this report might contain tables or illustrations that an ordinary letter would not have. The letter-report format is useful for short, informal reports comprising several pages. For example, an organization's board of directors often will make use of the letter report to present pertinent changes and developments to its membership. The tone or wording of this type of communication may be of a personal nature.

The first page of the letter report is typed on company letterhead stationery; matching plain bond paper is used as continuation sheets for reports of several pages. The headings on the continuation sheets are the same as those on regular letters. Good use may be made of a subject line to focus attention on the main theme of the report. The body of the letter report is also interspersed with headings and subheadings positioned at strategic points for emphasis, clarity, and ease of reference. The following illustration shows one way to style the headings and subheadings so that the topics of greater and lesser importance will be clear to the reader:

TITLE (centered)
(space down 3 times)
MAIN HEADINGS (centered)
(space down 3 times)
Subheadings (centered)
(space down 3 times)
Marginal Side Heading (flush with left margin)
(space down 2 times)
Paragraph Heading. (indented and run in with rest of text)

The short business report Short business reports differ from memorandum reports and letter reports in content and in format. Short reports deal informally with topics that are typically limited in scope and are uncomplicated. The format of the short report may include all or some of the following elements: a title page, a preliminary summary with emphasis on conclusions and recommendations, any applicable authorization information, a statement of the problem at hand and its scope, findings presented in relation to the problem, the conclusions, and the recommendations. In addition, other special parts (as tables or graphics) may be added whenever they are needed to illustrate and highlight specific aspects of the report.

Either single- or double-spacing is appropriate for the short business report according to the company's style or the writer's preference. Headings such as the ones used with letter reports that are illustrated in the foregoing section may be used to focus attention on certain aspects of the report and to make it easy to locate information quickly.

The short report may assume one of three physical forms: (1) unbound, (2) top-bound, or (3) side-bound. The typist needs to be mindful of the appropriate typewriter settings for the actual form that the report will take. Is is imperative that the typist adhere consistently to one chosen style throughout the report. A listing of appropriate machine settings will be helpful to the typist and will also save time. The following chart provides an example of standardization in machine settings.

A Guide to Typing Business Reports and Manuscripts

Job Specifications	Machine Settings for Binding Style	
	Unbound or Top-bound	*Side-bound*
Margin—top, first page	12 lines	12 lines
Margin—top, second page	6 lines	6 lines
Margin—bottom, all pages	6 lines	6 lines
Margin—left side, all pages	12 spaces elite 10 spaces pica	18 spaces elite 15 spaces pica
Margin—right side, all pages	12 spaces elite 10 spaces pica	12 spaces elite 10 spaces pica
Spacing—body	single or double	single or double
Spacing—long quotation	single	single
Spacing—footnotes	single	single
Indention—paragraphs	5 spaces	5 spaces
Indention—long quotations	5 spaces in from left and right margins	5 spaces in from left and right margins
Indention—tables and lists	5 plus spaces in from left and right margins	5 plus spaces in from left and right margins
Indention—footnotes	2 spaces for the first line of each footnote	2 spaces for the first line of each footnote
Pagination—title fly	Assign Roman numeral *i;* it is *not typed*	Assign Roman numeral *i;* it is *not typed*
Pagination—title page	Assign Roman numeral *ii;* it is *not typed*	Assign Roman numeral *ii;* it is *not typed*
Pagination—all other preliminary parts of the report up to the first page of the body, e.g., letters, acknowledgments, table of contents, lists of figures, tables or charts, and synopsis or summary	Assign continuous Roman numerals *iii* and above in succession; center and type each numeral 3 to 6 lines from the bottom of the page	Assign continuous Roman numerals *iii* and above in succession; center and type each numeral 3 to 6 lines from the bottom of the page
Pagination—first page of body	Assign Arabic numeral *1;* it is *not typed*	Assign Arabic numeral *1;* it is *not typed*
Pagination—all other pages in the body of the report, the appendix, the bibliography, and the index	Assign Arabic numerals 2 and above in succession; center and type each numeral 3 to 6 lines from the bottom of the page	Assign Arabic numerals 2 and above in succession; type each numeral at the right margin either 3 to 6 lines from the top of the page or 6 lines from the bottom of the page

NOTE REGARDING MULTIPLE-FOOTNOTE SPACINATION
If there are two or more footnotes on a page, single-space each footnote; however, double-space between footnotes.

The title page contains the title of the report; the name, title, and address of the person to whom the report is submitted; and the name, title, and address of the preparer of the report. The date is also included on the title page. Long report titles are divided, centered, and typed on several lines in the upper third of the page. Each line of the divided main title should be shorter than the line above; thus, the total format will resemble an inverted pyramid. A pleasing effect will result from this format. In contrast, extremely brief report titles may be spread or typed with an extra space between each letter and with several spaces placed between each word; the amount of space between words will depend on the typestyle used. Experimentation ahead of time on a separate piece of paper will aid the typist in determining the proper spacination between spread words.

The formal report Although the formal report may be characterized in many ways, it has three unique features that distinguish it from all other types of reports: (1) it typically follows a sophisticated style of presentation similar to that contained in the list shown below (2) it is generally complex in its scope and content, and (3) it is usually lengthy. A formal report may contain all or some of the following elements, each of which is illustrated and discussed in detail in subsequent sections of this chapter.

Cover
Flyleaf
Title fly
Title page
Letter of authorization
Letter of transmittal
Foreword *or* Preface
Acknowledgments
Table of contents
List of tables (if any)
List of figures or illustrations (if any)
Synopsis *or* Summary
Body *or* Text
Footnotes
Appendix
Bibliography
Index

Note: Some of the elements listed above may be combined, e.g., the letter of transmittal can be coalesced with the synopsis.

Because of the length and the complexity of the formal report, headings are used to divide the report in such a way that readability and reference will be enhanced. The various subtopics in the report follow a predetermined pattern to aid the reader. It is imperative that a consistent style be used throughout the report.

Good-quality bond paper is used for the typing of the formal report; either single- or double-spacing may be used. The prefatory section (including the title fly through the synopsis but excluding the title page) of a side-bound report is usually paginated with lowercase Roman numerals which are centered from three to six lines from the bottom of the paper. The rest of the report, including the body and all appended sections, is paginated with Arabic numerals positioned at the right marginal setting, generally one inch from the top of the page at the right margin or one inch from the bottom of the page at the right margin. Additional suggestions for arranging the various parts of a report may be found in the preceding chart entitled "A Guide to Typing Business Reports and Manuscripts."

Extreme care should be taken to follow a uniform typing style when preparing the headings and subheadings throughout the report (see the suggested typewriting styles for headings that are illustrated on page 290). Many formal reports feature the decimal system of subdividing report topics. Or, the writer may prefer to use the traditional outline listings of alternate numbers and letters. The decimal system of outline enumeration is handled in this way:

1. The first subdivision at this level . . .
  1.1 The next subdivision at this level . . .
    1.11 The next subdivision at this level . . .
      1.111 The next subdivision at this level . . .
      1.112 The second point in this subdivision . . .
    1.12 The second point in this subdivision . . .
  1.2 The second point in this subdivision . . .
2. The second subdivision at this level . . .

The format of topic subdivisions listed in outline style with numbers and letters used alternately is as follows:

I. The first subdivision at this level . . .
  A. The next subdivision at this level . . .
    1. The next subdivision at this level . . .
      a. The next subdivision at this level . . .
        (1) The next subdivision at this level . . .
          (a) The next subdivision at this level . . .
            (i) The next subdivision at this level . . .

ELEMENTS OF THE FORMAL REPORT

The cover The cover, which is sometimes called the binder, should adequately protect the report, should be attractive, and should contain the title and the author's name. The title may be typed in all-capital letters either directly on the cover or on a gummed label that is then affixed to it. Formal report covers are generally conservative; however, a bright or even an illustrated cover may sometimes be preferred. A very short report without a cover may be stapled. If one staple is used, it should be placed diagonally in the upper left corner.

The flyleaf A flyleaf is a blank sheet of paper. Formal reports have two flyleaves—one at the beginning and the other at the end. They dress up the report, contribute to its formality, and provide space for written comments.

The title fly The title fly if used contains only one item: the report title typed in all-capital letters and usually positioned in the upper third of the page. This title is identical to the one on the title page.

The title page This page typically contains the title and subtitle if there is one; the name, corporate title, department, and/or address of the writer; the name, title, department, firm name, and address of the recipient; and the completion date of the report. If a report does not have a cover and title fly, the title page can be typed on heavier paper and thus serve as the cover. If the report has a copyright, the fact is recorded on the reverse title page. See the illustration on the following page which shows the title page of an engineering report.

Letter of authorization If the writer has received written authorization for the investigation, that memorandum or letter may be included in the report as the letter of authorization. If the writer has received oral authorization to produce the report, this authorization should be cited in the letter of transmittal or the introduction to the report. A typical letter of authorization is shown on page 295.

Title Page of a Long Report

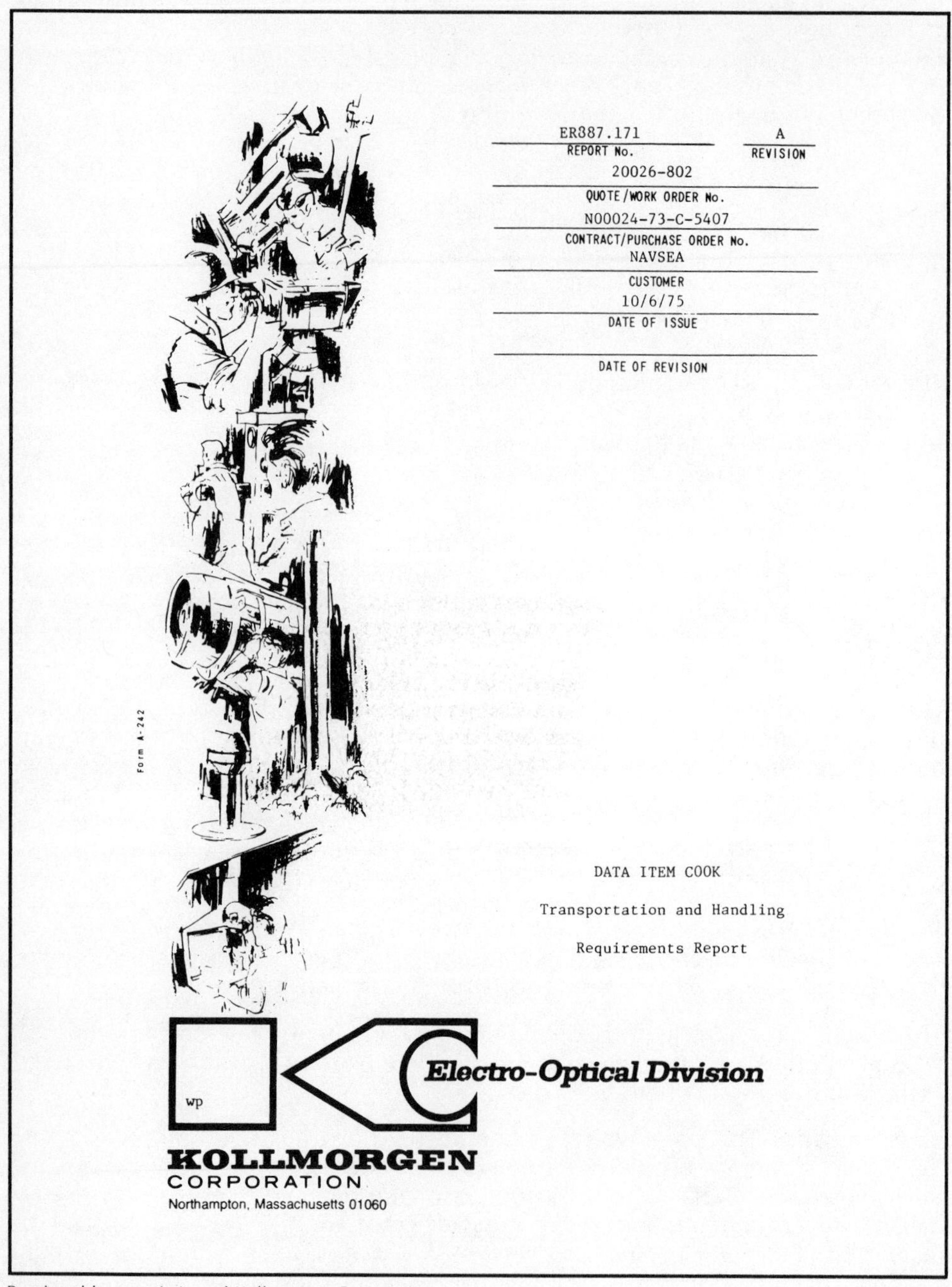

ER387.171
REPORT No.

A
REVISION

20026-802
QUOTE/WORK ORDER No.

N00024-73-C-5407
CONTRACT/PURCHASE ORDER No.

NAVSEA
CUSTOMER

10/6/75
DATE OF ISSUE

DATE OF REVISION

Form A-242

DATA ITEM COOK

Transportation and Handling

Requirements Report

wp

Electro-Optical Division

KOLLMORGEN
CORPORATION
Northampton, Massachusetts 01060

Reprinted by permission of Kollmorgen Corporation.

A Letter of Authorization

TO: Anne Carter, Assistant Director
Secretarial Services

FROM: Alice Harper, Director
Secretarial Services Department

DATE: April 3, 19—

SUBJECT: Report Authorization

You are hereby authorized to write a research study on The Format of Formal Reports. It is to comprise no more than fifty pages and should provide definitive information on report writing (selecting a topic, writing the outline, and gathering information), and on report format. The study should also provide specific information concerning techniques of report writing.

The completion date of the report is May 29, 19—.

If you have any questions concerning this investigation, do not hesitate to contact me.

A. H.

coc

cc Constance Sullivan

iii

Letter of transmittal A letter of transmittal often accompanies a report and also may serve as its preface or foreword. The writer conveys to the recipient (often the person who assigned the report) the purpose, scope, and limitations of the report, its authorization, the research methods employed, special comments, acknowledgments, and the main idea or ideas contained therein. (See also the illustration of acknowledgments on page 298). The letter of transmittal usually ends with a statement that expresses the writer's appreciation for having received the assignment and that exhibits a willingness to provide additional information or answer any questions concerning the report. The tone of the letter should be sincere and cordial. The letter of transmittal is typed on letterhead stationery and is signed. A typical letter of transmittal is illustrated on page 297.

Acknowledgments Acknowledgments may be made either in the letter of transmittal or in the introduction. If there are many acknowledgments, a special page for them may be included. It is considered proper to acknowledge those individuals, companies, or institutions assisting in the preparation of the report. The illustration on page 298 is typical of the acknowledgment section of a report.

Table of contents The table of contents, also called contents, is essentially an outline of the report showing its pagination. It indicates major and minor divisions of the material by showing pertinent headings and subheadings. Leader lines (periods typed horizontally across the paper to connect headings and page numbers) may be typed consecutively (one after the other), or a space may be left between periods. If a space is left between periods, the periods must align vertically; this may be accomplished by typing on odd or even numbers only as indicated by the alignment scale of the typewriter (see the Punctuation/Spacination Table on pages 227 and 228 of Chapter 7 for an illustration of properly positioned leaders). The table of contents is centered horizontally and vertically on the page. The illustration on pages 299–300 shows a rather elaborate table of contents used in a technical report. Notice how the continuation sheet of the table of contents is typed; its styling and margins match the first sheet exactly. The continuation-sheet heading is simply: TABLE OF CONTENTS (Cont'd). The second illustration of a table of contents (page 301) shows the use of the Roman-numeral outline styling that is followed in the text of the report. Spaced leaders are used in this particular format. It should be reemphasized that the table of contents in any formal report should follow exactly the internal style chosen by the writer. Therefore, if the writer has selected the decimal system of topic presentation within the text, the table of contents should reflect this system; if, on the other hand, the writer has used the Roman-numeral system of topic presentation, the table of contents should show the Roman numerals and the proper topical headings. If numbers and letters (or some other system) have been used within the text to divide and subdivide topics, the contents page should follow this pattern, too.

List of illustrations If the number of illustrations is somewhat limited, a list of them may be appended to the table of contents. If there are numerous illustrations, a special list of them may be included on a separate page in the report. The figure on page 302 shows a list of illustrations in a technical report where each illustration has been assigned a number. These numbers as well as the page numbers are included in the list of illustrations. The figure on page 303 shows a shorter list of illustrations that features Roman numerals for tables and Arabic numerals for graphics. Leader lines are also featured in this setup. In general, the styling of the list of illustrations should follow the pattern used in the table of contents.

A Letter of Transmittal

SMITHVILLE COLLEGE
678 Dow Drive
Smithville, ST 56789

School of Business
Department of Business Education

413-536-1306

completion date May 29, 19—

recipient | Ms. Sarah Lee, Director
Secretarial Services Department
Southern Engineering Company
678 Dow Industrial Park
Smithville, ST 56789

salutation Dear Ms. Lee

report title | The research study entitled The Format of Formal Reports is now complete. As you suggested, the report is limited
limitations | to those formats that we believe would be best suited to the particular requirements of Southern Engineering.

purpose | Specific information is provided on the mechanics of report writing, the essential parts of a report, and special formats for engineering reports and studies that are to be submitted to the United States Department of
sources of information | Defense. The report is based on extensive library research, field trips, and the latest United States government publications relevant to this subject.

acknowledgments | I would like to acknowledge the assistance of Mr. Howard Smith of the Department of Art who prepared the graphics.

cordial closing | Thank you for the opportunity to work on this interesting project. It is always a pleasure for those of us in Business Education to interface with our counterparts in private industry. If you have any questions regarding the report, do not hesitate to call me.

complimentary close Respectfully submitted

signature |

Joyce A. Browining
Assistant Professor | writer's identification

typist's initials coc

iv small Roman numerals

An Acknowledgments Section of a Report

ACKNOWLEDGMENTS

The author is indebted to the many individuals that assisted in this study.

Ms. Anne Etterman made several trips to the Stevens Engineering Company research library to obtain vital information.

Mr. Joseph Brock assisted in the preparation of the graphics.

Ms. Helen Jones edited the manuscript, and Ms. Amy Roth typed the manuscript.

A.C.

Table of Contents in a Long Technical Report Reflecting the Decimal System of Topic Presentation

Electro-Optical Division ■ Northampton, Massachusetts 01060

KOLLMORGEN
CORPORATION

REPORT ER887.171 PAGE i

CONTINUED ON PAGE ii REV. A

TABLE OF CONTENTS

Form A-244

Reprinted by permission of Kollmorgen Corporation.

KOLLMORGEN CORPORATION

Electro-Optical Division ■ Northampton, Massachusetts 01060

REPORT ER887.171 PAGE ii

CONTINUED ON PAGE iii REV. A

Table of Contents (Cont'd)

Form A-244

A Sample Table of Contents Reflecting the Roman-numeral System of Topic Presentation

TABLE OF CONTENTS

vi

List of Illustrations in a Long Technical Report

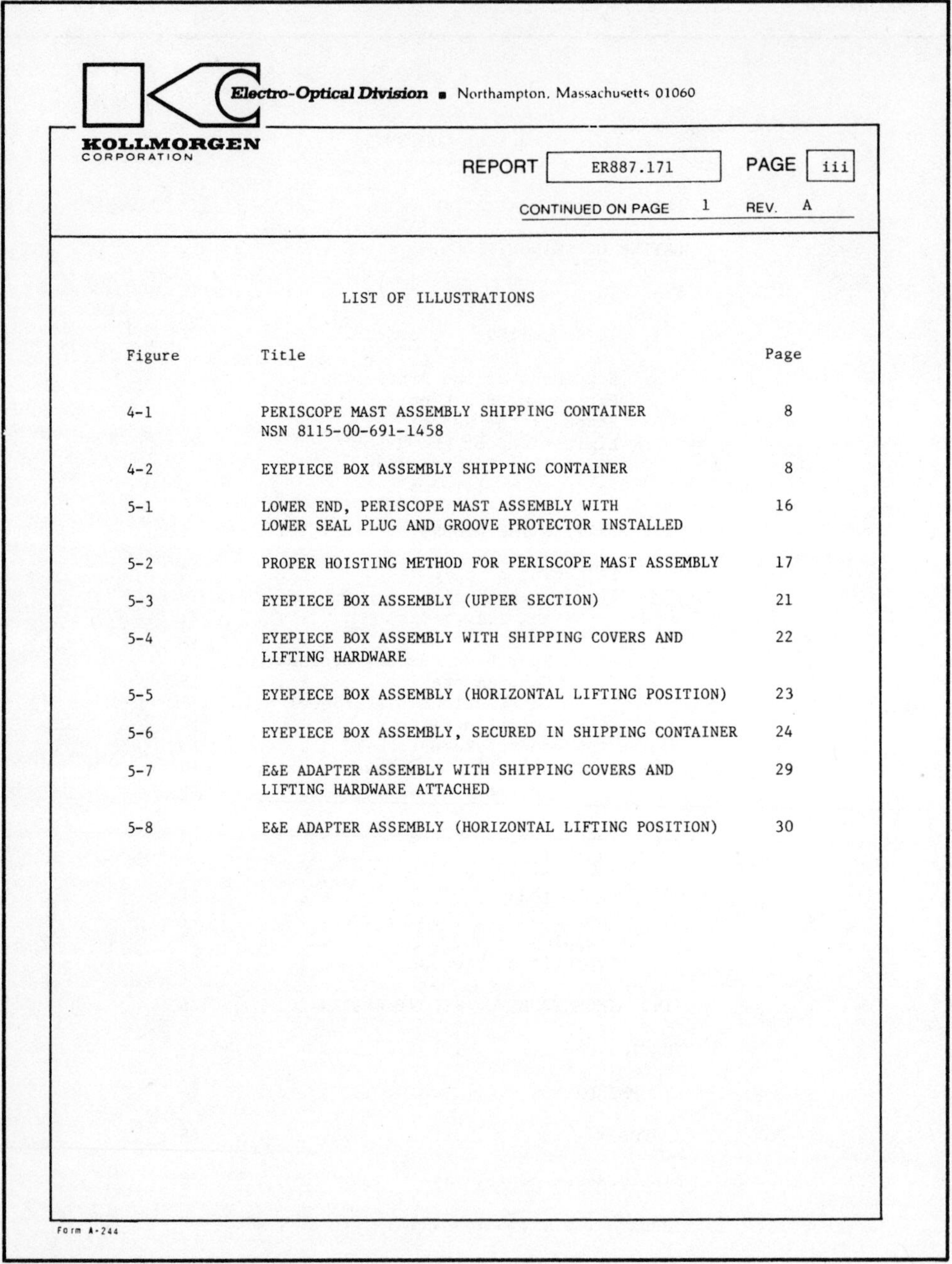

Electro-Optical Division ■ Northampton, Massachusetts 01060

KOLLMORGEN
CORPORATION

REPORT ER887.171 PAGE iii

CONTINUED ON PAGE 1 REV. A

LIST OF ILLUSTRATIONS

Form A-244

A Sample List of Illustrations

LIST OF ILLUSTRATIONS

Synopsis The synopsis (also called the abstract, summary, digest, précis, brief, epitome, scope, or introduction) is a condensation of the entire report. Most busy executives prefer a summarization at the beginning of a report in order to obtain a quick, concise overview of the significant findings of the study. If additional information is needed, the reader can then review the body of the report in detail. The synopsis usually appears on a page by itself. In some offices, additional copies of the synopsis are distributed separately from the report itself, thus permitting wide circulation of the report findings at little cost. The illustration on page 305 shows the format for a one-page synopsis.

Report body The body of the report usually comprises three parts: a brief introduction summarizing the report and/or indicating its conclusions, a lengthy general text section, and terminal section reporting conclusions and recommendations in detail. The introduction presents the report to the reader. The purpose of the study, a clear definition of the problems or matters to be considered, the scope of the study, any limitations imposed on the study, and any pertinent background information may be discussed. The main thrust of the report is often presented in this initial part to provide a quick overview for the busy executive. The core of the report is found in the body of the text. Here, all data essential to the study are presented. While the writer may need to analyze and interpret these data, the material should still be discussed with as much objectivity as possible. In addition, conciseness, brevity, clarity, and completeness should characterize this and all other sections of the report. Conclusions are derived from the facts or findings of the study. It is imperative that the conclusions be relevant to the findings. As an aid to the reader, the conclusions are often enumerated: 1, 2, 3, 4 . . . . The recommendations are derived from the writer's interpretations of the conclusions and should be sensibly related to them. Certain courses of action may be indicated here. The recommendations are usually enumerated.

Footnotes Since a great deal of research is based on secondary sources, not only the writer but also the typist should know how to acknowledge quoted and paraphrased material with footnotes. Footnotes are used by writers to acknowledge and document material borrowed from other writers or sources. Acknowledgment and documentation are essential for the following two reasons:

1. It is dishonest to borrow and not credit material that has been written by another person or persons. Failure to acknowledge such material is called plagiarism.
2. Documentation enables the reader to locate more source material on a subject or subjects that he may wish to investigate in greater depth or detail.

Footnotes should be used to document material that has been quoted or paraphrased. To quote is to reproduce exactly a text, passage, sentence, or phrase that originates from another writer or source. To paraphrase is to restate a text, passage, sentence, or phrase by giving the essential meaning in a form somewhat different from the original. Another writer's ideas are just as much his as are his exact words and their use deserves to be acknowledged. One should also use footnotes when referring or alluding to important source material even though that material may not have been quoted or paraphrased.

A secretary who understands the basic mechanics of footnote style can be of great assistance to the writer both in setting up and proofreading the manuscript. The placing of footnotes on the page and the styling of the notes themselves often vary with the writer's company, institution, or academic field. Many corporations and institutions have developed their own style manuals and guidelines for such documentation; consequently, the secretary should be familiar with these details

A Sample Synopsis in a Formal Report

SYNOPSIS

This study concerns the preparation of formal reports in a style best suited to the needs of a particular company.

The report topic or subject is usually designated in a formal letter of authorization. First, an outline of the report should be carefully constructed. Next, research data are gathered from primary and/or secondary sources. Finally, the report itself is written.

The three major sections of a formal report are the introduction, the findings or the text, and the terminal section (containing conclusions and recommendations). The physical components are the cover, flyleaves, prefatory sections, body, and appended sections.

The writer should be objective (except in the recommendations section), concise, clear, and accurate. Meticulous documentation, including footnotes and a bibliography, is required.

The report should be typed on bond paper, 8½" x 11". Carbon copies should be typed on onionskin paper. A film ribbon or a black medium-inked fabric typewriter ribbon should be used. Additional copies may be prepared on a copy machine.

The report should be submitted with a letter of transmittal that serves as its preface.

viii

before attempting to type an article, paper, or report. In any case, one of the important things to keep in mind is the selection of and adherence to one footnote styling throughout a project for the sake of uniformity, coherence, and clarity. The fact that the footnote conventions of the *MLA Style Sheet* (published by the Modern Language Association of America) are the basis for some of the illustrations in this book in no way disparages or invalidates any other reasonable approach that may be used by some other organization.

A full footnote contains all or some of the following elements:

books

author's name(s) (if more than three authors, the first author's name is followed by *et al.*)

title of the work and subtitle, if any

editor, compiler, or translator, if applicable

name of the series in which the book appears and volume number within the series, if applicable

edition, if other than the first

number of volumes, if applicable

publishing data (geographical location of the publisher, name of publisher, publication date)

page number(s)

periodicals

author's name(s) (if more than three authors, the first author's name is followed by *et al.*)

title of article in quotation marks

name of periodical underlined or in italics

volume of the periodical

number of the periodical

issue date (month, day, year)

page number(s)

unpublished materials

author's name if known

title of document in quotation marks, if known

the nature of the material (as a letter or a dissertation)

folio number or other identification number

name of collection in which the material appears

geographical location of collection

date if known

Footnotes may be placed at the bottom of the page on which the quoted or paraphrased material appears (see page 308 for an example), at the end of each chapter in a list, or at the end of the entire work in a list (see the next illustration). If a quoted passage is very brief, its source may be enclosed in parentheses and included in the running text; however, the first reference to a work should appear in a full footnote.

Footnotes to a text are indicated by Arabic superscript (*or* superior) numerals placed immediately after the source material with no intervening space. If a terminal quotation mark appears (as at the end of a very short quotation that is included in the running text), the numeral is placed outside the final quotation mark with no space intervening:

". . . nearly 4500 tons in that year."[9]

This numbering may be consecutive throughout the paper, article, report, or book; however, renumbering with the beginning of a new chapter is also common.

The first line of a footnote begins with the applicable superscript Arabic numeral separated from the first letter of the author's first name by one space and indented from one to six spaces from the left margin, according to the writer's preference or the style manual being followed. Subsequent lines of the footnote are aligned flush with the left margin. The illustrations in this section show the various indentations. The notes themselves are usually single-spaced internally but double-spacing is used between notes when the material appears in final printed form. When the secretary is typing a manuscript before publication, however, the notes should be double-spaced internally with triple-spacing between notes.

The following illustration, reprinted from *Webster's New Collegiate Dictionary* shows a cross section of typical full footnotes based on the *MLA Style Sheet,* which may be consulted for more detailed information on manuscript preparation:

Sample Footnotes

BOOKS

one author — [1] Albert H. Marckwardt, *American English* (New York: Oxford University Press, 1958), p. 94.

multiple authors — [2] De Witt T. Starnes and Gertrude E. Noyes, *The English Dictionary from Cawdrey to Johnson 1604–1775* (Chapel Hill: University of North Carolina Press, 1946), p. 119.

translation and/or edition — [3] Simone de Beauvoir, *The Second Sex*, trans. and ed. H. M. Parshley (New York: Alfred A. Knopf, 1953), p. 600.
[4]William Shakespeare, *The Complete Works of Shakespeare*, ed. George Lyman Kittredge (Boston: Ginn and Company, 1936), p. 801.

second or later edition — [5] Albert C. Baugh, *A History of the English Language*, 2nd. ed. (New York: Appleton-Century-Crofts, 1957), p. 300.

a work in a festschrift or collection — [6] Kemp Malone, "The Phonemes of Current English," *Studies for William A. Read*, ed. Nathaniel M. Caffee and Thomas A. Kirby (Baton Rouge: Louisiana State University Press, 1940), pp. 133–165.

corporate author — [7] *Report of the Commission on the Humanities* (New York: American Council of Learned Societies, 1964), p. 130.

book without publisher, date, or pagination — [8] *Photographic View Album of Cambridge* [England], n.d., n.p., n. pag.

ARTICLES

from a journal with continuous pagination throughout the annual volume — [9] Daniel Cook, "A Point of Lexicographical Method," *American Speech*, 34 (1959), 20–25.

from a journal paging each issue separately — [10] Donald K, Ourecky, "Cane and Bush Fruits," *Plants & Gardens*, 27, No. 3 (Autumn 1971), pp. 13–15.

from a monthly magazine — [11] William Irwin Thompson, "Planetary Vistas," *Harper's*, Dec. 1971, pp. 71–78.

from a weekly magazine — [12] Eric F. Goldman, "A Sort of Rehabilitation of Warren G. Harding," *New York Times Magazine*, 26 Mar. 1972, p. 42.

from a daily newspaper — [13] Haskell Frankel, "Observing the Theater: 'Night Watch' Is First-Class, And Mum's the Word," *National Observer*, 11 Mar. 1972, p. 23, cols. 1–2.

letter to the editor — [14] Arthur M. Cohen, "Letters," *Change*, May 1972, p. 4.

a signed review — [15] Harry Hoijer, rev. of *A Leonard Bloomfield Anthology*, ed. Charles F. Hockett, *Language*, 47 (1971), 911–13.

The following illustration shows one how to document sources on a page of running text.

Footnotes Placed at the Bottom of a Page

21

If a "quoted passage is four lines or less in length, it is typed with the report text and is distinguished from the normal text by quotation marks."[17] However, a different procedure is used for longer quotations:

> But if a longer quotation (five lines or more) is used, the conventional practice is to set it in from both left and right margins (about five spaces) but without quotation marks. . . . the quoted passage is further distinguished from the report writer's work by single spacing . . .[18]

A series of usually three periods called ellipsis are used to indicate omissions of material from a passage.[19]

Footnotes may be placed "at the bottom of the page . . . separated from the text by a horizontal line. If a line is used, it is typed a single space below the text and followed by one blank line."[20] Lesikar prefers the separation line to be 1½ or 2 inches.[21] From a typing standpoint, reserve three lines of blank typing space per footnote at the bottom of the page. Generally, typewriting textbooks state that a 2-inch line is adequate (20 pica strokes; 24 elite strokes). The line is constructed by striking the underscore key.

---

17 Report Writing for Business (Homewood: Richard D. Irwin, Inc., 1973), p. 187.

18 Loc. cit.

19 Ibid., p. 188.

20 The Administrative Secretary: Resource (New York: McGraw-Hill Book Company, 1970), p. 391.

21 Lesikar, op. cit., p. 189.

When the same source is cited repeatedly, shortened footnotes may be used as space-saving devices. The following simplified footnote styling for repeated sources represents a general consensus of several modern style manuals:

1. If the author's name occurs in the running text, it need not be repeated in footnote references to the work after the first one:

   first reference

   [1]Albert H. Marckwardt, *American English* (New York: Oxford University Press, 1958), p. 94.

   repeated reference

   [2]*American English* (New York: Oxford University Press, 1958), p. 95.

   or

   [3]*American English,* p. 95.

2. If the author's name does not appear in the running text prior to a repeated reference, either of these stylings may be used:

   repeated reference

   [4]Marckwardt, *American English,* p. 95.

   or

   [5]Marckwardt, p. 95.

   The styling of footnote 4 should be followed, however, if more than one work by the same author is being cited.

3. In repeated references to books by more than one author, the authors' names may be shortened:

   first reference

   [6]DeWitt T. Starnes and Gertrude E. Noyes, *The English Dictionary from Cawdrey to Johnson 1604–1775* (Chapel Hill: University of North Carolina Press, 1946), p. 120.

   repeated reference

   [7]Starnes and Noyes, *The English Dictionary from Cawdrey to Johnson 1604–1775,* p. 126.

   or

   [8]Starnes and Noyes, p. 126.

   The styling of footnote 7 should be followed, however, if more than one work by the same authors is being cited.

4. A long title may also be shortened if it has already been given in full in an earlier footnote:

   [9]Starnes and Noyes, *The English Dictionary,* p. 126.

5. A shortened reference to an article in a periodical that has been cited earlier should include only the author's last name, the title of the article which can be shortened if it is a long one, and the page number(s).

While the simplified and shortened footnote stylings have now gained wide currency, some writers still prefer to use the traditional Latin abbrevations *ibid., loc. cit.,* and *op. cit.* as space-savers in repeated references to sources cited earlier. Current usage indicates that these abbreviations may be typed or printed in either Roman or italic type, depending on the preference of the writer or publisher. For convenience they are shown in italic in the examples below. When a page reference follows one of these abbreviations, it may or may not be set off by a comma:

Ibid. pp. 95–98.
or
Ibid., pp. 95–98.

These Latin abbreviations are capitalized when they appear at the beginning of a footnote, as shown on page 309, but not otherwise.

The first of the abbreviations—*ibid.* (for *ibidem,* "in the same place")—is used when the writer is referring to the work cited in the immediately preceding footnote. This abbreviation may be used several times in succession. Examples:

first reference

[1]Simone de Beauvoir, *The Second Sex,* trans. and ed. H. M. Parshley (New York: Alfred A. Knopf, 1953), p. 600.

repeated reference (immediately following note 1)

[2]*Ibid.,* p. 609.

repeated reference (immediately following note 2)

[3]*Ibid.*

When *ibid.* is used without a page number, it indicates that the same page of the same source is being cited as in the footnote immediately preceding. Thus, note 3 above cites page 609 of *The Second Sex.*

The abbreviations *loc. cit.* (for *loco citato,* "in the place cited") and *op. cit.* (for *opere citato,* "in the work cited") may be used only in conjunction with the author's name, which may occur in the running text or at the beginning of the first reference. When the writer cites a book or periodical, he should include its complete title the first time he refers to it in a footnote. In subsequent references, *loc. cit.* or *op. cit.* with or without page numbers may be substituted for the title, depending on the type of citation. Examples of the use of *loc. cit.* are as follows:

first reference

[1]DeWitt T. Starnes and Gertrude E. Noyes, *The English Dictionary from Cawdry to Johnson 1604–1775* (Chapel Hill: University of North Carolina Press, 1946), pp. 119–122.

repeated reference (other footnotes intervening)

[4]Starnes and Noyes, *loc. cit.*

Note 4 without a page reference indicates that pages 119–122 are being cited again.

repeated reference (other footnotes intervening)

[7]Starnes and Noyes, *loc. cit.,* p. 119.

Examples of the use of *op. cit.* are as follows:

first reference

[1]Albert H. Marckwardt, *American English* (New York: Oxford University Press, 1958), p. 94.

repeated reference (other footnotes intervening)

[3]Markwardt, *op. cit.,* p. 98.

In short, *loc. cit.* may be used only when referring to the same page or pages of the same source cited earlier with other footnotes intervening, while *op. cit.* may be used when referring to a source cited earlier but not to the same page or pages of that source. The title of the work rather than the abbreviation should be used if the writer is using material from more than one work by the same author.

Appendix If an appendix is required, it appears before all other back-matter sections (such as footnotes listed at the end of the report, a glossary, a bibliography, or an index that may have been included in the report). An appendix contains supplementary material consequential enough to be included with but not in the body of the report. It may include reproduced correspondence, texts of documents such as laws that amplify points already made in the text itself, checklists, questionnaires, tabular data, or illustrations. An appendix should not, however, be forced to serve as a catchall for miscellaneous details that the writer should have been able to incorporate into the body of the report.

An appendix is introduced by a half-title, typically centered and typed all in capital letters on a recto (right-hand) page:

APPENDIX
THIRD-QUARTER SALES FIGURES

When more than one appendix appears in a report, each of them should be separately and sequentially introduced either by letters (as APPENDIX A, APPENDIX B) or by numbers (as APPENDIX 1, APPENDIX 2). Each appendix should be introduced on a recto page and should contain a half-title as shown in the first example. They may be paginated separately.

Bibliography A bibliography is an alphabetical list of the sources used by a writer in a report or other work. A bibliography entry may contain all or some of the following elements:

books
author's name(s), surname first (if more than three authors, the first author's name is followed by *et al.*)
title of the work and subtitle, if any
editor, compiler, or translator, if applicable
name of the series in which the book appears
volume number if any
edition, if other than the first
number of volumes if more than one
publication data (geographical location of publisher, name of publisher, publication date)

periodicals
author's name(s), surname first (if more than three authors, the first author's name is followed by *et al.*)
title of article in quotation marks
name of periodical underlined or in italics
volume of the periodical
number of the periodical
issue date (month, day, year)
page number(s)

unpublished material
author's name if known, surname first
title of document in quotation marks, if known
nature of the material (as a letter or dissertation)
folio number or other identification number
name of collection in which the material appears
geographical location of collection
date if known

Annotated bibliographies, intended to direct the reader to other works for additional information or further reading on a particular subject, contain brief comments about each entry in addition to the data shown above. These comments may be typed on another line two spaces below the last line of an individual entry or they may be run in on the same line. Very long bibliographies may be subdivided into subject categories, with each category introduced by subheads (see the illustration on page 314).

Bibliography entries are similar but not identical to footnotes, with the main difference between them being a reversal of the authors' names so that the bibliography may be alphabetized and the use of hanging indentation for the first line of a bibliographic entry so that the authors' names are emphasized. The internal punctuation in a bibliography entry also differs from that of a footnote (compare the footnote and bibliography stylings shown in the following illustration).

A Comparison of Footnote and Bibliography Stylings

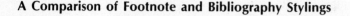

footnote styling

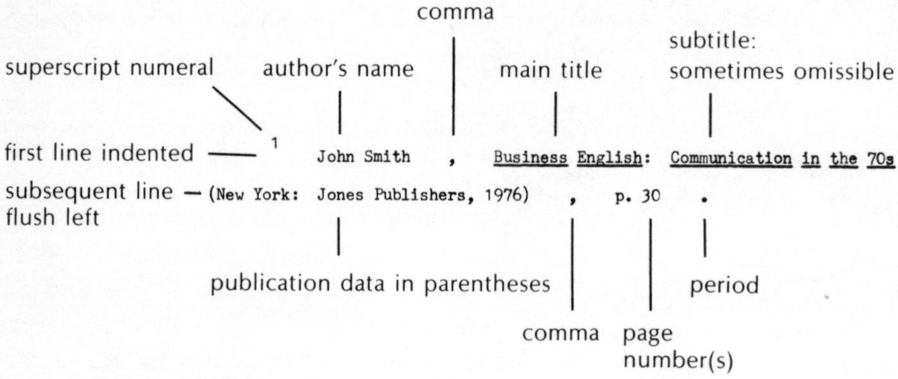

bibliography styling

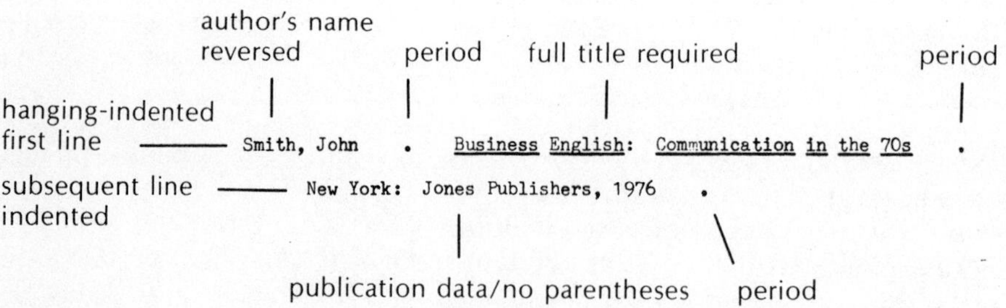

Note: Sample footnotes and a sample bibliography are shown elsewhere in this chapter; consult these illustrations for examples of proper spacination with punctuation. The setup of footnotes and bibliography entries for periodicals is shown in these illustrations, also.

Bibliography entries are unnumbered but are arranged alphabetically by first element. The first line of an entry is aligned flush with the left margin; subsequent lines are indented from one to seven spaces depending on the style being used or on organizational typing guidelines. Bibliography entries are single-spaced internally, and double-spacing is used between entries when they appear in final form. However, when a secretary is typing material in prepublication manuscript form, the bibliography entries should be double-spaced internally with triple-spacing between entries to allow space for possible corrections.

While page numbers of entire books are not included in bibliography entries, inclusive page numbers of articles and parts of books are shown, as in the following sample entries:

periodical

Doe, Jane. "Simplified Letter Styling."
Business Magazine, March 1974, pp. 3–10.

part of a book

Jones, Robert. "Problems in Office Management."
The Secretary. Ed. Joseph Smith. New York:
Alpha Press, 1975, pp. 452–652.

entire book

Smith, John. *Business English: Communication in the 70s.*
New York: Jones Publishers, 1976.

Several works by the same author are alphabetized by title. The author's name is included in the first bibliography entry. Subsequent entries citing works by that same author are introduced by a 3-em dash (or three typed hyphens) followed by a period with no space intervening, followed by one space before the first letter of the title, as

Smith, John. *Business English: Communication in the 70s.* New York: Jones Publishers, 1976.

---. *Effective Letter Writing.* Chicago: XYZ Press, 1973.

The full title of a work must be given in its bibliography entry: this includes the main title and the subtitle, as is shown in the first of the pair of entries above. As with footnotes, styling details of bibliographies vary according to the style manual being consulted or with individual corporate and institutional guidelines. The sample bibliography on page 314 represents a consensus of several current handbooks of style, and does not attempt to illustrate every possible variation.

Index An index, which lists alphabetically all of the topics as well as the page numbers where they appear, is included in lengthy reports and studies. It may be omitted from shorter reports, where the table of contents will serve as a guide. An index to a long report or study should be detailed and complete: it ought not to be just an expanded table of contents. Every major subject, topic, idea, or sentence in the text should have proper index entry.

The writer constructs an index by meticulously screening the text and underlining all items that are to be included. Each item and its page number or numbers is accurately recorded on a separate 3″ × 5″ card. The writer then sorts the cards alphabetically and rechecks them. The secretary types the index by following the alphabetically ordered cards. It is well for the typist to check each card before typing the material to ensure that all items are in the proper order and are styled consistently. The typist should also understand beforehand exactly how the writer desires the index to be styled. If the writer wishes to see the typewritten index in draft form first so that all entries, page numbers, and cross-references can be rechecked, the secretary should double-space the material and present the draft to the writer for approval. Final copy of an index (as one appearing in a report) that is not intended for outside publication should be single-spaced in a two-column page layout. On the other hand, if the index is a component of a manuscript that will be published, the typist should double-space the index entries in a single-column format.

A Sample Bibliography

BIBLIOGRAPHY

Reference Works

reference work — Webster's New Collegiate Dictionary. Springfield: G. & C. Merriam Company, 1975.

Books and Pamphlets

book, more than 3 authors — Anderson, Ruth I., et al. The Administrative Secretary: Resource. New York: McGraw-Hill, 1970. pp. 357-410.

book, 2 authors — Aurner, Robert R., and Morris Philip Wolf. Effective Communication in Business. Cincinnati: South-Western Publishing Company, 1967.

Graves, Harold F., and Lyne S. S. Hoffman. Report Writing. Englewood Cliffs, N. J.: Prentice-Hall, 1965.

Himstreet, William C., and Wayne Murlin Baty. Business Communications. Belmont, Cal.: Wadsworth, 1973. pp. 305-396.

book, 1 author — Lesikar, Raymond V. Report Writing for Business. Homewood, Ill.: Richard D. Irwin, Inc., 1973.

book, author unknown — A Manual of Style. 12th ed. Chicago: University of Chicago Press, 1969.

Murphy, Herta A., and Charles E. Peck. Effective Business Communications. New York: McGraw-Hill, 1972.

Articles

article in professional journal — Williams, Patricia. "Compositional Problems at the Typewriter." Business Education Review, 52 (1972), 22-23.

Handbooks, Bulletins, and Reports

handbook — Connecticut Business Education Handbook, Revised Edition. Connecticut State Department of Education, Bulletin No. 43. Hartford: 1966.

bulletin — FBE Bulletin, Foundation for Business Education, Vol. 14, No. 52. New York: 1968.

report — Financing the Lodging Industry: A Survey of Lender Attitudes. Laventhol and Horwath. Philadelphia: 1975.

Although there are several kinds of indexes having varying formats, two of the more common stylings are the *run-in* and the *indented.* While the former is more economical in terms of space, the latter is easier for a busy reader to scan quickly because the eye can move vertically down the page to pick out both entries and subentries, which are set apart from each other. With the run-in index styling, the reader's eye must scan horizontally a number of entry and subentry lines, many of which may be incomplete, i.e., the entry may be on one line, but its page number may have been run in on a subsequent line. The following are examples of these two index stylings:

run-in

Inside address: abbreviations in, 33; page placement of, 27–28; punctuation of, 13–14; Simplified Letter, 27; street address styling in, 32–34; ZIP Codes in, 33. *See also* Letters.

indented

Inside address. *See*
    also Letters.
  abbreviations in, 33
  page placement of, 27–28
  punctuation of, 13–14
  Simplified Letter, 27
  street address styling
   in, 32–34
  ZIP Codes in, 33

The most basic elements of an index are as follows:

1. **entry** This is a main subdivision of an index. It includes a heading and a page number or numbers and is typically typed flush left. The first letter of the first word in an entry is capitalized; all other words are lowercased unless they are proper nouns or adjectives, or unless they are normally lowercased words that have been arbitrarily capitalized in a particular work. In the examples above, *Inside address* is an entry.

2. **subentry** This is a secondary subdivision of an index; it is a subheading positioned beneath an entry. A subentry is typically indented one space. It consists of a subheading and a page number or numbers, and it enables the reader to locate specific points or discussions that are related to or fall within the larger subject encompassed by the entry. A subentry is lowercased unless it is a proper noun or adjective or unless it is composed of normally lowercased words that have been arbitrarily capitalized in a particular work. In the examples above, *abbreviations in, Simplified Letter,* and *ZIP Codes in* are subentries under the entry *Inside address.* The subentry *Simplified Letter* is an example of a compound that has been arbitrarily capitalized since it designates a particular style of business letter.

3. **sub-subentry** This is a tertiary entry that marks off a narrower category related and subordinate to a subentry. Its styling parallels that of a subentry. See the illustration on page 316 for an example.

4. **cross-references** These are devices that direct the reader through the text to all points, discussions, and subjects related to the one he is interested in. The two most common cross-references in indexes are the *see* cross-reference and the *see also* cross-reference. A *see* cross-reference may direct the reader to a parallel entry where more complete information is found. Example:

   Stationery, quality of. *See*
       Paper.

   A *see also* cross-reference, on the other hand, will direct the reader from one subject to a related subject. Example:

   Inside address. *See also*
       Letters.

   Cross-references are introduced by the italic or underscored words *See* or *See also.* Only the first letter of the first word of the entry cross-referred to is capitalized unless the entry is a proper noun or adjective. Regardless of its positioning within the entry, the cross-reference is terminated by a period. If there are multiple references within a single cross-reference, they are separated by semicolons. Example:

Salutation, 37–40. *See*
also Courtesy titles;
Letters.

Punctuation should be kept to a minimum in indexes. Periods are used at the ends of lines only if the lines end in cross-references. A comma is used between an entry or a subentry and any word or words modifying it, as

Correction fluid, use of,
in correspondence, 25

The following illustration shows the page layout and typewriting format for an indented index.

An Example of an Indented Index

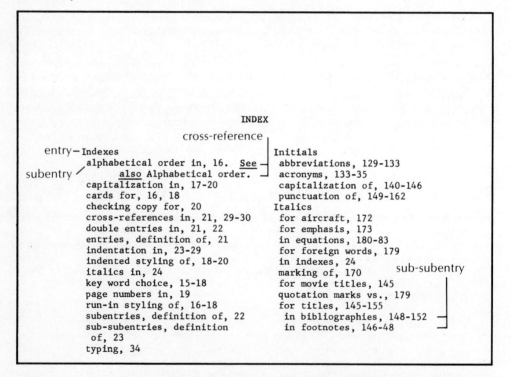

```
                              INDEX
                    cross-reference
entry—Indexes                                  Initials
        alphabetical order in, 16.  See         abbreviations, 129-133
subentry  also Alphabetical order.              acronyms, 133-35
        capitalization in, 17-20                capitalization of, 140-146
        cards for, 16, 18                       punctuation of, 149-162
        checking copy for, 20                  Italics
        cross-references in, 21, 29-30          for aircraft, 172
        double entries in, 21, 22               for emphasis, 173
        entries, definition of, 21              in equations, 180-83
        indentation in, 23-29                   for foreign words, 179
        indented styling of, 18-20              in indexes, 24
        italics in, 24                          marking of, 170      sub-subentry
        key word choice, 15-18                  for movie titles, 145
        page numbers in, 19                     quotation marks vs., 179
        run-in styling of, 16-18                for titles, 145-155
        subentries, definition of, 22            in bibliographies, 148-152
        sub-subentries, definition               in footnotes, 146-48
         of, 23
        typing, 34
```

It should be emphasized that indexing is a highly specialized area—an area that cannot be covered in detail in a book of this type. The foregoing material is, then, a general presentation tailored mainly to report typing. Readers interested in detailed discussions of indexing procedures may consult pages 76–96 of *Words into Type,* 3rd ed. (Englewood Cliffs, N.J.: Prentice-Hall, Inc., 1974) or Chapter 18 of *A Manual of Style,* 12th ed. (Chicago: University of Chicago Press, 1974).

GRAPHIC AIDS

Graphic aids or illustrations are essential components of many reports in that they aid in depicting material in a concise, understandable, and interesting way. Tables, bar and line charts, pie charts, maps, or pictograms are commonly included. They should be neatly executed and may be in color. Graphic aids are numbered sequentially: tables may be captioned by Roman numerals (Table I, Table II, Table III, etc.), and figures by Arabic numerals (Figure 1, Figure 2, Figure 3, etc.). Bar charts and pictograms may be drawn by a graphic artist in the company, but tables are usually typed by a secretary. Such tables and charts are placed near the point of reference (as "Please see Table 5 for additional evidence") or they may occupy an entire page. Other tables that are not essential to the text may be placed in an appendix. When a table is to be included in the report text, three blank spaces (top and bottom) should separate the table from the running text. Each table should be numbered consecutively and tabulated with equal space between columns.

8.6

TYPING MINUTES OF MEETINGS

The secretary who types the minutes of any meeting has an important responsibility. She should keep in mind that because minutes serve as the *official* record of a meeting, accuracy on her part is essential. Modern tape-recording devices are of great value. They may be used in checking the precise wording of motions, the order of business, and so forth. Even though meetings vary in size, degree of formality, scope, and function, it is imperative that the wording of minutes be factual, brief, and devoid of editorial opinion and comment. Acceptable minutes capture the gist or substance of the meeting and follow the agenda closely; as a rule, verbatim record is made only of main motions and resolutions. Whenever one's superior is the presiding officer of a meeting, he or she will frequently want to see a rough draft of the minutes before the final copy is typed.

PREPARATION FOR TYPING MINUTES

A little organizational forethought is needed before beginning the actual typing of the minutes. Being well-organized makes the task easier and saves time and effort—thus increasing one's productivity. The following items should be assembled:

A copy of the agenda of the meeting
Attendance information; an absentee list; a roster
Previous minutes of the group or organization
Reference books on style and parliamentary procedure
Copies of reports and materials distributed at the meeting
A copy of motions and/or resolutions
An up-to-date dictionary
A copy of the constitution and/or bylaws of the organization
Official printed stationery and continuation sheets
Other data pertinent to the minutes

Before starting to type the minutes, all details should be carefully checked: the spelling of names, the correct use of titles, and other items. (See also Chapter 3, pages 51–54, for further information on meetings and minutes.)

THE FORMAT OF THE MINUTES

Since the format of the minutes is determined in most cases by the standards set by one's organization, one should carefully examine the setup of minutes that have been previously typed. Some organizations provide special printed stationery designed especially for the first page of the minutes. Printed continuation sheets are also often provided. If special printed paper is not available, the secretary should then select the appropriate quality of plain white bond stationery. (See Chapter 3, pages 53–54, for minutes typed on plain stationery.)

Format for Minutes Typed on a Printed Form

ADMINISTRATIVE MANAGEMENT SOCIETY

OFFICIAL MINUTES

AMS

OF THE BOARD OF DIRECTORS

Chapter Hartford
Date October 14, —
Date of Meeting October 13, 19—
Number on Board 14
Number Present 12

A meeting of the Board was called to order by President Ted Corvair at the Towers Hotel at 4:45 p.m., Monday, October 13, 19—.

Attendance: All members were present except Messrs. Curtis and Larson.

1. Treasurer's Report
____
____
__________________.

2. Membership
____
______________________________:
____
____
____
____
____

3. Area Director Nominations
____
____
____
__________________________.

4. November Meeting
____
______________.

5. Directors' Reports
Education - ______________________________
____
_____________________________.

____
Secretary

COPIES OF THIS REPORT SHOULD BE IN THE HANDS OF THE AREA DIRECTOR AND THE INTERNATIONAL AMS OFFICE WITHIN TWO WEEKS OF THE DATE OF THE MEETING.

6-71

EVERY CHAPTER SHOULD PARTICIPATE IN THE MERIT AWARD PLAN

Form 110

Printed in U.S.A.

Form 110 courtesy of the Administrative Management Society.

OFFICIAL BOARD MINUTES (continued)

Chapter, AMS Hartford ______ Date October 14, 19- Page 2

Special Programming - ______________________________
____
______________________________.

Systems and Information - ______________________________
____
______________________________.

Financial Management - ______________________________
______________________________.

6. Other Business

____
____
______________________________.

7. Comments from Officers

____
____
______________________________.

There being no further business, the meeting was adjourned at 5:35 p.m.

Margaret L. Tinsley

Secretary

Form 114 6-71

Printed in U.S.A.

The arrangement of the typed minutes should closely parallel the agenda or order of business of the meeting. Some of the common elements found in minutes are:

meeting identification

name of the organization or group, its address;
type of meeting: regular or special

start of the meeting

call to order: time, date, presiding officer;
attendance information;
previous minutes—referral to these, and corrections;
reports—by whom, title, subject;
unfinished business (if any)—motions, by whom, votes;
program—speaker's name and title;
announcements

close of the meeting

adjournment, time

TYPING THE MINUTES

With a preprinted meeting form, it is an easy task for the secretary to fill in the needed information while at the same time taking care not to type directly on the printed lines so that the typescript will be obscured. Since the style in which minutes are recorded varies greatly, the illustration on pages 318–319 of this chapter shows an example of a styling that has been tailor-made for the Administrative Management Society. Such a styling can be modified or adapted by a forms designer so that it will fit a company or organization's particular requirements. The company logo can be imprinted at the top of the page.

Typing Guides For Minutes Some suggested format guides for minutes—especially those that are to be typed on plain paper—are as follows:

1. Leave a two-inch top margin.
2. Type the title all in capital letters on line 13.
3. Center the date two lines beneath the title; the date may be typed in capital and lowercase letters.
4. Use all-capitalized side headings or side headings that are in underscored capital and lowercase letters. Choice of side-heading style (such as ATTENDING or ATTENDANCE/ *Attending* or *Attendance*) will usually vary according to organization guidelines; hence, several stylings are shown in the illustrations in this book.
5. Single-space the text paragraphs for the sake of saving space.
6. Use a 60-space typing line for textual matter.
7. Include a complimentary close (as *Respectfully submitted*) followed by the secretary's and the chairman's signatures.
8. Make the necessary copies for distribution and filing.

A facsimile of a full set of minutes typed on plain stationery is shown in Chapter 3 on pages 53–54. It is accompanied by textual discussion on the machanics of composing minutes. The following illustration is a facsimile of a meeting summary. Notice that the word *summary* is typed all in capital letters one inch from the top left edge of the page. Since this facsimile illustrates a confidential meeting, the word *confidential* is typed one inch from the top right edge of the page, also all in capital letters. The rest of the material is formatted according to the guidelines given above, except that the complimentary close and signature lines, which are unnecessary in most meeting summaries, are omitted.

Format of a Meeting Summary

SUMMARY CONFIDENTIAL

XYZ CORPORATION

CONSUMER PRODUCTS DIVISION FINANCE COMMITTEE MEETING

October 22, 19—

ATTENDANCE	Messrs. Adams, Bowen, Carter, and Dann; Ms. Eagleton
TREASURER'S DEPARTMENT	Mr. Adams submitted liquidity forecasts, budget allocations, and figures representing long-term investment transactions. Forty million dollars of cash flow still is not committed for 19— disbursement, which will result in $45 million of surplus liquidity at year's end if the situation continues.
COMMON STOCK DEPARTMENT	Ms. Eagleton discussed and analyzed current performance and reviewed recent transactions. Cash reserves continue to be held at the 30% level while the Department awaits a more auspicious opportunity to deploy them into stocks.
TRANSACTIONS	All transactions for the period October 1 - November 1 of this year were approved.

8.7

HOUSE ORGANS

Company newsletters, newspapers, and magazines are called *house organs.* They contain news and general information about individual employees, company activities, and accounts of miscellaneous happenings or events. The general purpose of a house organ is to maintain and boost good interpersonal relations and employee morale by establishing a channel of communication among the various echelons of the organization. A secretary may be responsible for writing, typewriting, or reproducing the material that will appear in this kind of publication. Although each organization will have its own editorial house-organ guidelines for layout and content, there are, nevertheless, a few general points that can be set forth regarding the preparation of the material that will be reproduced.

THE NEWSLETTER/NEWSPAPER LAYOUT

The layout of the newsletter-type house organ is often similar to that of a regular newspaper: it is characterized by headlines, articles set up in columnar formats, and illustrations. An easy way to set up the typed material for a company newsletter or newspaper follows. A sheet of 8½" × 11" paper is divided vertically into two columns. A proportionally-spacing typewriter may be used to great advantage in order to obtain even (or *justified*) right-hand margins (see Chapter 5 "Automated and Specialized Typewriting with Stylization," pages 92–93, for right-margin justification). On the other hand, if a conventional typewriter is used, the secretary can still attain even right-hand margins by using manual justification:

1. First, the material is typed in columnar format. Diagonal lines (or virgules) are then typed to fill in the unused spaces at the ends of the lines:

```
Mr. David R. Duncan of the Person-
nel Department has announced that on/
July 4 there will be a company picnic
for employees and their families at//
```

2. Next, the final draft is prepared after the text has been rechecked for accuracy and completeness. In the final draft, the typist inserts extra spaces for each virgule between words within the text. In this way, even (or justified) right margins are achieved:

```
Mr. David R. Duncan of the Person-
nel Department has  announced that on
July 4 there will be a company picnic
for employees  and their  families at
```

See also Chapter 5, pages 91–95, for a discussion of the special effects that can be achieved by use of automated typewriting—effects that can be used to great advantage in the typewriting of newspapers and newsletters. Further, the reader should scan Chapter 12 for detailed information on the reprographics equipment and processes that may be employed in setting up and reproducing house-organ materials.

THE MAGAZINE LAYOUT

Some organizations—especially very large corporations having broad-based domestic and foreign operations—prefer to use the magazine format for their house organs. This type of publication often contains articles of a general nature (such as a piece on a foreign country where the company may have a subsidiary) as well as specific information and news about corporate goals and operations and items about individual divisions and particular employees. Company magazines often feature a number of photographs and other illustrations.

A secretary ordinarily will not be responsible for the editorial policies, format guidelines, and the actual reproduction of this type of publication. Rather, she would be responsible for following the typewriting guidelines established by the organization for manuscripts and other material that will be reproduced in the magazine. Since format policies vary widely from organization to organization, the most that can be said here is that all manuscripts and news items should be neatly and accurately typewritten on plain bond paper with ample (1½" × 2") margins all around. The text should be double-spaced. All organizational style guidelines should be adhered to.

8.8

PROOFREADING TECHNIQUES

Regardless of whether the material is a news release, a report, minutes, or other document, it should be carefully proofread for typographical errors or mistakes in format. The most commonly used proofreaders' marks are shown in the illustration below, which is reprinted from page 922 of *Webster's New Collegiate Dictionary.*

PROOFREADERS' MARKS

- delete; take it out
- close up; print as one word
- delete and close up
- caret; insert here (something
- insert a space
- eq# space evenly where indicated
- stet let marked text stand as set
- tr transpose; change order the
- / used to separate two or more marks and often as a concluding stroke at the end of an insertion
- set farther to the left
- set farther to the right
- set æ or fl as ligatures æ or fl
- straighten alignment
- straighten or align
- imperfect or broken character
- indent or insert em quad space
- ¶ begin a new paragraph
- Sp spell out (set 5 lbs as five pounds)
- cap set in capitals (CAPITALS)
- sm cap or s.c. set in small capitals (SMALL CAPITALS)
- lc set in Lowercase (lowercase)
- ital set in italic (*italic*)
- rom set in roman (roman)
- bf set in boldface (**boldface**)
- = or -/ or or /H/ hyphen
- 1/N or en or /N/ en dash (1965–72)
- 1/M or em or /M/ em — or long — dash
- superscript or superior (3 as in πr^2)
- subscript or inferior (2 as in H_2O)
- centered (for a centered dot in $p \cdot q$)
- comma
- apostrophe
- period
- ; or ;/ semicolon
- : or colon
- or quotation marks
- (/) parentheses
- [/] brackets
- OK/? query to author: has this been set as intended?
- push down a work-up[1]
- turn over an inverted letter[1]
- wf wrong font; a character of the wrong size or esp. style[1]

[1] The last three symbols are unlikely to be needed in marking proofs of photocomposed matter.

Proofreading involves the location of the error and the notation of the error for subsequent correction. A light pencil notation in the margin of the paper will make it easy to find the error when it is time to correct the copy. Later, a soft eraser can easily be used to remove the penciled notation. An alternate notation technique is to list errors on a separate sheet of paper; then, they can be checked off one by one as corrections are made.

BASIC APPROACHES TO PROOFREADING

There are two basic approaches to proofreading: the solo method and the team method. More often than not, the secretary works alone and has to accept the full responsibliity for detecting and correcting any errors in the copy. Often errors will be overlooked unintentionally because of blind spots in reading. Normally, a second reading will serve to catch any remaining problems.

On the other hand, the team method of proofreading involves the assistance of another person in the process of combing and sifting through the copy for possible omissions, deletions, and corrections. One person usually reads aloud from the original copy while the other carefully compares the typescript with the words of the reader concerning placement, format, and content. In the case of long, difficult, or highly technical copy, the team may decide to exchange positions, e.g., the former reader becomes the observer and vice versa.

TRIPLE-CHECK PROOFREADING SYSTEM

After typing a document or any page of copy, the secretary will want to be sure that the work is letter-perfect and that it is ready for the executive's signature and/or for distribution. The application of the following three-way proofreading system will point up any needed changes or corrections in the completed copy before it leaves the typewriter:

1. Check the material for correct format and style.
2. Read the text for accurate content.
3. Scan the document for minor imperfections in typescript.

Check the material for correct format and style Major style errors can be discovered immediately if the typist inspects the format of the typed document first of all. For example, failure to indent a paragraph or the omission of a heading would be obvious at first glance. In such cases, there is no need to proofread the material further; a retype is clearly needed.

Read the text for accurate content If the copy is read once or perhaps twice for content and meaning, hidden errors (such as the omission of an article, a preposition, or some other word) will surface. Sometimes if similar words or phrases are used in two consecutive lines in copy, the typist will inadvertently skip a line of copy. Often a word ending will be incorrectly typed; and *-ing* instead of a *-tion* may have been used. These or other such errors that will seriously affect the usefulness of the document should be detected early. In some instances, crowding and/or spreading may be used to make the necessary corrections. (See also Chapter 5, pages 99–100, for further details on crowding and spreading techniques.)

Scan the document for imperfections in typescript A careful inspection should be made of the copy to catch errors in the quality of the typescript: check for light or pale letters or figures, be sure that underscoring and markings (if used) are clear and complete (often the typewriter will malfunction and a hyphen or an underscore will not print), judge the quality of the corrections, and look for any smudges or extraneous marks on the page. Then, proceed to correct all of the problems.

9

CHAPTER NINE

LETTERS COMPOSED BY THE SECRETARY

CONTENTS

9.1

INTRODUCTION

Communication is unquestionably essential to the success of any business. Today, the administrative secretary should know how and when to respond to written communications addressed to the executive. The administrative secretary takes on this responsibility with executive consent. Competent fulfillment of this task depends on the secretary's thorough knowledge and understanding of the employer's role within the corporate structure. Thus has evolved the concept of the secretary as an executive extender. The secretary renders a quasi-managerial service in performing certain letter-writing functions that release the employer's time for additional projects and decision-making. Also, answering correspondence during the employer's absence is a major facet of secretarial responsibility.

9.2

THE WRITING OF LETTERS: General Pointers

An administrative secretary in a large corporation can best utilize dictation skills by dictating letters to word processing centers. (For additional information, see Chapter 4, "Dictation and Transcription: Input and Output.") The secretary in a smaller office lacking a word processing center may compose and type certain letters that have been delegated to her by the executive.

GETTING READY TO WRITE

Composing a good business letter involves some pre-writing preparations. The following seven steps, suggested for preparing a business communication, might serve as a checklist for the secretary who is interested in achieving maximum efficiency and productivity:

1. Consult the executive on procedure.
2. Classify and sort incoming letters.
3. Assemble needed materials.
4. Make marginal notes.
5. Underscore important facts.
6. Outline the content of the reply letter.
7. Compose the reply letter.

Consult the executive on procedure A cooperative decision should be made by the secretary and the executive regarding certain procedures (as the opening and reading of the mail—e.g., the handling of priority, confidential, routine, and other communications). It is important to know whether the executive would like to see all of the mail or whether the secretary should screen the mail and immediately route certain communications to subordinates. Setting up a modus operandi for handling correspondence is vital to smooth office work flow. Above all, the employer should explicitly indicate those types of letters to be answered by the secretary.

As soon as possible each day, the secretary should present to the executive all correspondence in the *priority* or *immediate attention* classification—a category that includes urgent business letters, international messages, telegrams, and Certified, Registered, or Special Delivery mail. One should be aware of the executive's preferences with respect to the handling of such items. For instance, is this mail to be opened and arranged in the order of its importance or is it to remain unopened?

Classify and sort incoming letters Among the wide variety of communications coming to an executive office may be material relating to banking, finance, insurance, and investment—material that may arrive labeled and classified as CONFIDENTIAL. The secretary must use good judgment in deciding which of these communications may be opened and acted upon for the executive.

Having been opened, the mail may then be subdivided and placed in file folders for easy reference. Identifying the folder labels by color, numerical sequence, and type of correspondence should prove helpful to the busy executive. An illustration follows:

Classifications of Executive Correspondence

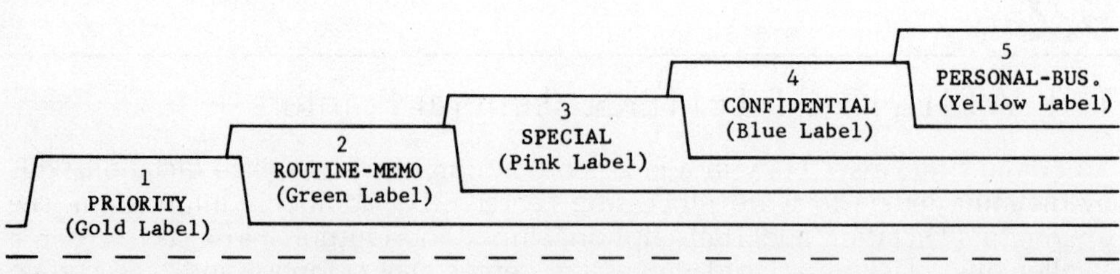

Assemble needed materials Frequently one must refer to previous correspondence from a client before a reply can be sent. Tabular information, reports, printouts, catalogs, reference books, manuals, and other items also may have to be assembled in advance for dictation readiness. Choice of the appropriate stationery size is important: Which type will be required—the full size, the executive size (Monarch), or the half-sheet (Baronial)?

Make marginal notes The secretary will find it helpful to make marginal notes on letters to be answered. Several types of information may be needed for the typed response such as conference dates, appointments, and titles of brochures. Jotting down this information in advance will ensure a speedier reply.

Underscore important facts It is useful to employ a yellow felt-tip pen or a red auditor's pen to underscore the significant facts in a letter which are pertinent to the reply. Color will highlight this information and make it easy to identify when the response is later being written.

Outline reply letter content One should put all the facts together, have a clear-cut idea of what one wants to say, jot down the major topics that will be treated in the reply letter, and examine examples of previous correspondence for guidance in drafting the reply.

Compose the letter If one plans and prepares carefully before writing, the actual composition of the reply should be easier. One should also remember to use in the letter expressions that are popular with the executive. See pages 332 and 337 of this chapter for examples of letters written by a secretary.

THE MAKEUP OF A GOOD LETTER

A well-written managerial communication delivers a positive first-glance impact on the reader or on the audience (as with letters or memorandums addressed to several persons). By the same token, a favorable corporate image can also be achieved with letters delegated to and composed solely by the secretary if she is cognizant of the mechanics of good letter makeup. An analysis of the basic makeup of the modern business communication follows.

Setting the stage The full view of a letter, like one's first look at the stage when the curtain is opened, should evoke a favorable reader response. The backstage preparations which contribute to a positive effect are:

1. Correct size of impressive bond stationery
2. Sharp, dark, clean-cut typescript
3. Attractive letter style (see Chapter 6)
4. Picture-frame letter placement (see Chapter 6)

Creating the opening Since the corporate image can be enhanced or tarnished through one's choice of words, the secretary must be certain that just the right words are used. This statement is especially applicable to the opening paragraph of a communication. Remember—waken the reader's interest; capture his attention. Openings that have the reader's point of view in mind will bring him pleasure, satisfaction, and personal involvement in the matters being discussed. The following is an example of a good opening paragraph:

How lucky we are that you said "Yes" to our invitation to appear before a group of new secretaries at our annual "Get-Acquainted Day" on Thursday, October 2! After hearing you speak at the CPS meeting in April, I am convinced that we couldn't find a better speaker.

Cues to the reader The secretary should regard every business-communication reader as a critic of corporate letter production. Thus, each communication to a client or to a potential customer provides an opportunity to epitomize the very best in company service, goodwill, and helpfulness. Here are some ways to create a positive impression on the reader:

1. Use tactful, easy-to-understand language. Short words, clear-cut and direct, are easier to read and to understand than lengthy words. Write as you speak, using natural everyday expressions. Example:

   It is a real pleasure to know that you will lead our Transactional Analysis Seminar on May 14.

2. Organize your language carefully and concisely. Time is a precious commodity, and the busy executive wants to get the gist of the message on the first reading. Interesting messages contain sequences that vary in length and in internal structure. Coherence and continuity are other prime requisites of modern communications. (See also Chapter 7, pages 263–269, for sentence and paragraph strategy.)
3. Construct sentences correctly. Technical correctness in writing is a worthy goal for any secretary. In order to attain it, one should proofread the material and make sure that none of the following infelicities—among many others—is present: misplaced commas, misspelled words, incorrect word division, numbers written incorrectly, hackneyed and stilted expressions, a lack of agreement between subjects and verbs, and other such grammatical and stylistic pitfalls. (Details concerning written expression may be found in Chapter 7.)
4. Give accurate, precise information. The omission of one important detail can spell the difference between order and confusion in the reader's mind. This is an example of a letter written by a secretary to a woman executive accepting a speaking engagement for a secretarial conference (note the questions in paragraph two):

   Thank you for your gracious invitation to participate in your secretarial conference on October 19 at Sanford Hall. It is thoughtful of you to include me in your program.
   Would you please send along a map showing the best driving route to your campus, and also mention the amount of time allotted for my message?

   If the writer of the letter had checked the outgoing letter carefully for details, it would not have been necessary for the guest to politely request information on the length of the address and on conference location.

5. Write clearly to avoid any hint of double meaning. It has often been said that if a statement can be misunderstood, it will be! By scanning all written messages for unintended hidden meanings, the writer can avoid many problems. For example, which way will the following statement be interpreted?

   One and two-page photos are needed for this year's annual report.

   reader's questions
   How many photos are needed?
   Is one two-page photo needed?
   Is the need for one one-page photo and one two-page photo?

   A careful rewording of the original statement will prevent any misunderstanding:

   Please prepare one full-page photo and one double-page photo for use in this year's annual report.

6. Respond to questions raised. It is a serious omission when one neglects to answer a question that has been raised in previous correspondence. Here is another safeguard that will ensure good secretarial writing: double-check to see that no such omissions have been made, by rereading relevant previous correspondence and then comparing it with your response.
7. Introduce an unfavorable comment with a favorable one. It is helpful to present all the positive aspects of a situation first and then to lead into any negative or unfavorable comments. Find points of agreement with the reader and mention them before talking about an unfavorable fact. Example:

   Your complimentary copy of *Better Letter Dictation* is on its way to you. Your kind comments about the usefulness of this brochure are greatly appreciated.

   Popular demand for copies of the brochure within recent weeks has depleted our supply, unfortunately. However, please feel free to reproduce temporary copies for use by your staff. When our new shipment arrives, we'll speed a dozen copies to you.

Devising a friendly way to close a letter Give the reader a pleasant closing thought in the final paragraph of the letter, as in this example:

Again, thank you for giving us permission to reprint the article on your company's research in the field of pollution control. This information will provide excellent material for next month's issue of *The Executive*.

One should avoid thanking someone for something in advance. It is really rather impertinent to assume beforehand that one's request will be honored. Wait until the service is rendered; then, make an appropriate acknowledgment for it. (See also Chapter 7, pages 271–279, for a list of business clichés that should be avoided, especially in letters.)

The secretary's signature on a letter written for an executive When the secretary composes a letter for the employer, there should be an understanding between them about whose signature is to be used at the end of the communication. In general, a good rule to follow is that only the letters of general information (such as those regarding conference dates, report titles, and others) may bear the secretary's signature unless the secretary has been otherwise instructed by the employer. When the executive is away from the office for several days, the secretary may be authorized to sign the executive's name on outgoing correspondence. In this case, the secretary's initials may be written beneath the executive's name, as shown in the first example below, or the secretary may sign the letter under her own name if her name and professional title are typed in the signature block as shown in the second example below:

Sincerely *Ellen Barnes* *al* Ellen Barnes President	**or**	Sincerely *Sara Wiley* Sara Wiley Secretary to Ellen Barnes

9.3

THE SECRETARY WRITES ROUTINE LETTERS, FORM LETTERS, AND MEMORANDUMS

Routine correspondence containing general information may, subject to the executive's approval, go out over the secretary's signature. Such routine letters that the experienced secretary may expect to be called on to answer include many involving acknowledgment, inquiry, introduction, order, remittance, reservation, and transmittal. Particularly important is the acknowledgment of correspondence during an employer's absence since this not only lets the correspondent know that the letter will receive prompt attention upon the employer's return, but to some degree establishes the tone of the later correspondence. The secretary should follow closely the executive's writing style, especially in such acknowledgments. Illustrations of some types of routine letters along with letter-writing guides may be found in this chapter on pages 332 and 337.

FORM LETTER CONSTRUCTION

An expedient way to handle routine mail is the use of form letters to standardize responses. A ring binder might be used to categorize certain types of letters that are frequently written. By using appropriate index tabs on the various divisions of the ring binder, one can locate information quickly. Thus, when one writes such letters as those of announcement and acknowledgment, one may refer to similar or prototypal letters—a trick that expedites composition. The notebook might also contain a stock of ready-made paragraphs labeled as A, B, C, D, and so on. In this way, the secretary might delegate to other secretaries the responsibility of constructing certain letters by referring them to specific combinations of stock paragraphs in the ring binder. Form letters are often printed in advance. The secretary then adds the date and the inside address; sometimes other data are also added to the body of the form letter. Automated letter production or word processing is a popular way to reproduce a form letter because it lends the letter the appearance of an original. (See also Chapter 5 for detailed information on this technique.)

THE WRITING OF OFFICE MEMORANDUMS

The office memorandum is another type of routine communication which the secretary may compose. *Webster's New Collegiate Dictionary* defines *memorandum* as " . . . a usually brief communication written for interoffice circulation." As such, its topics may include general messages (as notices, announcements, procedures, or inquiry). Memorandums are usually circulated freely among corporate branch offices located in distant cities. Large companies have standardized memorandum forms. There is a wide variety in the printed styling of memorandums; however, the basic parts of most memorandums are the headings (TO, FROM, SUBJECT, DATE) and the body (message). (See also Chapter 8, "Special Typing Projects," for a detailed discussion of memorandum writing and styling.)

The memorandum audience The memorandum is a fast, economical, and efficient way to relay important news that should reach all or a significant fraction of the corporate staff. Today an office copier can, in a few minutes, reproduce multiple copies of a memorandum, thus making it ready for wide distribution to a large reader audience. On the other hand, a memorandum may also be addressed solely to one person.

Preparing the heading of the memorandum One of the popular features of the office memorandum is the ease with which its message may reach office personnel. For example, the TO line may be addressed to one individual or to many persons at the same time:

TO: Frances Rummel, Secretarial Services Supervisor
or
TO: Office Services Personnel
or
TO: Secretarial Staff, School of Business

Usually, the other heading components consist of the following: the FROM line which includes the name of the writer, and his or her title or position; the DATE line; the SUBJECT line; and the LOCATION (floor, extension, or branch) line, which is optional.

The subject line of the memorandum The SUBJECT line in the heading of the memorandum is very important, for it gives the reader an overview of the message content. The secretary needs to compose a subject line that really encapsulates the message. The SUBJECT line also is useful for filing purposes. Examples of typical SUBJECT lines are as follows:

SUBJECT: April Meeting of the Secretarial Forum
or
SUBJECT: NEED FOR A NEW ELECTRIC TYPEWRITER
or
SUBJECT: Transportation Rates on Iron or Steel Bars

Composing the message (or body) of the memorandum Brevity, courtesy, factualness, and tact are four requisites of message content in office memorandums. The main idea of the message is usually contained in the first paragraph, while additional or supporting data may be added in succeeding paragraphs. The final part of a memorandum may close with a courteous request for action or further information. In some instances the request for service, action, or specific information may be found in the opening paragraph with supporting data located in subsequent paragraphs.

A sample memorandum One kind of interoffice communication frequently written by the secretary is a meeting notice. A sample of a typical memorandum serving as a meeting notice is found on page 339.

THE SECRETARY HANDLES SPECIAL CORRESPONDENCE

Apart from the normal stream of office mail, there is a segment of correspondence that might be called *special.* Such correspondence is so designated because one or more of the following situations exist: (1) only the executive has the complete understanding of the situation needed to make a correct response (2) the executive alone has the technical know-how to respond properly (3) complex questions and/or problems may be answered best by the executive, or (4) the respondent is a close personal friend and knows the executive's style of writing too well to accept any substitute for it.

On occasion, the executive may outline a response to a *special* letter or write or dictate certain sections of it and then turn it over to the secretary for completion. Some types of *special* communications are letters of adjustment, application, reservations, appreciation, cancellation, collection, or sales. Examples of these letters, together with letter-writing guides that should assist one in composing similar letters may be found on the following pages.

Acknowledgement During the Employer's Absence

COMMUNICATIONS MEDIA CORPORATION
345 Jones Street
Jonesville, ST 12345

February 15, 19--

Ms. Nancy Voelker
President, Secretaries Club
Carter Secretarial College
1234 Smith Street
Smithville, ST 56789

Dear Ms. Voelker:

Thank you for your gracious invitation to Mr. Moore to be the keynote speaker at the annual meeting of the Secretaries Club on May 26, 19--.

Mr. Moore will be returning from a business trip in Western Europe next week. On his return, you can be sure that your letter will receive his prompt attention.

Cordially yours,

Lillian Ayala

Lillian Ayala
Secretary to
William Moore

Letter-writing Guides:
Acknowledge the request.
Explain the reason for the delay.
Use a courteous close.

Order

Rodriguez, Inc.
2255 West 189th Street
New York, NY 11250

November 13, 19--

Mr. George Holmes, Manager
Baxter and Halloway, Inc.
Smithville, ST 56789

Dear Mr. Holmes:

Please accept this order for immediate shipment to Rodriguez, Inc., Wood Products Division, 2255 West 189th Street, New York, NY 11250.

Quantity	Description	Unit Price	Total
1800	No. 202 T. Hinges, Brass Plate	$1.00 pr.	$900.
600	No. 78 Corner Braces, Brass Plate	1.25 ea.	750.
		Total	$1,650.

An unexpected flurry of orders has depleted our stock. Therefore, any assistance that you can give in expediting our order and delivery will be greatly appreciated.

Sincerely,

Paul Thomas

Paul Thomas
Purchasing Agent

PT:ls

Letter-writing Guides:
Notice the urgent need for the order and shipping address.
List the quantity, description and price of the ordered items.
Emphasize the reason for the rush order and the need for prompt delivery.

Inquiry

ACME EQUIPMENT COMPANY
42 Grove Street
Johnsonville, ST 23456

September 17, 19--

Mr. Harold Thomas
Sales Manager
Laprade Industries
1525 State Street
Smithville, ST 56789

Dear Mr. Thomas

Presently we are planning to add yard and garden tractors to our line of leased equipment. It is my pleasure to announce that we shall feature Harris Tractors.

Would you please send us a complete list of models and specifications for Harris Tractors. It would be helpful to have the following data as soon as possible:

1. Horsepower/range of job function.
2. Commercial/homeowner equipment.
3. Contract samples/sale terms.

Since the publication date for our catalog is slated for November, your early reply will be appreciated.

Sincerely yours

Thomas Domizio

Thomas Domizio
Marketing Manager

TD:ls

Letter-writing Guides:
Give the needed information.
Detail the request.
Mention the due date.
Close the letter politely.

A Letter of Introduction

BILLINGSLEY AND NEVINS
Attorneys-at-law
100 Ellory Boulevard
Masonville, ST 45678

June 26, 19--

Mr. Hillory Atkins
Atkins and Atkins
43 Downs Avenue
Smithville, ST 56789

Dear Mr. Atkins:

This is a letter of introduction for Miss Lillian Collins who has served ably as our secretary for more than two years.

We learned from Miss Collins a few days ago that she will be married next month. She and her husband plan to move to Smithville.

While we are happy for Miss Collins, we are sorry to lose her. She has courteously and efficiently handled a multitude of tasks in our office. Her loyalty and dedication are admired by all. We feel that our loss will be the gain of the firm that is fortunate enough to obtain her services.

If there is additional information that you should like to have concerning Miss Collins, please do not hesitate to call us at 248-9711.

Yours sincerely,

Howard Billingsley

Howard Billingsley
Attorney

HB:ls

Letter-writing Guides:
Make the introduction.
Present personal data.
Give an evaluation.
Offer more information upon request.

Response to an Invitation

UNIVERSAL MILLS, INC.
54 Main Street
West Bend, ST 34567

October 22, 19--

Dr. Samuel Ross, President
Jones University
165 Royston Drive
Smithville, ST 56789

Dear Doctor Ross:

It isn't every day that one is honored by an invitation to give a commencement address! I was extremely pleased to have received your kind invitation to address your graduates on Friday, May 20, 19--, at 5 p.m. in Smith Hall.

After reflecting on a topic, perhaps "Environment Concerns in Today's World" would be of interest to your graduates. As you know, our firm has done considerable research in this area.

As soon as my travel arrangements are confirmed, I shall send further information to you.

Thank you, once again, for the opportunity to participate in your 100th Commencement. May I offer my congratulations to you for the splendid contributions that Jones University has made to the field of education.

Sincerely,

Harrison Takington

Harrison Takington
President

HT:ls

Letter-writing Guides:
Respond graciously to the invitation.
Supply additional relevant information.
Acknowledge the honor of being invited to the event.

Letter of Transmittal

FAIRMONT STAINLESS STEEL CORPORATION
1480 Hamilton Road
Fairmont, ST 67890

March 18, 19--

Professor James Wilhelm
DePaul Technical College
Smithville, ST 56789

Dear Professor Wilhelm:

It is good to know of your interest in the Annual Report of the Fairmont Stainless Steel Corporation for use by the students in your research seminar.

As you requested, a dozen copies of Fairmont's Annual Report were mailed to you today. Since these reports were labeled Priority Mail, you will have them well in advance of the target date for their use.

Each year, if you will let us know the number of these reports that you will need, it will be our pleasure to send them. We feel that the material will be our contribution to the business and economic understanding of your students.

Sincerely yours,

Jean Linamen

Jean Linamen
Secretary to Mr. Fulton

Letter-writing Guides:
Acknowledge interest in the item.
Give details on transmittal.
Use a friendly closing.

Subscription Letter

HOLLISTON AND BEEM ASSOCIATES, INC.

68 Industrial Park Drive
Macon, GA 30724

October 14, 19--

The Jenkins Press
95 High Ridge Road
Smithville, ST 56789

Gentlemen:

A check for $18.50 is enclosed for a two-year subscription to Monthly Management Reports.

Since we shall be moving to our new offices in December, please use the following address:

Mr. Henry Holliston
Senior Consultant
Holliston and Beem Associates, Inc.
27 Cranston Lane
Macon, GA 30724

It is my understanding that by subscribing now, we will be sent a bonus issue of Word Processing Implementation. This report sounds most interesting.

Sincerely yours,

Henry Holliston

Henry Holliston
Senior Consultant

les

Enclosure: Check

Letter-writing Guides:

Mention the amount of the enclosed check or money order.
Mention the name of the publication being subscribed to.
Give any other pertinent information (as a change in address).
Reconfirm subscription terms if necessary.

Memorandum

TO: Ms. Alt
Ms. Rasmusson
Ms. Stanislawczyk
Ms. Walden

Messrs: Anderson
DiAngelo
Guilford
Perez
Timkins

FROM: Richard Farnsworth, Secretary

DATE: July 15, 19—

SUBJECT: EXECUTIVES' ROUNDTABLE MEETING NOTICE

There will be a meeting of all members of the Executives' Roundtable on Thursday, July 25, 19—, at 11 a.m. in the Beacon Room of the Tower Building in Chicago.

Luncheon will be served at 12:15 p.m. If you cannot be with us, please call 247-9521 no later than July 14.

An agenda is enclosed. Also, you will find a map with complete travel directions and a description of the parking facilities at the Tower Building.

It will be a pleasure to welcome all members to this important planning session of our organization.

Richard Farnsworth
Richard Farnsworth

RF:les

Enclosures: Agenda
Map

Letter of Adjustment

Sagarino Flower Company
One Maywell Street
Palm Sands Beach, ST 56789

August 15, 19--

Mrs. Richard Katz
425 Belmont Street
Smithville, ST 56789

Dear Mrs. Katz:

Thank you for letting us know about the roses that arrived at your home in less than perfect condition. Enclosed please find a check refunding your full purchase price.

An unexpected delay in the repair of our loaded delivery van, coupled with an unusual rise in temperatures last Thursday, caused the late delivery of your roses. Please accept our apology for it and our assurance that steps will be taken to prevent a repetition of this.

During the past fifteen years, it has been our pleasure to number you among our valued customers. Customer satisfaction is the goal we strive to achieve.

Please let us know how we may be of greater service to you.

Yours sincerely,

Thomas Sagarino

Thomas Sagarino
President

les

Enclosure: Check

Letter-writing Guides:
Acknowledge the error or the complaint and explain the measures being taken to rectify the situation.
Explain the reason for the mistake or error, extend an apology, and reassure the customer that it will not happen again.
Express appreciation for having the person as a customer and offer future service.

Letter of Application (*as for a franchise*)

PERRETTA AND SONS HARDWARE STORE
1510 Long Street
Kansas City, ST 56789

October 19, 19--

Mr. David Lindberg
Credit Manager
The Harkins Company
100 Lake Street
Smithville, ST 56789

Dear Mr. Lindberg:

After inspecting your recent exhibit of fine hardware at the International Hardware Convention in San Francisco last week, we should like to add your line of merchandise.

Please consider this letter an application for a charge account within the $800 to $1,000 range. Credit references will be supplied upon request.

We should appreciate the opportunity to handle the Harkins franchise in Kansas City.

Very truly yours,

Howard Perretta

Howard Perretta
President

les

Letter-writing Guides:
Present the request or the application.
Give necessary supportive data.
Use a courteous closing.

Reservations Letter

PINELAND PAPER COMPANY, INC.
608 South Street
Portland, ST 56789

March 20, 19--

Reservations Manager
Willoughby Hotel
674 Dennis Drive
Smithville, ST 56789

RESERVATIONS FOR A BRANCH MANAGERS' CONFERENCE

Please reserve your largest three-room executive suite for June 16 and 17, 19--. After seeing your fine facilities last week, our representative, Mr. Howard Martin, has recommended the Willoughby Hotel as this year's conference site for our branch managers.

We shall need conference table arrangements using the "U" formation for 20 persons for one room, space for large product displays in another, and an informal social meeting room.

An early confirmation of this reservation would be appreciated.

Robert Anderson

ROBERT ANDERSON - MANAGER

RA:ls

Letter-writing Guides:
Give the name and dates of the event.
List the details of required room arrangements.
Tactfully request an early written confirmation.

Appreciation *(as for new business)*

CHEN LUMBER COMPANY

650 Main Street
Manchester, ST 56789

August 6, 19--

Mr. and Mrs. George Parent
68 Cottage Street
Smithville, ST 56789

Dear Mr. and Mrs. Parent:

Congratulations on your decision to become a new home owner! Thank you for the confidence you have shown in us through opening an account and placing your order at the Chen Lumber Company.

It will be a pleasure to supply all the lumber and millwork needs for your beautiful home. You can build with confidence knowing that only quality lumber materials and supplies are being used.

Mr. Ralph Fu will be glad to be of service to you in any aspect of planning or designing your new home.

Please let us know if there is any way in which we may be of further assistance.

Sincerely,

Larry Chen

Larry Chen
President

ls

Letter-writing Guides:
Express appreciation for the order.
Reinforce the reader's self-esteem.
Offer further services.
Close in a friendly but not effusive way.

Letter of Cancellation

KELLEY ELECTRICAL SUPPLY SHOP
6802 Eastern Highway
Smithville, ST 56789

November 5, 19--

Mr. Howard Harris
Universal Electrical Service
4628 Southern Boulevard
Smithville, ST 56789

Dear Mr. Harris:

Over the past seven years, we have valued your account with us and considered it one of our best.

Recently with the turndown in business, we have noticed that your practice of discounting your bills every thirty days has ceased. Your last payment was ninety days late.

It is imperative that we keep current on our accounts receivable; therefore, regretfully, it is necessary to ask you to make future purchases on a cash only basis until your account is cleared.

Please accept the enclosed Special Courtesy Discount card for future cash purchases. It will entitle you to a three percent cash discount to help you through this transition period.

May we hear from you soon, Mr. Harris.

Very sincerely,

Albert Terranova

Albert Terranova
Credit Manager

AT:les

Enclosure

Letter-writing Guides:
Commend the reader for past positive actions.
Point out the current problem as politely as possible.
Suggest a solution.
Offer special assistance if possible.
Request a response soon and word the request firmly but politely.

Collection Letter

KINGSTON KOMPACT CARS
129 Fulton Boulevard
Smithville, ST 56789

November 5, 19--

Ms. Franceen Hopkins
46 West Lincoln Street
Smithville, ST 56789

Dear Ms. Hopkins:

Have you ever had to write a reminder letter? This is the situation with us now.

You have sent your monthly installments to us promptly for almost a year. However, we find that your Kompact Car payments of $50.50 for September 1 and October 1 have not come in as yet.

Perhaps your payments are already on their way to us. If this is the case, won't you please overlook this letter. On the other hand, in the event that some difficulty has arisen, just let us know. Perhaps we can offer some helpful suggestions.

Won't you let us hear from you soon.

Sincerely yours,

Joseph Thomas

Joseph Thomas
Credit Manager

les

Letter-writing Guides:
Use a novel opening—one that will catch the reader's attention immediately.
Mention something positive.
Point out the problem tactfully but firmly.
Suggest possible alternatives.
Ask politely for a response.

A Sales Letter

PARSONS OFFICE MANAGEMENT SERVICES
15 EVERGREEN STREET
JONESVILLE, ST 12345

October 24, 19--

Mr. James Huntwell
Morris Office Supply
250 Maple Street
Smithville, ST 56789

WHAT'S NEW FOR THE OFFICE?

Today's office manager is challenged to constantly seek information on this question. Parsons Office Management Services is a recognized authority on the subject.

Each month a newsletter entitled Office Products Update summarizes new entries in the office supply and equipment arena to aid the beleaguered office manager in making the right decisions fast. This month's edition is enclosed. Please accept it with our compliments.

Gain an edge on your competitors by obtaining the latest office products information in summary form each month. It won't take long until your customers will recognize Morris Office Supply as a leader in What's New for the Office.

Office Products Update may be yours each month for the new subscriber fee of only $6 for the entire year. If you will make use of the enclosed special subscriber's card before the end of this month, you will receive two extra issues for the year at no extra cost. May we hear from you soon?

Daniel B. Parsons

DANIEL B. PARSONS - VICE-PRESIDENT

ls

Enclosures

Letter-writing Guides:

Use a unique opening that will attract the reader's attention.
Offer advantages of your product and describe your services.
Provide the reader with a chance to see the product himself.
Use a close that will encourage the reader to take positive action right away.

THE SECRETARY COMPOSES PERSONAL BUSINESS COMMUNICATIONS

Executives receive many invitations to speak at meetings and to attend social/business events—both formal and informal. Also, they extend many business invitations of their own. In addition, personal correspondence often comes to them from close business associates. With the permission and under the general guidance of the executive, the secretary can be of great service by providing responses to these communications. Some letters of this type (as letters of condolence, letters of congratulations, and invitations) are illustrated on pages 348–351.

Writing letters of condolence To be most effective, a sympathy letter should be written as soon as possible after the event. Therefore, the secretary should scan the newspapers and alert the executive concerning the loss or misfortune of business associates or close personal friends. A sympathy letter to a close personal friend should be written in longhand on the executive's personal stationery. Condolence letters to business associates may be typewritten on stationery in the executive/Monarch or the half-sheet/Baronial size. While the letter should be short, it should be worded so as to express sincere feelings of sympathy. If the situation warrants, offers of assistance may be included as illustrated in the letter on page 348.

Writing letters of congratulation Letters bearing words of congratulation relate to happy events such as weddings, anniversaries, authorship, promotion, births, and a host of others. Even though this kind of correspondence may be personal, it is also an indirect aid in developing goodwill for the firm. Here again, the secretary may be of invaluable assistance by keeping the executive abreast of happenings that should be noted. After receiving instructions on general procedures, the secretary may move ahead to respond with appropriate letters of congratulation. See the illustration on page 349.

Writing invitations Letters of invitation may be formal or informal. After securing specific information from the executive about the special event, the secretary may proceed with the invitations.

An informal invitation should be specific in detail, naming the occasion and giving the applicable day of the week, the date, the time of day, and the location of the event. Depending on the type of event, the invitation may also include a spouse or a friend. It is frequently requested that the invitee respond to the invitation by telephone. Other invitations might specify that the invitee call only if unable to attend. See the illustrations on pages 350–351.

A formal invitation is usually handwritten, printed, or engraved on fine stationery. Tradition calls for formal invitations to be written in the third person. All pertinent information such as the occasion, the day of the week, the date, the time of day, and the place, should be detailed. One should use the abbreviation *R.S.V.P.* (please reply) in the lower left-hand corner of the stationery. Reply cards which are often printed are normally included with formal business invitations. See page 352 for an example.

Acceptance or refusal of formal invitations Printed reply cards make it easy for the invited guests to respond to formal invitations. If a reply card is not included with a formal invitation, the reply should be handwritten and so should the envelope address. In the latter case, one should answer in the third person, repeating the name of the occasion, the day, the date, the time of day, and the place of the event. If accepting an invitation, one should express pleasure; if declining, one should do so with regret. Preferably one should give a reason for not being able to attend. Examples of handwritten formal invitations, acceptances, and regrets may be found on page 352 of this chapter.

Letter of Condolence

September 9, 19--

Dear Mr. Caroleen:

My staff and I wish to extend our heartfelt sympathy to you at this time of your bereavement since the passing of your wife, Helen.

Your many friends here at Parker Mills join me in offering assistance with special scheduling of your orders at this time. Please do not hesitate to let us know how we may help.

It must be a comfort to have your family so near at this time. May your faith sustain all of you and bring you strength and peace.

Sincerely,

Randolph Parker

Mr. Gunnar Caroleen
President
Universal Products, Inc.
Everett, ST 56789

Letter-writing Guides:
Extend sympathy.
Offer assistance if possible.
Try to end on a note of comfort.

Letter of Congratulation

January 3, 19--

Dear Mr. Duchesne:

Yesterday's Statesville *Recorder* announced the pleasant news of your appointment as General Manufacturing Manager at Ace Precision Tools. Congratulations!

It is well known that great strides were made at Ace Precision Tools while you were Materials Manager. The recognition you are now receiving is certainly well deserved.

Again, you have my sincere congratulations and best wishes for continued success.

Cordially,

Mary Lawrence

Mr. Herbert Duchesne
General Manufacturing Manager
Ace Precision Tools
Statesville, ST 56789

Letter-writing Guides:
Commend the recipient of the honor or promotion.
Make additional comments on the nature of the achievement.
Close the letter with good wishes.

In-house Informal Invitation on Executive Stationery

NEW ENGLAND GENERAL LIFE INSURANCE COMPANY / Patrick R. O'Toole
Hartford, CT 06115
(203) 249-8981

April 7, 19—

Mr. Herbert D. Sheridan
Director of Public Relations - 272

With Mae Davis and Howard Kaiser winding up their New England General Careers this spring, Herb, I am planning a get-together in their honor at the end of this month.

You are invited to join some of our Officers and our Directors in extending best wishes to Mae and Howard in the Director's area on the sixth level from five to six on Wednesday, April 27.

I hope you can be there.

Pat

Patrick R. O'Toole

For regrets only, please call Extension 2036

Letter-writing Guides:
Mention the occasion.
Extend a cordial invitation.
Add a personal line.
Provide for response.

Outside Business Invitation on Executive Stationery

GLOBAL HARDWARE ASSOCIATES

84 Highland Drive
Chicago, Il 60147

June 26, 19—

Mr. William Mann
Baker Company
14 Bank Street
Bartlett, IL 60432

YOU'RE CORDIALLY INVITED:

to come to our Industrial Hardware Exhibits to be held on July 10, 19—, at the Civic Center, 25 High Boulevard, Chicago, Illinois, from 9 a.m. to 3 p.m.

The newest industrial hardware will be on display. Representatives from leading hardware manufacturers will be on hand to answer your questions.

Parking facilities will be available at the Civic Center Garage. Travel directions and a map are enclosed for your convenience.

Won't you join your business associates for an interesting and rewarding day at the Civic Center's Industrial Hardware Exhibits on July 10.

Wayne D. Thoren

Wayne D. Thoren, Sales Manager

coc

Enclosures (2)

Letter-writing Guides:
Open in a cordial way.
Give motivation for attendance.
Include directions and other details.
Encourage action in the final paragraph.

The Formal Invitation

Mr. and Mrs. Robert Lee Floyd
request the pleasure of
Mr. and Mrs. John Francis O'Donnell's
company at dinner
on Thursday, the fifth of July
at eight o'clock

Colony Club
River Room
R.S.V.P. Newport

The Formal Acceptance of an Invitation

Mr. and Mrs. John O'Donnell
accept with pleasure
the kind invitation of
Mr. and Mrs. Robert Lee Floyd
for dinner
on Thursday, the fifth of July
at eight o'clock
at the Colony Club, River Room
Newport

The Formal Declination of an Invitation

Mr. and Mrs. John O'Donnell
regret that they are unable to accept
the kind invitation of
Mr. and Mrs. Robert Lee Floyd
for dinner
on Thursday, the fifth of July

The following example of a printed reply card might be used with a printed or engraved business invitation:

Please respond on or before

August 5, 19--

M ________________________

will _____ attend.

10

CHAPTER TEN

THE OFFICE MAIL AND THE POSTAL SERVICE

CONTENTS

10.1

INTRODUCTION

This chapter deals with the efficient processing of office mail and the utilization of postal services to speed up mail handling and delivery. Since the United States Postal Service is very much concerned with the increasing volume of mail and its expeditious delivery, it has devised sophisticated optical character readers, ZIP Codes, and new services and procedures to facilitate the handling of the mail. It is suggested that the reader first thumb through this chapter for an overview of office mail procedures and postal services; then, pertinent sections can later be studied in detail.

10.2

OFFICE MAIL: Incoming

Efficient processing of incoming mail is one of the tasks the secretary is expected to perform. The steps outlined in the following pages are applicable to mail processing in small, medium-sized, or large offices.

PRELIMINARY SORTING
It is generally expeditious to sort mail in piles before it is opened. This is particularly true of large-volume mail deliveries. The mail may be sorted by these categories: telegrams, first class, second class (newspapers and magazines), third class

(circulars, booklets, catalogs, and other printed materials), fourth class (domestic parcel post), priority mail (air parcel post), international mail, and memos.

OPENING THE MAIL

Letters marked *personal* or *confidential* should not be opened by the secretary unless special authority to do so has been delegated by an appropriate superior. (If a letter is opened unintentionally, the secretary should mark the envelope "Opened by mistake," initial it, and reseal the envelope with tape.) Second- and third-class mail should be opened neatly: remove all protective covers and flatten any rolled items.

The secretary should tap the bottom edge of each envelope to ensure that the contents are not at the top. Checks and important items have been damaged through neglect of this procedure. One should first open all the envelopes by slitting the top edge with a letter opener or by using an automatic letter-opening machine. The contents must be removed carefully. One ought to be sure that everything is removed from the envelope. The enclosure notations on letters must be checked. If an enclosure is missing, the secretary should make a note of this fact on the letter. When practicable, enclosures may be fastened to their letters with paper clips or staples.

Some offices require that envelopes be fastened to letters. If this is not the practice, the secretary should check to see if the sender's address is on the letter before throwing the envelope away. Some experienced secretaries save all the envelopes for the day in order to recheck for missing enclosures, addresses, or other items.

DATING THE MAIL

A hand or automatic date stamp is used to record the date and sometimes the time when the mail was received. (Date and time received are often matters of critical importance in law offices, for example.) If mechanical devices are not available, the secretary should write "Received" and the date on the letter. In some offices, just the date in numerical form will suffice.

SECONDARY SORTING

The next step is the secondary sorting of mail for presentation to the executive. At this time, mail is arranged by priority so that the executive may deal with the most important mail first. Correspondence (such as telegrams and Registered or Special Delivery mail) should be placed on the top of the pile. Some offices have special file folders such as *urgent, important, routine, information,* and *advertising.*

READING THE MAIL

In some offices, the secretary reads the letter and underlines important passages for the executive. Notes to the executive (as "Refer to file," or "See invoice") may also be written in the side margins. The secretary also provides any additional information that the executive may need in responding to the letter. The file of previous correspondence may be particularly helpful in accomplishing this task. If a piece of mail is to be brought to the attention of several people, it can be circulated by a routing slip or it can be photocopied and distributed. If time is of the essence, photocopying greatly expedites matters, since routing slips may circulate slowly and may sometimes be misplaced.

RECORDING THE MAIL IN A REGISTER

The final step in handling incoming mail in some offices is making a record of it in a register or log. All important mail is recorded in this register, but items as circulars and ads are omitted. The following data are usually recorded: the date and time of day received, the date of the letter itself, the writer, the addressee, a brief description (as of the subject), and the disposition of the letter.

Mail Register or Log

REC'D	DATED	TIME	FROM	ADDRESSEE	DISPOSITION	DATE
7/2/76	7/1/76	9a.m.	Barker Bros.	President	Letter-Info	7/2/76
7/2/76	4/30/76	9a.m.	Acme Corp.	T. Cooke	Price List	7/6/76
7/2/76	7/1/76	2p.m.	Cole, Inc.	Personnel	Letter-Chart	7/4/76
7/3/76	7/2/76	9a.m.	R. Dow	S. Smythe	Letter-Info	7/5/76

10.3

OFFICE MAIL: Outgoing

The secretary's duties in processing outgoing mail are usually related to the size of the business. While a large business office may have a special mailing department including a messenger service and an automobile mail service that will relieve its secretaries of some mailing duties, nevertheless, the mail must still be prepared for the mail room. This duty usually falls to a secretary. In a smaller office, a secretary may have to take on total responsibility for mailing—i.e., the secretary may have to assume the duties of the mail room as well as preparatory responsibilities. The five common checking tasks in both a large and a small office are discussed below.

CHECKING ADDRESSES

The data in the inside address typed on the letter itself and that of the address on the envelope should be the same. To reduce the chance of error and to speed up the mailing process, some companies prefer to use window envelopes, thus eliminating the need for typing the address on the envelope. If a window envelope is used, it is imperative that the inside address be complete: it should include the complete name, street address, city, state, and ZIP Code. The post office box and room number should also be included if applicable. In this case, the ZIP Code of the box number should be used and not that of the street address. The all-capitalized and unpunctuated two-letter state abbreviations are preferred by the post office (see page 366 for a table of two-letter state and dependency abbreviations). The responsible secretary keeps an up-to-date mailing list that should contain correct addresses and ZIP Code numbers.

CHECKING MAILING NOTATIONS

Two types of notations may be typewritten on an envelope: (1) on-arrival reminders such as CONFIDENTIAL or PERSONAL and (2) mailing service reminders such as CERTIFIED MAIL or SPECIAL DELIVERY, all of which are typically typed entirely in capital letters. The secretary should ensure that every letter having an attention line, a special mailing notation, or an on-arrival notation should also have the same notation or notations on its envelope. On-arrival reminders or notations are typically typed four lines below the return address or nine lines below the top edge of the envelope, starting at least one-half inch in from the left edge of the envelope.

On-arrival notations other than PERSONAL and CONFIDENTIAL (for example, Please Forward) are generally typed in capitals and lowercase letters and are underscored; however, their envelope placement is the same as any other on-arrival notation. Postal directions or special mailing notations are placed on the same line (line 9) as the on-arrival notations and are typed all in capital letters, one-half inch from the right edge of the envelope. See also Chapter 6, "Style in Business Correspondence," pages 145-146, for detailed envelope addressing instructions, and page 147 for an envelope facsimile.

CHECKING SIGNATURES

It is the secretary's responsibility to check all letters for proper signatures. If the secretary is authorized to sign letters with an executive signature, it must be initialed by the secretary (See also Chapter 6, page 130 and Chapter 9, page 329). A letter is an invalid document without a signature in ink.

CHECKING ENCLOSURES

It is very important that the secretary check carefully to see that all enclosures cited in the enclosure notation at the bottom of the letter are included with the letter. Some secretaries note enclosures by using visual reminders such as three hyphens or three periods typed in the left margin opposite each line in which mention is made of the item or items to be enclosed. In this way, the secretary is alerted to include the enclosures with the letter. It is frustrating for an addressee to receive a letter without the intended enclosure or to receive the wrong enclosure. Therefore, it cannot be overemphasized that their inclusion be double-checked.

CHECKING CARBON COPY NOTATIONS

The carbon copy notation (cc) indicates to whom additional copies of the letter should be sent. The secretary should check carefully to see that envelopes have been addressed to the individuals mentioned in regular (cc) and blind carbon copy (bcc) notations. The blind carbon copy notation usually appears only on the carbon copies in the upper left-hand corner of the sheets; however, it may also be placed below reference and enclosure notations. These carbons should be checked for such notations. An extra carbon copy should be available for filing.

GENERAL POINTERS

Sorting the mail Mail that must reach its destination the next day requires special separation and sorting from normal, routine correspondence or mailings. (See pages 362-365 for information concerning special mail services such as Express Mail, which guarantees next-day delivery for mail sent before 5 p.m.) So that one's office will receive faster service, the Postal Service suggests that the secretary or mailing department separate and presort mail as follows:

1. Separate the mail. Your mail can skip an entire sorting operation at the post office if you separate it into major categories such as *local, out-of-town, state,* or *precanceled.* The mail is usually bundled with an identifying label indicating the applicable category.
2. Use postage meters. Many businesses—both large and small—use postage meters to expedite the movement of mail (postage meters are explained in more detail on page 359). Five or more pieces of metered mail must be faced and bundled. The post office provides the needed printed bands. Large numbers of metered or permit mail may be placed in trays provided by the post office. Trayed mail should have addresses and postage faced in one direction to speed postal sorting and dispatching.
3. Presort your mail by ZIP Code. Large mailings are further expedited if sequenced by ZIP Code numbers with the lowest number first and the highest number last. Mail can be bundled by ZIP Code number if there are ten or more pieces destined for a single zone.

Stamping the mail After checking and sorting it, the secretary must weigh and stamp or meter all outgoing mail; however, in large offices the mail room assumes this responsibility. Mail is collected from the outgoing mailbox.

When to mail The Postal Service suggests early mailings to alleviate the usual congestion at the close of the business day. If possible, mailings should be made throughout the day. One large mailing at the end of the business day is to be avoided.

ZIP CODES

To handle the ever-increasing volume of mail, the Postal Service has automated mail handling by introducing optical character readers (OCRs) that can "read" a ZIP Code—a five-digit number which encodes the following information:

the first digit designates one of ten national areas; each area is given a number (0–9)

the first three digits designate a large city or sectional center; there are 552 sectional centers in the United States

the last two digits designate a delivery area or post office within a sectional center

For example, the ZIP Code 06117 indicates the following:

first digit 0 one of the states in the Northeast
first three digits 061 Greater Hartford, Connecticut, area
last two digits 17 Bishops Corner Post Office in West Hartford, Connecticut

The secretary can refer to three basic sources for ZIP Code information:

1. The *National ZIP Code Directory* lists all the five-digit numbers in use in the United States. The directory is available at some post offices for purchase. It may also be obtained from:
   Superintendent of Documents
   Government Printing Office
   Washington, DC 20420
2. The classified section of the telephone directory usually has a map indicating local postal zones and a complete listing of area ZIP Code numbers.
3. The Postal Service will willingly answer questions concerning ZIP Code numbers. Post offices in large cities have a special telephone listing for ZIP Code information, found under "United States Government, United States Postal Service" in the telephone directory.

Business firms that address mail by computer may use without charge the "Zip-A-List," a magnetic computer tape providing ZIP Code listings. One can make application for the list through one's main post office.

FOLDING AND INSERTING LETTERS INTO ENVELOPES

The following diagrams depict the correct procedures for folding and inserting letters:

Small Envelope

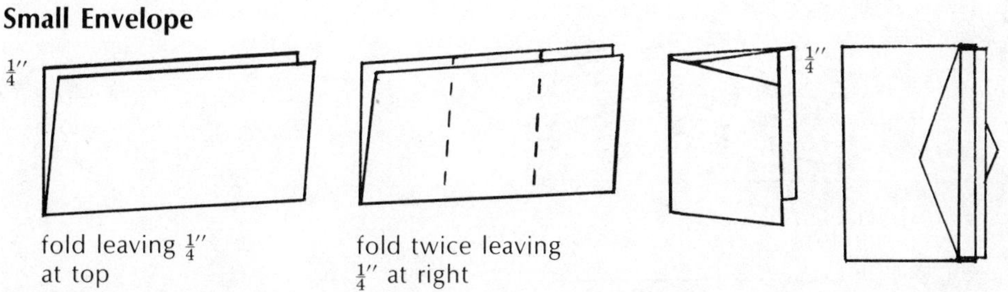

Large Envelope

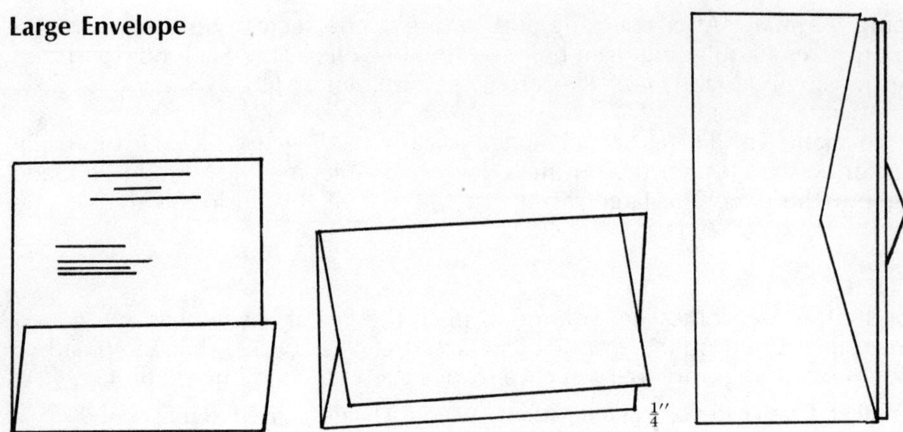

Window Envelope

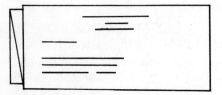

Some stationery has a fold line indicating where to fold for insertion in window envelopes.

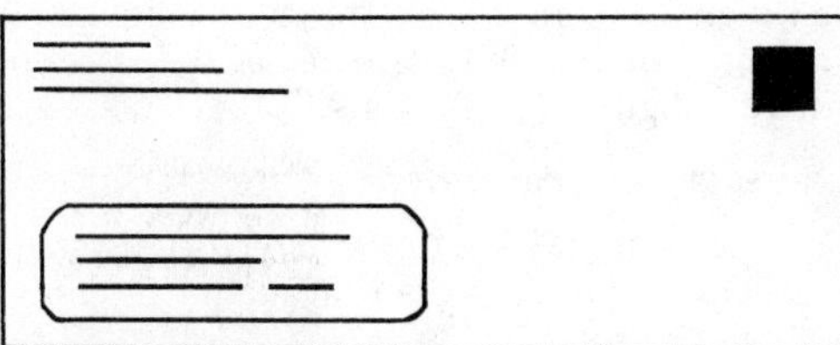

Insert so that at least $\frac{1}{4}''$ is left between the side and bottom edges of the address and the window.

The following are some suggestions for sealing and stamping envelopes by hand:

1. Use a moist sponge or moistening device.
2. Never lick envelopes or stamps as this practice is both unsanitary and hazardous. The secretary can be cut by the sharp edge of the envelope flap.
3. Moisten envelopes and stamps over a blotter. The blotter will absorb excess water and avoid a messy situation.
4. A large quantity of envelopes can be moistened quickly by placing them one behind the other as follows:

Press down the flap of each envelope as it is moistened.

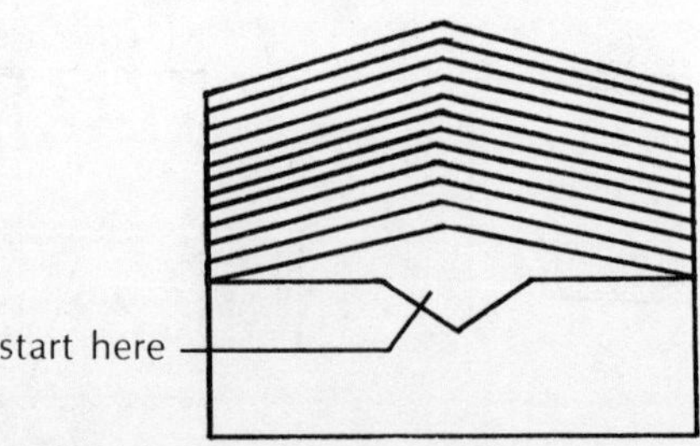

Envelopes can similarly be stamped in quantity:

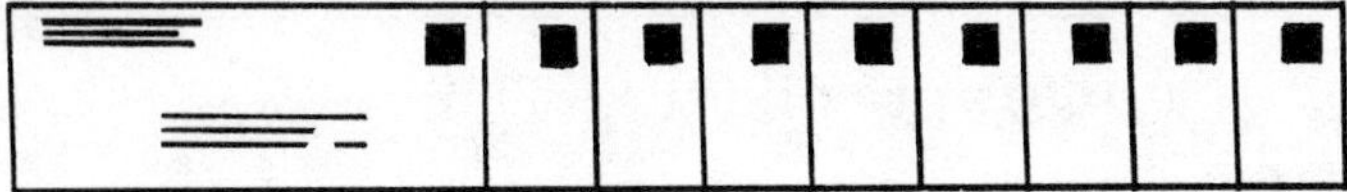

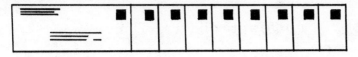

METERED MAIL

Mailing can be systematized by the use of modular mailing units. The number of machines employed in any modular system is relative to the size of the mailing operation. The following is a listing of mailing equipment that can be combined in modules to increase mailing efficiency:

postage meter machine (prints postage, seals and stacks envelopes)
mailing scale
mail opener
folding and inserting machines
address printer
embossing machine

Some examples of modular mailing equipment are listed below:

small mailing operation
postage meter machine
mailing scale
mail opener

medium-sized mailing operation
postage meter machine
mailing scale
high-speed mail opener

large mailing operation
postage meter machine
mailing scale—computerized
mail opener
folder/inserter
addresser/printer
embossing machine
copying machine
collating machine
counting and imprinting machine

Mail that bears an imprinted meter stamp is called *metered mail.* A postage meter is a useful convenience for many mailers. The postmark, date, and cancellation are imprinted by the meter directly onto the envelope, or onto an adhesive strip that is then affixed to large envelopes or packages. The meter may also seal and stack envelopes. Meters are leased or rented from the manufacturer, and the mailer must obtain a meter permit from the post office. Payment for postage is made in a lump sum to the post office. The meter is then set for that amount of postage in advance. For a fee, a Postal Service representative will set the postage meter at one's office. The following are some of the advantages of metered mail:

1. Accurate postage accounting eliminates the theft of stamps.
2. Stamp and envelope flap wetting are eliminated.
3. Mail processing at the post office is speeded: envelopes do not have to be faced and stamps do not have to be canceled.
4. Personalized meter ads may be used.
5. Trips to the post office to purchase stamps may be avoided.

10.4

EFFICIENT AND ECONOMIC USE OF THE POSTAL SERVICE

DETERMINING THE MAIL CLASSIFICATION

If one's office does not have a mail room, it is the secretary's responsibility to send the mail out efficiently and economically. Since postal rates change frequently, it is suggested that the secretary write or call the post office for a brochure of current rates. Since a secretary may have to determine the proper classification of the outgoing mail, the various classes are discussed below.

First-class mail This category includes handwritten and typewritten messages, bills and statements of account, postcards and postal cards (postal cards are the ones printed by the Postal Service), canceled and uncanceled checks, and business reply mail. First-class mail is sealed and may not be opened for postal inspection. Within a local area, overnight delivery can ordinarily be expected. Your post office will designate what constitutes your local area. To qualify for overnight delivery, one must deposit letters by 5 p.m., or at a mail processing facility by 6 p.m.

Second-day delivery is standard for other points within 600 miles. Third-day delivery is standard for other points within the 48 contiguous states. It should be noted that mailable envelopes, cards and self-mailers can be no smaller than 3″ x 4¼″. First-class postage is required for cards exceeding 4¼″ x 6″. Large envelopes or packages sent as first-class mail should be stamped FIRST CLASS to avoid confusion with third-class mail by postal employees.

Second-class mail This category includes magazines and newspapers issued at least four times a year. A permit is required to mail material at the second-class rate. A mailer other than a publisher can mail individual, complete copies of a publication. The publication should be clearly marked SECOND CLASS.

Third-class mail This category consists of circulars, booklets, catalogs, and other printed materials (as newsletters or corrected proof sheets with manuscript copy). Merchandise, farm and factory products, photographs, keys, and printed drawings may be sent third class. Some people refer to third-class mail as "advertising mail." This mail class is limited in weight to less than 16 ounces; should it exceed 16 ounces, it is classified as fourth-class mail or parcel post. The two categories of third-class mail are single piece and bulk. This type of mail is usually not sealed so that it can be opened easily for postal inspection.

Fourth-class mail (parcel post) This category consists mainly of domestic parcel post. Also included in it are special catalog mailings, special fourth-class mailings, and library mailings. It is mostly used to send packages or parcels weighing 16 ounces or more. Parcels mailed at, and addressed for delivery to, a first-class post office in the 48 contiguous states may not exceed 40 pounds in weight or 84 inches in combined length and girth. The parcel post regulations specify that all other parcels may not be more than 70 pounds or 100 inches in combined length and girth. Parcel post postage rates are based on the weight of the package and the delivery distance. The minimum weight is 16 ounces per parcel. Parcels under 16 ounces are mailed according to third-class, first-class, or priority regulations.

Overnight delivery can be expected within the local area if parcels are mailed by 5 p.m. at post offices or receiving platforms. Second-day service can be expected for distances up to 150 miles. Service time depends on the distance the parcel must travel; for example, service time may be as long as eight days for distances beyond 1,800 miles. An envelope may be taped to the outside of a parcel if first-class postage is paid.

Priority mail or air parcel post This type of mail is given full airmail handling. All first-class mail exceeding 13 ounces is rated as *priority mail.* The maximum weight for priority mail is 70 pounds.

International mail This category includes letters, letter packages, printed matter, small packages of merchandise and samples, and parcel post destined for foreign countries. However, overseas military mail, i.e., APO (Army Post Office) and FPO (Fleet Post Office), is not classified as international mail. Aerogrammes are a convenient form of stationery for international correspondence. Their price includes prestamped stationery that folds into a self-enclosed envelope. International postal cards and parcel post service are available to most foreign countries.

Since there is a great deal of information concerning international mail too voluminous to include in this book, it is suggested that the secretary obtain a copy of Publication 42, *International Mail,* from the U.S. Government Printing Office, Superintendent of Documents, Washington, DC 20402. The publication is a handy reference source for those who must handle much outgoing office mail in this category.

The United States Postal Service also provides Publication 51, *International Postage Rates and Fees.* It includes an overview of international mail services as well as specific information about rates and fees, and it can be obtained without charge.

International mail consists of two sub-categories: postal union mail and parcel post. *Webster's Third New International Dictionary* defines *postal union* as "an international agreement to observe uniform regulations governing international mail." Postal union mail is divided into LC mail (letters and cards) and AO mail (other articles). LC mail consists of letters, letter packages, aerogrammes, and postcards; on the other hand, AO mail comprises printed matter, matter for the blind, and small packets. Postal union articles should be addressed legibly and completely. Roman letters and Arabic numerals should be used. The name of the post office and country of destination should appear entirely in capital letters. The sender should be sure to use the ZIP Code or postal delivery zone if available. It is permissible to use a foreign-language address, provided that the names of the post office, province, and country are in English. The envelopes or wrappers of postal union mail should be endorsed ("Printed Matter," "Printed Matter—Catalogs," "Printed Matter—Books," "Letter," "Par Avion," or "Exprès") to show the mail classification. The maximum size permissible for articles not in the form of a roll is 36 inches in combined length, breadth, and thickness. The greatest length allowed is 24 inches. For articles in the form of a roll, the maximum length permitted is 36 inches. The maximum length plus twice the diameter permitted is 42 inches. Very small articles should have a strong, rectangular address tag.

All postal union articles except letters and letter packages must remain unsealed. The Postal Service requires that registered letters and registered letter packages be sealed. Neither insurance nor Certified mail service is available for postal union mail. However, Special Delivery is available to most countries. It is possible to obtain a return receipt. Mail going to most countries can be registered. There is daily airmail delivery to practically all countries.

All articles should be correctly prepaid in relation to weight in order to avoid delays. The proper postage should be affixed. If an article is returned for additional postage, the proper amount should then be affixed and the "Returned for postage" endorsement should be crossed out. A mailer can also send his correspondent international reply coupons that are used to prepay reply letters. Postal union mail is generally returned to the sender if delivery cannot be made.

Parcel post service is available to almost all countries. The greatest length allowed is 3½ feet. The greatest combined length and girth allowed is 6 feet. Parcels may measure 4 feet in length if not more than 16 inches in girth when mailed to some countries. Prohibited articles include items that may damage the mail or cause injury to postal employees, such as matches and most live or dead creatures; and communications having the character of current correspondence (which means in effect that one cannot enclose a letter in a parcel post package). There are restrictions on firearms that can be concealed, on flammable liquids, and on radioactive materials. In addition, any country may prohibit or restrict various articles that it wishes to control.

Parcels should be packed very securely in strong containers made of good-quality material that will withstand often radical climatic changes and repeated or rough handling. Insured or registered parcels must be sealed. Some parcels, even though they may be unregistered and uninsured must be either sealed or unsealed depending on the postal regulations of the countries to which they are sent.

Form 2966-A—a customs declaration—is required for parcel post packages mailed to other countries. A dispatch note (Form 2972 or Form 2966) may be required for mail going to some countries. Insurance is available for mail being sent to many countires; however, registration is available only for material being sent to a few countries. Although C.O.D. and Certified Mail are not available, air service and Special Handling are.

In conjunction with the foregoing discussion of international mail, it should be mentioned that there are private companies licensed by the U.S. government that help importers prepare the Customs documents required for imported packages and articles. Other services that may be included are: export crating, reforwarding, delivery to and from airports and ocean ports, and bonded warehouse marking and distribution. These companies are called *customhouse brokers.* They offer savings on import/export charges, and they expedite delivery.

SPECIAL SERVICES

In addition to determining the mail classification (first class, second class, etc.), a secretary may have to select and use special services. The special services provided by the Postal Service are listed alphabetically and examined in detail below:

aerogrammes
Business Reply Mail
Certificate of Mailing
Certified Mail
Collect-on-Delivery
Controlpak
Express Mail
insured mail
Mailgram
money orders
passport applications
post office boxes
Registered Mail
self-service postal centers
Special Delivery
Special Handling

Aerogrammes An economical means of communicating abroad is the use of a combined letter and envelope called the *aerogramme.* (See the section on international mail, page 361, for additional information about aerogrammes.)

Business Reply Mail A mailer may wish to pay the postage for those responding to his mail—an important factor when one is trying to sell something through the mail. To use the Business Reply service, one makes an application on Form 3614.

This form can be obtained from a local post office. There is no charge for the permit; however, the mailer must guarantee that he will pay the postage for replies. Postage may be collected when the reply is delivered; also, an advance deposit may be required under certain conditions. Business Reply Mail must be clearly identified on the envelope. In addition, the permit number, the post office issuing the permit, the words "No Postage Stamp Necessary if Mailed in the United States," and the words "Postage Will be Paid by Addressee" (or "Postage Will be Paid by" over the name and address of the person or firm) must appear on the envelope.

Certificate of Mailing An original Certificate of Mailing for individual pieces of mail is issued for a fee. The post office keeps no record of such certificates. A Certificate of Mailing is used by a mailer to prove that an item was actually mailed.

Certified Mail This designation provides that a record of delivery be maintained by the addressee's post office. The carrier obtains a signature from the addressee on a receipt form which is kept by the post office for two years. There is a fee for this service. A return receipt will be provided the sender for an additional fee.

Collect-on-Delivery With Collect-on-Delivery—commonly referred to as C.O.D.—both the postage and the value of the contents of a parcel or letter are collected from the addressee. The maximum amount that can be collected is $200. The fee charged for C.O.D. includes insurance against loss or damage and failure to receive payment. First-, third-, and fourth-class mail can be sent C.O.D., the regular postage being paid in addition to a C.O.D. fee. The addressee may not examine the contents of the letter or parcel in advance of charges paid. Parcels sent must be based on bona fide orders or on agreement between the mailer and addressee. For an additional fee, the mailer of C.O.D. letters or parcels will be notified of nondelivery. First-class mail sent domestic C.O.D. may be registered at an additional charge.

Controlpak To assure maximum security of credit cards and other valuable items, the postal service has developed Controlpak. The mailer addresses the envelopes, affixes first-class postage, sorts the mail by ZIP Code, and packages it in special Controlpak plastic bags which are heat-sealed against theft. The bag is then transported to the supervisor of the ZIP Code delivery unit from which distribution is made. It is opened under controlled conditions and the mail is delivered by carrier.

Express Mail Express Mail is a fast, intercity delivery system linking 58 major metropolitan areas in the United States. It is used for the reliable delivery of important products or documents. Overnight delivery of letters and parcels is guaranteed. This service is used for urgent mail. A 95 percent reliability record of on-time delivery for Express Mail has been established. These are the five service options:

1. *Door-to-door* Your Express Mail is picked up at your office and is taken to the airport. On arrival, a Postal Service driver delivers it to the addressee.
2. *Door-to-destination airport* Your Express Mail is picked up at your office and is taken to the airport. The addressee picks up the shipment at the airport.
3. *Originating airport to addressee* You deliver the Express Mail to the airport postal facility. On arrival, the Postal Service driver delivers it to the addressee.
4. *Airport-to-airport* You take the Express Mail to your airport postal facility; the addressee picks it up on arrival at his airport.
5. *Regular Express Mail service* Your shipment is sent to a designated postal facility by 5 p.m. It is picked up at the destination office by 10 a.m. the next business day or it is delivered by 3 p.m.

Insured mail Third- and fourth-class mail can be insured against loss and damage up to $200. Items of greater value should be sent by Registered Mail. There are two kinds of insured service: unnumbered and numbered insured mail. A minimal fee is charged for unnumbered insured mail; delivery is by parcel post. With numbered insured mail, a receipt is given to the mailer at the point of origin. A signature is required on delivery. There is an additional fee for this service. One may obtain a return receipt as proof of delivery for insured mail exceeding $15 in value.

Mailgram The Mailgram is a special mail-via-satellite service offered jointly by the United States Postal Service and Western Union. These letter-telegrams are delivered the next business day by U.S. letter carriers to virtually any address within the 48 contiguous states. Small offices can use this service by supplying the Mailgram message to a Western Union office by telephone (toll-free) or in person. Fees are paid to Western Union for this service. Rates are based on 100-word units in the message. Within larger firms, up to 50 common or variable-text messages can be typed directly from the company's teleprinter into the Western Union computer on a single connection. A basic fee is charged for each message, in addition to the telex/TWX usage charges. (Instructions may be found in the firm's telex/TWX directory.) Mailgrams in volume may be handled by putting mailing lists on computer tape, which can hold up to 10,000 address lines on a single tape. There is a basic fee for each message of 600 characters or less, and a fee for each additional 600 characters, plus a minimum charge for each tape. The most economical way to input a Mailgram is from the company's computer directly into Western Union's computer. In this case, a basic fee is charged for each message, in addition to a minimum fee for each tape.

Money orders Money can be sent through the mail by purchasing Postal Money Orders up to $300 that are redeemable at any post office. International Money Orders can be purchased for amounts up to $100 at large, i.e. first-class, post offices.

Passport applications The Postal Service, working in conjunction with the United States Department of State, accepts applications for passports from those wishing to travel abroad (see also Chapter 15 for detailed information on passport application).

Post office boxes Boxes and drawers may be rented in post offices. These boxes and drawers facilitate the receiving of mail, since mail can be obtained at any time that the post office lobby is open.

Registered Mail Domestic first-class and priority mail may be registered to protect valuable items. This is the safest way to mail valuables. The fee for this service is based on the declared value of the mail, and the indemnity limit is $10,000. The customer is given a receipt at the time of mailing; therefore, Registered Mail cannot be dispatched from a regular collection box. The post office keeps record of the mailing through the number it has been assigned. For an additional fee, a proof-of-delivery receipt will be returned to the mailer. Registered Mail is transported under lock and is kept separate from other mail.

Self-service postal centers Self-service postal centers are located in convenient places such as post office lobbies, shopping centers, or automobile drive-ups. They supplement existing postal services by providing around-the-clock service seven days a week. Automatic vending machines dispense stamps, postal cards, stamped envelopes, and minimum parcel insurance. These stamps are sold at face value, unlike those from the private stamp vending machines.

Special Delivery This designation virtually assures delivery on the day mail is received at the destination post office. As soon as the mail is received there, it is delivered by Special Delivery messenger. An extra fee in addition to the regular postage is charged for this service. Special Delivery may be used for all classes of mail. Although Special Delivery does not speed mail transportation from the post office of origin to the destination post office, it does assure rapid delivery from the destination post office to the intended addressee.

Special Handling This designation assures preferential, separate handling for third- and fourth-class mail. There is an extra fee for Special Handling.

ADDRESSING FOR AUTOMATION

So that the secretary can take full advantage of the post office's computerized sorting equipment (including new optical character readers that can scan and sort many thousands of pieces of mail an hour), the United States Postal Service recommends that <u>all</u> envelopes be addressed properly for automation. All typescript should be clear and easy to read. The basic procedures in addressing envelopes are as follows:

1. Use rectangular envelopes no smaller than 3½″ × 5″ and no larger than 6⅛″ × 11½″. There should be good color contrast between the paper and the type impressions.
2. The address should be single-spaced and blocked (straight left margin). The address must be at least 1″ from the left edge of the envelope and at least ⅝″ up from the bottom. There should be no print to the right or below the address.
3. Additional data (as the attention line, account number, or date) should be part of the blocked address; these data should be positioned above the second line from bottom. Envelope addresses should be typed entirely in capital letters without punctuation marks. Use type fonts other than script, italic, or proportionally-spaced fonts. Do not type the address at a slant.

   C REEVES CORP
   ATTN MR R C SMITH
   XXX XXXX XX XXX XXX
   XXXXXXXX XX XXXXX

4. If mail is addressed to occupants of multi-unit buildings, the unit number should appear after the street address on the same line.

   C REEVES CORP
   ATTN MR R C SMITH
   186 PARK ST ROOM 960
   XXXXXXXX XX XXXXX

5. The bottom line of the address should contain the city, state, and ZIP Code number (see the table of two-letter state abbreviations, page 366).

   C REEVES CORP
   ATTN MR R C SMITH
   186 PARK ST ROOM 960
   HARTFORD CT 06106

6. A Post Office box number is typed on the line above the last to assure delivery to this point. (Use the ZIP Code for the box number, not the street address.) The box number precedes the station name.

   C REEVES CORP
   186 PARK ST
   PO BOX 210 LINCOLN STA
   HARTFORD CT 06106

7. At least ¼″ should be left between the address and the sides and bottom edges of the opening on window envelopes.

One can save typing time and facilitate computerized sorting by using the following capitalized and unpunctuated two-letter state abbreviations:

Two-letter State Abbreviations for the United States and its Dependencies

Alabama	AL	Kentucky	KY	Oklahoma	OK
Alaska	AK	Louisiana	LA	Oregon	OR
Arizona	AZ	Maine	ME	Pennsylvania	PA
Arkansas	AR	Maryland	MD	Puerto Rico	PR
California	CA	Massachusetts	MA	Rhode Island	RI
Canal Zone	CZ	Michigan	MI	South Carolina	SC
Colorado	CO	Minnesota	MN	South Dakota	SD
Connecticut	CT	Mississippi	MS	Tennessee	TN
Delaware	DE	Missouri	MO	Texas	TX
District of Columbia	DC	Montana	MT	Utah	UT
Florida	FL	Nebraska	NE	Vermont	VT
Georgia	GA	Nevada	NV	Virginia	VA
Guam	GU	New Hampshire	NH	Virgin Islands	VI
Hawaii	HI	New Jersey	NJ	Washington	WA
Idaho	ID	New Mexico	NM	West Virginia	WV
Illinois	IL	New York	NY	Wisconsin	WI
Indiana	IN	North Carolina	NC	Wyoming	WY
Iowa	IA	North Dakota	ND		
Kansas	KS	Ohio	OH		

Two-letter Abbreviations for Canadian Provinces

Alberta	AB	Newfoundland	NF	Quebec	PQ
British Columbia	BC	Northwest Territories	NT	Saskatchewan	SK
Labrador	LB	Nova Scotia	NS	Yukon Territory	YT
Manitoba	MB	Ontario	ON		
New Brunswick	NB	Prince Edward Island	PE		

A maximum of 22 strokes or positions is allowed on the last line of an envelope address. The Postal Service suggests the following maximum number of positions:

13 positions for the city
 1 space between the city and state
 2 positions for the state
 1 space between the state and ZIP Code number
 5 positions for the ZIP Code number

22 total positions allowed

Many cities exceed the suggested maximum number of 13 positions. The Postal Service suggests that these abbreviations be used to facilitate mail processing:

Abbreviations for Street Designators and for Words that Appear Frequently in Place Names

Academy	ACAD	Bend	BND	Bypass	BYP
Agency	AGNCY	Big	BG	Camp	CP
Airport	ARPRT	Black	BLK	Canyon	CYN
Alley	ALY	Bluff	BLF	Cape	CPE
Annex	ANX	Bottom	BTM	Causeway	CWSY
Arcade	ARC	Boulevard	BLVD	Center	CTR
Arsenal	ARSL	Branch	BR	Central	CTL
Avenue	AVE	Bridge	BRG	Church	CHR
Bayou	BYU	Brook	BRK	Churches	CHRS
Beach	BCH	Burg	BG	Circle	CIR

City	CY	Hot	H	Road	RD
Clear	CLR	House	HSE	Rock	RK
Cliffs	CLFS	Inlet	INLT	Rural	R
Club	CLB	Institute	INST	Saint	ST
College	CLG	Island	IS	Sainte	ST
Corner	COR	Islands	IS	San	SN
Corners	CORS	Isle	IS	Santa	SN
Court	CT	Junction	JCT	Santo	SN
Courts	CTS	Key	KY	School	SCH
Cove	CV	Knolls	KNLS	Seminary	SMNRY
Creek	CRK	Lake	LK	Shoal	SHL
Crescent	CRES	Lakes	LKS	Shoals	SHLS
Crossing	XING	Landing	LNDG	Shode	SHD
Dale	DL	Lane	LN	Shore	SHR
Dam	DM	Light	LGT	Shores	SHRS
Depot	DPO	Little	LTL	Siding	SDG
Divide	DIV	Loaf	LF	South	S
Drive	DR	Locks	LCKS	Space Flight Center	SFC
East	E	Lodge	LDG	Spring	SPG
Estates	EST	Lower	LWR	Springs	SPGS
Expressway	EXPY	Manor	MNR	Square	SQ
Extended	EXT	Meadows	MDWS	State	ST
Extension	EXT	Meeting	MTG	Station	STA
Fall	FL	Memorial	MEM	Stream	STRM
Falls	FLS	Middle	MDL	Street	ST
Farms	FRMS	Mile	MLE	Sulphur	SLPHR
Ferry	FRY	Mill	ML	Summit	SMT
Field	FLD	Mills	MLS	Switch	SWCH
Fields	FLDS	Mines	MNS	Tannery	TNRY
Flats	FLT	Mission	MSN	Tavern	TVRN
Ford	FRD	Mound	MND	Terminal	TERM
Forest	FRST	Mount	MT	Terrace	TER
Forge	FRG	Mountain	MTN	Ton	TN
Fork	FRK	National	NAT	Tower	TWR
Forks	FRKS	Neck	NCK	Town	TWN
Fort	FT	New	NW	Trail	TRL
Fountain	FTN	North	N	Trailer	TRLR
Freeway	FWY	Orchard	ORCH	Tunnel	TUNL
Furnace	FURN	Palms	PLMS	Turnpike	TPKE
Gardens	GDNS	Park	PK	Union	UN
Gateway	GTWY	Parkway	PKY	University	UNIV
Glen	GLN	Pillar	PLR	Upper	UPR
Grand	GRND	Pines	PNES	Valley	VLY
Great	GR	Place	PL	Viaduct	VIA
Green	GRN	Plain	PLN	View	VW
Ground	GRD	Plains	PLNS	Village	VLG
Grove	GRV	Plaza	PLZ	Ville	VL
Harbor	HBR	Point	PT	Vista	VIS
Haven	HVN	Port	PRT	Water	WTR
Heights	HTS	Prairie	PR	Wells	WLS
High	HI	Ranch	RNCH	West	W
Highlands	HGLDS	Ranches	RNCHS	White	WHT
Highway	HWY	Rapids	RPDS	Works	WKS
Hill	HL	Resort	RESRT	Yards	YDS
Hills	HLS	Rest	RST		
Hollow	HOLW	Ridge	RDG		
Hospital	HOSP	River	RIV		

11

CHAPTER ELEVEN

RECORDS MANAGEMENT SYSTEMS

CONTENTS

11.1

STORAGE AND RETRIEVAL OF RECORDS: The Equipment

An administrative secretary must be familiar with all records containing information that the executive will need in order to make decisions. This information can be in the form of a letter, an interoffice memorandum, or a directive; it can be on microfilm or in microform; and it can be on computer tape or in a reference book. It also can be stored in various containers or locations: in vertical, lateral, or visible filing cabinets; on open shelves; on cards filed in cabinets or in retrievers; in a central storage center; in an inactive storage center; in a computer center; in a company library; or in storage centers located off the premises of the company or organization.

RECORDS MANAGEMENT: A Secretarial Overview

With an efficient records and information management program, one must assume that only records of value are kept in storage. A record can be considered of administrative, historical, legal, or research value. For instance, records that are needed for day-to-day or long-term decision-making are of administrative value to an organization and thus often need to be retained for future executive-level decisions. In addition, firms interested in compiling or maintaining corporate history either for their own needs or for public, university, or private libraries would surely wish to preserve those records in which all important company-related events have been chronicled. The company legal counsel recommends those records which must be kept for the company's own protection. All deeds, long-term contracts, articles of incorporation or charters, and other legal papers are examples of records having long-term legal value. Those records that might be of assistance to a researcher in various areas of a company's operations are also very important and should be kept over the long term. In dealing with this material, the company's records administrator and his or her assistants should be guided by top management.

All other records are of short-term value and are usually kept in an organization's central records center, if there is one, or in an executive office. The dates on which these records should be destroyed are determined by the individual company or the organization; the secretary only needs to observe them. Guidelines are established by top management, individual executives, the organization's legal counsel, and the records manager regarding which records can be destroyed immediately after action has been taken on them, which records should be retained for a specified time period and then destroyed, and which records should be kept indefinitely. The secretary's responsibility is to know the proper storage location of each type of record that is retained and the length of time it is to be kept. The term *record* may refer to a series of like documents, e.g., boxes of invoices, reports, or checks, as well as a single document.

STORAGE OF RECORDS

A secretary's office or work station will usually house vertical, lateral, or visible filing cabinets. Many information managers are of the opinion that within a few years the vertical filing cabinet will have become passé. The lateral cabinets have the length of the file against the wall and may or may not be fitted with drawers. They are generally believed to provide more accessibility and offer speedier storage and retrieval. In most cases, the folders themselves will provide easy reference, and guides are not necessary except for major breakdowns of filing subdivisions. Other means of storage such as open shelves, card files, microfilm, and computer tape are likely to be found in central records. Only the records that are necessary for day-to-day operations are needed in an executive's or a secretary's office; these are records that are used at least once a month. Material not referred to at least once each month is considered inactive and should be moved to central storage to allow for more space in the office. Requests for material in central storage can be made when such material is needed.

Vertical and lateral cabinets Vertical storage cabinets can be from two to five drawers in height, depending on the amount of material that must be stored for active use. Each drawer in the cabinet should be labeled to indicate its contents and should contain guides that will provide easy, quick reference and adequate physical support for the folders. All folders, whether hanging or conventional, should have pressure-sensitive or self-adhesive labels that have been neatly and consistently typewritten. Letters should be filed in folders with the left side of the letter against the crease in the folder, and the most recent letters should be filed at the front of the folder. Each drawer should have from 20 to 25 guides. No folder should contain more than 50 sheets of paper; at this point, a new folder for the individual, company, or subject in question should be set up.

The order of the guides and folders from the front to the back of the drawer is shown in the illustration on page 371: main guide (CAL), individual folders (arranged alphabetically), permanent cross-reference guides, OUT guides or folders and special name guides (placed in proper alphabetical location), and a miscellaneous folder (CAL) at the end of that section for material not yet considered active. Some records managers think miscellaneous folders should not be used at all. However, if they are used, records should be kept in the miscellaneous folders only until five pieces to, from, or about the same subject, organization, or person have accumulated. Then, individual folders should be set up. Individual folders should be used only for names of specific persons, organizations, or subjects.

In the vertical cabinets, hanging folders may be used. Hanging folders differ from regular folders in that they are more expandable, they have several possible tab positions, and they can hold larger numbers of records. The sides of hanging folders have hooks which enable the folders to rest on a frame that has been inserted in the file drawer. The tabs can be placed at any position desired.

Lateral storage cabinets have the same features and functions as vertical cabinets except that the length of the cabinet is against the wall and the drawers extend only about one foot toward the operator. The fronts of the folders face the left side of the drawer, and the sides instead of the fronts of the folders face in the direction of the operator. The back ledge of the lateral storage cabinet may be moved forward to accommodate letter-size folders, and backwards to accommodate legal-size folders. The lateral storage cabinets can be from two to five drawers in height.

Arrangement of Materials within a Folder

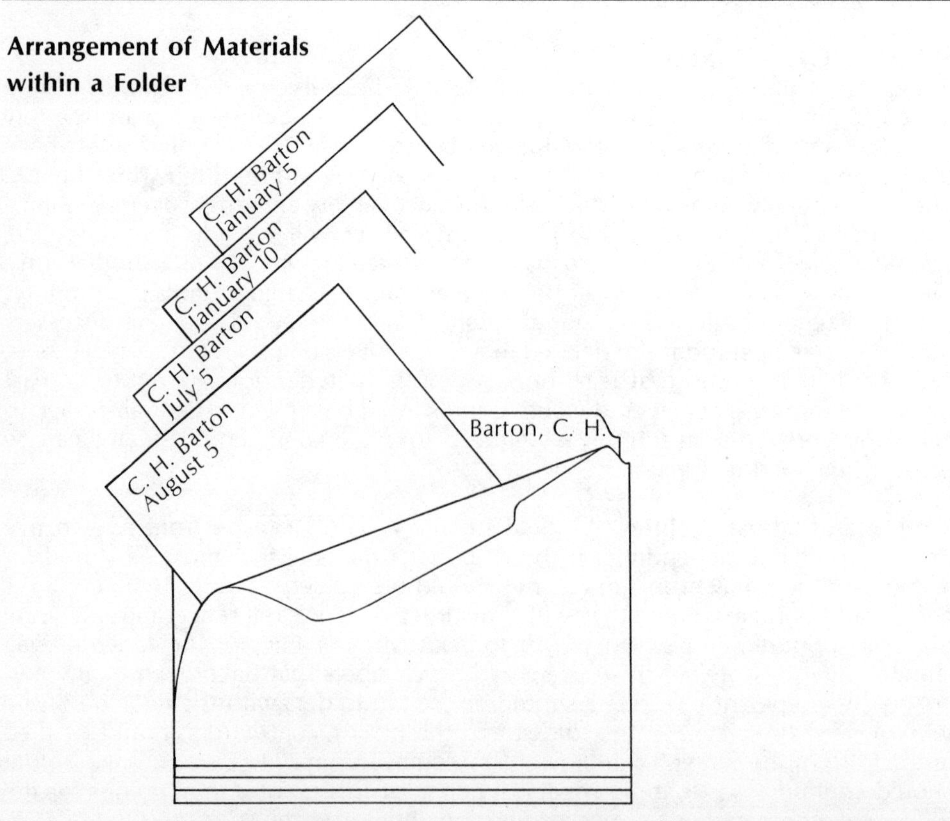

Guide and Folder Arrangement for Cabinet Files

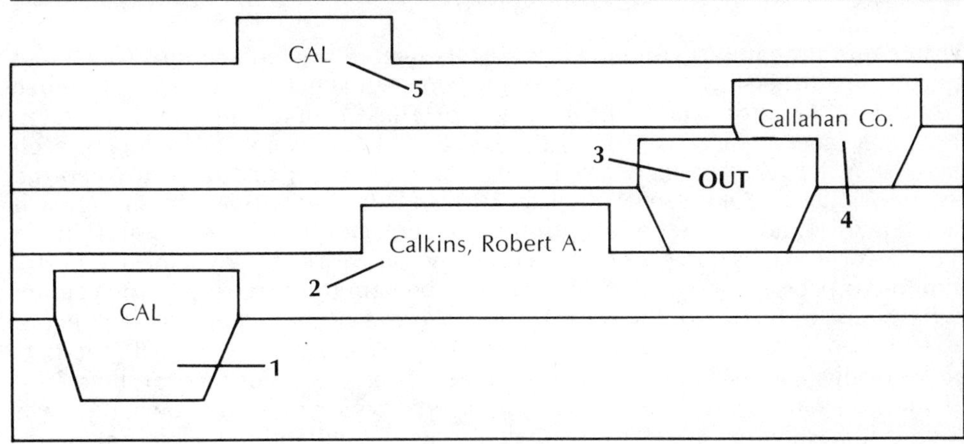

1. *Alphabetical Caption Guides* The natural position for primary reading is at the left of the guiding area. These caption guides exhibit the basic breakdown of the material that has been filed.
2. *Individual Account Folders* The heaviest account correspondence or data regarding a company's most important clients is kept here. Individual account folders are placed directly behind the alphabetical captions.
3. *Out Guides* Out guides or substitution cards located at the extreme right of the file control material that has been removed from the file. Their boldface lettering and distinctive position render them highly visible.
4. *Special Name Guide* Guides can be inserted at the far right for very active accounts. Special name guides carry the names of those entries that have more than one folder or that require special handling.
5. *Miscellaneous Folders* These folders hold material not of sufficient quantity and activity to warrant use of an individual account folder. Miscellaneous folders are placed at the end of each letter-caption category, and they bear the same caption identification as the alphabetical caption guides.

Open-shelf storage Open shelves are becoming very popular because of the savings in space (up to 50 percent) and the quick and easy reference that they offer. The shelves are adjustable and are tilted forward slightly—most of them have boxes (containing the materials pertaining to one subject or correspondent) which attach to the shelf and which are removable. Only in areas where there is neither air conditioning nor air filtration would the use of open-shelf storage be questionable. The dust accumulation and the lack of control over the humidity would make this equipment difficult to use in such conditions. Within the last few years, open-shelf storage cabinets have been constructed on tracks for movability. For this reason, they require less space and make fast work of filing and retrieving. The great advantage of these cabinets becomes clear when one realizes that an employee can stand in one position and still work with three cabinets.

Card cabinets Information about a person or subject can be housed in card cabinets of various sizes. The most often used card sizes are 3″ × 5″, 4″ × 6″, and 5″ × 8″. Card cabinets can be wide enough to hold only one series of cards such as 3″ × 5″ cards, or the cabinets can be partitioned and set up in different widths to hold two or three rows of cards. The most modern card cabinets are those in automatic retrieval units, which, at the touch of a button, bring needed information from a storage cabinet or a vault of one or more stories (or about 30 feet) in height to an operator in one stationary position.

Visible filing cabinets Visible filing cabinets feature small drawers usually about two inches in height and five to 12 inches in width that house cards on which detailed lists of information are typically kept. These cabinets are usually in stacks and house cards which reveal only the identifying or descriptive heading of each card. Each drawer is partially covered with a metal cover that helps to keep the records lying flat. One can easily gain access to the desired data by lifting each card. Such cabinets are especially useful as receptacles for indexes to locations of other records. For example, one large company uses visible filing cabinets to house information about every record that has ever been in the company records center from the incorporation of the company to the present time. When a certain record is requested, records management employees can look at the visible file cabinets at the receiving desk to determine such information as the location of the record in question, whether it was destroyed or placed on microfilm, and how long it was kept, if it was kept at all. This company also uses visible files in an automatic retrieval unit so that the location of a vital record can be determined.

Microfilm storage The use of microfilm has markedly reduced storage space requirements. When hard copy is converted to microfilm, only two percent of the original space taken up by the material is necessary for the microfilm: savings of up to 98 percent are gained. Microfilm can be filed on 16-mm. and 35-mm. rolls in color or in black and white, and housed in cartridges or magazines. Other microforms (microfilm forms) are jackets, tab cards, microfiche, and strip holders. Storage cabinets, binders, and small tubs are available for storing microfilm and microforms. See also section 11.8 of this chapter.

Computer tape storage Computer tapes which hold a tremendous amount of information, save large amounts of space, and afford fast information retrieval. Special cabinets can be used to store these tapes. The storage device may actually be a closed cabinet, or it may be a rack which is kept in a closed area. In addition to these devices, there are also storage boxes designed so that the tapes slide forward as one is taken out, thus facilitating retrieval. The tapes are indexed, and a record is kept of the location of each tape so that information can be located fast.

Tickler files A tickler file is used as a reminder. It is usually in 3″ × 5″ card-file form and is handy as a follow-up file, since it contains reminders and copies of material that may be used in following up something (as a project or a meeting). A typical tickler file has 31 guides (or folders, if it is not a card file)—one for each day of the month and 12 guides (or folders) for each month. The guide for the current month is at the front of the file with the 31 daily guides behind it. As a reminder becomes necessary, a card is made out containing the required information, a reminder date is written at the top, and the card is filed behind that date. Each morning, the secretary should look at the tickler file to see what is to be done that day. At the end of a month, that month's guide is placed at the back of the file, and the new month and the same guides (numbered appropriately for the month) are placed at the front of the file. When the tickler file is in the form of a tub file on wheels instead of a 3″ × 5″ card file, guides and folders (12 guides for the months and 31 folders for the days) are set up. The letters that need following up are placed in folders behind the dates or months on which action must be taken. Special folders are also available with sliding signals which indicate the dates on which follow-up action should be taken.

SUMMARY

Many organizations have libraries that house records of historical value as well as reference books and other materials needed by executives and managers. A secretary should be aware of the functions and availability of the types of records and information that are kept in such libraries. It is also important for a secretary to know what types of documents are restricted—i.e., available only to authorized persons. For instance, project notebooks filled out by scientists in an industrial firm may be available only to members of the research and development division of that company, even though they may be stored in the company's library. Government contracts, including classified documents or confidential papers, will need to be stored in vaults or cabinets with locks and/or combinations that meet government security specifications. A secretary who handles these kinds of documents will be briefed on procedures outlined by the Department of Defense.

A knowledge of the records considered important and the appropriate kinds of equipment for housing them as well as an awareness of proper and efficient information processing techniques and procedures will make the administrative secretary a valuable asset to any executive, whatever the organization.

11.2

TYPES OF FILING SYSTEMS

A knowledge of the various filing systems that are commonly used and the reasons for their selection is essential to the administrative secretary. Each alphabetic, nonalphabetic, and combination filing system is designed to fit a specific office requirement, and the administrative secretary needs to know not only when to use a particular system but also how to use it most effectively.

STORAGE SYSTEM SELECTION

The most important questions that must be asked are these: How is the information to be requested? Under what name, subject, or code number will the information be found? What is the means of access to it? Earlier filing systems were based solely on the names of individuals. Later, names often became less important than the subject of the correspondence or the location of the addressee. When an element of confidentiality became important, code numbers were introduced. Code numbers and color codes are now recognized as catalysts to speedy filing and retrieving. The use of numbers has also facilitated the storage and retrieval of information with computer systems.

ALPHABETIC FILING SYSTEMS

During the time when spindles were used for storing, when papers were piled in desk drawers or on desk tops, and even later when vertical filing cabinets had become a part of an office, filing *alphabetically* by an individual's name was easy. To eliminate unnecessary time for searches, files were arranged according to surnames. When several individuals had the same surname, the material was secondarily arranged by the first name or initial, and then by the middle name or initial. If a further breakdown was necessary, a city, a state, a street name, a house number, an individual's age, or some other data were used. The same method of alphabetic filing is followed today using strict alphabetic sequence for placing records in storage. The illustration on page 374 shows the *C* through *CRO* sections of an alphabetic system. Although detailed rules for indexing vary with one's organization,

Guide and Folder Arrangement for an Alphabetic Filing System

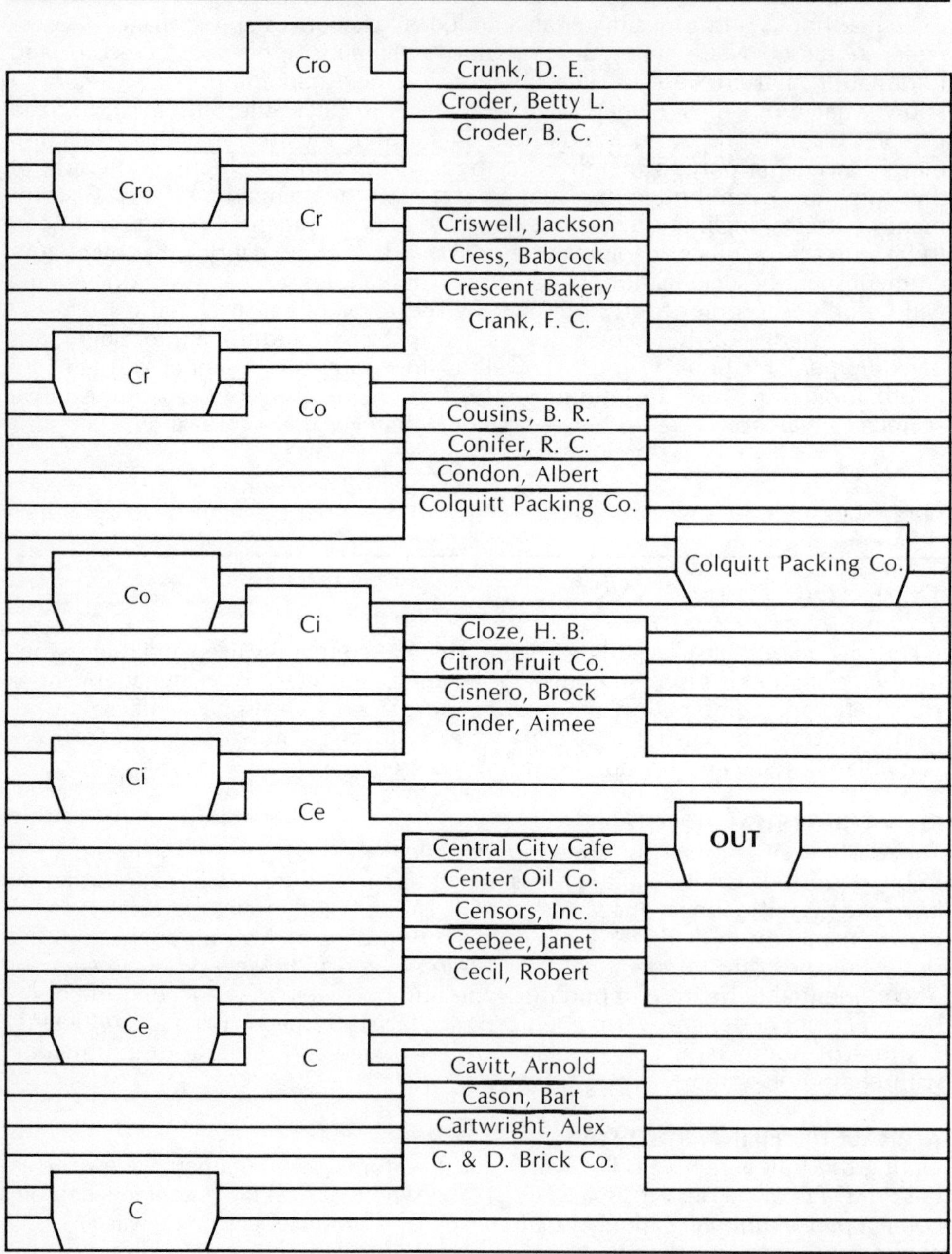

some rules are published by the Association of Records Managers and Administrators (ARMA). Indexing rules are discussed in more detail in section 11.5.

Subject filing When the name of the individual is not so important as the subject of the record, the *subject* becomes the filing unit for reference. The most important subject name becomes the first unit, the second most important subject is selected

Alphabetic Subject Filing System

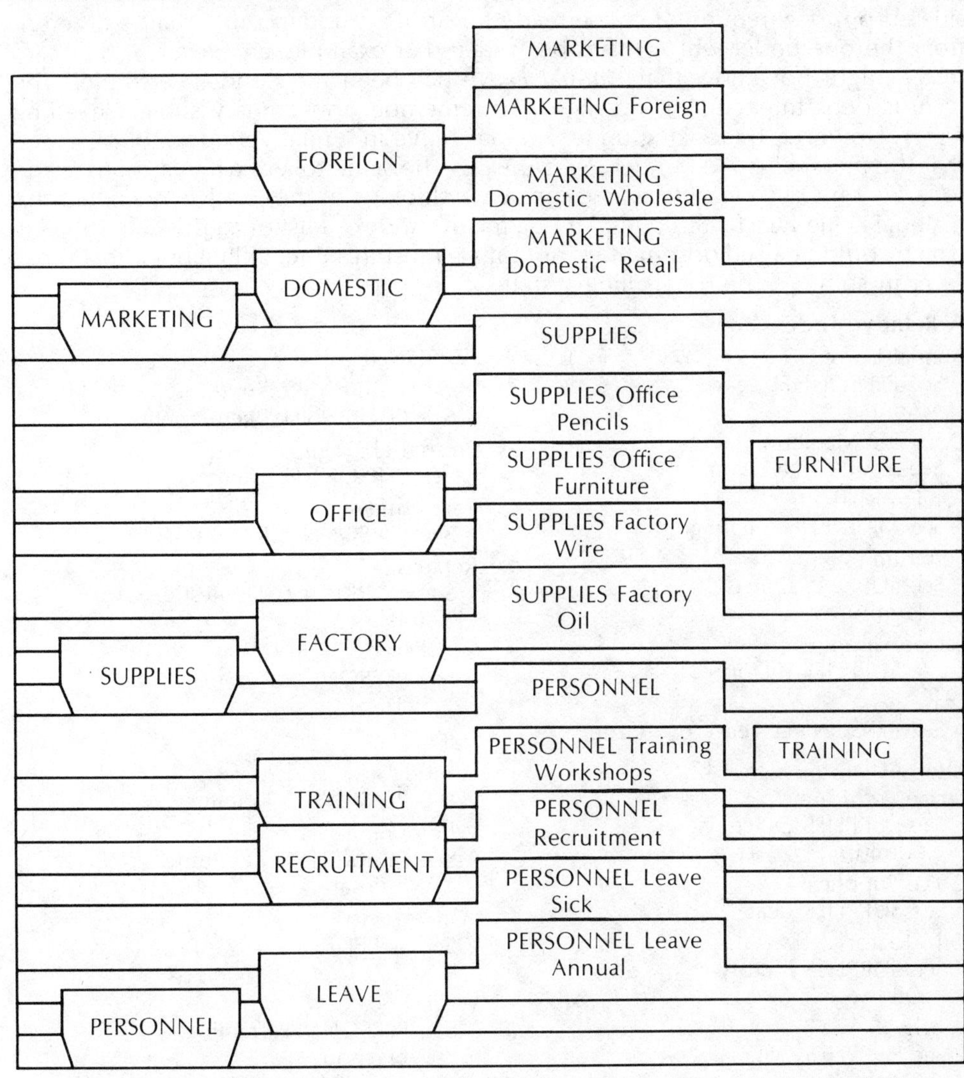

as the second unit, and so on. This process is continued as far as is necessary to sort the material alphabetically. Subject filing is a variation of the alphabetic system.

A subject system is difficult to set up because there is an absolute need to select the proper subjects, and yet one may be uncertain just which ones are truly important. Each reference begins with the most important subject title. The subject titles can be best selected by setting up an outline. After the outline has been thoroughly planned and checked by those who have selected the subject headings, the list of subjects must be furnished to all the departments and individuals using the services of the records center. In some cases, secondary titles can be cross-referenced back to primary titles (i.e., the most important titles) for faster reference. (The cross-reference procedure is more fully explained on page 381 of this chapter.) The illustration above shows a section of an alphabetic filing system arranged by subjects.

An important addition to the subject system is the *relative index* (see the next illustration). Because of the difficulty in deciding which subjects should be considered primary, requests may be made for an item under a title that is different from the one under which it has been filed. For example, an executive or a secretary might not know that *Annual Leave* has been filed under *Personnel.* The records department might not know or remember the primary subject heading either. However, by looking under *Annual Leave* in a relative index, they can see that the material is filed under *Personnel.* By the same token, when a call is made for a file on *Office Furniture,* one can see by looking at the relative index that the material is filed under *Supplies.* Thus, a relative index—a list of all possible subjects which could be used or sought—is not only a must in subject filing but also a timesaver in some of the other filing systems.

A Relative Index

Annual Leave
  See PERSONNEL Leave
    Annual
Domestic Marketing
  See MARKETING Domestic
Foreign Marketing
  See MARKETING Foreign
Furniture
  See SUPPLIES Office
    Furniture
Factory Supplies
  See SUPPLIES Factory
Leave
  See PERSONNEL Leave
MARKETING
Office Furniture
  See SUPPLIES Office
    Furniture
Office Supplies
  See SUPPLIES Office
Oil - Factory
  See SUPPLIES Factory
    Oil
Pencils
  See SUPPLIES Office
    Pencils
PERSONNEL
Personnel Recruitment
  See PERSONNEL Recruitment
Personnel Training
  See PERSONNEL Training
Recruitment
  See PERSONNEL Recruitment
Retailing
  See MARKETING Domestic
    Retail
Sick Leave
  See PERSONNEL Leave
    Sick
SUPPLIES
Training
  See PERSONNEL Training
Wholesaling
  See MARKETING Domestic
    Wholesale
Wire - Factory
  See SUPPLIES Factory
    Wire
Workshops
  See PERSONNEL Training
    Workshops

Geographic filing When the location of a correspondent or subject is of more importance to the user than a name or subject, the *geographic* system of filing may be preferred. Although the geographic system is seldom used on a general basis, it is, nevertheless, helpful to mail-order companies interested in sales activities in different parts of the world or in a particular country, state, or city. This system is also helpful to utility companies concerned with the locations of their installations and customers. Again, the most important title becomes the first or primary unit, the second most important title becomes the secondary unit, and so on. When it is evident that a record may be requested under more than one title, a cross-reference procedure is necessary for ease in locating the material (see the illustration on page 381). For example, a company might be operating in more than one city. In that case, the *main office* or the *most active office* would be the geographic filing unit used. In the event that information about the Hodges Foundry in Smithville, State, was needed, a cross-reference would be placed under *State, Smithville, Hodges* to refer the searcher to the proper main-office location under *State, Jonesville, Hodges.* As all units are arranged alphabetically by location, the geographic filing system is really another variation of the alphabetic filing process.

Combination subject filing Variations of subject filing (shown in the following illustrations) are the *subject-numeric* in which numbers are assigned to a subject outline, the *duplex-numeric* in which a combination of numbers is used, the *alpha-numeric* in which a combination of letters and numbers is assigned from the subject outline, and the *decimal* system which is derived from the subject outline. In all of these variations, an outline is built from the most important subject headings; numbers or letters are assigned to primary and secondary units. Likewise, numbers and letters are delegated to third- and fourth-level units. The numbers and letters assigned to these units may be either alternating or consecutive. In some cases, numbers are assigned to each unit and are divided by hyphens, with the first number being the primary unit; the second number the secondary, and so forth.

Subject-numeric Filing System

COMMUNICATIONS
1 Telegraph - Telephone
1-1 rates - charges
2 Mail
2-1 registered - insured
2-1-1 receipts

FORMS
1 Design - Development
1-1 standards
2 Distribution

MEETINGS
1 Local
1-1 Federal agencies
1-1-1 Bureau of Economics
2 National
3 International

Duplex-numeric Filing System

1 COMMUNICATIONS
1-1 Telegraph - Telephone
1-1a rates - charges
1-2 Mail
1-2a registered - insured
1-2a-1 receipts

2 FORMS
2-1 Design - Development
2-1a standards
2-2 Distribution

3 MEETINGS
3-1 Local
3-1a Federal agencies
3-1a-1 Bureau of Economics
3-2 National
3-3 International

Alpha-numeric Filing System

A ADMINISTRATION
A1 COMMUNICATIONS
A1-1 Telegraph - Telephone
A1-1-1 rates - charges
A1-2 Mail
A1-2-1 registered - insured
A1-2-1-1 receipts
A2 FORMS
A2-1 Design - Development
A2-1-1 standards
A2-2 Distribution
A3 MEETINGS
A3-1 Local
A3-1-1 Federal agencies
A3-1-1-1 Bureau of Economics
A3-2 National
A3-3 International

Decimal Filing System

100 ADMINISTRATION
110 COMMUNICATIONS
111 Telegraph - Telephone
111.1 rates - charges
112 Mail
112.1 registered - insured
112.11 receipts
120 FORMS
121 Design - Development
121.1 standards
122 Distribution
130 MEETINGS
131 Local
131.1 Federal agencies
131.11 Bureau of Economics
132 National
133 International

In summarizing these systems, one can conclude that the straight alphabetic, the subject, the geographic, the subject-numeric, the duplex-numeric, the alpha-numeric, and the decimal systems are all variations of the basic alphabetic system.

NUMERIC FILING SYSTEMS

A second filing system is the *numeric*. The numeric also has variations such as the terminal-digit and phonetic systems. The straight numeric system is used by attorneys, physicians, or others who require that records be continually added for new customers, patients, or clients. The straight numeric system begins with the first numbered folder used for the first account. As new folders are required, new numbers in strict numeric sequence are added. As the system develops, new records are first kept in *miscellaneous* folders and maintained separately. When five records are received about an individual or firm, an *individual* folder is made up and a number assigned to it with the name of the individual or company on the label and maintained in another location.

Numeric system components The numeric filing system is made up of the following four parts:

1. the miscellaneous alphabetic folders that hold only those records that are inactive
2. the individual numeric folders that hold only those records which are active and those to which numbers were sequentially assigned and kept separate from the miscellaneous folders
3. an accession register that houses a record of the numbers assigned
4. a card file (relative index) that indicates whether correspondence is located in miscellaneous or individual files; it is a complete list of correspondents and could include addresses for a mailing list

The accession register, either in book form or card form, is a complete list of correspondents in numeric order beginning with 1. In the event that a number cannot be remembered when one calls for a record, the card file which is arranged alphabetically by correspondent will then furnish the number assigned to the individual or indicate that the data or correspondence is filed in the miscellaneous file.

Numeric variation: terminal digit The *terminal-digit* system, a variation of the numeric, includes only those folders that have preassigned numbers. This system can be used very effectively by organizations such as hospitals or insurance companies, and in other situations such as those that have been listed under the numeric system. The difference between this system and the straight numeric is that the numbers are read from right to left and that significance is attached to the numbers in this order. The first two numbers at the right are considered primary, the next two numbers (third and fourth from the right) are considered secondary, and the remaining numbers are considered tertiary. Instead of reading the policy No. 61534 from left to right, records department employees would read the folder as 34 15 6. They would look under the 34 section of the file first, then under the 15, and finally under the 6 in order to file or retrieve the material. The terminal-digit system is considered very easy to work with because numbers are easier to remember than personal names or names of organizations, because locating folders by number is very rapid, and because filing is very fast. Greater accuracy is also achieved by use of this method.

PHONETIC FILING SYSTEM

A third system, one not used frequently but important in certain situations, is called the *phonetic* system, although it involves some attention to letters as well as to sounds. The system is used in such organizations as large hospitals, Social Security offices, police departments, and offices dealing with state motor vehicle records. It is especially effective when a very large number of records (especially in card form) are used, when calls for records come over telephones or intercoms (that is, when names are only heard and not seen), and when retrieval must be quick. When this system is used, the records department employee is able to translate the name heard into a letter and number code without knowing exactly how the name is spelled. By means of this code, the record that is needed can be located rapidly.

SUMMARY

Alphabetic filing either by name or by subject is the system most often used. The terminal-digit system is rapidly gaining popularity, however, because new folders can be distributed quickly and easily. The secretary should consult a records expert (as the company records manager) for assistance in setting up the system that will be most efficient for the office.

11.3

PLANNING AND SETTING UP FILING SYSTEMS

CHOOSING A SYSTEM

First of all, the secretary must know how filed materials will be requested; then it will be easy to recommend the filing system that will be most appropriate for the office. If records are asked for by name, the alphabetic system should be used; if they are requested by subject, then the subject system or a variation of it should be used; if location is the most important factor, then the geographic system should be selected. If one's office requires a filing system in which cases or patients are referred to by number, a numeric system should be used; in offices where large files are used with which numbers would be more efficient, a variation of the subject and alphabetic systems would be best employed. In organizations where records are most often requested by telephone, the phonetic system should be used.

EQUIPMENT SELECTION

Before actually setting up the files, an estimate must be made as to the equipment and supply items that will be needed. Some of these items are file cabinets, guides, folders, staplers (no paper clips or pins should be used in storing papers), two-hole perforators (to attach papers to a folder), desk trays (to hold incoming materials and materials to be filed), filing shelves (to attach to a file drawer or an open shelf for use in holding material to be filed), filing stools, and sorters. Sorters range from notebook size (8½″ x 11″) marked with file tabs containing letters from A to Z, to the large tub-size portable cabinets. The most often used sorters are those that are movable; they are typically six inches wide and from three to four feet long. As the operator sits in a stationary position, the sorter is moved back and forth to permit the operator to sort material for filing into the same arrangement as the cabinets that will hold it, e.g., into alphabetic, subject, geographic, or some other filing arrangement.

SOURCES OF ASSISTANCE

If the company has a records management program, the records administrator is the most likely person to consult concerning the establishment of a filing system.

If a company-wide program is not in effect, then the consulting of secretaries in similar offices elsewhere would be an alternative source of information. However, the most efficient source would be an outside consultant familiar with the particular types of records being analyzed. If one considers the value of an expert's advice and the resultant time savings, one realizes that employment of such a consultant is often well worth the cost. In most large cities, records information consultants are listed in the Yellow Pages of the telephone book. Information may also be sought from those office supply and equipment firms that employ consultants.

11.4

STEPS IN FILING

The most important step in handling records is to determine whether or not the record can be destroyed immediately after the information in it has been disseminated or whether it should be retained for a certain period of time. Retention schedules, set up with the cooperation of the records administrator, a representative from top management, the organization's legal counsel, and department heads, are a necessity in establishing and maintaining control over records. The retention schedule lists names of records, the department or division responsible for the originals, the records retention periods and the place where the records are to be stored, microfilming and microfilm storage instructions where they are relevant, and possibly an indication of the method of destruction.

PREPARATION OF DOCUMENTS FOR STORAGE

Procedures to be observed when preparing for the storage and retrieval of those records which must be retained include the following:

1. Read or scan the letter, memorandum, card, report, or other communication.
2. If your records management system permits it, place a mark or code on the record to indicate to records personnel where the material should be stored. [Some records administrators, however, prefer to take this step themselves.]
3. Place on the record a letter or some other indication that will indicate to records personnel the length of storage. [Again, some records administrators prefer to do this task themselves.]
4. Check to see whether or not the record needs cross-referencing. Will it be called for by a title or titles other than the one already coded? See the illustration on page 381.
5. Place a release mark or code on the document to indicate that the record is ready for filing.
6. Sort the material in the same order in which it will be stored so that it may be filed quickly.

Since approximately 25 percent of the records crossing a secretary's desk each day can be destroyed immediately or passed on to some other person in the company for disposition, those records can be processed with no thought for storage.

Reading, scanning, and coding After mail which has no retention value has been discarded, after information has been disseminated to proper departments or persons, or after the material has been routed to those interested in it, the records which are left can be made ready for filing. In reading or scanning a record, the secretary should look for the name or subject which is the most important; the secretary should underscore or encircle the name or subject in pencil or write or code the subject or name onto the letter if it has not already been mentioned in the text itself. The name could be in the inside address, signature line, or the body of the letter. The code would include a number if the filing system being used is numeric or a combination of numeric and alphabetic. Examples: if the system is terminal digit, the code would be 123456; if the system is an alpha-numeric combination, 1A2b would be the code; or, if the system is straight numeric, the code would be 45632.

Much care should be taken to select the proper title. Some records administrators prefer that a secretary not code records which are being sent to central records, as the records personnel will be more familiar with the titles which should be used for storage. A secretary can, of course, code the records that she will store herself.

The secretary should indicate to the filing personnel that the letter is ready to be filed; this can be done by initialing the material or by using some symbol for release such as a stamp marked "File" or "Release." The release mark or stamp is typically placed in the upper right-hand corner of the record.

Retention codes As a help to the filing personnel, each document should be marked with a code indicating the retention period of the material (such as 30 days, 60 days, 90 days, one year, two years, or longer). The retention schedule will indicate whether the records are to be transferred to inactive storage, microfilmed, or placed in computer storage in accordance with established company policy.

Cross-references Too many offices do not use the cross-referencing procedure which is so essential to quick retrieval. When a record might be called for under titles other than the one under which it is filed, a cross-reference sheet should be filed under the possible title, referring searchers to the proper storage location. For example, when correspondence is filed under the legal name of a married woman, as *Jones, Carrie M.* (*Mrs.*), a cross-reference sheet should be filed under her husband's name, as *Jones, John H.* (*Mrs.*) and reference made to the proper position for filing (see the next illustration). Cross-referencing is also useful when the first filing order of departments or bureaus of government agencies might not be readily recalled, when a company has offices with different addresses, and when a periodical is filed under its name but a cross-reference under its publisher's name would be timesaving.

Example of a Cross-reference Sheet

CROSS-REFERENCE

JONES, JOHN H. MRS.

Letter pertaining to purchase of shoes dated 5/21/76

SEE

JONES, CARRIE M. MRS.

When it is evident that a customer is becoming active in correspondence (i.e., when five cross-references have accumulated), the procedure is stopped and a permanent cross-reference guide is set up. This guide is similar to a regular guide, but the tab is prepared in this fashion: *Jones, John H.* (*Mrs.*) SEE *Jones, Carrie M.* The guide is then filed under the cross-referenced title, thus saving time and supplies by making it unnecessary to prepare additional cross-reference sheets.

Follow-up When an executive anticipates that he or she will want to see a record in the near future, the executive or the secretary will indicate on the record the date on which the executive would like it to be returned. If the record is being sent to the records center, the secretary or the records personnel will use a tickler file to remind themselves that this record must be pulled for the executive on the indicated date.

Presorting for storage Instead of taking material to the cabinets or shelves in disarray, sorting it in the same arrangement that is used in the cabinets or on the shelves will save a great deal of time. If this procedure and the other procedures mentioned earlier are observed, great savings in time and money will result.

11.5

INDEXING SYSTEMS

Indexing systems are used to determine how a record is to be filed so that it can be found when needed. Codes facilitate filing and retrieving information.

BASIC RULES FOR INDEXING

Some basic rules for indexing are generally observed, but specific rules usually vary with one's organization. The most important rule is to be consistent—treat each piece of information in the same manner. A respected source for indexing rules is the book *Rules for Alphabetic Filing* which can be obtained for a nominal fee by writing to the Association of Records Managers and Administrators (ARMA), P.O. Box 281, Bradford, RI 02808. ARMA recommends rules for three classifications: (1) Names of Individuals (2) Names of Business Establishments, and (3) Governmental/Political Designations. A principle of the greatest importance is to decide what is the most important unit and to use it as the primary unit.

Indexing individual names With the name of an individual, the surname is of primary importance. The first name or initial is of secondary importance and is considered as the second unit and the middle name or initial is the third unit. Records relating to individuals who have nicknames are filed in the same manner, except that a cross-reference is used to direct searchers to the complete name, if it is known. If no surname is known, then the name is filed as written: *Alfred the Great, Alfred* being the first unit and *Great* the second, as *the* is ignored in all cases. Names with prefixes such as *de, des, le,* or *Mac* include the prefixes in the first unit; thus, *MacDonald* is considered as one unit. Similarly, hyphened names are treated as one unit; for example, with a name like *John Smith-Jones, Smith-Jones* comprises the first unit and *John* the second. Titles made up of several important elements and not followed by a name are filed in the order of these elements: in *Prince of Wales, Prince* is the first unit, *Wales* is the second, and *of* is ignored. Other titles or degrees are not used in filing unless they are essential in identification or in distinguishing sex, marital status, or numerical sequence (as *Junior, Third,* or *III*).

Indexing names of organizations or businesses When one is indexing the names of organizations or businesses, rules similar to the ones just described are observed. For example, in a company name composed of the full name of an individual, the name is inverted so that the surname appears first. For example, in the name *Ted Corvair, Inc., Corvair* is first unit and *Ted* is second. When no complete name of an individual is used, the company name is indexed as it is ordinarily written. If the company name is *Corvair Construction Company,* the name appears on the file just as it is written here. Companies operating under two different names are indexed under the name that is used most often, and they are cross-referenced under the other name. When a compound word or a hyphened name occurs, it is treated as one unit. The same is true of coined expressions. For instance, the *A-1 Manufacturing Company* would be filed under *A-1,* assuming that this expression is used when calling for records under that name. Compound geographical names are treated differently, however. *The Los Alamos Construction Company* would be filed under *Los* as the first unit, under *Alamos* as second unit, and under *Construction* as third unit, with *The* being ignored as is done with all prepositions, conjunctions, and articles. Punctuation within a name is ignored: *Smith's Grocery* would be filed under *Smiths.*

When indexing names that have compass points as essential elements (such as *Northwestern Life Insurance Company* or *North West Real Estate Company*), each directional word is filed separately: *North* as the first unit in both cases; *-western* and *West* as second units, respectively; and so forth. Single letters in names such as those used in radio or television stations are treated as separate units. *KXYZ* has four units and is filed at the beginning of the *K* section of the files. Names of companies containing numbers in figure form are filed in numerical order at the front of the entire file. If the numbers are spelled out, however, the written-out number is retained and is filed alphabetically. For example, *2015 Main Building* would be filed in the front of the complete files in the *2015* position, while *One Main Street* would be filed alphabetically under the *O*'s. Names of foreign firms as well as titles included in them are filed as they are normally written unless elements of them are identifiable as surnames or as complete names, in which case they are treated like their English counterparts.

Indexing governmental and political designations When indexing government correspondence, one uses the most important word. In all federal communications or records, the first three units are always *United States Government.* Then the name of the department, bureau, or commission becomes the next succeeding unit or units for filing. The same approach is taken with states and cities: the official name of the state such as *Texas, State of* or *Virginia, Commonwealth of* is used first, followed by the applicable department, bureau, or division within the state government. Military installations are first filed under *United States Government* and then under the name of the installation (as a fort, station, or base). Foreign governments are treated like states and cities. A record from a department of the government of South Korea would be filed first under *Korea, Republic of* and then under the department's name.

For a complete treatment of indexing rules, the ARMA *Rules for Alphabetic Filing* should be consulted. However, a secretary should first of all be familiar with the particular indexing system used by the organization. The records manager should be able to brief the secretary on the guidelines established to cover all of the major indexing categories discussed earlier in this section. Finally, the secretary should be sure to follow these guidelines consistently so that misplacement or loss of material will be minimized and so that retrieval can be accomplished expeditiously.

11.6

CONTROL OF CONFIDENTIAL AND CLASSIFIED DOCUMENTS

No matter how records are filed or when they are stored, a system for controlling their location and movement must be established and observed by all personnel. If there is no control, records may be missing when they are needed or may fall into the wrong hands. When a secretary has accepted a record for safekeeping, every precaution must be taken to protect that record so that it will be available when needed. By the same token, when a records center accepts a record for storage, it must take similar precautions to protect the material so that it is available when it is called for.

A simple method of exercising normal protection over the company records is not to permit anyone except an authorized secretary or the filing personnel to withdraw material from the files. Cutting down on the number of people working with the files will provide greater control.

Special precautions must be exercised when confidential or classified documents are in the possession of a secretary for safekeeping or when they are stored in the records center. In addition to the normal protection just mentioned, an organization can use a safe or a built-in vault large enough for holding storage equipment. Another method of protecting confidential or classified documents is to duplicate or microfilm the material and then place it in the hands of an attorney or a bank for safekeeping.

Private firms holding government contracts either to manufacture, distribute, or store classified government materials or products are required by the Department of Defense to assign special control numbers to each of the classified documents that may be kept on company premises. Communications (as letters and memorandums) regarding these contracts or projects also require control numbers. Although the responsibility for maintaining records for these classified documents is in the hands of a special department within the firm, secretaries should be aware of the necessity for control numbers; similarly, secretaries and other office personnel should recognize all other identification that may be placed on classified documents. The Department of Defense typically classifies documents as TOP SECRET, SECRET, or CONFIDENTIAL. Stamps are used to note the appropriate security classification of a document (see Chapter 6, page 193, for examples of these stamps.) The National Security regulation warning against unauthorized disclosure of classified material is also stamped or typewritten on the document (see Chapter 6, page 191). In addition to following the special storage procedures for such documents, care must be taken not to leave classified documents uncovered on desks. Also, one should be sure that cover pages are attached to the documents, and that the documents are kept in drawers or locked areas when they are not being used. Classified documents may not be released to a person unless proof has been furnished that the individual is cleared to handle the documents. Other precautions that a records department could use would be red-bordered envelopes indicating that classified information is within, the hand-carrying of documents instead of the use of interoffice mail, and the retention of receipts that have been signed by the person charging out the materials.

CHARGE-OUT PROCEDURES

Assuming that all retained records are valuable regardless of whether they are classified, common sense dictates that they must be protected and that their whereabouts must be controlled. Removal of a record from the files should not be permitted until it has been properly charged out. A record can be charged out to a person after he or she has officially requisitioned it for a previously agreed-on length of time. A special form should be available for this purpose. An official requisition which includes the description of the record, the date of the record, the kind of record, and the signature of the person requesting it can often serve as a charge-out form. It can fit into a pocket on the OUT guide. If only one record is removed for charge-out, then an OUT guide or Substitution Card containing the same information about the record can replace the charged-out record in the file. If another request is made for that record, the secretary or the filing personnel will be able to tell the person requesting the material exactly where the record is and for what length of time it has been requisitioned. An OUT folder is preferred when an entire folder has been charged out; the OUT folder also serves as a receptacle for records that are to be stored while the original folder is charged out. However, OUT guides (with or without pockets) can be used for an entire folder.

Charge-out Form

______________________________	__________
Name or Subject	Date
______________________________	
Description of material charged out	
______________________________	
______________________________	
______________________________	__________
Signature	Dept.

An ON CALL guide could be placed in the same position as the OUT folder. The ON CALL guide directs the filing personnel to send related material on to the person listed on the ON CALL guide when the original folder is returned. Only when the material is returned can the OUT guide or folder be removed for reuse in a similar procedure. This records control procedure is absolutely essential. Some companies establish a policy that a record can be kept out for only two weeks; others, for a month. In any case, a policy should be determined, agreed on, and adhered to by all. Examples of OUT folders, OUT guides, and ON CALL guides are found in the group of drawings on pages 386–387.

CONTROL OF CORRESPONDENCE

As another aspect of records/information management, a secretary can contribute to the reduction of records costs by encouraging oral instead of written communication whenever possible. Since the cost of processing a single letter is now about five dollars, telephone calls or even telegrams can often be used to convey or obtain information more cheaply. This procedure is a time-saver as well.

Records Control Devices

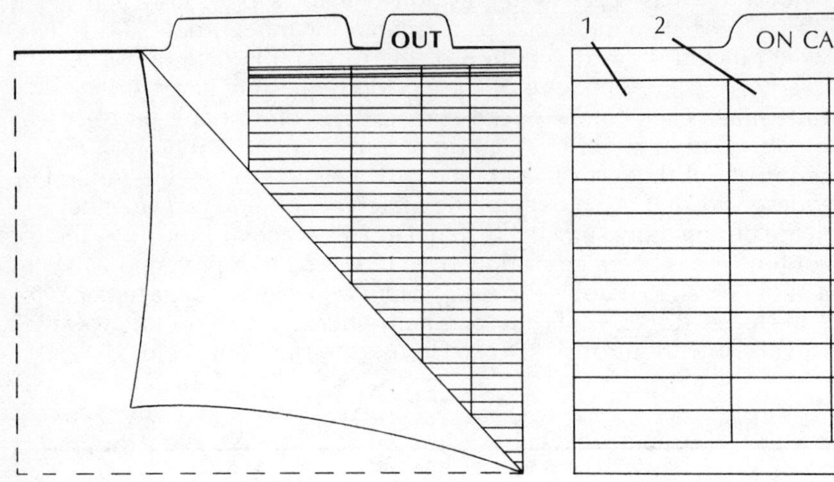

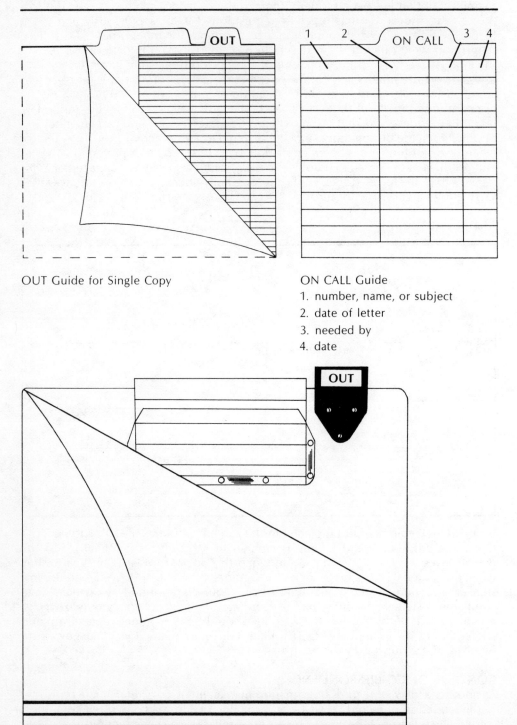

OUT Guide for Single Copy

ON CALL Guide
1. number, name, or subject
2. date of letter
3. needed by
4. date

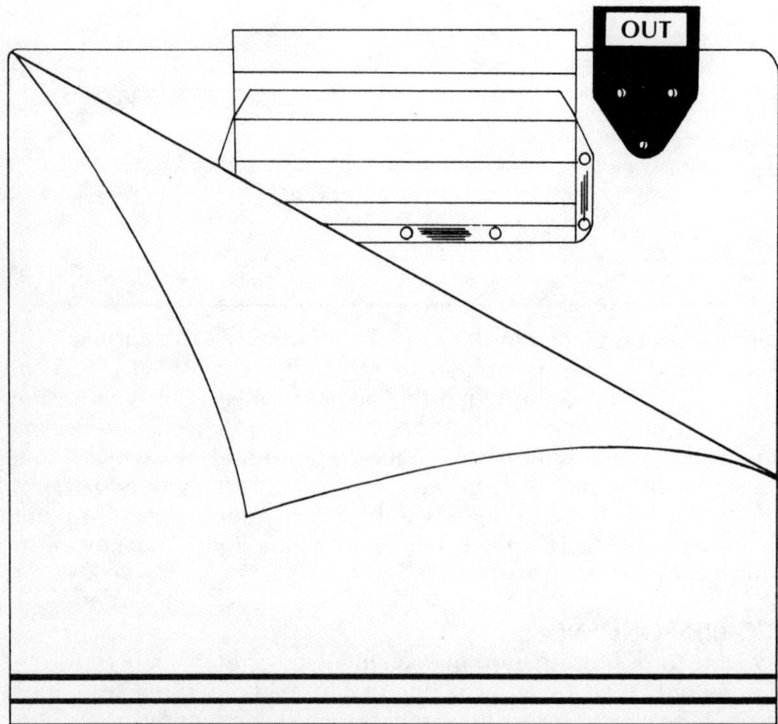

OUT Folder with Pocket

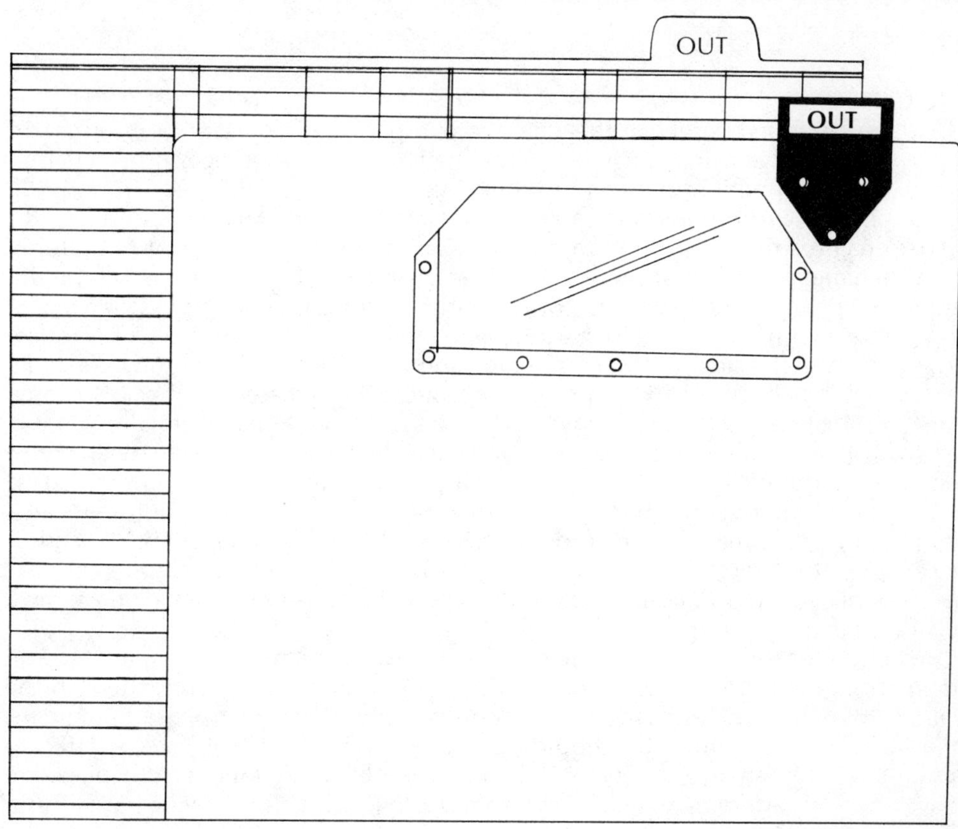

OUT Guide for an Entire Folder

11.7

CENTRALIZED AND DECENTRALIZED FILES

Information storage can be either centralized or decentralized. If information is centralized, all records of any kind are kept in a central storage area. Authorized personnel charge out records and other resource materials at this location. Information concerning the records system is available in the center also. Certain departmental records are retained within the department itself for 30-60 days or sometimes as long as one year before being forwarded to the central storage area. Other records are sent on as soon as they are no longer useful to a particular department or division on a daily or monthly basis.

A decentralized system, on the other hand, provides that all records be kept in individual departments within an organization. There is no central records area. When the records have served their purpose in the departments, they are then sent to an inactive storage center if they must be kept.

11.8

MICROGRAPHICS

MICROFILM

Microfilm, as stated earlier in this chapter, is especially important in information processing and handling because of the space saved in storage, the increased amounts of information that can be stored, and the facility and speed in retrieval. When obtaining information for an executive today, a secretary will often have to refer to records that are either on microfilm or in some other type of microform.

When microfilm first became available to businesses, many firms used it for the storage of their records. With use of the early microfilm technology, storage area and retrieval time were often wasted, and high costs were the result. Today, however, an increasing number of organizations are using microfilm because its technology has been greatly improved and because a greater number of records must be retained (as for tax or inventory purposes) over longer terms.

Microfilm lasts as long as the best bond paper and occupies only two percent of the space required for hard copy. Material is easily and speedily converted to microfilm by photographing the hard copy of any size manually or automatically. Microfilm clerks prearrange records for filming, remove staples or welds, and, if necessary, attach records of unusual sizes to 8½″ x 11″ sheets for automatic feeding. A duplicate roll of film can be made for security purposes (storage may be in a location other than a records center).

The various forms in which microfilm may be used are roll film, a unit stored on an aperture card or cards with other identifying information keypunched on the card, strips of film and units mounted in transparent jackets, microfilm strip holders, and microfiche. The roll film should be used for records that will be referred to infrequently. When information is sought frequently, the roll film can be placed in magazines or cartridges which enable one to load a reader for viewing without touching the film. A 35-mm. microfilm (of such things as engineering drawings or parts of drawings) can be stored on a tab punch card. The keypunched card has identifying information concerning the drawing, and the drawing (approximately 1½″ x 2″) is attached to the card by a special machine. The punch cards are easily inserted into a reader where the film portion of the card is enlarged and then read. (Small microfilm readers are now standard desk equipment in some offices where this system is used continually. One only has to request a copy of a particular microfilm which will then be sent directly to the person requesting it for viewing.)

Microfilm strips can be stored in special plastic jackets having horizontal pockets to hold this kind of strip film. The film is inserted into the jacket by use of a special instrument that will pull out a micro unit and substitute an updated one for it. As many as 100 pages can be stored in one jacket. Jacketed microfilm is used for catalogs of parts, student records, medical records, or for similar records containing detailed information.

Strips of microfilm stored in narrow plastic holders are especially useful for retention of telephone numbers, credit ratings, rate tables, ZIP codes, and similar data. The strip holder is easily inserted into a reader for viewing.

Although the roll film is still the most commonly used form, microfiche is also widely popular for business uses. Microfiche—a set of microimages grouped together for efficient use or reference—is a duplicated copy of microfilm images. The microfiche is easily mailed to a customer (as to a distributor for updating pages of catalogs with parts and prices) or circulated throughout a company for the fast dissemination of much information. With the use of modern records processing equipment, the updating of microfiche is greatly simplified with resultant savings in time and money.

The range of reduction ratios currently available make microfilming especially helpful in reducing letters, drawings, maps, and other material to sizes that are convenient for storage. The reduction ratio is the difference between the size of the record and its size in microfilm. For instance, a record that is 17″ x 17″ may be reduced to an image measuring 1″ x 1″, with the reduction ratio thus being 17:1. Reduction ratios range from 5:1 up to 48:1 or higher.

Computer Output Microfilm The newest method of microfilming is called Computer Output Microfilm (COM), in which data stored in a computer are transferred directly to film instead of being printed out on paper by means of the impact-printing system. This method affords speedy information retrieval, considerable savings in computer time, easier information distribution via film instead of printouts, an elimination of paper-handling bottlenecks (such as collating, bursting, and binding), accurate copy, and a great saving of storage space.

For a time, the paper impact-printing (PIP) system was thought to be the ideal means of handling information until large volumes of printout paper began to accumulate in offices. In the PIP system, magnetic tape (on which the original records have been microfilmed) transmits images to a computer in computer language. Then from the computer, the information is printed, decollated, bursted, assembled, bound, and sent by volumes to offices or to archives for storage.

Now COM picks up the data from the magnetic tape and transfers it to the recorder by way of cathode-ray tubes which scan the data page by page. A camera records the pages onto microfilm at speeds of 15,000 to 20,000 pages per hour. (With the impact-printing methods, a speed of 1,000 pages per hour was considered very fast.) After recording is completed, the COM film is processed in the usual way and ends as roll film, microfiche, or aperture cards. At one stage in the process, if hard copies are needed, they can be provided. Extra copies of the microfiche can easily be duplicated at low cost.

When the COM system is compared with the impact-printing system, the difference in cost is so great that it would be unwise not to consider this system for processing information. If, however, a company does not feel that having this equipment is economical, especially if it will not be kept in use continually, service centers for various companies can be contracted to do specific COM film processing jobs. Information required in updating the output can be furnished to the centers each day and the updated material can be picked up the next day.

The administrative secretary should become acquainted with this aspect of records handling and should keep up-to-date on the technological advances which are making possible more efficient handling of records and are reducing costs.

11.9

TRANSFER AND DISPOSAL OF FILES

An active record is one which is referred to at least once a month. Other records are regarded as inactive and should be considered for transfer unless they must be kept in their present location for administrative or security reasons.

TRANSFER OF RECORDS

Records that are no longer useful in an office should be sent to central records or to an inactive storage area. A secretary or the records personnel are responsible for preparing such material for transfer. Transfer boxes, transfer forms, and instructions for labeling should be available from the inactive or central storage center. Transfer boxes are typically composed of paperboard and will accommodate either letter- or legal-size papers. Guides are not transferred since the folders which are transferred serve as the means for locating the material; also, guide support is not so necessary during transfer. Transfer forms indicate which records are scheduled to be moved, their codes, inclusive dates or series, and the length of time that the records are to be kept in the inactive area. The transfer boxes as well as the transfer forms should have labels and identification that conform to the requirements of the records administrator.

Regardless of whether the secretary takes an active part in the transfer and disposition of the files, she must surely be aware of various methods of transfer and the specific transfer process required by the records administrator. The secretary needs to know where every record in her office is, and if it is not accessible within 30 seconds, she must be able to report what has happened to it: Is it being used by someone in the office? Has it been transferred to the records center on a certain date with a specific location code? Was it transferred to the records center for a definite length of time for storage? Or, was it destroyed on a certain date?

Periodic transfer Transfer can be made at the end of a certain time (as at the end of six months or a year). This method is called the *periodic method of transfer.* Active material can be kept in the middle drawers of a cabinet, but the inactive material to be transferred can be kept in the bottom and top drawers which are the least accessible areas. Sometimes every other cabinet is reserved for inactive records. Even if inactive material is kept in separate cabinets, a difficulty in the use of the periodic transfer method may arise when the material is requested and it has to be retrieved from a place where it is not expected to be. And many times the material is transferred out of the office to the inactive area at the end of a designated period. Thus, this difficulty can become very pronounced.

Continuous transfer A more effective method of transfer is the *continuous transfer method.* The records personnel or the secretary sets aside time occasionally to look through the records and pull those that are ready for transfer. (They are already coded as described in section 11.4 of this chapter.) This method allows a continuous flow of inactive records out of the space that is active and provides space for new records, thereby precluding the need to purchase more filing equipment.

RETENTION SCHEDULES

The retention schedule is a printed form which lists all the company records and indicates the time periods for which they should be kept and provides instructions for their disposition and/or destruction. The retention schedule is made up by the records administrator and is approved by departmental managers, the company attorney, and a vice-president or someone else representing top management. Copies of the retention schedule should be in the hands of all persons involved in the handling of company information. The secretary should have a copy of this schedule and should be aware of all updates or changes that have been made in the schedule. Nonessential records can be destroyed shortly after being received and not be filed at all. On the other hand, records needed for 60/90 days, for a year, for two years, or for some other period of time will need to be retained for those periods and then destroyed. Other records might be kept in a particular department for certain time periods and then transferred to an inactive center to be kept for longer periods and then destroyed or microfilmed. And still other records might become a part of the five to ten percent which are kept permanently. Included in this small percentage are vital records—those records which are necessary in order for the company to conduct business from day to day. Examples of vital records—in addition to the legal records such as deeds, contracts, and articles of incorporation—are personnel lists, bank statements, accounts payable and accounts receivable records, daily balance sheets, and so on. Special care must be given to these records in case of fire or other disaster by sending copies of them to another location. Some companies have underground storage facilities or use commercial underground storage facilities.

RECORDS DISPOSAL

The retention schedule may also provide for disposal or destruction of records. Some records that are no longer valuable can be torn and discarded in a wastebasket; others may need to be boxed for shredding in the records center or in the inactive storage center; and still others might carry instructions for disposal by other means (as burial or chemical decomposition). *Records disposal* does not necessarily mean *destruction*. The retention schedule could also require that certain records be microfilmed and then stored in that form. The destruction of confidential or classified company records must be witnessed by the records administrator, and in some cases, a representative from top management. Forms must be made out and signatures obtained to indicate that these records were destroyed and that the proper approval for destruction was given beforehand.

Secretaries employed by companies having government contracts (and especially contracts with the Department of Defense) must be very careful when discarding shorthand or longhand notes taken in connection with classified documents. Carbon ink or film ribbons used on typewriters, carbon paper, and scratch paper that have been used in typing classified information must be totally destroyed in a manner that renders the information absolutely unusable and/or unreadable. The disposition of government classified documents or those which have been declassified but still need to be destroyed must be done by methods prescribed by the Department of Defense. The methods used may be similar to those employed when a firm's own confidential documents are destroyed, e.g., they may be burned, shredded, or chemically decomposed. The secretary should refer to the Department of Defense Manual No. 5200.1-R *Information Security Program Regulation* (obtainable from the Superintendent of Documents, U.S. Government Printing Office, Washington, D.C. 20402) for more detailed instructions on the handling of government classified and confidential documents.

12

CHAPTER TWELVE

OFFICE EQUIPMENT SYSTEMS: How to Make Them Work for You

CONTENTS

12.1

REPROGRAPHICS EQUIPMENT AND PROCESSES

INTRODUCTION

Today's society depends on paper-based communications. An estimated 15 trillion pieces of paper are presently in circulation in U.S. business offices, and another million new pages are added each minute of each working day. Not only the influx of original material but also the constantly increasing use of multiple copies of documents have fundamentally altered the business scene. The production and handling of this paper barrage is dependent on the ever-increasing technological evolution of office machines which goes on at an almost unbelievable pace. Every issue of the business magazines and newspapers bombards its readers with "the newest" and "the best" in office copiers. The term designating this field is *reprographics*: this includes all the processes, techniques, and equipment employed in the multiple copying or reproduction of documents in a graphic form—hence *repro* plus *graphics*.

Not only have technological advancements created considerable impact on offices, but they have also altered the responsibilities and duties of secretaries. The secretary's role has been expanded; now the secretary must understand the capabilities of each reprographic process, and must know how to operate commonly used copying equipment. Since the office function affects the profit-and-loss statement of a business, the secretary also needs to be aware of the costs of each copying process. Often a secretary selects the reprographics equipment for the office; therefore, it is vital that the secretary understand which process will provide the office with the best copy quality in minimum time and at minimum cost.

No single office reproduction method can be described as the best for handling all situations, and requirements of each particular situation will suggest the appropriate reprographic process. However, the selection of a reprographic process should be based principally on quality/quantity/budget requirements with consideration given to one or more of the following factors:

1. **Appearance of copy desired**
   If the copy will be distributed within an organization, generally a lower quality of reproduction is acceptable; however, if the copy is mailed to someone outside the business, a higher quality product is usually desired.
2. **Quantity needed**
   Most decisions involve the number of copies needed. If only a few copies are required, one process may be better than another. But if a large number of copies is needed, a process specifically applicable to large-volume reproduction requirements would probably be used.
3. **Cost**
   In general, the higher the quality of the copy, the higher the cost in materials and labor. However, some of these costs can be substantially lowered where a large output is usual.
4. **Time demands**
   If a copy is needed instantly with no setup time, this limitation will determine the reprographic method to be used.
5. **Additional considerations**
   Any unusual requirements will affect the method of reproduction, since standard equipment cannot always accommodate unusual jobs. Such additional factors might include unusual sizes of copy, special copy design, and the need for color reproduction.

These factors are seldom considered separately, but rather in various combinations, depending on the requirements of each job. Though the priority of the factors may be determined by the business organization, it is the secretary who often must determine the most appropriate method in each situation.

Reprographics encompasses five basic processes of duplication:

1. Carbon Process (conventional and film)
2. Fluid Process
3. Stencil Process
4. Printing Process
5. Photocopy Process

In addition, the five basic processes have been integrated in a variety of ways to serve additional needs. Each of the processes is described in the following paragraphs.

CARBON PROCESS

The carbon process can be effectively used to make from 2 to 15 copies of a document. Two types of carbon are available—conventional carbon paper and carbon film. Conventional carbon paper has long been a staple supply in offices. The selection of the grade and weight of conventional carbon paper depends on the number of copies that are required. The table below provides guidelines for the selection of conventional carbon paper.

Carbon Paper Recommendations for Typewriters

Electric Typewriters		**Manual Typewriters**	
Number of Copies	Weight Recommended	Number of Copies	Weight Recommended
1–5	Heavy (standard)	1–3	Heavy (standard)
6–8	Medium	4–5	Medium
8–10	Light	6–8	Light

The weight of carbon paper is often expressed as *heavy, medium,* or *light;* and the weight indicates the number of copies that can be successfully reproduced with one typing. A lighter-weight carbon paper should be used as the number of copies increases. Manufacturers usually suggest that conventional carbon paper can be used satisfactorily from five to eight times, but many secretaries stretch its reuse considerably.

Film carbon is a newer development that is gaining enthusiastic acceptance in the office. Film carbon is a tough polyester film coated with a plastic solvent. The increased durability of film carbon prevents tearing and eliminates wrinkling and curling. This strong but pliant carbon will produce up to 15 legible copies. Film carbon has the added advantage of not smearing or smudging hands or paper.

Additional factors affecting the suitability of carbon paper or carbon film include the weight of the original stationery and the second sheets, the sharpness of the typewriter typeface, the kind and condition of the typewriter platen, and the touch of the typist, particularly if a manual typewriter is being used.

An impression control device on electric typewriters regulates the pressure of the typeface striking the paper. This mechanism allows for a setting of one to ten, with the *one* setting being suitable for typing one or two copies and the *five* (or more) setting appropriate when the secretary is making many copies. Electric typewriters also have a carbon copy lever which interacts with the impression control regulator to ensure that multiple copy impressions are properly made.

Carbon pack A carbon pack contains the original, the carbon paper, and the copy sheets. Two methods can be used when assembling a carbon pack:

1. **Desk Assembly Method**

   a. Assemble the materials by placing the copy (sometimes called the *second sheet*) on top of your desk; then place one sheet of carbon paper on top with the carbon side down.

   b. Add another copy sheet and the carbon paper to the stack. (A copy sheet topped with a carbon sheet should be added for every extra copy needed.)

   c. Place the original sheet of letterhead or bond paper on the top of the pack.

   d. Pick the carbon pack up carefully and straighten the edges by tapping the pack gently on the desk.

   e. Turn the pack until the glossy carbon side of the carbon paper is facing you.

   f. In order to keep the carbon pack from slipping, insert the pack into the fold of an envelope or into the crease of a folded piece of paper before inserting it into the typewriter.

   g. Insert the pack and the envelope or the folded paper into the typewriter with a quick turn of the cylinder, roll it around, and then remove the envelope or the folded paper from the pack.

   h. Use the paper-release lever on the typewriter after you have partially inserted the carbon pack to avoid wrinkling the carbon pack and to allow you to straighten it.

2. **Machine Assembly Method**

   a. Assemble one sheet of letterhead or bond stationery in front of the required number of copy sheets and begin inserting them into the typewriter.

   b. Turn the cylinder to a point where all of the sheets are gripped securely by the feed rolls. (Approximately seven-eighths of the paper will not have entered the typewriter.)

   c. Then, flip all of the sheets except the last sheet of copy paper toward you over the top of the typewriter.

   d. Place one sheet of carbon paper (with the glossy carbon side facing you) between each of the sheets of paper. Lay each sheet back as the carbon sheet is added.

e. After all carbon sheets have been inserted, continue rolling the pack into the regular typing position.

f. Use the paper-release lever on the typewriter to avoid wrinkling the carbon pack and to allow you to straighten it.

Note: Previously assembled carbon sets may be purchased. These sets consist of a lightweight sheet of carbon paper attached to the top of a sheet of copy paper. These carbon sets may be stacked to make several copies at one typing. Although the cost of the preassembled carbon sets is somewhat higher than the do-it-yourself packs, many secretaries believe the savings in time more than compensate for the added cost.

After the typing is completed, the carbon pack can be removed from the typewriter by pulling the paper bail forward and using the paper-release lever. The carbon paper can be removed in one swift motion by giving the pack a quick downward shake. If the machine assembly method is used, the carbon extensions may be grasped and the carbon sheets pulled out all in one motion.

Correction of errors Quality typing demands careful correction of errors. Although some typists follow the practice of correcting an error on all copies of a document, a growing trend today is to correct the errors only on the original and on those copies being sent outside the business firm. An exception to this practice occurs when an error is made on a number or date, or when the error might cause the message to be misunderstood. In those cases, corrections should be made on all copies. Errors should be corrected on all copies of statistical/technical typing.

A hard, abrasive typing eraser works best when one is correcting errors on an original, and a soft pencil eraser is most effective when one is correcting carbon copies. Erasures will be neat if the typist (1) makes sure that the hands are clean before making an erasure (2) checks to see that the eraser is clean (one can clean it by rubbing it on a rough surface such as sandpaper or an emery board) (3) erases with the grain of the paper, and (4) erases each letter separately with a light, short stroke (5) camouflages the erased area by applying a white charcoal film or by using a special white charcoal pencil. Also, a good quality white liquid correction fluid can be used to cover up difficult corrections, punctuation marks, and others. Tinted liquid correction fluid is available to match colored shades of stationery, but should be ordered at the time the stationery order is placed. If an erasing shield is used, it should be placed in front of the carbon paper. When correcting subsequent copies, the typist should transfer the shield, making sure that it is placed in front of the carbon each time.

When errors are discovered after the carbon pack has been removed from the typewriter, the typist inserts each sheet into the machine individually to make the correction. If it is important to keep the shading similar, a small piece of carbon can be placed over the erased spot before the correction is typed on the copy.

The typist ought to use the typewriter alignment scale and the variable line spacer to align the typing when reinserting typewritten work into the machine for correction. A good practice is to check the positioning of the typewriter typeface in relation to the alignment scale by first typing a few words on a sheet of scratch paper.

Use of colored carbon paper Carbon paper is available in several colors. There may be occasions when one will want to highlight a word, a sentence, or a symbol in a second color. The typist inserts a small piece of colored carbon paper behind the typewriter ribbon (which affects the original) and additional pieces behind each sheet of carbon. The colored carbon pieces are removed as soon as the typist has completed typing the word(s) that are to be highlighted.

Disposal of carbon paper Carbon paper should be discarded as soon as it no longer makes good, clean copies. The life of carbon paper varies, and this feature should be evaluated before the paper is purchased. The secretary should check carbon copies after typing numbers to be sure that the numbers can be easily read. Wrinkled carbon paper should not be used, since any characters striking the wrinkled section will be distorted.

Storage of carbon paper Carbon paper should be stored in a flat folder with the carbon side down and away from heat. Used carbon paper should be put away as soon as possible to avoid the possibility of getting carbon marks on other papers, on clothing, or on the desk top.

Problem-solving tips for working with conventional (non-film) carbon paper The following table describes some of the more common problems encountered with conventional (non-film) carbon paper and suggests some ways these problems may be solved (note that the characteristics of film carbon differ markedly from those of conventional carbon; therefore, the table that follows does not apply to film carbon):

Problem-solving Tips—Carbon Process

Condition	Probable Cause(s)	Guideline(s)/Solution(s)
Curling	usually the result of a change in temperature or humidity	Store carbon paper face down in a flat folder away from extreme temperature or excessive moisture; purchase curl-free carbon paper.
Limited durability	possibly due to poor-quality carbon paper or a soft finish on the carbon paper, or excessive wear caused by the use of the high impression settings on the typewriter	Select carbon paper having a hard finish; alternate the carbon sheets within the carbon pack for more even wear.
Illegibility	often due to excessive use of carbon paper beyond the manufacturer's recommendations	Typewriter may need cleaning; discard worn carbon paper and replace it with unused sheets; determine whether the finish and weight of the carbon paper are suitable for the number of copies being typed.
Cutting	results when the typewriter's typeface is excessively sharp	Use a heavier weight of carbon paper; if lightweight bond paper is used for the original, insert a second sheet of bond between the original and the first carbon.
Slippage	may be caused by using copy sheets with a slick finish	Slip the carbon pack into the fold of an envelope before inserting it into the typewriter; when typing near the bottom of a page, insert an extra sheet of bond paper between the last copy and the cylinder.

Smudging	may be caused by careless handling of carbon copies; may be aggravated by using glossy copy paper	Use carbon paper having a hard finish; select copy paper that will absorb carbon.
Treeing	results from wrinkled carbon paper	When inserting or removing a carbon pack, use the paper-release lever. This procedure tends to smooth out potential wrinkles.
Offsetting image	usually caused by excessive pressure on the carbon pack	Adjust the impression control mechanism on the typewriter; use lightweight carbon paper and copy paper; discourage roller marks by moving the rollers to the edge of the paper.

Advantages and disadvantages of the carbon process Every reprographic process has superior features as well as limitations, and the carbon process is no exception. The following table describes some of the advantages and disadvantages most evident in this process:

Advantages
1. a relatively inexpensive method of producing copies
2. process can be used on a wide variety of papers relative to color, quality, and weight
3. all copies made at same time as original
4. entire process completed in one location; secretary does not have to leave work station
5. additional equipment not needed to make copies
6. file copies reproduced on lightweight paper, creating less bulk in files

Disadvantages
1. only a limited number of copies reproduced from one typing
2. time needed to make corrections on the original and all copies

Although reprographics is often associated with copier equipment, the secretary should recognize the suitability of the use of carbon paper or film in preparing a small number of copies. This process is often superior to any other for many office requirements.

FLUID PROCESS

Fluid duplicating is one of the older reprographic processes. Other well-known terms for this kind of duplication include *liquid, spirit,* and *direct-process.* (The newer thermal spirit masters are discussed on page 413.) The fluid process involves the interaction of five elements: the carbon sheet, the master sheet, the moistening fluid, the duplicating paper, and a duplicator machine. The material is typed directly onto the spirit master. After the carbon sheet is removed, the master sheet is placed on the outside of the machine cylinder (sometimes called the *drum*) with the carbon copy side up. The paper is then fed through the moistening unit and between the cylinder and impression roller. As each sheet of moistened paper makes contact with the master on the cylinder, the moistening fluid on the paper dissolves a thin layer of the carbon deposit from the master. The copy that appears on the sheet of paper is the result of this layer of carbon deposit.

The master unit The master unit consists of the original sheet of special glossy white paper (*master*) attached to a sheet of paper coated with a waxlike substance (*direct process/hectograph carbon*) which gives the appearance of carbon. Typewriting, handwriting, drawing, or printing on the face of the master causes this waxlike carbon to be transferred to the back of the master. A protective tissue slipsheet separates the master from the carbon sheet and must be removed before any impressions are made on the master. After the master sheet has been completed, the protective sheet should be replaced behind it to protect its content and to avoid unwanted carbon transfer that will stain other surfaces. Master units are available in the following range of sizes: 8½" × 11", 11" × 8½", 8½" × 14", 17" × 11", and 17" × 14". Special master units which provide printed guidelines to assist the typist in positioning the copy can be purchased for routine jobs.

Master units can be purchased in several colors, but purple is considered the standard color. Other available colors are red, green, blue, and black. These colors are often used to highlight words or pictures. Two or more colors can be used on the same master unit. Different colors can be obtained by inserting the color of carbon that has been selected behind the white glossy master, and then by typing, writing, or drawing the desired material. These colors will be reproduced on the final copy. Duplicating paper is available in white and also in a variety of colors; however, the most common colors are pink, green, blue, and yellow.

The fluid process is used primarily for work to be distributed within a business organization. This process tends to produce adequately legible, but not high-quality copy. Each master is capable of making about 300 legible copies. The fluid duplicating process is the most economical process for duplicating up to 300 copies.

Preparation of a typed spirit master The typeface on the typewriter must be clean. The ribbon should be left in the normal typing position. Then, the typist should experiment with several pressure settings to decide which one will result in the sharpest carbon image on the back of the master. Normally, the lowest pressure setting is the most effective; however, the highest pressure setting is better on some typewriters.

After removing the protective tissue sheet, the typist should insert the open end of the master unit into the typewriter to allow for easier correction of errors. The master unit is positioned in the same way that it is when one is typing on a regular sheet of bond paper. Allow a one-half-inch margin at the top of the master unit for clamping the master sheet onto the cylinder of the duplicator. Push the rollers on the paper bail to the side so they do not ride on the master. (If the platen is worn, a plastic backing sheet inserted under the master unit will produce a sharper copy.)

Preparation of artwork on a master A ball-point pen, a stylus, or a pencil with hard lead should be used to draw on a master unit. Use firm, even pressure and work on a flat, smooth surface. It may be helpful to fold the carbon sheet back and sketch the proposed drawing in pencil on the master in order to position the sketch. Then replace the carbon sheet behind the master sheet and trace over the sketch. When making a sketch, one may prefer to fold the master unit carbon back and then insert a sheet of regular typing carbon between the master and the design one wishes to copy. After the design has been traced, the typing carbon is removed, the master unit carbon is slipped back into place, and the design is recopied on the master.

A shading plate may be used to provide the characteristics of halftone work on a drawing. Shading plates are made of thin pieces of plastic on which a pattern has been etched. The shading plate should be placed beneath the master unit. Then the master is rubbed with a stylus wherever the shading pattern design is desired. Lettering guides and tracing sheets can also be used to achieve the desired appearance.

Correction of errors Errors can be corrected so that they are undetectable on final copies. For example, a scratcher or fiberglass brush eraser can be used to lightly scrape the carbon from the back of the master. However, care must be exercised to avoid damaging the surface of the master. Any remaining carbon crumbs should be removed by blowing or brushing them away.

Transparent tape, special correction tape, or strips of self-sticking labels can be used to block out a large area on the master. Press the tape over the material to be corrected, insert an unused strip of carbon over the tape and then redo the material. The master can be cut apart and taped back together—a feature that can be used to good advantage when the typist needs to add or delete any section of the master.

After an error in copy has been corrected on the master, place a new piece of carbon face-up under the spot where the error was removed. (Cut—do not tear—a small section from an unused corner of the master carbon since only a small piece of carbon is needed.) Type the correct letter and remove the extra piece of carbon. Check the back of the master to see that the correction is satisfactory. The correction on the front of the master will appear as a strikeover but will not affect the duplicated copies.

Reproduction of a master The following procedure should be followed in running a spirit master:

1. Prepare the duplicator. Check to make sure an adequate supply of fluid is in the machine. Turn on the fluid feeding mechanism. Place paper (felt side up) neatly on the feed tray. Adjust the paper guides for the width of paper being used. Check the receiving tray to confirm that the position is suitable to receive the length of paper being used.
2. Set the pressure control knob or lever. Almost all runs use a medium setting. If larger quantities are to be run, start with a light pressure setting and increase the pressure setting periodically. This procedure will allow a gradual wearing of the master so that all copies will be similar in shading.
3. Set the counter at zero before running the copies.
4. Open the master clamp lever; insert the master in the cylinder. Place the master with the carbon side up (reverse image). Close the master clamp. Avoid touching the carbon on the master.
5. Turn on the electric motor and activate the paper feeder mechanism. Run a few test copies to check copy quality; make any needed adjustments in the machine; complete the runoff of copies. (If a manual machine is used, turn the handle clockwise to run the copy.)
6. Remove the master by opening the clamp lever and lifting the master off the cylinder. Close the clamp lever. If the master will be used again, attach it to the protective tissue sheet; otherwise, fold the master with the carbon side inside and discard it.
7. It is very important to remember to turn the machine off. Set the pressure knob or lever on zero. Be sure to check to see that the clamp on the cylinder is also closed. Turn off the fluid feeding mechanism.
8. Clean up the work area. It is quite inconsiderate to leave the work area in a state of disarray for the next person who will use it.

Problem-solving tips for working with master units The table below shows the possible reasons for copying problems when one is using a fluid duplicator. Possible solutions to these problems are also provided.

Problem-solving Tips—Fluid Process

Condition	Probable Cause(s)	Guideline(s)/Solution(s)
Wrinkled master	result of not loading the master squarely into the clamp of the duplicator	Remove the master from the drum and reinsert it into the clamp while making sure it is clamped squarely; press the master down where it fits into the clamp; gently pull the edges of the master in the area of the wrinkle and put a piece of transparent tape on the front of the master. This procedure may require a second person to help.
Wrinkled copy	impression paper possibly not feeding properly, due to moisture absorption in humid conditions	Use paper from a different ream.
	corner separators may be binding	Adjust the corner separators to cover the feed edges of the paper.
	feed table possibly overloaded	Check to determine if too much paper was loaded on the feed table.
Offsetting image	impression roller may contain excessive deposits from the direct-process carbon caused by the absence of paper during machine operation	Clean any carbon deposits from the impression roller periodically (use duplicating fluid as a cleaning agent).
	dark shadows or roller marks may appear down the sides of the copy	Discourage roller marks by moving the rollers to the ends of the paper bail.
Streaked copy	can be caused by a lint-covered wick	Wipe any accumulated lint from the moistening roller and wick. Change the wick if necessary.
	duplicator possibly not level, resulting in uneven distribution of fluid	Check to see that the duplicator is level. Revolve the drum several times without the master to ensure that the wick is uniformly coated with fluid.
Typing appearing on tissue	protective tissue not removed from master unit before typing	Place the protective tissue instead of master onto the drum. Usually a limited number of copies can be run from this protective tissue sheet.

Advantages and disadvantages of the fluid process The following table shows some of the advantages and disadvantages of using the fluid process for duplicating materials.

Advantages

1. an inexpensive process, with each copy costing less than one cent
2. master usable on a variety of paper weights and colors
3. several colors usable simultaneously on a single copy
4. copies that can be made at a rate of over 100 a minute
5. equipment that is easy to use and that requires a minimum of training time

Disadvantages

1. a master must be prepared before any copies can be made
2. about 300 copies can be made from one master
3. copies not having a high-quality appearance when compared with more sophisticated copy work
4. copies not usually legible enough to be satisfactorily reproduced on a photocopying machine
5. carbon is messy and requires careful handling
6. black masters tend to reproduce in a dull, gray shade rather than in black

STENCIL PROCESS

One of the better-known reprographic processes involves the use of a stencil and is technically referred to as the *stencil process.* This method of duplication is more versatile than the carbon paper process or the fluid process because electronic stencil-cutting equipment that allows one to reproduce photographs is available. The stencil process relies on four elements: the stencil, the ink, the paper, and the stencil duplicator machine. The stencil is prepared and placed on the cylinder of the stencil duplicator over an ink pad. Ink flows from the inside of the cylinder onto the ink pad and through the openings in the stencil. As paper is fed between the cylinder and the impression roller, the roller causes the paper to touch the stencil. Simultaneously, the ink flows from the ink pad through the openings in the stencil and produces a copy on the paper.

Stencil selection Stencils are available to accommodate varying conditions relative to copies required, durability, guide markings, cushion coating, and preprinted designs. Because of the variety of stencils available, it is important that the intended use of a stencil be carefully considered. For instance, if 1,000 copies or less are required, an average-run stencil is suitable; however, if more than 1,000 copies are planned or if the stencil will be run at a later time, it is advisable to select a long-run stencil which can produce 5,000 or more satisfactory copies. If drawings are planned, the use of an artist stencil is more appropriate. Stencils are available in different colors, an option which can be helpful for color-coding certain kinds of jobs. For example, all sales invoices might be typed on green stencils while shipping notices might be typed on yellow stencils.

Special stencils Manufacturers offer a variety of special stencils designed for specific kinds of jobs. Some of the more important special stencils available are:

1. **Addressing stencil** This stencil provides 33 grid spaces in which names and addresses are to be typed. The stencil can be run off on regular paper or on sheets of gummed labels.
2. **Bulletin stencil** This stencil is helpful in typing bulletins or double-page forms that would normally require a typewriter with a long carriage. Guidelines are provided for cutting the stencil apart, typing the copy, and cementing the stencil together before running.

3. **Continuous stencil** This stencil has control holes punched along one or both sides and is used with automated data processing printout machines.
4. **Document stencil** This stencil is intended for use when typing oversized documents.
5. **Electronic stencil** This stencil is electronically produced and permits the reproduction of letterheads, office forms, and bulletin or memo headings with the use of an electronic scanner.
6. **Four-page folder stencil** This stencil provides printed guidelines to help the typist avoid copy-positioning errors.
7. **Handwriting stencil** This stencil is equipped with guides so that the secretary can keep the handwriting straight and well-spaced on it.
8. **Music stencil** This stencil provides precut music staffs.
9. **Newspaper stencil** This stencil is divided into two and three columns to aid the typist when typing copy for newspapers or newsletters.
10. **Outline map stencil** This stencil contains a precut geographical outline map. Outline map stencils are available for states and many countries. Locations and other data may then be typed or marked on the stencil.
11. **Thermal stencil** This stencil is cut by running an original copy with a stencil through a special thermal photocopier, thereby eliminating the need to type the stencil.

Stencil pack A stencil pack usually has four parts: (1) the stencil sheet, (2) the backing sheet, (3) the cushion sheet, and (4) the typing film (optional). The stencil sheet is made of a fine but tough fibrous tissue covered on both sides with a wax coating that will not allow ink to pass through the surface. This coating is pushed aside when the typewriter key or stylus strikes the stencil. The backing is the heavy, smooth sheet on which the stencil is mounted. The cushion sheet is placed between the stencil and the backing sheet. It supports the stencil, cushions the blow of the typeface, and makes the typed stencil easier to read. The typing film, considered an optional feature, is a thin sheet of plastic film lightly attached to the top of the stencil sheet. Use of the typing film sheet tends to make the copy more bold in appearance and minimizes the cutting out of letters on the stencil sheet.

Preparation of a stencil The following steps are involved in the correct typing of a stencil:

1. Place the ribbon control lever on the typewriter in the "white" or "stencil" position.
2. Clean the typewriter keys with a stiff brush. Certain liquid type cleaners may be used only on conventional typebars, but never on elements or fonts.
3. Push the paper bail rollers to the sides of the paper bail.
4. Insert the cushion sheet between the stencil sheet and the backing sheet (glossy side up, if the cushion sheet is coated).
5. Insert the stencil pack into the typewriter and straighten it, using the paper-release lever on the typewriter.
6. On manual typewriters, use a firm, even, staccato touch; on electric typewriters, adjust the pressure regulator (starting with lowest pressure setting).
7. Proofread the material after typing has been completed.

Correction of errors Errors can be corrected on a stencil by following these directions:

1. If you are using a coated (glossy) cushion sheet in the stencil pack, apply a thin coat of correction fluid to each character individually with a vertical, upward brushstroke.
2. If you are using a film-topped stencil, detach the film from the stencil and apply the correction fluid directly onto the stencil sheet.
3. If a tissue cushion sheet is being used, burnish (i.e., flatten out) the error first by rubbing it gently in a circular motion with the rounded end of a glass burnishing rod or a

paper clip. Then insert a pencil between the stencil sheet and the cushion sheet and apply the correction fluid; this creates an air pocket that will thoroughly seal off the error and will pave the way for a good correction.

4. Allow the correction fluid to dry and then type over the corrected error with a slightly lighter-than-normal touch.

Using stencil duplicating machines Though the kinds of stencil machines vary in minor details, their basic features are the same and the same procedures will ordinarily be followed with all machines. These procedures are given below:

1. Adjust the paper on the paper table. The left guide of the paper table should be set according to the scale indicated on the metal table, and the right guide should be moved in toward the paper stack until it lightly touches the right edge of the paper. Push the paper in until the corners are under the separators.
2. Raise the paper table to the correct height for the feed rollers.
3. Adjust the receiving tray to accommodate the size of paper being used.
4. To attach the stencil pack, move the right end clamps to release the right end of the protective cover on the ink pad. Then, open the left end clamp and remove the protective cover. Attach the stencil pack to the left end of the cylinder by hooking the stencil stub over the stencil hooks. Close the left clamp and remove the backing sheet by tearing it from the pack. Lay the stencil smoothly over the ink pad, ease out any wrinkles in the stencil, and attach the end of the stencil under the right cylinder clamps.
5. Release the brake, turn on the motor switch, raise the feed lever, and set the copy counter mechanism. Run the number of copies desired.
6. Turn off the copy counter mechanism and the motor switch.
7. When you have finished using the stencil duplicator, remove the stencil and cover the ink pad with a protective cover. Be sure that the ink cylinder is placed in the "Stop Here" position. This allows the ink to settle in the bottom of the cylinder and eliminates the possibility of the ink seeping through the ink pad.
8. Set the brake and clean up the work area.

If the position of the image on the paper is unacceptable, the stencil duplicator can be adjusted to correct the situation. When the copy image must be moved one-half inch or more horizontally from one side of the paper to the other, move the paper table guide rails and the paper supply in the same direction that the copy must be moved. The lateral adjustment knob can be used to make minor horizontal copy adjustments of less than one-half inch. Copy may be raised or lowered by using the vertical adjustment lever on the stencil duplicator. If the duplicated image is crooked, use the angular adjustment lever to correct this problem.

Color copies Multiple colors can be used with the stencil process. Either of the following two methods is acceptable when the addition of color is desired:

1. Use colored ink pads. It should be emphasized that this method is effective when used for short runs only, because the various colors of ink eventually overlap and blend. Cover the cylinder with a special wax-coated cover to prevent the black ink from flowing; attach a multicolor ink pad over the coated cover; outline the image area of the stencil with one or more colors of ink. Then, stretch the stencil over the ink pad to show where additional ink is needed. Pull the right edge of the stencil off the ink pad. Apply colored ink directly to the pad with a small brush. Paint on additional ink as needed. Fasten the loose end of the stencil and run off the copies.
2. Use colored ink cylinders for long runs. Some stencil duplicators allow the entire cylinder to be removed and replaced with another cylinder that is filled with a different color of ink. With this method, only the copy to be printed in any given color is cut in each stencil. Change the ink cylinder and the stencil after each run of copy until the desired result is obtained.

Drawing on a stencil An illuminated drawing board designed for stencil preparation is available to hold the stencil. The drawing to be traced should be placed on top of the drawing board. A flexible writing plate—a textured, translucent, plastic sheet—goes on top of the drawing. The backing sheet of the stencil pack is inserted through an opening at the top of the drawing board. The stencil is clipped to the frame of the drawing board. By using the light under the drawing board, one can easily trace a drawing onto the stencil. The proper drawing tools include an assortment of styli, plastic shading plates, and lettering guides.

Storage of stencils Stencils that will be used again should be stored individually in stencil folders (sometimes called *filing wrappers*) and ought to be kept in a cool, dry area. The stencil should be placed in the folder with the ink side up. The stencil must be carefully straightened to avoid wrinkling. Any excess ink on the stencil will be absorbed by closing the folder and firmly rubbing the outside of the folder. After five minutes, the folder should be opened and the stencil turned over to prevent it from sticking to the folder when it dries. Stencils may be cleaned with various special preparations or they may be washed (depending on the kind of ink used) so that handling and storage are facilitated (washed stencils may be hung on racks). The contents of each stencil folder should be identified for filing purposes. Simple techniques for doing so are these: (1) run the stencil folder through the stencil duplicator before removing the stencil for storage (2) remove the stencil and blot it on the stencil folder, thus reproducing a copy, or (3) tape one copy from the stencil duplication on the outside of the folder.

Stencil maker This piece of equipment will automatically transfer printed, typewritten, or pasted-up copy to an electronic stencil. The original and a blank electronic stencil are placed side-by-side on the cylinder of the stencil maker. When the machine is activated, the image of the original is transferred to the blank stencil.

Problem-solving tips for working with stencils The table on page 405 offers some solutions to the problems that are often encountered when one uses a stencil duplicator.

Advantages and disadvantages of the stencil process The following table lists some of the advantages and disadvantages of the stencil process.

Advantages

1. inexpensive process
2. stencil duplicator generally uncomplicated; operator can be easily trained
3. easy-to-type stencils; corrections easy to make
4. legible copies with excellent contrast between black ink and paper
5. stencils repeatedly usable on paper of different weights and colors
6. from 11 to 5,000 or more copies may be made from one stencil at a production rate of 7,500 to 12,000 copies an hour

Disadvantages

1. stencil must be prepared before copies can be made
2. color can be produced, but the process is time-consuming and untidy
3. machine operation somewhat difficult if operator is improperly trained
4. stencils may be cleaned for later runs, but doing so is a messy process

The stencil process is used primarily in small or medium-sized businesses. Considerable use of this process is also made by educational institutions, religious organizations, and social groups.

Problem-solving Tips—Stencil Process

Condition	Probable Cause(s)	Guideline(s)/Solution(s)
Visible corrections	excess keystroke pressure applied when correcting error	Type all corrections using normal keystroking pressure.
	error not completely covered with correction fluid	After correcting an error, see that all parts of the error have been covered with correction fluid.
	error typed over before correction fluid dried	Allow time for the correction fluid to dry properly.
Closed characters	dirty typewriter typeface	Clean the typewriter typeface.
Cut-out characters	excessively sharp typeface	Type on a typing film sheet placed on top of the stencil.
	keys struck too hard or machine impression lever set too high	Use a gentle stroke when typing; lower the impression setting.
Uneven quality	stroking possibly inconsistent or too light	Use a firm, even, staccato touch on a manual machine or adjust the pressure on an electric.
	strokes not printed clearly due to improper machine adjustments	Adjust the multiple copy control so that the stencil is held securely.
Setoff	newly-run sheets dropped into the receiving tray before the ink had dried on previous sheets—often caused by the use of a slow-drying ink	Check to see that the stencil duplicator is not overinked; use an ink that is quick-drying (oil-based inks are slower drying). Add a blank clean sheet or an inter-tray sheet as a separator between each printed sheet.
Poor signature(s)	signature(s) not cut deeply enough into the stencil	Write slowly with a uniform, heavy pressure on the stylus; use a rollpoint stylus; write the signature over a writing plate or on a hard surface.
Light spots	inadequate inking	Measure the ink supply in the cylinder for adequacy, adding ink if needed. Paint additional ink on the ink pad to ink especially dry areas on the pad, or change/agitate the ink pad.
	stencil duplicator not level	Place levelers under the stencil duplicator so that it is perfectly balanced.
	impression roller in poor condition	Replace the impression roller.
Copy in margins	typing extended beyond the guidelines on the stencil	Keep all the typing and drawings within the printed guidelines.

PRINTING PROCESS

The five basic printing methods are: (1) letterpress (2) gravure (3) engraving (4) screen, and (5) offset. Since the offset process is the one most often used in business offices, it is described here. The popularity of offset duplicating equipment has soared in the last few years. Probably this great popularity has been due to the availability of smaller, tabletop offset units. Tabletop offset machines are capable of producing quality copies, and they are relatively simple to operate. Some models are self-cleaning.

The fundamental parts of an offset duplicator are the master (or the *plate*) cylinder, the blanket cylinder, the impression cylinder, the ink fountain, and the water fountain. When the offset duplication process is begun, the master contacts the blanket cylinder leaving a mirror image. When paper passes between the blanket cylinder and the impression cylinder, the image is mirrored a second time and appears on the copy in correct, original form.

Classification of offset masters The offset duplicating master may be paper, plastic, or metal. Paper masters are less durable and are normally used for short runs (from 50 to 1,000 copies) while plastic masters are designed for producing as many as 25,000 copies. Metal masters are the most durable, and the same metal master may be used repeatedly over a period of several years to produce 50,000 and more copies. Masters are available in a variety of sizes and weights, mountings (as straight-edge, slotted, or pin), and come in rolls, individual sheets, and fan-fold pockets. Each of these is designed for specific applications.

Imaging offset masters Several methods can be used to transfer an image to a paper offset duplicating master:

1. **Direct image** The image is made on an offset master by writing, drawing, or typing directly on the offset master. Special tools containing an oil-based substance that will attract ink must be used. Special pencils, crayons, ball-point pens, and rubber stamps can be purchased for this purpose. Typewriter ribbons suitable for use in the offset process are carbon ribbons (paper, polyethylene, and Mylar) or fabric ribbons (cotton, nylon, and silk).
2. **Electrostatic** This method uses a copying feature available on many photocopying machines. The original copy is inserted into the machine and is projected onto a positive-charged photoconductive plate. This plate is passed through a toner solution and the emerging image is transferred, and then fused by the application of heat, onto a master. Many machines have the capability to produce paper and plastic masters, and several models of photocopying machines can also image metal masters. Masters can be made in seconds from any printed, typed, drawn, or bound original and will produce a minimum of 100 high-quality copies.
3. **Transfer** This method uses a photographic camera process without the use of a separate negative. An image from an original is projected onto a light-sensitive sheet by way of gelatin transfer and photo-transfer methods. This process images a master. Self-contained photocopy units can deliver several masters a minute using this method.
4. **Pre-sensitized** A photocopying machine is utilized in this process. An original and a special pre-coated master sheet are inserted into the machine. This master sheet has been pre-coated with a highly sensitive substance which is acted on by the photocopying machine and results in a master ready for use on an offset duplicator.

Two methods can be used to produce an image on a metal master:

1. **Pre-sensitized** A graphic camera is used to make a film negative of an original. This film negative is exposed to a concentrated light source and onto a metal master. These film negatives can be stored and used many times to make additional metal masters when needed. Metal masters produce very high-quality copies. Photographs

can be effectively reproduced through the capability of this method to reproduce halftones.

2. **Transfer** This method is basically the same as the one described for imaging paper and plastic masters. Photocopying machines can produce metal masters of the same size as the original, while a camera process can accommodate the enlargement or reduction of the original before imaging the metal master.

Typing paper offset masters Secretaries are directly involved in writing or typing on paper offset masters. A discussion concerning the correct procedures to follow when typing paper offset masters is included in this section. Paper offset masters must be handled with care. The following steps outline a satisfactory procedure in preparing typewritten offset masters:

1. Clean the typeface on your typewriter.
2. Check the typewriter fabric ribbon to make certain that it is suitable for typing on a paper offset master; certain kinds of film ribbon may be used in offset master preparation.
3. Push the paper bail rollers to the margin area of the master.
4. Type directly on the paper master with the same amount of pressure that is used in regular typing, but at a slightly slower pace. (A heavy touch tends to encourage the appearance of hollow characters on copies.)
5. The paper master should be handled with the utmost care. One's fingers should touch only the edges of the master to avoid smearing. Hand lotion containing lanolin or nail polish can produce smudge marks on copies. Also, paper offset masters should never be folded or creased.
6. If the paper master must be reinserted into the typewriter, slip a clean sheet of paper over the master to prevent it from being smudged by the feed rollers.
7. After typing the master, allow it to rest for a minimum of 30 minutes. This waiting period will provide time for the image to become fixed so that the master will produce a darker, sharper image when run on the offset duplicator.

Special offset pens, pencils, and crayons should be used when drawing, writing, or ruling on an offset master. When one is tracing a design on a paper master, offset carbon paper must be used. (The manufacturer of the offset duplicating equipment can provide the necessary information concerning the drawing tools needed for preparing various kinds of artwork on an offset master.)

Correction of errors on a paper offset master For best results, errors should be corrected with a special eraser designed for use on paper offset masters. Offset erasers are very soft and do not contain abrasives that will mar the surface of the master. (If absolutely necessary, any soft nonabrasive eraser may be substituted; however, this practice is not recommended.) A light, quick stroke should be used in erasing an error. The eraser should be cleaned after each stroke by rubbing it on a clean sheet of paper or on a piece of sandpaper. One should not erase too heavily since the carbon deposit is removed rather easily. A slightly visible ghost image may remain on the master, but this image will not be reproduced on the copies. Only the surface ink should be removed. Deep erasures will remove the surface coating on the paper master, and these spots will reproduce in black. Offset deletion fluid can be used to make a correction which covers a large area of the master. The secretary can then type over the erased area with the same pressure used originally. Only a single erasure can be made in any one spot.

Storage of offset masters Offset paper masters should be filed and stored in a plain paper folder and placed in a flat position. If more than one master is stored in a folder, each of the paper masters should be separated with a sheet of paper to prevent them from absorbing ink from each other. A cotton pad moistened with water can be used to remove any smudges left on the edges of a master before it is stored. If proper care is taken of paper offset masters, they can be rerun many times with excellent results. The same methods that have been suggested on page 404 for identifying the folders in which stencils are stored can be used in filing paper offset masters. Plastic and metal masters can be stored in paper folders in the same manner as paper masters; however, special cabinets are available in which these plates may be hung so that there is little danger of their touching each other.

Problem-solving tips for working with offset masters Some of the more common problems encountered in working with offset masters are identified in the following table.

Problem-solving Tips—Offset Process

Condition	Probable Cause(s)	Guideline(s)/Solution(s)
Black correction smudges	errors erased too deeply on offset master, thereby removing surface coating	Typist must prepare a new offset master.
	dirty eraser	Use fountain solution on the eraser to try to clean the master error area.
Fingerprints	improper handling of offset master	Only the edges of the offset master should be touched; avoid using hand lotion with lanolin before touching the offset master.
Roll marks	excess pressure from typewriter rollers	Push the paper bail rollers to the margin area of the offset master; if reinserting the master, place a sheet of paper over the master.
Light image	offset master run immediately after preparation	Allow the offset master to rest from 30 minutes to two hours to allow the image to set.
	typing strokes too light	Type the master using a slightly heavier pressure or install a new offset fabric ribbon.
Uneven drawing	uneven pressure used when making outlines	Make all drawings on a flat, hard surface; use a firm, even pressure when making lines; use the artwork tool that is appropriate for the desired effect.

Advantages and disadvantages of the offset process The following table lists the advantages and disadvantages of the offset process.

Advantages

1. high-quality printing closely resembling original
2. all copies of equal quality
3. copy reproducible on both sides of the paper

Disadvantages

1. equipment relatively expensive when compared with that used in fluid and stencil processes
2. more training required for operating personnel

4. printing can be in color
5. hourly production rate of 9,000 or more copies
6. only one metal master needed for more than 50,000 copies

3. equipment requires more maintenance than fluid and stencil process equipment
4. higher material costs than those used in fluid and stencil processes
5. more time needed both in preparing the machine for operation and in cleaning the machine after copies have been run off

Use of the offset printing process can result in excellent reproduction. If appearance is a primary requirement, offset duplication offers many advantages, particularly for business communications that will be distributed outside one's organization.

PHOTOCOPY PROCESS

The copying machine has rapidly become a necessity in the office. Copiers are now used in virtually all offices, large or small. These photocopying machines reproduce directly from original documents. No intermediate master is needed.

Copiers are usually classified in two ways. One classification is based on the chemical process by which the copier works; the second, which is used more frequently, concerns the type of paper used for making copies. The newest innovation in copying machines is the capability to produce copies in a variety of colors, including a range of seven colors. The major copier classifications are the *wet process* and the *dry process*. These are divided into a number of secondary processes. There are four basic wet processes and three dry processes. The wet processes are: (1) diazo (2) diffusion transfer (3) stabilization, and (4) dye transfer.

1. **Diazo process** uses a coated paper that is sensitive to light. After exposure to the original, the coated paper passes through a developing process which converts the coating into a duplicate of the original. Copies reproduced in this way are inexpensive. An added advantage is that oversize documents can be copied on diazo process equipment. This feature is often used for special applications such as copying engineering drawings. The equipment is rather complicated and generally requires considerable maintenance. Unfortunately, copies cannot be made from originals printed on both sides or from opaque paper.

2. **Diffusion transfer** is sometimes called a photo transfer. The original sheet and a negative sheet are rolled around a light source so that the light passes through the photo paper. The negative is then exposed by the reflection from the original. After exposure, the negative is placed with a sheet of positive sensitized paper and is developed. Both sheets emerge slightly dampened from the copier, and the negative sheet is peeled off and discarded. This process has the capacity to make very clear copies and can also reproduce colors. Although the equipment itself is relatively inexpensive, the per-copy cost tends to be expensive and the process is somewhat wasteful. Since the copies emerge from the machine in a damp condition, some drying time must elapse before the copies can be handled.

3. **Stabilization** exposes the original to a sheet coated with a silver-sensitive emulsion mixed with a developing agent. These sheets are then passed through a special solution which activates the developing agent and results in an emerging image. Next, the sheets are bathed in a stabilizing solution so as to set the image. This image is a reverse negative and produces a white-on-black copy. To obtain a more usable black-on-white copy, the reverse negative must be reinserted into the machine with a second coated sheet, and the entire process must be repeated a second time. The negatives can be filed and reused many times. The general complexity and increased costs associated with this photocopy process has diminished its use. The necessary repetition of steps as well as the time needed to dry the dampened copies is a disadvantage of the process.

4. **Dye transfer** uses an incandescent light source to expose a sensitized master (sometimes called a *matrix*) to the original. The master is developed in an activating solution and is then placed with a sheet of ordinary paper and passed through rollers. The rollers apply sufficient pressure to transfer the dye image from the master to the copy paper. This process requires that the two sheets be separated after they emerge from the machine. This process allows the copying of colors. Each master can reproduce about eight copies. Unfortunately, copies tend to be brownish in appearance. Copies are expensive unless several copies are made from each master: the more copies made from a master, the lower the cost per copy.

Dry photocopying processes are: (1) thermal (2) dual spectrum, and (3) electrostatic.

1. **Thermal** is a process by which an original and a heat-sensitive sheet are joined and exposed to an infrared light source. Because dark material absorbs more heat than light material does, this exposure images the dark outlines and produces a copy. Unfortunately, the copies made with this process have a tendency to become brittle as time passes.
2. **Dual spectrum** is a process in which a light-sensitive copy paper and a heat-sensitive copy paper are both needed to produce a copy. The original and the light-sensitive paper are exposed to a light source. Then, the original is removed and the light-sensitive copy paper and the heat-sensitive copy paper are placed together and are exposed to a source of heat. This step transfers the image to the heat-sensitive paper which becomes the final copy.
3. **Electrostatic** involves a *transfer* electrostatic process which is based on light reflecting an original through lenses and exposing a charged drum. The resulting particles of toner left on the drum become the image, which is then transferred and fused by heat onto the copy. A *direct* electrostatic process follows the same principles as the transfer electrostatic process except that the image appears directly on the copy paper and does not need to be transferred.

Photocopying machines are sometimes categorized as *coated-paper copiers* or *plain-paper copiers*, depending on the copy paper required for duplication. Earlier machines used coated papers, and although these photocopiers are still very prevalent, the present trend is definitely toward an increased use of plain-paper copying equipment. Some of the reasons given for the current popularity of plain-paper copiers include the following:

1. The appearance of the copies closely resembles the original, since the same grade and weight of paper is used in the duplication process.
2. Plain-paper copies can be produced on letterhead stationery.
3. The slightly higher per-copy cost of plain-paper copies is often considered to be justified, because of the higher quality copies that can be made. The appearance of plain-paper copies is especially suitable and desirable for documents that will be sent outside the company.
4. Photocopying equipment manufacturers continue to develop special peripheral equipment used with plain-paper copiers that can easily and quickly produce offset masters, transparencies, and two-sided copies; that can automatically sort and collate copies; and that can provide for the cassette-loading of paper. Other available features include: slitters, perforators, folders, staplers, stitchers, and binding devices. Often, these mechanisms can be operated independently of the copier.
5. The ease of operating a plain-paper copier is appealing to office employees.
6. Special supply requirements are kept to a minimum.

Though coated-paper copiers are used in many offices, the copies made with these machines do have some limitations: (1) coated-paper copies do not resemble or feel like bond stationery, (2) writing is difficult on coated-paper copies, and (3) equipment tends to be complex and requires special materials for its use. Efforts are being made by manufacturers of coated-paper copiers to overcome some of these disadvantages. Even though the present costs of plain-paper copies are higher than the coated-paper copies, predictions are that by 1980, six out of every seven copies made will be reproduced on plain paper. Another apparent trend is towards the use of hybrid copier/duplicators. These machines can automatically develop masters and run copies in one step.

Control of photocopying machines The total volume of copies produced on an individual copying machine depends on the size of the office, the type of material copied, the availability of the copier, and whether or not use of the machine is supervised. The duplicating costs associated with a copier can be astonishingly high. An abnormally large part of an organization's reprographics budget is often spent on photocopiers. When copiers are very convenient and easy to operate, their use is often diverted to activities unrelated to business. One director of a large corporation has estimated that over ten percent of the copies made on unattended copiers was for the personal use of the employees. Several plans have been devised to discourage the personal use of copying machines as well as the indiscriminate copying of business communications. The following copy control systems are in use today:

1. **Key control plan** A key must be inserted into the photocopying machine in order to make copies.
2. **Card control method** A small card (plastic or computer) must be placed into the photocopier before it will function properly and produce copies.
3. **Coin control method** A pay-as-you-go practice is followed by which the insertion of a coin is required in order to activate the machine.
4. **Supervisory control plan** One person is placed in charge of the copying machine(s), and all work to be copied must be submitted to this person before copying is allowed.
5. **Audit system** A machine-recorded tally is kept of all work being processed on the copier. An audit system can be used independently or in conjunction with any of the previously mentioned plans.

Problem-solving tips for working with copiers Although most copiers work quite satisfactorily, an occasional problem may arise during their operation. The table on page 412 lists a few problems associated with some photocopiers, offers possible causes of the trouble, and suggests a few solutions.

Advantages and disadvantages of the photocopying process The following table provides an overall view of some of the strengths and weaknesses often associated with using a photocopying process.

Advantages

1. copies easy to make
2. copies reproducible very quickly
3. machine that is easy to operate and requires little training
4. no master needed—only a legible original
5. quality on all copies remains the same throughout a run
6. pages from the firm's catalogs and from books (with copyright permission) can be copied on many machines

Disadvantages

1. higher costs per copy than with other duplicating processes
2. very attractive for copying material for personal use
3. tendency toward making too many unnecessary copies of material
4. rather slow functioning of some copiers

Problem-solving Tips—Photocopying Machines

Condition	Probable Cause(s)	Guideline(s)/Solution(s)
Feeding difficulties	dimensional stability and tolerance of the paper affected feeding—perhaps paper was too stiff	Use 20-pound paper for best results; lighter paper is more difficult to handle.
	moisture content in the paper too high	Check your packaging and storing facility—humidity must be controlled.
Paper curls	inadequate weight of paper being used	Read the instruction manual to determine whether the proper kind of copy paper is being used. If so, call the sales office of the firm selling the equipment for further advice.
Poor duplication	attempting to copy show-through originals	Use only opaque originals.
Machine malfunction	any one of many mechanical difficulties	Call the authorized service representative.

A chart entitled "Summary of Methods of Copying and Duplicating" that shows some of the characteristics of the various reprographic processes is presented on pages 414 and 415 of this chapter.

IN-HOUSE REPROGRAPHICS CENTERS

The immense popularity of photocopiers as well as many new developments in the reprographics field have resulted in the initiation of some changes in the reprographic approaches used by many companies. After studying the reprographic needs of their firms and the availability and the costs of various kinds of equipment, many managers have determined that economies could be effected by the formation of departments committed to copying and printing, rather than relying on the reproduction services of an outside firm. Those business firms with medium-volume or high-volume reproduction needs have discovered that they can often lower their reprographics budget to a substantial extent and yet continue to maintain a high level of service by following such practices as: (1) comparing available pricing plans of equipment and selecting the one that is most reasonable for the firm's operation (2) centralizing all duplication equipment in one area in order to more fully use the greater volume capacity and faster equipment available (3) switching from plain-paper copiers to the lower-cost coated-copy systems for all internal company documents (4) purchasing copying machines or leasing them from a third party not directly associated with the manufacturer, and (5) instituting a copy control system which encourages a chargeback policy to the user department. Experience indicates that greater savings have resulted from the installation of a copy control system than any other single procedure.

Advantages of an in-house copy center include: (1) the increased flexibility in scheduling production jobs (2) the convenient on-site availability of reprographics equipment (3) internal control over reprographics costs, and (4) a lower cost per copy through the controlled use of high-volume equipment and the observance of management supervision.

Reprographics departments have been organized in several ways to meet the needs of the companies. Some firms prefer to have one centralized reprographics center in which all duplication work is done. Other businesses employ one center for the principal reprographics workload but have installed satellite copy areas throughout the building(s) to provide fast service for lower-volume jobs. Such satellite copy areas may be attended or unattended by operators, depending on the extent of their use. Other companies prefer to continue employing the services of an outside firm for major high-volume work but install satellite copy centers easily accessible to the office personnel in the immediate vicinity of each center for lower volume work. Satellite installations have been popular for companies having buildings separated by considerable distances. The continued improvement in reprographics equipment, the availability of auxiliary machines, and the lowering of per-copy costs will eventually cause many companies to establish their own reprographics departments.

NEW DEVELOPMENTS IN REPROGRAPHICS

Technological developments cause frequent changes in reprographic techniques; even the best copying method for a particular office application may become obsolete or too expensive overnight. A few of the technological developments that in time will probably change or alter office copying procedures are described here.

Thermal spirit masters Photocopying machines that use the heat-transfer process can also be used to make thermal spirit masters. Of course, a special thermal spirit master pack is required, but these packs are not expensive. The original to be copied is inserted into the thermal carbon pack; then the pack is passed through the photocopying machine. This flexibility allows thermal spirit masters to be made of typewritten copy, letters, magazine articles, or handwritten copy. The master made by this process will produce from 40 to 50 legible copies.

Electronic stencil scanner This office machine can create a stencil that produces up to 10,000 copies. The electronic scanner copies any original copy including typewritten copy, line drawings, hand lettering, and photographic halftones. Simple scanners recognize all colors as black, but more expensive models can be set to ignore specific colors in the original copy. Although these devices may require as much as 12 minutes to make one stencil, the machine can be left unattended.

Thermal stencils The thermal photocopying process has also been incorporated into a special machine for making stencils. The machine requires a special, heat-sensitive stencil. This process can reproduce copy which is prepared in black ink. Photographic halftones cannot be reproduced. Care must be taken in order not to smudge the original copy, since this process reproduces all shades of any color as definite black impressions.

Facsimile copying Images of telegram-size messages have been transmitted between offices over teletype telephone lines for years. The recent application of laser technology has broadened the size and volume capabilities as well as the speed with which messages can be transmitted. Facsimile copiers are designed for use anywhere that a telephone and an electric outlet are available. One master at the source office can cause single or multiple copies to be transmitted to many other offices which may be geographically separated. Documents, charts, and pictures can be transmitted or received within two to six minutes. (See also Chapter 14, "Telecommunication Systems.")

Summary of Methods of Copying and Duplicating

Factors to Consider	Carbon Paper	Fluid Duplicating
COPY APPEARANCE One of the first points to consider is what you want your copies to look like. Some methods are limited to one-color reproduction only. Others permit you to use multicolors economically and/or reproduce pictures and illustrations.	single-color reproduction	multicolor reproduction
ECONOMICAL LENGTH OF RUN The copy ranges listed here do not represent the maximum length of run, but the most economical range for each method. There is usually a point where an economical length of run dictates the method used unless it is overruled by other considerations.	1 to 10 copies	11 to 300 copies
PAPER SIZE RANGE The size of the original to be copied or the size of the paper to be duplicated or printed will help determine the methods that you should use.	letter size legal size	11″ x 15″ maximum 3″ x 4″ minimum image: 11″ x 14″
COPY COST RANGE (8½″ x 11″) Cost per copy will vary with the method of master preparation, the types of supplies and paper used, and the length of the run. Because quantity purchasing can also affect costs, approximate copy cost ranges are shown.	1¢ and more	⅗¢ to 1¢ per copy
SPEED Speed is an important factor to consider because it is related to your investment in people and also to the urgency of the material to be duplicated. If it takes too long to get copies, costly minutes or hours can be lost.	copies made as original is typed	up to 120 copies/minute, or 7200 copies/hour
MASTERS The type of master will directly reflect on all of the above factors. Each process varies with the flexibility afforded by various methods of master generation.	none	*Direct Image* It is imaged by typing, writing, or drawing. Available in various colors: blue, black, red, and green; and in various lengths of run: long = 300+ copies, medium = 200+ copies, short = 100+ copies. *Thermal* With a faxable original copy, a short run spirit master can be created by a single pass through a thermal copier. Purple and black are available.

Stencil Duplicating	Offset Duplicating	Copier
multicolor reproduction	full-color reproduction	single-color reproduction or multicolor reproduction (up to 7 colors)
11 to 5000 or more copies	11 to 50,000 or more copies	1 to 10 copies
9″ x 15″ maximum 3″ x 5″ minimum image: 7⅝″ x 14″	11″ x 17″ maximum 3″ x 5″ minimum maximum image: tabletop 9½″ x 13″ console 10½″ x 16½″	up to 10″ x 15″
⅓¢ to 1⅖¢ per copy	⅓¢ to 1½¢ per copy	2¢ to 5¢ and more
fluid inks: up to 200 copies/minute, or 12000 copies/hour *paste inks*: up to 125 copies/minute, or 7500 copies/hour	up to 9000 copies/hour	first copy in 3 to 10 seconds; various ranges of output up to 8,000+/hour
Stencil It is imaged by any combination of typing, writing, or drawing. Various types are available for specific applications. It will produce thousands of copies. *Thermal Stencil* With a faxable original copy, a stencil can be created by a single pass through a thermal copier. It will produce thousands of copies. *Electronic Stencil* In a matter of minutes, a stencil can be produced from most originals including halftone photographs. It will produce thousands of copies.	*Direct image* It is imaged by any combination of typing, writing, or drawing. Lengths of run are from 50 to several thousand. *Electrostatic* It is imaged on an electrostatic copier. Copies are available in seconds. It will produce a minimum of 100 copies. *Metal Plate* With a photographic negative and concentrated light source, a metal plate is exposed and duplicated. Short run = 10,000 copies/side; long run = 25,000+ copies/side. *Camera/Processor* It is a photographic process using a separate negative. Self-contained units deliver several masters/minute. Length of run is in the thousands. All of the above masters will duplicate in any of hundreds of colors.	no master involved, as copying is not a transfer process unless teamed with offset duplicating; copy and masters are prepared from an original copy

Micrographic copies Many offices have used microfilm as a relatively inexpensive method of storing large files. This photoreduction process allows individual records to be retrieved, viewed, and copied. The term *micrographics* merely indicates a variety of microfilm record-storage processes. Photographs or architectural-engineering drawings are usually recorded on film that is larger than the kind used for standard letters. Each film exposure can be attached to a computer punch card for filing. An alternative is a plastic jacket that can contain one exposure or a strip of exposures. Modern computers can record their output on either microfilm or microfiche when a microform camera is attached directly to the computer. Computer Output Microfilm (COM) is gaining rapid acceptance because of its low storage cost coupled with its speed and the easy retrievability of the records it produces. Computer Output Microfilm stores pages of printed copy on rolls of film. Computer microfiche output stores pages of copy on sheets of film approximately 4″ x 6″ in size. While standard microfiche ratios store 100 or 220 exposures per film sheet, ultrafiche can store two to three times this number of exposures on the 4″ x 6″ film sheet. Each exposure on the fiche is a picture of an 8½″ x 11″ document. The stored information on fiche may be retrieved through the use of a microfiche reader. This reader is attached to some models of photocopying machines and printed copies may be made.

12.2

DATA PROCESSING WITH CALCULATORS

The term *data processing* covers much more than computers or punch cards. Many times our notion of data processing includes only computer programs, expensive equipment, and reports printed on special paper. The daily typewriting and routine arithmetic calculations performed in offices are also forms of data processing. This section describes the calculating machines used in typical offices to process data.

Most desk calculators perform only arithmetic operations; therefore, they are used for addition, subtraction, multiplication, or division problems. Other calculating machines may be quite complex: they perform arithmetic and logical operations, and they may have the ability to store and retrieve those data from machine-readable files. Although modern electronic data processing equipment may perform both arithmetic and logical operations, their arithmetic calculations utilize the same principles as their predecessors—the manual and electric adding machines.

ELECTRIC ADDING MACHINES

The electric adding machine is still available in some offices for basic arithmetic functions. However, this full-bank keyboard is becoming less popular than the newer 10-key model. The arithmetic function keys (the PLUS and the MINUS keys) are used as the data entry keys on the electric adding machine. The operator depresses the numeric keys that represent the number desired; that number is entered into the machine by next depressing either the plus (addition) or the minus (subtraction) keys. Multiplication on most electric adding machines is performed by depressing the addition key a repeated number of times. For example, to multiply the number 674 by 4, the operator would enter 674 and depress the addition key 4 times. Some electric adding machines require that a REPEAT key be held down while the addition key is depressed in order to perform multiplication. A paper tape is used on this machine. Each entry is shown on the tape. For example, with the depression of a TOTAL key, an accumulated total will print on paper tape. Usually, electric adding machines can perform only addition, subtraction, multiplication, and division.

ELECTRONIC CALCULATORS

Electronic calculators are much smaller and faster than electric adding machines; their operation is facilitated by a 10-key numeric keyboard. Electronic calculators perform all arithmetic functions rapidly as well as sequential operations, which are often stored in the calculator's memory. Some calculators print numbers and totals on paper tape, but other models display numbers and totals on a digital readout window.

Electronic printing calculators These printing calculators are useful for accounting purposes when complex addition or multiplication problems must be verified for accuracy. Electronic printing calculators have a 10-key numeric keyboard for entering the values *zero* through *nine;* numbers and totals are printed on a paper tape. Some models may have a display (digital readout) window as well. (Dual-feature electronic printing calculators have both paper tape and digital readout windows.) On the keyboard a separate key is available for each of the basic arithmetic functions: addition, subtraction, multiplication, and division.

Many electronic printing calculators have additional function keys that allow such operations as the automatic calculation of percentages or of square roots. A separate key may facilitate chain arithmetic operations, such as repeated multiplications with different multiplicands. An additional key will allow a constant value to be stored in the machine's memory in order that the same value can be used in different, separate calculations. Most of the machines provide for a total to be accumulated in the machine's memory and that total can be increased as a result of separate additional calculations.

Electronic display calculators The electronic display calculator is characterized by a digital readout window for displaying numbers and totals; there is no printing capability in this instance. Numbers are displayed as they are entered and totals are displayed as they are calculated. The keyboard is the typical 10-key numeric keyboard along with an assortment of function keys. The electronic display calculator is similar in most respects to the electronic printing calculator, except for the manner in which the data are displayed. The electronic printing calculator prints data on paper tape, while the electronic display model has only a digital readout window; however, some models offer both of these features. Since the electronic display calculator provides no audit tape or printed record of the numbers entered or the totals accumulated, the operator must verify these values by observing the display window. Although the lack of printed entries and totals may be a disadvantage, this model's purchase price is usually less than that of the electronic printing calculator.

There are few moving parts in this calculator; usually the result is fewer service calls and correspondingly lower maintenance costs. The relatively low cost of these machines often makes it more economical to discard a broken electronic display calculator rather than to have it repaired.

While the printing calculator usually draws its power from a standard electrical outlet, most display calculators are also equipped with a rechargeable battery.

PROGRAMMABLE ELECTRONIC CALCULATORS

A unique feature of the programmable electronic calculator is its ability to store a complex program in its memory. A programmable calculator can be directed by a series of instructions to perform sequential calculations automatically. The operator merely (1) feeds the instructions into the calculator (2) enters any values required, and (3) starts the calculation series. These instructions are often called a *program*. Programs may be recorded on strips of magnetic tape which are inserted into the calculator whenever the program is required. The use of a program relieves the operator of the responsibility for making several repeated calculations in the proper, logical sequence.

Calculator vendors usually have libraries containing several routines or programs commonly used in business. In fact, many times the library accompanies the calculator without any additional payment. Additional programs are available with the calculator for a small additional fee. Customized programs designed especially for a particular office operation may also be acquired from most vendors. A common arrangement provides for a specific number of customized programs to be delivered with the calculator, and additional programs to be prepared at a later date for a specific programming fee. Some business offices have staff members who are able to write programs for these calculators.

Programmable display calculators vary in size and sophistication. Hand-held programmable calculators feature the typical 10-key numeric keyboard with additional function keys. These calculators usually perform the common arithmetic functions as well as additional calculations such as sine, cosine, square root, and percentage. These functions may be used by depressing the proper function key.

There are larger programmable calculators that may be called *minicomputers*. The desktop minicomputer usually has a typewriter keyboard and an additional cluster of 10 numeric keys together with special function keys. The desktop model is approximately the size of an electric typewriter. Programs for this calculator are often stored on a cassette tape similar to those used on dictating and transcribing machines. Many programs may be stored on one cassette tape. Some calculator keyboards may have as many as 10 function keys which are applicable to specific office calculations. These function keys initiate stored programs that automatically perform the arithmetic calculations and sequential processing steps that are frequently used in business offices. One example of such a program is the calculation of a repeated number of specified chain discounts. Such a program is helpful when there are as many as five chain discounts applied to any purchase, and when each discount is different. A long series of discounts can be recorded as a program, and the entire program can be used by merely depressing one function key. Another example of a program initiated by a function key is the calculation of payroll values. The payroll program can be stored on a cassette tape, and the individual function keys are used to calculate overtime pay, withholding tax, and social security tax. In each case, the calculation of payroll deductions requires several arithmetic steps. The program is the collection of these arithmetic steps in the proper sequence. The steps may be executed by depressing the proper function keys.

A calculator that is classified as a minicomputer obviously requires more memory than a hand-held calculator. A programmable desktop calculator usually has about 4,000 positions of memory storage, and the memory can be expanded by adding additional units of 4,000 storage positions.

COMMON FEATURES OF ELECTRONIC CALCULATORS

All electronic calculators have 10 number keys representing the values 0-9. These keys are used to enter numbers into the calculator's memory. Calculators also have separate function keys for each of the arithmetic functions—addition, subtraction, multiplication, and division. Another feature common to all electronic calculators is a key that will cause the total to be displayed or printed. This key—a TOTAL key—may be labeled TOTAL, T, =, or *.

Electronic calculators have a memory for storing numbers. The memory is divided into three separate parts: (1) keyboard memory, (2) operating memory, and (3) storage memory. The keyboard memory (sometimes called a *keyboard register*) contains the number entered from the keyboard. The operating memory handles addition, subtraction, multiplication, and division. The storage memory retains data that may be recalled in the future. The following calculator keys may be depressed in order to make changes in numbers stored in these three memory registers:

CLEAR ENTRY **CE**	This key will erase any number entered into the machine (keyboard register) if the CE key is depressed before striking the arithmetic function key. The CLEAR ENTRY key is used to erase a number entered in error. A typical error occurs when the operator accidentally depresses the wrong numeric key.
CLEAR **C**	The CLEAR key erases the keyboard register and the operating register, but not the storage memory. However, when a calculator does not have a CLEAR ALL key, this key will erase all three sections of memory.
CLEAR ALL **CA**	This key will erase the keyboard register, the operating register, and the storage memory. The CLEAR ALL key should be depressed before beginning each new calculation in order to clear all previous totals and numbers from the calculator.
MEMORY PLUS **M+**	This key will cause the number entered on the keyboard to be added to whatever value is in the storage memory.
MEMORY MINUS **M−**	This key will cause the number entered on the keyboard to be subtracted from the contents of the storage memory.
MEMORY RECALL **MR**	This function recalls the value in the storage memory in order that the recalled value may be displayed or used in an arithmetic calculation. The use of this key does not change or erase the value in the storage memory.

The following function keys are more commonly found on electronic calculators. These keys execute complete calculations:

ROUND OFF **R/O**	This key will cause all calculated answers to be rounded off to a selected decimal position. Some calculators have a ROUND OFF switch that may be set to round off all calculations. Other calculators have a key that may be depressed to round off only the answer stored in the storage memory—this answer is the last value calculated or the value displayed on the screen.
CONSTANT **K**	The CONSTANT key permits the calculator to retain a value and to use that same value in separate arithmetic operations. This function is usually used for repeated multiplication or division. An example of the use of the CONSTANT key is the calculation of a chain of discounts, when each discount is identical (5% − 5% − 5%).
PERCENT %	The PERCENT key converts the number entered into a decimal value (expressed in hundredths—.00), and it multiplies the accumulated total by that decimal value. The resulting answer is expressed as a percentage.
PERCENT OF CHANGE % **CHG**	Although this key is not found on small calculators, large calculators often provide this automatic function. The procedure for using this function is: (1) enter the base number (2) depress the PERCENT OF CHANGE key, and (3) enter the second number. The calculator will automatically show the amount of change and the % of change between the base number and the second number.

VERIFICATION OF ARITHMETIC

Since it is so easy to depress an incorrect key when entering numbers, all arithmetic should be verified. Because electronic calculators without a printed output tape display only the number entered and the accumulated total, there is no record of separate entries so that the accumulated total can be verified.

Verification with output tape The paper output tape produced by electronic printing calculators lists each entry as well as the accumulated total. Many calculators will also print a sign representing the arithmetic function applied to each entry, such as a *plus* (+) sign representing addition and a *minus* (−) sign representing subtraction. Verification of a calculator's paper tape simply involves a comparison of each entry number on the paper tape with the number that the operator had intended to enter. When the number on the paper tape is correct, the operator can place a check mark next to that number. The check mark helps the operator return to the proper checking location if interrupted. When all numbers on the paper tape have been verified by this procedure, the operator can be confident that the accumulated total is correct.

Verification with a display screen Electronic display calculators do not produce a printed record of the numbers entered. A number entered is shown on the display screen only until the arithmetic function key is depressed; then, the accumulated total is displayed. The procedure for calculating and verifying totals on an electronic display calculator is listed below:

1. Clear the machine's total.
2. Enter all numbers together with the desired arithmetic functions.
3. Write the *final* accumulated total on a sheet of paper.
4. Repeat Steps 1 and 2 by entering all numbers a second time.
5. Compare the second *final* accumulated total with the total already written on the sheet of paper (Step 2).
6. If the two totals are identical, the total is correct. In case the two totals are not identical, the operator should repeat Steps 1, 2, and 3 until at least two (2) consecutive *final* totals are identical.

HAND POSITIONS FOR THE CALCULATOR KEYBOARD

Since an operator often has many numbers to enter into a calculator, the operating speed is important. Practice will help anyone develop the skill necessary for touch operation of the keyboard. Calculators, like typewriters, have a home row for the index, middle, and ring fingers. The home row keys are the 4, 5, and 6 keys. Normally, the 5 key contains a bump or depression to assist the touch operator in locating the home row. The third of the following four illustrations shows the proper fingers placed on the home row keys. The second illustration shows the thumb reaching the zero key. Each of the fingers moves independently from its home row position immediately up to reach the top row of keys, and immediately down to reach the bottom row of keys. For example, the index finger moves up to reach the 7 key; the middle finger moves up to reach the 8 key; and the ring finger moves up to reach the 9 key, as shown in the fourth illustration. The first illustration shows the proper finger positions for the 1, 2, and 3 keys. Practice in keying numbers into a calculator will develop touch operation similar to touch typing.

ROUNDING NUMBERS

Electronic calculators contain electronic circuits that calculate answers; these answers are retained in the calculator's memory. The memory of an electronic calculator is sometimes called a *register.* Most calculators are designed so that any

Fingering Techniques

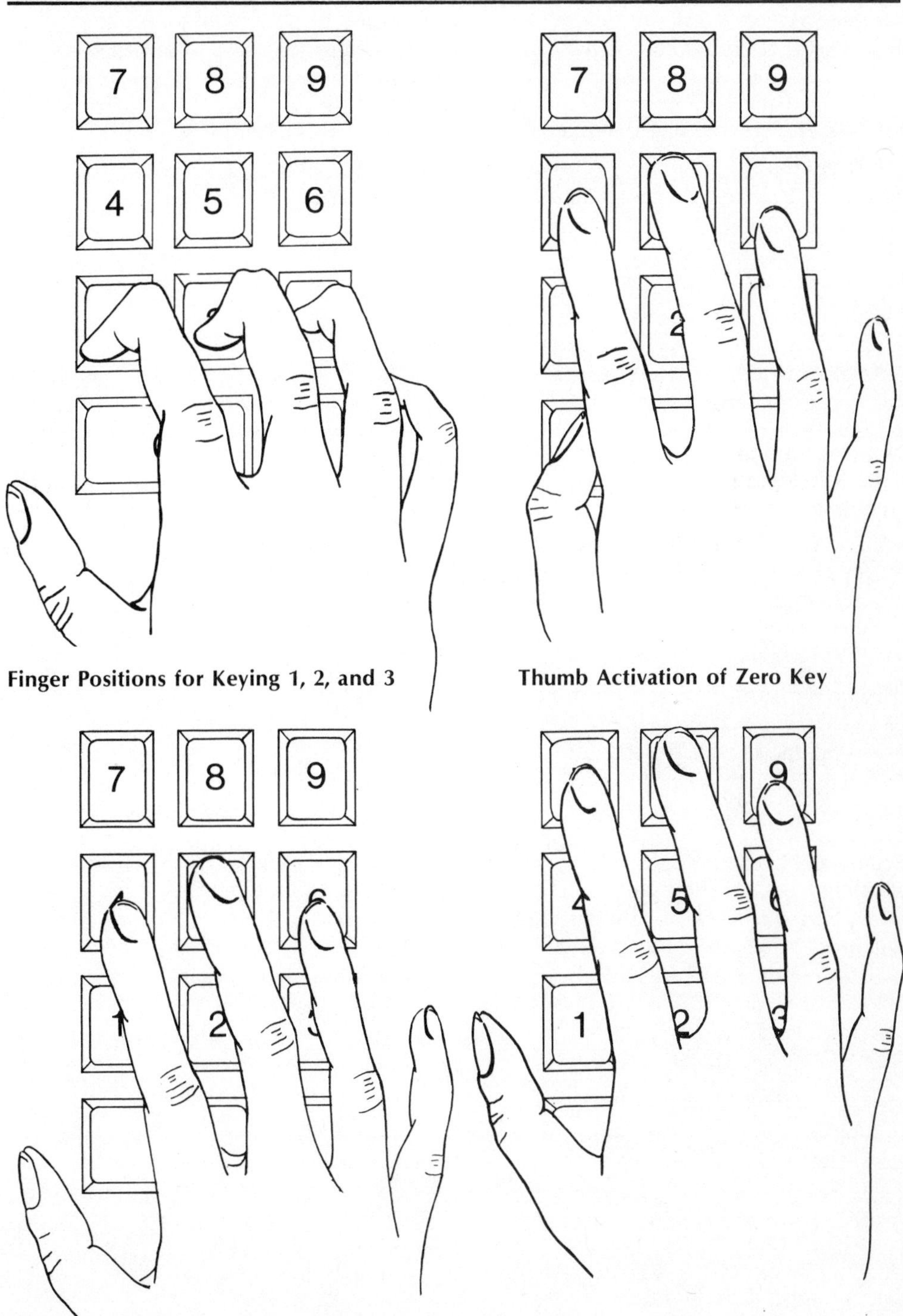

Finger Positions for Keying 1, 2, and 3

Thumb Activation of Zero Key

Proper Finger Position on Home Row Keys

Finger Positions for Keying 7, 8, and 9

calculated answer completely fills a memory register; therefore, a calculated answer may contain more numbers than are needed by the operator. For example, an 8-digit calculator will calculate answers containing 8 digits, regardless of the operator's need. Some calculators automatically suppress zeroes to the right of the desired answer, even though they are calculated and retained in the machine's memory. The following illustration shows the difference between an expected answer and the answer calculated and retained in the machine's memory.

Problem Multiply $2.42 by 11 (desired answer in dollars and cents)

Manual Calculation	**Machine Calculation (8-digit Machine)**	
2.42	2.42	enter
× 11	×	enter
2 42	11	enter
24 2	26.620000	machine register contents
26.62	26.62	right zeroes suppressed

While some calculators will automatically position the decimal point in the proper place, others depend on the operator to position the decimal point. The calculator in the example shown above retains an 8-digit answer in its register (26.620000) even though a 4-digit answer (26.62) is as accurate.

The operator is often required to *round* numbers to a desired length. Numbers that are to be rounded are calculated (or *carried*) two places beyond (to the right) of the rounding position. This rule is illustrated below:

When Rounding To	Number Desired	Carry To
Thousandths	.746	.74611
Hundredths	.57	.5724
Tenths	.6	.643

The procedure for rounding numbers is as follows:

1. Begin rounding with the right-most digit (this is called the *test digit*).
2. When the test digit is 5 or more, add 1 to the digit immediately to the left of the test digit.
3. Discard the test digit.
4. Repeat Steps 1, 2, and 3 until the number contains the digits required.

Problem Round 457.7561 to an accuracy of two places to the right of the decimal point (hundredths).

Solution			
	Step 1	457.7561	Test digit is 1.
	Step 2	1	is not equal to or more than 5.
	Step 3	457.756	Discard the test digit.
	Step 4	457.756	New test digit is 6.
	Step 5	6	is greater than 5.
	Step 6	457.76 (6)	Add 1 to the digit left of the test digit.
	Step 7	457.76	Discard the test digit.

Example Problem Round $756.4227 to the nearest cent.

Solution			
	Step 1	756.4227	Test digit is 7.
	Step 2	7	is more than 5.
	Step 3	756.423(7)	Add 1 to the digit left of the test digit.
	Step 4	756.423	Discard the test digit.
	Step 5	3	is the new test digit.
	Step 6	3	is not equal to or more than 5.
	Step 7	756.42	Discard the test digit.

CALCULATION OF PERCENTAGES

Business mathematics employs percentages rather than fractions in expressing relationships between numbers. A percentage is a fraction expressed in hundredths; for example, 1/2 is 50% or 50/100, which is written .50. A few commonly used business fractions with their decimal equivalents are shown in the table on page 426. It is common to use percentages and not fractions in business letters, business reports, and invoices. For example, invoices typically show a percentage of the total amount due as deductible for prompt payment. Examples of common business discount percentages with their decimal equivalents are shown in the table on page 426. This table also includes the *complement* of each decimal equivalent, since complements are sometimes used in calculating chain discounts. The use of complements in calculating chain discounts is explained on page 424.

Calculating a simple percentage The percentage relationship can be calculated by using the following formula:

Percentage Amount = Base Number × Percentage

Problem What is 12% of $647?

Solution ? = $647 × .12
$77.64 = $647 × .12
$77.64 is 12% of $647.

Calculating the percentage of change Sometimes two amounts are known, but it is important to know the percentage that represents the relationship between the two amounts. This relationship is the *change* or *difference* between one amount and the base amount. The following formula and examples may help illustrate this procedure:

Percentage of Change = Amount of Change ÷ Base Amount

Problem Profits last year were $5000; this year profits were $8500.
What is the percentage representing the increase?

Solution *Step 1* $3500 (Amount of Change) = $8500 − $5000 (Base Amount)
Step 2 Percentage = $3500 ÷ $5000
.70 (70%) = $3500 ÷ $5000
Profits increased by 70%

Problem Sales last month were $1500; this month sales were $950.
What is the percentage representing the decrease?

Solution *Step 1* $550 (Amount of Change) = $1500 (Base Amount) − $950
Step 2 Percentage = $550 ÷ $1500
.3666 (37%) = $550 ÷ $1500
Sales decreased by 37%

CALCULATING CHAIN DISCOUNTS

A *discount* is expressed as a percentage and it is deducted from the amount of an invoice. A *chain discount* is a series of discounts which are calculated separately. Each discount in the chain (series) is deducted from the remaining invoice amount so that each discount percentage is applied against a reduced value. The following example may help explain the procedure for calculating the net invoice amount after a chain of discounts has been deducted from the beginning invoice amount.

Net Invoice Amount = Invoice Amount − (Invoice Amount × Discount)

Problem Calculate the New Invoice Amount for a $1000 invoice with a
5% - 3% - 2% chain discount.

Solution *Step 1* Net Invoice Amount = \$1000 − (\$1000 × .05)
\$950 = \$1000 − \$50 * (5% discount)
Step 2 Net Invoice Amount = \$950 − (\$950 × .03)
\$921.50 = \$950 − \$28.50 * (3% discount)
Step 3 Net Invoice Amount = \$921.50 − (\$921.50 × .02)
\$903.07 = \$921.50 − 18.43 * (2% discount)
The Net Invoice Amount is \$903.07

*Notice how the amount of the discount is calculated by multiplying the next discount percentage in the chain by the remaining invoice amount. This procedure is repeated for each discount in the chain.

Calculating chain discounts with complements Some secretaries prefer to combine chain discounts into a single value that may be multiplied by the invoice amount to obtain the net invoice amount. A complement is useful in this procedure. A complement is calculated by subtracting the discount percentage from 1.00. For example, the complement of 5% is 95% (1.00 − .05 = .95), and the complement of .15 is .85 (1.00 − .15 = .85). The table on page 426 shows the complements of several common discount amounts.

Chain discounts may be combined by multiplying discounts by each other in order to obtain a single discount, and then by applying the single discount to the invoice amount. The following example illustrates the use of complements in combining chain discounts:

Problem An invoice for \$500.00 provides for chain discounts of 10% and 5%. Calculate the net invoice amount.

Solution Net Invoice = (Complement × Complement) × Invoice Amount
Step 1 The complement of .10 is .90; the complement of .05 is .95.
Step 2 Net Invoice Amount = (.90 × .95) × \$500.00
Step 3 Net Invoice Amount = .855 × \$500.00
Step 4 \$427.50 = .855 × \$500.00
The Net Invoice Amount is \$427.50

CALCULATING MERCHANDISE MARKUP

The basic calculation for retail sales firms is the application of a markup percentage to either the cost or the selling price of merchandise. These two methods of calculating markup are usually designated as: (1) calculating selling price with markup based on cost, and (2) calculating selling price with markup based on the selling price.

Markup based on cost This method of calculating the markup involves multiplying the cost of the merchandise by the markup percentage desired and then adding the calculated markup amount to the cost:

Selling Price = Cost + (Markup Percentage × Cost)

Problem When an article costs \$20 and the desired markup percentage is 40%, what is the selling price?

Solution *Step 1* Selling Price = \$20 + (.40 × \$20)
Step 2 Selling Price = \$20 + \$8
Step 3 \$28 = \$20 + \$8
The Selling Price is \$28

Markup based on selling price This method of calculating the markup is somewhat more complicated than using a markup based on cost. In this case it must be remembered that the selling price is 100% of the amount we wish to calculate. Therefore, the cost plus the markup must equal 100% or the selling price. For example, if the markup is to be 40% of the selling price, then the cost must be 60% of the selling price (selling price–100% = markup–40% plus cost–60%). The selling price is determined by dividing the cost by its percentage relationship to the selling price. (Selling Price = Cost ÷ .60). The following example illustrates this point.

Selling Price = Cost ÷ Cost's percentage of Selling Price
Markup = Selling Price − Cost

Problem When an article costs $30 and the desired markup is 20% of the selling price, what is the markup amount and what is the selling price?

Solution *Step 1* Selling Price (100%) = Cost (80%) + Markup (20%)

Step 2 Selling Price = Cost ÷ .80
Selling Price = $30 ÷ .80

Step 3 $37.50 = $30 ÷ .80

The Selling Price is $37.50

Step 4 Markup = Selling Price − Cost
Markup = $37.50 − $30
$7.50 = $37.50 − $30

The Markup is $7.50

The following steps may be followed in order to verify the calculation of the Markup.

Step 5 Markup = .20 × Selling Price
Markup = .20 × $37.50

Step 6 $7.50 = .20 × $37.50

The Markup is $7.50

ELECTRONIC DATA PROCESSING WITH COMPUTERS

Complex data processing procedures and problems are usually handled by computers. The technology for computers and electronic calculators is the same; however, there are several differences between computers and electronic calculators. Three of these differences are: (1) computers have larger memories than calculators (2) computers have the ability to make decisions and branch to alternative programs, and (3) computers have the ability to repeat operations a controlled number of times. Most modern offices use computers for some data processing. While specialists operate computers, the input data for computer programs is often prepared by secretaries and clerical employees. The preparation of accurate input data is very important, since the computer is not likely to detect errors in the input data until after a great deal of expensive processing has been completed. The most common computer input medium is the punch card. Data are transferred from source documents such as invoices and orders to the punch card.

The standard punch card has eighty columns and one character can be punched in each column. The computer input card is punched by a keypunch machine. This machine has a keyboard arranged like a typewriter's keyboard. The keypunch machine has only uppercase letters; therefore, the *Shift* key will cause numbers and special characters to be punched in the card. Although there is more than one manufacturer producing keypunch machines, all machines use a standard code for punching characters in the 80-column card. This code is known as the Hollerith Code, and it is shown in the illustration on page 427.

Table of Fractions with Decimal Equivalents

commonly used fractions	decimal equivalent	commonly used fractions	decimal equivalent
½	.5	1/9	.1111
		2/9	.2222
⅓	.3333	3/9	.3333
⅔	.6667	4/9	.4444
		5/9	.5556
¼	.25	6/9	.6667
¾	.75	7/9	.7778
		8/9	.8889
⅕	.2		
⅖	.4	1/12	.0833
⅗	.6	5/12	.4167
⅘	.8	7/12	.5833
		11/12	.9167
⅙	.1667		
⅚	.8333	1/16	.0625
		3/16	.1875
1/7	.1429	5/16	.3125
2/7	.2857	7/16	.4375
3/7	.4286	9/16	.5625
4/7	.5714	11/16	.6875
5/7	.7143	13/16	.8125
6/7	.8571	15/16	.9375
⅛	.125		
⅜	.375		
⅝	.625		
⅞	.875		

Table of Representative Decimal Equivalents With Complements

%	decimal equivalent	complement
.5 (½ of 1%)	.005	.995
1.0	.01	.99
2.0	.02	.98
2.5	.025	.975
3.0	.03	.97
4.0	.04	.96
5.0	.05	.95
7 ⅛		
7 ¼		
7 ½	.075	.925
7 ¾	.0775	.9225
10.0	.10	.90
12.0	.12	.88
12 ½	.125	.875
15.0	.15	.85
20.0	.20	.80
85.0	.85	.15
90.0	.90	.10

A Card Punched with the Hollerith Code

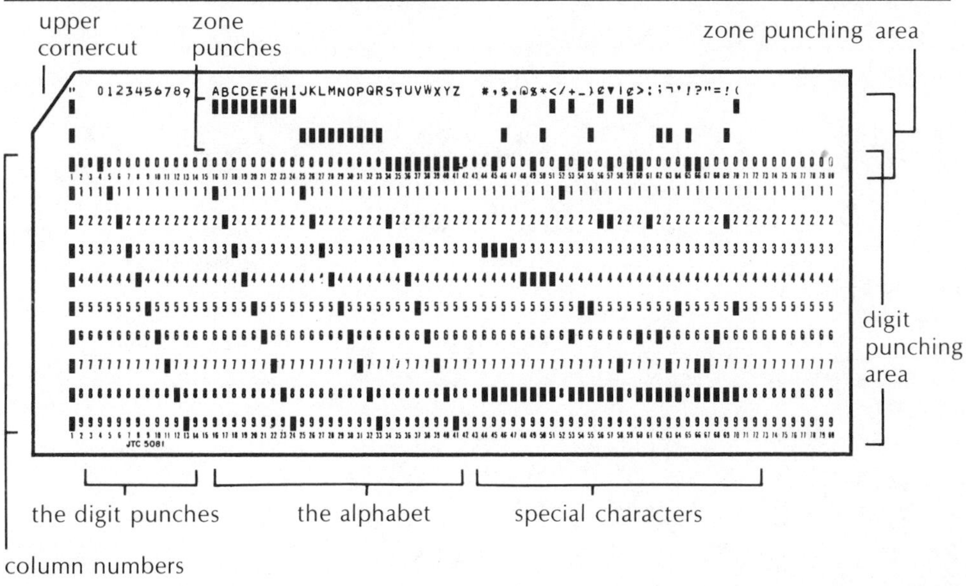

Two popular models of the keypunch machine are the Direct-punch machine and the Buffered machine. The difference between these two machines is in the punching of cards. The Buffered machine holds all characters entered into its memory until the operator activates the punching sequence. Then, all stored characters are punched into the card in a rapid sequence. In contrast, the Direct-punch machine punches each character in the card as that character's key is depressed by the operator. The Buffered machine allows the operator to correct any keystroke errors by merely backspacing and reentering the proper character.

CATHODE-RAY TUBE TERMINAL

With the advent of computers, an additional data input device is now a part of the modern office scene. This new device is a terminal connected to a computer through a telephone line. Although there are many styles of computer terminals, two types are common: the typewriter terminal, and the cathode-ray tube (CRT) terminal. The typewriter terminal is usually a teletype machine or a modified typewriter. The CRT looks like a TV screen with a typewriter keyboard. All computer terminals are operated like a typewriter. The CRT allows the operator to enter data directly into the computer without using punch cards. Since the computer may be shared by many offices with CRTs, it is economical to share computer programs that perform long, complex calculations. Accountants or statisticians may write computer programs that are used by office personnel. The CRT is a data entry device that allows a secretary to use a large powerful computer as easily as a calculator to solve complex statistical or accounting problems. The CRT operator does not really need to know how the calculations are performed; all that is needed is the ability to feed input data to the computer.

13

CHAPTER THIRTEEN

BASIC ACCOUNTING SYSTEMS FOR THE SECRETARY

CONTENTS

13.1

AUTOMATED ACCOUNTING AND SECRETARIAL APPLICATIONS

Though today's secretary may not maintain financial records for a firm, the means by which such records are produced must be understood. Large and moderate-sized companies use sophisticated equipment to process accounting information at great speeds and in unusually large quantities. The secretary who knows this equipment and what it can do is prepared to deal with the many reports, statements, and forms that are generated.

AUTOMATION AND DATA PROCESSING

The terms *automation* and *data processing* are used interchangeably here and involve the handling of business information with a minimum of human involvement. Once data have been prepared, they can be processed automatically to give management a variety of facts for speedy decision-making.

Extent of use A few examples will suffice to show the wide uses of data processing equipment: insurance companies review millions of policies overnight for appropriate billing and updating the next morning; payrolls for thousands of employees are prepared within a matter of hours; airlines know instantly the number of seats available on future flights and produce tickets on the spot; inventory, sales, and purchase records are maintained simultaneously, with built-in capacities for reordering required merchandise and for pinpointing slow-moving stock; banks process millions of checks daily with unheard-of accuracy.

Importance to the secretary With so much information available at such quick speeds, the secretary must decide when to use it for maximum executive efficiency. An acquaintance with new storage devices is essential for the immediate retrieval of vital facts. Conventional filing systems have been replaced by new ones containing tapes, cards, discs, and drums, while printouts of accounting reports require a knowledge of format and application.

ADP, IDP, EDP These terms are used to describe systems for the processing of information. ADP stands for *automated data processing* and involves the processing of data by automatically operated mechanical or electronic equipment. IDP means *integrated data processing,* a system in which equipment such as accounting machines and typewriters are provided with special attachments to produce punch cards and perforated tapes as by-products of the information processed. EDP is an abbreviation for *electronic data processing,* in which computers are used to handle information.

SOURCE DOCUMENTS

Regardless of the complexity of a data processing system, a basic record is required to start the accounting process. Such records are called *source documents,* examples of which are bills, time cards, checks, and notes. The information contained in source documents is put into a form that can be used by data processing equipment.

UNIT RECORD EQUIPMENT

Data can be processed by the use of punch cards on equipment that can sort, count, merge, select, match, duplicate, perform arithmetic operations, and print. As a group, the machines are called *unit record equipment* because each punch card contains information about one particular item, be it an employee's payroll data, a sale, or a purchase. The components of the system include:

Name of Machine	*Function*
Keypunch	to punch alphabetic and numeric information from source documents into punch cards
Verifier	to check the accuracy of cards already punched
Sorter	to sort, count, and select cards
Interpreter	to print on the punch cards information already punched onto the cards in the form of holes
Reproducer	to duplicate cards and to punch holes on cards containing graphite pencil marks (this is called *mark sensing*)
Collator	to match, select, and merge cards
Accounting Machine (Tabulator)	to add and subtract, and to print reports and documents

Unit record equipment is used to process data such as payrolls, inventories, sales, purchases, and commission payments; it is also utilized for a variety of other accounting functions.

COMPUTERS

The most advanced means of processing data is through the use of computers. These machines perform arithmetic and decision-making operations at tremendous speeds and with great accuracy. They provide executives with up-to-the-minute reports in easily read form.

Hardware A computer system consists of:

Component	*Function*
Input	to convert information from punch cards or punched paper tape into a form for computer processing
Control	to interpret instructions and to direct all computer operations
Storage	to retain instructions and data
Arithmetic	to add, subtract, multiply, divide, and compare; to select the sequence of processing operations
Output	to provide results of operations in the form of printed reports and documents or as data on punch cards, punched paper tape, magnetic tape, magnetic discs, and cathode-ray tubes

Software This term is used to describe the instructions that guide a computer. A *program* is a set of instructions, and the person who devises the instructions is known as a *programmer.*

Computer program languages Programs are written in a variety of ways, but computers must convert these forms into their own languages. Examples of program languages used by programmers are COBOL (Common Business Oriented Language) and FORTRAN (Formula Translation).

Magnetic Ink Character Recognition (MICR) The numbers and symbols at the bottom of a typical check are magnetic ink characters that enable computers to process checks at great speeds.

Applications Firms owning or renting computers process most of their business transactions on this equipment. Specific applications include customer and creditor control, insurance policy updating, car rental inventory maintenance, warehouse receiving and issuing, and stock market transactions. As a result of the wide applicability of computers in business, secretaries must be aware of their uses and potential.

AUTOMATION AS AN AID TO PROFESSIONALS

The ability of computers to retrieve information within very short time periods makes them valuable tools for attorneys, physicians, engineers, educators, and other professionals. Enormous quantities of information can be stored in miniature devices for ready access in printed form. This contrasts sharply with conventional filing systems which require much space and equipment and expensive clerical time.

SPECIAL EQUIPMENT

Adding, accounting, and calculating machines, as well as typewriters, can be provided with attachments to create tapes as by-products of their operations. A typewriter with this feature is called a Flexowriter. The tapes are used as input sources to computers. Teleprinters and teletypewriters are machines that operate over long distances to transmit written messages in the form of punched tape. They also reproduce messages in written form and generate as many copies as are desired.

SERVICE BUREAUS

Firms that do not have computers may contract with service bureaus to process their records. In many instances, this may be less expensive than owning or renting a computer. Service bureaus provide reports, statements, and documents promptly in whatever form is stipulated. Fees for this service depend primarily on operational complexity and quantity and are developed on a contractual basis. Medium- and small-sized firms frequently avail themselves of this service.

TIME-SHARING

Because computers can be very expensive, some firms purchase time from computer owners instead of possessing their own equipment. In other cases, a company may require computer time that its own overburdened computer cannot provide. Time-sharing is also desirable for the time seller because it provides income during periods when the computer is not being utilized.

IMPACT OF AUTOMATION ON THE SECRETARY'S POSITION

Though the secretary may not be versed in data processing techniques, involvement in data processing matters cannot be avoided. It may be necessary to deal with programmers, computer operators, data typists, computer operations supervisors, and systems analysts. The secretary should know how the firm's data processing department relates to other departments and should be familiar with computer printout forms and computer terminology. It is important, too, to understand how unit record equipment and special automated equipment fits into the firm's overall processing system.

13.2

BANKING FOR THE FIRM

Bank services include checking accounts, collection of notes, loans, money orders, and many others. Business activities are so intertwined with banking that the secretary must be aware of how these services are used by their firms. Secretaries in corporations and secretaries in moderate- to small-sized companies are often called on to perform such duties as writing checks, depositing funds, paying bills, and arranging travel finances.

CHECKING ACCOUNTS

A checking account is opened at a commercial bank upon deposit of funds and the completion of bank forms listing the bank's rules and regulations. A signature card must be completed containing the signature(s) of anyone empowered to sign checks for the firm. The depositor is known as the *drawer,* the bank is the *drawee,* and the company or individual to whom a check is made out is the *payee.* A check made out to CASH can be cashed by anyone in possession of it.

Deposit slip Funds deposited in the bank are accompanied by a deposit slip in duplicate containing the types and amounts of money being deposited. This money includes coins, bills, checks, and money orders. Interest coupons may be included, too. The duplicate is retained by the depositer.

The checkbook A company's checkbook usually contains three checks to a page, with prenumbered stubs attached by perforation to the prenumbered checks. Information about the check—date, payee, amount, and reason for the disbursement—is written on the stub prior to preparation of the check, thus assuring a permanent record of the payment. In larger companies, checks are printed by computers which store information about the checks internally for quick reference.

Writing checks Checks may be typed, printed, or written in ink. The signature should be written or printed in facsimile. Erasures and deletions are not permitted. If an error is made, the word VOID should be written on both the stub and the check. The symbols at the bottom of the check are printed in magnetic ink, and through the magnetic ink character recognition system, computers process large numbers of checks quickly and efficiently.

Voucher checks Checks may be printed with attached stubs that contain information about the checks. The stubs (vouchers) are used by the payees for recording and reference purposes.

Overdrafts Despite the best of intentions, or through an oversight, company checks may occasionally be written for sums greater than the amount on deposit. As a customer service, the bank may honor the overdrawn check(s) and ask the company to deposit sufficient funds to cover the checks. On the other hand, it may refuse to honor the checks. Since the latter action can cause great embarrassment to the company, overdrafts should be treated seriously, and good relations with the bank should be cultivated. Dishonored checks may be returned to a depositor with a bank notice indicating the reason for its return. The term NSF (Not Sufficient Funds) is usually written on the notice.

Stop payments Should a depositor want to stop payment on an issued check, the bank must be notified immediately. However, the bank cannot stop the check if it has already been cleared. Stop payments are usually requested on stolen or lost checks and on those that contain errors.

Checkwriters These machines write check amounts so that they are difficult to change. They also reduce the time it takes to write checks.

Check endorsements In order to negotiate a check, the payee must endorse it on its reverse side. When endorsed in *blank,* only the payee's name appears as the endorsement. This may be done by a payee who is a private individual, but it is a dangerous practice because the bearer of the endorsed check can cash it or negotiate it further. A *full* or *special* endorsement contains the name of the company or person to whom the check is being given, followed by the payee's signature. Only the new payee can negotiate the check further. A *restrictive* endorsement indicates the condition of endorsement and limits the negotiability of the check. The words *For Deposit Only* followed by the payee's signature mean that the check is to be deposited in the payee's bank account. It cannot be negotiated again.

Types of Endorsements

Blank Endorsement	Full Endorsement	Restrictive Endorsement
Barbara Dee	Pay to the order of George May Martin Lander	For Deposit Only Sue Foreman

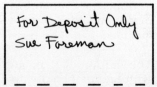

BANK STATEMENTS AND BANK RECONCILIATIONS

Depositors receive monthly statements from their banks which indicate the previous month's beginning balance, deposits made and checks paid during that month, other charges or additions, and the ending balance. Because it is likely that certain transactions have not been entered on both the bank's and the depositor's books by the last day of the month, their respective end-of-month balances will not coincide. A bank reconciliation statement must be prepared indicating the reasons for the disparity. The statement is prepared by the computer, an accountant, or a bookkeeper.

Canceled checks These are checks that have been paid by the bank and are returned in the envelope containing the bank statement. Banks are developing systems that eliminate the return of canceled checks, at no inconvenience to the depositor.

Outstanding checks If a depositer's check has not cleared the bank by the end of the previous month, it is considered outstanding.

Deposits-in-transit Depositors may enter receipt amounts in their records which do not reach the bank as deposits by the last day of the previous month and are therefore not included on the bank statement. Such deposits are said to be late or in transit.

Bank service charges Banks may charge depositors for services such as the collection of notes and stop payments. These charges are listed on the bank statements.

Bank memos Deductions and additions indicated on bank statements are sometimes explained in debit and credit memos sent along with the statement to the bank customer.

OTHER BANK SERVICES AND FEATURES

The secretary should be acquainted with the variety of services offered by banks. Such information is invaluable for use in assisting a busy executive.

Cashier's check A bank's customer who does not have a checking account may purchase a cashier's check from the bank by paying for the amount of the check plus a service charge. Also known as a *treasurer's check* or an *official check,* it is written by the bank on its own funds. The check is used in the same manner as an ordinary check.

Bank draft Similar in purpose to a cashier's check, a bank draft is a check written by a bank on funds it has in another bank. The customer pays for the amount of the draft plus a service charge.

Sight or time draft This instrument is used in instances where a seller is not certain of a buyer's credit rating. The seller gives the bank both the draft and a bill of lading, which has been prepared by a transportation company and specifies the nature of the merchandise sold. The buyer receives the bill of lading from the bank upon payment of the draft. The buyer then presents the bill of lading to the transportation company and receives the goods. The bank remits the payment to the seller. If the draft is due at the end of a certain time period, it is called a *time draft.* If it is due on sight, it is known as a *sight draft.*

Personal money order For customers requiring small sums, banks sell money orders similar to those sold by post offices. These bank money orders are negotiable and serve the same purpose as business or personal checks.

Certified check Should a payee require guaranteed payment, a bank will certify that a depositor's account contains sufficient funds to pay for the check. The amount is subtracted from the depositor's balance and the check is stamped "Certified."

Certificate of deposit Banks pay interest on short-term deposits (a minimum of 30 days) to customers who do not want cash to lie idle. The bank issues a promissory note to the depositor which can be negotiated to other parties or cashed at the end of the time period.

Short-term checking account A depositor can open a temporary checking account for a particular purpose. As soon as that purpose has been accomplished, the account is closed.

Bank discounting If a company wants to secure cash for a draft or note it is holding, it may do so by discounting the instrument at a bank. After deducting interest, the bank gives the company the proceeds and collects on the instrument at the specified time.

Foreign payments Firms doing business in foreign countries may send funds through banks in the form of cable money orders, bank drafts, and currency.

Safe-deposit box For a fee, a firm or an individual may rent a safe-deposit box from a bank for the storage of valuable papers and other items. The amount of the fee is charged according to the size of the box.

Transportation bill processing A firm can arrange for the bank to pay its freight bills by having transportation companies send the bills directly to the bank. The firm receives monthly statements from the bank showing the amounts paid.

Miscellaneous services Banks provide special payroll processing help, dividend collections, banking by mail, and a wide variety of investment services.

13.3

CASH TRANSACTION RECORDS

Accounting for cash is an extremely important part of a firm's financial recordkeeping system. Controls must be devised to protect receipts and to account for payments. Responsibilities for handling cash must be assigned to personnel in a way that minimizes the opportunities for theft and collusion.

CASH RECEIPTS AND PAYMENTS

Although specific procedures for the receipt and payment of cash depend on the nature of a company's business, there are fundamental rules to which most enterprises adhere. The rules are devised either by the accounting firm that audits the company's books or by the company's internal accounting department.

Types of cash Most people consider cash as being coins and currency only. From an accounting viewpoint, however, cash also includes checks, money orders, bank drafts, and bank deposits.

Accounting for cash receipts Firms that do business with consumers use cash registers for cash sales. Some registers are provided with paper tapes that record sales and sales tax information. Other registers are tied to computers to provide automatic cash totals, sales distributions as a by-product, and inventory updating. Cashiers should be trained to operate their registers properly and to make change correctly. Procedures must be devised for periodic daily collections of cash from the registers. Cash received by mail is usually in the form of checks or money orders. Occasionally, currency and coins are included. Personnel responsible for opening the mail prepare lists of the receipts which are used for making bank deposits and accounting entries. Whether cash is put into a register or received by mail, those who handle the cash should not make the accounting entries in the firm's books. This separation of functions is an effective means of minimizing the chances of collusion and fraud. Recording of cash receipts is made in a cash receipts journal, which may be a handwritten book, a form used on an accounting machine, or a magnetic tape on a computer.

Accounting for cash payments Except for very small amounts, payments are made by check. As with cash receipts, personnel responsible for authorizing payments should not sign checks. All checks should be supported by invoices or other documents explaining the disbursements. Recording of cash payments is made in a cash payments journal, also called a *cash disbursements journal* or a *check register.*

Cash short and over The busy activities involved in cash register transactions frequently cause cashiers to make errors in giving change. An end-of-day shortage as compared with the amount on the register's tape is considered an expense, while an overage is listed as income.

Cash basis vs. accrual basis of accounting Professionals and many small businesses maintain their accounting records on a cash basis. This involves recording expenses and income only when cash is paid or received. Larger firms use the accrual basis, which provides for charging expenses and listing income during the period in which they occur, regardless of when cash is paid or received.

PETTY CASH FUND

Since it is impractical to pay small expenses by check, firms maintain petty cash funds for that purpose. Items such as carfares, postage, and small quantities of office supplies are paid from the fund.

Starting a petty cash fund To start the fund, a check is written and cashed. The cash is kept in a locked office drawer or box and is maintained by the person (frequently the secretary) designated to disburse the funds. The amount of the fund depends on the size of the business and the frequency of small payments.

Petty cash receipt A disbursement from the fund is recorded on a petty cash receipt (written authorization) which indicates the date, receipt number, amount, and purpose of the expenditure. It also contains the signature of the person receiving the money. The receipts are kept in the petty cash box, so that at all times the total of cash and receipts equals the original amount. Where a bill has been received, it is attached to the petty cash receipt.

Petty Cash Receipt

PETTY CASH RECEIPT

Date June 3, 19-- No. 25
Paid to Lloyd Baron
Reason Car fare | 4 | 20 |
Account charged Travel Expenses Amount
Received payment:
Lloyd Baron

Replenishing the fund When the fund is low, a check is cashed to restore the fund to its starting amount. The petty cash receipts are given to the accounting department for entry in the financial records.

TRAVEL FUNDS

The secretary must be certain that sufficient funds are available to the executive on foreign or domestic trips. Advance preparations involve visits to banks and offices to secure cash substitutes (or foreign money denominations if the trip involves leaving the country) and documents.

Letter of credit This document is available from the firm's bank. It contains the name of the person who will be requesting the funds and the maximum amount that can be secured. This amount is deducted from the company's account with the bank. When the traveler needs funds in a foreign country, the letter of credit is presented to a designated bank and the amount received is listed on the document. A letter of credit usually involves a large amount of money.

Traveler's checks For smaller amounts, traveler's checks can be purchased at banks, Western Union, American Express, and some travel agencies. They come in denominations of \$10, \$20, \$50, and \$100 and cost \$1 for each \$100 purchased. The checks must be signed at the time of purchase by the person who will use them. The user's signature on the checks is required when they are cashed.

Express money orders These may be purchased by a secretary and either given or sent to the traveler, who is designated as the payee. As with regular checks, the traveler may either cash the money orders or transfer them to other parties.

Foreign currency Banks sell foreign money in \$10 packages which may be used by the traveler as starter funds upon arrival in a foreign country.

Expense record Since business expenses are deductible for income tax purposes, the traveler should maintain careful records. The firm's accounting department supplies the proper expense record forms and uses them upon the traveler's return to make appropriate entries in the books.

The voucher system Although all business organizations require controlled cash accounting systems, the opportunity for fraudulent practices is greater in larger firms. The voucher system, whereby all liabilities are listed as soon as they arise, is used extensively to eliminate the possibility of unauthorized payments. All checks are supported by vouchers, which are numbered forms containing details about the liabilities and subsequent expenditures.

13.4

PAYROLL PROCEDURES

All business organizations are required to conform to federal and state payroll laws and to maintain accurate payroll records. Federal and state tax forms must be filed showing employee names, amounts earned, and payroll deductions. Management too, requires information about payroll costs and taxes, while employees must be paid promptly. Since executives are often involved in payroll matters, secretaries must provide them quickly with pertinent data. A knowledge of payroll laws and procedures is, therefore, essential to the secretary.

TYPES OF COMPENSATION

An employee is one who works for a business firm and is subject to the company's directions and supervision. An employee is distinguished from an independent contractor who performs services for a company but is not directly under its control. Payroll laws relate to employees only.

Salary This term is generally used to describe compensation for administrative-level employees who are paid periodically, usually for a month or longer.

Wages Employees who work on an hourly or piecework basis are said to receive wages. Such employees may be skilled or unskilled. Many people use the terms *salary* and *wages* interchangeably.

Commissions Salespeople whose compensation is based wholly or in part on their sales totals receive commissions on those sales and are considered employees.

GROSS PAY AND NET PAY

The salary, wages, or commissions earned are called *gross pay.* For those on an hourly basis, gross pay is computed by multiplying hours worked by the hourly rate. For example, someone who makes $4 an hour and works 30 hours earns a gross pay of $120. If an employee works more than 40 hours during a week (overtime), the federal Fair Labor Standards Act requires that payment be made at the rate of time-and-a-half for all hours above the 40. The following case illustrates the computation of gross pay where overtime is involved.

Roz Benson earns $5 an hour and worked 42 hours during the week of February 8. The computation is as follows:

Hours Worked		×	*Rate of Pay*	=	*Gross Pay*
Total	40	×	5.00	=	200.00
Overtime	2	×	7.50	=	+15.00
					215.00

Net pay is another term for take-home pay and is determined by subtracting certain payroll deductions from gross pay. If Ms. Benson's deductions in the example above came to $50, her net pay would be $165.

Payroll deductions While some types of payroll deductions vary from company to company, there are some that are common to all business organizations. They are:

1. FICA—this term stands for Federal Insurance Contributions Act and is used more frequently by accountants and payroll departments than the term *so-*

cial security. The FICA rate is set by Congress and has been changed several times over the years. FICA deductions support the old-age, survivors, and disability insurance program (OASDI) and the medicare program. The actual deduction for an employee can be determined from FICA tax tables supplied by the government or purchased from stationers, or by multiplying gross pay by the current FICA rate. Each year, Congress sets a tax rate and the maximum amount of gross pay from which FICA taxes are to be deducted. The law also requires employers to match the taxes deducted from employees' pay by remitting a like amount.

2. FWT—this term stands for Federal Withholding Taxes. It refers to the income taxes which employers must withhold from their employees' salaries or wages as the money is earned. The withheld funds are sent to the federal government periodically. FWT is determined from tax tables that may be obtained at federal tax offices or from stationers. The FWT deduction is based upon the employee's gross pay for the payroll period and the number of exemptions (dependents) claimed. Some states have their own income tax programs and require employers to deduct these taxes from salaries and wages.

Other deductions may be made for union dues, U.S. Savings Bonds, health insurance, loans, pension funds, company stock purchase plans, and charitable contributions.

PAYROLL RECORDS

Some companies design their own payroll forms to conform to computer or accounting machine specifications. Other firms use standard records which can be purchased from stationery suppliers.

Time cards These cards are used to maintain records of employee arrival and departure times and as an indication of the amount of time spent by employees on specific work assignments. The data on the cards are the basis for the hours worked in a gross pay computation.

Payroll register Information is copied from the time cards onto a payroll register, which also includes employees' names, the number of exemptions claimed, pay rates, gross pay, taxable earnings for FICA and unemployment insurance computations, deductions, net pay, and check numbers. The register includes all employees who work during a payroll period.

Payroll Register

PAYROLL PERIOD January 8-14, 19--													
NAME				EARNINGS			TAXABLE EARNINGS		DEDUCTIONS				
	No. Exemp.	Hrly. Rate	Hours Wkd.	Reg.	Over-time	Total	FICA	Unemp. Ins.	FICA	FWT	Total	Net Pay	Chk. No.
Bart, Gwen	2	5.60	40	224.00	—	224.00	224.00	224.00	13.10	40.00	53.10	170.90	65
Evans, Sid	1	7.40	42	310.80	7.40	318.20	318.20	318.20	18.62	80.00	98.62	219.58	66
Murray, June	3	10.00	44	440.00	20.00	460.00	460.00	460.00	261.91	69.00	95.91	364.09	67
Sokol, Larry	2	4.00	36	144.00	—	144.00	144.00	144.00	8.42	24.00	32.42	111.58	68
				1118.80	27.40	1146.20	1146.20	1146.20	67.05	213.00	280.05	866.15	

Employee earnings record The federal Wages and Hours Law requires employers to maintain an individual record for each employee. The employee earnings record contains the employee's name, address, social security number, number of exemptions claimed, date of birth, marital status, rate of pay, hours worked, earnings, deductions, net pay, check numbers, and year-to-date earnings.

Employee Earnings Record

NAME Bart, Gwen
ADDRESS 14 Pawling Avenue
Troy, New York 12180
NO. OF EXEMPTIONS 2

SOCIAL SECURITY NO. 046 12 1930
DATE OF BIRTH June 5, 19--
MARITAL STATUS Married
HOURLY RATE $5.60

Line No.	Week Ended	Hours Wkd.	EARNINGS			DEDUCTIONS			Net Pay	Check No.	Year-to-date
			Reg.	Over-time	Total	FICA	FWT	Total			
1	1/7	41	229.60	2.80	232.40	13.60	41.00	54.60	177.80	22	232.40
2	1/14	40	224.00	—	224.00	13.10	40.00	53.10	170.90	65	456.40

TAX FORMS

Employers are required to file certain payroll tax forms at different times of the year. Information on the forms is derived from the payroll register.

Federal Tax Deposit (Form 501) This form is filed at a commercial bank along with funds withheld for FICA and FWT whenever these amounts plus the employer's FICA contributions amount to more than $200 during a month.

Employer's Quarterly Federal Tax Return (Form 941) Amounts remitted with Forms 501 plus amounts not yet remitted are summarized on Form 941, which is filed during the month following the payroll quarter. The form also contains employees' names, social security numbers, taxable FICA wages, and FWT and FICA taxes deducted.

Reconciliation of Income Tax Withheld and Transmittal of Wage and Tax Statements (Form W-3) Income taxes withheld and listed on Forms 941 are summarized on Form W-3. The form is accompanied by copies of W-2 forms for all employees.

Wage and Tax Statement (Form W-2) This statement is sent by employers to employees no later than January 31 and contains the previous year's gross pay, federal income taxes withheld, FICA taxes withheld, and total FICA wages paid. Where state income taxes are deducted, an additional copy is sent. The employee files a copy of the W-2 statement attached to the federal income tax form by April 15.

Employee's Withholding Exemption Certificate (Form W-4) This form is completed by the employee and filed with the employer at the time of employment. It lists the number of exemptions to which the employee is entitled and becomes the basis for the employer's use of FWT tables. A new form is filed when the employee's exemptions change.

EMPLOYERS' PAYROLL TAXES

As indicated earlier, employers match their employees' FICA deductions and pay these FICA taxes to the federal government. The Federal Unemployment Compensation Tax Act also requires employers to pay taxes on gross payrolls, with the tax based on an employee earnings maximum set by Congress. Unemployed people receive benefits from these tax funds. Employers pay premiums for Workmen's Compensation Insurance, too, which provides benefits for workers injured on their jobs.

Federal Unemployment Insurance Tax (FUTA) This tax is used for the administration of unemployment insurance programs. Except for a few states, only employers are required to pay the tax. The employer files an annual Federal Unemployment Tax Return (Form 940) by January 31 of the year following the taxable year and remits the tax with the form.

State Unemployment Insurance Tax (SUTA) The funds that are accumulated from this tax are used to pay unemployment insurance benefits. Merit-rating plans reduce the taxes for employers with stable payrolls. The form is filed quarterly and its contents vary with the state. Other data that are usually required on this form include: employees' names, social security numbers, taxable wages, and tax computation. As with federal unemployment insurance, most states tax the employer only.

Workmen's Compensation Insurance Qualifying employers pay an estimated premium for this insurance, which is adjusted upwards or downwards at the end of the year. The insurance rate depends on the type of work performed by the employees.

PAYROLL AIDE SYSTEMS

Secretaries should familiarize themselves with the different methods by which payrolls are processed. The payroll system that a particular company, organization, or institution uses is geared to the number of its employees and to the complexity of the payroll itself.

Computers Firms using computers process their payrolls in amazingly short times and receive printouts (and other media such as magnetic tape) of payroll registers, employee earnings records, employee checks, and payroll tax forms. The computers also maintain journals, ledgers, schedules, and other records that are essential to the firm's operations.

Service bureaus Some companies have their payrolls processed by private service bureaus which produce a variety of forms and documents. Input payroll data, of course, is provided by the companies.

Unit record equipment Payrolls are processed by some firms through the medium of the punch card. Though slower than computers, this equipment can generate most of the payroll items produced by computers.

Pegboard systems Payrolls can be so processed by hand that an employee's earnings record, payroll register line, and check are produced with one writing. The use of a pegboard aligns the three records so that, with carbon interleaves, the information appears simultaneously. Pegboard systems save a great deal of time and are also used to record cash, sales, and purchase transactions.

13.5

THE EMPLOYER'S TAX RECORDS

Every business organization pays taxes, but not all companies pay the same types of taxes. Taxes are imposed by all levels of government: federal, state, and local. Records must be maintained for information on which tax rates are based, and completed tax forms must be available for ready reference. Accounting journals, ledgers, business papers, and report forms are designed by accountants, office managers, forms design specialists, and systems analysts. Record books and other forms can also be secured from stationers and printers in preprinted bound or loose-leaf stylings.

THE FEDERAL INCOME TAX

While corporations and individuals pay federal income taxes and must file annual tax returns, proprietorships and partnerships do not. However, single owners and partners must report business profits on their personal income tax returns. In addition, partnerships are required to file informational returns annually. (Some states require corporations and individuals to pay state income taxes.)

Impact of decision-making on taxes Business decisions often affect a company's tax liability. For this reason, tax planning is an essential part of a firm's policies. Accountants, tax specialists, and attorneys provide advice to boards of directors, corporate officers, and proprietors on a fee or retainer basis.

Tax rates The United States Congress establishes tax rates for corporations and individuals. The rates increase as income increases. Because of this feature, the income tax is sometimes called a *progressive* tax. Dividends received by a stockholder are taxed on the stockholder's personal income tax return. This results in double taxation for the stockholder since the corporation of which he or she is an owner is also taxed. Of course, incorporation offers advantages which may offset this double taxation feature.

THE SALES TAX

Most states and many cities impose sales taxes on tangible personal property sold at retail as well as on services furnished at retail. Although this means that consumers are charged the tax, business concerns act as tax collectors by remitting the taxes collected to the government. This requires companies to maintain sales records that include sales tax collections. Depending upon the requirements of the particular state or city, sales tax reports are filed monthly or quarterly along with the remittances.

THE PROPERTY TAX

Local governments impose property taxes on businesses according to the latters' property (assessed) values. Once its budget needs for the year have been determined, the government establishes a tax rate. The assessed valuation for each business is then multiplied by the tax rate to arrive at its tax liability. Accurate records of business property holdings must be maintained to assure the establishment of fair assessed values.

THE SECRETARY'S DUTIES

Due to the confidential nature of tax returns, particularly income tax returns, the typing of these forms is frequently the private secretary's responsibility. Care must be taken to see that all figures are correct, that all required signatures have been affixed, that payments due are included, and that the forms are mailed on time. However, many tax returns are now prepared and printed by computers.

13.6

FINANCIAL STATEMENTS

Since businesses are organized on a profit basis, they must be able to evaluate their financial operations. They do this through the preparation and analysis of statements for varying time periods. The statements are prepared by accountants, but they may be used by a number of people in the firm for different purposes.

OFFICE BUDGETS

As a key employee, the secretary must be able to provide office cost data and may be asked to help in the preparation of the office budget.

Development Office cost elements include personnel, equipment, and supplies. With proper record maintenance and with an awareness of prior years' expenses, a budget can be developed to reflect the new year's plans. Though unexpected expense items will occur, an attempt should be made to anticipate needs. Contingency funds should be included to provide for the unexpected expenditures.

Operation Budgets are effective only if they are controlled through proper record keeping. If funds in one category are running low, it may be necessary to shift funds from another category to that one. Situations may arise where funds are eliminated because of cancellation of an expense category. Periodic statements of budget expenditures will enable the secretary to judge how well the office is adhering to budget allowances.

THE INCOME STATEMENT

A company determines its profits (and its losses, too) by means of a financial report called an *income statement.* Prepared by an accountant, the income statement provides management with information about its income and expenses. The income statement is also a key document for decision-making by stockholders, creditors, and lending institutions.

Time period Although the income statement can be prepared monthly, quarterly, or semiannually, a formal statement for income tax purposes and for the corporation's annual report is prepared at the end of the fiscal year. An income statement covers a specific period of time.

Components For a service business, two basic elements appear in the income statement: income and expenses. For a trading concern, an additional element is required: cost of goods sold. Manufacturing firms also include an element called cost of goods manufactured.

Format The statement on page 443 shows how the profit for 19-- was calculated for the law firm (a service business) of Bell and Bar. The heading contains information about the firm's name, the type of statement, and the time period. The expense section lists a variety of expenses normally incurred by a law firm. The last line indicates the amount of profit for the year.

Income Statement

BELL AND BAR
INCOME STATEMENT
FOR THE YEAR ENDED DECEMBER 31, 19--

Income from Services		$25,000.00
Expenses:		
Salary Expense	$15,000.00	
Rent Expense	2,400.00	
Office Supplies Used	1,600.00	
Utility Expense	500.00	
Process Service Expense	300.00	
Miscellaneous Expense	200.00	
Total Expenses		20,000.00
Net Profit		$ 5,000.00

The following illustration shows an income statement for a trading company. The heading is similar to that in the first statement. The cost of goods sold section shows the goods on hand on the first day of the year ($420,000), additional purchases of goods made during the year ($560,000), the total amount of goods available for sale during the year ($980,000), the goods on hand on the last day of the year ($260,000), and the cost of goods sold. The gross profit is the profit before deducting expenses. Except for the cost of goods sold section, this format is the same as the one shown in the previous illustration.

Income Statement for Trading Concern

HARROW-DALE CORPORATION
INCOME STATEMENT
FOR THE YEAR ENDED DECEMBER 31, 19--

Sales		$900,000.00
Cost of Goods Sold:		
Merchandise Inventory—1/1	$420,000.00	
Add: Purchases	560,000.00	
Goods Available for Sale	980,000.00	
Less: Merch. Inv.—12/31	260,000.00	
Cost of Goods Sold		720,000.00
Gross Profit on Sales		180,000.00
Operating Expenses:		
Salary Expense	$ 40,000.00	
Rent Expense	7,200.00	
Supplies Expense	6,400.00	
Advertising Expense	5,000.00	
Depreciation Expense	4,000.00	
Miscellaneous Expense	3,500.00	
Total Expenses		66,100.00
Net Profit [before tax]		$113,900.00

Analysis It is more valuable to analyze financial statements using percents than it is to use dollars. For example, it makes more sense to say (in the first income statement) that the net profit is 20% of the income ($5,000 ÷ $25,000) than that the net profit is $5,000 of the $25,000 income. It is also easier to compare net profits of different years by using percents. Similarly, we can make better judgments about expense trends by comparing them in terms of percents.

Tax impact Since corporations pay income taxes on net profits, they constantly analyze their expenses in order to minimize their tax liability. Stockholders receive dividends from net profits and must report the dividends on their personal income tax returns.

THE BALANCE SHEET

This statement shows the financial condition of a business at a particular time. Accountants prepare balance sheets to enable management and stockholders to assess the financial health of their business. Balance sheets are also of interest to creditors and tax agencies.

Components Three basic elements appear on a balance sheet:

1. Assets—items owned by a business
2. Liabilities—amounts owed by a business
3. Equity—the value of the business: it is the difference between the assets and the liabilities.

Format The statement in the following illustration shows how the components of a balance sheet are presented for convenient reading by those who may not understand accounting. The assets appear on the left-hand side. The liabilities and stockholders' equity are listed on the right-hand side and represent claims by creditors and stockholders on the firm's assets. The asset "Cash" includes money, checks, and money orders. The asset "Accounts Receivable" shows how much the company's customers owe. The liability "Accounts Payable" shows how much the firm owes its creditors.

Analysis Accountants use ratios to provide management with useful information. For example, the assets cash, accounts receivable, merchandise, and office supplies—totaling $32,000—would be compared with the $8,000 of accounts payable to indicate how well the company is able to meet its current debts. The current ratio of ($32,000 : $8,000) shows that $4 could be available quickly to pay each $1 of current debt. Other ratios enable management to project future activities.

Balance Sheet

DEVON COMPANY
BALANCE SHEET
DECEMBER 31, 19--

Assets		*Liabilities*	
Cash	$ 4,000.00	Accounts Payable	$ 8,000.00
Accounts Receivable	8,000.00		
Merchandise	19,000.00	*Equity*	
Office Supplies	1,000.00		
		James Devon, Capital	24,000.00
Total Assets	$32,000.00	Total Liabilities and Capital	$32,000.00

Statement of account to a customer This statement is sent by a company to its customers monthly and indicates the transactions for the month. The next illustration shows that the Ace Products Company (the customer) owed $1500 on June 1, that it paid that balance on June 11, that it purchased additional amounts of $200 and $300 on June 15 and June 28, and that its closing balance was $500.

Statement of Account

STATEMENT

Devon Company
181 Main Street
Statesville, ZZ 45678

To: Ace Products Co.
758 Third Avenue
Jonesville, ST 56789

Date	Explanation	Charges	Credits	Balance
June 1			Opening Bal.	1500.00
11	Cash		1500.00	00.00
15	Sale	200.00		200.00
28	Sale	300.00		500.00

13.7

CORPORATIONS AND SECURITIES

A profit corporation is organized under a charter issued by a state. Although stockholders are the corporation's owners, business policies and decisions are made by a stockholder-elected board of directors. The following illustration contains a typical corporate table of organization.

Corporate Table of Organization

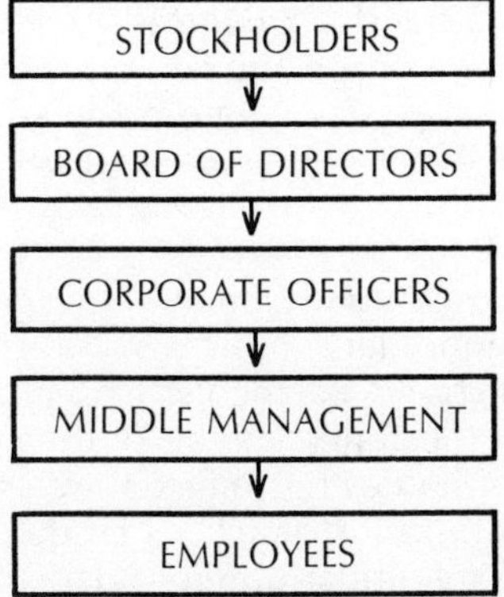

Decisions made by the board of directors are recorded in a minutes book, and accountants rely on these minutes for making entries in the financial records.

STOCKHOLDERS' RIGHTS

Depending on the class of stock owned, a stockholder may posses the following rights:

1. To vote
2. To share in the distribution of earnings
3. To purchase shares of new stock issues so that the same fractional ownership will be maintained (preemptive right)
4. To share in the distribution of assets if the corporation goes out of business.

CAPITAL STOCK

Corporations sell stock to secure operating funds. Ownership of stock is represented by stock certificates, each certificate representing a number of shares owned. An updated record of stockholders' names and number of shares owned is maintained in a stockholders' ledger.

Common stock This class of stock often carries all the four rights mentioned previously. Since voting rights are regularly provided, those who own a sufficient number of common shares can control the corporation. It is also the class of stock that rises or falls in price most rapidly.

Preferred stock This class of stock receives dividends (distributions) from earnings before common stock does. In the event a corporation is liquidated (goes out of business), it is also entitled to a share of the assets before common stock. However, a preferred stockholder does not usually have the right to vote.

Dividends These are distributions to stockholders of corporate profits, usually on a quarterly or annual basis. Dividends may be given in the form of cash or additional stock. Only the board of directors has the right to declare dividends.

Market prices of stock Stock is bought and sold through stockbrokers on stock exchanges. Stock prices are affected by such things as corporate earnings, the condition of the nation's economy, government policies, world problems, and other factors. People and institutions trade stock in the hopes of making profits and also in order to receive dividends.

BONDS

Corporations may secure additional funds by issuing bonds. A *bond* is a written promise by a corporation to repay a loan to a creditor at a specific rate of interest at certain time intervals. Most corporate bond interest payments are made semiannually. Bonds are long-term obligations, e.g., for 10, 20, 30 years, and sell in minimum denominations of $1000.

Types of bonds Secured bonds, such as collateral trust bonds, chattel mortgage bonds, and real estate mortgage bonds, provide bondholders with claims on specific corporate property in the event of default on bond payments. Unsecured bonds are called *debenture bonds* and are based on the general credit of the corporation. Registered bonds provide for bondholders' names to be listed with the corporation, whereas coupon (bearer) bonds do not. Bonds which come due at one time are called *term bonds,* while those which mature at different dates are known as *serial bonds.* Callable bonds give the corporation the right to redeem the bonds before maturity, and convertible bonds allow bondholders to exchange their bonds for corporate stock.

Bond interest rates The interest rate printed on the bond certificate is called the *contract,* the *nominal,* or the *coupon rate.* The actual rate at which a bond is sold is known as the *market* or the *effective rate.* Market rates are affected by conditions similar to those that affect stock prices. For a particular bond issue, the contract and market rates may be the same or different, depending on business conditions.

Bond redemption Bonds may be redeemed by the corporation at maturity or, in the case of callable bonds, whenever it is to the corporation's advantage. The corporation may also repurchase its own bonds in the open market.

PROMISSORY NOTES

As defined by the Negotiable Instruments Law, a *promissory note* is a promise in writing to pay a sum of money to a payee or a bearer of the note upon demand or at a fixed or determinable future time. A note is an important medium of exchange and may be used for short- or long-term purposes. Notes may or may not provide for interest payments and can be discounted (the proceeds can be secured earlier) at banks. The person who promises the money is called the *maker* of the note and the one who receives it is known as the *payee.* To the maker it is a note payable, while the payee considers it a note receivable. A note is negotiated by delivery when it is made out to "bearer" (no payee's name appears on the note). When a payee's name is written on the note, it is negotiated by endorsement. Note forms can be purchased from commercial stationers.

14

CHAPTER FOURTEEN

TELECOMMUNICATION SYSTEMS

CONTENTS

14.1

INTRODUCTION

The first practical telephone office became operational in January, 1878, in New Haven, Connecticut. This manually operated switch served 21 locations over eight open wire lines. With it, the telecommunication network of the United States was born.

Today, this telecommunication network reaches more than 90 percent of American homes and virtually every business establishment. It adds up to 240 million circuit miles of wire and cable, 435 million circuit miles of microwave radio, 19,000 switching centers, and 10 million billion possible connections. There are presently over 150 million telephones in use today, and it is predicted that approximately 20 million more telephones will be added by the year 1988. This phenomenal growth has caused the state of the art to undergo constant change. New technologies, greater transmission speeds, and new concepts are continually changing the procedures under which we operate today. Management demands that responsible employees keep informed of these new technologies and that they anticipate the need for new and future telecommunication facilities. We live in a competitive market, and it is mandatory that we familiarize ourselves with the ways and means of increasing the efficiency of telecommunication service while at the same time holding a tight reign on our budgetary expenditures to ensure overall economy.

The new competitive nature of the telephone industry has brought forth new products and new ideas that were unheard of ten years ago. In 1968, the Federal Communications Commission (FCC) made a monumental decision which ended the prohibition of interconnecting privately owned telephone equipment to the Bell System. The Carterfone decision, as it is generally known, presently permits customer-owned telephone equipment to be attached to the Bell network. The types of equipment may be large PBXs, key systems, recording devices, data sets, and individual telephones. Specialized common carriers are installing telecommunication networks via microwave and satellite in competition with the Bell System. They are supplying services for voice, data, and customized forms of telemetry requiring point-to-point transmission. Economies must be weighed, and overall service efficiency must be studied when making a decision to interconnect one's own telephone equipment, to buy service from a specialized common carrier, or to lease from the Bell Telephone System. Communications costs continue to spiral and the rules of the game continue to change. This chapter will attempt to explain some of the systems, methods, and devices that are used in business telecommunication today so that you may become more efficient in using this medium.

14.2

TELEPHONE COMMUNICATIONS

Telephones are the life blood of good business. They not only provide instant communication but also give reliability and economy when used properly.

LOCAL CALLING

Usually local calls have been charged at a flat rate for unlimited usage in a local area; however, this method is fast disappearing and is being replaced by message units which allot a certain number of calls for a fixed fee. Most large cities throughout the United States are now using message units.

LONG-DISTANCE CALLS

The United States is presently divided into 14 rate steps based on distances ranging from one mile to 3,000 miles. Calls are classified as *station-to-station, operator station-to-station* and *person-to-person*. Rates are based on the time of day when the call is placed and the rate mileage. The Day Rate period is Monday through Friday from 8:00 a.m. to 5:00 p.m.; the Evening Rate (currently a 35 percent discount of the Day Rate) is Sunday through Friday from 5:00 p.m. to 11:00 p.m., and the Night & Weekend Rate (currently a 60 percent discount of the Day Rate) is every night from 11:00 p.m. to 8:00 a.m. and all day Saturday and all day Sunday except for the hours 5:00 p.m. through 11:00 p.m.

Station-to-station calls (Direct-Distance Dialing) This is the fastest and least expensive way to place telephone calls. The charge is based on a one-minute minimum with an additional charge for each succeeding minute.

Operator station-to-station calls These calls can be categorized into *credit card, collect,* or *bill-to-third-party* calls. Based on a three-minute minimum with an additional charge for each succeeding minute, these calls are much more expensive than station-to-station calls. They usually range from a $.15 to a $1.15 increase for a six-minute telephone call.

Person-to-person calls The charge for these calls is also based on a three-minute minimum plus an additional charge for each succeeding minute. Person-to-person is by far the most expensive way of calling and its use certainly should be minimized.

Conference calls Some telephone systems are capable of setting up conference calls with three to eight outside parties by means of the direct-distance dialing network. The telephone company operator can manually arrange for conference calls in which each call is charged at the operator-handled rate. It should be noted, however, that this rate is expensive.

Zero Express Dialing (ZED) ZED is commonly used for credit card calls, collect calls, or bill-to-third-party calls. Dial 0 followed by the telephone number. The telephone operator will request your credit card number or other instructions and then your call will be connected; the call will be charged as an operator-handled call.

Wide Area Telephone Service (WATS) WATS is a bulk-use tariff available to large users of telephone service throughout the United States and Canada. The United States is divided into five bands excluding the state in which you are located; Canada is divided into three bands. Presently, each system is independent of the other. Band 1 encompasses all surrounding states and especially bordering states; Band 5 includes the entire United States. Each band is inclusive of the preceding band; that is, Band 4 service includes Bands 4, 3, 2, and 1. Service may be purchased for your own state or for any of the five bands based on a Full Business Day Rate or a Measured Rate. Full Business Day Rates for Bands 1 through 5 are based on a minimum of 240 hours use per month plus overtime. The Measured Rate is for a minimum of ten hours a month plus an overtime rate. Rates vary from state to state depending on the location and distance.

WATS is designated as *inward* or *outward*. Outward WATS will let you place as many calls as you wish, one after another, to a specific band up to the allotted time that you have purchased. Inward WATS permits you to receive as many calls as are needed, one after another, over a specific line. To the number of your inward WATS line is prefixed an 800 Area Code number. With the purchase of inward WATS, the telephone company gives you an additional facility which allows you to receive another call when the primary inward WATS is busy. This call is charged at the overtime rate.

WATS calls are handled over the same telephone switch network as other direct-distance calls. There is no difference in transmission characteristics, since the same telephone network is used. The big difference is that with WATS, a significant reduction in cost can be gained by large-volume telephone users. Most businesses take advantage of the service and use it not only for telephone voice transmission but for data transmission as well.

Towards the end of 1976, AT&T and Bell of Canada will be offering WATS service covering not only the mainland United States but also Canada, Alaska, and Hawaii. With this new offering, WATS coverage will be extended so that Band 6 will include 50 percent of the Canadian telephones nearest your state. Band 7 will include the remaining 50 percent.

International dialing Generally, in order to place a telephone call overseas, you must call the local telephone operator and give the name of the city and country that you wish to call. You will then be connected with the overseas telephone operator who will place the call. The initial charge is for a three-minute minimum, and for each additional minute the charge is approximately one third of the three-minute rate. Rates are determined by the time the call originates and are categorized as *Day* and *Night/Sunday*. The time period may vary for some countries but the Day Rate most often extends from 5:00 a.m. to 5:00 p.m.; the Night Rate, from 5:00 p.m. to 5:00 a.m. Sunday rates apply all day Sunday.

United States Time Zone Map

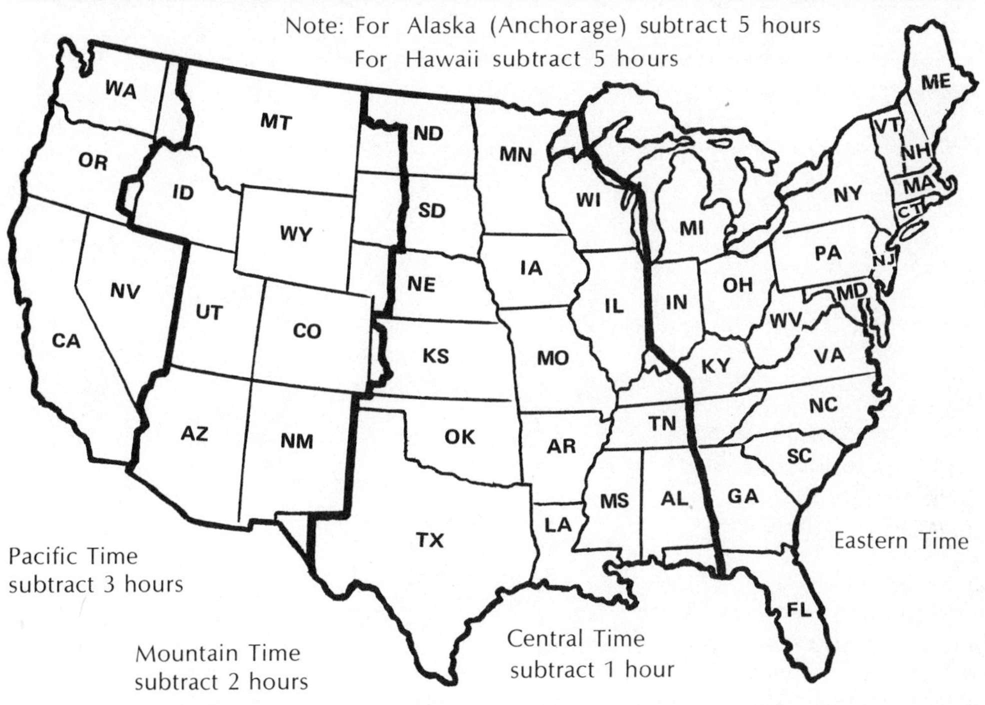

Some areas throughout the United States have access to the International Direct Distance Dialing Service (IDDD). This expands your direct-dialing capability without operator assistance to over 32 countries overseas. IDDD is by far the simplest, fastest, and least expensive way to call abroad. If you have access to an area which has IDDD, you can dial 011 + the country code + the city routing code + the local telephone number and be connected without operator assistance. As an example—a six-minute call to the United Kingdom dialed directly would currently cost about $7.20; a call made with operator assistance, about $10.80; and a collect or person-to-person call about $15.00.

Mobile Calls Telephones can be used to communicate with automobiles, trucks, aircraft, and ships. Calls are connected via land-line telephones through radio circuits.

CONTROLLING TELEPHONE EXPENSES

The least expensive and most efficient way of calling is to do it yourself. Direct-distance dialing (DDD) gets you there faster without operator assistance, via the most direct route. Incoming calls should be answered yourself without any other secretary screening the call. It is very difficult to teach people to use the phone efficiently, especially since many persons believe that it is prestigious to have someone else place calls or answer calls for them; however, this method is also very expensive. Time is being added to the use of your company's telephone facilities and time is money in this instance. Therefore, you should place your own calls and answer your own telephone, rather than relying on another secretary or a receptionist to do it for you.

Area Codes—by States

State	Area Code	State	Area Code
Alabama	205	Minnesota	218, 507, 612
Alaska	907	Mississippi	601
Arizona	602	Missouri	314, 417, 816
Arkansas	501	Montana	406
Bahamas	809	Nebraska	308, 402
California	209, 213, 408, 415, 707, 714, 805, 916	Nevada	702
		New Hampshire	603
Canada	204, 306, 403, 416, 418, 506, 514, 519, 604, 613, 705, 709, 807, 819, 902	New Jersey	201, 609
		New Mexico	505
		New York	212, 315, 516, 518, 607, 716, 914
Colorado	303	North Carolina	704, 919
Connecticut	203	North Dakota	701
Delaware	302	Ohio	216, 419, 513, 614
District of Columbia	202	Oklahoma	405, 918
Florida	305, 813, 904	Oregon	503
Georgia	404, 912	Pennsylvania	215, 412, 711, 814
Hawaii	808	Rhode Island	401
Idaho	208	South Carolina	803
Illinois	217, 309, 312, 618, 815	South Dakota	605
		Tennessee	615, 901
Indiana	219, 317, 812	Texas	214, 512, 713, 806, 817, 915
Iowa	319, 515, 712		
Kansas	316, 913	Utah	801
Kentucky	502, 606	Vermont	802
Louisiana	318, 504	Virginia	703, 804
Maine	207	Washington	206, 509
Maryland	301	West Virginia	304
Massachusetts	413, 617	Wisconsin	414, 608, 715
Mexico	903	Wyoming	307
Michigan	313, 517, 616, 906		

Personal calls or nonbusiness-related calls could amount to 20 to 45 percent of an organization's total daily telephone traffic. In no way can this be eliminated totally, but it certainly can be curtailed. Pay phones located in the lobby or in the cafeteria can help. Timing devices can be installed into telephone systems so that an audible signal reminds an individual that he or she is talking too long. Automatic message accounting systems can record on magnetic tape all digits dialed, and association of this information with a station user can certainly assist a manager in analyzing the telephone bills of the organization. The best method of cutting telephone costs is for management to make all personnel cognizant of the cost of telephone service. Any medium or large user of telephone services would certainly like to know where the calls are going, who is making them, and how more calls can be realized economically. Automatic identification of outward dialing equipment and traffic analyzers are becoming quite common, as they are very beneficial in reducing communications expenses, especially if the telephone service comprises a mixture of trunks such as FX service, tie lines, WATS, and toll trunks. These systems can:

1. Identify incoming and outgoing calls on magnetic tape
2. Allocate telephone costs by extension number and cost center
3. Analyze traffic data trunk groups to ensure the best and cheapest mix of service
4. Eliminate manual ticket handling.

Area Codes—by Numbers

Area Code	State	Area Code	State	Area Code	State
201	New Jersey	413	Massachusetts	703	Virginia
202	District of Columbia	414	Wisconsin	704	North Carolina
203	Connecticut	415	California	705	Ontario, Canada
204	Manitoba, Canada	416	Ontario, Canada	707	California
205	Alabama	417	Missouri	709	Newfoundland
206	Washington	418	Quebec, Canada	712	Iowa
207	Maine	419	Ohio	713	Texas
208	Idaho	501	Arkansas	714	California
209	California	502	Kentucky	715	Wisconsin
212	New York City	503	Oregon	716	New York
213	California	504	Louisiana	717	Pennsylvania
214	Texas	505	New Mexico	801	Utah
215	Pennsylvania	506	New Brunswick, Ca.	802	Vermont
216	Ohio	507	Minnesota	803	South Carolina
217	Illinois	509	Washington	804	Virginia
218	Minnesota	512	Texas	805	California
219	Indiana	513	Ohio	806	Texas
301	Maryland	514	Quebec, Canada	807	Ontario, Canada
302	Delaware	515	Iowa	808	Hawaii
303	Colorado	516	New York	809	Bahamas, Puerto Rico, Virgin Islands
304	West Virginia	517	Michigan	812	Indiana
305	Florida	518	New York	813	Florida
306	Saskatchewan, Ca.	519	Ontario, Canada	814	Pennsylvania
307	Wyoming	601	Mississippi	815	Illinois
308	Nebraska	602	Arizona	816	Missouri
309	Illinois	603	New Hampshire	817	Texas
312	Illinois	604	British Columbia, Canada	819	Quebec, Canada
313	Michigan	605	South Dakota	901	Tennessee
314	Missouri	606	Kentucky	902	Nova Scotia
315	New York	607	New York	903	Mexico
316	Kansas	608	Wisconsin	904	Florida
317	Indiana	609	New Jersey	906	Michigan
318	Louisiana	612	Minnesota	907	Alaska
319	Iowa	613	Ontario, Canada	912	Georgia
401	Rhode Island	614	Ohio	913	Kansas
402	Nebraska	615	Tennessee	914	New York
403	Alberta, Canada	616	Michigan	915	Texas
404	Georgia	617	Massachusetts	916	California
405	Oklahoma	618	Illinois	918	Oklahoma
406	Montana	701	North Dakota	919	North Carolina
408	California	702	Nevada		
412	Pennsylvania				

NOTE: Your telephone directory contains an Area Code map specifying Area Codes for particular states and locales, including those states (as California) that have more than one Area Code.

As local and long-distance rates increase regularly, the need for such control systems increases. Companies such as ESL, Phonetel, Inc., Vidar, and Extel can provide your company with the system best suited for its needs. Costs and methods of attachment to your company's present telephone system vary, so it is best to check with the manufacturers of these systems. Some advantages of the systems offered by the companies mentioned above and by other such companies are that they:

1. Eliminate manual control of trunk calls
2. Reduce telephone abuse
3. Utilize trunk facilities to the utmost
4. Reduce billing errors
5. Make management more cognizant of telephone costs, since individual station billing is used.

Some hints for reducing telephone expenses are as follows:

1. Management should designate one individual within the organization to be responsible for ordering telecommunication equipment. This individual should be the only contact with telephone company personnel and other telecommunication suppliers. The secretary should know who this person is and should direct inquiries to him or her, if problems arise with the system.
2. When you are calling from the East Coast to the West Coast, keep in mind that there is a three-hour time difference. Whenever possible, place your call after 5:00 p.m. and take advantage of the Evening Rate. It is only 2:00 p.m. in San Francisco. This procedure is also applicable in reverse to calls being placed from the West Coast to the East Coast.
3. When you have to call Europe, get up early. Place your call before 5:00 a.m. if possible. When it is 5:00 a.m. in the United States, it is 11:00 a.m. in much of Europe. Your call will also go through at a much cheaper rate. In addition, you should check time zones to make sure that the overseas party is likely to be in his or her office.
4. Review telephone equipment details (line 1 of your telephone bill) every month to make sure that all equipment is accounted for. The telephone company is required to make a physical inventory of all equipment every year. However, errors are known to occur.
5. Review your toll statement and make an attempt to account for all calls listed. In a small office, you should pass it along to your executive for further scrutiny. For a large office, the telephone company can provide a magnetic tape of your monthly tolls so that you or your executive can analyze this information. The telephone company will gladly investigate any discrepancies that are found, and will make whatever adjustments are called for.
6. Report all service disruptions immediately to the telephone company.
7. When changes in service are requested, make sure that the work is done to your satisfaction and that the equipment is installed exactly as you or your superior have specified. Make sure that service terminations are carried out as required and that the billing coincides with the removal of the equipment. The telephone company is known for its expert workmanship, but remember you and your company are the customer and are entitled to satisfaction.
8. Make sure that credits are applied when your service is interrupted or when you have misdialed a number.
9. Management should install pay phones for company customers to use for business as well as for personal calls. A pay phone booth may collect enough revenue to give your company a commission.
10. Telephone locks can be installed which will stop unauthorized persons from using the equipment.
11. The trend to charge for Directory Assistance is becoming quite common among telephone companies. It would therefore be wise to keep a supply of telephone directories for major metropolitan areas on hand so that you can look the numbers up yourself.
12. Telephone company personnel are always willing and able to perform usage studies and will provide free training for management and employees.

TELEPHONE EQUIPMENT

Telephones are basically made up of three parts: a transmitter, a receiver, and an electrical circuit that produces energy. Modern technology has produced thousands of uses for this simple device ranging from ordinary voice conversation to high-speed data transmission at a rate of over 50,000 bits per second. Business people encounter many types and styles of telephones, some of which are described here.

Single line telephones The single line telephone is the basic telephone set that we are all familiar with—it can come in many colors, sizes, and types. It may be a dial or a pushbutton telephone. Its configuration may be desk, wall, Trimline, Candlestick, Cradle, or Ericofon.

Multi-button telephones The multi-button telephone can feature 6, 10, 20, or 30 buttons. It is typically used by secretaries or small business offices to answer, transfer, or screen calls. Various signals and intercommunications can be installed within these telephone sets.

Hands-free telephones The hands-free telephone is commonly referred to as a *speakerphone*. Various types of hands-free telephone devices are available: some have individual receivers and transmitters, while others form an integral part of the telephone set. Hands-free devices are ideal when one is having a telephone conversation with three or four people at once. These devices are also helpful to one who is checking data and talking over the telephone at the same time.

Automatic answering device Telephone answering and receiving devices, such as Electronic Secretary and Code-A-Phone, to name two, answer incoming calls automatically with prerecorded announcements. These automatic systems can tell the caller to leave a message, they can tell the caller where the person being called is or when he or she will be back. Advantages of these devices include the following: (1) the telephone is covered 24 hours a day (2) the expense of an office clerk is saved, and (3) telephone ordering and reporting procedures are speeded up.

Automatic dialer With the use of an automatic dialer, a repertoire of telephone numbers can be stored on magnetic tape or prepunched on plastic cards so that you may poll many locations or continually dial the same number automatically.

Radio paging Two types of radio paging equipment are available: *tone only* or *tone and voice*. Access is effected by dialing the paging equipment to tone-alert or voice-page pocket radio receivers that are carried by individuals. A common type that is offered by AT&T is called the Bellboy.

Telephone aids For noisy environments, "push to talk" handsets are very helpful. A Confidencer or amplifier is also widely used today. Such an aid can assist you in a noisy environment so that you can be understood by a distant party or it can amplify the voice of the calling party so that you can hear better.

Videophone This device is available in some areas of the United States but its use is very limited at the present time. It can be used for face-to-face conferences or group conferences.

Automatic call distributor This device is used primarily by large department stores for taking orders or by banks for obtaining credit information. A recorder informs you that you are in queue and that your call will be answered shortly.

TELEPHONE SYSTEMS

The wide variety of telephone systems on the market and the great flexibility in features offered today give the customer complete freedom of choice to select the system that suits his or her company best. With stored-program electronic switching and the use of small minicomputers and detailed message accounting techniques, these new telephone systems offer more features and benefits than have ever been available before. The Dimension R of the Bell System and the electronic switches of the interconnect industries such as the Danray CBX 2000, the Northern Telecom Ltd. Pulse, the Rolm CBX, the North Electric NX-1E, and the ITT and Stromberg-Carlson Electronic PABXs, to name a few, give high reliability, are easily maintained, and can provide excellent service. The features of the available telephone systems are numerous and varied. Along with the standard Direct Inward Dialing (DID), Direct Outward Dialing (DOD) and station-to-station calling, the following are some of the more exotic features that are offered to customers:

1. Local Automatic Message Accounting (LAMA)—a service providing a magnetic-tape record of all telephone calls except station-to-station calls; information such as the station calling, the number called, the time and length of the call, the trunk used, and the charges may be captured on tape. This is an excellent tool to control a company's toll costs.
2. Automatic Route Selection—the routing of calls over the least expensive trunk (as tie line, WATS, or FX); and the automatic stepping up to the next most expensive route (DDD) if all primary routes are busy.
3. Traffic Analysis—a system by which trunk loading statistics assist in an analysis to determine the number of facilities needed to handle the particular call load.
4. Call Transfer—the ability to transfer to another party inside or outside the telephone system an established incoming or outgoing call without the assistance of an attendant.
5. Add-On Conference—an option that permits the telephone user to add a third party to any established conversation without the assistance of an attendant.
6. Call Forwarding—the capability to have incoming calls rerouted automatically to another telephone number; this feature is activated by dialing a forwarding code and then the number to which the calls are to be forwarded.
7. Camp On Busy—the ability of an operator to camp on an incoming call to your telephone while it is in use; a short burst of tone may be sent to your line to notify you that a call is waiting for your attention.
8. Call Pick-Up—the ability to answer an incoming telephone call directed to another telephone.
9. Abbreviated Dialing—the ability to program one's telephone to accept a set of abbreviated numbers to replace certain telephone numbers; this is a feature that speeds up outside dialing.
10. Automatic Call Back—by dialing a code into the system, the user programs the system to continue to attempt to accept a call on a busy telephone; the first instant that the line is free, the system will automatically put the call through.
11. Outgoing Trunk Queuing—if all outgoing trunks are busy, the system will remember the station being dialed and will call back as soon as a trunk is free; this feature can be programmed into the system upon request.

The solid-state stored programmable switch in use today has taken giant steps within the past 20 years. The original step-by-step mechanical switcher which still is the foundation of the telephone switching network is slowly being phased out. The Crossbar switch, which is the next step in the switching hierarchy, is an electromechanical device using a vertical and horizontal matrix.

Centrex is a word for equipment generally described as an automatic switching system providing PBX service and offering Direct Outward Dialing, Direct Inward Dialing, and Identification of Outward Dialing. The vehicle for Centrex service offered today can either be step-by-step, Crossbar, or electronic, depending on the size of the system required and the geographic location. The trend today is naturally toward the concentration on electronic PBX systems.

SPECIAL TELEPHONE EQUIPMENT SYSTEMS AND SERVICES

Foreign Exchange Service Foreign Exchange (FX) provides the user with flat-rate service to other locations for outgoing or incoming calls. FX service can be purchased from the Bell System or from specialized common carriers at a 24-hour monthly rate.

Tie line service Point-to-point full-time leased service can be provided using tie line service. With this arrangement, service can be engineered for alternate voice and data transmission, thereby providing full utilization of this line. Service can be purchased on a 24-hour monthly basis and is available from the Bell System as well as from specialized common carriers.

Telpak Telpak service provides a wide-band communications channel between two points. Within the wide band are many voice-grade lines that can be used in any way that the subscriber wishes—for tie lines, FX service, data service, teletype, etc. There are four basic Telpak services available:

Telpak "A"—equivalent to 12 voice-grade lines
Telpak "B"—equivalent to 24 voice-grade lines
Telpak "C"—equivalent to 60 voice-grade lines
Telpak "D"—equivalent to 240 voice-grade lines

Electronic transceivers These can be used for credit card authorization, check verification, and other funds-transfer functions. The equipment includes a unique telephone having a single slot through which magnetically striped cards are passed and read by a centralized computer. These phones can then be dialed into a centralized computer for verification. Another type uses the Touch-Tone pad on a regular telephone as a computer input device.

Answering services Check the Yellow Pages of your telephone directory where there are various answering service advertisements which will help you in your selection. Most answering services are available 24 hours a day and can answer the telephone in your name or your company's name or by any other identification that you designate. The types of answering services that are available range from relaying messages to two-way radio dispatching or radio paging. An answering service can be contracted for on a month-to-month basis.

Telephone dictation service Centralized dictation systems have been installed by most large companies today. These systems are usually available from any telephone within a PBX telephone system allowing anyone within the system to dictate. When an access code is dialed, a recorder is seized. By following a prescribed procedure, the document that the user dictates is recorded on tape or on a magnetic disk and is ready for transcription. Playback, correction, stop, and operator assistance features are also available. The advantages of these systems are many: dictation can take place at any time of the day, centralized secretarial help reduces a company's clerical staff, and centralized dictating equipment reduces the cost of having such equipment installed and operational in individual offices.

Facsimile transmission High-speed facsimile transmission over regular telephone lines is finally coming of age. Manufacturers presently have on the market the equipment to transmit an 8½″ × 11″ page in a time span ranging from 35 seconds to two minutes. This is a far cry from the four- to six-minute transmission time we have been accustomed to. Granted that the high-speed facsimile equipment is more expensive, but it can often be justified by the economies that can be gained by the decreased telephone toll costs. Most equipment is available in either a manual or an automatic mode, thus making it an ideal transmission device between two points after working hours. Documents can be stacked and transmitted automatically over tie lines or WATS facilities that are often idle in the late hours of the working day.

Some manufacturers offer "store and forward" features which can record documents on magnetic tape and transmit them on command. Automated facsimile devices can broadcast a single document to many locations or poll other minicomputers and request automatic transmission of documents from distant points. New technology is also being introduced to explore facsimile transmission of multicolored documents. At the present time, only black and shades of gray can be recorded, but the next step will be color transmission. Overseas facsimile transmission has always been a problem because of equipment incompatibilities and the reluctance of some governments and carriers to agree on transmission methods. However, these problems are being overcome and facsimile transmission overseas will be common in the near future.

Data communication Of great and ever-growing importance for telecommunication systems is the concept of data communication. Data communication involves the transmittal of electric signals from one point to another at speeds of up to 250,000 bits per second. Data can be transmitted over ordinary telephone lines or via specialized point-to-point facilities by means of data sets (called *modems*) which convert the digital signal from one's business machine to an analog signal. Digital signals can simply be described as the transmission of a fixed set of symbols as "ones" and "zeroes." Analog signals can assume an indefinite number of symbols—the softness or loudness of a speaker's voice over the telephone is an example. The telephone network is designed to transmit analog signals; thus, data sets are required to *modulate* and *demodulate* the signals. Various types of data sets are available today that can handle any specific function and can transmit at a specific speed. These data sets can be connected directly to the direct-distance dialing network or they can be arranged for private line point-to-point transmissions. They can be used as store-and-forward systems, management information systems, inventory control systems, airline or hotel reservation systems, or they can fulfill any specialized data collection requirements that a business may have. Data-Phone Digital Service (DDS) is a new network being constructed by the Bell System for the exclusive use of transmitting data. This network eliminates the need for conversion from digital to analog signals and thus offers a more reliable and economical data transmission network. The service was first offered between Boston, New York, Chicago, Washington, and Philadelphia. By the end of 1975, it had been expanded to 24 major cities throughout the United States. In the future, it will expand to serve many more points. Computer technology will continue to expand at an explosive rate because of the business sector's need for instant information. Data communication facilities will eventually play a major part in our private as well as in our business needs.

SPECIALIZED COMMON CARRIERS

Specialized common carriers can also provide a wide range of telecommunication services. Companies such as MCI Telecommunications Corporation, Datran, and others specialize in voice and data transmission facilities and services similar to those offered by the Bell System. Companies like these transmit over private microwave and satellite transmission facilities to approximately 80 major cities throughout the United States. The range of services offered include the following:

Voice Tie Lines	Voice Plus Data
Foreign Exchange Service	Multi-point Service
Data Channels	Share Use Service
Measured Time & Part-time Service	

The circuits offered by these carriers can interface with those of the local telephone company and can eliminate the need for two independent terminals at one's office. These carriers serve selected segments of the communications market that need point-to-point transmission of voice or data. They do not share the overall responsibility of serving the entire public. Because of this, their services are not all-encompassing as are those of the Bell System; however, they can offer a company tailor-made services that may fulfill budgetary requirements.

14.3

TELEGRAPH COMMUNICATIONS

DOMESTIC SYSTEMS AND SERVICES

Western Union provides us with a simple and convenient method of transmitting the written word from one point to another. All one has to do is to telephone one's local Western Union office and dictate the message that is to be transmitted. The cost for this service will be billed to the customer by the local telephone company. Telegrams and cablegrams can also be transmitted from one's business office by using the office teletype equipment or FAX machine. If the volume is sizable, one may want a direct line to the Western Union office. Telegrams provide three basic types of service:

Day Letter—usually reaches its destination within two hours. A 15-word minimum charge not including the address and signature is applicable; this service is fast but expensive.

Night Letter—usually delivered to its destination early the following morning on or before the opening of business; the minimum charge is for 100 words, excluding the address and signature. (Keep the three-hour time difference in mind when sending a telegram from the East Coast to the West Coast, and vice versa. It may be to your advantage to send a Day Letter in place of a Night Letter.)

Telegraph Money Order—a service which enables money to be transmitted swiftly between Western Union offices at a nominal charge. Most companies have special arrangements with Western Union so that there is no need for a cash advance. Money Orders are transmitted as telegram Day Letters and can reach their destination within a few hours.

Word count is very important in telegrams, because you pay for exactly what you write. The following guidelines may be helpful in the writing of economical messages:

1. The only free words are the address and signature.
2. Dictionary words are counted as one word.
3. Non-dictionary words longer than five letters are counted as two words or more.
4. Abbreviations of less than five letters are counted as one word.
5. Proper names are counted according to the way they are normally written.
6. Punctuation marks are not chargeable, but signs and symbols such as $, &, #, ' (for *feet*) and " (for *inches*) are counted as part of a mixed group used in conjunction with other numbers and letters. Every five characters equals one word.

OTHER TELEGRAPH SERVICES AND SYSTEMS

New automated systems are fast replacing the telegraph service which at one time was the primary means of transmitting the written word. The transmission of administrative traffic—namely, short instructions, purchase orders, inquiries, or information requests—can now be accomplished in many other ways. Private systems can be installed using high-speed teletypewriters or CRT (cathode-ray tube) devices using the direct-distance dialing network. Store-and-forward minicomputers can store administrative traffic and forward information to other locations during non-prime time, thus enabling the user to take advantage of lower telephone rates.

Devices such as AT&T's Dataspeed 40, Texas Instruments' Silent 700, Western Union's Data Services, or General Electric's TermiNet printers can be used in any number of ways. These systems can be built in any configuration for data and administrative message handling in order to accommodate AT&T or Western Union line circuits. The systems can also access TWX and telex equipment serving domestic as well as worldwide facilities. Some of the message switching systems currently in operation service the airlines for passenger reservations, state governments for criminal information systems, the American Stock Exchange, or large manufacturers who have developed ways of combining all services into one total system. The following paragraphs give an overview of some of the telegraph systems and services that are available to American business offices.

Telex service Telex is a service offered by Western Union to give the customer a low-cost worldwide communications system. This service is available in a manual and/or an automatic mode. Most subscribers prefer the automatic unit which can perforate and transmit prepunched tape at a maximum speed of 66 words per minute. Incoming messages as well as hard copy can be received simultaneously on perforated tape. All telex teletypewriters are automatically activated and will automatically respond to a unique preselected identification code. Charges are based on distance and time used. There is no minimum charge. Telex is compatible with the worldwide communication network covering 120 nations throughout the world. Telex equipment can also send messages to TWX equipment by means of a computer interface. In addition, a telex can send multiple address messages and telegrams. Refer to the *Telex Directory* published by Western Union for further details on TWX and a full explanation of current operational procedures.

TWX Service TWX service is the companion service of telex and is also offered by Western Union. This service also can transmit in a manual or an automatic mode up to a speed of 100 words per minute. Both services can communicate with each other by means of a computer interface. The difference between the two lies in the speed: TWX is faster. There is also a distinct difference in the method of charging: TWX rates are based on a one-minute minimum. This service also can be used in combination with data transmission, since it offers a four-row keyboard very similar to the typewriter keyboard. In contrast, the telex service offers a three-row keyboard limiting the number of charcters that the user can transmit. Both teletypewriters can either be leased through Western Union or purchased from Western Union or another manufacturer. Many models presently on the market can satisfy the needs of a company.

INFOCOM This is a computerized message-data service that offers its subscribers an administrative private transmission network and the economies of a nationwide shared system. Each location operates as a member of a private system exchanging messages. Members of the system may also send and receive telegrams and exchange messages with any telex or TWX subscriber.

Datagram This is a subscriber service providing a one-way voice answering service that converts these messages into teletypewritten records, which in turn are transmitted to one's home office via telex or TWX. Datagram is ideal for sales people who are constantly on the road.

Telepost This is a word processing and business communications system developed by Western Union. The system is capable of storing frequently used business letters and address lists so that one need only select any combination for transmission. These letters are handled domestically via Mailgram service and via cablegram service for overseas. Next-morning delivery is guaranteed.

Mailgram The Mailgram was developed jointly by Western Union and the U.S. Postal Service to speed written communications. A Mailgram can be prepared at one's teletype terminal, computer terminal or by facsimile machine; or it may be telephoned into one's local Western Union office for transmission. The message is dispatched to the nearest post office and is delivered to the addressee in the first mail the following morning. In addition, a business reply envelope can be incorporated in the Mailgram to ensure a quick response in the shortest time possible. A Mailgram is charged at the standard Western Union rate, plus a special delivery charge.

News Alert This is a subscriber service that automatically delivers major news bulletins to one's office over the telex or TWX systems.

FYI News Service One can dial the latest news on one's telex or TWX for a regular usage charge. Some of the categories that may be selected are News, Finance, and Marketing.

INTERNATIONAL SYSTEMS

There are two basic ways of transmitting a message overseas, either by cablegram or by International Telex Service. The major international common carriers that can provide this service are as follows:

French Telegraph Cable Company
ITT World Communications, Inc.
RCA Global Communications, Inc.
Western Union International, Inc.

International telegrams (cablegrams) International telegrams can be sent by way of your local Western Union office to any location in the world. Western Union will file the message with an international carrier of your choice which will then transmit the message overseas. It will then be delivered by the local telegraph company, post office, or government agency of the destination country. The two types of cablegram rates most commonly used are Full Rate Service, which has a seven-word minimum, and Letter Rate, which has a 22-word minimum. Full Rate Service is the most expensive and the message is transmitted immediately. This type of service should be used sparingly. Remember that there is a five- to six-hour time difference between the U.S. and Europe. Don't send a message by Full Rate Service to Europe in the late afternoon or evening. Cablegrams sent by Letter Rate are 50 percent cheaper than the ones sent by Full Rate. These cablegrams usually arrive at the destination after 8:00 a.m. local time the next morning.

Word count is always important, especially if you are sending a Full Rate cable. Rates vary from country to country, of course. *Every word is counted,* including the address and signature as well as the text. Words longer than 10 letters are counted as two words, and each punctuation mark or symbol is counted as one word. Most companies have registered cable addresses: use them. This procedure will certainly reduce word charge. Specify the routing (i.e., the name of the international common carrier of your choice) and give delivery instructions (if desired).

International telex Direct teletype connection can be made to more than 150 countries from any teleprinter that is connected directly to an international carrier. The message can be either directed by keyboard or prepared on punched paper tape and transmitted to your overseas correspondent. You can also have two-way written communication which provides you with instant confirmation and verification that your message has been received and understood. Rates are about one fifth those for cablegrams but they vary from country to country. Most European and South American countries are on a one-minute minimum (or approximately 60 words). All others are on a three-minute minimum. Most overseas teletypes are equipped with automatic answer-back features so that no matter what time of day it is, the printer that you call is ready to receive your message.

Leased channels and data/voice service Private teletype circuits ranging in speed from 16½ words to 100 words per minute can be leased from an international carrier. These circuits can be leased on a full-time monthly basis. High-speed data circuits that handle up to 9,600 bits per second can transmit voice-grade or any combination of teletype, voice, or data services simultaneously, thus providing a full complement of overseas services. Rates and types of service offered vary from country to country. Consult your overseas carrier for further information.

14.4

TERMINOLOGY

Area Code
a three-digit number that, for the purpose of direct-distance dialing, designates one of the geographical locations within a country

area, local service
the area within which are located the stations that a customer may call at local rates according to the local tariff

ASCII
the abbreviation for *American Standard Code for Information Interchange;* this code represents alphanumeric information established as a U.S. standard by the American National Standards Institute

Automatic Calling Unit (ACU)
a dialing device supplied by the communication common carriers which permits a business machine to automatically dial calls over the communication networks

Automatic Dialing Unit (ADU)
a telecommunication device that is capable of automatically generating dialing digits; *compare* AUTOMATIC CALLING UNIT (ACU)

automatic message switching center
a center in which messages are automatically routed according to the information in them

auxiliary handset
a handset that, when used with a data set, allows the user to maintain voice communication with another party; the handset is no different from any other telephone when used this way

baud
a variable unit of data transmission speed that is usually equal to one bit per second

Baudot code
a code for the transmission of data in which five bits represent one character; it is named for Emile Baudot, a pioneer in printing telegraphy

bit
a contraction of *binary digit;* it is the smallest unit of information which has two possible states: *one* or *zero*

bps
an abbreviation for *bits per second;* in serial transmission, it is a measure of the speed with which a character is transmitted by a machine or a channel

buffer
a temporary storage unit used to compensate for a difference in the rates of information flow of two devices, or for the time of the occurence of events

busy hour
the peak 60-minute period during a business day when the largest volume of communications traffic is processed

cable
an assembly of one or more conductors within an enveloping protective sheath that has been constructed so as to permit the use of conductors separately or in groups

camp on
a method of holding a call for a line that is in use and signaling when the line becomes free

central office
the place where communications common carriers terminate customer lines and locate the equipment which interconnects those lines

Centrex Service
an automatic switching system service providing PBX service and also Direct Inward Dialing and Identified Outward Dialing

channel
a path for electrical transmission between two or more stations or channel terminations in telephone or telegraph company offices that is furnished by wire or radio, or by a combination of both; *compare* CIRCUIT

channel, two-wire
a two-way circuit for transmission in either direction

character
a symbol (as a letter or number) that represents information; *also:* a representation of such a character that may be accepted by a computer

circuit
a physical, metallic connection between two points; *compare* CHANNEL

circuit, multipoint
a circuit interconnecting several locations where information transmitted over the circuit is available at all locations simultaneously

coaxial cable
a cable consisting of one conductor, usually a small copper tube or wire, that is insulated from another conductor of larger diameter—usually copper tubing or copper braid

communication
the transmission of information from one point to another

communication, data
the transmission of data from one point to another

conditioning
the addition of equipment to a leased voice-grade channel to provide the ability for data transmission

Crossbar switch
a switch having a plurality of vertical bars or paths, a plurality of horizontal paths, and an electromagnetically operated device for interconnecting any one of the vertical paths with any of the horizontal paths

crosstalk
interference in a communication channel that comes from adjacent channels

data, analog
information represented by a physical quantity (as voltage) such that the representation bears an exact relationship to the original information; for example, the electrical signals on a telephone channel are analog data representation of the original voice

data, digital
information that is represented by a code consisting of a sequence of discrete elements

data set
a modulation/demodulation device that provides compatibility between input/output equipment and communications facilities by conditioning data signals for transmission

dial-up
a service through which a dial telephone can be used to make a station-to-station telephone call

direct-distance dialing
a service that enables the caller to dial toll calls without operator assistance; *called also* DDD

duplex, full
operation of a communication facility whereby each end can both transmit and receive data simultaneously.

duplex, half
operation of a communication facility whereby each end has the ability to alternately transmit or receive data in only one direction at a time

ESS (Electronic Switching System)
a Bell System term for computerized telephone exhange; ESS 1 is a central office and ESS 101 gives private branch exchange (PBX) switching that is controlled from the local central office

exchange
a defined area that is served by a communications common carrier within which the carrier furnishes service at the exchange rate and under the regulations applicable in that area as prescribed in the carrier's filed tariffs

exchange, central office
the place where a communications common carrier locates the equipment which interconnects incoming subscribers and circuits

exchange, private automatic (PAX)
a dial exchange that provides private telephone service to an organization, and that does not allow calls to be transmitted to or from the public telephone network

facsimile (FAX)
the transmission of pictures, maps, diagrams, etc., by wire or radio; the image is scanned at the transmitter and reconstructed at the receiving station

FCC
abbreviation for *Federal Communications Commission,* the agency which regulates common carrier interstate communications service offerings

foreign exchange service (FX)
that service which connects a customer's telephone to a telephone company central office not serving the customer's location

holding time
the length of time a communication channel is in use for each transmission; this includes both message time and operating time

jack
a connecting device to which a wire or wires of a circuit may be attached and which is arranged for the insertion of a plug

keyboard send/receive
a combination teletypewriter transmitter and receiver with transmission capability from keyboard only

leased line
a telephone line reserved for the exclusive use of a single customer

line, long
a circuit arrangement designed to extend the range of a subscriber line, tie trunk, or PBX extension line with respect to one or more functions such as supervision, dialing, or ringing

local channel
a channel connecting a communications subscriber to a central office

local line, local loop
a channel connecting the subscriber's equipment to the line terminating equipment in the central office exchange; it is usually a metallic two-wire or four-wire circuit

microwave
radio transmission using short wavelengths in the ultrahigh to extremely high frequency classes of the radio spectrum ranging from 1,000 to 300,000 megahertz

off-hook
activated (in regard to a telephone set); by extension, a data set automatically answering on a public switched system is said to go "off-hook"

on-hook
having been deactivated (in regard to a telephone set); for example, a telephone not in use is "on-hook"

PABX
private automatic branch exchange; *compare* PRIVATE BRANCH EXCHANGE

poll
a flexible systematic centrally-controlled method that permits stations on a multipoint circuit to transmit without contending for the line

private branch exchange (PBX)
a telephone exchange serving an individual organization and having connections to a public telephone exchange

private line
a circuit leased by a customer for his sole use

punched paper tape
a strip of paper on which characters are represented by combinations of punched holes

pushbutton dialing
the use of keys or pushbuttons instead of a rotary dial on a telephone set to generate a sequence of digits that establish a circuit connection; the signal form is usually multiple tones

routing
assignment of the communications path by which a telephone call will reach its destination

speed
the rate of transmission by a terminal or channel that is usually expressed in words per minute (WPM), characters per second (CPS), or bits per second (bps)

station
one of the input or output points of a communications system

step-by-step switch
a switch that moves in synchronism with a pulse device (as a rotary telephone dial); each digit dialed causes the successive selector switches to carry the connection forward until the desired line is reached

subscriber's line
the telephone line that connects the exchange to the subscriber's station

switch hook
a switch on a telephone set, associated with the structure supporting the receiver or handset; it is operated by the removal or replacement of the receiver or handset on the support

switching center
a location in which incoming data from one circuit are transferred to the proper outgoing circuit

switching center, automatic message
a location where an incoming message is automatically directed to one or more outgoing circuits according to intelligence contained in the message

tariff
the published schedule of regulated charges for common carrier services and equipment

telecommunication
transmission or reception of signals, writing, sounds, or intelligence of any nature by wire, radio, visual, or other electronic or electromagnetic systems

telex
a communication service involving teletypewriters connected by wire through automatic exchanges

tie line
a leased communication channel or circuit

time-sharing
a method of operation in which a computer facility is shared by several users for different purposes; although the computer actually services each user in sequence, the high speed of the computer makes it appear that the users are all handled simultaneously

toll
a charge for making connection beyond the extended area service zone

toll center
a central office where channels and toll message circuits terminate; while this is usually one particular central office in a city, larger cities may have several central offices where toll message circuits terminate

transmission
the electrical or electromagnetic transfer of a signal, message, or other form of intelligence from one location to another

trunk
a channel connecting switching centers of exchanges; a communication channel used as a common artery for traffic between switchboards or other switching devices

TWX
an abbreviation for teletypewriter exchange service provided by Western Union

voice-grade channel
a channel suitable for transmission of speech, digital or analog data, or facsimile

Wide Area Telephone Service (WATS)
a service providing a special line allowing the customer to call a certain zone or certain zones on a direct-distance dialing basis for a fixed monthly fee

wide band channel
a channel wider in bandwidth than a voice-grade channel

WPM (words per minute)
a common measure of speed in telegraph systems

15

CHAPTER FIFTEEN

TRAVEL AND THE MULTINATIONAL CHARACTER OF MODERN BUSINESS

CONTENTS

15.1

INTRODUCTION

Modern business is, of course, global in its scope and thrust. Domestic and international competition is now so acute that it is vital for business people to be extremely aggressive in protecting, maintaining, and expanding the national and international markets that they have established for their products and services. It is equally vital that executives be vigilant and imaginative in searching out and capturing new potential growth markets for their products, both on the home front and in other countries. To accomplish these and other related objectives, executives must keep up-to-date on national and international economic and monetary trends, on U.S. foreign policy as it affects commerce, on continually changing national and international political situations, and on general corporate and technological developments throughout the world. In short, executives have to be able to react fast, decide fast, and move fast in order to maintain their positions in the world market. A sharp increase in business-related travel, especially in international travel, is one of the logical results of this multinationally based and heightened competitive pattern. Consequently, the secretary's role has been extended in yet another direction to reflect additional specialized executive requirements. No longer is it enough for the secretary just to make plane reservations and type up itineraries. The secretary now must have a fairly broad understanding of what types of trade and travel information are needed for various kinds of business trips, must know where to obtain current information quickly, and must be competent enough to sift out and discard extraneous and irrelevant data from the essential data that must be presented to the executive. In short, a secretary ought to be able to facilitate and expedite a business trip from the initial planning stages through the post-trip follow-up. Good secretarial support during all stages of a trip can sometimes mean the difference between a smooth-running success and a fouled up, confused failure.

It is worth reemphasizing the need to help keep one's executive informed of developments in the countries with which he or she may be dealing. With the ever-increasing number of joint ventures between U.S. and foreign companies, it is essential that the American executive be kept continually abreast of those international developments that may affect his or her business. American executives must also have a measure of understanding of the cultures and social structures of countries that are important to them in order to establish and maintain friendly working relationships with their foreign counterparts. A secretary who can supply in-depth information pertinent to the society and the customs of the countries can be of great value to the executive and to the company. It is with these considerations in mind that this chapter provides an overview of domestic and multinational travel and business and the secretary's expanded role in facilitating and supporting them.

15.2

SETTING UP A TRIP

Sending the traveler to his or her destination on a predetermined schedule requires careful preparations carried out in a methodical manner. Even though an in-house travel department might be available, a truly efficient secretary already knows where information may be obtained and what information will be needed in each instance.

TRAVEL AGENTS

Reputable travel agencies are staffed with skilled employees who can assist international and domestic travelers. A call to a travel agent will save time and will assure a minimum of confusion from the beginning to the end of the trip. Travel agents make travel reservations; issue airline, ship, and rail tickets; recommend hotels and make hotel reservations; arrange for car rentals; and assist travelers in obtaining passports and visas. The agents sometimes give additional help with incidentals such as tickets for the theater, the opera, or sporting events. Travel agents have at their fingertips data about major as well as regional and local airlines and their flight schedules, air distances and travel times to principal cities around the globe, luggage limitations, and air freight.

Even if one arranges an itinerary oneself, one can plan it by working directly with the airlines, because many international air carriers make hotel as well as plane reservations for passengers. Hotel reservations made through the airlines should, however, be confirmed by the secretary. Travel guides are also excellent aids in planning overseas trips. For example, the differences between European and American hotel classifications are discussed in these guides. (See page 504 of this chapter for a list of travel guides.)

ITINERARY AND SCHEDULE MAKEUP

In planning an itinerary, the secretary must confer with the executive and make careful notes about the date and time of departure and the date and time of arrival at the destination, about intermediate stops, and about the date and time of the return. Errors in planning can result in costly delays and needless confusion.

Dates and schedules of any conferences, planned attendance at special events (such as trade fairs), and free time for personal matters are additional data that the secretary should know about and plan for in advance when making up an itinerary. All of this information should be kept in a file from which the itinerary and an appointment schedule are then typed. Itineraries should be logically and neatly arranged so that the executive can review them at a glance. Dates should be listed, followed by specific times and brief descriptions of planned activities; departure and arrival details should be specified; airports, ports, or railway stations should be named; hotels should be listed and confirmed reservations should be indicated; and social engagements should be itemized with a mention of suggested or required dress. These are examples of the kinds of information that, if set down in a complete and orderly way, will make executive travel better organized and thus easier. (See also Chapter 3, page 47, for a sample itinerary.)

The itinerary supplied by a travel agent should be reviewed carefully and supplemented with any other information essential for the executive's trip. Making up a separate appointment schedule might also be advisable if the itinerary itself has been planned by the travel agent. This schedule can be invaluable as a means of guiding the executive through a busy day in a distant city. It might contain pertinent data about individuals to be contacted, prescheduled appointments, reference to briefcase folders on reports and correspondence, reminders to reconfirm flight reservations and business luncheon arrangements, suggestions for social amenities in accord with the customs of the country, as well as other significant items.

Assembling take-along materials also demands careful attention. Items such as agreements, contracts, speeches, formats for meetings, reading materials, or special instructions should be precisely labeled with the dates when and the places where they will be needed by the executive. A set of manila folders or clasp envelopes could be helpful in organizing and packing the take-along materials.

VACCINATIONS AND REQUIRED IMMUNIZATIONS

The International Health Regulations adopted by the World Health Organization stipulate that vaccinations against smallpox, cholera, and yellow fever may be required for entry to a given country. Up-to-date information must be obtained by the traveler before the trip. For return to the United States, a smallpox certificate is required only if in the preceding days the traveler has visited a country in which smallpox has broken out. Required immunizations must be recorded on approved forms such as those included in the booklet PHS-731 "International Certificates of Vaccination," available through most local health department offices. Details concerning the immunizations and prophylaxis recommended or required for travel to all areas of the world can be obtained from any local, county, or state health department. The sequence of countries that the executive intends to visit should be set down on paper well in advance of the trip in order that required immunizations not be overlooked. Entry into and exit from some countries might require special immunizations. Exemptions from immunizations can be obtained if a physician thinks one or more immunizations should not be given on medical grounds. In this case, the traveler should be given a signed and dated statement of these reasons written on the physician's stationery. Smallpox and cholera shots may be given by a private physician; however, the physician must give the traveler an official written statement that he has administered the shots so that they can be approved by the proper public health authorities. Yellow fever shots can be given only by a local, county, or state health department. Allowing ample time for a traveler to complete all necessary shots before departure is of the utmost importance. The secretary should call the health department to arrange for the executive's shots, since in some departments certain shots are given only on specific days of the week.

A publication entitled *Health Information for International Travel* can be obtained from the U.S. Department of Health, Education and Welfare, Public Health Service, Center for Disease Control, Bureau of Epidemiology, Atlanta, GA 30333. This publication is designated as DHEW Publication No. (CDC) 75-8280 (formerly 74-8128 and 73-8216).

PASSPORTS AND VISAS

To find information about passports in your community, use the telephone directory; in the directory look up "United States Government, Passports, U.S." If a passport is required, a person can apply for one at a Passport Agent's office; the applicant can also go to a clerk of a federal court, a clerk of a state court of record, a judge or clerk of a probate court, or a postal clerk designated by the Postmaster General. Passport agencies are located at the following addresses:

Boston, MA 02203: Room E 123, John F. Kennedy Bldg., Government Center

Chicago, IL 60604: Room 331, Federal Office Bldg., 230 South Dearborn Street

Honolulu, HI 96813: Federal Bldg., 335 Merchant Street

Los Angeles, CA 90261: Room 2W16, Hawthorne Federal Bldg., 15000 Aviation Blvd., Lawndale

Miami, FL 33130: Room 812, Federal Office Bldg., 51 Southwest First Avenue

New Orleans, LA 70130: Room 400, International Trade Mart, 2 Canal Street

New York, NY 10020: Room 270, Rockefeller Center, 630 Fifth Avenue

Philadelphia, PA 19106: Room 4426, William J. Green, Jr. Federal Bldg., 600 Arch Street

San Francisco, CA 94102: Room 1405, Federal Bldg., 450 Golden Gate Avenue

Seattle, WA 98101: Room 225, Logan Bldg., 500 Union Street

Washington, DC 20524: Passport Office, 1425 K Street, N.W.

Except in extraordinary circumstances, all U.S. citizens need passports to depart from or reenter the United States and to enter most foreign countries. Even though a passport is not required by U.S. laws for travel to North, South, and Central America or adjacent islands except for Cuba, a passport is still recommended. Travelers who visit countries in these areas without a passport should carry a birth certificate or some other documentary evidence showing U.S. citizenship. Information about passport requirements for travel to and from specific countries can be obtained from the embassies or consulates of these countries, or directly from the Passport Office (Department of State) publications M-264 "Visa Requirements of Foreign Governments," and "You and Your Passport" (Revised September, 1974).

The traveler should apply early for a passport, preferably several weeks before the planned departure. To apply for a first passport, the traveler should present a completed Passport Application at one of the issuing offices. A second passport can be applied for by mail if the conditions stated on the application are met. Several items are needed for filing an application for a passport:

1. **Evidence of citizenship** A previously issued passport provides this evidence. Evidence in lieu of a previously issued passport is a certified birth certificate, which is considered primary evidence. However, secondary evidence such as a baptismal certificate is acceptable if no birth certificate is available.
2. **Two passport photos taken within six months of the date of application** Photos should be at least 2½" × 2½" and not more than 3" × 3". The photos should be front view and full-faced. Color shots are acceptable.

3. **Proof of identification** Personal identity must be established to the satisfaction of the person executing the application. If the applicant is personally known by the executor, no further identification is required. Items generally accepted for identification are as follows: a previously issued U.S. passport, a driver's license, a certificate of naturalization or citizenship, or a government (federal, state, or municipal) card or pass. Social security cards and credit cards are not acceptable, however.

Business firms contracting with U.S. government agencies to carry out missions abroad should carefully check with the contracting agency about special requirements for passports.

New passport applications may be made by mail if the applicant has held a U.S. passport for not more than eight years prior to the date of application. Passports are valid for five years from the date of issuance unless they are specifically limited by the Secretary of State. Lost or stolen passports should be reported immediately to the Passport Office, Department of State, Washington, DC 20524, or to the nearest American consular office. Stolen passports should also be reported to local police authorities. Every precaution should be taken to prevent loss or theft of passports, for considerable delay may be experienced before a new passport can be issued.

A visa is permission granted by the government of a country for an alien to enter that country and remain there for a specified period of time. Stamped notations to this effect are usually entered in passports. The traveler is responsible for obtaining necessary visas before going abroad. Visas should be obtained well in advance from the nearest embassy or consular office of the country or countries to which one is going. The addresses of foreign consular offices in the U.S. may be obtained by consulting directories which are available in most libraries, or by consulting local telephone directories.

Information about both visas and passports is in the government publications already referred to in this section. Because information about visas does change in many countries, up-to-date information should be obtained before each trip. Even in countries not requiring visas, the traveler should carry evidence of U.S. citizenship and personal identification. The following examples of passport and visa requirements will alert the secretary to the necessity of checking requirements whenever a trip is being planned because these requirements differ from country to country and because requirements for any one country are subject to change:

Bahrain—A passport and visa are required. Apply to the Permanent Mission of the State of Bahrain to the U.N., 605 Third Avenue, NY 10016, for specific requirements.

Brazil—A passport is required. A visa is not required for a tourist stay of up to 90 days. Tourists must have return tickets or bank introduction letters attesting to their financial capability. A smallpox vaccination is required. Children from three months to six years of age must have polio vaccinations. Check with the Brazilian Embassy or Consulate for information on stays that will last more than 180 days.

Canada—A passport or a visa is not required for tourists, but evidence of citizenship (as a valid or expired passport, birth certificate, or a certificate of naturalization), and personal identification (as a driver's license or an employee I.D. card) should be available. A passport is required for immigration, employment, or residence. Check with the Canadian Embassy, Washington, DC 20036, or with the nearest Canadian Consulate for specific requirements regarding nonimmigrant entry.

LUGGAGE

For international travel, the free baggage allowance is 66 pounds for first-class passengers and 44 pounds for coach/economy passengers. The airline carrier may be consulted for the exceptions that are in effect between some cities. Excess weight on international flights is charged at the rate of one percent of the one-way first-class fare per kilogram (2.2 pounds) regardless of the class of service. No limit is placed on the number of bags per passenger. Generally, carry-on luggage must be placed under the seats. The approximate dimensions of space under seats are 9″ × 13″ × 23″

Unless an excess valuation is declared before the flight departure, the airline's maximum liability for baggage and claims on such baggage is strictly limited. Therefore, the passenger should inquire about the airline's liability limitations for checked and unchecked baggage and other property. Claims for damage must be filed in writing within 7 days and claims for loss or delay must be filed in writing within 21 days of the incident.

CUSTOMS DECLARATIONS

Travelers should pay special attention to duty-free imports and items that must be declared. Articles acquired abroad and brought into the United States are subject to applicable duty and internal revenue tax; however, as a returning resident, a traveler is allowed certain exemptions from duties on items obtained abroad. Articles totaling $100 (based on fair retail value in the country where they were purchased) may be entered duty-free, except for liquor and cigars. Travelers should heed the following warnings:

1. The understatement of an article's value or the misrepresentation of the nature of an article may lead to its seizure and forfeiture. Duty must be paid even if an article is seized.
2. Failure to declare an article may lead to its seizure and forfeiture, and to an additional liability equal in amount to the value of the article in the U.S.
3. Advice from those outside the United States Customs Service should be avoided.
4. If doubt exists about whether an article is dutiable, the article should be declared and the customs inspector queried.
5. The invoice or the bill of sale that has been provided abroad must reflect the true value of the article that has been purchased there.

Detailed pamphlets on customs regulations are available from a District Director of Customs. District customs offices are located in the following cities:

Anchorage, AK 99501
Baltimore, MD 21202
Boston, MA 02109
Bridgeport, CT 06609
Buffalo, NY 14202
Charleston, SC 29402
Chicago, IL 60607
Cleveland, OH 44199
Detroit, MI 48226
Duluth, MN 55802
El Paso, TX 79985
Galveston, TX 77550
Great Falls, MT 49403
Honolulu, HI 96806
Houston, TX 77052
Laredo, TX 78040
Los Angeles—San Pedro, CA 90731
Miami, FL 33132
Milwaukee, WI 53202
Minneapolis, MN 55401
Mobile, AL 36602
New Orleans, LA 70130
New York, NY 10004
(Write: Area Director of Customs)
Nogales, AZ 85621
Norfolk, VA 23510
Ogdensburg, NY 13669
Pembina, ND 58271
Philadelphia, PA 19106
Port Arthur, TX 77640
Portland, ME 04111
Portland, OR 97209
Providence, RI 02903
St. Albans, VT 05478
St. Louis, MO 63101
St. Thomas, VI 00801
San Diego, CA 92101
San Francisco, CA 94126
San Juan, PR 00903
Savannah, GA 31401
Seattle, WA 98104
Tampa, FL 33601
Washington, DC 20018
Wilmington, NC 28401

FILM AND RECORDINGS

Before departure, the traveler should register cameras, tape recorders, and other articles that can be readily identified by serial numbers or other markings. All foreign-made articles are subject to duty each time they are brought into the United States unless the traveler has acceptable proof of prior possession. Certificates of registration can be obtained at the nearest customs office. If such certificates for any reason cannot be obtained, one can use bills of sale, insurance policies, or purchase receipts as proof of prior possession. Exposed film that a traveler has purchased abroad may be released without examination by Customs if it is not to be used for commercial purposes and if it does not contain objectionable matter. Developed or undeveloped U.S. film exposed abroad is duty-free and need not be listed in customs exemptions. Motion-picture film to be used for commercial purposes is, however, dutiable when returned to the United States. Foreign film purchased abroad as well as prints developed there are subject to duty, but they may be included in customs exemptions. U.S.-manufactured film may be mailed to the United States; if it is, the traveler should use the proper mailing envelopes obtainable from film manufacturers or processing laboratories. The outside wrapper should be marked as follows: *Undeveloped photographic film of U.S. manufacture—Examine with care.*

INTERNATIONAL AMENITIES

The American executive who conducts business abroad should be familiar with the business and social customs of the host countries; otherwise, he or she risks offending the foreign business people and the government officials with whom he or she confers or negotiates. Acceptable behavior is often based more on experience, instinct, or a feel for good manners than on written protocol. Although social practices and behavior in homes and restaurants do vary from country to country, tact, subtlety, courtesy, and geniality are always in order. Foreign business executives, and particularly those whose educational ties are European, are impressed if a visitor understands the cultural heritage and the language spoken in their country. The American executive going abroad should, therefore, take the time and make the effort to become well-informed about the country or countries that will be visited. It would also be in order for the executive to brush up on the languages of these countries if he or she has had training in them.

The American who is invited to a foreign business associate's home for an evening should take the invitation seriously. The invitation to a home, however, is more likely to be strictly social than business. The American executive who can talk intelligently about the arts, music, theater, and world politics will make a favorable impression. If an executive is a guest in a foreign colleague's home, a small present might be given to the host or hostess. The guest should be discreet about choosing gifts; certainly the selection should not be ostentatious. Flowers are always appropriate. No gift should be taken if one is a guest at a private club; however, if the entertainment is a golf game, the guest might present the host with golf balls imprinted with the company name and its logo.

Business behavior is as important and as varied as social behavior in different countries; for example, Austrians are formal in their business associations, but less so than Germans. Shaking hands is a polite gesture when greeting or leaving throughout continental Europe. In countries such as Denmark and the Soviet Union, visiting cards are exchanged among executives. In some countries business is conducted during lunch; in others, it is not. Business hours differ from country to country, and from summer to winter. For example, office hours in Italy are customarily from 8:00 a.m. to 1:00 p.m. and from 4:00 p.m. to 7:00 p.m. (Monday through Friday); in Denmark, summer hours are from 8:30 a.m. to 3:00 p.m. (Monday through Friday), but winter hours are from 9:00 a.m. to 5:00 p.m. Banking hours also vary from country to country. Punctuality is important in many countries; in fact, delays of more than five minutes in some countries might be considered rude. These examples point out to the secretary how important such details are in helping executives prepare for trips abroad and in setting up daily work schedules.

Customs for making appointments and for dress also should be adhered to. The American custom of making spur-of-the-moment appointments by telephone is looked upon with disapproval in many countries. Foreign business people are accustomed to receiving requests for appointments by letter well in advance, and in these letters they expect to see the corporate titles of their visitors. They also prefer that the nature of the visit be explained. Americans may make a habit of working lunches, but European luncheons are more frequently a time for building personal relationships than for discussing business.

Executives should be familiar with the dress conventions of the countries they visit. For instance, a dark business suit may be masculine uniform in one country, but casual attire may be acceptable in another. Some countries have strong notions about feminine attire; for example, pantsuits may be considered inappropriate in many countries. It is therefore the traveler's responsibility to be informed on social and business customs before embarking on a trip. The secretary should try to provide appropriate background material for the executive so that he or she will be an exemplary representative of both company and country abroad. An annotated list of helpful books may be found on pages 503–509 of this chapter.

Holidays in foreign countries affect the American executive's travel and appointment schedule abroad. The secretary can help the executive by supplying a list of holidays observed in the countries that will be visited so that appointments will not be made on such days (see pages 476–489 of this chapter for a list of worldwide holidays); holidays should also be included in the itineraries prepared for executives. For instance, Moslem, Christian, or Jewish holidays all might affect the schedule of an executive traveling in the Middle East during a particular time period. Indeed, there are very few days in the year when there is no holiday somewhere in the world. Because many holidays based on the lunar calendar have variable dates from year to year, the secretary should check with foreign embassies or consulates in the United States about exact dates for holidays with varying dates. American travelers also must consider U.S. holidays when scheduling appointments with U.S. government representatives and American business people stationed overseas.

In some countries such as France and Italy, business activity is sharply curtailed in July and August when people go on vacation. It is, therefore, wise to avoid traveling in these countries on business during the summer months unless one is sure that one's business colleagues will not be on vacation. The practice of taking long weekends is also customary in many countries; therefore, it is useless for an executive to plan a Thursday arrival in a particular country followed by a full Friday schedule of appointments if foreign business associates will not be in their offices on Friday.

The following material, such as the list of worldwide holidays, will be of help to the secretary in scheduling travel and appointments for the executive conducting business abroad.

WORLDWIDE HOLIDAYS

Several hundred civil and/or religious holidays are celebrated each year in countries throughout the world. American business people ought to consider these dates when planning overseas travel because many holidays effect business- and government-office closings in the celebrating countries. The following chart of worldwide holidays begins on January 1 of a typical year and ends on December 31. It comprises three columns:

column 1
contains the date

column 2
lists the holiday(s) occurring on that date followed by a code or codes describing each holiday:
C = civil
R = religious
C/R = civil and religious

column 3
lists in alphabetical order those countries celebrating the holiday or holidays occurring on each date

While this chart is comprehensive, it is not all-inclusive. The reader should use it, all the time keeping in mind the following limitations:

1. Some holidays are observed only locally or regionally in a country. Such holidays are not listed in this chart.

2. Holiday schedules for a given country may vary from year to year; dates may be changed by law; new holidays may be added; and established holidays may be renamed, curtailed, or dropped altogether. When in doubt about the date or dates of a holiday in a particular country, the secretary should telephone the consulate or embassy of that country to confirm the information. Other alternatives are to consult the international division of a large bank (as Morgan Guaranty Trust Company or the Chase Manhattan Bank) or call the United States Department of State in Washington, DC.

3. Holidays occurring on Saturdays and especially on Sundays are often celebrated on the preceding Friday or on the following Monday. It would therefore be wise to avoid scheduling appointments on days which may be so affected by weekend holidays.

4. The celebration of some holidays often begins at noon or 1:00 p.m. on the day preceding, at which time businesses, government offices, and banks close for the duration of the holiday. In some instances, stores, banks, and offices will remain closed until about noon of the day following the holiday. These customs should be taken into consideration when itineraries and appointments are planned.

5. Most Israeli holidays (except for ones such as New Year's Day and Independence Day/May 5) occur according to the Jewish religious calendar. In Israel, banks, government offices, and businesses are closed on Saturday.

6. Countries in which the Muslim religion is predominant (Saudi Arabia, Egypt, Indonesia, Iran, Jordan, Tunisia, Morocco, Pakistan) observe the Muhammadan religious holidays, which are based on the lunar calendar and are therefore variable. In predominantly Muslim countries, banks and other offices and businesses are usually closed on Friday but are open on Saturday and Sunday. Some other countries (as Guyana and Nigeria) observe both Muslim and non-Muslim holidays. And still other countries—especially those in Asia—observe holidays based on the Buddhist and other Eastern religious calendars. All of these varying customs should be considered when one is planning a trip abroad.

Note: Variable holidays are signaled by an asterisk * positioned immediately before the name of the holiday. Half-day holidays and holidays that usually comprise a half a day are signaled by a double asterisk ** positioned immediately before the name of the holiday.

Worldwide Holidays

Date		Holiday and Type	Country
January	1	New Year's Day (C)	all countries except Afghanistan, Bangladesh, Bhutan, Burma, Cambodia, Ethiopia, Iran, Libya, Nepal, Pakistan, Saudi Arabia, Sri Lanka, Tanzania, Vietnam, People's Democratic Republic of Yemen
		Independence Day (C)	Cameroon, Haiti, Sudan, Western Samoa
		Founding of the Republic of China (C)	Republic of China (Taiwan)
		Celebration of the Revolution (C)	Cuba
		Bank Holiday (C)	Egypt
	2	Second day of New Year (Bank Holiday) (C)	Bulgaria, Republic of China (Taiwan), Czechoslovakia, German Democratic Republic (East Germany), Grenada, Japan, Mauritius, New Zealand, Rumania, Seychelles, South Korea, Western Samoa, Yugoslavia
		Ancestors Day (C)	Haiti
	3	Third day of New Year (Bank Holiday) (C)	Republic of China (Taiwan), Japan, South Korea
	4	Independence Day (C)	Burma
		Martyrs of Independence (C)	Zaire
	6	Epiphany (R)	Andorra, Argentina, Austria, Canary Islands, Colombia, Cyprus, Federal Republic of Germany (West Germany), Greece, Italy, Liechtenstein, Spain, Sweden, Switzerland, Uruguay, Venezuela, Virgin Islands of the U.S.
		Army Day (C)	Iraq
	7	Ethiopian Christmas (R)	Ethiopia
		Pioneers Day (C)	Liberia
	9	Day of Mourning (*or* Martyrs Day) (C)	Panama
	12	Hostos's Birthday (C)	Puerto Rico
		Zanzibar Revolution Day (C)	Tanzania
	13	National Redemption Day (C)	Ghana
		Liberation Day (C)	Togo
	14	Bank Holiday (C)	Nepal
	15	Adults Day (C)	Japan
		Martin Luther King Day (C)	Virgin Islands of the U.S.
	18	Remembrance Day (C)	Tunisia
	19	Ethiopian Epiphany (R)	Ethiopia
	20	Army Day (*or* Holiday of the National Army *or* Mali Army Day) (C)	Mali

Date		Holiday and Type	Country
	21	Altagracia Day (R)	Dominican Republic
	26	Australia Day (C)	Australia
		Duarte's Day (C)	Dominican Republic
		Republic Day (C)	India
	30	**Martyrs Day (C)	Nepal
	31	National Holiday (C)	Hong Kong
February	2	Candlemas Day (R)	Liechtenstein
	3	Federal Territory Holiday (C)	Malaysia
		St. Blas Day (R)	Paraguay
	5	Constitution Day (C)	Mexico
	6	New Zealand Day (C)	New Zealand
	7	Independence Day (C)	Grenada
	8	Ramadan Revolution (*or* Fourteenth Day of Ramadan Revolution) (C)	Iraq
	9	St. Maron's Day (R)	Lebanon
	10	St. Paul's Shipwreck (R)	Malta
	11	Youth Day (C)	Cameroon
		National Foundation Day (C)	Japan
		Armed Forces Day (C)	Liberia
	12	Union Day (C)	Burma
	18	National Day (C)	Gambia
	21	National Mourning Day (*or* Shaheed Day) (C)	Bangladesh
	23	Republic Day (C)	Guyana
	25	National Day (C)	Kuwait
	27	Independence Day (C)	Dominican Republic
March	1	Battle of Aduwa Day (C)	Ethiopia
		Independence Day (C)	South Korea
		National Day for Veterans and War Victims (C)	Laos
		Heroes Day (C)	Paraguay
	3	Martyrs Day (C)	Malawi
		Throne Day (C)	Morocco
		Unity Day (*or* Unity Celebration *or* Southern Accord Anniversary) (C)	Sudan
	5	National Day (C)	Equatorial Guinea
	6	Independence Day (C)	Ghana
	8	Revolution Day (C)	Egypt
		International Women's Day (C)	U.S.S.R.
	9	Baron Bliss Day (C)	Belize
	10	Teachers Day (C)	Laos
	12	Renovation Day (C)	Gabon
		Moshoeshoe's Day (C)	Lesotho
		Independence Day (C)	Mauritius
	15	J. J. Roberts' Birthday (C)	Liberia

Date		Holiday and Type	Country
March	17	St. Patrick's Day (C/R)	Northern Ireland, Republic of Ireland
	19	St. Joseph's Day (R)	Canary Islands, Colombia, Costa Rica, Italy, Liechtenstein, Malta, Spain, Venezuela
	20	*Vernal Equinox Day (C)	Japan
		Independence Day (C)	Tunisia
	22	Arab League Day (C)	Jordan, Lebanon
		National Tree Planting Day (C)	Lesotho
		Emancipation Day (C)	Puerto Rico
	23	*Armed Forces Day (C)	Laos
		Pakistan Day (C)	Pakistan
	25	Greek Independence Day (C)	Cyprus, Greece
		Annunciation Day (R)	Liechtenstein
	26	Independence Day (C)	Bangladesh
	27	Resistance Day (C)	Burma
	29	Youth Day and Chinese Martyrs Day (C)	Republic of China (Taiwan)
		Memorial Day (C)	Malagasy Republic (Madagascar)
	31	Bank Holiday (C)	Indonesia
		*Transfer Day (C)	Virgin Islands of the U.S.
April	1	Bank Holiday (C)	Burma
		National Day (C)	San Marino
	4	Ching Ming Festival (*or* National Festival of the Sweeping of the Tombs) (C)	Republic of China (Taiwan)
		Liberation Day (C)	Hungary
		Independence Day (C)	Senegal
	5	Day following Ching Ming Festival (C)	Hong Kong
		Arbor Day (C)	South Korea
	6	Victory Day (*or* Patriots Victory Day) (C)	Ethiopia
		Chakri Day (C)	Thailand
	9	Bataan Day (C)	Philippines
		Martyrs Day (C)	Tunisia
	11	Juan Santamaría Day (Battle of Rivas Day) (C)	Costa Rica
		Fast and Prayer Day (R)	Liberia
	13	National Day (C)	Chad
		Songkran Day (C)	Thailand
	14	Day of the Americas (C)	Honduras
	16	De Diego Day (*or* Diego's Birthday) (C)	Puerto Rico
	17	Evacuation Day (*or* Independence Day) (C)	Syria
	19	Landing of the Thirty-three (C)	Uruguay
		Independence Day (C)	Venezuela

Date		Holiday and Type	Country
	21	*The Queen's Birthday (C)	Belize, Hong Kong
		Tiradentes Day (C)	Brazil
	22	*First Day of Summer (C)	Iceland
		**National Sovereignty Day (C)	Turkey
	23	National Sovereignty Day (C)	Turkey
	25	Anzac Day (C)	Australia, New Zealand, Western Samoa
		Portugal's Day (C)	Azores
		Liberation Day (C)	Italy
		National Flag Day (C)	Swaziland
	26	Union Day (C)	Tanzania
	27	Independence Day (C)	Togo
	29	St. Peter, Martyr (R)	Canary Islands
		The Emperor's Birthday (C)	Japan
	30	The Queen's Birthday (C)	Netherlands
May	1	May Day (C)	Albania, Algeria, Bangladesh, Benin, Burma, Czechoslovakia, India, Malta, Pakistan, Sri Lanka, Yemen Arab Republic
		Labor Day (C)	Andorra, Argentina, Austria, Azores, Belgium, Belize, Bolivia, Brazil, Burundi, Cameroon, Cape Verde, Central African Republic, Chad, Chile, People's Republic of China, Colombia, Congo, Costa Rica, Cuba, Cyprus, Denmark, Dominican Republic, Ecuador, El Salvador, Ethiopia, Federal Republic of Germany (West Germany), Finland, Gabon, German Democratic Republic (East Germany), Greece, Guatemala, Guinea, Guyana, Haiti, Honduras, Hungary, Iceland, Iraq, Ivory Coast, Jordan, Kenya, Laos, Lebanon, Liechtenstein, Luxembourg, Malaysia, Mali, Malagasy Republic (Madagascar), Mauritius, Monaco, Mongolia, Morocco, Mozambique, Nicaragua, Niger, Norway, Panama, Paraguay, Peru, Philippines, Poland, Portugal, Rumania, Rwanda, Senegal, Singapore, Somalia, Spain, Surinam, Sweden, Syria, Tanzania, Togo, Tunisia, Uganda, Upper Volta, Uruguay, Venezuela, People's Democratic Republic of Yemen, Yugoslavia, Zaire, Zambia
		Saint Joseph the Worker Day (R)	Canary Islands, Equatorial Guinea, Vatican City State

Date		Holiday and Type	Country
May	1	Spring Feast (C)	Turkey
	1, 2	Labor Day (C)	Bulgaria, U.S.S.R.
	3	Constitution Day (C)	Japan
		The King's Birthday (C)	Lesotho
		Bank Holiday (C)	Scotland
	5	*Independence Day (C)	Israel
		Children's Day (C)	Japan, South Korea
		Anniversary of the Battle of Puebla (C)	Mexico
		Coronation Day (C)	Thailand
	6	Martyrs Day (C)	Lebanon
	9	Victory Day (C)	U.S.S.R.
	11	Constitution Day (C)	Laos
	14	Prayer Day (R)	Denmark
		Anniversary of Guinean Democratic Party (C)	Guinea
		Unification Day (C)	Liberia
		Kamuzu Day (C)	Malawi
	14, 15	Independence Day (C)	Paraguay
	17	Constitution Day (*or* Independence Day) (C)	Norway
	18	Battle of Las Piedras Day (C)	Uruguay
	19	Youth and Sports Day (C)	Turkey
	20	Constitution Day (C)	Cameroon
	21	Battle of Iquique Day (*or* Navy Day) (C)	Chile
	22	National Sovereignty Day (*or* Day of Sovereignty) (C)	Haiti
		Republic Day (C)	Sri Lanka
	23	*Labor Day (C)	Jamaica
	24	Commonwealth Day (C)	Belize, Bermuda, Lesotho
		National Education Day (*or* Day of Slavonic Culture) (C)	Bulgaria
		*Victoria Day (C)	Canada
		Battle of Pichincha Day (C)	Ecuador
		African Freedom Day (C)	Zambia
	25	Anniversary of the 1810 Revolution (*or* May Revolution Day) (C)	Argentina
		African Liberation Day (C)	Chad, Liberia, Mali, Mauritania, Zambia
		Independence Day (C)	Jordan
		Anniversary of the May Revolution (C)	Sudan
	26	*Memorial Day (C)	Puerto Rico
		**National Holiday (C)	Turkey
	27	Independence Day (C)	Afghanistan
		Army Day (C)	Nicaragua
		National Holiday (C)	Turkey

Date		Holiday and Type	Country
	31	President's Day (C)	Botswana
		National Day (C)	Brunei
		Republic Day (C)	Republic of South Africa
		Bank Holiday (C)	United Kingdom (*except* Scotland)
		Memorial Day (C)	Virgin Islands of the U.S.
June	1	Madaraka Day (C)	Kenya
		Muslim Supreme Council Day (C)	Uganda
	1-3	Independence Holidays (C)	Western Samoa
	2	Tuen Ng Festival (*or* Dragon Boat Festival) (C)	Republic of China (Taiwan), Hong Kong
		Republic Day (*or* Proclamation of the Italian Republic) (C)	Italy
		Birthday of the Yang di-Pertuan Agong [Head of State] (C)	Malaysia
	3	Martyrs Shrine Day (R)	Uganda
	5	**Constitution Day (C)	Denmark
	6	Memorial Day (C)	South Korea
	7	The Queen's Birthday (C)	New Zealand
	10	Portugal's Day (*or* Camoes Day) (C)	Azores, Cape Verde, Portugal
		Public Holiday (C)	Guinea-Bissau
	12	*The Queen's Birthday (C)	Fiji
		Armistice Day (C)	Paraguay
		Independence Day (C)	Philippines
	17	Day of National Unity (C)	Federal Republic of Germany (West Germany)
		Independence Day (C)	Iceland
	18	Evacuation Day (C)	Egypt
	19	Awakening for National Recovery (*or* National Day) (C)	Algeria
		Labor Day (C)	Trinidad and Tobago
		Artigas Day (C)	Uruguay
	20	Flag Day (C)	Argentina
	22	Army Day (C)	Congo
		*Organic Act Day (C)	Virgin Islands of the U.S.
	23	The Grand Duke's Birthday (C)	Luxembourg
	24	**Agricultural Day (C)	Peru
		Battle of Carabobo Day (C)	Venezuela
		New Constitution Day (C)	Zaire
	25	*Midsummer Eve (C)	Finland, Sweden
		Independence Day (C)	Mozambique
	26	Independence Day (C)	Malagasy Republic (Madagascar), Somalia
		Midsummer Day (C)	Sweden
	29	Sts. Peter and Paul Day (R)	Andorra, Canary Islands, Colombia, Costa Rica, Italy, Malta, Peru, Spain, Venezuela

Date		Holiday and Type	Country
June	29, 30	Bank Holidays (C)	El Salvador
	30	Army Day (C)	Guatemala
		Independence Day (C)	Zaire
July	1	Bank Holiday (C)	Bangladesh, Iraq, Pakistan
		Independence Day (C)	Burundi
		Dominion Day (C)	Canada
		Republic Day (C)	Ghana
		*Half-year Holiday (C)	Hong Kong
		Independence Day (C)	Rwanda
		Union Day (C)	Somalia
		Emancipation Day (C)	Surinam
	2	*Family Day (C)	Lesotho
	3	Emancipation Day (C)	Virgin Islands of the U.S.
	4	Philippine-American Friendship Day (C)	Philippines
		Independence Day (C)	Puerto Rico, Virgin Islands of the U.S.
		Fighters Day (C)	Yugoslavia
	5	Independence Day (C)	Algeria
		Caribbean Day (C)	Barbados
		Caricom Day (C)	Guyana
		Peace Day (C)	Rwanda
		Independence Day (C)	Venezuela
		Heroes Day (C)	Zambia
	5-7	Republic Celebrations (C)	Malawi
	6	Unity Day (C)	Zambia
	7	National Day (C)	Equatorial Guinea
		Saba Saba Day (C)	Tanzania
	9	Independence Day (C)	Argentina
	10	Independence Day (C)	Bahamas
	12	July Holiday (C)	Northern Ireland
		Rhodes Day (C)	Rhodesia
	13	Founders Day (C)	Rhodesia
	14	Bastille Day (C)	France
		1958 Revolution (C)	Iraq
		National Holiday (C)	Monaco
		Day of National Dignity (C)	Nicaragua
	16	Bank Holiday (C)	Nepal
	17	1968 Revolution Day (*or* July Revolution Day) (C)	Iraq
		Constitution Day (C)	South Korea
	17-19	Republic Days (C)	Afghanistan
	18	National Uprising (C)	Spain
		Constitution Day (C)	Uruguay
	19	Martyrs Day (C)	Burma
		Independence Day (C)	Laos
	20	Independence Day (C)	Colombia

Date		Holiday and Type	Country
	21	Independence Day (C)	Belgium
	22	National Day (C)	Poland
		The King's Birthday (C)	Swaziland
	23	National Day (C)	Egypt
		Arab Revolution Day (C)	Syria
	24	Bolívar's Birthday (C)	Ecuador, Venezuela
		Lourenço Marques City Day (C)	Mozambique
	25	Annexation of Guanacaste (C)	Costa Rica
		Santiago Day (R)	Spain
		Republic Day (C)	Tunisia
	26	Cuban Revolution Day (*or* The Assault of Fort Moncaba) (C)	Cuba
		Independence Day (C)	Liberia
		Supplication Day (C)	Virgin Islands of the U.S.
	27	Barbosa's Birthday (C)	Puerto Rico
	28, 29	Independence Days (C)	Peru
	29	Cup Match Day (C)	Bermuda
	30	Somers Day (C)	Bermuda
August	1	Independence Day (C)	Benin
		*National Holiday (C)	Botswana
		*Independence Day (C)	Jamaica
		National Day (C)	Switzerland
		Parents Day (C)	Zaire
	2	Emancipation Day (C)	Bahamas
		Feast of Our Lady of the Angels (R)	Costa Rica
		*Bank Holiday (C)	Fiji, Iceland, Ireland, Malawi
		Commonwealth Day (C)	Guyana
		*Liberation Day (C)	Hong Kong
		*Discovery Day (C)	Trinidad and Tobago
	3	Independence Day (C)	Niger
		The President's Birthday (C)	Tunisia
	5	Constitution Day (C)	Iran
		*Renaissance Day (C)	Jordan
	6	Independence Day (C)	Bolivia
	7	Battle of Boyacá Day (C)	Colombia
	9	National Day (C)	Singapore
		Youth Day (C)	Zambia
	10	Independence Day (C)	Ecuador
	11	Independence Day (C)	Chad
		Coronation Day (C)	Jordan
	12	The Queen's Birthday (C)	Thailand
	13	Women's Day (C)	Tunisia
	14	Independence Day (C)	Pakistan
	15	Independence Day (C)	India, South Korea
		Founding of the City of Asunción (C)	Paraguay

Date		Holiday and Type	Country
August	16	Restoration Day (C)	Dominican Republic
	17	Death of General San Martin (C)	Argentina
		Independence Day (C)	Gabon
		Independence Day (C)	Indonesia
	20	Constitution Day (C)	Hungary
		Beira City Day (C)	Mozambique
	23, 24	National Days (C)	Rumania
	24	Flag Day (C)	Liberia
	25	Constitution Day (C)	Paraguay
		Independence Day (C)	Uruguay
	30	National Holiday (*or* Liberation Day) (C)	Hong Kong
		St. Rose of Lima Day (R)	Peru
		Victory Day (C)	Turkey
		*Bank Holiday (C)	United Kingdom (*except* Scotland)
	31	Pashtunistan Day (C)	Afghanistan
		National Day (C)	Malaysia
		Independence Day (C)	Trinidad and Tobago
September	1	*Labor Day (C)	Canada, Puerto Rico, Virgin Islands of the U.S.
		Libyan Revolution Anniversary (C)	Egypt
	3	Liberation of Monaco (C)	Monaco
		Commemoration of Sept. 3, 1934 (C)	Tunisia
	4	*Independence Day (C)	Qatar
	6	Fall Fair (*or* Schobermess) (C)	Luxembourg
		Defense Day (C)	Pakistan
		Settlers Day (C)	Republic of South Africa
		Independence Day (C)	Swaziland
	7	Independence Day (C)	Brazil
	8	National Holiday (C/R)	Andorra
		Patron Saint's Day (R)	Canary Islands
		Commemoration of Two Sieges (C)	Malta
	9	National Assembly Day (C)	Afghanistan
		Liberation Day (C)	Bulgaria
	10	National Day (C)	Belize
	11	Ethiopian New Year (C)	Ethiopia
		Jinnah Day (*or* Death Anniversary of Quaid-i-Azam) (C)	Pakistan
	12	Pioneers Day (C)	Rhodesia
	14	Battle of San Jacinto Day (C)	Nicaragua
	15	Independence Day (C)	Costa Rica, El Salvador, Guatemala, Honduras, Nicaragua
		Respect for the Aged Day (C)	Japan

Date		Holiday and Type	Country
	16	Independence Day (C)	Mexico
		Independence Day (C)	Papua New Guinea
	18	Victory of the Uprona Party (C)	Burundi
		Independence Day (C)	Chile
	19	Day of the Armed Forces (C)	Chile
	20	Thanksgiving Day (C)	Laos
	22	Independence Day (C)	Mali
	23	*Autumnal Equinox Day (C)	Japan
	24	Feast of Our Lady of Mercy (R)	Dominican Republic
	24–27	Sheker Bairam (*or* Feast of Sugar) (C)	Turkey
	25	Frelimo and FPLM Day (C)	Mozambique
		National Day (C)	Yemen Arab Republic
	26–28	Revolution Days (C)	People's Democratic Republic of Yemen
	28	Birthday of Confucius (C)	Republic of China (Taiwan)
		Referendum Day (C)	Guinea
	29	Victory of Boquerón Day (C)	Paraguay
	30	Botswana Day (C)	Botswana
October	1	Bank Holiday (C)	Burma
		National Sports Day (C)	Lesotho
		National Day (C)	Nigeria
	1, 2	Founding of the People's Republic of China (C)	People's Republic of China
	2	Independence Day (C)	Guinea
		Mahatma Gandhi's Birthday (C)	India
	3	*Francisco Morazán's Birthday (C)	Honduras
		National Foundation Day (C)	South Korea
	4	Independence Day (C)	Lesotho
	5	Republic Day (C)	Azores, Guinea-Bissau, Portugal
	6	Armed Forces Day (C)	Egypt
	7, 8	Republic Day (C)	German Democratic Republic (East Germany)
	9	Guayaquil Independence Day (C)	Ecuador
		Alphabet Day (C)	South Korea
		National Day of Dignity (C)	Peru
		Independence Day (C)	Uganda
	10	Double Ten Day (*or* Double Tenth Day) (C)	Republic of China (Taiwan)
		Kruger Day (C)	South Africa
	11	*Thanksgiving Day (C/R)	Canada
		Fiji Day (C)	Fiji
		Sports Day (C)	Japan
		Revolution Day (C)	Panama
		Columbus Day and Puerto Rico Friendship Day (C)	Virgin Islands of the U.S.
		National Holiday (C)	Western Samoa

Date		Holiday and Type	Country
October	12	Columbus Day (*or* Day of the Race) (C)	Argentina, Colombia, Costa Rica, Chile, Ecuador, Mexico, Nicaragua, Paraguay, Puerto Rico, Uruguay, Venezuela
		Discovery Day (C)	Bahamas, Honduras
		Our Lady of Pilar Day (R)	Canary Islands
		Independence Day (C)	Equatorial Guinea
		Hispanic Day (C)	Spain
		Sudan Republic Day (C)	Sudan
	13	Assassination of the National Hero (*or* Murder of Prince L. Rwagasore) (C)	Burundi
	14	Independence Day (C)	People's Democratic Republic of Yemen (Southern Yemen)
		President Mobutu's Day (C)	Zaire
	15	Deliverance Day (C)	Afghanistan
		Evacuation of Bizerte Day (C)	Tunisia
	16	*National Heroes Day (C)	Jamaica
	17	Dessalines' Day (C)	Haiti
		Mothers Day (C)	Malawi
	18	*Republic Day (C)	Rhodesia
		*Thanksgiving Day (territorial) (C/R)	Virgin Islands of the U.S.
	20	Revolution Day (C)	Guatemala
		Kenyatta Day (C)	Kenya
	21	Armed Forces Day (C)	Honduras
	21, 22	Revolution Anniversary (C)	Somalia
	23	Chulalongkorn Day (C)	Thailand
	24	United Nations Day (C)	Afghanistan, Barbados, Botswana, Haiti, South Korea, Swaziland
		Popular Resistance Day (C)	Egypt
		Independence Day (C)	Zambia
	25	*Restoration Day (C)	Republic of China (Taiwan)
		Labor Day (C)	New Zealand
		Veterans Day (C)	Puerto Rico
	26	National Holiday (C)	Austria
		Revolution Day (C)	Benin
		Birthday of the Shah (C)	Iran
		Armed Forces Day (C)	Rwanda
	27	Anniversary of Zaire (C)	Zaire
	28	Greek National Day (C)	Cyprus
		National Day (C)	Greece
	29	Turkish National Day (C)	Cyprus
		Independence Day (C)	Turkey
	31	Birthday of Chiang Kai-shek (C)	Republic of China (Taiwan)

Date		Holiday and Type	Country
November	1	Revolution Day (C)	Algeria
		All Saints' Day (R)	Andorra, Argentina, Austria, Azores, Belgium, Benin, Burundi, Canary Islands, Cape Verde, Chad, Chile, Colombia, Congo, Equatorial Guinea, France, Gabon, Guatemala, Guinea-Bissau, Haiti, Italy, Ivory Coast, Lebanon, Liechtenstein, Luxembourg, Malagasy Republic (Madagascar), Malta, Mauritius, Monaco, Mozambique, Paraguay, Peru, Poland, Portugal, Rwanda, Senegal, Seychelles, Spain, Sweden, Togo, Upper Volta, Vatican City State, Venezuela
		National Holiday (C)	Hong Kong
	2	All Souls' Day (R)	Belgium, Bolivia, Brazil, Ecuador, France, Haiti, Luxembourg, Mexico, Uruguay
	3	Cuenca Independence Day (C)	Ecuador
		Culture Day (C)	Japan
		Independence Day (C)	Panama
	4	Imam Reza's Birthday (C)	Iran
		Unity Day (C)	Italy
		*Thanksgiving Day (C/R)	Liberia
	5	First Call for Independence (C)	El Salvador
	7	Anniversary of the October Revolution (C)	Bulgaria, Hungary, U.S.S.R.
	9	Muhammad Iqbal's Birthday (C)	Pakistan
	11	Veterans Day (C)	Belgium, France, Virgin Islands of the U.S.
		Remembrance Day (C)	Bermuda, Canada
		Cartagena Independence Day (C)	Colombia
		Victory Day (C)	Monaco
		Independence Day (C)	Rhodesia
	12	Sun Yat-sen's Birthday (C)	Republic of China (Taiwan)
	13	The King's Birthday (C)	Laos
	14	Prince Charles's Birthday (C)	Belize, Fiji
		King Hussein's Birthday (C)	Jordan
	15	Dynasty Day (C)	Belgium
		Proclamation of the Republic Day (C)	Brazil
	17	Repentance Day (C)	Germany
		Armed Forces Day (C)	Zaire
	18	Armed Forces and Veterans Day (C)	Haiti
		Independence Day (C)	Morocco
		National Day (C)	Oman

Date		Holiday and Type	Country
November	19	Liberation Day (C)	Mali
		Discovery Day (C)	Puerto Rico
	20	Anniversary of the Revolution (C)	Mexico
		Prince of Monaco Holiday (C)	Monaco
	22	*Independence Day (C)	Lebanon
	23	Labor Thanksgiving Day (C)	Japan
	24	Anniversary of the New Regime (C)	Zaire
	25	*Thanksgiving Day (C/R)	Puerto Rico, Virgin Islands of the U.S.
		Independence Day (C)	Surinam
	27	National Day (C)	Burma
	28	Independence Day (C)	Mauritania
		Republic Day (C)	Burundi, Chad
		Independence from Spain (C)	Panama
	29	William V. S. Tubman's Birthday (C)	Liberia
		Day of the Republic (C)	Yugoslavia
	30	Independence Day (C)	Barbados, People's Democratic Republic of Yemen (Southern Yemen)
		Bonifacio Day (C)	Philippines
December	1	Independence Day (C)	Azores
		Restoration Day (C)	Cape Verde, Portugal
		National Day (C)	Central African Republic
		Matilda Newport Day (C)	Liberia
	2	National Day (C)	United Arab Emirates
	5	Anniversary of the Discovery of Haiti (C)	Haiti
		The King's Birthday (C)	Thailand
		Constitution Day (C)	U.S.S.R.
	6	Foundation of Quito (C)	Ecuador
		Independence Day (C)	Finland
	7	Independence Day (*or* National Day) (C)	Ivory Coast
	8	Immaculate Conception Day (R)	Andorra, Argentina, Austria, Azores, Canary Islands, Cape Verde, Chile, Colombia, Costa Rica, Guam, Italy, Liechtenstein, Malta, Mozambique, Nicaragua, Panama, Paraguay, Peru, Portugal, Seychelles, Spain, Venezuela
		Day of the Beaches (C)	Uruguay
	9	Independence Day (C)	Tanzania
	10	Constitution Day (C)	Thailand
	11	National Holiday (C)	Upper Volta
	12	Independence Day (*or* Jamhuri Day) (C)	Kenya

Date	Holiday and Type	Country
13	National Day (*or* Republic Day) (C)	Malta
15	Constitution Day (C)	Nepal
16	National Day (*or* Victory Day) (C)	Bahrain, Bangladesh
	Day of the Covenant (C)	Republic of South Africa
18	Republic Day (C)	Niger
24	**Christmas Eve (R)	observed in many countries
25	Christmas (C/R)	observed in most countries
	Constitution Day (C)	Republic of China (Taiwan)
26	*Boxing Day (C)	Australia, Bahamas, Barbados, Belize, Bermuda, Botswana, Canada, Fiji, Gambia, Ghana, Guyana, Hong Kong, Jamaica, Kenya, Lesotho, Malawi, New Zealand, Nigeria, Rhodesia, Sierra Leone, Republic of South Africa, Swaziland, Trinidad and Tobago, United Kingdom (*except* Scotland)
	St. Stephen's Day (R)	Austria, Belgium, Cyprus, Greece, Hungary, Iceland, Ireland, Italy, Liechtenstein, Switzerland
29	The King's Birthday (C)	Nepal
30	Rizal Day (C)	Philippines
31	New Year's Eve (C)	a bank holiday in many countries

FOREIGN COUNTRIES

A list of foreign countries with their capitals, nationalities, and official language(s)—information frequently used by the secretary in multinational firms—follows. When more than one language appears at an entry, the listing is alphabetical.

Country	Capital	Nationality	Official Language(s)
Afghanistan	Kabul	Afghan	Persian, Pushto
Albania	Tirana	Albanian	Albanian
Algeria	Algiers	Algerian	Arabic, French
Andorra	Andorra la Vella	Andorran	Catalan
Angola	Luanda	Angolan	Portuguese
Arab Republic of Egypt	Cairo	Egyptian	Arabic
Argentina	Buenos Aires	Argentine	Spanish
Australia	Canberra	Australian	English
Austria	Vienna	Austrian	German
Azores	Ponta Delgada	Azorean	Portuguese
Bahamas	Nassau	Bahamian	English
Bahrain	Manama	Bahraini	Arabic
Bangladesh	Dacca	Bengali	Bengali

Country	Capital	Nationality	Official Language (s)
Barbados	Bridgetown	Barbadian	English
Belgium	Brussels	Belgian	Flemish, French
Belize	Belmopan	Belizean	English
Benin (*formerly* Dahomey)	Porto-Novo	Beninese	French
Bermuda	Hamilton	Bermudian	English
Bhutan	Thimbu	Bhutanese	Bhutanese
Bolivia	La Paz	Bolivian	Spanish
Botswana	Gaborone	Botswana	English
Brazil	Brasília	Brazilian	Portuguese
Brunei	Brunei	Bruneian	English
Bulgaria	Sofia	Bulgarian	Bulgarian
Burma	Rangoon	Burmese	Burmese
Burundi	Bujumbura	Burundian	French, Rundi
Cambodia (Khmer Republic)	Phnom Penh	Cambodian	Khmer
Cameroon	Yaoundé	Cameroonian	English, French
Canada	Ottawa	Canadian	English, French
Canary Islands	Las Palmas	Canarian	Spanish
Cape Verde	Praia	Cape Verdean	Portuguese
Central African Republic	Bangui	Central African	French
Ceylon—*see* SRI LANKA			
Chad	Ndjamena	Chadian	French
Chile	Santiago	Chilean	Spanish
China, People's Republic of	Peking	Chinese	Chinese
China, Republic of	Taipei	Chinese	Chinese
Colombia	Bogotá	Colombian	Spanish
Comoro	Moroni	Comoro	French
Congo	Brazzaville	Congolese	French
Costa Rica	San José	Costa Rican	Spanish
Cuba	Havana	Cuban	Spanish
Cyprus	Nicosia	Cypriot	Greek, Turkish
Czechoslovakia	Prague	Czechoslovak	Czech, Slovak
Dahomey—*see* BENIN			
Denmark	Copenhagen	Danish	Danish
Dominican Republic	Santo Domingo	Dominican	Spanish
Ecuador	Quito	Ecuadorean	Spanish
Egypt—*see* ARAB REPUBLIC OF EGYPT			
El Salvador	San Salvador	Salvadoran	Spanish
England—*see* UNITED KINGDOM			
Equatorial Guinea	Malabo	Equatorial Guinean	Spanish
Ethiopia	Addis Ababa	Ethiopian	Amharic
Fiji	Suva	Fijian	English

Country	Capital	Nationality	Official Language(s)
Finland	Helsinki	Finnish	Finnish
France	Paris	French	French
Gabon	Libreville	Gabonese	French
Gambia	Banjul	Gambian	English
Germany, East (German Democratic Republic)	East Berlin	East German	German
Germany, West (Federal Republic of Germany)	Bonn	West German	German
Ghana	Accra	Ghanaian	English
Great Britain—*see* UNITED KINGDOM			
Greece	Athens	Greek	Greek
Grenada	St. George's	Grenadian	English
Guatemala	Guatemala City	Guatemalan	Spanish
Guinea	Conakry	Guinean	French
Guinea-Bissau	Bissau		Portuguese
Guinea, Equatorial—*see* EQUATORIAL GUINEA			
Guyana	Georgetown	Guyanese	English
Haiti	Port-au-Prince	Haitian	French
Honduras	Tegucigalpa	Honduran	Spanish
Hungary	Budapest	Hungarian	Hungarian
Iceland	Reykjavík	Icelandic	Icelandic
India	New Delhi	Indian	English, Hindi
Indonesia	Jakarta	Indonesian	Bahasa Indonesia
Iran	Tehran	Iranian	Persian
Iraq	Baghdad	Iraqi	Arabic
Ireland (*or* Irish Republic)	Dublin	Irish	English, Irish
Israel	Jerusalem	Israeli	Arabic, Hebrew
Italy	Rome	Italian	Italian
Ivory Coast	Abidjan	Ivory Coaster	French
Jamaica	Kingston	Jamaican	English
Japan	Tokyo	Japanese	Japanese
Jordan	Amman	Jordanian	Arabic
Kenya	Nairobi	Kenyan	English, Swahili
Khmer Republic—*see* CAMBODIA			
Korea, North	Pyongyang	North Korean	Korean
Korea, South	Seoul	South Korean	Korean
Kuwait	Kuwait	Kuwaiti	Arabic
Laos	Vientiane	Laotian	Lao
Lesotho	Maseru	Basotho	English
Liberia	Monrovia	Liberian	English
Libya	Tripoli	Libyan	Arabic
Liechtenstein	Vaduz	Liechtensteiner	German

Country	Capital	Nationality	Official Language(s)
Luxembourg	Luxembourg	Luxembourger	French, German
Malagasy Republic (Madagascar)	Tananarive	Malagasy	French, Malagasy
Malawi	Lilongwe	Malawian	English, Nyanja (*or* Chewa)
Malaysia	Kuala Lumpur	Malaysian	Malay
Maldives	Male	Maldivian	Maldivian
Mali	Bamako	Malian	French
Malta	Valletta	Maltese	English, Maltese
Mauritania	Nouakchott	Mauritanian	Arabic, French
Mauritius	Port Louis	Mauritian	English
Mexico	Mexico City	Mexican	Spanish
Monaco	Monaco	Monacan (*or* Monegasque)	French
Mongolia	Ulan Bator	Mongol	Mongolian (Khalkha)
Morocco	Rabat	Moroccan	Arabic
Mozambique	Maputo	Mozambican	Portuguese
Nauru		Nauruan	English
Nepal	Katmandu	Nepalese	Nepali
Netherlands	Amsterdam (*official*) The Hague (*de facto*)	Dutch	Dutch
New Zealand	Wellington	New Zealander	English
Nicaragua	Managua	Nicaraguan	Spanish
Niger	Niamey	Nigerois	French
Nigeria	Lagos	Nigerian	English
North Korea—*see* KOREA, NORTH			
North Vietnam—*see* VIETNAM, NORTH			
Norway	Oslo	Norwegian	Norwegian
Oman	Muscat	Omani	Arabic
Pakistan	Islamabad	Pakistani	Bengali, English, Urdu
Panama	Panama	Panamanian	Spanish
Papua New Guinea	Port Moresby	Papua New Guinean	English
Paraguay	Asunción	Paraguayan	Spanish
Peru	Lima	Peruvian	Spanish
Philippines	Quezon City	Filipino	English, Pilipino
Poland	Warsaw	Polish	Polish
Portugal	Lisbon	Portuguese	Portuguese
Puerto Rico	San Juan	Puerto Rican	English, Spanish
Qatar	Doha	Qatari	Arabic
Rhodesia	Salisbury	Rhodesian	English
Rumania (*or* Romania)	Bucharest	Rumanian (*or* Romanian)	Rumanian (*or* Romanian)
Russia—*see* UNION OF SOVIET SOCIALIST REPUBLICS			
Rwanda	Kigali	Rwandan	French, Ruanda
Samoa, Western—*see* WESTERN SAMOA			

Country	Capital	Nationality	Official Language(s)
San Marino	San Marino	San Marinese	Italian
São Tomé and Principe	São Tomé		Portuguese
Saudi Arabia	Riyadh	Saudi Arabian	Arabic
Senegal	Dakar	Senegalese	French
Seychelles	Victoria	Seychellois	English
Sierra Leone	Freetown	Sierra Leonean	English
Singapore	Singapore	Singaporean	Chinese, English, Malay, Tamil
Somalia	Mogadishu	Somali	Somali
South Africa	Pretoria (*administrative capital*), Capetown (*legislative capital*), Bloemfontein (*judicial capital*)	South African	Afrikaans, English
South Korea—*see* KOREA, SOUTH			
South Yemen	Aden	South Yemeni	Arabic
Spain	Madrid	Spanish	Spanish
Sri Lanka (*formerly* Ceylon)	Colombo	Sri Lankan	Sinhalese
Sudan	Khartoum	Sudanese	Arabic
Surinam	Paramaribo	Surinamese	Dutch
Swaziland	Mbabane	Swazi	English
Sweden	Stockholm	Swedish	Swedish
Switzerland	Bern	Swiss	French, German, Italian, Romansh
Syria	Damascus	Syrian	Arabic
Tanzania	Dar es Salaam	Tanzanian	English, Swahili
Thailand	Bangkok	Thai	Thai
Togo	Lomé	Togolese	French
Tonga	Nukualofa	Tongan	English, Tongan
Trinidad and Tobago	Trinidad and Tobago	Trinidadian and Tobagonian	English
Tunisia	Tunis	Tunisian	Arabic
Turkey	Ankara	Turkish	Turkish
Uganda	Kampala	Ugandan	English
Union of Soviet Socialist Republics (U.S.S.R.)	Moscow	Russian	Russian
United Arab Emirates	Abu Dhabi	Arabic	Arabic
United Kingdom	London	British	English
Upper Volta	Ouagadougou	Upper Voltan	French
Uruguay	Montevideo	Uruguayan	Spanish
Vatican City State			Italian

Country	Capital	Nationality	Official Language (s)
Venezuela	Caracas	Venezuelan	Spanish
Vietnam (*formerly* North Vietnam)	Hanoi	Vietnamese	Vietnamese
Western Samoa	Apia	Western Samoan	English, Samoan
Yemen	San'a	Yemeni	Arabic
Yugoslavia	Belgrade	Yugoslav	Macedonian, Serbo-Croatian, Slovenian
Zaire	Kinshasa	Zairian	French
Zambia	Lusaka	Zambian	English

EXPENSE ACCOUNT RECORDS

Reimbursable and tax deductible items are key listings in any record of business expenses. Forms for recording expense records can be prepared by the forms designers and analysts in corporations; such forms should be designed to comply with U.S. Internal Revenue Service requirements. Conditions underlying deductions on federal income tax returns for travel, entertainment, and gifts are set forth in the Internal Revenue Service's Publication 463, "Travel, Entertainment, and Expenses." Copies of this booklet can be obtained from one's local Internal Revenue Service office or from the Superintendent of Documents, U.S. Government Printing Office, Washington, DC 20402. Record-keeping rules are included in this document, and some of the ones listed on page 14 are quoted as follows:

"No deductions will be allowed for any travel expenses (including meals and lodging while away from home), for any items concerning a type of activity generally considered entertainment, amusement, or recreation, or a facility used in connection with such activity, or for any expenses for gifts, unless the taxpayer substantiates the following elements:

1) The amount of the expense or other item;
2) The time and place of the travel, entertainment, amusement, recreation, or use of the facility, or the date and description of the gift;
3) The business purpose of the expense or other item; and
4) The business relationship to the taxpayer of the persons entertained, using the facility, or receiving the gift.

"No deduction will be allowed for approximations or estimates, or for expenses that are lavish or extravagant."

For travel, one must be prepared to prove the following, according to page 14 of the same document:

"1) The amount of each separate expenditure for travel away from home overnight (such as the cost of your transportation or lodging) but the daily cost of your breakfast, lunch, dinner, and other incidental elements of such travel may be totaled, if they are set forth in reasonable categories (such as for meals, gasoline and oil, and cab fares);
2) The dates of your departure and return home for each trip, and the number of days spent on business away from home overnight;
3) Your destinations or the locality of your travel, described by name of city, town, or similar designation; and
4) The business reason for your travel or the business benefit derived or expected to be gained from your travel."

For entertainment, the following must be proved, according to Publication 463:

"1) The amount of each separate expenditure for entertaining, except that incidental items like cab fares and telephone calls may be totaled on a daily basis;

2) The date the entertainment took place;
3) The name (if any), address or location, and the type of entertainment (such as dinner or theater) if such information is not apparent from the name or designation of the place;
4) The reason for the entertainment or the nature of the business benefit derived or expected to be gained from entertaining and, except for *certain business meals* . . . the nature of any business discussion or activity that took place; and
5) The occupation or other information about the person or persons entertained, including name, title, or other designation, sufficient to establish his business relationship to you."

Business people bringing home gifts from abroad must be able to substantiate the following information: the cost, date of purchase, a description of the gift, the reason for giving it, and the occupation of or other information about the recipient including his name, title, or other designation.

METRIC EQUIVALENTS

Many secretaries in multinational firms work with metric measures; other secretaries will of necessity be required to become familiar with the metric system as the United States converts to these standards of measurement. The following metric system table is reprinted from page 724 of *Webster's New Collegiate Dictionary;* see also page 502 of this chapter for a weights and measures table.

METRIC SYSTEM[1]

LENGTH

unit	*abbreviation*	*number of meters*	*approximate U.S. equivalent*
myriameter	mym	10,000	6.2 miles
kilometer	km	1,000	0.62 mile
hectometer	hm	100	109.36 yards
dekameter	dam	10	32.81 feet
meter	m	1	39.37 inches
decimeter	dm	0.1	3.94 inches
centimeter	cm	0.01	0.39 inch
millimeter	mm	0.001	0.04 inch

AREA

unit	*abbreviation*	*number of square meters*	*approximate U.S. equivalent*
square kilometer	sq km *or* km²	1,000,000	0.3861 square mile
hectare	ha	10,000	2.47 acres
are	a	100	119.60 square yards
centare	ca	1	10.76 square feet
square centimeter	sq cm *or* cm²	0.0001	0.155 square inch

VOLUME

unit	*abbreviation*	*number of cubic meters*	*approximate U.S. equivalent*
dekastere	das	10	13.10 cubic yards
stere	s	1	1.31 cubic yards
decistere	ds	0.10	3.53 cubic feet
cubic centimeter	cu cm *or* cm³ *also* cc	0.000001	0.061 cubic inch

CAPACITY

unit	*abbreviation*	*number of liters*	*approximate U.S. equivalent* *cubic*	*dry*	*liquid*
kiloliter	kl	1,000	1.31 cubic yards		
hectoliter	hl	100	3.53 cubic feet	2.84 bushels	
dekaliter	dal	10	0.35 cubic foot	1.14 pecks	2.64 gallons
liter	l	1	61.02 cubic inches	0.908 quart	1.057 quarts
deciliter	dl	0.10	6.1 cubic inches	0.18 pint	0.21 pint
centiliter	cl	0.01	0.6 cubic inch		0.338 fluidounce
milliliter	ml	0.001	0.06 cubic inch		0.27 fluidram

MASS AND WEIGHT

unit	*abbreviation*	*number of grams*	*approximate U.S. equivalent*
metric ton	MT *or* t	1,000,000	1.1 tons
quintal	q	100,000	220.46 pounds
kilogram	kg	1,000	2.2046 pounds
hectogram	hg	100	3.527 ounces
dekagram	dag	10	0.353 ounce
gram	g *or* gm	1	0.035 ounce
decigram	dg	0.10	1.543 grains
centigram	cg	0.01	0.154 grain
milligram	mg	0.001	0.015 grain

[1] For metric equivalents of U.S. units see Weights and Measures table.

TABLE OF AIR AND ROAD DISTANCES

A complete list of air mileage from cities in the United States to foreign cities is shown in the *Official Airline Guide.* This guide, commonly called the *OAG,* also lists complete airline schedules and is updated frequently. It is an essential reference for the executive who travels regularly.

TABLES OF AIRLINE DISTANCES

All Distances in Statute Miles

Between Principal Cities in the United States

FROM/TO	Albuquerque, N. Mex.	Atlanta, Ga.	Baltimore, Md.	Boise, Idaho	Boston, Mass.	Brownsville, Tex.	Buffalo, N. Y.	Chicago, Ill.	Cincinnati, Ohio	Cleveland, Ohio	Denver, Colo.	Des Moines, Iowa	Detroit, Mich.	El Paso, Tex.	Fargo, N. Dak.	Fort Worth, Tex.	Galveston, Tex.	Hastings, Nebr.	Hot Springs, Ark.	Houghton, Mich.	Jacksonville, Fla.	Kansas City, Mo.	Los Angeles, Calif.
Albuquerque, N. Mex.	....	1273	1670	774	1967	838	1577	1126	1248	1417	332	833	1360	228	968	561	803	588	773	1252	1492	717	663
Atlanta, Ga.	1273	....	575	1830	933	960	695	583	368	550	1208	738	595	1293	1112	750	688	901	498	947	286	675	1935
Baltimore, Md.	1670	575	....	2055	358	1525	273	603	423	305	1505	913	398	1750	1143	1239	1245	1154	964	808	682	962	2313
Boise, Idaho	774	1830	2055	....	2266	1610	1872	1453	1663	1754	637	1155	1671	969	975	1263	1538	934	1384	1367	2098	1158	663
Boston, Mass.	1967	933	358	2266	....	1881	398	849	737	550	1766	1159	613	2067	1304	1574	1598	1415	1302	922	1015	1250	2590
Brownsville, Tex.	838	960	1525	1610	1881	....	1575	1234	1184	1402	1047	1102	1398	682	1445	471	287	1013	650	1543	1025	923	1370
Buffalo, N. Y.	1577	695	273	1872	398	1575	....	454	392	175	1368	762	218	1690	923	1221	1289	1019	956	560	880	862	2195
Chicago, Ill.	1126	583	603	1453	849	1234	454	....	249	307	918	310	236	1249	571	820	954	566	585	367	861	413	1741
Cincinnati, Ohio	1248	368	423	1663	737	1184	392	249	....	218	1090	509	234	1333	818	839	897	742	569	589	628	541	1892
Cleveland, Ohio	1417	550	305	1754	550	1402	175	307	218	....	1223	617	94	1521	838	1046	1116	871	787	518	768	700	2044
Denver, Colo.	332	1208	1505	637	1766	1047	1368	918	1090	1223	....	607	1153	554	642	643	925	353	749	970	1468	555	828
Des Moines, Iowa	833	738	913	1155	1159	1102	762	310	509	617	607	....	545	980	397	640	851	256	488	458	1024	180	1433
Detroit, Mich.	1360	595	398	1671	613	1398	218	236	234	94	1153	545	....	1475	745	1018	1111	800	761	427	832	643	1976
El Paso, Tex.	228	1293	1750	969	2067	682	1690	1249	1333	1521	554	980	1475	....	1161	543	723	757	802	1422	1481	836	702
Fargo, N. Dak.	968	1112	1143	975	1304	1445	923	571	818	838	642	397	745	1161	....	973	1218	440	875	393	1400	548	1426
Fort Worth, Tex.	561	750	1239	1263	1574	471	1221	820	839	1046	643	640	1018	543	973	....	283	544	273	1093	943	460	1212
Galveston, Tex.	803	688	1245	1538	1598	287	1289	954	897	1116	925	851	1111	723	1218	283	....	808	375	1277	799	677	1423
Hastings, Nebr.	588	901	1154	934	1415	1013	1019	566	742	871	353	256	800	757	440	544	808	....	513	666	1178	226	1177
Hot Springs, Ark.	773	498	964	1384	1302	650	956	585	569	787	749	488	761	802	875	273	375	513	....	901	728	326	1437
Houghton, Mich.	1252	947	808	1367	922	1543	560	367	589	518	970	458	427	1422	393	1093	1277	666	901	....	1216	633	1787
Jacksonville, Fla.	1492	286	682	2098	1015	1025	880	861	628	768	1468	1024	832	1481	1400	943	799	1178	728	1216	....	952	2153
Kansas City, Mo.	717	675	962	1158	1250	923	862	413	541	700	555	180	643	836	548	460	677	226	326	633	952	....	1352
Los Angeles, Calif.	663	1935	2313	663	2590	1370	2195	1741	1892	2044	828	1433	1976	702	1426	1212	1423	1177	1437	1787	2153	1352	....
Louisville, Ky.	1174	317	498	1623	823	1093	483	268	92	309	1035	477	315	1253	818	751	807	693	480	636	595	480	1825
Memphis, Tenn.	938	335	792	1506	1133	777	802	481	410	627	878	485	621	978	882	448	492	591	176	830	591	370	1602
Miami, Fla.	1710	610	958	2368	1258	1100	1184	1190	957	1088	1732	1338	1156	1662	1721	1150	941	1468	983	1545	328	1247	2355
Minneapolis, Minn.	980	905	948	1140	1125	1335	733	356	603	632	699	235	542	1156	219	870	1087	399	722	272	1192	413	1522
Missoula, Mont.	895	1790	1947	252	2124	1706	1740	1348	1578	1640	670	1074	1552	1115	819	1312	1595	891	1385	1208	2070	1117	910
Nashville, Tenn.	1117	218	597	1631	941	952	626	394	239	456	1018	523	468	1169	900	643	666	697	370	760	502	472	1777
New Orleans, La.	1030	427	1001	1713	1359	536	1087	831	708	922	1079	825	938	986	1221	470	288	870	358	1187	511	678	1675
New York, N. Y.	1810	747	170	2153	188	1695	291	711	568	404	1628	1023	483	1902	1213	1398	1415	1275	1125	849	838	1097	2446
Norfolk, Va.	1696	507	167	2137	467	1465	435	696	474	429	1562	983	522	1755	1258	1226	1195	1216	955	946	548	1009	2352
Oklahoma, Okla.	518	753	1173	1138	1490	659	1117	689	755	946	503	469	905	578	786	188	456	357	260	926	988	293	1182
Omaha, Nebr.	718	815	1026	1044	1280	1061	883	432	620	738	485	122	666	875	390	590	828	135	490	547	1098	165	1312
Philadelphia, Pa.	1748	663	90	2113	268	1614	278	664	501	343	575	972	444	1834	1186	1324	1335	1222	1051	827	758	1037	2388
Phoenix, Ariz.	330	1592	2002	733	2295	1023	1904	1451	1578	1745	585	1154	1685	347	1225	858	1065	901	1094	1550	1800	1045	357
Pittsburgh, Pa.	1498	520	194	1863	478	1424	178	411	258	115	1320	718	208	1592	952	1097	1140	967	825	530	703	784	2135
Portland, Me.	2015	1022	446	2282	100	1961	438	892	802	603	1803	1197	657	2126	1313	1642	1678	1454	1371	924	1113	1300	2631
Portland, Oreg.	1107	2172	2367	349	2553	1944	2167	1765	1987	2063	985	1479	1975	1286	1248	1612	1885	1271	1733	1638	2442	1397	825
Richmond, Va.	1628	470	128	2060	471	1428	375	618	399	353	1488	905	445	1695	1180	1170	1154	1142	897	870	953	937	2283
St. Louis, Mo.	938	467	731	1389	1036	975	662	259	308	490	793	270	452	1033	658	568	697	455	325	591	755	238	1585
Salt Lake City, Utah	483	1580	1858	292	2099	1317	1701	1260	1450	1567	372	952	1490	689	865	977	1249	708	1116	1242	1840	922	577
San Francisco, Calif.	893	2133	2451	516	2696	1675	2298	1855	2037	2163	946	1547	2087	993	1447	1454	1693	1297	1648	1833	2375	1500	345
Schenectady, N. Y.	1823	840	278	2120	150	1770	249	702	605	408	1618	1012	467	1930	1157	1445	1487	1267	1175	776	960	1107	2445
Seattle, Wash.	1178	2180	2341	405	2508	2015	2130	1743	1974	2035	1020	1470	1945	1373	1206	1658	1938	1288	1759	1588	2450	1505	956
Shreveport, La.	764	548	1064	1433	1410	510	1080	725	688	904	799	624	891	752	1002	209	233	615	142	1043	733	326	1420
Spokane, Wash.	1028	1960	2110	290	2279	1852	1900	1514	1746	1804	827	1243	1715	1238	976	1470	1753	1061	1552	1360	2239	1286	939
Springfield, Mass.	1889	863	282	2196	79	1805	325	774	659	473	1692	1085	540	1990	1240	1495	1524	1340	1224	860	957	1173	2515
Vermillion, S. Dak.	742	917	1083	973	1314	1161	916	479	694	785	468	187	705	920	284	689	938	167	605	510	1203	280	1291
Washington, D. C.	1648	542	33	2045	392	1493	290	594	403	303	1490	895	397	1726	1141	1210	1214	1139	936	813	647	943	2295

Reprinted from **Webster's Atlas and Zip Code Directory** courtesy of Hammond, Incorporated.

These tables showing airline distances between principal cities of the United States, between representative cities of the United States and Latin America, between principal cities of Europe, and between principal cities of the world are reprinted from pages 346 and 347 of *Webster's Atlas and Zip Code Directory* (Springfield: G. & C. Merriam Company, 1973), a book prepared by the staff of Hammond, Inc.

Louisville, Ky.	Memphis, Tenn.	Miami, Fla.	Minneapolis, Minn.	Missoula, Mont.	Nashville, Tenn.	New Orleans, La.	New York, N. Y.	Norfolk, Va.	Oklahoma, Okla.	Omaha, Nebr.	Philadelphia, Pa.	Phoenix, Ariz.	Pittsburgh, Pa.	Portland, Me.	Portland, Oreg.	Richmond, Va.	St. Louis, Mo.	Salt Lake City, Utah	San Francisco, Calif.	Schenectady, N. Y.	Seattle, Wash.	Shreveport, La.	Spokane, Wash.	Springfield, Mass.	Vermillion, S. Dak.	Washington, D. C.
1174	938	1710	980	895	1117	1030	1810	1696	518	718	1748	330	1498	2015	1107	1628	938	483	893	1823	1178	764	1028	1889	742	1648
317	335	610	905	1790	218	427	747	507	753	815	663	1592	520	1022	2172	470	467	1580	2133	840	2180	548	1960	863	917	542
498	792	958	948	1947	597	1001	170	167	1173	1026	90	2002	194	446	2367	128	731	1858	2451	278	2341	1064	2110	282	1083	33
1623	1506	2368	1140	252	1631	1713	2153	2137	1138	1044	2113	733	1863	2282	349	2060	1389	292	516	2120	405	1433	290	2196	973	2045
823	1133	1258	1125	2124	941	1359	188	467	1490	1280	268	2295	478	100	2553	471	1036	2099	2696	150	2508	1410	2279	79	1314	392
1093	777	1100	1335	1706	952	536	1695	1465	659	1061	1614	1023	1424	1961	1944	1428	975	1317	1675	1770	2015	510	1852	1805	1161	1493
483	802	1184	733	1740	626	1087	291	435	1117	883	278	1904	178	438	2167	375	662	1701	2298	249	2130	1080	1900	325	916	290
268	481	1190	356	1348	394	831	711	696	689	432	664	1451	411	392	1765	618	259	1260	1855	702	1743	725	1514	774	479	594
92	410	957	603	1578	239	708	568	474	755	620	501	1578	258	802	1987	399	308	1450	2037	605	1974	688	1746	659	694	403
309	627	1088	632	1640	456	922	404	429	946	738	343	1745	115	603	2063	353	490	1567	2163	408	2035	904	1804	478	785	303
1035	878	1732	699	670	1018	1079	1628	1562	503	485	1575	585	1320	1803	985	1488	793	372	946	1618	1020	799	827	1692	468	1490
477	485	1338	235	1074	523	825	1023	983	469	122	972	1154	718	1197	1479	905	270	952	1547	1012	1470	624	1243	1085	187	895
315	621	1156	542	1552	468	938	483	522	905	666	444	1685	208	657	1975	445	452	1490	2087	467	1945	891	1715	540	705	397
1253	978	1662	1156	1115	1169	986	1902	1755	578	875	1834	347	1592	2126	1286	1695	1033	689	993	1930	1373	752	1238	1990	920	1726
818	882	1721	219	819	900	1221	1213	1258	786	390	1186	1225	952	1313	1248	1180	658	865	1447	1157	1206	1002	976	1240	284	1141
751	448	1150	870	1312	643	470	1398	1226	188	590	1324	858	1097	1642	1612	1170	568	977	1454	1445	1658	209	1470	1495	689	1210
807	492	941	1087	1595	666	288	1415	1195	456	828	1336	1065	1140	1078	1885	1154	697	1249	1693	1487	1938	233	1753	1524	938	1214
693	591	1468	399	891	697	870	1275	1216	357	135	1222	901	967	1454	1271	1142	455	708	1297	1267	1288	615	1061	1340	167	1139
480	176	983	722	1385	370	358	1125	955	260	490	1051	1094	825	1371	1733	897	325	1116	1648	1175	1759	142	1552	1224	605	936
636	830	1545	272	1208	760	1187	849	946	926	547	827	1550	630	924	1638	870	591	1242	1833	776	1588	1043	1360	860	510	813
595	591	328	1192	2070	502	511	838	548	988	1098	758	1800	703	1113	2442	953	755	1840	2375	960	2450	733	2239	957	1203	647
480	370	1247	413	1117	472	678	1097	1009	293	165	1037	1045	784	1300	1397	937	238	922	1500	1107	1505	326	1286	1173	280	943
1825	1602	2355	1522	910	1777	1675	2446	2352	1182	1312	2388	357	2135	2631	825	2283	1585	577	345	2445	956	1420	939	2515	1291	2295
....	319	923	605	1550	153	623	650	528	675	579	580	1512	345	892	1953	457	242	1400	1983	695	1945	598	1720	745	663	473
319	....	878	700	1483	195	358	953	778	422	529	878	1264	660	1205	1852	722	242	1250	1800	1010	1867	279	1652	1055	642	763
923	878	....	1516	2359	821	681	1095	802	1233	1402	1023	1998	1014	1357	2716	831	1067	2098	2603	1229	2740	950	2528	1210	1510	927
605	700	1516	....	1010	695	1050	1019	1047	692	291	985	1279	745	1145	1435	968	464	988	1585	975	1403	859	1173	1056	238	936
1550	1483	2359	1010	....	1582	1733	2030	2045	1162	978	1997	932	1754	2133	430	1967	1331	435	762	1978	395	1457	170	2060	887	1940
153	195	821	695	1582	....	470	758	586	602	604	683	1445	472	1015	1970	526	253	1390	1958	820	1973	470	1752	863	704	567
623	358	681	1050	1733	470	....	1173	932	575	845	1090	1318	923	1445	2063	899	599	1433	1923	1259	2098	280	1898	1287	960	968
650	953	1095	1019	2030	758	1173	....	293	1324	1144	83	2142	313	277	2455	287	873	1972	2568	142	2419	1230	2190	120	1189	204
528	778	802	1047	2045	586	932	293	....	1186	1095	220	2027	316	565	2458	79	771	1925	2510	426	2440	1037	2211	411	1166	145
675	422	1233	692	1162	602	575	1324	1186	....	405	1256	843	1013	1550	1488	1122	456	862	1386	1354	1523	297	1324	1412	502	1150
579	529	1402	291	978	604	845	1144	1095	405	....	1094	1032	837	1318	1373	1020	352	833	1425	1133	1372	617	1149	1205	115	1012
580	878	1023	985	1997	683	1090	83	220	1256	1094	....	2079	254	360	2419	205	808	1923	2518	205	2388	1153	2159	201	1143	122
1512	1264	1998	1279	932	1445	1318	2142	2027	843	1032	2079	....	1829	2345	1007	1960	1270	504	652	2152	1112	1067	1020	2220	1043	1980
345	660	1014	745	1754	472	923	313	316	1013	837	254	1829	....	545	2174	242	561	1670	2264	350	2145	939	1918	400	891	188
892	1205	1357	1145	2133	1015	1445	277	565	1550	1318	360	2345	545	....	2563	565	1094	2127	2725	197	2513	1484	2285	159	1345	480
1953	1852	2716	1435	430	1970	2063	2455	2458	1488	1373	2419	1007	2174	2563	....	2381	1723	636	536	2405	143	1783	295	2488	1293	2360
457	722	831	968	1967	526	899	287	79	1122	1020	205	1960	242	565	2381	....	699	1850	2436	406	2362	985	2133	407	1089	96
242	242	1067	464	1331	253	599	873	771	456	352	808	1270	561	1094	1723	699	....	1158	1738	898	1722	466	1500	958	450	710
1400	1250	2098	988	435	1390	1433	1972	1925	862	833	1923	504	1670	2127	636	1850	1158	....	592	1950	697	1155	548	2027	785	1845
1983	1800	2603	1585	762	1958	1923	2568	2510	1386	1425	2518	652	2264	2725	536	2436	1738	592	....	2548	680	1655	730	2625	1383	2437
695	1010	1229	975	1978	820	1259	142	426	1354	1133	205	2152	350	197	2405	406	898	1950	2548	....	2363	1290	2139	86	1165	313
1945	1867	2740	1403	395	1973	2098	2419	2440	1523	1372	2388	1112	2145	2513	143	2362	1722	697	680	2363	....	1820	229	[illegible]	1282	2335
598	279	950	859	1457	470	280	1230	1037	297	617	1153	1067	939	1484	1783	985	466	1155	1655	1290	1820	....	1621	1333	726	1035
1720	1652	2528	1173	170	1752	1898	2190	2211	1324	1149	2159	1020	1918	2285	295	2133	1500	548	730	2139	229	1621	....	2216	1055	2105
745	1055	1210	1056	2060	863	1287	120	411	1412	1205	201	2220	400	159	2488	407	958	2027	2625	86	2445	1333	2216	....	1242	321
663	642	1510	238	887	704	960	1189	1166	502	115	1143	1043	891	1345	1293	1089	450	785	1383	1165	1282	726	1055	1242	....	1073
473	763	927	936	1940	567	968	204	145	1150	1012	122	1980	188	480	2360	96	710	1845	2437	313	2335	1035	2105	321	1073	....

Between Principal Cities of the World

FROM/TO	Azores	Bagdad	Berlin	Bombay	Buenos Aires	Callao	Cairo	Cape Town	Chicago	Istanbul	Guam	Honolulu	Juneau	London	Los Angeles	Melbourne	Mexico City	Montreal	New Orleans	New York	Panama	Paris	Rio de Janeiro	San Francisco	Santiago	Seattle	Shanghai	Singapore	Tokyo	Wellington
Azores	....	3906	2148	5930	5385	4825	3325	5670	3305	2880	8985	7421	4715	1562	5034	12190	4584	2548	3718	2604	3918	1617	4312	5114	5718	4720	7324	8338	7370	11475
Bagdad	3906	....	2040	2022	8215	8618	785	4923	6490	1085	6380	8445	6180	2568	7695	8150	8155	5814	7212	6066	7807	2385	7012	7521	8876	6848	4468	4443	5242	9782
Berlin	2148	2040	....	3947	7411	6937	1823	5949	4458	1068	7158	7384	4638	575	5849	9992	6119	3776	5182	4026	5902	540	6246	5744	7842	5121	5323	6226	5623	11384
Bombay	5930	2022	3947	....	9380	10530	2698	5133	8144	3043	4831	8172	6992	4526	8810	6140	9818	7582	8952	7875	9832	4391	8438	8523	10127	7830	3219	2425	4247	7752
Buenos Aires	5385	8215	7411	9380	....	1982	7428	4332	5598	7638	10516	7653	7964	6919	6148	7336	4609	5619	4902	5295	3319	6891	1230	6487	731	6956	12295	9940	11601	6341
Callao	4825	8618	6937	10530	1982	....	7870	6195	3765	7666	9760	5993	5806	6376	4155	8196	2619	3954	2990	3633	1450	6455	2400	4500	1548	4964	10760	11700	9740	6696
Cairo	3325	785	1823	2698	7428	7870	....	4476	6231	780	7175	8925	6352	2218	7675	8720	7807	5502	6862	5701	7230	2020	6242	7554	8100	6915	5290	5152	6005	10360
Cape Town	5670	4923	5949	5133	4332	6195	4476	....	8551	5210	8918	11655	10382	5975	10165	6510	8620	7975	8390	7845	7090	5732	3850	10340	5080	10305	8179	6025	9234	7149
Chicago	3305	6490	4458	8144	5598	3765	6231	8551	....	5530	7510	4315	2310	4015	1741	9837	1690	750	827	727	2320	4219	5320	1875	5325	1753	7155	9475	6410	8465
Istanbul	2880	1085	1068	3043	7638	7666	780	5210	5530	....	7015	8200	5665	1540	6895	9189	7160	4825	6220	5060	6797	1390	6420	6770	8230	6124	5084	5440	5649	10790
Guam	8985	6380	7158	4831	10516	9760	7175	8918	7510	7015	....	3896	5225	7605	6255	3497	7690	7840	7895	8115	9220	7675	11710	5952	9946	5785	1945	2990	1596	4206
Honolulu	7421	8445	7384	8172	7653	5993	8925	11655	4315	8200	3896	....	2825	7320	2620	5581	3846	4992	4305	5051	5347	7525	8400	2407	6935	2707	5009	6874	3940	4676
Juneau	4715	6180	4638	6992	7964	5806	6352	10382	2310	5665	5225	2825	....	4496	1835	8162	3210	2647	2860	2874	4456	4700	7611	1530	7320	870	4968	7375	4117	7501
London	1562	2568	575	4526	6919	6376	2218	5975	4015	1540	7605	7320	4496	....	5496	10590	5605	3370	4656	3500	5310	210	5747	5440	7275	4850	5841	6818	6050	11790
Los Angeles	5034	7695	5849	8810	6148	4155	7675	10165	1741	6895	6255	2620	1835	5496	....	8098	1445	2468	1695	2466	3025	5711	6330	345	5595	961	6598	8955	5600	6806
Melbourne	12190	8150	9992	6140	7336	8196	8720	6510	9837	9189	3497	5581	8162	10590	8098	....	8599	10553	9455	10541	9211	10500	8340	7970	7130	8330	4967	3768	5172	1655
Mexico City	4584	8155	6119	9818	4609	2619	7807	8620	1690	7160	7690	3846	3210	5605	1445	8599	....	2247	940	2110	1532	5800	4810	1870	4122	2339	8120	10495	7190	7003
Montreal	2548	5814	3776	7582	5619	3954	5502	7975	750	4825	7840	4992	2647	3370	2468	10553	2247	....	1390	340	2545	3490	5110	2557	5461	2309	7141	9280	6546	9206
New Orleans	3718	7212	5182	8952	4902	2990	6862	8390	827	6220	7895	4305	2860	4656	1695	9455	940	1390	....	1161	1600	4846	4798	1960	4553	2137	7830	10255	6993	7950
New York	2604	6066	4026	7875	5295	3633	5701	7845	727	5060	8115	5051	2874	3500	2466	10541	2110	340	1161	....	2211	3600	4810	2606	5134	2440	7460	9617	6846	9067
Panama	3918	7807	5902	9832	3319	1450	7230	7090	2320	6797	9220	5347	4456	5310	3025	9211	1532	2545	1600	2211	....	5440	3311	3349	3000	3680	9430	11800	8560	7580
Paris	1617	2385	540	4391	6891	6455	2020	5762	4219	1390	7675	7525	4700	210	5711	10500	5800	3490	4846	3600	5440	....	5710	5680	7300	5080	5855	6730	6132	11865
Rio de Janeiro	4312	7012	6246	8438	1230	2400	6242	3850	5320	6420	11710	8400	7611	5747	6330	8340	4810	5110	4798	4810	3311	5710	....	6655	1852	6945	11510	9875	11600	7510
San Francisco	5114	7521	5744	8523	6487	4500	7554	10340	1875	6770	5952	2407	1530	5440	345	7970	1870	2557	1960	2606	3349	5680	6655	....	5960	692	6245	8440	5250	6800
Santiago	5718	8876	7842	10127	731	1548	8100	5080	5325	8230	9946	6935	7320	7275	5595	7130	4122	5461	4553	5134	3000	7300	1852	5960	....	6466	11850	10270	10850	5925
Seattle	4720	6848	5121	7830	6956	4964	6915	10305	1753	6124	5785	2707	870	4850	961	8330	2339	2309	2137	2440	3680	5080	6945	692	6466	....	5780	8200	4863	7310
Shanghai	7324	4468	5323	3219	12295	10760	5290	8179	7155	5084	1945	5009	4968	5841	6598	4967	8120	7141	7830	7460	9430	5855	11510	6245	11850	5780	....	2395	1095	6080
Singapore	8338	4443	6226	2425	9940	11700	5152	6025	9475	5440	2990	6874	7375	6818	8955	3768	10495	9280	10255	9617	11800	6730	9875	8440	10270	8200	2395	....	3350	5360
Tokyo	7370	5242	5623	4247	11601	9740	6005	9234	6410	5649	1596	3940	4117	6050	5600	5172	7190	6546	6993	6846	8560	6132	11600	5250	10850	4863	1095	3350	....	5730
Wellington	11475	9782	11384	7752	6341	6696	10360	7149	8465	10790	4206	4676	7501	11790	6806	1655	7003	9206	7950	9067	7580	11865	7510	6800	5925	7310	6080	5360	5730	....

Between Principal Cities of Europe

	Amsterdam	Athens	Baku	Barcelona	Belgrade	Berlin	Brussels	Bucharest	Budapest	Cologne
Amsterdam	....	1340	2218	770	875	365	105	1100	710	128
Athens	1340	....	1395	1160	500	1112	1292	460	698	1200
Baku	2218	1395	....	2427	1487	1867	2240	1220	1562	2127
Barcelona	770	1160	2427	....	998	925	658	1210	924	692
Belgrade	875	500	1487	998	....	618	850	295	205	750
Berlin	365	1112	1867	925	618	....	401	798	425	300
Brussels	105	1292	2240	658	850	401	....	1110	700	110
Bucharest	1100	460	1220	1210	295	798	1110	....	295	982
Budapest	710	698	1562	924	205	425	700	295	....	590
Cologne	128	1200	2127	692	750	300	110	982	590	....
Copenhagen	381	1320	1960	1085	840	225	475	970	629	400
Istanbul	1360	350	1070	1380	502	1068	1345	272	650	1240
Dresden	385	1022	1837	860	530	95	407	725	345	292
Dublin	468	1765	2490	919	1327	815	480	1560	1176	585
Frankfort	228	1113	2055	665	652	268	198	890	504	93
Hamburg	232	1250	2020	910	760	165	301	950	572	228
Leningrad	1090	1535	1570	1740	1165	815	1175	1080	965	1090
Lisbon	1140	1770	3050	610	1555	1410	998	1842	1515	1126
London	220	1476	2435	707	1040	575	202	1285	900	308
Lyon	458	1100	2238	327	752	601	352	1025	680	370
Madrid	912	1463	2742	316	1235	1149	807	1518	1214	875
Marseilles	627	1025	2238	211	750	730	521	1020	718	528
Milan	517	900	2028	450	540	570	435	819	476	390
Moscow	1325	1388	1175	1852	1160	995	1392	920	965	1285
Munich	415	925	1912	648	475	310	372	725	350	282
Oslo	568	1610	2118	1330	1112	520	672	1245	920	635
Paris	257	1300	2335	518	890	540	170	1152	770	250
Riga	820	1310	1590	1440	855	520	900	870	685	805
Rome	808	650	1900	530	440	730	730	700	500	675
Sofia	1073	335	1360	1072	231	810	945	194	395	945
Stockholm	695	1495	1862	1410	1005	503	793	1080	820	722
Toulouse	625	1215	2425	156	930	815	515	1210	883	875
Warsaw	673	990	1555	1150	510	320	720	580	342	602
Vienna	580	795	1700	830	300	322	568	520	128	460
Zurich	375	1000	2050	513	590	410	312	855	498	259

	Copenhagen	Istanbul	Dresden	Dublin	Frankfort	Hamburg	Leningrad	Lisbon	London	Lyon
Amsterdam	381	1360	385	468	228	232	1090	1140	220	458
Athens	1320	350	1022	1765	1113	1250	1535	1770	1476	1100
Baku	1980	1070	1837	2490	2055	2020	1570	3050	2435	2238
Barcelona	1085	1380	860	919	665	910	1740	610	707	327
Belgrade	840	502	530	1327	652	760	1165	1555	1040	752
Berlin	225	1068	95	815	268	165	815	1410	575	601
Brussels	475	1345	407	480	198	301	1175	998	202	352
Bucharest	970	272	725	1560	890	950	1080	1842	1285	1025
Budapest	629	650	345	1176	504	572	965	1515	900	680
Cologne	400	1240	292	585	93	228	1090	1126	308	370
Copenhagen	....	1240	315	768	412	180	708	1520	590	760
Istanbul	1240	....	995	1830	1150	1222	1292	2005	1540	1238
Dresden	315	995	....	852	236	238	885	1380	592	540
Dublin	768	1830	852	....	671	668	1440	1015	300	720
Frankfort	412	1150	236	671	....	250	1075	1160	392	350
Hamburg	180	1222	238	668	250	....	880	1301	448	580
Leningrad	708	1292	885	1440	1075	880	....	2235	1300	1420
Lisbon	1520	2005	1380	1015	1160	1301	2235	....	975	850
London	590	1540	592	300	392	448	1300	975	....	455
Lyon	760	1238	540	720	350	580	1420	850	455	....
Madrid	1272	1690	1100	902	888	1098	1980	313	777	557
Marseilles	906	1205	655	875	492	730	1540	810	620	170
Milan	720	1030	435	880	323	570	1315	1350	595	210
Moscow	970	1180	1200	1728	1240	1100	391	430	1540	1560
Munich	520	975	227	855	193	378	1100	1208	526	352
Oslo	303	1505	620	786	675	445	670	1690	720	1005
Paris	634	1390	523	480	295	459	1335	890	210	248
Riga	453	1115	585	1210	780	600	300	1940	1035	1122
Rome	948	840	630	1175	698	810	1440	1150	890	462
Sofia	1010	315	730	1525	860	954	1218	1685	1235	928
Stockholm	330	1340	598	1010	730	502	435	1848	885	1080
Toulouse	962	1400	762	761	560	780	1635	640	550	228
Warsaw	415	852	325	1130	550	462	640	1700	890	850
Vienna	538	790	235	1040	370	460	975	1415	762	562
Zurich	595	1090	342	768	193	432	1225	1058	480	206

	Madrid	Marseilles	Milan	Moscow	Munich	Oslo	Paris	Riga	Rome	Sofia	Stockholm	Toulouse	Warsaw	Vienna	Zurich
Amsterdam	912	627	517	1325	415	568	257	820	808	1073	695	625	673	580	375
Athens	1463	1025	900	1388	925	1610	1300	1310	650	335	1495	1215	990	795	1000
Baku	2742	2238	2028	1175	1912	2118	2335	1590	1900	1360	1862	2425	1555	1700	2050
Barcelona	316	211	450	1852	648	1330	518	1440	530	1072	1410	156	1150	830	513
Belgrade	1235	750	540	1160	475	1112	890	855	440	231	1005	930	510	300	590
Berlin	1149	730	570	995	310	520	540	520	730	810	503	815	320	322	410
Brussels	807	521	435	1392	372	672	170	900	730	945	793	515	720	568	312
Bucharest	1518	1020	819	920	725	1245	1152	870	700	194	1080	1210	580	520	855
Budapest	1214	718	476	965	350	920	770	685	500	395	820	883	342	128	498
Cologne	875	528	390	1285	282	635	250	805	675	945	722	875	602	460	259
Copenhagen	1272	906	720	970	520	303	634	453	948	1010	330	962	415	538	595
Istanbul	1690	1205	1030	1180	975	1505	1390	1115	840	315	1340	1400	852	790	1090
Dresden	1100	655	435	1200	227	620	523	585	630	730	598	762	325	235	342
Dublin	902	875	880	1728	855	786	480	1210	1175	1525	1010	761	1130	1040	768
Frankfort	888	492	323	1240	193	675	295	780	698	860	730	560	550	370	193
Hamburg	1098	730	570	1100	378	445	459	600	810	954	502	780	462	460	432
Leningrad	1980	1540	1315	391	1100	670	1335	300	1440	1218	435	1635	640	975	1225
Lisbon	313	810	1350	430	1208	1690	890	1940	1150	1685	1848	640	1700	1415	1058
London	777	620	595	1540	526	720	210	1035	890	1235	885	550	890	762	480
Lyon	577	170	210	1560	352	1005	248	1122	462	928	1080	228	850	562	206
Madrid	....	394	728	2120	910	1474	645	1670	840	1385	1598	344	1410	1110	765
Marseilles	394	....	238	1642	445	1165	410	1238	372	895	1225	196	950	620	318
Milan	728	238	....	1408	215	1000	400	1010	295	715	1020	400	705	385	137
Moscow	2120	1642	1408	....	1220	1030	1538	520	1462	1100	770	1770	710	1028	1350
Munich	910	445	215	1220	....	810	425	800	430	672	811	570	500	222	158
Oslo	1474	1165	1000	1030	810	....	830	531	1242	1295	267	1140	653	835	869
Paris	645	410	400	1538	425	830	....	1050	690	1080	950	431	845	770	295
Riga	1670	1238	1010	520	800	531	1050	....	1155	985	276	1335	350	685	930
Rome	840	372	295	1462	430	1242	690	1155	....	545	1220	569	810	470	421
Sofia	1385	895	715	1100	672	1295	1080	985	545	....	1170	1080	662	500	780
Stockholm	1598	1225	1020	770	811	267	950	276	1220	1170	....	1281	500	770	908
Toulouse	344	196	400	1770	570	1140	431	1335	569	1080	1281	....	1062	725	425
Warsaw	1410	950	705	710	500	653	845	350	810	662	500	1062	....	345	640
Vienna	1110	620	385	1028	222	835	770	685	470	500	770	725	345	....	365
Zurich	765	318	137	1350	158	869	295	930	421	780	908	425	640	365	....

Reprinted from **Webster's Atlas and Zip Code Directory** courtesy of Hammond, Incorporated.

New York to	Miles	San Francisco to	Miles	Seattle to	Miles	Washington to	Miles
Buenos Aires	5,295	Buenos Aires	6,487	Buenos Aires	6,956	Buenos Aires	5,205
Bogota	2,474	Bogota	3,863	Bogota	4,166	Bogota	2,344
Caracas	2,100	Caracas	3,900	Caracas	4,100	Caracas	2,040
Guatemala City	2,060	Guatemala City	2,525	Guatemala City	2,930	Guatemala City	1,835
Havana	1,302	Havana	2,600	Havana	2,805	Havana	1,110
La Paz	3,905	La Paz	5,080	La Paz	5,110	La Paz	3,780
Panama	2,211	Panama	3,349	Panama	3,680	Panama	2,020
Para	3,281	Para	5,430	Para	5,550	Para	3,270
Managua	2,100	Managua	2,860	Managua	3,240	Managua	1,920
Rio de Janeiro	4,810	Rio de Janeiro	6,655	Rio de Janeiro	6,945	Rio de Janeiro	4,710
San Jose	2,200	San Jose	3,070	San Jose	3,430	San Jose	2,030
Santiago	5,134	Santiago	5,960	Santiago	6,466	Santiago	4,965
Tampico	1,880	Tampico	1,790	Tampico	2,200	Tampico	1,665

Between Representative Cities of the United States and Latin America

Chicago to	Miles	Denver to	Miles	Los Angeles to	Miles	New Orleans to	Miles
Buenos Aires	5,598	Buenos Aires	5,935	Buenos Aires	6,148	Buenos Aires	4,902
Bogota	2,691	Bogota	3,100	Bogota	3,515	Bogota	1,996
Caracas	2,480	Caracas	3,105	Caracas	3,610	Caracas	1,990
Guatemala City	1,870	Guatemala City	1,935	Guatemala City	2,190	Guatemala City	1,050
Havana	1,315	Havana	1,760	Havana	2,320	Havana	672
La Paz	4,130	La Paz	4,445	La Paz	4,805	La Paz	3,480
Panama	2,320	Panama	2,620	Panama	3,025	Panama	1,600
Para	3,820	Para	4,580	Para	5,110	Para	3,470
Managua	2,060	Managua	2,230	Managua	2,540	Managua	1,250
Rio de Janeiro	5,320	Rio de Janeiro	5,900	Rio de Janeiro	6,330	Rio de Janeiro	4,798
San Jose	2,100	San Jose	2,420	San Jose	2,725	San Jose	1,425
Santiago	5,320	Santiago	5,495	Santiago	5,595	Santiago	4,553
Tampico	1,460	Tampico	1,240	Tampico	1,470	Tampico	720

FOREIGN CURRENCY TABLE

The following money table, reprinted from pages 742 and 743 of *Webster's New Collegiate Dictionary,* lists countries, the names of their currencies, currency symbols and currency subdivisions. Because rates of exchange change so rapidly, they must be checked almost daily if current quotations are required. These rates, not shown here, can be obtained from most banks and some newspapers.

MONEY

NAME	SYMBOL	SUBDIVISIONS	COUNTRY
afghani	Af	100 puls	Afghanistan
baht *or* tical	Bht *or* B	100 satang	Thailand
balboa	B/	100 centesimos	Panama
bolivar	B	100 centimos	Venezuela
cedi	¢	100 pesewas	Ghana
colon	₡ *or* ¢	100 centimos	Costa Rica
colon	₡ *or* ¢	100 centavos	El Salvador
cordoba	C$	100 centavos	Nicaragua
cruzeiro	$ *or* Cr$	100 centavos	Brazil
dalasi	D	100 bututs	Gambia
deutsche mark	DM	100 pfennigs	West Germany
dinar	DA	100 centimes	Algeria
dinar	BD	1000 fils	Bahrain
dinar	ID	5 riyals 20 dirhams 1000 fils	Iraq
dinar	JD	1000 fils	Jordan
dinar	KD	1000 fils	Kuwait
dinar	LD	1000 dirhams	Libya
dinar	£SY	1000 fils	Southern Yemen
dinar	D	1000 millimes	Tunisia
dinar	Din	100 paras	Yugoslavia
dirham	DH	100 francs	Morocco
dollar	$	100 cents	Australia
dollar	B$	100 cents	Bahamas
dollar	$	100 cents	Barbados
dollar	$	100 cents	Bermuda
dollar		100 sen	Brunei
dollar	$	100 cents	Canada
dollar	Eth$ *or* E$	100 cents	Ethiopia
dollar	$F	100 cents	Fiji
dollar	G$	100 cents	Guyana
dollar	HK$	100 cents	Hong Kong
dollar	$	100 cents	Jamaica
dollar	$	100 cents	Liberia
dollar	M$	100 cents	Malaysia
dollar	NZ$	100 cents	New Zealand
dollar	S$	100 cents	Singapore
dollar	TT$	100 cents	Trinidad and Tobago
dollar	$	100 cents	United States
dollar — see YUAN, below			

NAME	SYMBOL	SUBDIVISIONS	COUNTRY
dong	D	100 xu	North Vietnam
drachma	Dr	100 lepta	Greece
escudo	E *or* E°	100 centesimos 1000 milesimos	Chile
escudo	$ *or* Esc	100 centavos	Portugal
florin — see GULDEN, below			
forint	Ƒ *or* Ft	100 filler	Hungary
franc	Fr *or* F	100 centimes	Belgium
franc	FBu	100 centimes	Burundi
franc	Fr *or* F	100 centimes	Cameroon
franc	Fr *or* F	100 centimes	Central African Republic
franc	Fr *or* F	100 centimes	Chad
franc	Fr *or* F	100 centimes	Congo (Brazzaville)
franc	Fr *or* F	100 centimes	Dahomey
franc	Fr *or* F	100 centimes	France
franc	Fr *or* F	100 centimes	Gabon
franc	Fr *or* F	100 centimes	Guinea
franc	Fr *or* F	100 centimes	Ivory Coast
franc	Fr *or* F	100 centimes	Luxembourg
franc	Fr *or* F *or* FMG	100 centimes	Malagasy Republic
franc	Fr *or* F	100 centimes	Mali
franc	Fr *or* F	100 centimes	Mauritania
franc	Fr *or* F	100 centimes	Niger
franc	Fr *or* F	100 centimes	Rwanda
franc	Fr *or* F	100 centimes	Senegal
franc	Fr *or* F	100 centimes *or* rappen	Switzerland
franc	Fr *or* F	100 centimes	Togo
franc	Fr *or* F	100 centimes	Upper Volta
gourde	₲ *or* G *or* Gde	100 centimes	Haiti
guarani	₲ *or* G	100 centimos	Paraguay
gulden *or* guilder *or* florin	F *or* Fl *or* G	100 cents	Netherlands
kip	K	100 at	Laos
koruna	Kčs	100 halers	Czechoslovakia
krona	Kr	100 aurar	Iceland
krona	Kr	100 öre	Sweden
krone	Kr	100 öre	Denmark
krone	Kr	100 öre	Norway
kwacha	K	100 tambala	Malawi
kwacha	K	100 ngwee	Zambia
kyat	K	100 pyas	Burma
lek	L	100 qintar	Albania
lempira	L	100 centavos	Honduras
leone	Le	100 cents	Sierra Leone
leu	L	100 bani	Rumania
lev	Lv	100 stotinki	Bulgaria
lira	L *or* Lit	100 centesimi	Italy
lira *or* pound	£T *or* LT *or* TL	100 kurus *or* piasters	Turkey
mark *or* ostmark	M *or* OM	100 pfennigs	East Germany
mark — see DEUTSCHE MARK, above			
markka	M *or* Mk	100 pennia	Finland
naira	₦	100 kobo	Nigeria
ostmark — see MARK, above			
pa'anga	T$	100 seniti	Tonga
pataca	P *or* $	100 avos	Macao
peseta	Pta *or* P (*pl* Pts)	100 centimos	Equatorial Guinea
peseta	Pta *or* P (*pl* Pts)	100 centimos	Spain
peso	$	100 centavos	Argentina
peso	$B	100 centavos	Bolivia
peso	$ *or* P	100 centavos	Colombia
peso	$	100 centavos	Cuba
peso	RD$	100 centavos	Dominican Republic
peso	$	100 centavos	Mexico
peso	₱ *or* P	100 sentimos *or* centavos	Philippines
peso	$	100 centesimos	Uruguay
piaster	Vn$ *or* Pr	100 cents	South Vietnam
pound	£	1000 mils	Cyprus
pound	£E	100 piasters 1000 milliemes	Egypt
pound	£	100 pence	Ireland
pound *or* lira	I£ *or* IL	100 agorot	Israel
pound	L£ *or* LL	100 piasters	Lebanon
pound	£	100 pence	Malta
pound	£	20 shillings 240 pence	Rhodesia
pound	£S *or* LSd	100 piasters 1000 milliemes	Sudan
pound *or* lira	£S *or* LS	100 piasters	Syria
pound	£	100 pence	United Kingdom
pound — see LIRA, above			
quetzal	Ꝗ *or* Q	100 centavos	Guatemala
rand	R	100 cents	Botswana
rand	R	100 cents	Lesotho
rand	R	100 cents	South Africa
rand	R	100 cents	Swaziland
rial	R *or* Rl	100 dinars	Iran
rial	R	1000 baizas	Oman
rial	YR	40 buqshas	Yemen
riel	Ɉ *or* CR	100 sen	Cambodia
riyal	R *or* SR	20 qursh 100 halala	Saudi Arabia
ruble	R *or* Rub	100 kopecks	U.S.S.R.
rupee	Re (*pl* Rs)	100 paise	Bhutan
rupee	Re (*pl* Rs)	100 cents	Sri Lanka
rupee	Re (*pl* Rs)	100 paise	India
rupee	Re (*pl* Rs)	100 cents	Mauritius
rupee	Re (*pl* Rs)	100 paise	Nepal
rupee	Re (*pl* Rs)	100 paisa	Pakistan
rupee	Re (*pl* Rs)	100 cents	Seychelles
rupiah	Rp	100 sen	Indonesia
schilling	S *or* Sch	100 groschen	Austria
shilingi *or* shilling	Sh	100 senti	Tanzania
shilling	Sh	100 cents	Kenya
shilling	Sh *or* So Sh	100 cents	Somalia
shilling	Sh	100 cents	Uganda
sol	S/ *or* $	100 centavos	Peru
sucre	S/	100 centavos	Ecuador
taka		100 paisa	Bangladesh
tala	WS$	100 senes	Western Samoa
tical — see BAHT, above			
tugrik		100 mongo	Outer Mongolia
won	W	100 jun	North Korea
won	W	100 chon	South Korea
yen	¥ *or* Y	100 sen	Japan
yuan	$	10 chiao 100 fen	China (mainland)
yuan *or* dollar	NT$	10 chiao	China (Taiwan)
zaire	Z	100 makuta (*sing:* likuta) 10,000 sengi	Zaire
zloty	Zl *or* Z	100 groszy	Poland

WEIGHTS AND MEASURES[1]

UNIT	ABBR. OR SYMBOL	EQUIVALENTS IN OTHER UNITS OF SAME SYSTEM	METRIC EQUIVALENT
		WEIGHT	
		avoirdupois	
ton			
short ton		20 short hundredweight, 2000 pounds	0.907 metric tons
long ton		20 long hundredweight, 2240 pounds	1.016 metric tons
hundredweight	cwt		
short hundredweight		100 pounds, 0.05 short tons	45.359 kilograms
long hundredweight		112 pounds, 0.05 long tons	50.802 kilograms
pound	lb *or* lb av *also* #	16 ounces, 7000 grains	0.453 kilograms
ounce	oz *or* oz av	16 drams, 437.5 grains	28.349 grams
dram	dr *or* dr av	27.343 grains, 0.0625 ounces	1.771 grams
grain	gr	0.036 drams, 0.002285 ounces	0.0648 grams
		troy	
pound	lb t	12 ounces, 240 pennyweight, 5760 grains	0.373 kilograms
ounce	oz t	20 pennyweight, 480 grains	31.103 grams
pennyweight	dwt *also* pwt	24 grains, 0.05 ounces	1.555 grams
grain	gr	0.042 pennyweight, 0.002083 ounces	0.0648 grams
		apothecaries'	
pound	lb ap	12 ounces, 5760 grains	0.373 kilograms
ounce	oz ap *or* ℥	8 drams, 480 grains	31.103 grams
dram	dr ap *or* ʒ	3 scruples, 60 grains	3.887 grams
scruple	s ap *or* ℈	20 grains, 0.333 drams	1.295 grams
grain	gr	0.05 scruples, 0.002083 ounces, 0.0166 drams	0.0648 grams
		CAPACITY	
		U.S. liquid measure	
gallon	gal	4 quarts (231 cubic inches)	3.785 liters
quart	qt	2 pints (57.75 cubic inches)	0.946 liters
pint	pt	4 gills (28.875 cubic inches)	0.473 liters
gill	gi	4 fluidounces (7.218 cubic inches)	118.291 milliliters
fluidounce	fl oz *or* *f* ℥	8 fluidrams (1.804 cubic inches)	29.573 milliliters
fluidram	fl dr *or* *f* ʒ	60 minims (0.225 cubic inches)	3.696 milliliters
minim	min *or* ♏	1/60 fluidram (0.003759 cubic inches)	0.061610 milliliters
		U.S. dry measure	
bushel	bu	4 pecks (2150.42 cubic inches)	35.238 liters
peck	pk	8 quarts (537.605 cubic inches)	8.809 liters
quart	qt	2 pints (67.200 cubic inches)	1.101 liters
pint	pt	1/2 quart (33.600 cubic inches)	0.550 liters
		British imperial liquid and dry measure	
bushel	bu	4 pecks (2219.36 cubic inches)	0.036 cubic meters
peck	pk	2 gallons (554.84 cubic inches)	0.009 cubic meters
gallon	gal	4 quarts (277.420 cubic inches)	4.545 liters
quart	qt	2 pints (69.355 cubic inches)	1.136 liters
pint	pt	4 gills (34.678 cubic inches)	568.26 cubic centimeters
gill	gi	5 fluidounces (8.669 cubic inches)	142.066 cubic centimeters
fluidounce	fl oz *or* *f* ℥	8 fluidrams (1.7339 cubic inches)	28.416 cubic centimeters
fluidram	fl dr *or* *f* ʒ	60 minims (0.216734 cubic inches)	3.5516 cubic centimeters
minim	min *or* ♏	1/60 fluidram (0.003612 cubic inches)	0.059194 cubic centimeters
		LENGTH	
mile	mi	5280 feet, 320 rods, 1760 yards	1.609 kilometers
rod	rd	5.50 yards, 16.5 feet	5.029 meters
yard	yd	3 feet, 36 inches	0.9144 meters
foot	ft *or* ′	12 inches, 0.333 yards	30.480 centimeters
inch	in *or* ″	0.083 feet, 0.027 yards	2.540 centimeters
		AREA	
square mile	sq mi *or* m²	640 acres, 102,400 square rods	2.590 square kilometers
acre		4840 square yards, 43,560 square feet	0.405 hectares, 4047 square meters
square rod	sq rd *or* rd²	30.25 square yards, 0.006 acres	25.293 square meters
square yard	sq yd *or* yd²	1296 square inches, 9 square feet	0.836 square meters
square foot	sq ft *or* ft²	144 square inches, 0.111 square yards	0.093 square meters
square inch	sq in *or* in²	0.007 square feet, 0.00077 square yards	6.451 square centimeters
		VOLUME	
cubic yard	cu yd *or* yd³	27 cubic feet, 46,656 cubic inches	0.765 cubic meters
cubic foot	cu ft *or* ft³	1728 cubic inches, 0.0370 cubic yards	0.028 cubic meters
cubic inch	cu in *or* in³	0.00058 cubic feet, 0.000021 cubic yards	16.387 cubic centimeters

[1] For U.S. equivalents of metric units see Metric System table

15.3

BACKGROUND RESEARCH PRIOR TO TRAVEL

Executives who travel and work in foreign countries need a great deal of background information before going abroad, and by the same token the executives who are based in the United States and who work with those in other countries also need the same type of background. Economics, marketing, management, language, culture, politics, history, and geography are all important facets of this background. A knowledge of the changing policies of the United States and other nations is also vital, because foreign relations do affect the operations of multinational firms.

Company, municipal, and university libraries house source materials (such as federal government publications) on the subjects that have just been mentioned. Where does the researcher look for other materials in libraries? Basic to the search are indexes to current information and publications, travel guides, encyclopedias, and atlases.

INDEXES

Using indexes is a practical way for one to identify periodicals in print and to research current topics discussed in them. Finding the headings under which full articles are listed might be a little difficult for an uninitiated person until he learns the system of topical indexing that these books feature. Librarians can assist researchers in finding the required headings in these books, which are usually located together in the reference-book sections of libraries. Some of the most useful indexes are listed below together with some brief explanations of their scope and utility.

Business Periodicals Index. ed. Bettie Jane Third (Bronx, N.Y.: H. W. Wilson Company) This publication indexes English-language periodicals in the fields of accounting, banking, labor, and management; it also includes listings for specific businesses, industries, and trades. The researcher should look for the heading "multinational" which will direct him or her to more specific headings.

International Executive. ed. John Fayerweather (Hastings-on-Hudson, N.Y.: The Foundation for the Advancement of International Business Administration, Inc.) This index contains references to over 200 periodicals, and it highlights material that is basic to international business operations. Books and articles are listed with descriptive notes. *International Executive* is published three times a year.

Monthly Catalog United States Government Publications (Washington: U.S. Government Printing Office) This catalog lists current publications (particularly those originating in the Commerce Department) many of which are of interest to executives in multinational firms. Instructions for ordering publications and paying for them are included in this catalog.

New York Times Index (New York: Quadrangle/The New York Times Company) The researcher should refer to "Economic Conditions and Trends (General)" for general material on world conditions and especially conditions in underdeveloped areas and for information on private foreign investments. The researcher should see "Foreign Aid" for general material on government. Other headings that may prove helpful are "United Nations," "Agriculture," and "Labor." One should refer to "Commerce" for news about continents, groups of countries, or specific countries.

Reader's Guide to Periodical Literature. ed. Zada Limerick (Bronx, N.Y.: H.W. Wilson Company) The researcher is referred from the "Multinational" heading to more specific headings such as the one entitled "Corporations—International." Of the total number of periodicals indexed, relatively few are strictly business-oriented; however, many general periodicals carry articles of interest to business people.

Social Sciences Index. ed. Joseph Bloomfield (Bronx, N.Y.: H. W. Wilson Company) This publication, though not primarily oriented to business, does index some periodicals (such as *Asia, Business History Review, Far Eastern Economic Review, Foreign Affairs,* and *The Journal of Economic History*) that are important to the internationally-minded executive.

Ulrich's International Periodicals Directory (New York: R. R. Bowker Company) This is a yearly index of the names of approximately 57,000 periodicals that are in print throughout the world. Under the heading "Business and Industry" are the subdivisions "Chamber of Commerce Publications" and "Commerce and Trade." "Banking and Finance" and "Economics" are also main headings.

Wall Street Journal Index (New York: Dow Jones & Company, Inc.) This index separates corporate-news references from general information references. If the researcher is interested in foreign countries, he or she should look under the name of the appropriate country. The International Monetary Fund and the World Bank are specifically indexed.

TRAVEL GUIDES

Travel guides—also important sources of information because of their frequent updating—are likely to be especially valuable to those who travel on a regular basis. The following annotated list is representative of these books.

All Asia Guide. ed. William Knox (Hong Kong: The Far Eastern Economic Review, Ltd., 1974) This guide contains a chapter apiece on countries east of Afghanistan. Each chapter begins with a brief description and history of the country under discussion. Topics covered are the languages (national and others) that are spoken, surveys of weather conditions throughout the year, suggestions regarding clothing appropriate for local conditions, working hours for government and business offices, and hotels and restaurants. The last section of each chapter is a chronological list of the local festive seasons and a list of public holidays.

Businessman's Guide to Europe: Country-by-Country Including Eastern Europe and U.S.S.R. (Boston: Cahners Books, 1974) An introduction to Europe is followed by an overview of each European country. The book discusses the history, people, topography, climate and mode of dress, and the economy and industry of each country. It also describes the ways of doing business in each country. A brief bibliography of references is included.

Fielding's Travel Guide to Europe by Temple Fielding (New York: Fielding Publications) This guide contains information on travel preparations as well as sections covering the attitudes of Europeans toward tourists. It also offers details on money and prices, food, hotels, and tipping.

Fodor's Europe. eds. Eugene Fodor and Robert C. Fisher (New York: David McKay Company, Inc., 1974) This guide, which is updated annually, covers 35 countries. In addition to travel tips, it contains historical sketches of each country as well as information about the people of each country, art, food and drink, and weather. A tourist's vocabulary in English with equivalents in 12 European languages is found in the appendix of this guide.

Michelin Red Guides (Roslyn Heights, N.Y.: Michelin Tire Corporation) These guides rate hotels, motels, and dining service in various European countries. They include maps, tables of distances between cities, and points of interest.

ENCYCLOPEDIAS

Encyclopedias are also helpful to the researcher, particularly *Encyclopaedia Britannica* (published by Encyclopaedia Britannica, Inc.) and *Encyclopedia Americana* (International Edition published by Grolier, Inc.). A one-volume encyclopedic reference book is the *News Dictionary* which is updated annually and contains topics of interest to the international executive. The researcher will usually find topics dealing with international finance and trade.

ATLASES

Atlases may often be helpful to the secretary. Some of them are listed below.

Britannica Atlas (Chicago: Encyclopaedia Britannica, Inc., 1970) This international atlas features world, ocean, and continent maps; regional maps; and selected metropolitan area maps. Populations of cities and towns are shown in tabular form. A section entitled "The World Scene" includes data on world political changes, religions and languages of the world, agriculture, national resources, manufacturing, gross national products, directions of trade, commodities traded, intercontinental air connections, continental transport routes, time zones, and others.

Commercial Atlas and Marketing Guide (Chicago: Rand McNally, 1972) This atlas contains information primarily about the United States, but it also has a gazetteer of countries, regions, and political divisions around the world for which information regarding land areas, populations, forms of government, capitals and largest cities, and predominant languages is presented. Principal rivers, lakes, and mountains are also treated. This atlas, however, is not truly commercial in a literal sense because it does not contain data such as the value of commodities.

The International Atlas from Rand McNally (Chicago: Rand McNally, 1974) This volume is designed for those whose native languages are English, German, Spanish, and French. Map labels are in the languages of the countries being illustrated, but English is used for the names of major features extending across international borders. Metric measures of distances as well as distances in miles are shown for map scales.

The *National Geographic Atlas of the World* (Washington: National Geographic Society, 1975) This book contains good maps of various geographical regions of the world. The texts accompanying the maps contain vignettes of the political subdivisions in the regions being illustrated. These descriptive passages include names of rivers, amounts of rainfall, descriptions of landscape, and assorted historical facts.

[London] *Times Atlas of the World: Comprehensive Edition* (London: Times Newspapers Ltd., 1972) Preceding the maps section of this international atlas is a list of states, territories, and principal islands of the world including a description of each, the location and land area of each, and the population of each. In addition, the book contains a table of geographical comparisons, a textual discussion of world resources supplemented with maps, and text/map coverage of the solar system, spaceflights, and satellites. (This atlas may be obtained by writing to Quadrangle/The New York Times Co.)

Webster's Atlas and Zip Code Directory (Springfield, Mass.: G. & C. Merriam Company, 1973) This atlas, prepared by the staff of Hammond, Inc., contains maps of Europe, North and South America, Africa, and Asia with indexes of cities and populations, lists of local currencies in foreign countries, lists of the major religions of the world, and indications of the languages spoken in various countries. The resource maps of the countries of the world include indications of dominant land uses, minerals indigenous to particular areas, and manufacturing features of the regions under discussion. As its title implies, it contains ZIP Code maps of America's largest metropolitan areas.

STATISTICAL REFERENCES

Three useful statistical sources of interest to executives in multinational firms follow.

Commodity Yearbook. ed. Seymour Gaylinn (New York: Commodity Research Bureau, Inc.) This annual publication contains statistical tables regarding numerous commodities. For example, the treatment of copper includes information on world copper production starting with 1961 and world smelter production for the major copper-producing countries, United States imports of copper from and exports of copper to selected countries, and refined copper stocks outside the United States. The statistical data are preceded by a brief discussion of the particular commodity market for the year covered in the book. Both agricultural and mineral commodities are included in this yearbook.

Direction of Trade. ed. Leonello Boccia (Washington: International Monetary Fund) This monthly volume reports statistics on exports and imports. Values of trade are given in U.S. dollars. Not all countries of the world are included in each issue.

Highlights of U.S. Export and Import Trade (Washington: U.S. Government Printing Office) This is a monthly compilation of statistical data on U.S. exports and imports that is prepared by the Bureau of the Census and the United States Department of Commerce. Statistics are grouped under headings such as individual commodities by unit of quantity for all methods of transportation collectively as well as separately for water and for air shipments. Data concerning each commodity for the current year and month and for the previous year and month are included. Cumulative amounts for prior years and months are also shown.

PAMPHLETS

"Background Notes on the Countries of the World" is actually a series of pamphlets published by the Bureau of Public Affairs, United States Department of State. They are available from the Superintendent of Documents, Washington, DC 20402. Written by officers in the State Department's Geographic Bureau, the pamphlets offer the reader a quick look at various countries and territories. Each pamphlet contains information on a country's land, its people, its history, its government, its political situations, its economy, and its foreign relations, as well as a map and a brief bibliography for the country under discussion.

PERIODICALS

Secretaries who do research for executives can also find information pertinent to multinational business in a variety of daily, weekly, monthly, and quarterly periodicals. If a secretary wants to review business topics in foreign publications, likely sources can be found under appropriate headings in *Ulrich's International Periodicals Directory,* described earlier in this chapter. Some of the periodicals that will assist executives in keeping up-to-date with international business and economics are listed below.

Barclays International Review (London: Barclays Bank International Limited) This monthly economic and trade review contains summaries of news as well as reports on specific countries around the world and on diverse topics as the European Economic Community, Middle East oil, and international monetary developments. The economic situation in countries such as Botswana, Guyana, Japan, the United Kingdom, and the United States are discussed.

Business International (New York: Business International Corporation) This weekly report is addressed to managers of worldwide business and industrial operations. Topics such as personnel and labor, foreign trade, government and politics, and the European Economic Community are covered in short articles. Some articles discuss economic conditions in specific countries.

Business Week (New York: McGraw-Hill, Inc.) This important weekly business news magazine discusses current business topics as well as other related subjects listed under headings such as "International Economics," "Finance," and "International Business."

Finance and Development (Washington: International Monetary Fund and International Bank for Reconstruction and Development) This quarterly journal is published in English, French, and Spanish (some editions are also printed in German and Portuguese). Its articles reflect the changing global economic scene, explain the workings and the policies of the Fund and the Bank, and discuss activities of the Fund such as assistance to countries in short-term balance-of-trade difficulties. Another section of the journal offers reviews of books on topics such as exchange and trade controls, international trade policies, and international monetary reform.

[London] *Financial Times* (London: Financial Times Ltd.) This daily British equivalent of *The Wall Street Journal* typically contains coverage of bank base rates, company news, foreign exchange quotations and rates, international company news, labor news, mining news, the state of the money market, overseas markets and news, stock exchange reports, and world trade news.

Forbes (New York: Forbes Inc.) This periodical is published twice monthly. It carries articles on topics such as domestic and foreign business, and presents its viewpoint on investments. The past performance of and outlook for specific firms are also featured.

Fortune (Chicago: Time, Inc.) This monthly magazine typically carries some long, in-depth articles related to domestic and foreign business operations, firms, and executives. The "Fortune Directory" of the largest industrial corporations outside the U.S., commercial-banking companies and life insurance companies, and utilities companies are features of this magazine.

IMF Survey (Washington: International Monetary Fund) This weekly publication briefly summarizes articles pertaining to organizations such as the European Economic Community, the Inter-American Development Bank, and the International Monetary Fund. It also contains articles on individual countries of the world and on commodities.

Nation's Business (Washington: Chamber of Commerce of the United States) Articles in this monthly periodical relate strictly to the American domestic business scene.

Survey of Current Business (Washington: Bureau of Economic Analysis, Social and Economic Statistics Administration, U.S. Department of Commerce) This monthly periodical publishes current business statistics arranged on a monthly and an annual pattern under headings such as "General Business Indicators," "Commodities," "Prices," "Labor Force," "Employment," and "Earnings." Articles on topics such as balance of foreign payments and foreign trade are also found in this publication.

The Commercial and Financial Chronicle (New York: National News Service, Inc.) This is a weekly newspaper which, in addition to articles on business topics, features a digest of market letters. It also offers its readers a digest of financial news appearing in other financial publications, a listing of letter stock, a list of sales and purchases of stock by officers of firms, stock records from stock exchanges, and listings of securities offered by the U.S. government and its agencies.

The Economist (London: 54 St. James Street SW1A 1JT) *The Economist* is a weekly journal that deals not only with business and economics, but also contains thorough coverage of world events. Its primary function, however, is to provide its readers with current economic and business news on the Continent, and throughout the rest of the globe.

The Wall Street Journal (New York: Dow Jones & Company, Inc.) This daily (except Saturday and Sunday) newspaper primarily covers current financial and business news in areas such as foreign trade, investments, stocks, bonds, and commodity markets. Coverage of foreign business news is limited. Two or three front-page by-line articles (on miscellaneous topics) are carried in each issue of the *Journal.*

UN Monthly Chronicle (New York: United Nations Publications) This periodical which is issued irregularly summarizes the activities of the United Nations and its specialized agencies such as the Economic Commission that concerns itself with Latin America, Western Asia, and other geographic areas of the world. It is a useful source for the researcher who is interested in obtaining information related to international business because it contains articles on multinational corporations, the International Monetary Fund (IMF), and monetary systems.

BOOKS

A brief list of books relating to international business and multinational enterprises follows. Of course, the researcher who investigates these volumes will find bibliographies in them which will lead to many other sources.

A Primer on the Dollar in the World Economy by Robert Warren Stevens (New York: Random House, 1972) This book, which focuses on the dollar in the world economy, begins with an explanation of what the role of balance of payments is and how a statement of balance of payments is organized. Along the way, it discusses exchange rates, the gold standard, and the International Monetary Fund.

Commodity Exports and African Economic Development by Scott R. Pearson, John Cownie, et. al. (Lexington, Mass.: Lexington Books, D. C. Heath and Company, 1974) The volume contains the principal results of study funded by the Joint Committee on African Studies of the Social Science Research Council of the American Council of Learned Societies. It discusses specific African commodities and their impact on the economic development of African nations. The involvement of multinationals is discussed on factual, not philosophical bases.

Conflicting Constraints on the Multinational Enterprise: Potential for Resolution by Jack N. Behrman (New York: Unipub, Inc., 1974) This monograph discusses the difference between United States government policies and those of Latin America, less developed countries, and European countries. It assesses the pressures for international controls to resolve differences in national policies and predicts changes in the structure of the multinationals as they respond to national and international pressures.

Global Companies. ed. George W. Ball (Englewood Cliffs, N.J.: Prentice-Hall, Inc., 1975) This book considers the multinational corporation not just from an industrial or commercial standpoint, but also from a political viewpoint. It provides a general overview of the multinational company as it fits into the global economy.

International Management Practice: An Insider's View by Gunnar Beeth (New York: American Management Association, Inc., 1973) This book contains guidelines for executives of American corporations and a brief overview of international business. The author states personal opinions on the use of export managers and licensees, the building of strong subsidiaries, the funding of distributors, and the financing of foreign operations.

Multinational Business Strategy by William A. Dymsza (New York: McGraw-Hill, Inc., 1972) This book defines the international firm and the multinational company, describes managerial organization and international marketing strategy, and examines the framework of international investments for this type of firm. With its discussion of these and other topics, the book offers its readers a broad view of the international enterprise system.

Multinational Corporations by Nasrollah S. Fatemi and Gail W. Williams (New York: A. S. Barnes and Company, 1975) This study examines labor's view on the impact that multinationals have had on employment problems centering on the transfer of technology abroad. It discusses the controversy on the taxation of multinationals, and it examines the impact of multinationals on the balance of payments. The historical development of multinational corporations is also covered by the authors.

Multinational Corporations, Trade and the Dollar. eds. Jules Backman and Ernest Block (New York: New York University Press, 1974) This volume contains a series of lectures which focus on the problems and challenges of United States international economic relations. As opposed to the usual discussion of American firms abroad, the *foreign* multinational company is covered in one of the lectures. The future of the American dollar, the growth of world trade, and the Common Market are also discussed in these lectures.

Planning for International Business Negotiations by Ashok Kapoor (Cambridge, Mass.: Ballinger Publishing Company, 1975) This book focuses on business negotiations between international companies and the host governments of developing nations. It is based on four case studies involving various corporations and the governments of countries such as India, Iran, and the Philippines. The chapter "Analysis of Negotiation" covers characteristics of international business analysis and suggests considerations for planning negotiations between the international company and the host government.

List of publishers The following is a list of publishers' addresses that might be helpful to a researcher in ordering the titles that appear in the foregoing section:

American Management Association, Inc.
135 W. 50th Street
New York, NY 10020

Ballinger Publishing Company
17 Dunster Street
Harvard Square
Cambridge, MA 02138

Barclays Bank International, Ltd.
54 Lombard Street
London EC3P 3AH
England

A. S. Barnes and Company
P.O. Box 421
Cranbury, NJ 08512

R. R. Bowker Company
1180 Avenue of the Americas
New York, NY 10036

Business International Corporation
One Dag Hammarskjold Plaza
New York, NY 10017

Cahner's Books
89 Franklin Street
Boston, MA 02110

Chamber of Commerce of the United States
1615 H Street, NW
Washington, DC 20006

Commodity Research Bureau, Inc.
One Liberty Plaza
New York, NY 10006

Dow Jones & Company
22 Cortland Street
New York, NY 10007

NOTE:
for subscriptions to *The Wall Street Journal:*
Dow Jones & Company, Inc.
200 Burnett Road
Chicopee, MA 01021

NOTE:
for *The Wall Street Journal Index:*
Dow Jones Books
P.O. Box 300
Princeton, NJ 08540

Economist
54 St. James Street
London SW1A 1JT
England

Encyclopaedia Britannica, Inc.
425 North Michigan Avenue
Chicago, IL 60611

Facts on File, Inc. (*News Dictionary*)
119 W. 57th Street
New York, NY 10019

Fielding Publications
105 Madison Avenue
New York, NY 10016

[London] Financial Times Ltd.
Bracken House, Cannon Street
London EC4
England

Forbes Inc.
60 Fifth Avenue
New York, NY 10011

Foundation for the Advancement of International Business Administration, Inc.
64 Ferndale Drive
Hastings-on-Hudson, NY 10706

Grolier, Inc.
575 Lexington Avenue
New York, NY 10022

International Monetary Fund
19th & H Streets, NW
Washington, DC 20431

Lexington Books
D. C. Heath and Company
125 Spring Street
Lexington, MA 02173

McGraw-Hill Book Company
1221 Avenue of the Americas
New York, NY 10036

David McKay Company, Inc.
750 Third Avenue
New York, NY 10017

G. & C. Merriam Company
47 Federal Street
Springfield, MA 01101

Michelin Tire Corporation
P.O. Box 188
Rosyln Heights, NY 11577

National Geographic Society
17th & M Streets, NW
Washington, DC 20036

National News Service, Inc.
110 Wall Street
New York, NY 10005

New York Times Company
229 W. 43rd Street
New York, NY 10036

New York University Press
Washington Square
New York, NY 10003

Prentice-Hall, Inc.
Englewood Cliffs, NJ 07632

Quadrangle/The New York Times Co.
10 E. 53rd Street
New York, NY 10022

Rand McNally & Company
P.O. Box 7600
Chicago, IL 60680

Random House
201 E. 50th Street
New York, NY 10022

Time Inc.
541 North Fairbanks Court
Chicago, IL 60611

Unipub, Inc.
P.O. Box 433
Murray Hill Station
New York, NY 10016

United Nations Publications
Room LX-2300
New York, NY 10017

United States Government Printing Office
Superintendent of Documents
Washington, DC 20402

H. W. Wilson Company
950 University Avenue
Bronx, NY 10452

15.4

INTERNATIONAL TRADE

INTRODUCTION

To increase its awareness of expanding foreign markets and to obtain assistance in developing these markets, private enterprise can look to the United States Department of Commerce, the United States Department of State, and the Chamber of Commerce of the United States, as well as to commercial banking institutions for encouragement and assistance. For American firms, the international scene involves more than just exports: it includes cooperative ventures with foreign corporations and foreign governments, it includes consulting agreements with them, and it includes joint developmental projects. Government assistance programs are varied and specialized, but taken together they form the pattern of a planned program of great importance to American business. Assisting and encouraging foreign governments and enterprises underlies much of the development of international trade for American firms; financing exports, the end result, makes this trade possible.

Secretaries who familiarize themselves with the services available for developing and financing world trade can offer an executive great help in ways that go beyond facilitating travel, conferences with foreign executives and government officials, and business and social relationships abroad. Secretaries in firms that have never exported their services and products can play an important role in helping to develop foreign markets for their firms by selectively collecting information on procedures for conducting business abroad and on sources of assistance, development of overseas markets, and ways of financing exports. This material can be invaluable to executives who are interested in penetrating foreign markets. Secretaries in firms already active in these markets can continue to lend valuable assistance to their executives by keeping up-to-date on developments related to world trade.

The discussion which follows is intended to introduce some of the most important sources of information and assistance in the area of international trade, including several areas of the United States government, the Chamber of Commerce of the United States, and American banks.

THE DEPARTMENT OF COMMERCE

This government agency has internal organizations and programs which offer specific types of assistance to multinational corporations and firms desiring to compete in foreign markets. Aid is available to firms launching new programs abroad and to firms expanding their existing international programs. Such help is available through the Department's 43 district offices in the United States and Puerto Rico as well as through the Domestic and International Business Administration and its four operating bureaus. Experienced trade specialists assist U.S. firms to expand exports and develop projects overseas, and they furnish information on the Department's programs and services as well as information from other federal agencies engaged in business-related activities.

The Domestic and International Business Administration (DIBA) This agency is headed by an assistant secretary of commerce. It carries out its international trade mission through the Bureau of International Commerce, the Bureau of East-West Trade, and the International Economic Policy and Research Staff. However, the Bureau of Domestic Commerce, the Bureau of Resources and Trade Assistance, and the International Economic Policy and Research Staff also contribute to the total operation of the DIBA.

1. The Bureau of International Commerce (BIC), whose chief responsibility is the development of the Department's export expansion programs, encourages nonexporting firms to become exporters, assists firms that are already in the export business, maintains an Export Information Reference Room, and helps executives cut through red tape in order to penetrate foreign markets and finance shipments abroad. In discharging its responsibilities, BIC offers the following programs:

a. The Major Projects Program helps companies capture a bigger share of the major construction, engineering, and development projects around the world. To qualify for the program, contracts for such projects must have an export value of at least $5 million. American companies equipped to bid on contracts for worldwide projects such as airports, dams, hydroelectric power systems, mass transit systems, and industrial plants are notified of impending projects and are offered various kinds of assistance such as aid from the U.S. Embassy in the project country or suggestions on how to secure financial aid. Information about future construction abroad is carried in two Department of Commerce publications: *Commerce America* (formerly *Commerce Today*) and *Commerce Business Daily*. For further information about the Major Projects Program, one should write to the Major Export Project Division, Office of Export Development, U.S. Department of Commerce, Washington, DC 20230.

b. The Overseas Product Sales Program assists firms in bidding against foreign competitors for products and equipment. Further information can be obtained from the Major Export Project Division, Office of Export Development, U.S. Department of Commerce, Washington, DC 20230.

c. The Foreign Investment Service assists U.S. firms in investigating, evaluating, and acting on overseas investments and licensing opportunities. It helps U.S. executives find potential foreign partners and licensees; it helps executives to research investment data and to find sources of capital needed to develop overseas projects. Further information can be obtained from the Foreign Services Staff, Overseas Business Opportunities Division, Office of Export Development, U.S. Department of Commerce, Washington, DC 20230.

d. The Trade Opportunities Program is an informational service that sends specific leads on export sales to U.S. subscribers. This information is collected from the State Department's commercial posts throughout the world. Subscribers receive only the information fitting the particular specifications which they have already submitted to the Program.

e. The Foreign Buyer Program assists U.S. executives in making contacts with foreign buyers who are visiting the United States. This program helps to set up business appointments, to schedule visits to plants, and to arrange itineraries for foreign buyers. It also promotes foreign attendance at domestic trade shows. For further information, one may write to the Domestic Export Programs Division, Office of Export Development, U.S. Department of Commerce, Washington, DC 20230.

f. The Export Promotion Multiplier Program, an information program, publishes *World Traders Data Reports* which contain information about the history, operations, sales, territory, business connections, regulations, and names of chief executives of foreign companies. The program also offers the *Export Mailing List Service* which provides mailing lists of overseas firms together with such information as their export potential, their agents and distributors, and/or their licensees; and *Foreign Market Reports,* which describe markets in foreign countries for specific products. These reports are listed in the *Index to Foreign Market Reports,* a monthly publication. For information about subscriptions to this *Index* or about buying specific *Foreign Market Reports,* one should write to the National Technical Information Service, Box 1553, Springfield, VA 22151.

g. The BIC Target Industry Program matches the more advanced and competitive U.S. industries with foreign markets for products of these U.S. firms.

h. Trade fairs, trade centers, and trade missions provide U.S. firms with opportunities to display, demonstrate, and market their products abroad. U.S. firms display and sell their products at trade fairs. Foreign trade centers are permanent showrooms where American products are displayed and sold. Trade missions are composed of U.S. business people who present proposals to foreign business people and government representatives. They confer, review counterproposals, and often work out with their opposite numbers the bases of later agreements. Yet basically their function is to present proposals and counterproposals. In essence, trade missions do not perform official State Department diplomatic functions. Further information about these activities of the Bureau of International Commerce is available from district offices of the Department of Commerce.

i. The Commerce Action Group for the Near East (CAGNE) serves as a focal point for the total Department of Commerce program in this particular geographical area. In addition, CAGNE coordinates Commerce Department participation in the special bilateral Joint Commissions formed with Near Eastern countries to assist them with industrialization and development. CAGNE organizes the participation of U.S. businesses including consulting, engineering, and construction firms. As CAGNE carries out these activities, U.S. equipment, products, and services are introduced into the Near Eastern countries' development programs.

2. The Bureau of East-West Trade helps to establish trade ties between the United States and countries in Eastern Europe and Asia with socialist economies. The executive who desires assistance in trading with East European and Asian countries can obtain advice from the Bureau's staff of specialists who are experienced in the fields of international business, market analysis, linguistics, and law.

THE DEPARTMENT OF STATE

The Department of State also assists American businesses that have international interests. It enhances international trade through commerce and navigation treaties and through bilateral and multilateral negotiations and agreements. It also provides overseas market data, helps companies gain access to foreign markets, and assists American business people while they are operating abroad. American business firms requiring overseas agents can obtain help through the Agent Distribution Service (ADS). The Department's assistance is not confined to our own shores, of course. American executives working or traveling in other countries often need briefings on the economy, changing political situations, trade opportunities, investments, export competition from other nations, trade restrictions, and exchange controls. This kind of information is available at our embassies abroad. Economic and political briefings for specific countries can be obtained from the State Department's desk officers.

United States embassies can often make appointments for American business people with government officials in the countries they are visiting. Another source of help and information for American executives traveling in other countries is the chain of commercial libraries which are attached to our embassies and consulates. Libraries are also operated at or near our embassies by the United States Information Service.

The State Department also offers overseas assistance to American business travelers by staffing foreign-based trade centers and by working with the Commerce Department in staging trade fairs, catalog shows, and technical sales seminars.

Although United States embassies cannot act as legal representatives for American executives or their firms in foreign countries, commercial officers stationed there can assist Americans by determining the facts of disputes that may arise and by recommending counsel when it is required.

Overseas, the State Department maintains a staff of commercial and economic officers who transmit commercial and economic information to business firms in the U.S. and to the Department of Commerce. Inquiries about the commercial services offered by the Department of State should be directed to its Office of Commercial Affairs, Washington, DC 20230.

The State Department's Publications Program furnishes a variety of valuable information for secretaries. Two of the titles listed with brief annotations below are of particular value:

Background Notes contains summaries on the economies, peoples, histories, cultures, governments, etc., of 164 foreign countries and territories. It is revised twice yearly, and is available from the Superintendent of Documents.

"Key Officers of Foreign Service Posts" is a pamphlet that provides the names of ambassadors, economic and commercial officers, consuls, and other section chiefs at American embassies and consulates. It is updated every four months and is available from the Superintendent of Documents.

UNITED STATES FOREIGN SERVICE POSTS

American consulates are located around the world. American business people traveling and working abroad can go to them for assistance in business and personal matters. U.S. embassies, legations, and consulates are located in the following countries:

Afghanistan
Kabul

Algeria
Algiers
Oran

Arab Republic of Egypt
Cairo
Alexandria

Argentina
Buenos Aires

Australia
Canberra, Australian Capital Territory
Brisbane, Queensland
Melbourne, Victoria
Perth, Western Australia
Sydney, New South Wales

Austria
Vienna
Salzburg

Azores—*see* PORTUGAL

Bahamas
Nassau

Bahrain
Manama

Bangladesh
Dacca

Barbados
Bridgetown

Belgium
Brussels
Antwerp

Belize
Belize City

Benin (*formerly* **Dahomey**)
Cotonou

Bermuda
Hamilton

Bolivia
La Paz

Botswana
Gaborone

Brazil
Brasília
Belém
Pôrto Alegre
Recife
Rio de Janeiro
Salvador
São Paulo

Bulgaria
Sofia

Burma
Rangoon
Mandalay

Burundi
Bujumbura

Cameroon
Yaounde
Douala

Canada
Ottawa, Ontario
Calgary, Alberta
Halifax, Nova Scotia
Montreal, Quebec
Quebec, Quebec
St. John's, Newfoundland
Toronto, Ontario
Vancouver, British Columbia
Winnipeg, Manitoba

Central African Republic
Bangui

Ceylon—*see* SRI LANKA

Chad
Ndjamena

Chile
Santiago

China, Republic of
Taipei

Colombia
Bogota
Cali
Medellin

Costa Rica
San Jose

Cyprus
Nicosia

Czechoslovakia
Prague

Dahomey—*see* BENIN

Denmark
Copenhagen

Dominican Republic
Santo Domingo

Ecuador
Quito
Guayaquil

Egypt—*see* ARAB REPUBLIC OF EGYPT

El Salvador
San Salvador

England—*see* UNITED KINGDOM

Equatorial Guinea
Malabo

Fiji
Suva

Finland
Helsinki

France
Paris
Bordeaux
Lyon
Marseilles
Nice
Strasbourg

French West Indies
Martinique

Gabon
Libreville

Gambia
Banjul

Germany (Federal Republic of Germany)
Berlin (West)
Bonn
Bremen
Dusseldorf
Frankfurt am Main
Hamburg
Munich
Stuttgart

Germany (German Democratic Republic)
Berlin (East)

Ghana
Accra

Greece
Athens
Thessaloniki

Guatemala
Guatemala City

Guinea
Conakry

Guyana
Georgetown

Haiti
Port-au-Prince

Honduras
Tegucigalpa

Hong Kong
Hong Kong

Hungary
Budapest

Iceland
Reykjavík

India
New Delhi
Bombay
Calcutta
Madras

Indonesia
Jakarta
Medan
Surabaya

Iran
Tehran
Isfahan
Shiraz
Tabriz

Ireland (Irish Republic)
Dublin

Ireland, Northern
—*see* UNITED KINGDOM

Israel
Tel Aviv

Italy
Rome
Florence
Genoa
Milan
Naples
Palermo
Trieste
Turin

Ivory Coast
Abidjan

Jamaica
Kingston

Japan
Tokyo
Naha, Okinawa
Osaka-Kobe
Sapporo
Fukuoka

Jerusalem
Jerusalem

Jordan
Amman

Kenya
Nairobi

Korea, South
Seoul

Kuwait
Kuwait

Laos
Vientiane

Lebanon
Beirut

Lesotho
Maseru

Liberia
Monrovia

Libya
Tripoli

Luxembourg
Luxembourg

Malagasy Republic (Madagascar)
Tananarive

Malawi
Blantyre
Lilongwe

Malaysia
Kuala Lumpur

Mali
Bamako

Malta
Valletta

Mauritania
Nouakchott

Mauritius
Port Louis

Mexico
Mexico, D. F.
Ciudad Juarez, Chihuahua
Guadalajaro, Jalisco
Hermosillo, Sonora
Matamoros, Tamaulipas
Mazatlan, Sinaloa
Merida, Yucatan
Monterrey, Nuevo Leon
Nuevo Laredo, Tamaulipas
Tijuana, Baja California

Morocco
Rabat
Casablanca
Tangier

Nepal
Katmandu

Netherlands
The Hague
Amsterdam
Rotterdam

Netherlands Antilles
Curaçao

New Zealand
Wellington
Auckland

Nicaragua
Managua

Niger
Niamey

Nigeria
Lagos
Ibadan
Kaduna

Norway
Oslo

Oman
Muscat

Pakistan
Islamabad
Karachi
Lahore
Peshawar

Panama
Panama

Papua New Guinea
Port Moresby

Paraguay
Asunción

Peru
Lima

Philippines
Manila
Cebu

Poland
Warsaw
Poznan
Krakow

Portugal
Lisbon
Oporto
Ponta Delgada, São Miguel, Azores

Qatar
Doha

Rumania (*or* **Romania)**
Bucharest

Russia—*see* UNION OF SOVIET SOCIALIST REPUBLICS

Rwanda
Kigali

Saudi Arabia
Jidda
Dharan

Scotland—*see* UNITED KINGDOM

Senegal
Dakar

Sierra Leone
Freetown

Singapore
Singapore

Somalia
Mogadiscio

South Africa
Pretoria, Transvaal
Cape Town, Cape Province
Durban, Natal
Johannesburg, Transvaal

South Korea—*see* KOREA, SOUTH

Spain
Madrid
Barcelona
Bilbao
Seville

Sri Lanka
Colombo

Sudan
Khartoum

Surinam
Paramaribo

Swaziland
Mbabane

Sweden
Stockholm

Switzerland
Bern
Zurich
Geneva

Syria
Damascus

Tanzania
Dar Es Salaam
Zanzibar

Thailand
Bangkok
Chiang Mai
Songkhla
Udorn

Togo
Lome

Trinidad and Tobago
Port-of-Spain

Tunisia
Tunis

Turkey
Ankara
Adana
Istanbul
Izmir

Union of Soviet Socialist Republics
Moscow
Leningrad

United Arab Emirates
Abu Dhabi

United Kingdom
London, England
Liverpool, England
Belfast, Northern Ireland
Edinburgh, Scotland

Upper Volta
Ouagadougou

Uruguay
Montevideo

Venezuela
Caracas
Maracaibo

Yemen Arab Republic
Sana

Yugoslavia
Belgrade
Zagreb

Zaire
Kinshasa
Bukavu
Lubumbashi

Zambia
Lusaka

THE CHAMBER OF COMMERCE OF THE UNITED STATES

This organization perceives private enterprise as a key contributor to world economic development. It believes that U.S. business people abroad have a dual role: they function both as unofficial ambassadors and as corporate representatives. The Chamber helps business executives adapt to the demands of this dual role, and it cooperates with the U.S. government agencies responsible for international policies and programs. It advocates a freer international flow of goods, services, and capital. The International Group of the Chamber of Commerce contributes to the Chamber's formulation of policies in major international trade, investment, energy, and monetary issues. Other activities of the International Group are:

1. Analyzing legislation which affects American business abroad and preparing testimony on bills before Congress
2. Maintaining close contact with key congressional staff and Executive Branch officials on matters which affect international business
3. Providing active support for an improved and expanded national export promotion program
4. Producing a variety of reports, surveys, and other publications (including audiovisual materials) on important international economic questions.

Inquiries related to multinational corporations and global business should be sent to the Chamber of Commerce of the United States, Washington, DC 20062.

FINANCING EXPORTS

In addition to developing foreign trade for American firms, U.S. government agencies facilitate the financing of the sale of goods and services to foreign buyers. Such financing is accomplished in cooperation with commercial banks. To reduce the risk for American exporters, credit insurance is available through the U.S. government in association with the insurance industry. Many exporters, however, obtain direct financing through U.S. banks having international banking departments.

The Export-Import Bank of the United States (Eximbank) This organization is an independent agency of the U.S. government that participates in financing America's exports by offering direct loans to overseas purchasers of American goods and services. It cooperates with commercial banks in the United States and abroad in providing financial arrangements that help U.S. exporters offer credit to their overseas buyers, it provides export credit guarantees to commercial banks which in turn finance export sales, and it offers export credit insurance.

Generally speaking, credit for direct loans is made available only to finance the dollar costs of capital goods and related services such as industrial and energy projects and the costs of the engineering, planning, and feasibility studies needed to prepare for the development of the projects. Medium-term loans—181 days to five years—are guaranteed to U.S. commercial banks and sometimes to American exporters to cover machinery, plant equipment, and other income-producing capital goods. The Eximbank, through its Cooperative Financing Facility, also extends financing to customers of financial institutions outside the United States; these loans to cooperating institutions cover one-half the funds necessary to make a purchase from the United States after a cash payment of at least ten percent of the cost of the purchase has been made. Cooperating institutions, in turn, lend the full amount of financing to their customers. For further information about Eximbank, secretaries should write to: Office of Export Development, Bureau of International Commerce, U.S. Department of Commerce, Washington, DC 20230.

APPENDIX: Suggestions for Further Reading

Accounting

Carson, Alexander B., et al. *Accounting Essentials for Career Secretaries.* Cincinnati: South-Western Publishing Co., 1972.

Palmer, Brock and Archer Binnion. *College Accounting for Secretaries.* New York: McGraw-Hill, 1971.

—*see also* CALCULATORS AND ELECTRONIC DATA PROCESSING

Administration

Anderson, Ruth I., et al. *The Administrative Secretary.* New York: McGraw-Hill, 1976.

Hanna, J. Marshall, et al. *Secretarial Procedures and Administration.* Cincinnati: South-Western Publishing Co., 1973.

Place, Irene, et al. *Office Management.* Scranton, PA: Canfield Press/Division of Harper & Row, 1974.

Neuner, John J., et al. *Administative Office Management.* Cincinnati: South-Western Publishing Co., 1972.

Winter, Elmer L. *The Successful Manager/Secretary Team.* West Nyack, NY: Parker Publishing Co., 1975.

Business Communication

Aurner, Robert R. and Morris P. Wolf. *Effective Communication in Business.* Cincinnati: South-Western Publishing Co., 1971.

Brock, Luther A. *How to Communicate by Letter and Memo.* New York: McGraw-Hill, 1974.

Murphy, Herta A. and Charles E. Peck. *Effective Business Communication.* New York: McGraw-Hill, 1972.

Poe, Roy W. and Rosemary T. Fruehling. *Business Communication: A Problem-Solving Approach.* New York: McGraw-Hill, 1973.

Reid, James M., Jr. and Robert M. Wendlinger. *Effective Letters: A Program for Self-Instruction.* New York: McGraw-Hill, 1973.

Sigband, Norman B. *Communication for Management and Business.* Glenview, IL: Scott, Foresman and Co., 1976.

Stewart, Marie M., et al. *College English and Communication.* New York: McGraw-Hill, 1975.

—*see also* STYLE MANUALS; WRITING

Calculators and Electronic Data Processing

Awad, Elias M. *Business Data Processing.* Englewood Cliffs, NJ: Prentice-Hall, 1974.

Carter, Juanita E. and Darrock F. Young. *Calculating Machines: A Ten-Key Approach.* Boston: Houghton Mifflin, 1975.

Laird, Eleanor. *Data Processing Secretary's Complete Handbook.* Englewood Cliffs, NJ: Prentice-Hall, 1973.

McCready, Richard R. *Solving Business Problems with Calculators.* Belmont, CA: Wadsworth Publishing Co., 1972.

Robichaud, B. *Understanding Modern Business Data Processing.* New York: McGraw-Hill, 1966.

Dictionaries and Other Reference Books

Arpan, Jeffrey S. and David A. Ricks. *A Directory of Foreign Manufacturers in the United States.* Atlanta, GA: Georgia State University Business Publications, 1976.

Crowley, Ellen T. and Robert C. Thomas. *Acronyms and Initialisms Dictionary.* Detroit: Gale Research Co., 1973.

Peegh, Eric. *A Dictionary of Acronyms and Abbreviations.* Hamden, CT and London: Archon Books and Clive Bingley, 1969.

Rybicki, Stephen. *Abbreviations; A Reverse Guide to Standard and Generally Accepted Abbreviated Forms.* Ann Arbor: The Pierian Press, 1971.

Spillner, Paul. *World Guide to Abbreviations* (3 Parts). New York: R. R. Bowker Co., 1972.

Webster's Atlas and Zip Code Directory. Springfield, MA: G. & C. Merriam Co., 1973.

Webster's Collegiate Thesaurus. Springfield, MA: G. & C. Merriam Co., 1976.

Webster's Instant Word Guide. Springfield, MA: G. & C. Merriam Co., 1972.

Webster's New Collegiate Dictionary. Springfield, MA: G. & C. Merriam Co., 1973.

Webster's Third New International Dictionary. Springfield, MA: G. & C. Merriam Co., 1961.

Engineering

Laird, Eleanor. *Engineering Secretary's Complete Handbook.* Englewood Cliffs, NJ: Prentice-Hall, 1967.

Lojko, Grace R. *Typewriting Techniques for the Technical Secretary.* Englewood Cliffs, NJ: Prentice-Hall, 1972.

English Grammar

Gorrell, Robert M. and Charlton Laird. *Modern English Handbook.* Englewood Cliffs, NJ: Prentice-Hall, 1972.

Irmscher, William F. *The Holt Guide to English.* New York: Holt, Rinehart and Winston, 1976.

Keithley, Erwin and Margaret H. Thompson. *English for Modern Business.* Homewood, IL: Richard D. Irwin, Inc., 1972.

Perrin, Porter G. and Jim W. Corder. *Handbook of Current English.* Glenview, IL: Scott, Foresman and Co., 1975.

—*see also* WRITING

Human Relations

Laird, Donald A., et al. *Psychology: Human Relations and Motivation.* New York: McGraw-Hill, 1975.

Nirenberg, Jesse. *Getting Through to People.* Englewood Cliffs, NJ: Prentice-Hall, 1968.

Law

Blackburn, Norma D. *Legal Secretaryship.* Englewood Cliffs, NJ: Prentice-Hall, 1971.

Brady, Patricia S. *Legal Secretary's Handbook.* Los Angeles, CA: Parker & Son, 1971.

Grahm, Milton, et al. *Legal Typewriting.* New York: McGraw-Hill, 1968.

Leslie, Louis A. and Kenneth B. Coffin. *Handbook for the Legal Secretary.* New York: McGraw-Hill, 1968.

National Association of Legal Secretaries. *Manual for the Legal Secretarial Profession.* St. Paul, MN: West Publishing Co., 1974.

Prentice-Hall Editorial Staff. *Legal Secretary's Encyclopedic Dictionary.* Englewood Cliffs, NJ: Prentice-Hall, 1962.

Mathematics

Huffman, Harry and J. Schmidt. *Programmed Business Mathematics.* New York: McGraw-Hill, 1975.

Medicine

Alcazar, Carol C. *Medical Typist's Guide for Histories and Physicals.* Flushing, NY: Medical Examination Publishing Co., 1974.

Bredow, Miriam. *Handbook for the Medical Secretary.* New York: McGraw-Hill, 1963.

Bredow, Miriam. *Medical Office Procedures.* New York: McGraw-Hill, 1973.

Davis, Phyllis E. and N. Hershelman. *Medical Shorthand.* New York: John Wiley & Sons, Inc., 1967.

Dennis, Robert L. and Jean M. Doyle. *The Complete Handbook for Medical Secretaries and Assistants.* Boston: Little, Brown & Co., 1971.

Eshom, Myreta. *Medical Secretary's Manual.* Englewood Cliffs, NJ: Prentice-Hall, 1966.

Kabbe, Elaine F. *Medical Secretary's Guide.* Englewood Cliffs, NJ: Prentice-Hall, 1967.

Siegfried, W. *Typing Medical Forms.* New York: McGraw-Hill, 1969.

Webster's Medical Speller. Springfield, MA: G. & C. Merriam Co., 1975.

Office Equipment Systems

Briggs, Robert and Eugene J. Kosy. *Office Machines - A Collegiate Course.* Cincinnati: South-Western Publishing Co., 1973.

Kupsh, Joyce. *Duplicating: Machine Operation and Decision Making.* Beverly Hills, CA: Glencoe Press, 1972.

Pactor, Paul and Mina M. Johnson. *Comprehensive Business Machines Course.* New York: Pitman, 1968.

Office Landscape

Duffy, Frank and A. Wankum. *Office Landscaping: A New Approach to Office Planning and Layout Planning.* New York: International Publications Service, 1969.

Robichaud, B. *Selecting, Planning, and Managing Office Space.* New York: McGraw-Hill, 1958.

Office Procedures

Dallas, Richard J. and James M. Thompson. *Clerical and Secretarial Systems for the Office.* Englewood Cliffs, NJ: Prentice-Hall, 1974.

Place, Irene, et al. *College Secretarial Procedures.* New York: McGraw-Hill, 1972.

Records Management

Johnson, Mina M. and Norman F. Kallans. *Records Management.* Cincinnati: South-Western Publishing Co., 1974.

Kahn, Gilbert, et al. *Progressive Filing and Records Management.* New York: McGraw-Hill, 1971.

Maedke, Wilmer O., et al. *Information and Records Management.* Riverside, NJ: Glencoe Press (distributed by Macmillan), 1974.

Place, Irene and E. L. Popham. *Filing and Records Management.* Englewood Cliffs, NJ: Prentice-Hall, 1966.

Place, Irene, et al. *Fundamental Filing Practice.* Englewood Cliffs, NJ: Prentice-Hall, 1973.

Tavernier, Gerard. *Basic Office Systems and Records.* New York: Beekman Publishers, 1971.

Shorthand and Transcription

Cleary, J. B. and J. Lacombe. *English Style Skill-Builders: A Self-Improvement Program for Transcribers and Typists.* New York: McGraw-Hill, 1974.

Style Manuals

Chicago Manual of Style. Chicago: University of Chicago Press, 1974.

Keithley, Erwin M. and Philip S. Schreiner. *Manual of Style for the Preparation of Papers and Reports.* Cincinnati: South-Western Publishing Co. 1971.

Skillin, Marjorie E. and Robert M. Gay. *Words into Type.* Englewood Cliffs, NJ: Prentice-Hall, 1974.

Writing

Brown, Leland. *Effective Business Report Writing.* Englewood Cliffs, NJ: Prentice-Hall, 1973.

Brusaw, Charles T. and Gerald J. Alred. *Practical Writing: Composition for the Business and Technical World.* Boston: Allyn & Bacon, 1973.

Janis, J. Harold. *Writing and Communicating in Business.* New York: Macmillan, 1973.

JOB APPLICATION LETTERS AND RÉSUMÉS

The job application letter A properly formatted and well-written letter of application will greatly assist in preselling you to a prospective employer. This type of letter is a concrete indication of your verbal and technical skills and of your general personality and intelligence. You should typewrite the letter on plain bond paper. (Do not use social stationery or personalized letterhead.) Exotic typefaces should be avoided. Either the Block, the Modified Block, or the Modified Semi-block styling is appropriate. The letter ought not to exceed one page. Under no circumstances should you prepare and photocopy a form letter to be sent to numerous firms. Such a practice will create a most unfavorable first impression on those evaluating your application. The applicant lacking the time and the common courtesy to write a personal letter to a firm will most probably not receive careful consideration.

Before typewriting the letter, you should plan your approach in detail. An outline or a draft of the points to be made will assist you. If the letter is solicited (i.e., you are responding to an advertisement), you should mention in the first paragraph the specific position for which you are applying and the date and source of the advertisement. If the letter is unsolicited (i.e., you are applying on your own initiative), you should say as much in the first paragraph and indicate why you are interested in working for the particular firm. Next, you ought to focus on and develop your best assets. A concise statement of your technical skills (as shorthand and typewriting rates) may be given, along with mention of your more specialized skills (as the ability to operate a media typewriter). Another sentence or even a paragraph expanding on some aspect of your education or on your previous employment experience not already developed fully in the résumé can be included in the letter. The tone throughout should be straightforward, yet modest and sincere. Of course, the material should be carefully proofread so that it will be devoid of grammatical and typographical errors. You should keep a copy of the letter for your records. See page 522 for a sample job application letter.

The résumé Your résumé is the balance sheet of your professional advancement and accomplishments to date. As such, it is a key factor in achieving your continued employment objectives. Although books have been written on this subject, there are elements essential to all well-written résumés which can be set down here. These elements are: (1) personal identification: your full name, address, and telephone number (home and/or office) typewritten at the top of the résumé (2) employment experience: each job that you have held listed chronologically from present to past, including the name and address of each firm, applicable employment dates, your job title and a brief job description if the responsibilities are not obvious from the title itself, and perhaps a concise summary of your special accomplishments in each position if space permits (3) educational background: a list of the institutions that you have attended or from which you have graduated, starting with the highest level (as graduate school or college) and concluding with high school (4) special skills: a list of special skills (as fluency in a foreign language or proficiency in the operation of electronic data processing equipment) that might prove a valuable asset to a prospective employer should you be hired, and (5) references: the sentence, "References will be provided on request," included at the end of the résumé. NOTE: If you have no previous employment experience, you can supplement your education category with a list of the business and secretarial courses that

A Letter of Application

123 Smith Lane
Jonesville, ST 98765
June 1, 19—

Ms. Ann Stone
Director, Personnel
ABC Insurance
81 Albany Towers Suite 12
Smithville, ST 12345

Dear Ms. Smith:

The ABC Insurance employment ad on page 48E of the May 30, 19— issue of the Sunday Republican has attracted my immediate interest. Because I believe that I am qualified for the executive secretarial position in your Medical Claims Department, I am sending you a copy of my résumé.

My shorthand rate is —— wpm; and my typewriting rate —— wpm. I am experienced in the use of machine dictation and transcription equipment — both cassette and belt. I am also thoroughly familiar with the use of electronic printing and display calculators.

As you can see from the attached résumé, I am currently employed as Medical Office Manager for Dr. Helen P. Thornton who is retiring from practice at the end of July. I believe that the experience gained in this position would be quite useful in medical claims work.

I look forward to a personal interview at your convenience, if you decide to follow up on this initial application. ABC Insurance is indeed a fine company — one for which I know I would enjoy working.

Sincerely yours,

Carol C. Mannington

Carol C. Mannington

Résumé

RÉSUMÉ

Carol Conners Mannington
123 Smith Lane
Jonesville, ST 98765
(300) 567-8910

Employment Experience

October 1974 - present	Helen P. Thornton, MD 129 Main Street Jonesville, ST 98765 Medical Office Manager
June 1965 - October 1974	BR Pharmaceuticals 12 Industrial Park Drive Smithville, ST 12345 Secretary to Dr. Kenneth Preston Group Leader, R&D
June 1960 - June 1965	Jonesville Municipal Hospital Jonesville, ST 98765 Director, Surgical Secretarial Services 1963 - 1965 Secretary, Surgical Services 1962 - 1963 Typist, Business Office 1960 - 1962

Education

1958 - 1960	Mason County Community College Jonesville, ST 98765	Associate in Arts Business Education
1954 - 1958	Jonesville High School Jonesville, ST 98765	Diploma

Special Skills

medical stenography
fluency in German

References

References will be provided on request.

you have successfully completed, you can mention your typewriting and transcription rates, and you can list any academic honors that you have been awarded. If you have completed any special free-lance secretarial projects (as the typing of manuscripts and theses), you can mention them under a heading "Special Projects" following the education section.

These data should <u>not</u> be given: (1) names and addresses of references: references should be selected separately for each prospective employer and should be provided by you at the interview or in an interview follow-up letter (2) salary: it is best to discuss salary requirements and ranges during the interview itself, since you will not want to undersell yourself ahead of time, or possibly price yourself out of a job market that you may be unfamiliar with (3) your reasons, if any, for changing jobs: since wording can often be misunderstood without personal clarification, it is best to discuss this matter with the interviewer <u>and only if you are asked</u>, rather than committing yourself on paper (4) your reasons for present unemployment, if applicable: this topic is also tricky and is therefore best dealt with in person; also, adequate explanations often require valuable page space that can be better used to highlight your assets, and (5) a photograph: a photo can work for or against you, depending on the subjectivity of the person evaluating your application; hence, it is best not to risk a premature negative reaction on the part of the employer before you have had a chance to present yourself in person.

Your résumé should not exceed one page. To achieve maximum brevity and at the same time attain comprehensiveness, you should plan the material and then write it out in draft form before typewriting it. All facts should be doubled-checked. Use plain, straightforward English devoid of technical jargon and superlatives. Tailor the material to the type of job you have in mind. Remember, you can write another résumé slanted toward a slightly different kind of job, if necessary. The material ought to be typewritten on plain, standard bond paper. Margins should be balanced on all four sides. Although there are many acceptable résumé formats, the simplest and cleanest treatment is to block all the material flush left. Entries should be single-spaced internally, with double- or triple-spacing between entries, depending on the page space available. Underscoring and capital letters may introduce main and secondary headings. Copies <u>must</u> be clean and legible: for this purpose, offset or Xerox copies are suggested. Avoid mimeographed copies and carbons. Your typewriter typeface must be sharp and clean. Avoid exotic typefaces (including italic). See page 523 for a sample résumé.

SIGNS AND SYMBOLS

Astronomy

SUN, GREATER PLANETS, ETC.

☉ the sun; Sunday
◐, ☾, *or* ☽ the moon; Monday
● new moon
☽, ◐, ☽, ☽ first quarter
○ *or* ⊛ full moon
☾, ◑, ☾, ☾ last quarter
☿ Mercury; Wednesday
♀ Venus; Friday
⊕, ⊖, *or* ♁ the earth
♂ Mars; Tuesday
♃ Jupiter; Thursday
♄ *or* ♄ Saturn; Saturday
♅, ♅, *or* ♅ Uranus
♆, ♆, *or* ♆ Neptune
♇ Pluto
☄ comet
✱ *or* ✳ fixed Star

ASPECTS AND NODES

☌ conjunction—indicating that the bodies have the same longitude, or right ascension
□ quadrature—indicating a difference of 90° in longitude, or right ascension
△ trine—indicating a difference of 120° in longitude, or right ascension
☍ opposition—indicating a difference of 180° in longitude, or right ascension; as, ☍ ♆ ☉, opposition of Neptune to the sun
☊ ascending node
☋ descending node

Biology

○ an individual, specif., a female—used chiefly in inheritance charts
□ an individual, specif., a male—used chiefly in inheritance charts
♀ female
♂ *or* ♁ male
× crossed with; hybrid
+ wild type
F_1 offspring of the first generation
F_2 offspring of the second generation
F_3, F_4, F_5, etc. offspring of the third, fourth, fifth, etc., generation

Business

a/c account ⟨in a/c with⟩
@ at; each ⟨4 apples @ 5¢ = 20¢⟩
/ per
c/o care of
number if it precedes a numeral ⟨track #3⟩; pounds if it follows ⟨a 5# sack of sugar⟩
℔ pound; pounds
% percent
‰ per thousand
$ dollars
¢ cents
£ pounds
/ shillings
(for other currency symbols see MONEY table)
© copyrighted
® registered trademark

Chemistry

+ signifies "plus", "and", "together with", and is used between the symbols of substances brought together for, or produced by, a reaction; placed above a symbol or to its right above the line, it signifies a unit charge of positive electricity: Ca^{++} denotes the ion of calcium, which carries two positive charges; the plus sign is used also to indicate dextrorotation (as +143°); it is sometimes used to indicate a base or alkaloid when placed above the initial letter of the name of the substance; (as $\overset{+}{M}$, morphine or $\overset{+}{Q}$, quinine)

— signifies a single "bond", or unit of attractive force or affinity, and is used between the symbols of elements or groups which unite to form a compound: H—Cl for HCl, H—O—H for H_2O; placed above a symbol or to its right above the line, it signifies a unit charge of negative electricity: Cl^- denotes a chlorine ion carrying a negative charge; the dash indicates levorotation (as −92°); it also indicates an acid, when placed above the initial letter of the name of the acid (as $\overline{C}$, citric acid); it is used also to indicate the removal of a part from a compound

/ often indicates valence (as $Fe^{//}$ denotes bivalent iron, $Fe^{///}$, trivalent iron); sometimes its use is restricted to negative ions so that it is equivalent to —

. is often used: (1) to indicate a bond (as H.Cl for H—Cl) or (2) to denote a unit positive charge of electricity (as Ca.. denotes two positive charges) or (3) to separate parts of a compound regarded as loosely joined (as $CuSO_4.5H_2O$)

○ denotes the benzene ring

= indicates a double bond; placed above a symbol or to its right above the line, it signifies two unit charges of negative electricity (as SO_4 =, the negative ion of sulfuric acid, carrying two negative charges)

≡ signifies a triple bond or negative charge

: indicates a double bond

⋮ indicates a triple bond

() mark groups or radicals within a compound [as in $C_6H_4(CH_3)_2$, the formula for xylene which contains two methyl radicals (CH_3)]

⌐ *or* ⌙ join separated atoms or groups in structural formulas, as in that for glucose:

$$CH_2OH\overset{\ulcorner\!-\!-O-\!-\!\urcorner}{CH(CHOH)_3CH}OH$$

= give or form

→ give, pass over to, or lead to

⇄ forms and is formed from

↓ indicates precipitation of the substance

↑ indicates that the substance passes off as a gas

≡ or ⇌ is equivalent—used in statements to show how much of one substance will react with a given quantity of another so as to leave no excess of either

1-, 2-, etc. used initially in names, referring to the positions of substituting groups, attached to the first, etc., of the numbered atoms of the parent compound

H^2 or ^2H deuterium

H^3 or ^3H tritium

Flowchart symbols

⬭ TERMINAL. Marks the beginning and the end of the flowchart.

▭ PROCESSING. Indicates the performance of a given task.

⏷ MANUAL OPERATION.

◇ DECISION. Indicates a juncture at which a choice must be made.

[ANNOTATION. Connected to the flowchart proper by a dotted line.

○ CONNECTOR. Used to indicate common points in the flow when connecting lines cannot be drawn.

▱ INPUT/OUTPUT. This is the general symbol for input/output. It may be replaced by one of the more specific symbols below.

PUNCHED CARD.

PUNCHED TAPE.

Q MAGNETIC TAPE.

MANUAL INPUT. Usually indicates a keyboard device.

DISPLAY OUTPUT. Indicates a video display.

DOCUMENT. Indicates output from a printing device (as a line printer).

ON-LINE STORAGE. Indicates a mass storage unit (as a drum or disk).

▽ or ▽ OFF-LINE STORAGE. Indicates data storage that cannot be accessed directly by a computer.

↑← DIRECTION OF FLOW. Arrowheads need not be used when direction of flow is from top to bottom or from left to right.

COMMUNICATION LINK. Indicates a transfer of data from one location to another (as by a telephone connection).

Mathematics

$+$ plus; positive $\langle a+b=c\rangle$—used also to indicate omitted figures or an approximation

$-$ minus; negative

$\pm$ plus or minus (the square root of $4a^2$ is $\pm 2a$)

$\times$ multiplied by; times $\langle 6\times 4=24\rangle$—also indicated by placing a dot between the factors $\langle 6\cdot 4=24\rangle$ or by writing factors other than numerals without signs

$\div$ or $:$ divided by $\langle 24\div 6=4\rangle$—also indicated by writing the divisor under the dividend with a line between $\langle \frac{24}{6}=4\rangle$ or by writing the divisor after the dividend with an oblique line between $\langle 3/8\rangle$

$=$ equals $\langle 6+2=8\rangle$

$\neq$ or $\ne$ is not equal to

$>$ is greater than $\langle 6>5\rangle$

$\gg$ is much greater than

$<$ is less than $\langle 3<4\rangle$

$\ll$ is much less than

$\geqq$ or $\geq$ is greater than or equal to

$\leqq$ or $\leq$ is less than or equal to

$\ngtr$ is not greater than

$\nless$ is not less than

$\approx$ is approximately equal to

$\equiv$ is identical to

$\sim$ equivalent; similar

$\cong$ is congruent to

$\propto$ varies directly as; is proportional to

$:$ is to; the ratio of

$\therefore$ therefore

∞ infinity

$\angle$ angle; the angle $\langle \angle ABC\rangle$

∟ right angle (∟ABC)

$\perp$ the perpendicular; is perpendicular to $\langle AB \perp CD\rangle$

$\parallel$ parallel; is parallel to $\langle AB \parallel CD\rangle$

$\odot$ or ○ circle

⌒ arc of a circle

△ triangle

□ square

▭ rectangle

$\surd$ or $\sqrt{}$ root—used without a figure to indicate a square root $\langle$as in $\sqrt{4}=2\rangle$ or with an index above the sign to indicate another degree $\langle$as in $\sqrt[3]{3}$, $\sqrt[5]{7}\rangle$; also denoted by a fractional index at the right of a number whose denominator expresses the degree of the root $\langle 3^{1/3}=\sqrt[3]{3}\rangle$

() parentheses, [] brackets, {} braces, — vinculum: indicate that the quantities enclosed by them are to be taken together

δ variation $\langle \delta x$; the variation of $x\rangle$

Δ increment

$\int$ integral; integral of $\langle \int 2xdx = x^2+C\rangle$

$\int_b^a$ the integral taken between the values a and b of the variable

σ standard deviation of a population

Σ sum; summation

$\bar{x}$ arithmetic mean of a sample of a variable x

μ arithmetic mean of a population

μ_2 or σ^2 variance

χ^2 chi-square

π pi; the number 3.14159265+; the ratio of the circumference of a circle to its diameter

Π product

$!$ factorial

e or ϵ (1) the number 2.7182818+; the base of the natural system of logarithms (2) the eccentricity of a conic section

$^\circ$ degree $\langle 60^\circ\rangle$

$'$ minute; foot $\langle 30'\rangle$—used also to distinguish between different values of the same variable or between different variables (as a', a'', a''', usu. read a prime, a double prime, a triple prime)

$''$ second, inch $\langle 30''\rangle$

^{2}, ^{3}, etc. —used as exponents placed above and at the right of an expression to indicate that it is raised to a power whose degree is indicated by the figure $\langle a^2$, the square of $a\rangle$

$^{-2}$, $^{-3}$, —used as exponents placed above and at the right of an expression to indicate that the reciprocal of the expression is raised to the power whose degree is indicated by the figure $\langle a^{-2}$ equals $1/a^2\rangle$

$\sin^{-1}x$ arc sine of x

$\cos^{-1}x$ arc cosine of x

$\tan^{-1}x$ arc tangent of x

$\cot^{-1}x$ arc cotangent of x

$\sec^{-1}x$ arc secant of x

$\operatorname{cosec}^{-1}x$ arc cosecant of x

f^{-1} the inverse of the function f

$|z|$ the absolute value of z

$\oplus$ an operation in a mathematical system (as a group or ring) indicating the sum of two elements

$\otimes$ an operation in a mathematical system (as a group or ring) indicating the product of two elements

$[x]$ the greatest integer not greater than x

(a,b) the open interval $a<x<b$

$[a,b]$ the closed interval $a\leqq x\leqq b$

$\aleph_0$ aleph-null

ω the ordinal number of the positive integers

$\cup$ union of two sets

$\cap$ intersection of two sets

$\subset$ is included in, is a subset of

$\supset$ contains as a subset

$\in$ or ϵ is an element of

$\notin$ is not an element of

Λ or 0 or ϕ or $\{\}$ empty set, null set

Medicine

A̅A̅, A̅, *or* a̅a̅ ana; of each
℞ take—used on prescriptions; prescription; treatment
☠ poison

APOTHECARIES' MEASURES

℥ ounce
f℥ fluidounce
fʒ fluidram

♏, ♍, ♍, *or* min minim

APOTHECARIES' WEIGHTS

℔ pound
℥ ounce (as ℥ i or ℥ j, one ounce; ℥ ss, half an ounce; ℥ iss *or* ℥ jss, one ounce and a half; ℥ ij, two ounces)
ʒ dram
℈ scruple

Miscellaneous

& and
&c et cetera; and so forth
" *or* " ditto marks
/ diagonal *or* slant *or* solidus *or* virgule; used to mean "or" (as in *and/or*), "and/or" (as in *dead/wounded*), "per" (as in *feet/second*), indicates end of a line of verse; separates the figures of a date (4/4/73)
☞ index *or* fist
< derived from — used in etymologies
> whence derived — used in etymologies
+ and — used in etymologies
* assumed — used in etymologies
† died—used esp. in genealogies
+ cross (for variations see CROSS illustration)
☧ monogram from Greek XP signifying Christ
卐 swastika
✡ Magen David
☥ ankh
℣ versicle
℟ response
✳ —used in Roman Catholic and Anglican service books to divide each verse of a psalm, indicating where the response begins
✠ *or* + —used in some service books to indicate where the sign of the cross is to be made; also used by certain Roman Catholic and Anglican prelates as a sign of the cross preceding their signatures
LXX Septuagint
f/ *or* f: relative aperture of a photographic lens
◉ civil defense
☮ peace

Physics

α alpha particle
β beta ray
γ conductivity, gamma, photon, surface tension
ϵ electric field intensity, electromotive force, permittivity
η efficiency, viscosity
κ kaon
λ wavelength
Λ lambda particle
μ magnetic moment, micro-, micron, modulus, muon, permeability, viscosity
μμ micromicron
ν frequency, neutrino, reluctivity
Ξ xi particle
π pion
ρ density, resistivity, rho particle
σ conductivity, cross section, surface tension
Σ sigma particle
τ transmittance
φ electric potential, luminous flux, magnetic flux
Ω ohm, omega particle

Reference marks

⁎ asterisk *or* star
† dagger
‡ double dagger
§ section *or* numbered clause
‖ parallels
¶ *or* ⁋ paragraph

Stamps and stamp collecting

★ unused
○ used
⊞ block of four or more
⊠ entire cover or card
△ on a piece of cover

Weather

barometer, changes of
⁄ Rising, then falling
⁄ Rising, then steady; or rising, then rising more slowly
/ Rising steadily, or unsteadily
✓ Falling or steady, then rising; or rising, then rising more quickly
— Steady, same as 3 hours ago
╲ Falling, then rising, same or lower than 3 hours ago
╲ Falling, then steady; or falling, then falling more slowly
╲ Falling steadily, or unsteadily
╲ Steady or rising, then falling; or falling, then falling more quickly
◎ calm
○ clear
◐ cloudy (partly)
● cloudy (completely overcast)
+ drifting or blowing snow
, drizzle
≡ fog
∾ freezing rain
▲▲▲ front, cold
warm
occluded
stationary
)(funnel clouds
∞ haze
● hurricane
6 tropical storm
↔ ice needles
• rain
⁑ rain and snow
¥ rime
S sandstorm or dust storm
▽ shower(s)
▽ shower of rain
▽ shower of hail
△ sleet
* snow
ꓘ thunderstorm
∽ visibility reduced by smoke

INDEX

K

L

T

U